CIW Site Designer
Certification Bible

CIW Site Designer Certification Bible

Chelsea Valentine and Natanya Pitts

Hungry Minds™

Best-Selling Books • Digital Downloads • e-Books • Answer Networks • e-Newsletters • Branded Web Sites • e-Learning

New York, NY ✦ Cleveland, OH ✦ Indianapolis, IN

CIW Site Designer Certification Bible

Published by
Hungry Minds, Inc.
909 Third Avenue
New York, NY 10022
www.hungryminds.com

Library of Congress Control Number: 2001092937

ISBN: 0-7645-4841-7

Printed in the United States of America

10 9 8 7 6 5 4 3 2 1

1P/RR/RS/QR/IN

Distributed in the United States by Hungry Minds, Inc.

Distributed by CDG Books Canada Inc. for Canada; by Transworld Publishers Limited in the United Kingdom; by IDG Norge Books for Norway; by IDG Sweden Books for Sweden; by IDG Books Australia Publishing Corporation Pty. Ltd. for Australia and New Zealand; by TransQuest Publishers Pte Ltd. for Singapore, Malaysia, Thailand, Indonesia, and Hong Kong; by Gotop Information Inc. for Taiwan; by ICG Muse, Inc. for Japan; by Intersoft for South Africa; by Eyrolles for France; by International Thomson Publishing for Germany, Austria, and Switzerland; by Distribuidora Cuspide for Argentina; by LR International for Brazil; by Galileo Libros for Chile; by Ediciones ZETA S.C.R. Ltda. for Peru; by WS Computer Publishing Corporation, Inc., for the Philippines; by Contemporanea de Ediciones for Venezuela; by Express Computer Distributors for the Caribbean and West Indies; by Micronesia Media Distributor, Inc. for Micronesia; by Chips Computadoras S.A. de C.V. for Mexico; by Editorial Norma de Panama S.A. for Panama; by American Bookshops for Finland.

For general information on Hungry Minds' products and services please contact our Customer Care department within the U.S. at 800-762-2974, outside the U.S. at 317-572-3993 or fax 317-572-4002.

For sales inquiries and reseller information, including discounts, premium and bulk quantity sales, and foreign-language translations, please contact our Customer Care department at 800-434-3422, fax 317-572-4002 or write to Hungry Minds, Inc., Attn: Customer Care Department, 10475 Crosspoint Boulevard, Indianapolis, IN 46256.

For information on licensing foreign or domestic rights, please contact our Sub-Rights Customer Care department at 212-884-5000.

For information on using Hungry Minds' products and services in the classroom or for ordering examination copies, please contact our Educational Sales department at 800-434-2086 or fax 317-572-4005.

For press review copies, author interviews, or other publicity information, please contact our Public Relations department at 317-572-3168 or fax 317-572-4168.

For authorization to photocopy items for corporate, personal, or educational use, please contact Copyright Clearance Center, 222 Rosewood Drive, Danvers, MA 01923, or fax 978-750-4470.

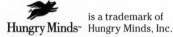

is a trademark of
Hungry Minds, Inc.

Credits

Acquisitions Editor
Melody Layne

Project Editor
Alex Miloradovich

Technical Editor
Robert Shimonski

Copy Editor
Alex Miloradovich

Editorial Manager
Ami Frank Sullivan

Project Coordinator
Jennifer Bingham

Graphics and Production Specialists
Beth Brooks, Sean Decker,
Jill Piscitelli, Brian Torwelle

Quality Control Technicians
John Greenough, Andy Hollandbeck,
Susan Moritz, Carl Pierce,
Dwight Ramsey

Permissions Editor
Laura Moss

Media Development Specialist
Greg Stephens

Proofreading and Indexing
TECHBOOKS Production Services

About the Authors

Chelsea Valentine is the lead markup language specialist at LANWrights, Inc., an Austin, TX-based training and consulting company. Chelsea has contributed to numerous Web- and markup-related titles for LANWrights including: the *Hip Pocket Guide to HTML 4.01, HTML 4 For Dummies,* 3rd Edition, *XHTML For Dummies,* and *XML For Dummies,* 2nd Edition, among others. She is a working participant at NetWorld + Interop and other trade shows, and consults with the occasional private client. She has taken — and passed — the CIW Site Designer exam. Contact her via e-mail at chelsea@lanw.com.

Natanya Pitts is a lead instructional designer and XHTML/XML specialist at Powered, an Austin, TX-based online training company. A former LANWrights employee, Natanya has contributed to over 25 Web-related titles for LANWrights, including: all editions of the *Hip Pocket Guide to HTML,* numerous editions of *HTML For Dummies* and *HTML 4 For Dummies, XHTML For Dummies,* and both editions of *XML For Dummies.* She has taken — and passed — the CIW Site Designer exam. Contact her via e-mail at natanya@io.com.

a moving target:
the Web changes as you watch
lifetime employment!

Preface

This book is designed to help you prepare for the CIW Site Designer Exam (1D0-420). CIW certification is recognized as a leading industry standard for the Internet industry, accredited by the Association of Internet Professionals (AIP), and endorsed by the International Webmasters Association (IWA). The CIW Site Designer Exam tests the candidate on a broad base of general knowledge related to designing, creating, developing, and managing public Web sites. CIW exams are currently offered at more than 1,000 testing locations worldwide.

This book not only serves as a comprehensive study guide for the CIW Site Designer Exam, but it also covers many topics in greater detail than the exam requires, and benefits from the authors' extensive, real-world experience in building and managing Web sites. For this reason, you'll find the book useful as a Web site planning, building, and managing guide long after you've passed the exam.

How This Book Is Organized

The main body of this book is comprised of 21 chapters subdivided into four parts. To get the maximum benefit — as these elements are arranged in a logical sequence — we recommend that you carefully study all of the material from beginning to end and complete all of the exercises and sample exam questions. In addition, there are seven appendixes, a glossary of terms, and a CD-ROM (loaded with useful software, tutorial files, and a comprehensive testing engine) to support your learning experience and help you prepare for the exam.

Exam Tip
The exam does a good job of measuring both "hard" and "soft" skills, but, because of the ever-changing nature of the practical matters, it tends (correctly, we feel) to put greater emphasis on testing your knowledge of the big picture.

The following sections give you a brief overview of the book's layout.

Part I: Exploring Web Site Design Methodology

This part begins by answering several fundamental questions, including:

✦ What is site design?

✦ Why must Web sites be designed?

✦ What kinds of tools and technologies can site designers use?

✦ Where is site design technology headed?

✦ How does the basic development process work?

In essence, the chapters in this part of the book define the fundamental terms and concepts, lay out the case for rigorous analysis and design, explore the principles of Web page layout and design, explain the various navigation tools and techniques at your disposal, investigate the effective use of graphics and multimedia, and review the entire Web site development process from inception to maintenance.

Part II: Understanding Web Site Design Technology

Here's where you tackle technical elements and markup languages your must master to do your job effectively. The primary focus of this part of the book is as follows:

✦ **Three chapters on HTML.** A review of current and emerging official standards that govern this markup language, the standards groups responsible for HTML in particular (and Internet technologies in general), a technical overview of HTML as a markup language, and more-advanced HTML topics — namely, tables, frames, and proper use of metadata.

✦ **A chapter on Cascading Style Sheets (CSS).** A presentation of the formatting controls that CSS provides for Web pages (and sites that use them).

✦ **A chapter on plug-ins.** An explanation of the important role that browser software components called plug-ins play in supporting access to enhanced, enriched forms of Web content, such as multimedia, audio, special text delivery formats, and animation.

Part III: Using Web Site Development Tools

This is where you strap on the site designer's tool belt, with separate chapters covering:

✦ Microsoft FrontPage 2000

✦ Macromedia Dreamweaver 3.0

✦ Allaire HomeSite 4.5 (now merged with Macromedia)

✦ Macromedia Flash 5.0 and dynamic media

You learn about HTML authoring tools, page publishing tools, link checkers, spell checkers, and a whole raft of visual editing techniques — including Flash animation — to help you create and manage not only individual Web pages but also entire Web sites.

Part IV: Applying Advanced Design Technology

Part IV explores the most advanced subject matter covered on the Site Designer Exam, including:

+ **JavaScript and client-side Web scripting.** An exploration of ways to enhance the interactivity or otherwise extend the capabilities of the Web sites you design and build

+ **Java Applets in Web pages.** A thorough look at this more powerful alternative to JavaScript

+ **Extensible Markup Language (XML) and authoring.** Takes a look at XML, upon which most cutting-edge Web applications and markup languages are based

+ **HTTP servers and cookies.** Investigates the workhorses of modern Web interactions with users in its coverage of HTTP (Web) servers and client-side data descriptions — innocuously known as "cookies"

+ **Web site publishing and database technology.** An examination of the methodologies for publishing your site and the benefits and capabilities to be gained by integrating Web sites with database engines

Appendixes

This book also contains several useful appendixes designed to provide references to more in-depth information on the topics covered in the book and to help you make the best use of this book as an exam preparation resource.

Of particular interest is Appendix C, the sample exam. We recommend that you don't look at this sample exam until you've read the entire book. If you can correctly answer at least 45 of the 60 questions in this sample exam, you're probably ready to take the real thing. If you need more help, the CD-ROM included with this book contains a testing engine with hundreds of sample exam questions to expand your knowledge of site design and to solidify your preparedness for the exam.

Also, Appendix D also gives you all the information you need to find a testing location, get signed up, and get certified.

How to Use This Book

This book is designed to provide you with the best possible learning and exam preparation experience. The structure of each chapter and the specific elements used are designed to present the exam material in a clear and easy-to-learn way.

The elements that you'll find in each chapter are:

✦ A list of exam objectives covered in this chapter

✦ A chapter pretest

✦ Clear, concise text on each topic

✦ Step-by-step instructions on how to perform specific tasks

✦ Screen shots and graphics to aid in your understanding

✦ A Key Point Summary

✦ A comprehensive Study Guide that contains:

  • Exam-style assessment questions

  • Scenario problems for you to solve

  • Lab exercises to perform on your computer

  • Answers to chapter pretest questions, assessment questions, and scenarios

✦ A list of resources for more information on the topics discussed

The suggested course of study

This book can be used either by individuals working independently or by groups in a formal classroom setting. The following study methods are recommended:

✦ **Read the book sequentially.** The chapters are designed to be studied in order, meaning that it's best to complete Chapter 1 before moving on to Chapter 2 (and so on). Some of the chapters can stand alone, but in many cases, the topics presented in a chapter are based on knowledge obtained in preceding chapters.

✦ **Approach each chapter systematically.** When studying each chapter, first, take the Chapter Pre-Test. Answer as many of the questions as you can. For those questions that you're unsure of, be on the lookout for the answers as you read the chapter. After you've read the chapter, use the Key Point Summary as a guide to what you have just learned. If any of the key points are unfamiliar to you, review that section of the chapter.

✦ **Complete the assessment questions.** If you're unsure of an answer, make your best guess. When you're done, check your answers. For any incorrect answers, review the topic by re-reading the appropriate section of the chapter.

✦ **Complete the scenario(s).** Here's where you test how you would apply the knowledge learned in the chapter to a real-world situation, and then compare your results with the answers provided.

✦ **Perform the lab exercises.** This is where you gain practical hands-on experience with the information you've acquired.

✦ **Use the CD-ROM test engine.** After you've completed your study of the chapters and reviewed the Assessment Questions in the book, use the test engine on the CD included with this book to get some experience answering practice questions. The practice questions will help you assess how much you've learned from your study and will also familiarize you with the type of exam questions you'll face when you take the real exam. Once you identify a weak area, you can restudy the corresponding chapter(s) to improve your knowledge and skills in that area.

Tip   Be sure to also test your knowledge with the sample exam, which is the subject of Appendix C.

Exam prerequisites

This book assumes the same level of knowledge that the CIW Site Designer Exam assumes — that is, a broad general knowledge of HTML and of basic Web site development and management topics and technologies. Just as the CIW Foundations Exam (1D0-410) is a prerequisite to the CIW Site Designer Exam, knowledge of the foundations of Web development are a prerequisite for readers of this book.

Hardware and Software You'll Need

Although we've tried to keep requirements to a bare minimum, you will need access to various hardware and software to be able to do the Lab Exercises in this book. Here are what we consider to be the minimum hardware requirements, although you may be able to get by with less if you're creative and patient:

✦ Intel-based computer with Pentium/133MHz processor, 64MB of RAM, and 2GB of hard disk space.

✦ CD-ROM drive

✦ Access to the Internet

Optional equipment that you might benefit from using includes:

✦ Network adapter card

✦ Printer

Here's a list of the software you'll need: Windows 98, Windows 2000, or Windows NT is recommended, but many of the exercises in the book can be completed with other operating systems as well.

Making the most of this book's features

This book uses a number of standards and conventions to help you process the material efficiently. It's helpful to familiarize yourself with the following items before reading the book:

✦ **New terms.** There are many terms unique to site design. These terms can be confusing to novices. New or potentially unfamiliar terms, such as *transactional,* are italicized in their first appearance in the book. In most cases, we define a new term right after its first mention.

Unfamiliar words and acronyms can always be looked up in the Glossary at the end of the book.

✦ **Code and other special listings.** All code listings, URLs, tags (elements), values, and attributes in this book are presented in typewriter font, like this `<tag>` or listings like this:

```
<time>6:00 A.M.</time>
```

✦ **Sidebars.** These elements are used to expand upon the information presented when it might prove beneficial for you, the reader, in your overall knowledge of site design, but may not relate directly to your quest to prepare yourself for the exam.

✦ **Icons.** Several types of icons are used throughout this book to draw your attention to matters that deserve a closer look:

This icon is used to highlight a common mistake that could be made in working with the technology or topic being discussed. It represents our effort to steer you clear of potential problems.

This icon points you to another place in this book for more coverage of a particular topic. It may point you back to a previous chapter where important material has already been covered, or it may point you ahead to let you know that a topic will be covered in more detail later.

This icon points out important information or advice for those preparing to take the CIW Site Designer Exam.

Sometimes things work differently in the real world than how they are described in books and on the CIW Site Designer Exam. This icon draws your attention to our real-world experiences, which will hopefully help you on the job, if not on the exam.

This icon highlights the particular exam objective (all of which are listed at the beginning of each chapter) that's covered in the section where the icon appears. Use this visual clue to focus your study.

Tip This icon is used to draw your attention to a little piece of friendly advice, a helpful fact, a shortcut, or a bit of personal experience that might be of use to you.

How to Contact Us

We've done our best to ensure that this book is technically accurate and free from errors. Our editors and technical reviewer have also worked their tails off to achieve this goal.

However, there will inevitably be some items that we have overlooked. So, if you find an error, or have a comment or insight you'd like to share, please send us an e-mail message at `CIW-SD@lanw.com`.

We promise to read all of our readers' e-mails and include corrections and ideas in subsequent editions, if possible. Because of the high volume of e-mail we receive, however, it may not be possible to respond to each message. Please don't take it personally if you don't receive a reply.

And one last request: For technical issues with the software used in this book, please contact the software vendor.

Good luck on the exam!

Acknowledgments

Thanks and praise must go to Mary Burmeister for keeping us on track and helping us sound good. To the gang at LANWrights for their constant encouragement, to my family and friends for putting up with me, and for Eun, wherever she may be.

—Chelsea Valentine

First and foremost, I'd like to thank my husband, Robby, and my daughter, Alanna, for supporting me in my writing endeavors. With you both in my life all things are possible. I'd also like to thank Ed Tittel for giving me yet another opportunity to put pen to paper—or hands to keyboard—and to contribute to a quality publication. Last, but certainly not least, I want to thank Mary Burmeister for her exceptional management skills, for fine-tuning my thoughts and ideas, and for working with me regardless of the situation.

—Natanya Pitts

We'd also like to thank the numerous other contributors to this book, including John Paul Ashenfelter, Alexis D. Gutzman, Max Miller, Mercury Shell Murphy, and Janet Valade.

Contents at a Glance

Contents

Exploring Web Site Design Methodology

Basic Design Concepts

+ Site design and Web development

+ Tools and technologies in site design

+ Knowledge of HTML

+ Emerging Web technologies

CHAPTER PRE-TEST

1. What are the roles tools and technology play in site design?

2. Why can the Web be described as a one-to-one medium that is transactional in nature?

3. What are some of the aspects of print and broadcast media that are incorporated into the Web?

4. What are at least two principles of good site design?

5. Why is a strong knowledge of HTML a prerequisite for good site design?

✦ Answers to these questions can be found at the end of the chapter. ✦

In the last several years — since its inception and subsequent commercialization — the Web has become a common and relied upon medium for the dissemination of information. A single Web site is just a drop in the ocean that is the World Wide Web, but for the owner of the site, it's a key communication and information delivery tool. A Web site functions as an effective information delivery tool when it's well designed and has useful content that meets users' needs and expectations.

This chapter introduces the basic principles of good site design and explores the role design plays in the overall development and maintenance of a Web site. You'll also find out why strong Hypertext Markup Language (HTML) skills are an absolute requirement for any good site designer and what the present and future of site design technologies and trends holds. At the end of the chapter, you'll have a good understanding of general site design principles — the driving force behind this book and the CIW Site Designer Certification test.

The Web as a New and Unique Information Media

The Web is now as powerful a communication medium as print or broadcast. A healthy percentage of everyday people have some sort of Internet connectivity — be it through work, home, or both — and surf the Web regularly. Companies and organizations consider the Web to be as integral a part of the messaging solution as storefronts or business cards.

The Web impacts both business and personal life in a variety of ways, the chief of which is making information available 24 hours a day, 7 days a week. Location and time are no longer barriers to doing business, and companies can leverage this to present a continued presence in cyberspace — even when employees are fast asleep. Because the Web is always open, companies have come to rely upon their Web sites as an extension of their offices, to provide both information and services to visitors around the clock.

As the Web has evolved from a geek-centered information system to a full-blown medium for delivering data and services of all types, individual users have come to have certain expectations about what a Web site will do and how it will perform. Customers expect that a retail store with a Web presence will also have an electronic store — a combination of retail options termed *click and mortar* — and that anything they can buy in a *bricks and mortar* store, they can buy online (at any hour of the day, of course). There was a time when simple catalog lists were acceptable; however, users have grown accustomed to online presences that mimic real world ones — in inventory, service, and style.

Even if a company, organization, or individual isn't in the retail business, Web site visitors still expect a well-designed experience; one that includes useful information that is easy to get to. For example, when a visitor goes to an auto or home loan-lending site, he or she expects to find online tools for calculating payments and percentage rates. The visitor also expects to be able to submit an application from the comfort of his or her own computer. In addition, when the owner of a software package visits the software vendor's Web site, he or she expects quick and organized access to software updates and support.

In the early days of the Web, most sites were not much more than online brochures. A quick visit to any medium to large Web site today tells a different story. Web sites are service centers, information kiosks, and online stores. The Web has come into its own as a dynamic media that can reach any user any time of day through his or her browser window.

How the Web is different from traditional media

Although early Web pages behaved much like mass market media — books, magazines, brochures and the like — the Web isn't a mass-market media. Some existing site design approaches continue to treat the Web as an electronic billboard, but successful and seasoned designers know better. They've learned to leverage the unique capabilities of the Web and take advantage of its dynamic nature.

The Web also has the unique capability of connecting to mass-market media formats, taking the best of each, and putting them all together in the following ways:

✦ **Print publications.** The Web is designed to make content available — either to mass audiences or to targeted audiences — just like print publications. Color, graphics, and design elements enhance and support content published on the Web, just as they do in print publications. Good Web sites use quality content as their focal point, just as successful print publications do.

✦ **Broadcast media.** Broadcast media uses audio and video to convey a message in a way that text and graphics alone cannot. Most Web designers have learned their lessons from broadcast media, and a well-designed site uses audio and video judiciously to disseminate information. The Web is a broadcast mechanism in many ways, because pages published on the Web are available for some or all to see, just as television and radio broadcasts are. Broadcast TV uses cable subscription services to require payment for special or high quality content. Some Web sites, such as Consumer Reports, have successfully adapted this model to sell content.

✦ **Traditional software.** The introduction of databases and programming to Web sites has made it possible for Web sites to evolve into Web applications that behave in many ways like traditional software packages. Bill payment services provide a bill payment application, much like features you find in Microsoft Money or Intuit's Quicken. Web-based human resources applications are available to run over a company's intranet. More and more traditional client/server applications are being moved to the Web because they work from any system on the Internet, not just from a company Local Area Network (LAN) or Wide Area Network (WAN), and because they're easier to update. Web-based applications use common software paradigms such as function buttons and drop-down menus, and often emulate the look and feel of software packages to create an environment users are comfortable with.

Although the Web has taken much from traditional media, it's still its own media with its own strengths and weaknesses. The Web is different from traditional media in a variety of ways, including:

✦ **Mass media is passive whereas the Web is active or transactional.** Mass media sends the same static message to everyone in an audience, even when the audience is targeted. Database and Web programming technologies make it possible to tailor a Web site to an individual user. The Web is also a two-way street, with the user sending information back to the server as well as receiving it. This transactional approach to requesting and receiving data makes the Web an active media — often called *transactional* — where users interact with sites and content.

✦ **Print is linear whereas the Web is non-linear.** You read books, magazines, and brochures from front to back in a linear fashion. Even when you jump around in a print document, you're just moving from one point on a line to another. The Web, by design, is non-linear; therefore, you can skip from page to page in a site or site to site. The non-linear nature of the Web makes it easier to insert new information into a site or remove outdated information by simply changing a few links. You don't have to reprint the entire publication as you would with a linear book or magazine.

✦ **The Web can be more quickly updated and changed.** Print media has to be published and that takes time. Fixing a typo in a book requires the republication of the entire book. Fixing a typo on a Web site simply requires the republication of the page or even a piece of information in a database.

Software, on the other hand, is an executable — a traditional client-server application built in a proprietary language and designed for a particular operating system. You can't load a PC application on to a Macintosh or vice versa, because each is built with a different set of code. You have to install the software on a computer, and it isn't accessible from any computer that doesn't have it installed. Web-based applications, however, are designed to run in any Web browser or a sub-set of all available Web browsers and don't have to be installed to be accessible from any computer. In addition, a Web-based application can be accessed from any platform so you don't have to write the software two or three times to make it available on two or three platforms.

Although Web-based applications have their limitations — low bandwidth can make them slow, they don't work flawlessly in all browsers, and it's difficult to maintain state on the Web — they have overcome some of the tactical problems associated with traditional software applications.

Unlike most traditional mass-market media, the Web is a one-to-one experience that involves a single user requesting content from one or more Web servers to drive their Web experiences. Users can submit information to a Web site to interact with it and better control their information destiny. In the broadcast world, you can navigate through a system of information at a very high level (think of television channel surfing). However, in the one-to-one world of the Web, you control your navigation at a very granular level by choosing the sites you want to visit and what information on those sites you want to see.

As you might expect, designing Web sites includes design principles from print, broadcast, and traditional software but still requires its own unique approach, meeting user's needs and expectations and accounting for the unique nature of the Web.

Exam Tip   Know that the Web is a one-to-one medium and transactional in nature. Be able to describe how it's different from traditional mass media and print mediums.

Personalization is the key

The Web is truly a unique medium that supports dynamic user experiences backed by databases and business logic. You can't get that from a printed piece of paper or even a television broadcast. When the Web was first developed, it was static in nature. Every visitor to a Web site saw the same information and navigated the same paths through the site. A primitive move towards creating a Web experience tailored to the user was creating graphic and non-graphic sites designed to accommodate users with low bandwidth connections or with graphics turned off. Frames and no-frames sites followed.

Early attempts to create tailored Web experiences were hampered by a lack of technology and high maintenance costs. Most sites with multiple user experiences were coded and maintained by hand. As more and more tools were developed to make it easier to build Web pages and to drive them with programming and databases, the easier it became to create sites that would mold themselves to the user.

In today's Web world, a personalized experience is the status quo. Users expect that they can visit a site, choose to register and log in, and have the site dynamically tailor itself to their needs. Gone are the days of static pages where "one size fits all" or even "one size fits most." A prime example of the effectiveness of personalization is the Amazon.com site (www.amazon.com).

The more active a user is on the site, the more personalized his or her experience. Users can edit a list of interests so they receive new recommendations each time they visit the site. As users are more active on the site — both browsing and buying — the recommendations become more targeted and useful. Amazon.com uses cookies to track users, so each time a registered user returns to the site, even if the user isn't logged in, he or she is welcomed by name and with a list of recommendations and interesting products.

Cross-Reference Perform Lab 1-1 in this chapter to see an example of personalization on the Amazon.com Web site.

As the user browses the site and moves from product to product, the site keeps track of all viewed pages and generates a dynamic personal page detailing recent activity, titled "The Page You Made." Visitors can better keep track of the products they're interested in and see related products.

Although this obviously presents more selling opportunities for Amazon, it also helps users navigate through their extensive product listings and find what they're looking for when a simple search just isn't enough. Although Amazon can't replicate the in-store shopping experience, personalization touches such as this make each visitor's shopping experience less generic and more productive.

The role of site design in Web development

Objective Site design and Web development

Web programming behind the scenes makes advanced Web sites function, but it's Web design on the front end that makes the sites usable and attractive. When Web sites were simple, site design focused on good document organization, and making the content readable and accessible to as many users as possible. The complex functionality that you seem to find in most Web sites these days requires well-planned and thoughtful design to help the user move through a dynamically changing site.

In a nutshell, the role of site design in Web development is to be sure the Web site conveys the site content to the intended recipient. If you think of content as a message to be sent, the site is the sender and the user is the recipient. In today's Web world, good site design sends a personalized message to all recipients in a consistent and easy to understand way.

Site design isn't just about look and feel and graphics. The design of a Web site is its *user interface* (sometimes abbreviated as UI) — the entire user-facing piece of the site. Users view and interact with the site through its design and rely on it to guide them to the information or product they're looking for. Site design is comprised of different components, including:

✦ Messaging

✦ Branding

✦ Supporting the user experience

In the following three sections, you take a closer look at these components of design and how they're used successfully in real world sites.

Messaging

As mentioned earlier, the content of a site is its message and it's your job as the site designer to be sure that the recipients — the users — get the message with little to no hassle. A site's messaging strategy is going to be unique to the organization that puts up the site and the goal of the site itself. For example, the Hungry Minds Web site (`www.hungryminds.com`) is a corporate Web site whose goal is to tell the world about Hungry Minds and the other brands it supports, such as Frommer's travel books and CliffsNotes. The direct goal of the Hungry Minds site, shown in Figure 1-1, is to provide information about the company, links to the different brand Web sites, and Hungry Minds University.

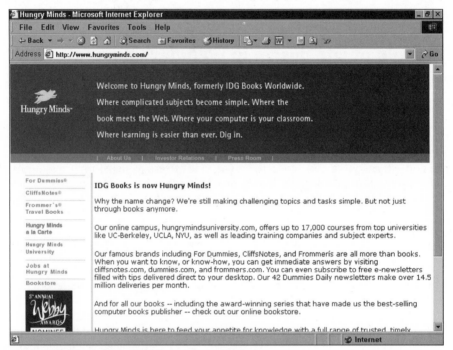

Figure 1-1: The Hungry Minds corporate Web site

The site design is very information driven. There are links at the top of the page to information about the company and for investors, as well as to press releases. Links to the company's brand sites are immediately visible on the left. Key information about who the company is and what it does is prominently displayed in the middle of the page. When you visit the site, you get an immediate snapshot of who the company is and what they do, and then you can choose where to go next to learn more.

Non-corporate sites have messages to convey as well and have the same design requirement to help guide users to pieces of the message. The World Wide Web Consortium (W3C) is a good example of a site that is very message driven and whose user interface is designed to facilitate information retrieval. The site's home page (www.w3.org), shown in Figure 1-2, uses a basic and clean design to facilitate linking to the vast resources on the site, as well as to provide information about the W3C itself.

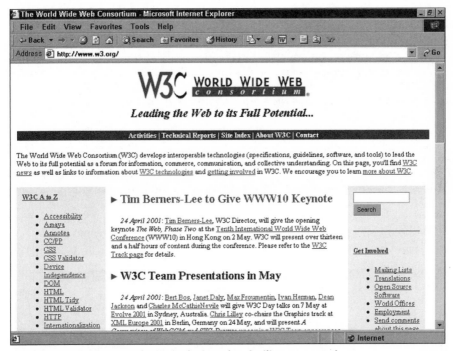

Figure 1-2: The W3C Web site is designed to facilitate messaging.

The navigation bar at the top of the page links to the most commonly accessed pieces of the site: activities, technical reports, a site index, an about page, and contact information. Chances are, users visiting the site can start in one of these key areas and find what they're looking for. A single paragraph following the navigation bar explains exactly what the W3C is and what its mission is.

The alphabetical list of links on the left side of the page are a substantial navigation tool that helps visitors to the site start down the right path to the information they're looking for. The search feature is prominently displayed at the top of the right-hand column for users who know what they're looking for. The middle portion of the page is devoted entirely to recent news. This is a boon for both new and repeat visitors. New visitors get an immediate idea of what the organization is about by reading about recent activities and events. Repeat visitors can quickly scan the news to keep track of the latest developments.

There's a saying on the Web that content is king, which can be translated to messaging is king. On all successful Web sites, the design elements work together to send a whole collection of messages to site visitors. However, there's often more to the site's message than the words on the page or the navigation scheme. Site branding goes a long way in conveying the organization's message.

Branding

Branding refers to a consistent look and feel of the Web site with the overall look and feel standards of the organization it represents. Although a Web site constitutes a considerable portion of a company's information delivery scheme, it isn't the only piece of the puzzle. All of the tools used to deliver a company's message need to be in synch and carry the same message — both textually and visually.

Microsoft is perhaps one of the best examples of branding done right. Regardless of what you get from them — software, computers, sales materials, newsletters, and even certification materials — you know at a glance it's from Microsoft. Its Web site carries the same kind of branding as all of its other communications tools and products. This further reinforces the Microsoft brand and message.

Another good example of a Web site where a company brand permeates all aspects of the site is the CliffsNotes site (www.cliffsnotes.com) shown in Figure 1-3.

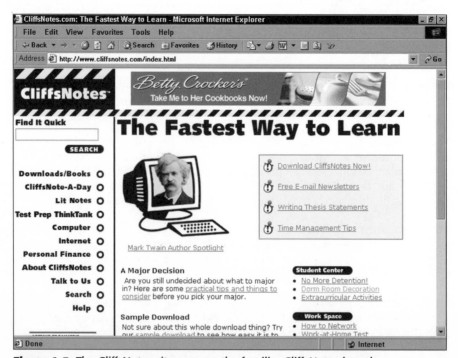

Figure 1-3: The CliffsNotes site conveys the familiar CliffsNotes brand.

The Web site itself feels like a CliffsNotes book thanks to the black, white, and yellow color scheme. But colors and graphics alone don't make the brand. The overall design of the site is compact and easy to move through — similar to the CliffsNotes we all remember so well from high school and college. Although the main focus of the site is to sell CliffsNotes, it includes useful information to promote the brand and help develop and retain customer loyalty.

The Lit Notes section of the site includes links to buy Adobe PDF versions of CliffsNotes as well as free resources on writing thesis statements, how to participate well in a course, and more. The Test Prep ThinkTank section has quick links to buy Test Prep books, and free information on test preparation and test taking strategies. The free information helps reinforce the CliffsNotes brand, because it's good information in an easy to digest format — what CliffsNotes strives to provide in all of its publications. The sample information on the site helps convince new customers that CliffsNotes publications are worth the money. The free information helps build brand loyalty by giving established customers a reason to come back to the site time and again. This gives the company an opportunity to showcase new products and drive repeat sales — which are the ultimate goals of branding.

Supporting the user experience

Beyond messaging and branding comes the user experience — which really ties messaging and branding together to help convey both to the user. The user experience is everything about how the site works as the user moves through it. Because the current trend in Web site development is towards heavily personalized Web sites that are driven by data, it can be difficult to create a cohesive design in which each user sees something different.

The key to designing a successful user experience for a dynamic site is thinking of the site as a collection of objects rather than a collection of pages. An object is something like a navigation bar or news story, and a page is built of a collection of objects. As a designer, you should concentrate on designing these objects so they work well together in different combinations, and their functions are intuitive to the user.

Creating a cohesive user interface that accommodates ever-changing content and advanced personalization is perhaps one of the most difficult design tasks a Web designer can face. The more you know about the technologies used to build a site, the easier it is to create a design that compliments the technology behind it. If you can exploit the strengths of the technologies to create a more useful user interface, you're well on your way to designing a successful site.

Just as it's useful for Web designers to have a working knowledge of the technologies that drive the site they're designing, it's equally as useful for technical developers to have a working knowledge of site design principles. A developer can build code that functions quickly and cleanly but doesn't support the design requirements of the site. If messaging, branding, and support for the user experience can't be easily accommodated by the technical design of the site, the site won't be successful. If technical developers know the user interface goals of the site and what it takes to create a successful user interface, they can better accommodate those goals.

User Interface Design Done Right

Amazon.com is a good example of a well-designed user interface for a very complex Web site with object driven Web pages. The top navigation unit of Amazon.com is consistent from page to page so users always have a familiar tool to guide them through the site.

Each page you visit on Amazon.com includes a collection of feature boxes, each of which holds a different feature or set of features, but that has a consistent look and feel. The title of the feature box is white text on a blue background and the top corners of the box are rounded. Standard icons show you what kind of merchandise you're looking at — books, music, electronics, etc. — even when the title doesn't. The middle of the page is always dedicated to content appropriate to where you are in the site.

Amazon also uses color changes to help keep users oriented as they move through the site. The prevailing color in the books section is Green and the feature boxes have a white text on a green background. The tabs are also green. The prevailing color in the DVD section is purple to give visitors a set of visual clues that they aren't in the book section anymore. Amazon.com is a good example of a site that uses consistent design features but with unique features for particular kinds of content.

There was a time when Web developers wore both the technical and design hats. As the technologies that drive Web sites have become more robust and complex, and the need for exceptional user interfaces has become evident, the technical and design development activities have split into two distinct activities. Developers work with designers to create an entire Web presence. When the two groups know a little bit about what the other is doing and can work together, the site has a better chance of success than when they develop their respective pieces of the site in a black box.

The evolution of site design

Our discussions of messaging, branding, and user interface design show that Web site design has evolved over time to include not only the look and feel of a site, but also all of its interactions with the user. Site designs are generally more refined and more complex than they were when the Web was a new medium. Designers don't build static pages that look the same to every user, but instead want to create a flexible interface that can change as personalization is applied to a site for each individual user.

Exam Tip   Know which specific areas have contributed to the growth of Web design and the Web in general in the last couple of years.

You've read about many of the factors responsible for the evolution of site design in the previous sections of this chapter. In reality, these factors have also contributed to the overall growth of the Web. You can distill them down into the following concise list:

✦ **Technology advances.** Not only is it possible to build Web sites based on complex logic, but new technologies such as Macromedia's Flash have made multimedia just another piece in the Web design puzzle. In the early days, it was difficult to integrate different media types into a Web site, but today the sky is the limit.

✦ **Data driven content.** Data stored in databases can be extracted and manipulated in hundreds of ways by computer programs rather than human hands. Data driven content makes personalization and dynamic Web sites possible. It also makes it more difficult to predict what users will see at any given time in their browser windows.

✦ **Transition from Web sites to Web applications.** The Web isn't just about displaying information anymore. Functional Web sites are the status quo now and require advanced user interface design to make them useful.

✦ **Sites have become specialized.** Web sites and even Web applications are no longer just about information. They are focused on a particular audience or function. Some of the most common site specializations are:

- E-commerce sites for selling goods and services

- Intranets that facilitate intra-organization communication

- Extranets that link select business partners and employees to a company's intranet using the Internet

Of all of the factors that have contributed to the significant change in the character of the Web and Web design, the specialization of sites is the most significant. Once the Web really got off the ground and organizations realized it wasn't just a passing fad, the application of Web technologies to a variety of business needs began in earnest. Intranets take advantage of Web technologies to help users in an organization access and share information. Whereas navigating a network or database may not be familiar to users, the Web site paradigm is, and intranets build on that familiarity.

Extranets are an extension of an intranet and allow select users outside of the organization to access the resources and information on an intranet. Resources can easily be shared among Internet, intranet, and extranet presences, because all three kinds of sites use the same technologies. You can easily leverage your intranet to create an extranet, or make approved company materials available to all users on both an intranet and a Web site.

Because there are so many different applications of Web technologies, the purpose of a site drives its design as much as the need to convey a message or branding. If you're designing a corporate intranet, the requirements and content will be different than if you're designing a Web site for the same organization. A good understanding of the purpose and goals of a site is crucial to a successful design.

The evolution of site design tools

The evolution of site design tools is as important to site design as the changes in site design requirements and theories. In the early days of the Web, a good text editor and graphics editor were the only two site design tools available to Web developers. All aspects of a site—HTML, graphics, and multimedia—had to be built by hand. Of course, this meant you had to know HTML to build Web pages, but it also meant that building and updating pages was a tedious process for even the most savvy developer.

Over time, site design and development tools have multiplied like proverbial rabbits. Today, you have a whole host of tools at your disposal to help you build and maintain Web sites. Many of these tools include a WYSIWYG (What You See Is What You Get) interface that hides HTML and even client-side scripting, such as JavaScript, and lets you concentrate on the business of design.

Caution   Because WYSIWYG development tools do all of the coding, you might be tempted to spend less time learning HTML and more time honing your design skills. Although we won't argue that the constantly changing world of site design makes it difficult to keep up as a designer, we highly recommend that you take the time to develop your HTML skills. You'll be a better designer for it and be able to pass the certification exams.

The early generation WYSIWYG tools were questionable at best. Many produced incorrect or messy HTML, and many would rewrite any HTML you'd crafted by hand. Although the intentions of the tool developers were good, the results weren't always usable. As the Web matured, so did the tools for building Web pages. The major development environments available today have been tuned over time to not only create good HTML, but also to provide you with a variety of features and functions that make the design, development, and maintenance processes easier and more efficient.

A good Web development tool has many benefits, including:

✦ **Access to a collection of technologies.** Most tools not only help you develop HTML, but also support JavaScript, possibly database connectivity, and even server-side programming, such as Common Gateway Interface (CGI). You can implement the right technology to meet your needs without becoming a guru in that technology.

✦ **A direct impact on productivity and efficiency.** Design tools tend to reduce the amount of time it takes to build a page, because coding by hand is usually slower than using the tool's buttons and pull-down menus. In most tools, you can quickly build a link using drag and drop and a complex table via a wizard. Support for templates in most tools makes it easier to create baseline HTML code that you or others can build on as you add new pages or objects to your site.

✦ **Access to the many different utilities required to develop and maintain a Web site.** A single Web development tool may include tools for managing files, editing graphics, uploading files to a remote server, and checking links. When these features are centralized in a single tool, development is faster simply because the tools are more accessible.

Two great examples of mature and feature-rich Web development tools are: Macromedia's Dreamweaver and Microsoft's FrontPage. Both are complete development environments that have support for both hand coding and WYSIWYG development. Both have utilities for managing all of the files in a site, checking links, and publishing the site to a Web server.

Later chapters in the book look at these two tools in detail. Chapter 13 focuses on FrontPage and Chapter 14 focuses on Dreamweaver. Chapter 21 includes information on how to use both tools to publish a site to the Web.

Even though tools such as Dreamweaver and FrontPage have matured over time and include a good collection of utilities to manage most aspects of a site, there's no perfect tool out there. Best practices in Web design include using a tool as just that, a tool, to supplement your own knowledge and make design activities more efficient. No tool is a substitute for knowledge. You need to know what you're trying to do before you use the tool to do it.

Be sure you have a working knowledge of the most common Web development tools, including FrontPage, Dreamweaver, HomeSite, and Flash. Ultimately, you'll most likely choose a tool or two that you use regularly. The goal of the test and this book, however, is to be sure you know what kind of tools are available, and how you combine them with your own knowledge and skills to design Web sites.

Choosing the right combination of tools and technology

Tools and technologies in site design

A central activity in Web site design is choosing the right combination of tools and technology to build your site. There's a whole host of technologies and tools to choose from, but the task can often be daunting. Should you build static HTML pages that incorporate some useful JavaScript code; build a dynamic, data-driven site that is heavily personalized; or do something in between? Which development tool or tools do you want to take the time to master?

Unfortunately, there are no right or wrong answers to these questions. The collection of tools and technologies that you use to build and drive your Web site is determined by your content, your audience, your available resources, and your goals for the site. When you evaluate tools and technology, remember that your goal is to create a messenger (the site) that can convey the message (the content) to the recipient (the visitor). If you keep this requirement firmly in your mind and let the principles of good site design lead you, you won't go wrong.

General Principles of Good Site Design

Surprisingly the principles of good site design aren't long or complex, but simplicity is always the safest path to travel. The previous sections of this chapter provided you with great detail on messaging, branding, interface requirements, and the type of site, and how they all affect the kind of site design you create. When you can mix those concepts with the following principles of good design, you'll be well on your way to a successful site:

✦ **Remember that the Web is its own media.** Even though the Web often resembles print or broadcast media, always remember that it's a one-to-one, transactional media that has its own advantages and issues. If you take advantage of the strengths of the media, as outlined earlier in the chapter, your design will be Web-centric.

✦ **All glitz and no content is bad (content is still king).** There was a time when creating multimedia was a difficult task that required a considerable amount of expensive equipment and knowledge. This simply isn't so any more. With a good computer, a digital video camera, and/or stereo audio system, you can create good quality multimedia and add it to your site. Tools such as Macromedia's Flash make it easy to build complex multimedia files and embed them in pages. However, if you get too lost in the glitz of multimedia and lose sight of the quality of the content, you sacrifice your brand and your message. Ultimately, people visit a site because they want to buy something or find something. Be sure they can find what they're looking for and that it was worth the effort to find it.

✦ **Give users what they want, not what you think they want.** A common mistake Web designers make is to build a site that reflects what they believe the users want but that isn't really what the users want. The intentions are good but the results are often bad. Remember that the site is about the users and their needs. As you design the site, focus on what you know about the users and their expectations of the site. If possible, talk to users and ask them to review your design ideas and give you feedback about what would make the site better.

✦ **Bandwidth is still a barrier.** The reach and speed of connectivity is growing by leaps and bounds, but not everyone has a Digital Subscriber Line (DSL) connection or a cable modem in his or her home. Some organizations still share T1 lines with others and there are even users out there that still use phone modems to dial up to the Internet. When you consider what design elements to use on your site—especially bandwidth heavy elements such as multimedia—consider your audience and what you know about their bandwidth. On a corporate intranet, bandwidth is not usually a problem, but if you're building a site for the general public, bandwidth is a key consideration. The more you know about your users and their connectivity, the better design decisions you can make.

✦ **Goal of the design should be to present a usable and intuitive user interface.** Always keep this principle firmly in the front of your mind as you design your site. Even when you're really ready to try a new technology or experiment with multimedia, always ask yourself if the design element is going to detract from the usability of the user interface or interfere with the user's experience in any way. If the answer is yes, try to think of a different way to use the element or save it for later phases of the project

In the Real World   As times change, so do the principles that guide good site design. The ones previously listed are appropriate to the current state of the Web and its role as an information dissemination tool. As Web technologies and applications change and evolve, so might some of these principles. We suspect, however, the idea of site design being all about creating a good user interface won't ever change.

Why You Need to Know HTML

Objective   Knowledge of HTML

Earlier in the chapter, you found out that it's very important—both for the purposes of the exam and for real-world design work—that Web designers know HTML. The ever-growing popularity of WYSIWYG tools, such as FrontPage and Dreamweaver, has fostered the idea that you don't need to know HTML. However, experience has taught us otherwise.

To build well-designed sites, you need an array of knowledge that encompasses a variety of topics, including:

✦ Web technologies, beginning with HTML

✦ Tools

✦ User interface design principles

✦ Content (messaging and branding)

All of these topics were discussed in other sections of the chapter, but it's important to understand that knowledge of HTML is a prerequisite for good site design. Regardless of the other technologies you use—JavaScript, multimedia, or server-side programming, to name a few—HTML forms the foundation of every Web page you create. When you're well versed in HTML, you can choose the right combination of markup to convey your message or drive your user interface.

Web browsers all display HTML just a little bit differently. When you're comfortable with HTML and the way different browsers handle it, you can tweak your HTML to work well in a variety of browsers. With your HTML knowledge, you can build complex pages and adjust them for performance — limiting nested tables, using height and width on images, and more — to make them download faster.

If you don't know HTML, you must rely totally on WYSIWYG tools, even if they build bad HTML or are out of date. When you want to adjust something in your HTML page, you have to work within the tool's parameters, which may not always support the changes you want to make. You also can't know if the HTML your tool is generating is well written or follows the latest specifications.

A knowledge of HTML can also help you choose the right design tool to meet your needs. Before you commit to a tool, you should use your knowledge of HTML to assess its functionality and output. You can evaluate the HTML it creates and the options you have for controlling that HTML. A good Web tool should allow you to leverage your knowledge and support the efficient and consistent development of Web pages. Before you use the tool to construct a page, you should have a good idea of how the page should behave and what HTML you want to use to drive that behavior.

As a final argument for learning HTML, remember that it isn't a programming language and it isn't really that difficult to learn. There are countless tutorials on the Web and a large selection of books available at your local or online bookseller. The time you spend learning HTML will be well spent and make you a better designer.

You'll find links to some of the HTML tutorials you can find on the Web in the "For More Information Section" at the end of this chapter.

The Future of Site Design

Emerging Web technologies

The state of Web design as we know it today won't last forever. Changing technologies, new applications of Web technologies, and new tools will all affect the way you design Web pages. Already on the horizon are collections of new technologies that are changing the way designers create a user interface. Among these technologies you will find:

✦ **Dynamic HTML (DHTML) and JavaScript.** DHTML combines HTML and client-side scripts written in JavaScript or VBScript to create HTML that users can interact with after the page is downloaded to their systems. A typical example of DHTML is images that change when a mouse pointer rolls over them. Other uses for DHTML are expanding and contracting menus and drag-and-drop objects on a page. Tools such as FrontPage and Dreamweaver have support for JavaScript and the responsibility for planning, and building DHTML falls often on the shoulders of the Web designer. DHTML can change your entire approach to designing a site and its features.

✦ **Cascading Style Sheets (CSS).** CSS is an advanced tool for defining the look and feel of a Web page. CSS has been around for a few years now, but only recently has it seen wholesale adoption by designers and browsers. CSS gives you more control over the layout of your pages than HTML alone can and is supported in mature design tools such as FrontPage and Dreamweaver.

✦ **Extensible Markup Language (XML).** XML is a markup language for defining markup languages. It lets you create your own markup tags that best fit your content and is the latest and greatest technology to hit the Web. Although you may not be building Web pages in XML any time soon, this technology has become a key part of many advanced Web solutions and may eventually replace HTML as the best way to create Web pages.

✦ **Browser advances.** Browser vendors have been adding new technologies and enhancing support for existing technologies almost since their inception. The capabilities of browsers will always drive changes in design methodologies, because the browser is responsible for the display of your design. You must walk a thin line between leveraging new browser advances and not leaving users who haven't upgraded to new browsers behind.

Cross-Reference We discuss JavaScript, CSS, and XML in more detail later in the book. Look to Chapter 11 for more information on CSS, Chapter 17 for information on JavaScript, and Chapter 19 for information on XML.

You don't have to use all (or any) of these technologies just because they exist. The technologies you choose for your site design should contribute to the overall usability of your site and help create a better user experience. Gratuitous technology doesn't impress users, especially if it hinders their ability to work with the site or find what they're looking for.

Key Point Summary

The topic of Web design is a rather large and complex one. Web design includes the look and feel of a site, the technology and tools used to create the site, and the message and branding the site needs to convey. Ultimately, site design is centered on creating an effective and attractive user interface that gives site visitors easy access to the information they're looking for. In this chapter you learned the following about site design concepts:

✦ The Web is a new and unique information media that has evolved over time from a rough information-posting system to a refined communication system that can be used for anything from customer support to retail sales.

✦ The Web integrates some elements of traditional print and broadcast media, such as a focus on conveying content, the use of graphics and layout to support content, and integration of multimedia elements. However, the Web is not a broadcast media but a one-to-one media that is focused on the individual user.

✦ Because users can request and send information to a Web server, the Web is transactional in nature rather than static like print or broadcast media.

✦ Most users expect personalized experiences when they visit Web sites; therefore, Web content must be able to mold itself to the user. Web programming makes personalized sites possible, but personalization presents a challenge to Web designers, because you never really know exactly what each user will see. Designing for personalized sites requires designing objects that can fit together in a way most meaningful to an individual user.

✦ Site design has a prominent role in Web development and is directly responsible for the delivery of the site's message, incorporation of branding, and presentation of an effective and intuitive user interface. Tools and technologies play a prominent role in site design, because they affect what mechanisms you have at your disposal for the creation of messaging, branding, and the user interface.

✦ Site design has evolved over time as the Web has evolved. The key factors that have driven the evolution of the Web — and subsequently site design — are technology advances, data driven content, Web applications, and specialization of Web sites as public facing, intranets, extranets, or e-commerce sites.

✦ New advances such as DHTML, XML, CSS, and browser improvements will further drive the evolution of site design.

✦ There are a few basic principles of good site design that should drive the development of the user interface for any site. Remember:

    • The Web is its own media.

    • Give users what they want and not what you think they want.

    • Bandwidth is still a barrier.

    • Always work to design the best possible user interface.

✦ To be a good site designer, you need to know HTML. WYSIWYG tools don't require knowledge of HTML for you to use them, but you need to know what drives the display of Web pages and how to manipulate it. You should use your knowledge of HTML to support your tool use and help you choose the best tools.

✦　　✦　　✦

STUDY GUIDE

Because site design is such a high-level topic, and there's so much to remember about it for the test, here's a study guide to help you practice what you've learned in this chapter. Use the assessment questions to test your knowledge, the scenarios to think about how you might use the knowledge in the real world, and the lab exercises to practice your skills. Be sure to look for the answers to the chapter pre-test questions, assessment questions, and scenarios in the "Answers to Chapter Questions" section at the end of this chapter.

Assessment Questions

1. What characteristic does the Web share with print media?

   A. It's linear in nature.

   B. It requires significant effort to fix typos and republish the content.

   C. It uses graphics and layout to enhance content.

   D. It's transactional in nature.

2. What factors affect the evolution of the Web and Web design?

   A. Technology advances

   B. Site specializations

   C. The evolution of Web applications

   D. All of the above

3. What is the role of site design in Web development?

   A. To convey the site's message using a well-developed user interface

   B. To create a site that provides a healthy contrast to an organization's standard brand

   C. To analyze ways to add as much multimedia as possible to a site

   D. To create the server-side code behind a data-driven site

4. What's the best approach to site design and development? (Choose the best answer.)

   A. Use a good WYSIWYG editor

   B. Combine a good WYSIWYG editor and your own knowledge of HTML

   C. Hand code all of the pages in a text editor

   D. Use either a WYSIWYG editor or a text editor but be sure not to mix the HTML they create

5. What should the primary goal of any Web site design be?

    A. To display the designer's technical and design skills

    B. To educate users about how a good user interface works

    C. To convey a different message to every user

    D. To create an intuitive interface that helps users find exactly what they're looking for

6. What technologies are already shaping the future of site design?

    A. XML

    B. CSS

    C. JavaScript

    D. All of the above

7. Which of the following is a benefit of knowing HTML?

    A. You can tweak the HTML a WYSIWYG editor creates to account for browser idiosyncrasies.

    B. You don't need any development tools to build Web pages.

    C. You can create server-side programs.

    D. None of the above.

Scenarios

You have a client who wants to build a new Web site that heavily utilizes multimedia elements, such as audio, video, and Flash. The site's primary audience is a group of educators who typically connect to the Internet with modems and older computers running older browsers. What arguments can you make to convey to the client why all glitz and no content is bad, and how do you begin steering site development in the right direction to create an effective user interface?

Lab Exercises

Lab 1-1: Evaluating Web site personalization

1. Go to www.amazon.com.

2. If you don't have an account with them, create one.

3. View items of interest in various categories — basically just shop around a little bit.

4. After you're done, close your browser.

5. Open your browser again and go back to the Amazon.com Web site.

6. If the "Your Recommendations" page doesn't appear, log in.

7. See what now appears as your recommendations and answer the following questions:

   • How does this personalization make you feel? Do you find it helpful, or does it make you uncomfortable?

   • Would you consider creating a site that has the same type of personalization functions?

Answers to Chapter Questions

Chapter pre-test

1. Tools help you use your knowledge to design sites. Technology provides you with a selection of mechanisms you can use to convey message and brand, and to build an effective user interface.

2. The Web is one-to-one because it delivers information to individual users on demand. The Web is transactional in nature because users can interact with the content on the Web, request only the parts they're interested in, and view dynamic content.

3. Similar to print, the Web uses graphics and layout to supplement content, and both are focused on content delivery. The Web is like broadcast media in that it can reach millions of users and can use audio and video to convey a message.

4. Good site design includes remembering that the Web is its own media, building an effective user interface that is focused on what most benefits the users, and remembering that heavy glitz and light content are not a good combination.

5. You need to know HTML because it's the foundation for all Web pages. When you know HTML, you're better prepared to make intelligent choices about what tools to use and to tweak the HTML the tool creates.

Assessment questions

1. **C.** The Web, like print, uses graphics and layout to enhance content. This information is covered in the section titled "How the Web is different from traditional media."

2. **D.** Technology advances, site specializations, and the evolution of Web applications all have an affect on the evolution of the Web and Web design. This information is covered in the section titled "The evolution of site design tools."

3. **A.** The role of Web design in Web development is to convey the site's message using a well-developed user interface. This information is covered in the section titled "The role of site design in Web development."

4. B. The best design development practice is using both a WYSIWYG, or other development tool, and your own knowledge of HTML to create HTML pages. This information is covered in the section titled "Choosing the right combination of tools and technology."

5. D. The primary goal of any Web site design should be to create an intuitive interface that helps users find exactly what they're looking for. This information is covered in the section titled "The role of site design in Web development."

6. D. XML, CSS, and JavaScript are all technologies that are already shaping the future of site design. This information is covered in the section titled "The Future of Site Design."

7. A. A benefit of knowing HTML is you can tweak the HTML a WYSIWYG editor creates to account for browser differences. This information is covered in the section titled "Why You Need to Know HTML."

Scenarios

Your best argument for convincing a client who wants to overdo glitz — sacrificing content and usability in the process — is to bring the client hard facts. Interview a small subset of the site's users or target users to find out what kind of Internet connectivity they have. You should also ask how they feel about a site that has a heavy multimedia focus and how that will affect the amount of time they spend on the site.

After you get feedback from users, put together a chart that shows how long different media pieces take to download, and then show the client what the users said about the affect long delays have on their visits to the site. As a next step, find out why the client wants to use a lot of multimedia, and find other solutions to the client's needs that are more audience appropriate. Create sample pages that show the client how your solution meets the client's needs and meets the user's needs. Focus on the elements of good site design the whole time and illustrate to your client how your design adheres to these elements.

For More Information

✦ **Information Architecture Tutorial.** http://hotwired.lycos.com/ webmonkey/design/site_building/tutorials/tutorial1.html

✦ **The Foundations of Web Design.** http://hotwired.lycos.com/ webmonkey/design/site_building/tutorials/tutorial3.html

✦ **Back to Basics.** www.webreview.com/1998/08_28/index.shtml: A compilation of basic Web design development articles.

✦ **Getting Started with HTML.** www.w3.org/MarkUp/Guide/

Page Layout and Design

EXAM OBJECTIVES

- ✦ Audience assumptions
- ✦ HTML tags for structure and formatting
- ✦ Web page layout
- ✦ Use of color in design
- ✦ Use of fonts in design
- ✦ Web usability

CHAPTER PRE-TEST

1. How is the Web different from the print medium?

2. How many seconds before users are likely to lose attention on a Web site?

3. What are a few of the basic layout components for a Web site?

4. What does the one and 10 second rule refer to?

5. How can you define color for a Web page?

6. How are fonts defined for a Web page?

7. What is a usability test?

8. What are the four usability elements?

Before you dive headfirst into the more specific topics in this book, it's important that you continue to build an understanding of Web design. Whether you're a Java programmer, or an HTML guru, you must be familiar with the design and page layout concepts that drive the Web. Expanding on the basic issues covered in the previous chapter, this chapter focuses more closely on the tools and technologies, with a view to getting your mind moving in the right direction.

Overview of Current Web Technologies

The Web has come a long way. Today, many people use the Web to find information necessary to their daily lives, rather than using other, more traditional means. It's not uncommon for you to reach for your browser instead of your telephone book to look up a telephone number. You may also go to `www.mapsco.com` before you take a trip to a new restaurant. Even trips to the grocery store may no longer be necessary because of the Web services available.

Businesses don't seem to mind this social transformation. With each new commercial or advertisement found in traditional media, you're likely to find a reference to a URL. It's easier for users to find businesses now, and that means it's easier for users to purchase products.

As a Web designer, you're in charge of "talking" to the users, and the design of a Web site is as important as the content. This idea may be upsetting to many, but it has become the norm. Bad designs scare users away.

To be competitive in the Web field — from the technical aspects to graphic design — you have to be familiar with Web design. There are technical and graphic design limitations that are direct results of design concepts. For example, a graphic artist may know how to create a perfect replication of the Mona Lisa, but without understanding the need for image optimization, users may never be able to see the Mona Lisa on the Web. Good design is essential for anything that makes its way onto a Web site. If you don't understand good design concepts, you're missing a big piece of the puzzle. This book is not just for those who want to make Web design their careers, it's also for those who work in other Web related fields that must understand how Web design might affect their work.

Web characteristics

 Audience assumptions

In the beginning, many Web designers thought of the Web as a way to broadcast their ideas or content to mass audiences. However, the nature of the Web allows you to take it a step further and establish one-to-one relationships with your users.

A user is more likely to have a more positive reaction to information or a product that is tailored for him or her, than a broadcast approach.

The *broadcast* approach is defined as a passive method, which means you hope to create enough interest so the viewer or reader will act on it. There's no interaction between the media and the user. For example, a commercial designer hopes that a viewer watches the commercial, and in turn, purchases the product. In this situation, there's a break between the two actions: first, the user watches the commercial; then, the user decides to purchase the product.

The Web is not passive, but transactional. It's interactive in that each move the user makes is based on the user's requests and server responses. For a company that sells a product on the Web, the experience is different for the user than it is with a commercial or other form of mass media. In this case, the user makes transactional decisions from within the site — from accessing the site, to navigating within the site, to shopping at the site, and then hopefully to returning to the site. At the same time, a user can decide to exit a site and visit another one at any time.

This book focuses on how to understand and use these transactional experiences to your benefit.

The direction of the Web

The Web is not what it once was. The direction of the Web has taken on a life of its own and is now moving in the following directions:

✦ Multimedia is taking on an expanding presence.

✦ The Web supports new types of data.

✦ Data-driven content is at the heart of many Web applications.

✦ Dynamic content allows Web pages to contain up-to-date information.

✦ E-commerce has taken the Web by storm.

The most notable of the previous items is e-commerce. The Web that once simply hosted documents, has become a mall.

Another direction of the Web is driven by intranets, which allow companies to "Webify" many of their in-house business processes. In addition, extranets are also attractive for business-to-business strategies.

Web technology and tools

Not too long ago, Web designers entered their HTML markup into plain-text editors by hand or by copying or pasting. There was speculation about creating a set of tools, such as WYSIWYG HTML editing tools, that would help the Web development process. Currently, there are many Web development tools in their fourth or fifth generations. For example, Dreamweaver is a WYSIWYG editor in its fourth generation. This complex HTML editor supports Dynamic HTML functionality, as well as complex forms and tables. Its newest relative, Dreamweaver UltraDev, supports the development of Active Server Pages (ASP), JavaServer Pages (JSP), and ColdFusion applications.

Tip   WYSIWYG stands for What You See Is What You Get, and is used to describe HTML editing tools that allow you to edit files as they would appear in the browsers, therefore, bypassing manual use of HTML. These tools have become highly popular; however, most serious Web designers like to do most of their markup by hand.

As a Web designer, you're expected to know at least a handful of these tools, many of which are covered in this book. More times than not, you're forced to manually create markup and use authoring tools. The main advantage to using WYSIWYG tools is that they are time savers.

Tip   The two HTML editors commonly used by designers are Macromedia's Dreamweaver (Chapter 14) and Microsoft's FrontPage (Chapter 13). Both of these tools, which are covered on the Site Designer exam, support basic and advanced HTML editing, as well as site management.

Moving beyond basic HTML editing, you'll find a treasure trove of multimedia authoring tools, such as Macromedia's Flash 5.0 and Adobe's After Effects. The most popular of these tools is Flash, which allows authors to create media-rich content that conserves bandwidth. Flash-based Web sites are popping up all over the Web.

Cross-Reference   Flash 5.0 and dynamic media are covered in Chapter 16.

Basic design concepts

The Web is in a constant state of creation. Unlike print media that has a tried and true methodology in place, the Web's rules and concepts continue to evolve. This is in large part because the Web is not static. Another reason is the relative age of the Web, which is fairly young.

As individuals begin to dive into the world of Web design, the first thought is to learn Flash, or some other multimedia tool, and get to work. The idea being that a truly great site is one that excites the user with the extensive use of multimedia. The truth is that multimedia, although exciting to many designers, can scare off the average user if not implemented carefully. Therefore, the most important element on any Web page is the content.

Content is king! Content is what users want, and it's why they visit a site in the first place. For some examples, visit the following sites:

✦ www.backrm.com/futrshws.htm

✦ http://nikebasketball.nike.com/nikebasketball/

The Battle between Mediums

Initial thoughts about Web design centered around print media. For example, if a company selling exercise equipment wanted to create a Web site, it would create a Web version of their product catalog.

The translation from print media to the Web did not work well. Print media is linear, and the Web is non-linear. Both mediums have different properties that require different approaches. The most significant property of the Web is that it's interactive. Whereas the print medium cannot personalize the experience for its users, the Web can. As designers, you'll be forced to think outside of the traditional print medium.

The first example does not use much multimedia, but what it does use is not effective. In addition to poor multimedia use, there's little organization to the content. Just trying to figure out what the site is all about can be quite a struggle.

The second example, found at Nike.com, uses tons of multimedia elements throughout the site. Each element tastefully adds to the user's experience. The site also allows the user to turn the sound on or off. In addition, the content is easy to find and navigate through.

When designing Web sites, you want to create a satisfying experience for your users. To simply excite them with multimedia, unless it's used wisely, is not going to help you achieve that goal. If you want to present your users with a satisfying experience, you need to plan for the following:

✦ Well-planned design

✦ Quality content

✦ Proper use of media

Reconciling design with technology

This book focuses on several tools and technologies available for designing Web sites. The technology available on the Web is constantly evolving, and the tools also constantly evolve to try to keep up. As a designer, and as you prepare for the CIW Site Designer exam, it's your job to keep up with the newest technologies and tools.

Later in this book, we focus on the following technologies:

✦ Cascading Style Sheets (CSS) — Chapter 11

✦ Extensible Markup Language (XML) — Chapter 19

✦ JavaScript — Chapter 17

We also focus on the following tools:

✦ Microsoft's FrontPage — Chapter 13

✦ Macromedia's Dreamweaver — Chapter 14

✦ Macromedia's Flash — Chapter 16

✦ Jasc's Paint Shop Pro — Chapter 4

Exam Tip The goal of this book is not to make you proficient in each technology and tool listed. For the exam, you're just expected to have an understanding of each technology and tool. You should be able to identify how each tool can benefit your company's goals.

HTML review

Objective HTML tags for structure and formatting

Before you prepare for the CIW Site Designer Exam, it's important that you already know your HTML. Because the CIW Foundations Exam is a prerequisite to the CIW Site Designer exam, you should already be familiar with the following:

✦ Basic document structure tags. `html`, `body`, `head`, and so on

✦ Formatting tags. `font`, `basefont`, `i`, `b`, and so on

✦ Hyperlinking and image tags. `a` and `img`

✦ Frame tags. `frame`, `frameset`, `iframe`, and `noframes`

✦ Form tags. `form`, `input`, `button`, and so on

Take a few seconds to look over the following markup. If you don't understand any of it, take some time out to review the HTML tag set at `www.w3.org/TR/html4/index/elements.html`.

Cross-Reference For a far more detailed look at HTML and the role it plays in successful Web site design, see Chapters 7 through 9 in Part II of this book.

```
<!DOCTYPE HTML PUBLIC "-//W3C//DTD HTML 4.0 Transitional//EN"
  "http://www.w3.org/TR/REC-html40/loose.dtd">
<html>
<head>
  <title>Sample HTML</title>
  <style type="text/css">
    body {
          font-family: Arial;
          color:gray;
          font-size:11pt;
          }
```

```
      td {
          background-color: blue;
          color:black;
          }
   </style>
</head>
   <body bgcolor="#ffffff">
      <img src="logo.gif" alt="Company Logo">
      <p>Providing over 100,000 people with online training!</p>

      <table width="97%" border="0" cellpadding="10">
        <tr valign="TOP">
        <td width="5%" align="CENTER">
          <a href="books.htm">
           <img src="graphics/books.gif" alt="Books" align=
           "RIGHT" border="0">
            </a>
          </td>
        <td width="45%">
          <p><a href="books.htm">Books</a><br></p>
          <p>Detailed descriptions of LANWrights' books, sorted
          by type,including pointers to associated Web sites.</p>
        </td>
        <td width="5%" align="CENTER">
         <a href="showcase.htm">
           <img src="graphics/showcase.gif" alt="Web Technology
           Showcase" border="0"></a>
</td>
<td width="45%">
<a href="showcase.htm">Web Technology Showcase</a><br>
   Java examples and demonstrations of recent adventures
        on the cutting edge.
</td>
</tr>
<tr valign="TOP">
<td width="5%" align="CENTER">
  <a href="training.htm">
  <img src="graphics/training.gif" alt="Training Center"
align="RIGHT" border="0">
  </a> </td>
<td width="45%">
   <a href="training.htm">The Training Center</a><br>
   Read about our classroom and online training offerings,
   demo our online training, and learn more about our
   Java-based, XML-driven test engine.
</td>
<td width="5%" align="CENTER"><a href="corporat.htm">
   <img src="graphics/corporat.gif"
   alt="Coporate Services" border="0"></a> </td>
<td width="45%">
<p><a href="lanw.htm">Corporate HQ</a><br>
</p>
```

```
<p>Learn more about LANWrights, including available services
and rates. Read staff bios, and review our corporate
history.</p>
</td>
</tr>
    </table>
      </body>
</html>
```

Effective Page Design and Layout Components

 Web page layout

When many of us think of page design and layout, a newspaper or magazine comes to mind. Most print media has distinctive layout features. For example, a magazine has a cover that provides headlines for the articles provided within the magazine. If you flip through some of the first few pages, you'll find the magazine's table of contents that provide a page number that references the associated article. The page references are similar to links.

This style of magazine or newspaper layout is often called an *inverted pyramid*. The first few pages provide an overview — arranged from the most significant to the least significant content elements — with references (or links) to the full story; and the lead sentences of each story also contain its most important elements, whereas the final sentences may contain links or references to related but non-essential topics and information.

 Exam Tip It's important that you understand the basic concept of the inverted pyramid for the exam.

Think of an online magazine, such as Slate.com (`http://slate.msn.com/`). The online design uses a similar layout to a print magazine. That is because the inverted pyramid design is perfect for the Web. Instead of references, the Web uses hyperlinks to link to additional information.

Layout components

As a Web designer, you must be familiar with all the basic Web page layout components, and how those components interact with each other. Page layout refers to how content is presented to the user. The layout should be structured and easy to follow. Your Web site should have a consistent structure throughout the site, using similar layout components on each page.

Each Web page will most likely include several of the following layout components:

✦ **Framesets.** Allow the designer to display multiple pages at the same time

✦ **Margins.** Control the amount of whitespace between the content and the browser window edges

✦ **Borders.** Provide a border for HTML tables and frames

✦ **Color.** Can be used to help define organization for a Web site

✦ **Navigation.** The component that helps users move through a Web site and locate information

✦ **Rules.** As in hard rules, can be used to divide content into sections

✦ **Whitespace.** Eliminates clutter on a Web page and can be used to separate content

✦ **Tables.** Present data in a tabular format or position elements on a Web page

✦ **Lists.** Provide content in a list format

✦ **Paragraphs.** Group blocks of text into logical sections

✦ **Divisions.** Divide sections of content into logical, larger sections

✦ **Headings.** Organize content in an outline format

✦ **Images.** Capture the user's attention or provide information

Layout formats

Users do not like to be surprised: the more familiar the layout, the easier your site is to navigate. If you're selling a product, your goal should be for the user to be able to locate a product in only a few clicks. Most Web sites use common layout components and a basic structure. For example, if you visit the following Web sites, you'll notice that they all use the same basic layout structure:

✦ www.amazon.com

✦ www.bn.com

✦ www.apple.com

Each document in these Web sites uses a tabbed layout, where the navigational elements are defined at the top of the document. There are several common navigational placements for a Web page, such as in the left-margin, the top-margin, and even in the bottom-margin.

There are other common layout components, such as white backgrounds, location of the company logo in the upper-left corner of the Web page, or blue underlined hyperlinks. Users have come to expect many of these common elements; therefore, you should consider each of them carefully.

The primary concern for layout decisions centers around the placement of the navigational elements. Depending on the type of content you're presenting, you'll most likely choose one of the following basic layout designs:

✦ **Left-margin.** The navigational elements are defined in the left-margin, allowing the content to take up the remaining width of the window. Figure 2-1 shows a real-world example.

Figure 2-1: www.cliffsnotes.com uses the left-margin layout.

✦ **Top-margin.** The navigational elements are defined in the top-margin, allowing the content to fill the remainder of the window. Figure 2-2 shows a real world example.

✦ **Left + Top-margins.** The navigational elements are defined in the left and top-margins. In many cases, general navigation, such as Help and Contact are defined in the top-margins, and page-specific navigation is identified in the left-margin. Figure 2-3 shows a real world example.

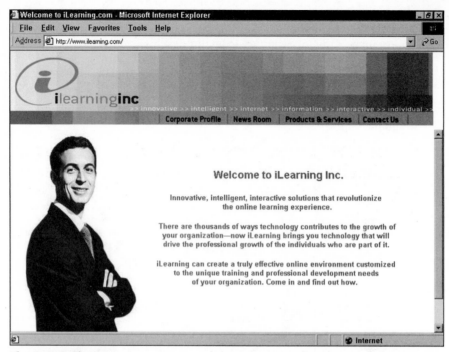

Figure 2-2: The www.ilearning.com home page uses the top-margin layout.

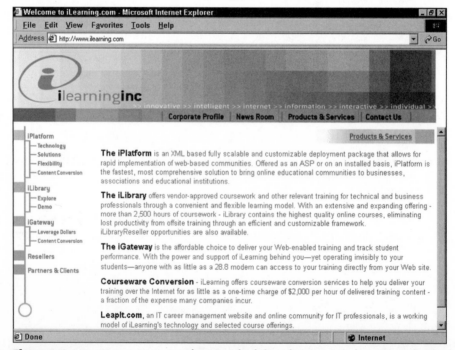

Figure 2-3: www.ilearning.com also uses the left and top-margin layout in sub pages.

✦ **Right-margin.** The navigational elements are defined in the right-margin, allowing the content to take up the remaining width of the window. We couldn't easily find a site with a right margin layout because it's not very common.

✦ **Distributed.** Last but not least, a distributed layout uses navigational elements in several sections of a Web page. This design is common for online news services, such as CNN.com. or CNet.com. Figure 2-4 shows a real world example.

Figure 2-4: `http://frommers.com/` uses the distributed layout.

User's attention

If your page does not download within 7 to 10 seconds, chances are you've lost your user's attention. After one second, user's are already feeling interrupted. Time is of the essence, and as a Web designer, time is not on your side.

In the Real World Many designers refer to the one and 10 second download times as the one and 10 second rule. If your page fails the 10-second rule, you should go back to the drawing board.

The Web is not a fast medium, regardless of bandwidth and processor speed, there are several steps involved in retrieving a Web page on the Web. First, the user must request the page. That request is then sent to a server, which collects the necessary content and sends it back to the client browser. Each time a user selects a hyperlink for the first time, this retrieval process is repeated. You can't control or circumvent that process; however, there are other elements to page design that you can control that will speed it up: namely, file size.

Exam Tip   Studies have shown that users feel interrupted after one second of download time and they lose attention after 10 seconds of download time. Keep these download statistics (the one and 10 second rule) in mind, because they may appear on the exam.

The key to a quick download is file size. Page size is the sum of all the file sizes for a given page. For example, if a Web page references five images, the images' file sizes factor into the overall page size. Images can really slow things down because they tend to be large and, therefore, add to your page size.

Cross-Reference   Various ways of optimizing images are covered in detail in Chapter 4.

The first step is to optimize all your images using a program such as Macromedia's Fireworks or Jasc's Paint Shop Pro. After your images are optimized, your page size will be significantly smaller. Table 2-1 demonstrates the maximum total page size that will result in the one or 10 second rule. Note that cable modems and Digital Subscriber Line (DSL) connections have a response time between the ISDN and T1 connections (closer to T1 connections).

Table 2-1 Page Size and Response Time		
Download method	*1-second response time*	*10-second response time*
Phone modem	2KB (kilobytes)	34KB
ISDN	8KB	150KB
T1	100KB	2MB (megabytes)

Exam Tip   It's important to note for the exam that a study conducted in 1997 found that the average Web page size was 44KB. That file size was even too large for optimal response times when users were accessing the Web with an ISDN connection.

If your pages download in one second, the user's experience is not interrupted and he or she will feel as if he or she can navigate freely throughout your site.

In the Real World One way to keep your download speed in perspective is to realize that users can find hundreds of sites just like yours. For example, if you sell coffee beans, you can be sure that a user can find at least a dozen other coffee bean distributors on the Web. If your site takes too long to download, the users will jump back to a search engine and find your competition.

Screen resolution

Although speed is crucial to keeping a user interested, screen resolution is a close second. It's best to design Web pages for a screen resolution of 640x480. This screen resolution prevents most users from having to scroll from left to right — something most users dislike.

This optimal screen resolution follows the design tactic of a "screen full." You want to prevent users from having to scroll at all. This is because studies have found that users rarely scroll; in most cases, they just scan the displayed content. For example, we've created two Web pages. The first, shown in Figure 2-5, demonstrates a screen resolution of 800x600. The second, shown in Figure 2-6, demonstrates the same Web page with a screen resolution of 640x480.

Figure 2-5: A screen resolution of 800x600 only requires users to scroll vertically.

Figure 2-6: A screen resolution of 640x480 requires most users to scroll horizontally and vertically.

The lesson here is that you want your pages to download in less than 10 seconds, and when they do, they should fill the user's screen with a screen resolution of 640x480. Therefore, our example needs to be modified to fill the 640x480 screen without the users having to scroll (horizontally at least).

Colors, Fonts, and Whitespace

Color is everywhere on the Web. Most users rarely notice the importance role color plays on the Web. However, as a designer, you'll come to use color for everything from grabbing your user's attention to providing an organizational feature for your site. There are several advantages to using color on your Web site:

✦ **Helps define a company's culture, style, and mood.** If you visit Macromedia at (www.macromedia.com/software), you'll notice that each product site (and each product package) has its own color. These are all bright colors such as pink, red, green, and yellow. Bright colors give the impression that the company is flashy, young, and exciting. However, more subdued colors, such as gray, navy, or white, tend to indicate more of a traditional and conservative corporate message. Check out www.hungryminds.com for an example.

✦ **Provides organization.** After you've selected your Web site color palette, you're ready to use the colors in your site. Color should be used consistently throughout your site. For example, all heading levels should use the same color scheme on each page. This allows the user to quickly identify your Web site's organization.

When planning color on a Web site, there are several questions you should ask yourself:

✦ Are my color choices complementary?

✦ How many colors should I use?

✦ Does the background color for the site work with the color scheme?

Color basics

 Use of color in design

There are several concepts that you must grasp when working with color. It would be ideal if you could choose your favorite periwinkle blue for your Web site; however, there are some limitations you should consider, such as computer monitor display limitations. That's right: computer monitors can limit what the user sees, so you must be familiar with how the computer monitor interprets color.

A computer monitor uses pixels, and each pixel displays one color at a time. When you're viewing an image, you're actually viewing a collection of pixels. Each pixel in the collection displays one particular color that when combined, creates the image on the screen.

Tip Pixel stands for "picture element," and it's a single dot on a display screen.

In the print media, all colors use a combination of cyan, magenta, yellow, and black. This color combination is known as CMYK. As you add more color to the mix, the CMYK inches closer to the color black. This combination of color is known as *subtractive*. To create a color other than black, you subtract color.

On the other hand, RGB is a color scheme that consists of red, green, and blue. This combination of color is known as *additive*. The more colors you add, the RGB inches closer to the color white. To create a color other than white, you subtract color.

The Web uses RGB as its color scheme. Each color can be described with a predefined color name, or by using one of the following two numeric color formats:

✦ RGB values

✦ Hexadecimal code

Tip The predefined color names are aqua, black, blue, fuchsia, gray, green, lime, maroon, navy, olive, purple, red, silver, teal, and yellow.

We cover both numeric formats in the following sections.

Color Models and Printing

CMYK is the standard color model used in offset printing for full-color documents. Because such printing uses inks of these four basic colors, it's often called four-color printing.

In contrast, display devices are generally RGB. One of the most difficult aspects of desktop publishing in color is color matching—properly converting the RGB colors into CMYK colors so that what gets printed looks the same as what appears on the monitor.

RGB values

Each RGB value works within base-10 numbers that range from 0 to 255. RGB values are additive, which means white is defined as:

- ✦ R=255
- ✦ G=255
- ✦ B=255

However, if you wanted to define red, it would be defined as:

- ✦ R=255
- ✦ G=0
- ✦ B=0

To use these values, you define them in a comma-separated list. For example, red would be defined as 255,0,0. To add these colors to HTML, you can use the following syntax:

```
<td bgcolor="255,0,0">
```

 In the Real World The HTML specification only permits the use of hexadecimal code or predefined color names. Because of this, many designers shy away from using RGB values.

What if you want to create periwinkle blue? Luckily, you don't have to figure out the RGB values in your head, someone has already done it for you. There are plenty of sites you can visit to find this information. We've listed some of our favorites at the end of this chapter.

Hexadecimal code

Hexadecimal code defines colors using a pound sign followed by 6 characters. The six characters are made up of three pairs of values ranging from 00 to FF (0, 1, 2, 3, 4, 5, 6, 7, 8, 9, A, B, C, D, E, F). The value of 00 represents no color, and on the opposite spectrum, the value of FF represents maximum color.

For example, the color white is defined as:

✦ Red=FF

✦ Green=FF

✦ Blue=FF

If you wanted to create the color red, it's defined as:

✦ Red=FF

✦ Green=00

✦ Blue=00

If you wanted to use hexadecimal code with an HTML document, you could add the following markup:

```
<td bgcolor="#FF0000">
```

You should notice a correlation between RGB color values and Hexadecimal code. Table 2-2 defines some of the Web's basic colors using both numeric values.

Table 2-2 Common Color Values		
Color	*RGB*	*Hexadecimal*
Red	255,0,0	FF0000
Green	0,255,0	00FF00
Blue	0,0,255	0000FF
White	255,255,255	FFFFFF
Black	0,0,0	000000

Using browser-safe colors

There are literally millions of color combinations you can define using RGB and Hexadecimal code; however, Netscape Navigator and Microsoft's Internet Explorer, only guarantee support for 216 colors. Each browser can only support up to 256 colors, and 40 of these colors are used by the operating system. This means that you should use the 216 colors to be safe.

What if you use a color that is not among the proud 216? Chances are the browser will engage in the process of *dithering*, by which it approximates the color to the closest browser-safe color that it supports. Table 2-3 defines a browser-safe color palette. The palette defines values that are supported by both browsers.

Table 2-3 Browser-Safe Color Palette	
RGB	*Hexadecimal*
0	00
51	33
102	66
153	99
204	CC
255	FF

To use the color-safe palette, you can select any combination of the defined values. For example, you could use any of the following combinations:

✦ #00FFCC

✦ #663300

✦ #33FF99

✦ #FF0033

✦ #CCFF66

Exam Tip   Color combinations are important for a Web site and a key issue on the exam. The most common color combination is black text on a white background, with other colors defining headings, images, and logos. The black text on a white background is thought to enhance readability because of its high contrast. Many usability studies support this theory.

Implementing fonts

Objective   Use of fonts in design

Now that you know about adding colors to the Web, it's time to turn your attention to fonts. As the Web has evolved, so has the use of fonts. There are several fonts to choose from; however, there are some that are consistently used in site design:

✦ Times New Roman and Arial for the PC

✦ Times and Helvetica for the Macintosh

In the Real World   If you use an obscure font that users might not have installed on their systems, you should provide a place for users to download the font.

There are some limitations to using fonts. Although there are many fonts to choose from, for users to view those fonts, they have to be registered on the user's system. If the user's system does not have a particular font, the browser will render its default font in its place (commonly Times New Roman for the PC and Chicago for the Mac).

Exam Tip   You can define fonts using the HTML `<font>` and `<basefont>` elements, as well as define fonts using Cascading Style Sheets (CSS). Keep this in mind as a possible exam topic.

Serifs

Serif fonts are defined by small decorative strokes at the end of a letter's main strokes (this is a serif font). They're readable in medium font sizes; however, readability suffers for small and large font sizes. There are four serif designs: Old Style, Transitional, Modern, and Slab Serif.

Sans serifs

Sans serif designs are those fonts that do not have serifs — the decorative strokes at the end of the letter's main strokes. These fonts work well in medium sizes, but are recommended for smaller and larger font sizes, such as copyright information and headings (this is a sans serif font).

Exam Tip   Whether you choose to use serif or sans serif fonts, it's important that you be consistent. For example, all navigation should be defined using the same font and all paragraph text should be in the same font.

Font size

HTML does not allow designers to define specific font sizes. Instead, you have to use numbers from 1 to 7. Most browsers define a default font size of 3. In addition to using sizes 1 to 7, you can define relative sizes using a plus (+) or minus (-) sign. Table 2-4 illustrates some examples.

Table 2-4 Font Size Examples	
Example	*Description*
`<font size="3">`	Because 3 is the default font size, there's no change in font size
`<font size="+1">`	Increases the font size to one higher than the base font
`<font size="-1">`	Decreases the font size to one lower than the base font

In the Real World There are some problems achieving consistent font sizes between the Macintosh and PC. Macintosh computers display font types at 72 dpi, whereas PCs display font types at 96 dpi. This translates into the Macintosh display being smaller than the same font displayed in a PC.

TrueType

A TrueType font is one that can be rendered in any font size without suffering from poor image quality. Developed by Apple Computer, TrueType is now used by both the Windows and Macintosh platforms. A few examples of TrueType fonts are Arial, Times New Roman, Georgia, and Verdana. Because they do not suffer when scaled, they increase readability.

Anti-aliasing

If you've used Photoshop or Paint Shop Pro, you're probably used to anti-aliasing. When graphics are used to represent letters, the *anti-aliasing* process smoothes the edges of each letter, thereby increasing readability. Although the file sizes tend to be larger, they sure make your page easier to look at.

Font tips

Here are some tips that will help you when you work with fonts:

✦ Avoid long horizontal line lengths.

✦ Consider how the font contributes to your design.

✦ One font cannot serve all purposes.

Whitespace and readability

Whitespace can make or break a Web page. Studies have shown that users only absorb 25 percent of what they see on a screen. The more cluttered the page, the less the user can absorb. Therefore, whitespace in your page layout is essential to good design.

Exam Tip Each Web page should contain 50 percent less content than a printed version of the same information. This is because users pick up less on the screen than they do on the printed page.

You also have to keep in mind that the screen is harder on the eyes than the printed page. Although there have been wonderful advances in monitors, they're not yet equal to the ease of reading the printed page.

Users are also less likely to read everything on a Web page. In fact, users typically just scan Web pages to grab the information they need.

To aid in readability, there are several techniques employed by designers:

✦ **Page layout using transparent GIFs.** Transparent GIFs can be inserted as a blank space place holder. You can manipulate the height and width of the transparent image to take up the exact amount of whitespace needed. For example, you can indent a section by adding the following tag:

```
<img src="transparent.gif" height="2" width="10"
alt="spacer">
```

✦ **Page layout using tables.** Designers have been using tables for layout for a long time now. All you have to do is turn the border off, and you have a layout tool ready for use. Although this is not what tables were intended for, it makes your life as a designer easier.

✦ **Page layout using frames.** Although frames are more commonly used to aid in navigation for a site, they can also be used for layout. You can turn frame borders on or off. When in the off position, the user can't tell that the frame is even there.

✦ **Page layout using positioning.** Although not all browsers support Cascading Style Sheets (CSS) positioning, it will one day make designers' lives a breeze. Currently, however, there's a compatibility problem, because Netscape Navigator uses the `<layer>` tag for positioning and Internet Explorer conforms to the W3C's CSS specification.

Defining and Executing Usability Tests

 Objective   Web usability

To some, usability is the most important concept to Web design. At the heart of creating a usable Web site is understanding your audience. For example, if you're selling hearing aids from your Web site, you'd most likely decide against using music as a multimedia element. However, if you're selling CDs, you might want to offer some music on your site.

One of the first steps in understanding your audience is to uncover its demographics, gathering information such as age, education, location, and income. In addition to gathering information about the users, you also need to ascertain the types of technology your users can support, such as connection speed, browser versions, and plug-ins.

Usability can be categorized into the following elements:

✦ **Quality control.** The quality of information is what the user is ultimately looking for.

✦ **Ease of navigation.** Users need to be able to navigate your site with ease. If users cannot navigate to their desired locations within three clicks, they're likely to leave your site.

✦ **Information architecture.** The organization of your information can make or break a site. A user needs to be able to locate your information.

✦ **Search capability.** Most users like the option of searching for their content; therefore, it's wise to include search capabilities on your site.

Each of these elements has equal importance and the combination of these elements is what makes up usability.

Technology

As the Web evolves, it appears that users are reluctant to follow. Studies have shown that as Web innovations increase, users favor the familiar and therefore, don't embrace the new innovations.

As the Web grows, it develops expectations for the user experience, and users are expecting that all Web pages conform to those expectations. For example, most users expect that blue underlined text is a hyperlink. If you decided that your hyperlinks should be defined in black, some of your users may not be able to identify your hyperlinks right away. Users have also come to expect an off trigger for any music that begins when the page downloads. Changing this behavior would confuse your audience.

One way to solve this problem is to advance Web design slowly. As you create a new site, it can follow conventions expected by users while still introducing some new innovations. As these new innovations take root, some will eventually be incorporated into standard Web design and, consequently, the expectations of users.

As for browsers, studies show that the amount of time it took users to upgrade their browsers from 3.x to 4.x took twice as long as upgrades from 2.x to 3.x. This means that users are not upgrading browsers nearly as quickly as they once did. There are several reasons for this slow upgrade rate:

✦ Upgrade download sizes have increased; therefore, upgrades require more time.

✦ The advantages to upgrading a browser have diminished from past upgrades.

✦ Many users don't know how to upgrade their browsers.

✦ Some browser upgrades require users to make software or hardware upgrades as well, and some users aren't financially able to make those upgrades.

✦ Newer users are not as technically adept as the early user base and are therefore more interested in content than upgrading their browsers.

Testing

The best way to make sure your site is usable is to conduct a usability test. Most designers like to think they can anticipate what a user will have trouble with, but that's just not the case. As the designer, you already know how to navigate the site.

A usability test will examine the site's effectiveness and should look at the four usability elements listed earlier.

Before testing, you need to make sure that your site is as close to finished as it can be. Testing on a site that is in production might not be that helpful or accurate.

Test pool

Your testing pool should be made up of participants (five or more is suggested) who have never visited your Web site before. This means that project team members should not be part of your testing pool. First, you need to determine your target audience's demographics, and then find participants who fall within that demographic. For example, if you're testing a site that sells networking products, you probably don't want any children in your testing pool.

Usability tasks

The usability test should be scripted with specific tasks. If users are not asked to participate in particular tasks that will mimic a real world scenario, they're not likely to locate significant problems. For the test, be sure to provide a list of tasks for each participant. However, be sure not to identify how to complete each task — remember that you're testing to see if a user can figure the *how* out for themselves. The test script should also ask each participant to jot down components they like and dislike.

Once the participants are ready to begin, leave the room. Although many of you probably want to watch participants' reactions, it's not helpful. As a matter of fact, it could disrupt the test and alter the results. If you must watch the participants, use a video camera or some other unobtrusive method. (Note that you should inform the participants if you're using a video camera.)

Analyzing the results

Before allowing your testing pool to walk out the door, be sure to follow up with a few questions to trigger any last minute observations. For example, you might want to include the following questions:

✦ What was your first impression?

✦ Was the site structure well organized?

✦ Can you remember the site's metaphors or theme?

When analyzing the results, it's important to look at trends in answers. Did multiple users note similar problems with the site design? If one user notes poor navigation, it's not that significant; however, if multiple users note poor navigation, you need to revisit the design.

After you analyze the results, it's time to make the necessary changes. It's rare to experience a usability test that doesn't produce some criticism or suggestions for change. Your first experience with a usability test may leave you feeling a tad defeated. Don't take it personally. After all, the feedback will only make your Web site better.

Key Point Summary

This chapter was chock full of practical information on page layout and design, all of which is aimed at preparing you for the rest of the book. The following concepts were covered in this chapter:

✦ Understanding your users is the key to defining your site, and selecting the appropriate technologies and tools.

✦ To complete this book and the CIW Site Designer exam you need to be comfortable with HTML.

✦ The use of color and fonts are important design elements and can also help set the mood for a Web site.

✦ There are several techniques for manipulating page layout, from adding transparent GIF images to using borderless tables.

✦ Usability testing should be conducted before taking a Web site live. A usability test analyzes a site's information architecture, content quality, search capabilities, and navigation elements.

✦   ✦   ✦

STUDY GUIDE

It's now time to study for your exam. Many of the questions included in the following section are basic preparatory questions—most of which are further defined in later chapters. The scenarios and labs will help you reinforce the theories presented in this chapter.

Assessment Questions

1. A newspaper uses which of the following layout designs?

    A. Back to front design

    B. Inverted pyramid

    C. Linear design

    D. Scalable pages

2. Which of the following is not a common layout design?

    A. Top-margin

    B. Left-margin

    C. Bottom-margin

    D. Right-margin

3. How many seconds does it take for a user to feel interrupted?

    A. 0

    B. 1

    C. 7

    D. 10

4. Which screen resolution should you design for?

    A. 640x480

    B. 480x600

    C. 800x480

    D. 800x600

5. The color scheme pink, red, and green implies which of the following company cultures? (Choose the best answer.)

    A. Conservative

    B. Strict

    C. Corporate

    D. Exciting

6. Which of the following is not a technique used to manipulate page layout?

    A. CSS positioning

    B. Tables

    C. Columns

    D. Frames

7. Which of the following is not a browser-safe color code?

    A. 00

    B. 22

    C. CC

    D. FF

8. Which of the following is not a common font?

    A. Times New Roman

    B. Times

    C. Arial

    D. Charcoal

9. What is the default font size for most Web pages?

    A. <font size="3">

    B. <font size="+1">

    C. <font size="-1">

    D. <font size="-3">

10. Which of the following is not a usability element?

    A. Search capability

    B. Ease of navigation

    C. Quality control

    D. Content

11. Which of the following browser generations saw the quickest upgrade time?

    A. 2.x to 3.x

    B. 3.x to 4.x

    C. 4.x to 5.x

    D. 5.x to 6.x

12. When testing for usability you should not do which of the following?

    A. Identify tasks for participants to complete

    B. Include some of the project team as participants

    C. Follow up with a few questions to trigger their memory

    D. Look for trends in the participants' answers

Scenarios

Your company has completed a Web site redesign. Your boss has asked that you solicit feedback from users about the redesign and conduct a usability study before the site goes public. He wants you to test for the following usability elements and determine the steps necessary to complete a usability test:

    ✦ Ease of navigation

    ✦ Quality control

    ✦ Search capability

    ✦ Information architecture

Lab Exercises

Lab 2-1: Conducting a usability test

For this lab, you must visit a Web site and conduct a usability test focusing on the four usability elements:

    ✦ Ease of navigation

    ✦ Quality control

    ✦ Search capabilities

    ✦ Information architecture

The following are tasks you're to complete as a part of the usability test. For each task, please identify any problems you discovered when completing the task. Open your Web browser and visit www.ilearning.com.

1. Identify the type of business.

2. Locate their contact information.

3. Define all products sold at iLearning.

4. Define all services provided by iLearning.

5. Locate the demo for one of their products.

Complete a summary analysis of the Web site. Please be sure to include information about the quality of the information provided and the navigational structure.

Answers to Chapter Questions

Chapter pre-test

1. Print media is linear and the Web is non-linear and interactive. An example of print media would be a product catalog. An example of a Web application would be an e-commerce site that allows users to purchase products.

2. Users are likely to lose attention after 10 seconds. It's even thought by some that seven seconds is too long for a page to download.

3. There are several layout components we could mention; however, a few of our favorites are tables, navigation, whitespace, and color. Any given Web page will have several layout components.

4. After a user has waited one second for a page to download, the user feels interrupted. After a user has waited 10 seconds for a page to download, the user loses attention and is likely to leave the site.

5. There three ways to define color for a Web page: RGB values, hexadecimal code, or predefined color names. The exam covers both RGB values and hexadecimal code. The official HTML specification, however, does not allow RGB values.

6. You can define a font for your page using Cascading Style Sheets, the <font> tag, or the <basefont> tag. Each of which allows you to use a font name, such as Times New Roman or Arial.

7. A usability test is necessary for every new Web site. It uses a testing pool to conduct a blind test on your Web site to assess your site's navigation, content, and organization.

8. The four usability elements are quality control, search capability, ease of navigation, and information architecture.

Assessment questions

1. **B.** A newspaper, like a magazine, follows an inverted pyramid design where the front page provides story summaries with page references that "link" to the full story. The Web has adopted this design. See "Effective Page Design and Layout Components."

2. **C.** There are five common layout designs: top-margin, left-margin, right-margin, left and top-margin, and distributed. Users have come to expect one of these layout designs. Depending on your content, you'll want to select one of these layout designs. See "Layout formats."

3. **B.** It only takes one second of download time for a user to feel interrupted. After 10 seconds, a user loses interest and is likely to leave your site. See "User's attention."

4. **A.** You should design pages that fill a typical screen full, with a screen resolution of 640x480. Although many users can support 800x600 screen resolution, you want to cater to the lowest common denominator. See "Screen resolution."

5. **D.** Colors such as pink, red, and green often make users think the company culture is exciting and young, whereas the colors gray, blue, and white make users think the company culture is more conservative and corporate. See "Colors, Fonts, and Whitespace."

6. **C.** There are several tactics for manipulating page layout. For example, a transparent image is oftentimes used to add a blank space. Tables are also used with a transparent border to manipulate layout. CSS positioning and frames are also used by designers to achieve their desired layout. See "Whitespace and readability."

7. **B.** There are six hexadecimal code pairs that are guaranteed to be browser safe, they are: 00, 33, 66, 99, CC, and FF. As a designer, you can use any combination of these pairs. For example, #003366 and #FF3300 are both browser-safe colors. See "Using browser-safe colors."

8. **D.** There are four fonts that you commonly see on Web sites: Arial, Times, Times New Roman, and Helvetica. These fonts are used because of their readability and browser support. Most browsers use one of these four fonts as their default font. See "Implementing fonts."

9. **A.** Browsers assume a default font size of 3. If you do not define a base font, all size values, such as -1 or +1, will be applied relative to the size of 3. See "Font size."

10. **D.** The four usability elements are quality control, ease of navigation, information architecture, and search capability. Each item is equally as significant and related to the others. For example, ease of navigation allows users to locate the content that is governed by quality control. See "Defining and Executing Usability Tests."

11. **A.** Users were quick to upgrade the earliest browser generation. See "Technology."

12. B. No participants should be familiar with the site in question. The goal of a usability test is to see how a first-time user reacts to a site's navigation, layout, and content. Because members of your project team already know the site design and navigational system, they will not produce significant results. See "Test pool."

Scenarios

The best way to solicit feedback from users is to conduct a usability study using a testing pool consisting of users that have never visited your site. Each user should be presented with a task sheet that mimics real-world user experiences. For example, if your Web site sells books, one task should be for the user to attempt to purchase a book. For each task, users should be asked to identify any problems they experienced when trying to complete each task.

Once the test is completed, be sure to follow up with some general questions about the Web site. It's helpful to jog the memory of your participants to catch anything they might have forgotten to document. The last step is to analyze the data collected, particularly focusing on trends in that data. Once the data is analyzed, it's time to modify the Web site accordingly.

For More Information

✦ **CNET.com.** `http://builder.cnet.com`: CNet's builder site provides Web developers with up to date articles on tools and techniques for building Web sites.

✦ **Useit.com.** `www.useit.com`: Jakob Nielsen's Web site that focuses on usability issues. There you will find articles and studies on Web site usability.

✦ **Webmonkey's color chart.** `http://hotwired.lycos.com/webmonkey/reference/color_codes/`: The Webmonkey color chart provides a full list of most colors available to Web designers.

✦ **RGB color chart.** `www.hypersolutions.org/rgb.html`: Another Web site that defines colors that can be used on the Web.

✦ **A List Apart.** `www.alistapart.com`: Articles by designers for designers. This Web site provides articles on usability and design issues.

Site Navigation

✦ The importance of Web site navigation

✦ Primary and secondary navigation

✦ Navigation hierarchy

✦ Site structure and information architecture

CHAPTER PRE-TEST

1. What are primary and secondary navigation?

2. What are familiar conventions?

3. What are some of the considerations for a navigation action plan?

As a Web designer, it's your duty to define a navigational system that is easy for users to use. Oftentimes, designers fail to plan accordingly, and navigation suffers. If there's one thing we've learned from developing Web sites, it's that users don't have patience for poor navigation. This chapter focuses on Web site navigation—from planning to implementation.

Why Is Navigation Important?

The importance of Web site navigation

The Web is based on navigation. Without navigation, the Web would be a vast system of unrelated pages. As a navigational system, the Web helps users locate a particular Web site or page from within this vast system.

Navigation does not translate into moving from one document to another. If it were that easy, you could close the book now and go take the exam. An effective Web navigation system allows you to move from one document to another in a controlled environment. Although total control is not possible, with a little planning, you'll be amazed at what you can achieve.

There are many analogies that can be used to illustrate the importance of navigation; however, the one most commonly used refers to driving directions. Here's an example: You move to Washington, D.C., and you've never been there before. You're likely to notice that finding your way through the district can be challenging at best. Thankfully, a friend is there to give you directions to the closest grocery store. As you hop in your car and make your way to the store, you second-guess yourself several times before you finally make it. The second trip to the store is easier because you recognize some of the turns. By the fourth or fifth time, you have the directions down pat.

Navigating within a Web site is much like navigating within an unfamiliar city. Most landmarks are unfamiliar, the street names are new, and even the grocery store names are different than where you're from. However, there are a few common elements to every city; for example, street signs are placed on street corners; major intersections have streetlights; and stop signs are all red with white lettering. The Web also has some common navigational elements. As a designer, it's your job to provide simple and direct navigation. Once a user is familiar with the navigation on your Web site, he or she is likely to come back.

You have about three clicks before a user gets frustrated or bored. This means if a user can't find what he or she needs in three clicks or less, the user will probably leave your site and not come back.

Navigation Strategies

Unfortunately, navigation is not up to only the designers. There are several important factors that play a vital role in any navigational design. Namely, browser interfaces are often used by users to bypass site-designed navigation. For example, instead of using site-designed navigational elements, users can select the browser's back button to jump to the previous page they visited. Another factor in navigation is the Web site's *hierarchy*, which is the structure of your Web site.

Each of these factors has a vital role in Web site navigation. Luckily, as designers, you control two of the factors on the following list. The second factor is already predefined, so you can plan around it.

✦ **Navigational elements on the page.** These elements are defined by you, as the designer, and are commonly referred to as primary and secondary navigational elements.

✦ **Browser navigation functionality.** As designers, browser navigation can be troublesome, and when the user decides to use the browser's navigational features over the site's navigation, you may have some problems. There are two key points here: First, you anticipate that some users will use a browser's navigational features, and plan accordingly. Second, you create a navigation system that is so usable and comfortable, that users will not want (or need) to use the browser's navigation.

✦ **Site structure.** The way you plan your site structure can make or break any navigation design. As the often under appreciated part of navigation design, a well thought out site structure is essential.

Primary and secondary

Primary and secondary navigation

Most navigation designs can be broken down and classified into two different categories: primary and secondary. Most Web sites have navigational elements that are accessible from the majority of the pages within the site. These common navigational elements are classified as *primary navigation.* On the other hand, a particular Web page from within a Web site may have navigational elements particular to that page, but not the entire Web site. These navigational elements are classified as *secondary navigation.*

For example, if you visit www.ilearning.com, you find several primary navigational elements, such as a hyperlink to Contact Us along the top of the page. If you navigate within the Web site, you find that very same hyperlink on each Web page. However, when you navigate to a particular page within that Web site (for example to the Contact Us page), you'll find hyperlinks that are specific to that page. On this site, the secondary hyperlinks appear on the left side of the screen as shown in Figure 3-1. These navigational elements are considered secondary navigation and are only relevant to the particular page.

Figure 3-1: The primary navigation appears at the top of the Web site and the secondary navigation is on the left side.

Exam Tip   Remember that most navigational elements defined by a Web site fall into one of these two categories: primary or secondary.

Browser navigation

Many Web browser interfaces are designed according to the following three levels of functionality:

✦ **Internet access layer.** Defines protocols for communicating with remote Web sites, ranging from the Hypertext Transfer Protocol (HTTP) to various encryption types, such as Secure Sockets Layer (SSL).

✦ **Navigation layer.** Tracks the users' actions; therefore, it knows where users have been and helps guide them to where they can go. Think about the address field, a browser's history function, or the back button.

✦ **Presentation layer.** This layer is the actual display of the Web page.

Most browsers share a few common features that allow us to anticipate user actions based on these common browser features. The common features found in most browsers include the following:

✦ **Bookmarks or Favorites.** If you're visiting a site that you need to remember, all you have to do is save the URL as a part of your bookmarks or favorites folder.

✦ **Browser history.** At times, this function can be a lifesaver. If you need to visit a site, but you can't remember the URL (and you didn't bookmark it), you can check your browser history. Any Web page you recently visited will be listed there. In Internet Explorer, the history entries are separated by date and are usually found in a folder such as C:\Documents and Settings\Administrator\ Local Settings\History. This location varies depending on your operating system and configuration, but this gives you a general idea of where to look.

✦ **Hyperlinks.** Browsers display hyperlinks in blue and underlined text. A user can change these default presentation preferences, but most users leave them alone.

✦ **Status bar.** The status bar is normally displayed in the bottom left portion of the browser window. The browser uses this space to display information about where you're navigating to, page loading, and more.

✦ **Toolbar back button.** The back button allows users to visit the previous page they visited. Most browsers keep track of users' actions. In this case, the user can select the back button to visit previous Web sites.

✦ **Toolbar forward button.** Similar to the back button, the forward button allows users to visit a site that they've already visited. Browsers keep track of Web sites users visit, and allow users to move forward and back between them.

✦ **URL address field.** The address field displays the current location of the Web page in the browser window. Users use this space to define URLs they want to visit.

✦ **URL drop-down menu.** You can use the drop-down menu in the address field to see the URLs you've recently visited. You can type **www.la**, for example, and the drop-down menu will display URLs you've visited that start with those letters, as shown in Figure 3-2.

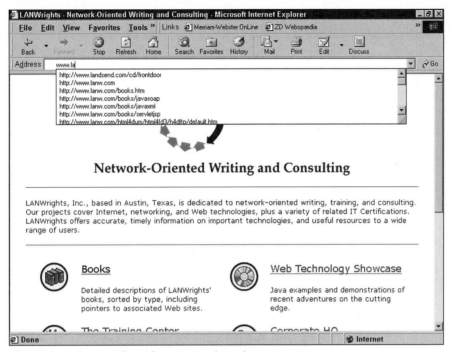

Figure 3-2: The URL drop-down menu in action

Site structure and hierarchy

Navigation hierarchy

Forget linear models because the Web allows you to mix things up a bit. When you read a book, you typically follow a linear path. When you drive to the store, you follow a linear path. However, when you want to visit a Web site, it's only one click away. The Web is not linear: You can jump from page to page without following a linear path. This is the good news. The bad news is that most of us still think linearly.

Take a second to think about some hierarchical relationships. Your family follows an organizational structure where your grandparents are at the top of the family tree and you are at the bottom. Businesses follow a hierarchical relationship as well. This is how a Web site is defined. The home page (the parent at the front door) is at the top of the organizational structure. At the next level, you find child pages. Each child page may have children of its own. Similar to a family tree, the Web site does not follow a linear structure, rather each branch of the structure can expand for as long as you would like.

Exam Tip

The organizational structure of a Web site is known as the *information architecture* of the site.

Positional awareness

 Site structure and information architecture

One of the first rules in navigation is to have a clear information architecture. Another rule is that your users also have to understand the information architecture. The last thing you want is a user trying to figure out where he or she is in your site. A user should always have a sense of where he or she is in your site. There are three questions a user should be able to answer while visiting your site:

✦ Where am I?

✦ Where have I been?

✦ Where can I go?

The five most common techniques you can use to help users answer these questions are:

✦ **Site map.** This may be the most obvious of the techniques. In this case, you provide a Web page that details the site structure. There you have it: Users know everything about your information architecture.

✦ **Breadcrumbs.** Breadcrumbs use arrows or slashes to provide the navigational path used to arrive at the current location. For example, you might use the following breadcrumb trail: LANW.com ⇨ training ⇨ login.htm. To see a working example of breadcrumbs, visit `www.useit.com` and select the All Alertbox columns hyperlink and a couple other links to see the breadcrumb navigation in action.

✦ **Images.** Many Web pages, such as Amazon.com and barnesandnoble.com, use tabs to provide positional awareness. The tab structure has become a hit on the Web. Each tab has a name and changes appearance when you visit it. This tells the users where they are and where they can go.

✦ **Color.** This is by no means our favorite method; however, using color to help define positional awareness is used throughout the Web. There are some drawbacks to this approach. The most obvious is that the user must first learn the color scheme and know what each color represents.

✦ **Headings.** Header information is a great way to let users know where they are within a Web site. Although this does not provide a page's relative position within a site, it does clearly identify the page. It's best to use headings in conjunction with several of the other techniques defined in this section.

Other navigational elements

We cannot possibly cover every conceivable navigational element; therefore, we cover what's covered on the exam. Please keep in mind that what is covered in this chapter is not an exhaustive list. The following three navigational elements, however, are covered on the exam:

✦ **Depth.** Be sure to stick to the *three-click rule*. A user should not have to click more than three times to locate a page on your site. Users are not patient, and will leave if they cannot locate information quickly.

✦ **Icons.** There are generally two types of navigational icons: labeled and unlabeled. If the icon is not obvious, it should be labeled. An obvious icon, for example, is a house icon to represent your home page. Otherwise, you should also add a label below the icon. Therefore, there's no confusion about the navigational element.

✦ **Toolbars.** Using toolbars has become common practice. Toolbars can consist of navigational icons or simply quick links. Toolbars are normally located at the top and/or bottom of your Web page. Because users read top to bottom, it would be wise to include your toolbar at the top of the page.

Other navigational elements are buttons, image maps and hot spots, table slices, rollovers, arrows, navigational bars and menus, and drop-down select menus.

Exam Tip   Don't forget about the *three-click rule,* it's likely to be on the exam.

Beyond the browser

Browser navigation is not exhaustive, so you cannot rely on it. Although many users will use browser navigation features to find their way through the Web, you should make your site easy to navigate so it can stand on its own. There are several limitations to browser navigation, so be sure to keep the following in mind:

✦ Use a site map to define your site hierarchy and provide links to the most important levels of your site.

✦ Use default hyperlink colors for your links. That means you should always use blue for unvisited links, and purple for visited links.

✦ Emphasize the site's information architecture. Users should be able to move one level up and one level down and understand where they are within your site structure.

✦ Don't use the `meta` element to automatically refresh your page when it's visited. This disables the back button and users can no longer visit the previous Web site. This will frustrate users and it's bad Web design.

✦ Home page navigation should be easy. You always want users to have quick access back to your home page

✦ Always use site identifiers to let users know just where they're visiting. If you use a corporate logo, be sure to add a hyperlink to the home page (that way you ensure that home page navigation is easy).

Defining and Implementing Site Navigation

After you understand the navigational terrain and are familiar with all the players, it's time to design and implement your site's navigation. There are many facets to the design and implementation phase. This section takes a look at the most important facets of navigational design.

Site structure, URLs, and file names

Think about the directories on your hard drive. No matter which operating system you're using, the directory structure is hierarchical. To locate a given document, you need to know in which folder it resides, and possibly any parent folders. You're probably familiar with the following syntax:

```
C:\Windows\documents\file.htm
```

This path locates a document in the documents folder that is found within the Windows folder. Now, take a look at the path that would locate a document on the Web:

```
http://www.lanw.com/books/default.htm
```

This path, formally called a Uniform Resource Locator (URL), locates a document in the books folder that is found within the Web site's root directory. The syntax and functionality is similar to the Windows path expression.

Site structure

Your Web site structure, much like the directories found on your hard drive, describes how your documents are stored on the Web server. On the Web server, your Web site will have one root directory. When users visit `http://www.lanw.com`, they're accessing the Web site's root directory. If users visit `http://www.lanw.com/books`, they're visiting the books folder found within the Web site's root directory.

The Web server houses the site's HTML files, images, and other site related documents. As the designer, you define the site structure. You name the folders, define the hierarchy of the folders, and populate them. For example, Figure 3-3 illustrates the site structure for the `www.lanw.com` Web site.

The structure is simple, with five folders.

Figure 3-4 illustrates what you would find if you expand the books folder.

Figure 3-3: Directory structure for www.lanw.com

Figure 3-4: Expanded directory structure for www.lanw.com

This expands the directory subfolders, which are found within the primary books folder. To access the ciw.htm file found in the books folder, you would enter the following URL in the browser's address field:

```
http://www.lanw.com/books/ciw.htm
```

URLs

URLs are used to define the location of a particular Web page; for example:

```
http://www.lanw.com/books/ciw.htm
```

This URL tells you:

✦ The exact location of the file

✦ Where it's located in relation to the site structure. In other words, you know how deep the file is within the Web site structure.

Because URLs can be used as navigational tools, you need to make sure that directory names are meaningful. The directory and file names in this example are not nearly as useful:

```
http://www.lanw.com/bhmciw/0112.htm
```

File names

Files names are the second part of a URL that users can rely on. The name of the document adds meaning to the URL and helps with navigation. As shown in the previous two sections, a file name can be either useless or helpful.

Many Web sites use their own lingo or nicknames to define both directories and files names. This is not wise. The more useful the file name, the easier it will be for your users to understand where they are within your site. The happier the users, the better chance that they will be back.

Familiar conventions

There are a few certainties about navigation, and one of those is that users like familiarity. The more familiar the navigational elements, the more comfortable the users' experience. Over time, the Web has become a collection of similar Web pages. Visit any Web page and you're likely to find: the navigation on the left, the company logo in the top right, hyperlinks in blue, and the primary content of the page to the right of the navigation.

Many of these navigational elements have specific meaning throughout the Web, and their familiarity has translated into predefined meanings. For example, if text is underlined and in blue font, it's assumed to be a hyperlink. Only an inexperienced Web designer would use a blue underlined font style for plain text.

Exam Tip   Common navigational elements are often referred to as *familiar conventions*.

Labels

Labels are commonly used to identify particular navigational elements. For example, you might call (or label) the pointer to your employment listings "Jobs" or "Job Listings." The key with labels is to be obvious. Clever labels will not work, and neither will long ones. For example, if you labeled the hyperlink to your corporate mission as "Us," users don't really know what they might find there. Likewise, long labels take too long to read. Always remember: Users like to be lazy, so plan accordingly.

Exam Tip   *Labels* are used to identify navigational elements and should be clear and concise.

Logos, searches, and much more

There are several common navigational traits: from having the company logo linked to the company's home page to including a Frequently Asked Questions (FAQ) page. Most users expect these traits, and you'd be wise to take advantage of them. Some of the most common are:

✦ **Logo.** The logo is commonly found in the upper-left corner of your Web site and linked to the home page.

✦ **Search.** Allows users to conduct a full site search.

✦ **FAQ.** Lists frequently asked questions along with their answers.

✦ **Site Map.** Defines the Web site structure and allows users to see the expanded structure and hyperlink to any page in that structure.

✦ **About Us.** Most Web sites have a page or two about the company. This is where users expect to find information about the company's mission and possibly contact information. Contact information may be defined in a separate link (for example, "Contact Us").

✦ **Help.** If you maintain a complex Web site, users like to request help finding what they need. The help hyperlink may point to a document that contains contact information, a hot line number, e-mail addresses for technical support staff, and/or even pointers to the FAQ.

Guided navigation

To guide a user through your Web site with arrows and labels such as "Next" is referred to as guided navigation. Although guided navigational elements may use some familiar conventions, the purpose is more defined. Think about purchasing a plane ticket on the Web. The first step is to select the departure city and then the destination city. After you enter all the required data, you hit a submit button. In many cases, you're presented with flights that fit your requests, as well as additional instructions for making a selection. After you choose your final flight, you're asked to select the submit button and are presented the detailed information of the flight you selected.

Keeping users on track is key. The links used to guide the user to the next step should be clearly marked. You'll also want to provide a link that allows the user to exit the navigational track. Think about another example, shopping at an online store. Most online retail outfits have some e-commerce system that guides you through the purchasing process. However, throughout that process you always have a way out or a way to return to the store. This is an important usability concept because you don't want to frustrate your users, or they may never return to your site.

 Exam Tip   Guided navigation must be intuitive and allow the user to navigate easily through a Web site. Links should be clearly marked and a way out should always be available.

Define a plan

A navigation plan is also referred to as a *navigation action plan*, because navigational designs should focus on the ease of movement from action to action. Because navigation usability can make or break your site, careful planning is a must. Navigation should be easy to follow, have a consistent look and feel, move smoothly from action to action, and most of all not confuse the user. Your plan of action should consider the following points:

✦ Determine site goals and needs

✦ Learn from tried and true navigation

✦ Plan navigation for several levels deep

✦ Provide shortcuts

✦ Assume users have different navigational behavior

The following sections take a look at each of these points in more detail.

Exam Tip   A navigation action plan requires that you consider several points. Be sure to remember each of the previous points.

Determine site goals and needs

The first step in defining navigational strategy is to understand your audience. More specifically, you want to understand your user's goals and needs. After you have an idea of what your users want, it will be easier to predict their possible actions. The heart of good navigational design is to understand your users' needs, and then build your site anticipating their actions based on these needs.

One step to determining your audience's goals and needs is to interview or survey the people that will visit your site. This means you have to get to work and actually talk to potential customers. Surveys are often a good tool to determine potential customer preferences; however, actually talking to them can provide more accurate information.

Learn from tried and true navigation

Previously in this chapter, we discussed common navigational elements formally referred to as familiar conventions. These common elements have evolved from several years of Web site navigation, and have become the de facto way to build navigational systems. This is not to say that you have to follow every familiar convention; however, it's smart to take a look around at other sites and learn a thing or two.

In the Real World   Web Pages That Suck.com has a portion of their site dedicated to bad navigation (called Mystery Meat navigation). For some good examples of bad navigation, see www.webpagesthatsuck.com/badnavigation.html.

Visit a site and perform a quick usability study. Can you navigate through the site easily? If so, what parts of the navigation do you like? If you find difficulty navigating the site, what were some of the obstacles to navigation?

According to many Web professionals, a well-designed navigation plan consists of one or several of the following characteristics:

✦ **Provides clear visual messages.** The rule with anything on the Web is that it must be clear and concise. This is particularly important with Web site navigation.

✦ **Defines alternatives for the user.** You don't want users to get stuck somewhere in your Web site, forcing them to either leave, or use the browser to navigate out of your site. Alternatives are important. The best way to decide on alternatives is to anticipate your users' possible actions.

✦ **Labels are understandable and clear.** Labels are meant to be short and quickly identifiable. If a user doesn't understand the label, he or she is not likely to select it. Likewise, labels should be clear. If a user selects a label expecting to find one thing, only to find something completely different, you can bet the user will be a tad frustrated.

✦ **A user's goals and behaviors should be anticipated.** You should anticipate and support most users' goals and behaviors.

✦ **Navigation should fit with the site's purpose.** The navigation should be a logical extension of the goals of the Web site. Don't get carried away defining navigational elements that have nothing to do with your Web site.

✦ **Navigation should appear in context.** Navigation should not be a surprise to the user, so be sure that it makes contextual sense.

✦ **Provides feedback for the user.** As mentioned in the "Positional awareness" section earlier, users like to be able to answer three questions: Where am I? Where have I been? Where can I go? Your navigational structure should do everything to answer each of these questions.

✦ **Defines a consistent look and feel.** Navigation must remain consistent for the user to feel comfortable while visiting your site.

✦ **Provides easy-to-learn navigation.** The navigational elements should be obvious and easy to remember.

Exam Tip

Of all of the previous characteristics, providing feedback is one of the most important. For example, if a user is purchasing a computer part from your Web site, he or she will want to know if the purchase was successful or if additional information is needed, and so on.

Plan navigation for several levels deep

For the most part, everyone gets the home page right — navigationally speaking that is. However, your navigational action plan should take interior pages into account as well. Detail is king in navigation, and you should plan your navigation from the home page to each individual content page. Most navigational nightmares occur because of poor interior navigational planning.

Provide shortcuts

Shortcuts, or quick links, allow users quick access to content such as search components, site maps, and FAQ lists. One of the main goals of Web site navigation is to define navigational elements that allow quick and painless access to content on your site. Quick links are an easy way to achieve this goal. A good shortcut is concise, clear, fast, and streamlined — and should never be confusing. For example, if you create a shortcut to your search component, you don't want to confuse the user with tons of options and selections. Remember to keep it simple.

Assume users have different navigational behavior

We all surf the Web differently. Some of us like to browse, whereas others like to search for exact pieces of information. No two users are alike, and as a designer, you have to take varying navigational behaviors into account. When you first design your site, look at different user perspectives.

Key Point Summary

This chapter presented the details of effective Web site navigation, from planning to implementation. The main points of this chapter were:

✦ The Web is based on navigation.

✦ The key players in the navigation of your Web site are the primary and secondary navigational elements, browser navigation functionality, and site structure.

✦ Navigational elements defined by a Web site fall into one of these two categories: primary or secondary.

✦ The organizational structure of a Web site is known as the *information architecture* of the site.

✦ The three questions a user should be able to answer while visiting your site are:

• Where am I?

• Where have I been?

• Where can I go?

✦ The most effective ways to help users answer these questions are a site map, breadcrumbs, images, colors, and headings.

✦ There are three navigational elements covered on the exam: depth, icons, and toolbars.

✦ A user should not have to click more than three times to locate a page on your site.

✦ URLs are used to define the location of a particular Web page. Be sure your navigation hierarchy (and hence your URLs) makes sense and is logical.

✦ Common navigational elements are often referred to as *familiar conventions*.

✦ Some of the most common navigational traits are as follows:

• Logo

• Search

• FAQ

• Site Map

- About Us

- Help

✦ Guided navigation should be intuitive and allow the user to navigate easily through a Web site.

✦ Your navigation action plan should consider the following points:

- Determine site goals and needs

- Learn from tried and true navigation

- Plan navigation for several levels deep

- Provide shortcuts

- Assume users have different navigational behavior

✦   ✦   ✦

STUDY GUIDE

This chapter covered the key concepts of site navigation that will be presented in the CIW Site Designer exam. However, your work is not done. The following sections contain multiple choice questions, labs, and scenarios to ensure your grasp of the fundamentals of the site navigation design process.

Assessment Questions

1. Good navigation allows for up to how many clicks before assuming a user will give up?

   A. 2

   B. 3

   C. 1

   D. 4

2. Of the following, what are two types of navigational elements?

   A. Primary and secondary

   B. Main and sub

   C. Menu and submenu

   D. Primary and sub

3. Which of the following is a useful tool to define positional awareness?

   A. Backgrounds

   B. Breadcrumbs

   C. Levels

   D. Instructions

4. What are common navigational elements also called?

   A. Guided navigation

   B. Fixed navigation

   C. Common navigation

   D. Familiar conventions

5. Controlling users' navigational steps is also called which of the following?

   A. Guided navigation

   B. Fixed navigation

   C. Common navigation

   D. Familiar conventions

6. A navigation action plan should consider which of the following points? (Choose the best answer.)

   A. Define navigation for only the home page

   B. Provide quick links for users

   C. Assume all users have the same backgrounds

   D. Test for only a few major browsers

Scenarios

You're asked to redesign your company's Web site and your boss wants you to focus on creating a better navigational structure. Before you get started, however, your boss wants you to complete the following tasks:

✦ Map out the company site structure

✦ Poll users about possible navigational needs

✦ Create a list of navigational concerns

Your boss then wants you to present your findings before you create the site. Answer the following questions as they relate to performing this task:

1. What is the easiest way to determine your company's current site structure?

2. How would you poll current users about navigational concerns?

Lab Exercises

Lab 3-1: Listing familiar conventions

For this lab, you need to visit several Web sites and identify a few common navigation elements:

1. Visit the following Web sites: www.w3.org, http://hotwired.lycos.com/webmonkey/, and www.useit.com.

2. Find the following familiar conventions (if they exist on the Web site):

- Logo with hyperlink
- Search feature
- FAQ
- Common Labels, such as "Contact"
- Help link
- Site map

Lab 3-2: Mapping out a site structure

For this lab, you need to visit www.useit.com and map out the site structure for the Web site. Your structure will not be exact—after all, you don't have access to their server—but try to identify at least two layers deep.

1. Visit www.useit.com.

2. Explore the site for a while. When exploring, be sure to note the URL found in the address field of your browser; it will let you know in which directory a particular file resides.

3. As you explore, take out a scratch sheet of paper and map out the various directories you find.

In the Real World   Although this Web site isn't the prettiest, note that Jakob Nielson is a big wig in the Internet usability community, so you'll find some very helpful information as you peruse this site.

Lab 3-3: Evaluate a Web site's navigation

For this lab, you should visit http://hotwired.lycos.com/webmonkey/ and evaluate the site's navigation according to the following points:

- ✦ Does this site identify the user's goals and needs?
- ✦ Does it provide tried and true navigation?
- ✦ Are the deep layers of navigation planned well?
- ✦ Does it provide shortcuts?
- ✦ Does it appeal to users with different navigational behavior?

Answers to Chapter Questions

Chapter pre-test

1. Navigation can oftentimes be divided into two different categories: primary and secondary navigation. Primary navigation is used to define navigational elements that are located on most pages in a Web site. For example, a Contact hyperlink is normally found on all pages on a Web site, and is an example of primary navigation. On the other hand, secondary navigation consists of all those hyperlinks on an interior page that are specific to that page (or subset of pages).

2. Familiar conventions are those common navigational elements that can be found on most any Web page. A few examples of familiar conventions would be a logo that is linked to the company home page, a search engine text box, or a site map hyperlink.

3. Although there are several aspects to navigational design that you should consider, a few of them are:

   • Determine site goals and needs

   • Learn from tried and true navigation

   • Plan navigation for several levels deep

   • Provide shortcuts

   • Assume users have different navigational behavior

Assessment questions

1. **B.** Usability studies have shown that users give up searching for a particular piece of information after three clickthroughs. Therefore, your navigational structure should allow users to locate any information on your Web site in three clicks or less. See "Why Is Navigation Important" and "Other navigational elements."

2. **A.** Most navigational elements fall within two categories: primary or secondary. Secondary navigational elements are those that are specific to a particular page. Primary navigation can be found on most pages in your Web site and are relevant to the entire site. See "Primary and secondary."

3. **B.** Breadcrumbs are one of many techniques used by Web designers to enhance positional awareness. Other techniques include using a site map, headings, colors, and images. See "Positional awareness."

4. **D.** Common navigational elements are known as familiar conventions. A familiar convention is a technique that is used by most Web sites. For example, positioning the logo in the top left corner of the Web site and having that logo hyperlinked. See "Familiar conventions."

5. A. Using guided navigation controls the user's steps. This is a useful technique if you're creating navigational elements for an e-commerce application or a sign up process. One word of warning, always provide your users with a way out. See "Guided navigation."

6. B. Defining an action plan involves many steps. One consideration is whether to include quick links to common pieces of information. Most Web sites use quick links and users are quick to understand them. Be sure to label them correctly. See "Provide shortcuts."

Scenarios

1. There are many ways to map out your current site structure. The key to Web design is to not make the solutions more difficult than they have to be. The quickest way to uncover your site structure is to go to the server and view the structure from there.

2. The second question is not as cut and dried. There are several ways to poll users. You can select a focus group to audit your site and provide you with feedback. You could also post a survey on your site requesting users to answer a few targeted questions. This one is a tad tricky because users have become wary of online surveys. Many companies now try to lure users to answer surveys by offering discounts and free gifts.

For More Information

✦ **World Wide Web Consortium (W3C).** www.w3.org: The W3C controls the HTML standard, as well as future versions of that standard. On their site, you have access to the standard itself, as well as an online validator that will check your documents for correct syntax and usage of tags.

✦ **Jakob Neilson's Alertbox.** www.useit.com: Jakob Neilson is the guru of navigational usability. He maintains this site and posts articles about usability on this site. You can also purchase his book titled, *Designing Web Usability* by New Riders Publishing, Indianapolis, 2000. ISBN 1-56205-810-X.

✦ **ZDNet's Developer site.** www.zdnet.com/developer/: The ZDnet developer Web site provides designers with tons of articles on Web design related issues. You're likely to find many articles on usability and navigation design. They even host some of Jakob Neilson's articles on this site.

✦ **Webreview.** http://webreview.com: Webreview provides the HTML community with articles about the business. They even have a section dedicated to designers.

Graphics

CHAPTER PRE-TEST

1. What are two types of digital images?

2. What role does user bandwidth play in the decisions you make about how to use images in page design?

3. What are some attributes of images?

4. How do transparent and animated GIFs work?

5. What are different ways to optimize images for display on the Web?

6. What kind of image-editing tool is Paint Shop Pro?

7. Explain what special effects are in Paint Shop Pro, how to apply them to images, and what preconditions your image's color depth must meet to use those special effects.

8. How do you increase or decrease color depth in Paint Shop Pro?

9. What are some of the options for controlling a screen capture in Paint Shop Pro?

✦ Answers to these questions can be found at the end of the chapter. ✦

Graphics are as essential to Web sites as text and markup. Graphics contribute significantly to the first impression a user has of a site and the usability of the site. Graphics also affect how quickly a site's pages are downloaded over the Web. Being able to use graphics effectively and having the right tools for working with graphics are key aspects of any site designer's skill set. In this chapter, you learn the role graphics play in site design, the fundamentals of how graphics are built, in which file formats you can store graphics, and how to optimize graphics for use on the Web. In addition, you learn how to use a common image development application — Paint Shop Pro 6.0 — to create and manipulate images for the Web.

Images and Site Design

 Role of Web graphics in site design

Rarely do you come across a Web site, or just a Web page for that matter, that doesn't use graphics as an integral part of its design. The graphics you choose for your Web site can have many different roles and contribute to many different aspects of the page, including:

- ✦ **Navigation.** Oftentimes, graphics are used as navigation devices. Users click on buttons and image maps to get from one place in a site to another. You can use text hyperlinks for navigation too, but graphics make the user interface more aesthetically pleasing and provide a richer experience for the user.

- ✦ **Overall look and feel.** A consistent look and feel and a consistent interface are important tenets of Web design. This consistency can be achieved using a collection of similarly themed graphics.

- ✦ **Branding.** In today's business world, consistent branding across all aspects of a company's collateral — products, Web sites, brochures, and the like — is considered a necessity. A standard color scheme and standard graphics contribute significantly to branding. When you incorporate these standard visual elements into a Web site, you can easily make it fit the brand of a particular company or product.

During the Web's infancy, graphics were used sporadically, were often not well designed, and didn't contribute significantly to a Web page's content. As the Web has matured and become a standard method of communication for all types of information, the role and quality of graphics have grown significantly.

To use graphics effectively as part of an overall Web design approach, you need to keep an eye on three elements of graphic design:

✦ **Image design and relevance.** Does the image fit with the page's overall theme and content?

✦ **Usefulness.** Is the image functional? Does it help users navigate or give them more information? Does it promote consistency or brand recognition?

✦ **Size.** Does the image download quickly?

Of these three elements, the most important and most often ignored is image size. In the following section, we examine the many issues associated with reducing image size without sacrificing the user's experience or image quality.

Exam Tip   It's important to know the characteristics of a good image.

Keeping an eye on image size

Second only, perhaps, to shoddy navigation, graphics can make or break a Web site. If your graphics don't compliment your site or they take too long to download, even the most dedicated user won't spend much time on your site. Unattractive graphics that detract from a site are problematic to say the least, but the bigger concern for designers is graphic size and download time.

You should strike a balance on your Web pages between aesthetics and file size. You want your pages to look good, to function well, and to promote a solid user experience. At the same time, you're subject to your users' bandwidth limitations. Images contain significantly more information than plain-text files, and, as a result, image files are usually bigger than the HTML pages that reference them. Every graphic that you add to your Web page adds to the total download time for the page. It's up to you, as a Web designer, to use graphics wisely so the pages you build don't take too long to download.

High-speed networks such as cable connections, Digital Subscriber Lines (DSL), and fiber-optic lines raise the bandwidth baseline. Fortunately, these high-speed networks are starting to reach the everyday user at home and work. However, many users still connect to the Internet with 28.8 Kbps modems and these users still expect Web pages to appear in relatively short order. This is the lowest common denominator that you have to think about when you're adding graphics to a Web page.

There are many different ways to test your Web pages to see how long they take to download over different bandwidth connections:

✦ Get a stopwatch and test the pages yourself if you have access to several different speed connections to the Internet. Be sure you test your pages at different times of the day as well. A page may take longer to load at 2:00 p.m. when the entire business world is online than it will at 10:00 p.m.

Tip

Note that this applies namely to users with dial-up connections. If you're developing a site for an intranet, testing the pages for download time isn't as crucial because intranets usually have dedicated lines with lots of bandwidth.

✦ Ask colleagues and friends to take a few moments to test a sample page or two. Ask them to supply you with the time of the test as well as what kind of connection they had to the Internet during the test.

✦ Run a test page through one of several online Web sites that test for load time. Our two favorites are Web Site Garage (http://websitegarage.netscape.com) and Doctor HTML (www2.imagiware.com/RxHTML).

If your first test of a page you've designed leaves you with frightening results, you should think about optimizing your images or removing some of the images in favor of text or form buttons. In general, you don't want your Web pages to take longer than 10 or 15 seconds to download at even the busiest time of day. The reality is that users simply won't stick around that long to wait for your page, no matter how compelling or useful your content is. The best way to get the most bang from your image buck is to have a solid understanding of how images work, which file formats are best suited for which particular kinds of images, and what you can do to optimize your images so their file size is smaller but you don't compromise quality.

Cross-Reference

Several sections in this chapter focus on the important topics of how images work, the ins and outs of file types, and optimizing images. The "Digital Images" section discusses image basics, the "Image File Formats" section covers all information related to choosing the correct format for a given graphic, and the "Optimizing Images for the Web" section discusses several techniques for reducing image file size.

Acquiring graphics for your Web pages

Before you can use images wisely on your pages, optimize images, or even choose an image file type, you need to have images. A common dilemma for many Web designers is where to get the images that are a prerequisite for a well-built Web site. You have several different options for acquiring images:

✦ Build them yourself

✦ Pay someone else to build them

✦ Use clip art

✦ Troll the Web for images

The following sections look at the pros and cons of each option as well as issues to think about as you weigh your options.

How to Calculate Download Time

It's important that you know how to calculate the download time for files to be copied remotely. (Normally, this means from the Internet.) This is important when dealing with images and various types of multimedia in your Web pages. The basic formula is to divide the size of the file(s) or object(s) to be downloaded by the usable bandwidth for your connection. To calculate the total size of files or objects, add up all the sizes of associated files and objects from your Web page; this total must include all images, the HTML document for the Web page itself, associated scripts, style sheets, and so forth. This calculation provides the dividend for your calculation (the number to be divided).

Calculating usable bandwidth for a connection means one of two things. The quick-and-dirty method is to assume the entire bandwidth is available, and to simply divide the total amount of data (the dividend) by the bandwidth of the connection (the divisor). A more accurate method is to use a bandwidth speed test (like the ones available at `http://computingcentral.msn.com/internet/speedtest.asp` or at `http://bandwidthplace.com/speedtest/`) and use the number reported as the divisor in your calculations.

To produce a meaningful result from your calculations, however, you must convert the file size and bandwidth numbers into some common unit of measure. This is typically bytes or bits. To convert your file size from kilobytes (KB) to kilobits (Kb), multiply the file size by 8 (1 byte = 8 bits). Bandwidth is normally reported in bps (bits per second), so this conversion will put both numbers into the same unit of measure. Now, divide the number of bits in the file by the number of bits per second for the usable bandwidth of your connection. For example, assume the Web page to download is 150K in size. Convert that to bits by multiplying 150 by 8 (to go from bytes to bits), then by multiplying by 1,024 (to go from kilobits to bits). This produces the formula 150 x 8 x 1024 and calculates to 1,228,800. Let's assume the target user has an ISDN line, running at full capacity at 128 Kbps. In bps, this actually calculates to 128 x 1024 or 131,072. Divide 1,228,800 by 131,072 to produce a result of 9.375, which means the target user can download the file in just a little over 9 seconds.

Build your own graphics

Building your own graphics requires some artistic savvy, a good tool set, and a good sense of design. Not everyone is an artist, but with a good tool set, as well as some practice and guidance from other Web designers, you can build solid graphics that can enhance your Web site. We know many Web developers who have become reasonably good at building their own images, so this is a viable option for just about any designer.

Hire a professional graphic artist

For high-end and corporate sites, the path to the best graphics is often through a professional. Professional Web graphic artists can create suites of graphics that can help maintain consistency and branding throughout an entire site. One of the greatest advantages of using a professional graphic designer is that he or she has access to many graphics resources that you don't. If you can afford to pay a professional, we highly recommend that you do.

A concern for many designers is that they feel once they hire a professional graphic artist, they're tied to that artist for all of their graphic needs. Although this is a valid concern, don't feel that it's insurmountable. If you're comfortable with graphic tools, you can usually take the base buttons and graphics the artist builds for you and repurpose them yourself as necessary. Be sure to get all pertinent information from the artist, including which fonts and any special color pallets they used during the creation of the graphics. Also, have the artist deliver all versions of the graphics to you, not just the ones optimized for the Web.

Work with clip art

Clip art has come a long way with the advent of the Web. You can buy clip art CDs with thousands of images on them for very little money. You can open and tweak the images in standard graphic editing programs such as Photoshop and Paint Shop Pro. Our biggest concern with clip art is that it may be difficult to gather a collection of images to present a consistent look and feel for your pages. However if your resources are limited and you don't want to build all of the graphics yourself from scratch, a good clip art collection will get you started. To find commercial clip art packages, visit your favorite search engine Web site and search for "clip art."

Download images from the Web

The Web is a wonderful resource for images of all kinds. There are entire Web sites devoted to providing free graphics to Web developers. If you choose to use images you download from the Web on your own pages, be sure to read the terms of use posted on the image distribution site (just about every graphics site has one). Often, sites restrict the use of graphics to personal use and require that you put a link back to the site from your Web site. If you want to use the graphics on a commercial site, contact the site's owner first to get permission.

Possibly the biggest concern you'll face when you choose to download images from the Web is that the images you use on your site may also be used on hundreds of other sites. It's difficult to create a customized look and feel for your site when you download graphics from the Web. In general, we recommend using graphics freely available on the Web for personal home pages but not for company sites in which branding is important.

Creating complete image elements

Not everyone on the Web can see images, and for those who don't, the use of images still impacts their Web experience. If a user has graphics turned off and is using a graphical browser such as Internet Explorer or Netscape Navigator, he or she will still see place holders for the graphics. If users browse the Web with a text browser, such as Lynx, they know graphics are in the page but they can't see them.

Images and Intranets

When you're designing for an intranet — as opposed to a Web site for general public consumption — the role of images and your image considerations change a bit. The goal of an intranet is to disseminate information efficiently over a network to a wide body of users. An intranet may serve a company of 5 or 5,000. Regardless of the size of an organization, its intranet is still designed to make information easily accessible.

Because the focus of an intranet is information dissemination and not promoting brand awareness, selling products, or spreading a marketing message, the look and feel of the intranet doesn't need to be as elaborate as it might be for a corporate Web site. Images on intranet pages should be functional and help guide users to the information they are looking for. Splashy logos or animated graphics don't really have a place on an intranet.

A benefit intranet designers get over Internet site designers is that you often know more about the standard computer and browser configurations the majority of users have. Most organizations standardize on one or two browsers and one or two operating systems. You can work with an IS department to get good information on the standard user setup, how many users have non-standard setups, and build your pages accordingly. In addition, intranets are often only available over closed networks; therefore, bandwidth is faster and modems are few and far between. The graphics you do use don't have to be as tightly optimized as those on an Internet site.

Because graphics can contribute to the content and functionality of the page, it's important that you provide alternative text for all images that you use in your page so their content and function aren't lost on those who don't or can't view images. Add alternative text to your image using the `alt` attribute in the `img` tag, like this:

```
<img src="corporate_logo.gif"
     alt="Computer Services, Ltd. - Computer Consulting Firm">
```

Although users may not be able to see the corporate logo embedded in the page with the previous `img` tag, they know what key information the logo conveys: the name of the company and what its primary business is. For images that display bullets or are designed to create white space, an asterisk or dash is a sufficient value for the `alt` attribute. All other images should have some sort of meaningful description stored in the attribute.

To test a Web page to be sure that your alternative text is meaningful and your pages are useful to users without images, clear the cache in your browser, turn off image display in the browser, and load the page. Try to navigate around the page and other linked pages without turning on graphics. If you can't get around or perform activities that you know the page supports, revisit your alternative text and general page layout to find ways to make the page more functional when images aren't displayed.

Digital Images

Creating and managing digital images effectively requires a good understanding of the different aspects of an image, including:

✦ The image type

✦ The image's attributes

✦ The image's file format

Once you're comfortable with how these different aspects work together to affect image quality and image size, you can use your knowledge and a good image-editing tool to optimize your image for both quality and size. The next several sections of this chapter introduce you to the ins and outs of these key aspects of digital images.

Image types

In general, there are two types of digital images:

✦ Vector images

✦ Bitmap images

The majority of Web graphics are bitmap images; however, vector images are becoming more prominent as new technologies emerge. In general, line art, shapes, and illustrations work best as vector images, whereas photographs, images with soft or blurry edges, and special effects such as drop shadows work best as bitmap images. The following three sections explain how images of each type are constructed and include tips on how to decide which type is the best one for any given image.

 Exam Tip   Be sure you're familiar with the differences between vector images and bitmap images.

Vector images

A *vector image* is essentially a collection of lines defined by mathematical equations. A vector image viewer interprets the mathematical equations and displays the image accordingly. For example, a vector graphic that describes a square simply needs to store information that identifies the square as a four-sided polygon with sides that are the same length. The actual length of the four sides is just a value stored in the graphic. A square that is five pixels in size has the same file size as a square that is five inches in size, because the size information is simply a value. Therefore, vector graphic file sizes are kept relatively small, which is a benefit when file size is important — as it is on the Web.

Graphical viewers that display vector graphics can quickly and easily resize the graphics because they only need to change the values that describe how the graphic should be displayed. Different size-display devices can display the same vector graphic at a size appropriate to the device's size without losing any of the graphic's information.

Because vector images are based on mathematical equations, they're best suited to clean graphics without much blurry or fuzzy information. The more transition from one line or color to another there is in a graphic, the more difficult it is to describe the graphic as a series of equations. As mentioned in the previous section, shapes, line art, and illustrations that are composed mainly of clean lines without much transition of color are good candidates for vector graphics.

Vector images are a relatively new kind of image and support for them across the major Web browsers and operating systems isn't complete. In fact, to view vector graphics in a Web browser, you usually need a special plug-in (the SVG Viewer from Adobe: `www.adobe.com/svg/main.html`). When vector graphics are more widely accepted, they can take the place of bitmap graphics where appropriate.

Bitmap images

Bitmap images are the most common type of images. You'll work with bitmap images frequently as you design Web sites. A bitmap image is a collection of squares, called *pixels,* of different colors that when merged create an image. The larger a graphic is, the more squares of color it needs to create the image. As mentioned, bitmaps are good for creating images with shadows, many transitions from one color to another, and that are generally complex.

In a bitmap graphic, varying shades of colors are used to make edges smooth and colors blend. For example, a black line on white background most likely includes gray bits to make a smooth transition from white to black. If you open a bitmap graphic in your image editor of choice and magnify it so you can see the individual pixels, you'll see that its edges are very rough. However, when you pull away from the individual pixels, the edges tend to be softer. A bitmap graphic can use as many or as few colors as the artist deems necessary. The more colors, the bigger the file size. The larger the graphic, the bigger the file size.

Tip   The bitmap way of developing graphics is not the same as the Bitmap file format (.bmp). File types such as GIF and JPEG are bitmap files supported by Web browsers.

The benefit of using bitmap images is that they're well supported by every major browser and all operating systems. Bitmap images can also be used to describe very complex images such as photographs. The only problem with using bitmaps is that they can become very large very quickly. Keeping bitmap file size down is possible when you use the right file format and optimizing techniques.

Cross-Reference   See the "Image File Formats" and "Optimizing Images for the Web" sections later in this chapter.

Choosing the right image type

For the time being, bitmap images are your best image solution simply because they're more widely supported by more image viewers, including the all-important Web browser. Because vector graphics have some significant benefits, including small file size and scalability, more work is being done in the vector graphic world. However, tools such as Adobe Illustrator can create vector graphics and then save them as bitmap graphics for use on the Web. This means you can experiment with vector graphics and still make sure all of your users can see them without needing special plug-ins or graphic viewers.

Image attributes

 Color depth and resolution

Given that the majority of Web graphics you create for your pages are bitmap graphics, this section is devoted to the different attributes of bitmap images. A good understanding of what aspects of an image each attribute controls is essential to learning how to create graphics that look good and download quickly. A bitmap image has a collection of attributes that affects its quality and file size. The most important are:

- ✦ Image size, measured in pixels

- ✦ Image resolution

- ✦ The number of colors used in the graphic

- ✦ The color pallet used for the graphic

These four attributes fall into two general categories: size and color. We examine the attributes by category in the following two sections.

Image size

An image's size is determined by more than just how much of your screen it takes up. Remember that the digital world has a variety of ways to display images — from computer screens to the printed page — so the actual size of an image is very much relevant to the device that displays it. The final display size of an image is based on the number of pixels, or squares of color, in the image and the resolution of the display device.

A display device that has a higher resolution and can display more pixels can handle bigger graphics and those graphics take up less of the display area, so the graphics look smaller on a screen with high resolution. A display device that has a lower resolution and can display fewer pixels can't handle extremely large graphics and the graphics they do display take up more of the display area and look larger.

Figures 4-1 and 4-2 show how the same image with the same number of pixels appear to be two different sizes when shown in displays with different resolutions. Figure 4-1 is displayed on a screen with a resolution of 800 x 600. Figure 4-2 is displayed on a screen with a resolution of 640 x 480. The image is 240 pixels wide by 123 pixels high.

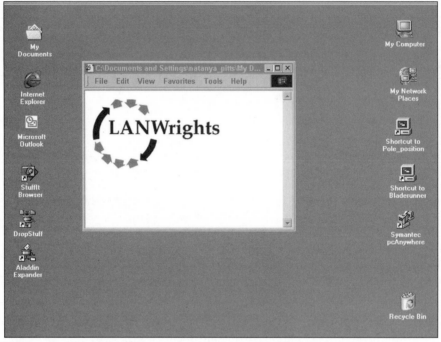

Figure 4-1: An image displayed on a screen with resolution set to 800 x 600 appears smaller than an image displayed on a screen set to 640 x 480.

Exam Tip   You can't anticipate the settings for every display device that your Web page will show up on, so it's best to build your graphics with a happy medium in mind: 800 x 600 screen resolution and 72 pixels per inch.

The other element of an image's size is how many pixels are in each displayed inch of the image. The more pixels there are in each inch, the sharper the image looks and the more detail you can include in the picture. High pixels-per-inch ratios make for better-looking graphics with significantly larger file sizes. If you're creating graphics for print, you want to set your pixel size to 300 or 600 pixels per inch. However, computer screens can only display 72 pixels per inch maximum, so using a larger ratio is a waste of file size.

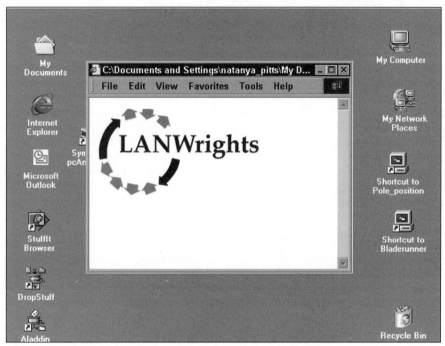

Figure 4-2: An image displayed on screen with resolution set to 640 x 480 appears larger than an image displayed on a screen set to 800 x 600.

You have more control over images during design when you have more pixels per inch to work with. When you're building images from scratch, start out at 300 pixels per inch and when you're happy with your image, reduce the pixel count to 72.

Image color

Images are all about color, and the color attributes for an image affect its final display and file size. The colors you see in an image are controlled by two different factors: color pallet and color depth. The color pallet is the collection of colors that you use to create an image. A color pallet can have as few or as many colors in it as you'd like. You can have a color pallet that is 150 different shades of blue or one that is 500 different shades of rainbow colors. The colors you have in your color pallet are the only options you have for creating an image.

Another attribute of an image is its color depth, which is simply the number of colors used to create the image. An image with a color depth of 256 colors has a limited collection of colors from which to draw. An image with a color depth of a million or more colors has a virtually unlimited collection of colors from which to draw. The larger your color depth, the larger the image file size.

Cross-Reference The "Optimizing Images for the Web" section later in the chapter discusses techniques for reducing the number of colors in your image to reduce file size.

When color pallets clash

Color pallets and color depth work together to display a digital image on a computer screen. A standard 8-bit monitor has a library of millions of colors from which to choose to form a display, but it can only show 256 of those colors at any given time. When you build a graphic in a graphics program, such as Paint Shop Pro, the system creates a pallet specifically for that image. The system also has its own default pallet that it uses for standard display. When the pallet for an image is different from the standard pallet, the system adjusts to display the image. If you have several different images open on the screen at once and they contain colors that are radically different from the system's pallet, you may see flashes on your screen as the system tries to adjust for each graphic.

To avoid screen flash and account for a collection of images built with different pallets, Web browsers use a technique called *dithering* to reconcile the differences between an image's color pallet and the system's color pallet. When the system dithers an image, it simply replaces colors in the image's pallet with system colors. Although this reduces screen flash, it can alter the display of an image drastically.

You can guard against dithering in two ways:

✦ Test your images in a Web browser on several different computers with different browsers running on different operating systems

✦ Use the colors in the Web-safe color pallet

The Web-safe color pallet

Not only do different operating systems have their own default color pallets, but Web browsers also have their own pallets that may be slightly different from the system pallet. Netscape Navigator's default pallet only includes 216 colors whereas the Windows operating system pallet has 256 colors.

The original Browser-Safe Pallet was created by Lynda Weinman and only includes the 216 colors common to the major Web browser pallets and the major operating systems. If you choose to use the safe pallet to create your graphics, you can be comfortable with the display of your graphics in just about any Web browser.

The downside to using the pallet is you only have 216 colors to work with, which may limit the quality and complexity of your images. You must decide on a case-by-case basis if you want to trade consistency of display for a limited pallet. You can read more about the safe applet and download a copy of the pallet to use with Photoshop or Paint Shop Pro at www.lynda.com/hex.html.

Image File Formats

 Graphic file formats

Understanding the ins and outs of the attributes of digital images is just one piece of the digital image puzzle. Another important piece is understanding the different file formats in which you can save your images and knowing when to use which format. There are a variety of file formats to choose from, but not all of them are supported by Web browsers. Each file format has its pros and cons as well as applications that it works best with. When you have a clear understanding of how file formats work, you can use them to your advantage to affect both image quality and file size.

File format options

There are different file formats simply because there are different image creation programs and different operating systems. In the infancy of digital images, each image-editing software application had its own proprietary image format. Eventually, it was clear that there needed to be formats that were supported by different applications so users could share images. Several different common file formats emerged, and over time, the list has been reduced to a handful of standard formats that just about every image-editing application supports. Table 4-1 lists the most common image file formats, their corresponding file extensions, and whether they're supported by most Web browsers.

Table 4-1
Common Image File Formats

Format	Extension(s)	Native browser support
Graphics Interchange Format (GIF)	.gif	Yes. In all versions of all browsers
Joint Photographic Experts Group (JPEG)	.jpg, .jpeg	Yes. In 3.0 browsers and later
Portable Network Graphics (PNG)	.png	Yes. In some 4.0 and later browser versions
Tag Image File Format (TIFF)	.tif	no
PostScript (PS)	.ps	no
Encapsulated PostScript (EPS)	.eps	no
Bitmap (BMP)	.bmp, .pcx	no
WordPerfect Graphics (WPG)	.wpg	no
Scalable Vector Graphics (SVG)	.svg	Only in testbed XML browsers

As Table 4-1 shows, many of the common file formats aren't supported by Web browsers. Therefore, when choosing the file format for your Web graphics, you're limited to a short list of graphic formats. The native file format you choose depends on what kind of image you're working with and your bandwidth limitations.

Native Web graphic formats

Not all graphic formats are created equal. Some formats are only designed to display on a particular platform, and others only work with particular kinds of software. When Web browsers were first developed, it was clear that they needed to support graphic formats that worked well on any computer and that had a relatively small footprint. The first file format to fit this category was GIF, which was followed shortly thereafter by JPEG. Recently, both PNG and SVG have emerged as options to GIF and JPEG, but neither is as well supported as the old standbys, GIF and JPEG. The following sections briefly describe the different native file formats, catalog the strengths and weaknesses of each, and include recommendations for what kind of images the file format is best suited.

Exam Tip   Be sure you're familiar with the features and drawbacks for each native Web image file format.

GIF

The Graphics Interchange Format (GIF) was created by CompuServe as a tool for displaying images in their pre-Web Internet access software. GIF files are platform independent and work in any graphical browser your users might use. GIF files are limited to a color-depth of 256 colors, which helps keep their file size down. In addition, part of the process of saving an image file to the GIF format is compression that creates a smaller file size than the original image had.

The limitations in color depth and the built-in compression of the file format make GIF files naturally smaller than other image files. However, limitations in color depth mean limitations in the quality of the graphic. Also, GIF is designed to be a *lossless* file format, which means that the graphic's quality doesn't suffer when the image is compressed. This may mean that the image file size won't be as small as other compressed file types (such as JPEG). As a designer, you can't control the level of compression in your file and must rely on the image-editing software tool you use to set the level of compression.

In general, the GIF file format is best used for line-art images and on graphic-rich Web pages. GIF is the best-supported file type and will work with even the oldest graphical browsers. Over time, GIF technology has evolved to support a variety of different image needs, including images that blend in with their backgrounds and animated images.

Transparent GIFs

A *transparent GIF* is one that blends in with its background. The background color of the Web page shows through as the background of the image, as shown in

Figure 4-3. Notice how the picture of Arthur in the "Arthur's Tip of the Day" section blends in with its background. The image's transparency makes this possible.

Tip   Only GIF files can have transparent elements.

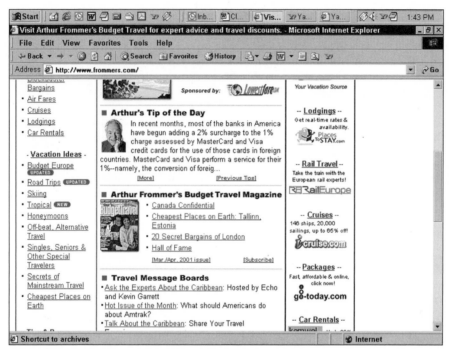

Figure 4-3: The picture of Arthur in the "Arthur's Tip of the Day" section is a transparent image.

Even when the background color of a page changes, transparent images continue to be transparent and show the current background color. This makes it easy to change the background color of a page, or reuse a single graphic on different pages with different backgrounds, without having to keep different versions of the graphic.

The technology behind transparent images is fairly simple. One particular color in the image is the transparent color. This information is saved as part of the graphic and when a browser displays the image, it ignores the transparent color and lets the background color on the page show through. A good image editor makes building transparent images a snap.

Cross-Reference   The "Creating transparent images" section later in the chapter details how to use Paint Shop Pro to make transparent images.

Animated GIFs

An *animated GIF* is a sequence of image files that are displayed one at a time to create a movie-like display. You can use animated GIFs to include short movies (animation) in your pages without requiring that the user download a special plug-in. However, animated GIFs can only contain GIF files and don't include a facility for adding sound.

Animated GIFs are saved in the GIF format and are comprised of images saved as GIFs. A Web page treats an animated GIF like any other image file and downloads the entire animation at once. If you have several, large animated GIFs on one Web page, they can greatly increase the time it takes to download the page. After the animated GIFs are downloaded to the user's browser, they can play repeatedly without being downloaded again.

The most difficult part of creating animated GIFs is creating the individual images that go into the final animation. For the GIF to flow smoothly, the images have to transition easily from one image to the next. You can use any standard image-editing tool to create the images for animated GIFs. However, you need a special tool to combine the images and create the animation. Animation tools have become very sophisticated and allow you to control the length of time between individual frames in a GIF and optimize the images in the final animation to help reduce file size.

Tip   The Animated GIFs page on Yahoo at `http://dir.yahoo.com/Entertainment/Comics_and_Animation/Animation/Computer_Animation/Animated_GIFs/` has links to several informative animated GIF sites.

JPEG

The Joint Photographic Experts Group (JPEG) file format is the other standard image file format most widely supported by Web browsers. JPEG was created as a way to overcome the color depth limitations of the GIF format. Image files are automatically compressed when they are saved as JPEG files and Web browsers decompress the images before they display them. You can control the level of compression when you create JPEG files.

The most significant benefit of JPEG files is that they support up to 16.7 million colors, as opposed to GIF's 256 colors. However, JPEG isn't a lossless format, and when you compress images with deep color depth into the JPEG format, the quality of the graphic may suffer. The more compressed the graphic is the fewer colors it maintains in its color pallet. One of the tricks of building good JPEG files is striking a balance between image quality and image size.

Although JPEG supports 16.7 million colors, remember that only 256 colors of those 16.7 million can be displayed at any time. You don't have any control over how the browser reconciles the myriad of colors in a JPEG with the 256 colors it can display. Dithering of JPEGs is the most common reason for degradation of image quality.

In general, JPEGs work best with digital photographs and on Web sites where graphic quality is extremely important and bandwidth isn't as much of an issue.

Some developers use JPEG for all of their images and build sites that look good and download quickly. If you choose to use JPEG as your file format to take advantage of the color depth, keep a close watch on the file size of individual graphics and for the entire collection of graphics on a Web page.

In the Real World   The need to have greater color depth without loss of quality is very important to Web design. JPEG 2000 is a new version of the JPEG format that should improve the loss associated with the JPEG format while maintaining the quality of images.

PNG

Portable Network Graphics (PNG) is the latest Web graphic file format and is a W3C specification. It was developed with the needs of designers and the drawbacks of GIF and JPEG in mind. PNG has several characteristics you commonly find in GIF or JPEG:

✦ PNG graphics are lossless

✦ PNG graphics can be transparent

✦ PNG graphics can be highly compressed

✦ PNG graphics can have great color depth

The main drawback of using PNG graphics is the lack of consistent browser support. Early versions of the major Web browsers (2.0, 3.0, and early 4.0) do not have support for PNG at all. The first PNG support appeared in Navigator 4.7 and Internet Explorer 5.0. As the 2.0 and 3.0 browsers are phased out, it will be safer to utilize the PNG file format.

The most effective use of PNG graphics is on intranet sites where you know more about your audience and the Web browsers they use. If you're fairly sure that your pages will be viewed with 4.0, 5.0, and later browsers, you can safely use PNG. Most major image-editing programs now support PNG, so you can convert old graphics from GIF or JPEG, build new graphics, and save them as PNG files.

SVG

Scalable Vector Graphics (SVG) is an attempt to bring vector graphics to the Web. SVG uses the Extensible Markup Language (XML) to describe the mathematical equations that make up vector graphics and is being developed by the W3C. As of July 2001, SVG is a Proposed Recommendation, which means that it should soon be a full-fledged specification. Support for SVG is emerging — albeit somewhat slowly.

A key benefit of SVG is that XML files are saved as plain-text files and are generally smaller than comparable binary image files. SVG files can also be added to HTML files as XML objects as well as take advantage of the XML object model in browsers that support it. In a browser that supports XML and the XML object model, you can link user events, scripts, and filters to the SVG object.

Although SVG represents the future of Web graphics, it's not very practical to use SVG for your graphics, because editing and display tools are still very limited.

Choosing the best image format

It's important to choose the correct image format for each image that you create, not for a Web site as a whole. A single Web page may contain images saved as both GIFs and JPEGs. When you're deciding which format to use, answer the following questions:

Exam Tip Knowing which graphic format to use based on graphic type, design specification, and user settings is an important topic on the exam.

✦ **What kind of Internet connection do the majority of your users have?** If your users generally have low bandwidth connections, small file size is imperative. If your users have the advantage of high bandwidth connections, you can sacrifice a bit of size for a bit of quality.

✦ **How important is image quality?** If rich graphics are fundamental to the success of your site, you want to choose an image format such as JPEG or PNG that supports rich color depth. If you need lossless graphics and can live with 256 colors, go with GIF.

✦ **What browsers do your users have?** If you need to support older browsers (2.0 and 3.0), GIF and JPEG are your best image format choices. If you know your users are on newer browsers (late 4.0 and 5.0), you can begin to take advantage of PNG.

✦ **Are you building a cutting edge solution?** If you want to put together a site that takes advantage of the most current technologies, as either a learning activity or demonstration, you should give some serious thought to trying your hand at SVG.

Cross-Reference The "Scenarios" section at the end of the chapter presents you with several different image requirements scenarios and asks you which image format you would use to meet the requirements.

Optimizing Images for the Web

Objective Image optimization

An optimized image strikes a careful balance between file size and quality. Optimized images use only the necessary number of colors or a reduced color pallet. In addition, optimized images should use the Web-safe color pallet. There are a variety of tools and techniques you can use to reduce the size of your image without impacting the quality of the image significantly.

Exam Tip An understanding of the different techniques for optimizing graphics is important for the exam.

When you want to add graphics to your Web pages, you can simply save them as a GIF or JPEG and go about your business. Chances are, however, that you could optimize your images so they look better and have a smaller footprint. There are a collection of relatively simple techniques that you can use to optimize your images for both appearance and speed:

✦ Reduce the number of colors

✦ Avoid anti-aliasing and gradients

✦ Slice your graphics into smaller pieces

✦ Reuse graphics

✦ Use `height` and `width` attributes

✦ Use optimization tools

We discuss these techniques in more detail in the following sections.

In the Real World The real goal of optimizing images is to find the happiest medium between file size and image quality. As you toy with the different optimizing techniques, you can watch your file size and image quality go from bad to worse and everything in between. Your goal is in between. The amount of file size or image quality you're willing to sacrifice depends entirely on your user's bandwidth limitations and the role images play on your site.

Reduce the number of colors

An image can utilize millions of colors and be megabytes in size. There's a direct correlation between the number of colors you have in your image and its file size. A good way to reduce your image's file size is to reduce the number of colors in the pallet you use to build your images. You can do this at two different times:

✦ **Before you build the image.** If you limit the number of colors you're working with from the get go, you can keep your image size down without having to worry about quality loss when you remove some of the colors. A down side to this approach is that some of the better tools in graphics programs require that you have a color depth of 16.7 million colors (24 bit) or more to use effects tools.

✦ **After you build the image.** After you're done building the image, get rid of the extra colors you aren't using. This will lighten your image's load and shrink its footprint. The only danger you face when you reduce the number of colors after you build an image is loss of some image quality. You may have to rework the image using fewer colors to get rid of any color at all.

Good image editors and image optimizing tools can help you quickly reduce the number of colors in an image and judge the effects the reduction has on the quality of the image.

Cross-Reference   The "Image Tools" section later in the chapter discusses such tools.

Avoid anti-aliasing and gradients

Anti-aliasing makes the transition between lines of color in a bitmap smoother by using varying shades of each color to blend the two colors. You get a smoother effect when you take advantage of anti-aliasing, but you add to the number of colors in the image's pallet to accommodate the transitions between colors. When possible, turn off anti-aliasing and create graphics with clean lines.

Gradients present the same problem as anti-aliasing does. Gradients are smooth transitions from a darker shade of a color to a lighter shade, or vice versa, and they require many different shades in between to make the gradient smooth. You can avoid a large color pallet by getting rid of the many and varying shades of colors needed to support anti-aliasing and gradients.

Slice your graphics into smaller pieces

Graphics that are large in file and display size can often be broken into a collection of smaller graphics that when reassembled, looks like the original large graphic. Even though you don't lessen the total file size when you break a large graphic into smaller graphics, you do make the download process less painful for the user. Instead of waiting for one large file to appear, the user can see smaller graphics pop onto the page as each one downloads.

The only drawback to this technique is that some browsers may add a bit of white space or even a line break between the images and not reassemble them into a duplicate of the large image. Be sure to test a collection of small images on several different browsers to be sure they reassemble correctly. Resize your browser window to see when images are forced onto new lines.

Reuse graphics

After a user downloads and views a graphic, a copy of the graphic is saved in the user's cache until it's cleared (either by the user or the browser). When you reference previously viewed graphics in other Web pages, the browser doesn't get a new version of the graphic from your Web site, it uses the one in the user's cache.

You can optimize graphic download time by simply reusing graphics wherever possible. Then the user only has to wait for the graphic to download once. This technique applies well to logos and navigation graphics. You want your users to have a consistent look and feel and this optimization technique is an added benefit.

Use height and width attributes

The `height` and `width` attributes let the browser know how much browser window space an image should take. The browser can use height and width information to create a place holder for the image in the window while it waits to receive the image. The browser can also display the image faster because it already knows how big the image really is.

 Caution Be sure that the height and width you specify for your images is accurate. If you provide the wrong height and width, the browser will scale your image to fit that height and width. The results are not usually good.

Use optimization tools

Our final optimization technique is to simply invest in an optimization tool that does all of what we've described in this portion of the chapter and more. Optimization tools are good because they show you how an image will look after it's optimized, give you several optimization options, and help you easily choose the happy medium between image quality and file size.

Many image-editing tools, such as Adobe Photoshop, Macromedia Fireworks, and Adobe ImageReady, have optimizing utilities built into them. You can also buy stand-alone optimizing tools or take advantage of Web-based optimizers. Most software optimizers are either shareware or commercial optimizers and cost anywhere from $20 to $150. Some of the best are:

- ✦ DeBabelizer (`www.debabelizer.com/`)
- ✦ GIF Cruncher (`www.spinwave.com`)
- ✦ Smart Saver Pro (`www.ulead.com/ssp/runme.htm`)

Online optimizers offer the same functionality as software optimizers, but you have to be connected to the Internet to use them. Online optimizers often charge a subscription fee so you can use them as often as necessary for a specific time period. Some good online services are:

- ✦ OptiView (`www.optiview.com/`)
- ✦ GifBot (`www.netmechanic.com/accelerate.htm`)
- ✦ GifLube (`http://websitegarage.netscape.com/O=wsg/turbocharge/gif_lube/index.html`)

A good resource for finding shareware and freeware image optimizing software is the C|Net's Image Editors section at:

```
http://download.cnet.com/downloads/0,10151,0-10077-106-0-
1-0,00.html?tag=dir.
```

If you own a professional image editor such as Photoshop, read through its help files to find out how to take advantage of its optimizing utilities. Online image optimizers are few and far between. Search your favorite search engine for "online image optimizer" to keep an eye out for new online services.

Cross-Reference   In Lab Exercise 4-1, you have the opportunity to optimize an image using an online service.

Image-Editing Tools

Image-editing tools come in all shapes and sizes with a variety of features and capabilities. Generally, the more you pay for an image editor, the more features it has. Image-editing tools fall into two categories:

✦ Drawing programs

✦ Paint programs

Not surprisingly, these two kinds of programs match up with the two kinds of graphics: Drawing programs are generally used to build vector graphics and paint programs are used to build bitmap graphics. Because bitmap graphics are the current graphic of choice for the Web world, most of the work Web designers do is in paint programs.

Drawing programs use mathematical equations to create vector graphics on a grid. Macromedia xRes and Adobe Illustrator are both examples of drawing programs and are most commonly used for schematics, charts, and other line-based images. Some graphic artists use drawing tools to build the foundation for Web graphics and then convert the vector images into bitmap images in their favorite paint program.

Paint programs such as Adobe Photoshop, Paint Shop Pro, and Image Composer create bitmap graphics and are the tools most commonly used by graphic artists and designers to create Web images. You can use paint programs to create original graphics, open and modify GIF and JPEG images from the Web, turn scanned images into Web-ready pictures, and even work with video frames to generate images.

Tip   Every Web designer should have at least one image-editing program in his or her tool set, but some of the higher-end tools such as Photoshop and Illustrator can be quite costly. Fortunately, tools are available that are affordable and rich in functionality, such as Paint Shop Pro. Choose your image-editing tool based on your resources and your needs.

As you might imagine, understanding how images work is only half the battle. To use your knowledge to create and optimize images for the Web, you need to know how to use a good tool. In the following section, you're introduced to the basic functionality of Jasc Paint Shop Pro 6 and you find out how to use it to build and optimize images.

Using Jasc Paint Shop Pro

 Objective Using Jasc Paint Shop Pro

Paint Shop Pro from Jasc software is a quality image-editing tool that is available at a reasonable price. Paint Shop Pro is a good addition to any designer's development toolbox because it's feature rich and has been tailored in the last few years to the development of Web graphics.

 Exam Tip Although Paint Shop Pro has many more features than are included in this chapter, the functionality highlighted here is the focus of the exam. Be sure you can perform these basic Paint Shop Pro activities before taking the exam.

The remainder of this chapter introduces you to Paint Shop Pro and walks you step by step through basic image creation and editing activities, including:

- ✦ Creating and saving new images
- ✦ Creating screen captures
- ✦ Adding text to image files
- ✦ Cropping images
- ✦ Changing an image's color depth
- ✦ Creating transparent GIFs
- ✦ Working with layers
- ✦ Adding special effects to your images
- ✦ Creating animated GIFs

 Tip If you own an older version of Paint Shop Pro, you can upgrade to the latest version for about half the price of a new copy. Because the latest version of Paint Shop Pro has new features designed to help you build better Web graphics, we encourage you to upgrade as soon as you can.

Before you can start using Paint Shop Pro, you need to download and install a copy of the software. You can try Paint Shop Pro free for 30 days, or purchase it for $99 as a download or $109 for the boxed copy. You can read more about Paint Shop Pro, download an evaluation copy, or purchase the software at `www.jasc.com/product.asp?pf%5Fid=001`.

 In the Real World The latest version of Paint Shop Pro is 7.0 but the exam covers version 6.0. If you already own 7.0, don't be alarmed if the screen shots you see in this chapter are slightly different from what you see in your version. The functions and techniques should be about the same.

A tour of Paint Shop Pro's menus and tool bars

After you install Paint Shop Pro, take some time to familiarize yourself with the software interface and tool bars, as shown in Figure 4-4.

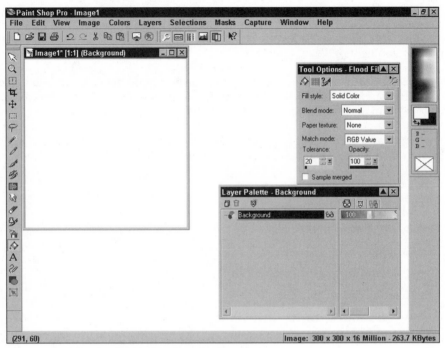

Figure 4-4: The standard Paint Shop Pro interface

Paint Shop Pro has standard Windows features such as a title bar; buttons for minimizing, maximizing, and closing the application; drop-down menus; and a collection of tool bars and tool pallets. The tool bars and pallets include:

✦ **Tool Bar.** This is the top tool bar immediately beneath the application menu. This tool bar includes links to standard functions (new file, save, cut, paste, etc.) as well as toggle options and a link to the Help menu.

✦ **Tool Pallet.** This is the collection of tools that runs vertically down the left side of the window. The Tool Pallet holds the standard tools for working with images, including selecting, adding text, painting lines and areas, adding text, and adding shapes.

✦ **Color Pallet.** This is the bar that runs vertically down the right side of the window. The Color Pallet includes a color picking tool, and the currently active background and foreground colors. Click on either the background or foreground box to launch a color window in which you can pick a new color for the background or foreground.

✦ **Tool Options.** This is a floating window whose display changes based on the tool you choose from the Tool Pallet. Look to this window to see which options are associated with each tool.

✦ **Layer Pallet.** This is a floating window that keeps track of the layers in your image.

We discuss layers in more detail later in the chapter in the "Working with layers" section.

✦ **Status Bar.** This bar runs horizontally across the bottom of the window. The Status Bar shows the size of the image, the color depth, and information on how to quickly access help.

To show or hide any of the tool bars and pallets, right-click on the tool bar or pallet and choose the tool bar or pallet you want to show or hide from the drop-down menu. To customize the Tool Bar that runs across the top of the window, right-click on the Tool Bar and choose Customize from the drop-down menu.

You may notice that some menu options or tools in bars and pallets are grayed out at different times. The tools and menu options that are available to you change based on a variety of factors. Until you open a graphic or open a new image window, most tools are grayed out. Many tools aren't available unless the image you're working on has a color depth of 16.7 million colors (24 bit).

To take advantage of Paint Shop Pro's many tools, we recommend that you build and edit your graphics at a color depth of 16.7 million colors. When you're done with your graphic, you can reduce the colors, as discussed later in this chapter in the "Changing color depth" section.

When you're comfortable with the Paint Shop Pro interface, you can start building and editing your own graphics with the software. The following two sections discuss basic image creation as well as some advanced techniques.

Basic image development

The basics of Paint Shop Pro activities include creating and saving images, and creating transparent images. We discuss these techniques and more in the following sections.

Opening, editing, and saving images

When you go to work on an image, you either work with an existing image or create a new one. To create a new image, choose File ➪ New. Next, you need to set the parameters for your new image in the New Image window, shown in Figure 4-5.

Figure 4-5: The New Image window

In the New Image window, you can specify the width of the image in pixels, inches, or centimeters, and set the resolution, background color, and the image type (color depth). As we mentioned earlier, it's best to create new images as 24-bit images with 16.7 million colors so you can access all of Paint Shop Pro's tool sets. Once you're happy with your settings, click OK to start working on your blank image.

To open an existing image, choose File ➪ Open. In the Open window, navigate through your file system until you locate the file you want to open and click Open. The Open window has a nice preview feature that allows you to preview images before you open them so you know you're opening the correct image.

To save an image with the same file name and file format choose File ➪ Save. Paint Shop Pro automatically saves the latest version of your file. If you want to save the image with a different name or in a different file format, choose File ➪ Save As. From the Save As window, you can specify a new name for the file and select the file format from a lengthy list of the most common file types.

Capturing screen images

In addition to creating your own images or working with images from clip art, graphic artists, or other sources, you may need to capture a display on your screen. This is a very common technique for creating software and Web site demonstrations. Paint Shop Pro has a wonderful screen shot utility that is easy to use and flexible. First, you configure the screen shot settings, and then you take the screen shot and save the file.

The behavior of Paint Shop Pro as it captures your screen shot is different depending on your settings. To configure the screen shot settings, choose Capture ➪ Setup. In the Capture Setup window, shown in Figure 4-6, specify exactly what you want to take a screen shot of, how you want to initiate the screen shot, and how you want cursors to look in the shot.

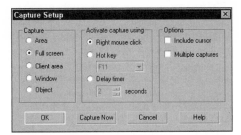

Figure 4-6: The Capture Setup window

In the Capture portion of the window, you can set what part of the screen you want to capture. The Full Screen, Client Area, and Window options automatically capture a particular part of the screen. If you choose Area or Object, you can use a cursor to draw a rectangle around the area to capture or select the object on the screen you want to capture.

In the Activate capture portion of the window, you specify how you want to activate the capture. The default is a right mouse click, but if you want to capture a drop-down menu that appears when you right mouse click on the screen, you'll need to choose a different way to activate the click. You can select the hot key of your choice or set a timer. In the Options portion of the window, you specify whether you want a cursor to appear in the screen shot or if you want multiple cursors — the cursor on the screen and Paint Shop Pro's cursor — to appear in the shot.

Tip   You can change the capture settings for every screen you shoot if necessary or use the same settings for every capture. The screen capture is taken based on the most recently set options in the Capture Setup window.

When you're done configuring your capture setup, click OK to save the settings for later screen shots or, if you want to take a screen shot immediately, choose Capture Now. To take a screen capture without changing the setup options, choose Capture ⇨ Start.

If your activator is a right mouse click, Paint Shop Pro disappears into the background and activates to take the screen shot the next time you right-click. If your activator is a hot key, the screen shot is taken when you next click the hot key. If a timer is the activator, the screen shot is taken however many seconds after Paint Shop Pro disappears into the background. The goal of the screen capture utility is to allow you to set up the capture, configure your screen display, and then take the screen shot.

Tip   If you usually set your screen display to larger than 800 x 600, you may consider resizing the display to a smaller size (under 800 x 600) to keep the image size, in both pixels and Kbps, to a minimum. It's also easier to see screen details when the screen resolution is larger.

Adding text to image files

A common practice for adding stylized text to a Web site is to build the text into a graphic. Adding text to a graphic is straightforward in Paint Shop Pro. Use the Text tool, shaped like an A and located on the Tool Pallet, to add text to a graphic and to edit text in a graphic.

Tip   You can only use the Text tool to edit text when you're using layers. Read more about layers in the "Working with layers" section, later in the chapter.

To add text to a graphic, select the Text tool and move the cursor to the approximate spot on the image where you want to add the text. Click on the graphic to bring up the Text Entry window, shown in Figure 4-7.

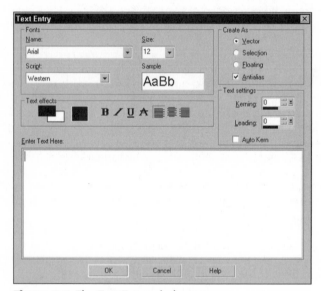

Figure 4-7: The Text Entry window

In the Text Entry window you can define the following for a block of text:

- ✦ Font face
- ✦ Font size
- ✦ Kerning
- ✦ Leading
- ✦ Effects such as drop shadow and line through
- ✦ Color
- ✦ Justification

✦ State (options are vector, selection, and floating)

✦ Antialias

After you set all of the attributes for a block of text, type the text and click OK. The text is added to the graphic and you can move it around as its own layer to finalize its position on the graphic. As long as the image is divided into layers, you can select the text with the Text tool to bring the Text Entry window back up and edit any of the text attributes as well as the text itself.

Cropping images

As you're working with new images or editing existing images, you may want to crop the image so it only contains a particular portion of the original image. This is an effective technique for reducing the file size and display size of images with extra white space. There are two ways to crop images in Paint Shop Pro:

✦ With the Cropping tool

✦ With the Selection tool

The Cropping tool on the Tool Pallet is the fastest way to crop an image but it only allows you to create a rectangular crop area. To use the Cropping tool, select the tool, click on the image, outline the area you want to crop, and double-click anywhere in the crop rectangle. You can resize or move the crop rectangle after you outline the crop area and before you double-click to actually crop the image.

If you want to crop an image using a shape other than a rectangle, you must use the Selection tool on the Tools Pallet to select the area and then crop the image. To choose which shape to use when you make your selection, click on the Selection tool in the Tool Pallet and choose the shape from the drop-down list in the Tool Options pallet, as shown in Figure 4-8.

Figure 4-8: Select the crop shape in the Tool Options pallet

Tip   If you choose an ellipse or circle as your crop area shape, Paint Shop Pro will still crop the image in the shape of a rectangle. Using a circle or an ellipse as the crop shape makes it easier to more specifically select the area you want to crop.

Changing color depth

We've mentioned several times that color depth is a key attribute of any image. There are times when you want to increase or decrease color depth. You can increase color depth if you want to use the full range of tools in Paint Shop Pro on a particular image or if you want to improve the quality of the image. You should decrease color depth when you're done building your image and want to optimize it for the Web.

To increase the color depth for an image, select Colors ➪ Increase Color Depth and choose the color depth you want from the sub-menu. Remember that when you increase color depth, you increase file size. To decrease color depth, select Colors ➪ Decrease Color Depth and choose the color depth you want from the sub-menu.

 Tip Decreasing color depth can change the quality of your image. As you experiment with color depth, be sure to save a copy of your color rich image as a baseline you can return to.

When you decrease your color depth to 256 colors, the Decrease Color Depth window pops up so you can specify how you want the color decrease to occur. You can choose which pallet to use (we suggest the Web-Safe pallet), how you want dithering handled, and other options, including whether you want to include Windows colors in your pallet.

Another way to decrease color depth is to save your image as a GIF file. Because GIF files only support 256 colors, Paint Shop Pro automatically reduces the color depth of the image as part of the process of saving to GIF.

Creating transparent images

Earlier in the chapter, we discussed the benefits of using transparent images and described how they work. You can use Paint Shop Pro's transparency functions to create transparent images quickly and easily. To make the background of an image transparent, choose Colors ➪ Set Pallet Transparency.

 Caution Only GIFs can have transparent backgrounds. If your image has layers in it or more than 256 colors, you'll receive a warning that the image will be converted to a "single, palleted, background layer." This has to occur before you can set a transparent color on the image. If you want to maintain the original version of the image, with layers and color depth intact, save a version of the graphic as a GIF and set the transparency on that image.

The Set Pallet Transparency window, shown in Figure 4-9, allows you to define which color you want to be transparent. You can select no transparency, the background color already assigned to the graphic (usually the color of choice), or any other color in the pallet that you'd like.

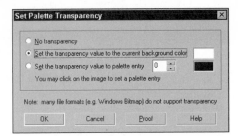

Figure 4-9: The Set Pallet Transparency window

Advanced techniques

After you get the hang of basic Paint Shop Pro activities, such as creating and saving images and creating transparent images, you can move on to more advanced techniques such as working with layers, using filters to apply special effects to images, and creating animated GIFs. The following sections discuss these techniques in detail.

Working with layers

Most images are made up of a collection of information that can be divided into layers. The background of an image may be one layer, a collection of shapes and photos might be several more layers, and a block of text yet another layer. You can use layers during the development of a graphic to keep the different elements of the image separate. You can move the contents of a layer around in the graphic independently of the other layers, delete layers, reorder layers to affect which pieces of the image are in the background and which are in the foreground, and more.

Using layers makes file sizes larger, so you generally don't want to maintain the layers in the images you optimize for the Web. In addition, GIF and JPEG files don't support layers. Combining all of the layers in an image into a single layer is called *flattening*. When you save an image as a GIF or JPEG, all of the layers are automatically flattened for you.

Tip

The flattening of layers means that you can no longer manipulate the different components of your image as individual elements. If you want to keep a layered version of your image for future tweaks and changes, save a version with layers as a Paint Shop Pro file and a separate version as a GIF or JPEG for display on a Web page.

When you're working with 24-bit images, a new layer is added to your image each time you add a component such as text or a shape to the image. To add a new layer manually, open the Layer Pallet and click the Create Layer button in the top, left corner, as shown in Figure 4-10.

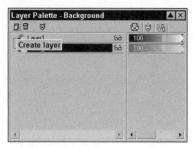

Figure 4-10: Adding a new layer
to an image

You can reorder the layers in your image by simply clicking on the layer name in
the Layer Pallet and dragging the layer up or down in the list. The layer listed at the
top of the pallet is the foremost layer, and the layer listed at the bottom of the list is
the back-most layer.

**In the
Real World**   Paint Shop Pro's layer functionality is extensive and allows you to control the opacity of layers, the transitions between layers, and more. Although advanced layer
functionality isn't on the exam, we recommend you take the time to read the help
topics on layers to become more familiar with how layers work. This way you can
take advantage of them as you build your own Web graphics.

Adding special effects by applying filters

More often than not, you want to apply special effects to your images to give them a
particular look. Paint Shop Pro has a collection of filters that help you apply special
effects to an entire image or portions of the image. You can use the Filter Browser,
shown in Figure 4-11 to see what kind of an effect the different filters have on a particular image.

Figure 4-11: The Filter Browser

To launch the Filter Browser choose Image ⇨ Filter Browser. You can automatically
apply a filter to an image from the browser. Select the filter you want to apply from
the list in the browser and click OK. To close the browser without applying a filter,
click the Cancel button.

Caution In Paint Shop Pro, your images need a color depth of 16.7 million colors to work with filters. Remember that you can always decrease your color depth later. Filters often use a wide spectrum of colors to achieve a particular effect; therefore, images with filters applied to them may be larger than the same image without the filter.

To add a filter to an image, select Image ➪ Effects and select the filter of your choice from the sub-menu. If you only want to apply the filter to a particular section of the image, use the Selection tool to select a portion of the image and then apply the filter. You can also apply a filter to a single layer in a layered image. Select the layer in the Layer Pallet and then apply the filter to the entire layer or a selection of the layer. You can use multiple filters on a single image and the effect of the filters is cumulative.

 Tip Most filters have a collection of settings you can tweak to specify how the filter affects the image. We suggest playing with the different filters and their settings to get a good idea of how you can use filters to enhance your images.

Creating animated GIFs

Earlier in the chapter, we discussed animated GIFs, which are a collection of images sequenced together in a sort of GIF-based movie that can run in any Web page without requiring special plug-ins. Paint Shop Pro includes a GIF animation utility called Animation Shop that you can use to build and edit animated GIFs. To launch Animation Shop, choose File ➪ Run Animation Shop.

 Tip Because animated GIFs are built with multiple images as well as instructions on how the animation should run, their file size can grow very rapidly. Before you create an animated GIF, be sure to optimize each of the images before you combine them in an animation.

The first step to creating an animated GIF is gathering all of the pieces of the animation and deciding in what order they need to appear. We recommend naming the images that will make up the animation in a sequential way (for example, fg01, fg02, fg03, and so on) so they're easy to assemble.

When all of your images are ready, you can use Animation Shop's Animation Wizard to put them together quickly. To launch the Animation Wizard, choose File ➪ Animation Wizard. The wizard walks you through the following steps so you can define attributes for the animation:

1. **Define the final size of the animation.** It can be the size of the first image included in the animation or a different size that you set.

2. **Set the background color for the animation.** This color shows through if the total size of your animation is larger than the size of the images you use to create it. You can create a transparent background or set a specific color. For example, if you create an animation that's 3 x 3 inches but the images inside of it are only 2 x 2 inches, you'll have a 1 inch background that's either set to a specific color or to transparent.

3. **Specify how images should be positioned in the animation.** If the images are different sizes, they all need to have the same starting position. Choose from upper-left corner or centered. You can also force the images to scale to fit the final size of the largest or smallest single image in the animation.

4. **Specify how many times the animation should loop.** You can identify the number of times or set the image to loop indefinitely. You can also specify how long each image should display (in 100ths of a second).

5. **Identify the images that should make up the animation.** You can choose as many images as you want and move them up and down in the animation sequence.

After you set all of these attributes for an animation, the wizard automatically generates the animation for you in GIF format, and you can add it to a Web page using a standard image (img) tag.

In the Real World   Animation Shop has a collection of functions for editing pre-assembled animated images. This information isn't required for the exam but is good to know if you plan to work with animated GIFs regularly. We suggest you read the Animation Shop help files for complete details on how to edit animated images with Animation Shop.

Key Point Summary

This chapter covered the many topics associated with using graphics in your Web page design. You learned the different kinds of digital images and their attributes, the different common file formats you can save images in, and how to choose the best format for your image and site needs. You were introduced to a variety of techniques for making your images smaller so they download quickly, and you found out how to use Jasc Paint Shop Pro to create and edit images and animated GIFs. The key points to remember about Web graphics are:

✦ Good Web graphics strike a balance between image quality and file size. A graphic on a Web page should contribute to the content of the page or be functional, or both.

✦ You should always consider your users' bandwidth limitations and the nature of your site — Internet or intranet — when deciding how to use images on your site.

✦ You can acquire Web graphics for your site from a variety of resources, including professional graphic artists, clip art collections, and Web-based image collections.

✦ The benefit of hiring a graphic artist is that the images are tailored to your needs. The benefit of using clip art images or images from the Web is that they're usually free or very inexpensive. Be sure you're aware of the copyright restrictions on any image you choose to use on your site.

✦ There are two kinds of digital images: vector images and bitmap images. Vector images are composed of lines defined by mathematical equations. Bitmap images are composed of blocks of color.

✦ Vector images are best suited to line art and diagrams. Bitmap images are best suited to photographs and other complex and color-rich images. Most Web graphics are bitmap images.

✦ The key attributes of bitmap images are image size, which is measured in resolution and pixels, and image color, which is measured in depth or the number of colors in the pallet used to create an image.

✦ Although an image can be built with millions of colors, a computer screen can only display 256 of those colors at any one time. Dithering is the process the computer uses to resolve differences in the colors and an image and the 256 colors it can display. A Web-safe color pallet of 216 colors is your best choice when you create Web graphics.

✦ Digital images can be saved in a variety of formats, but only GIF and JPEG are widely supported across the different versions of the major browsers.

✦ PNG is a new image format that combines the best of GIF and JPEG, but it isn't a well-supported format.

✦ SVG is an XML-based image format that is a new technology and not well supported by any mainstream browser.

✦ GIF files are lossless when compressed but are limited to 256 colors. Generally, the GIF format is best for images with a shallow color depth that need to download fairly quickly.

✦ JPEG files are compressed when they are saved and uncompressed by the browser for display. This may lead to some loss of quality but does lead to smaller file sizes. The JPEG format is usually best for images with a rich color depth where some loss of quality is acceptable and file size is crucial.

✦ There are two special kinds of GIF files: transparent GIFs and animated GIFs, which work as follows:

- Transparent GIFs allow the background of a Web page to show through.

- Animated GIFs are a sequence of image files combined into an animation. Animated GIFs don't require special plug-ins and are added to Web pages using the standard `img` tag.

✦ You can optimize images for display on the Web using a variety of techniques, including:

- Reducing the number of colors in the image

- Avoiding anti-aliasing

- Breaking large graphics into smaller images

- Reusing graphics across a series of pages

- Setting `height` and `width` attributes in the `img` tag
- Using image optimization tools to find the right balance between image quality and file size

✦ Image-editing tools come in two flavors: painting programs and drawing programs. Painting programs create bitmap images and drawing programs create vector images.

✦ Paint Shop Pro is a feature rich and moderately priced painting program that is a useful tool for any Web designer. You can use Paint Shop Pro to create new graphics, edit existing graphics, create transparent GIFs, take screen captures, change an image's color depth, and add text to a page. Advanced features such as layers and filters enhance an image's quality and appeal.

✦ You can use Animation Shop with Paint Shop Pro to create animated GIFs.

✦   ✦   ✦

STUDY GUIDE

This chapter contains quite a volume of information about the theory and practice of creating and optimizing digital images. In this section, you'll answer questions about images that are similar to the ones on the exam. You'll get the chance to work through some real-world image scenarios, and create and optimize images in the Lab Exercises.

Assessment Questions

1. How many colors are in the Web-safe color pallet?

    A. 256

    B. 216

    C. 156

    D. 116

2. Which of the following is *not* a characteristic of the GIF file format?

    A. You can control the level of compression with an image-editing or optimizing tool.

    B. The format is lossless.

    C. The color pallet is limited to 256 colors.

    D. You can designate one color in the GIF's pallet as a transparent color.

3. How can you reduce the number of colors in an image in Paint Shop Pro?

    A. Choose Colors ⇨ Decrease Color Depth and select a lower color depth from the sub-menu

    B. Choose Colors ⇨ Increase Color Depth and select a lower color depth from the sub-menu

    C. Save the file in the TIFF file format

    D. Save the file in the JPEG file format

4. When does dithering occur?

   A. When an image's color depth is increased from 256 colors to 16.7 million colors.

   B. When a browser has problems reconciling its color pallet with the system's color pallet.

   C. When a browser has problems reconciling an image's color pallet with its own color pallet.

   D. When two images are combined to create one image in an image-editing tool.

5. Which of the following is not a characteristic of a good Web image? (Choose the best answer.)

   A. It looks good and takes full advantage of rich color depth regardless of file size.

   B. It downloads quickly.

   C. It is functional.

   D. It is relevant to the content of the page.

6. What are some of the risks associated with using the JPEG file format?

   A. JPEG files can have a rich color pallet, which increases file size, and they aren't lossless.

   B. JPEG files aren't compressed so their file sizes are larger.

   C. JPEG files are lossless.

   D. JPEG files aren't well supported across multiple browsers.

7. Which of the following are *not* techniques for optimizing images?

   A. Use anti-aliasing and gradients regularly

   B. Reuse graphics across Web pages as practical

   C. Add the `height` and `width` attributes to your `img` elements

   D. Break large graphics up into collections of smaller graphics

8. In Paint Shop Pro, how do you specify which color should be transparent in a transparent GIF?

   A. Select the current background color

   B. Use the dropper to select any color in the image

   C. Set the transparency to no transparency

   D. All of the above

9. What role does user bandwidth play in image and page design?

    A. It should not affect how you design pages.

    B. It affects how long images take to download and affects how many images you use on any single Web page.

    C. It affects the speed of the user's connection.

    D. It should not affect how you combine images on a Web page.

10. Which of the following should you *not* expect from an image-optimizing tool?

    A. The tool may be available as a software package or as an online service.

    B. The tool requires that you choose which optimizing techniques you want to apply to the image.

    C. The tool will show you several optimized images with varying file sizes and quality so you can choose your level of optimization.

    D. The tool will apply several different optimizing techniques to an image at one time to control file size and maintain quality.

Scenarios

1. You're building a Web site that will be accessed by users with a variety of browsers and bandwidths. You want to use both line art and scanned photographs as images on the site. Which file formats should you consider for those images? What optimization techniques will you use to make the user experience a good one?

2. You're building a company intranet and you know that all of the intranet users have Internet Explorer 5.0 or later and will access the system with a high-speed connection. What role will graphics play on your site and which file formats should you consider for the images?

3. You're building a prototype Web site to test a collection of new technologies, including XML. The site won't be used regularly by everyday users but is instead a test bed for new directions for your company. What image formats would you want to explore as part of the prototype development?

Lab Exercises

Lab 4-1: Optimize a graphic using an online tool

1. Open the online optimizing service, OptiView, at `www.optiview.com/` in your browser.

2. In the section titled Try OptiView on your graphics and pages, type the URL for the company logo on the LANWrights, Inc. Web site at `http://www.lanw.com/graphics/lanwlogo.gif`.

3. Click the Try OptiView button.

4. Scroll down the results page to see how reducing colors and optimizing pallets affects the quality of the graphic.

5. Try OptiView on another graphic you've created that is available via a URL. If you're interested in signing up for the service, click on Click here to register next to the Demonstration Mode heading.

Lab 4-2: Create a new image in Paint Shop Pro

In this exercise, you'll open a new image, add text, add a special effect, reduce the color depth, and save the images as GIF files.

1. Launch Paint Shop Pro.

2. Create a new image (File ➪ New) that is 300x300 pixels in size and has a color depth of 16.7 million colors.

3. Set the foreground color in the Color Pallet to any shade of blue.

4. Click on the Text tool in the Tool Pallet and set the font to 36-point boldface Arial text that is centered. Set the Create As option to Floating.

5. Type **Certified Internet Web Master** with a hard return after each word in the phrase. Click OK.

6. Center the phrase on the image.

7. Use keyboard shortcut Ctrl+ D to set the text on the image.

8. Choose Image ➪ Effects ➪ Buttonize to turn the image into a button.

9. Reduce the number of colors in the image to 256.

10. Save the image in GIF format.

Lab 4-3: Create a transparent image

1. From the Examples folder for this chapter, which is on the CD that comes with this book, open the file butterfly.tif in Paint Shop Pro.

2. Choose Color ➪ Set Pallet Transparency.

3. Click Yes when the application asks you to reduce the image to a 256 color flat image, and click OK on the Decrease Color Depth dialog box.

4. In the Set Pallet Transparency dialog box, select the Set Transparency value to the Current Background Color option.

5. Click OK.

6. Save the image as a GIF file.

7. Build a basic Web page with the background set to navy blue and include an image (`img`) tag that references the butterfly.gif file you created in Step 6.

8. Open the Web page in a browser to test the image transparency. The navy blue background should show through.

Answers to Chapter Questions

Chapter pre-test

1. Vector graphics and bitmap graphics are two types of digital images.

2. User bandwidth should be a guiding factor in your image design activities. It should determine the maximum file size for each image, as well as the total file size of all of the images on a given page. The more images you have in a page, and the lower the user's bandwidth, the longer it takes for a page to download.

3. Image attributes include: color depth, resolution, and color pallet.

4. Transparent GIFs have a single color designated as transparent — usually the background color — which allows the Web page background to show through. Animated GIFs are a sequence of images compiled into an animation that behaves like a standard GIF file.

5. You can optimize images by reducing the color depth, avoiding anti-aliasing and gradients, breaking large graphics into smaller pieces, reusing graphics regularly, using `height` and `width` attributes, and using optimization tools.

6. Paint Shop Pro is a paint program for creating bitmap graphics.

7. Filters apply special effects to images or parts of images. Special effects include drop shadows, mosaic patterns, and other interesting visual effects. To apply filters to an image in Paint Shop Pro, the image's color depth must be 16.7 million colors.

8. You increase color depth in Paint Shop Pro by choosing Colors ⇨ Increase Color Depth. You decrease color depth by choosing Colors ⇨ Decrease Color Depth or saving the image as a GIF file.

9. You can control which portion of the screen is captured (whole screen, an area, a client window, an object, etc.), what key or time delay activates the capture, and whether you want cursors to be visible.

Assessment questions

1. **B.** The Web-safe color pallet contains 216 colors. This is covered in the section titled "The Web-safe color pallet."

2. **A.** You cannot manually control the level of compression in a GIF using a tool. The compression level is predetermined as part of the image format. The GIF format is lossless, has a limited pallet of 256 colors, and can be used to create transparent images. This is covered in the "GIF" section.

3. **A.** You can reduce color depth by using the Decrease Color Depth menu command or by saving the image as a GIF file. B is incorrect because increasing the color depth increases the size of the file. C and D are incorrect because the JPEG and TIFF formats do not require a reduced color pallet so the color depth isn't automatically reduced when you save to either format. This is covered in the "Changing color depth" section.

4. **C.** Dithering is an effect of the browser trying to reconcile its color pallet with the pallet of a particular image. A is incorrect because decreasing an images color depth with a tool does not cause dithering. B is incorrect because the browser doesn't have to reconcile its color pallet with the system's color pallet. D is incorrect because combining images increases the final image's color pallet but does not cause dithering. See "When color pallets clash."

5. **A.** Good Web graphics should always take user bandwidth into account and be optimized for quick download. A good Web graphic downloads quickly, is functional, and is relevant to the page. See "Digital Images."

6. **A.** The risks of using the JPEG format are that rich color depth can cause file size to increase and JPEG files aren't lossless, which can lead to degradation of image quality. B is incorrect because JPEG files are compressed. C is incorrect because JPEG files aren't lossless. D is incorrect because the JPEG format is well supported in the major browsers. See "JPEG."

7. **A.** Anti-aliasing and gradients can increase an image's file size instead of reducing it. B, C, and D are incorrect, because you can optimize graphics by: reusing them, adding height and width attributes to image tags, and breaking large graphics up into smaller graphics. See "Avoid anti-aliasing and gradients."

8. **D.** All of the options listed are ways to select the transparent color in Paint Shop Pro. See "Transparent GIFs."

9. **B.** User bandwidth affects how long images take to download and should be a consideration when you decide how many images to include on a page. C is incorrect because bandwidth does not affect the user's connection speed; the user's connection speed affects the bandwidth. A and D are incorrect because they do not take user bandwidth into account at all. See "Keeping an eye on image size."

10. **B.** Optimizing tools do not require that you manually choose which optimizing techniques to use on an image. A, C, and D are incorrect because an image-optimizing tool may be an online service or a software package, will show you

several options for optimizing your images, and will apply several standard optimizing techniques to an image at one time. See "Optimizing Images for the Web."

Scenarios

1. When you're building a Web site for mass consumption, you want to use as many well-optimized graphics as possible. GIF and JPEG are both well supported in all of the major browsers and are the file formats of choice. Make decisions about which file format to use for individual images based on the image's quality, content, and color depth requirements. To maximize the impact of your graphics, combine form and function to create navigation images and images that contribute to the content of the page. Reuse graphics across pages to take advantage of browser caching.

2. An intranet site is different from a Web site in that graphics aren't nearly as important for conveying a company brand. On an intranet, use graphics to increase functionality and to create a consistent user experience, but avoid gratuitous graphics — use HTML bulleted lists instead of graphical bullets, for example. Because you know that users on this intranet are using IE 5 or later, you might think about taking advantage of the PNG file format, which combines the best features of both the GIF and JPEG formats. You can, of course, use GIF and JPEG formats, and, because your bandwidth requirements aren't as constrained, you can use less compression to retain graphic quality.

3. A cutting-edge XML solution is a good place to experiment with the SVG file format. This will give you an opportunity to test SVG tools, examine issues associated with converting existing graphics to SVG, and converting SVG graphics to GIF or JPEG format for distribution on a mass consumption Web site.

For More Information

✦ **Graphics articles at Webmonkey.** http://hotwired.lycos.com/webmonkey/design/graphics/

✦ **Introducing Web Accessibility.** www.webreview.com/2001/03_02/webauthors/index03.shtml

✦ **Adobe SVG viewer.** www.adobe.com/svg/viewer/install/main.html

✦ **CNET Builder.com Spotlight on Web Graphics.** http://builder.cnet.com/webbuilding/0-3883.html

✦ **JPEG 2000 Links.** www.jpeg.org/JPEG2000.htm

✦ **W3C PNG site.** www.w3.org/Graphics/PNG/: find links to image editors that support PNG

✦ **W3C SVG site.** www.w3.org/Graphics/SVG/Overview.htm8

Multimedia

+ Multimedia design methodology
+ Current multimedia capabilities
+ Selecting multimedia elements
+ User interaction
+ Copyright issues

CHAPTER PRE-TEST

1. What are the three primary multimedia types?

2. What are the two primary ways audio files are delivered to the user?

3. What happens to an audio file when it is streaming?

4. What is the "spiral" model?

✦ Answers to these questions can be found at the end of the chapter. ✦

In this chapter, you learn how to effectively use multimedia within a Web site. Because Internet technology advances have allowed developers to integrate different media types within the same Web page, multimedia has gained popularity on the Web. Developers still have to plan carefully. There are several obstacles to using multimedia on the Web. To begin with, different browsers react to multimedia differently. Developers also must be aware of how media will react on different platforms. With a little planning, and a lot of patience, working with multimedia can be a worthwhile adventure.

Multimedia Design Methods

Objective
Multimedia design methodology

When multimedia first made its way to the Web, designers were ecstatic. Next thing you knew, audio and animation were popping up everywhere. After the glitz wore off, it became clear that multimedia could be annoying. No one wants to visit a site and have a hockey song blaring at him or her during the entire visit (especially if that person's surfing the Web at work). In addition, jerky animation isn't interesting to watch either.

When adding multimedia to a Web site, you should have a reason for doing so. Think of yourself as a user surfing the Web. What do you like? What annoys you? If you don't know where to find a site with animation or audio, visit the following sites to get a sense of what we are talking about:

✦ www.wallpaper.com

✦ www.nylonmag.com/04/index.html

A lot of what is liked by users comes from their personal tastes. However, there are some common themes that make multimedia engaging:

✦ **Identify goals for each multimedia element.** Don't just decide that music would be nice, and then add it to your company site. What is its purpose? Don't add animation because it looks cool. Is it illustrating a point?

✦ **Know the technology.** Don't decide that you want to add video and then jump in feet first. Take some time to research and investigate to find out what the current browsers support, what plug-ins would be needed, and what tools are needed to create the site.

✦ **Know your users.** Web design is all about targeting your audience. Be sure your audience is willing to download plug-ins.

The following sections take a closer look at defining multimedia design basics. This information will help you, as a Web designer, create engaging multimedia elements that advance the goals of your Web site.

Goals of a multimedia site

Developers tend to become overzealous when adding multimedia to Web sites. Just because you're no longer creating plain HTML pages, doesn't mean that usability should be thrown out the window. It's important to identify goals for the multimedia site before diving in. Remember that users want access to content; therefore, you need to plan carefully.

There are several items you have to identify when defining goals for your multimedia Web site:

✦ Your audience

✦ Your message

✦ Interface design

✦ Multimedia elements that complement the defined interface and message

✦ Tools needed

✦ Expertise needed

For example, if you create an online class environment, it might be nice to have a short Flash animation that takes your users through setting up their student accounts. In this case, you have to evaluate the previously defined items:

✦ **Your audience.** Students with a high technological understanding

✦ **Your message.** It's easy to sign up for one of our classes

✦ **Interface design.** Simple, clean, and informative

✦ **Multimedia elements that complement the defined interface and message.** Flash animation

✦ **Tools needed.** Flash 5 to create the animation and the students will need the Flash 5 plug-in

✦ **Expertise needed.** A Flash programmer

It seems like a great fit. Because a class environment is fairly controlled, you can request that users download the Flash 5 plug-in if they don't already have it. You shouldn't be worried that the users will have trouble downloading the plug-in because they have a high technological understanding. The Flash animation will take the student through the process of signing up before they have to do anything.

This is not to say that there aren't some considerations to make. Before you take any multimedia element live, you should test it on a focus group. What might work for some users, might not work for all users. After you've identified your goals and are ready to build your design, don't paint yourself into any corners. It's not uncommon to create a design, build it, and find that users don't like it, which means you have to go back to the drawing board.

Multimedia site design basics

With your goals identified, it's time to tackle some design basics. There are several issues to address when trying to create a functioning multimedia element that rises to the expectations of the user, such as:

✦ Outlining the navigational structure of the Web site.

✦ Deciding whether frames should be used.

✦ Determining whether plug-ins are necessary. If so, be sure they're easily accessible to your audience.

✦ Determining whether you'll offer a low-end version of the site that does not require high-resolution or plug-ins.

✦ Identifying your target audiences' average connection speed.

✦ Identifying your target audiences' viewing capabilities.

All of the previous issues are essential to creating an effective multimedia design. Remember: Multimedia is not just for fun; it must be effective in obtaining your goals.

Exam Tip Like a movie, it's important to create a mental model that users can interact with and relate to. There must be a common theme to your pages, where the content changes, but the setting does not. Users have come to expect familiarity, and if your navigation or layout scheme changes from page to page, you might lose your audience.

Multimedia Capabilities

Objective Current multimedia capabilities

Most designers come from the generation of too much TV, and most users want their monitors to turn into TVs — complete with audio. It seems like a perfect match, right? Well, there are several reasons that this is not yet the perfect match.

To create a truly effective multimedia experience, you need authoring, editing, and viewing tools. The problem is that the viewing world has not kept up with the creating world. This means that although you can create some killer multimedia experiences, the hardware (modem connections, bandwidth issues) and software (browsers, plug-ins) are not yet ready to play them.

This is not uncommon for technology. The principle has almost become central to the Web itself. As a designer, you have to be aware of what you can create, versus what your users can actually view.

Audio

Audio is different from most Web-based elements. An audio file is not affected by color palettes or monitor sizes. The three most common audio formats are:

✦ MIDI (musical instrument digital interface)

✦ WAV

✦ MP3 (MPEG, audio layer 3)

There are several ways to create and use audio files. The playback quality of the file depends on the recording process and file format used. For example, an MP3 audio format compresses audio files more than a WAV format. The MP3 file only loses a minor amount of audio quality, and it downloads quicker than a WAV file.

Developers can deliver audio files using two methods: downloading and streaming. If users select downloading as their option, they download the audio file to their hard drives and then playback the file. If the steaming method is used, the audio file is played as it's being downloaded. The following sections cover the most common file formats, followed by two sections dedicated to streaming and downloading audio files.

Exam Tip   The three most common audio file formats are: MIDI, WAV, and MP3.

MIDI

Musical Instrument Digital Interface (MIDI) is a digital audio standard originally created to allow sounds created on one keyboard to be played on another without losing any quality. MIDI is now used to enable electronic instruments and sound cards to communicate. The information contained in the audio file defines how the music should be produced. For example, it provides commands such as note-ons, note-offs, pitch bend, and key velocity. Because MIDI files don't contain actual notes (or sounds), the file size can be relatively small. The sound produced depends on the capability of the sound card and sound system to reproduce that sound. If you're interested in creating this type of audio file, all you need is the music, MIDI sequencing software, and a sound card. MIDI files have a .mid extension.

WAV

The WAV format was first developed by Microsoft and IBM to store audio files on a PC. The CDs you purchase of your favorite band use a WAV file format. When you hear people refer to "CD quality" sound, they're actually referring to the WAV format.

WAV files store the actual sounds in a wave pattern. Because each sound is stored in the file, the result can be large file sizes. If you intend to work with WAV files, get ready to share some space. About two minutes of this file type will consume about 20MBs of space. This means if a user has a 28.8 modem, it will take about 100 minutes for the file to download. WAV files have a .wav extension.

MP3

MPEG 1, audio layer 3, as it's formally known, is a rather new audio technology that has taken the Web by storm. Because WAV files are so large, and can take forever to download, the MP3 file format has emerged as a pleasant alternative. MP3 files are compression files that can compress CD-quality files to about 10 times less than their original size (this value is variable and can be as high as 17 times). What does compression mean for sound quality? The quality is definitely compromised, but because the human ear can only recognize certain frequencies, dumping those particular frequencies doesn't affect the user's experience. *Ripping* is the process of converting a WAV files to MP3s.

To learn more about tools that can create and rip MP3s, see the section titled "Tools for Creating Multimedia" later in this chapter.

Other audio formats

There are several other audio formats that are recognized by many personal computers. They are as follows:

✦ .aiff — Audio Interchange File Format (Macintosh native format)

✦ .au — UNIX native format

✦ .mov — QuickTime format

✦ .swf — Shockwave/Flash format

Downloading audio

Similar to images, an audio file can be embedded in an HTML file and then downloaded by the user. The user downloads the file, and then the media player plays the file. This process does come at a price. As discussed in the previous sections (see "WAV"), audio files can be quite large, requiring the users to wait during the long download process.

There's a significant disadvantage to requiring users to download large audio files: Users are not willing to wait long. To top it off, after a user downloads the file, the short playback length is likely to have stumped (and annoyed) the user. Remember that the key is to engage your users, not drive them away.

Similar to downloading audio files, you, as the Web designer, can embed a file that will play automatically, without giving the user the option to download. This is not recommended (at all). Remember that many people are viewing these pages while at work, and to surprise a user with song only ensures that they'll probably never visit your site again.

When using Flash, this recommendation is altered a bit. Flash allows designers more flexibility in controlling audio playback and timing. It's also common to find on and off buttons for music. We recommend that the default always be set to off, allowing the users the option of turning it on. You might be wondering about download time and quality. Well, Flash compresses audio files while preserving quality, as well as streams it to the user while it's playing.

Streaming audio

Streaming is a technology that allows audio files to be played as they arrive. Once the connection is made to the streaming audio server, the audio file is segmented and sent to a buffer on the server's hard drive. The buffer then packages the segments and produces a smooth, clean sound. This is an important breakthrough if you consider just how long it takes to download a WAV file.

Streaming significantly decreases the amount of time a user has to wait. RealNetworks was the first company to take this technology to the next level and is a leader in the streaming world. RealNetworks' RealPlayer can even play streaming media over connections as slow as 28.8 Kbps.

As a user, all you need is a media player such as RealPlayer; however, if you want to serve the media files, you need some server software that handles the outgoing streams. As you might assume, RealNetworks offers several versions of their server software — the first option being their Basic version. This version is free, but limited. The Basic version supports RealAudio 8, RealVideo 8, Flash animation, images, slides, and streaming text; however, it only supports 25 users at one time.

Exam Tip   The two ways an audio file can be delivered to users are the streaming and download methods.

Animation

Animation is all over the Web. There are several animation techniques you can use to spice up your Web site, and engage the user, such as:

✦ Animated GIFs

✦ Rollovers

✦ Flash

✦ Director/Shockwave

Exam Tip   This list is by no means exhaustive. In this section, we focus on the techniques that are covered on the exam.

There are several levels of animation — from simple, animated Graphic Interchange Format (GIF) files to complex virtual environments. No matter which animation technique you choose, the primary goal is to engage the user. Whether the animation's goal is to illustrate a concept, such as the images found at www.animated-teeth.com/, or to engage the user, the design must be meaningful and not distracting.

SVG and SMIL

There are two promising XML-based applications that are emerging multimedia standards:

✦ *Scalable Vector Graphics (SVG)*. A vector-based standard that allows for 2-D graphics and animations. There are several advantages to working with SVG, such as: Files can be created with a text editor; images are scalable (meaning they can be resized without losing any image quality); and images can be manipulated using scripts. For more information, visit `www.w3.org/Graphics/SVG`.

✦ *Synchronized Multimedia Integration Language (SMIL)*. This W3C standard allows authors to create presentations that integrate varying multimedia elements. For example, the author could integrate both audio and video and present a TV-like look. Integration is the key. Currently, HTML cannot define when an element should play in relation to another element. This means that it's difficult to synch two different multimedia elements. SMIL provides the author with the ability to define when each element should play in relation to another multimedia element. For more information, visit `www.w3.org/AudioVideo`.

Animated GIFs

Animated GIFs are simply a series of still images (or frames) set into motion at a designated sequence, speed, and repetition. For example, you can control the amount of time each still image displays, or the number of times the series of images loops. This method is one of the cheapest and easiest ways to flex your multimedia muscles.

If you're interested in cruising the Web to find this method in action, check out banner ads or animated logos. Most banner ads are created using simple animation. There are several benefits to working with animated GIFs:

✦ They are easy to create.

✦ The tools to create them are inexpensive.

✦ Browser support is good.

✦ They don't require plug-ins.

Although these are some compelling reasons to use animated GIFs, there are some glaring drawbacks, most of which are stylistic:

✦ Animated GIFs tend to be jerky; the transition between still images is not smooth like vector graphic animation (see "Macromedia Flash files" later in this chapter).

✦ The GIF color palettes can be limiting.

✦ GIF animation does not allow users to interact.

Exam Tip Animated GIFs can be used to add motion to a static page and to engage the user. Animated GIF creation is covered in Chapter 4.

Rollovers

You're probably familiar with rollovers, which are actions triggered when you scroll your mouse over a section of the page, and that trigger some action. The action is controlled by JavaScript. This approach is a simple alternative to the default underlined hyperlinks. The added event can capture a user's attention and provide additional content aimed to engage the user.

Cross-Reference For more information on creating rollovers in Dreamweaver, see Chapter 14.

Macromedia Flash files

If you've seen more than ten Web sites, you've seen Flash. Flash is a vector-based animation package that has swept the Web. To view Flash files, users must download a Flash plug-in for their browsers. This hasn't been a large hindrance to access to Flash files, but it's important to note that there are still users who are skeptical of downloading plug-ins from the Web.

In the Real World SVG and XML applications are the new standards for creating vector-based graphics and animation for the Web. Many of the big multimedia names have helped develop this standard, such as Adobe, Macromedia, Apple, Microsoft, IBM, Corel, and Kodak. Keep your eye out for this one. Read more at www.w3.org/Graphics/SVG/.

Flash-based Web sites are generally accepted by design and usability circles, and you can create usable sites if you're careful.

Caution One word of warning: Most users do not like scrolling text. Because of this, users are less likely to pay attention to scrolling text. Try to avoid this type of animation.

There are several aesthetic advantages to using vector animation. To begin with, vector graphics are responsible for the smooth, clean images you see in Flash movies. The edges of the images in Flash movies are smooth and non-pixelated. Therefore, the move from one frame to another isn't jerky like an animated GIF. File sizes are also rather small.

This is not to say that Flash is without its disadvantages. To begin with, there are still several usability concerns:

◆ Sites that are entirely Flash-based tend to focus more on the glitz and less on the navigation.

◆ There are accessibility issues because users are forced to download a plug-in, not to mention that users without graphical browsers will be left out completely.

✦ Some would argue that because Flash is a proprietary format, it's difficult for there to be a one-voice approach to vector-based images.

Cross-Reference

For more information on Flash, see Chapter 16.

Macromedia's Director

Some developers tend to get a tad confused when deciding between Macromedia's Director and Flash. You can use Director to create Shockwave files that can be viewed over the Internet. Director and Flash provide similar functionality. Director, originally designed to create interactive CD-ROMs, uses a scripting language called Lingo. Like Flash, this technology is viewed using a browser plug-in.

Exam Tip

It's not likely that the exam will cover Director. It's more likely that the exam will cover questions on Flash, rollovers, and animated GIFs.

Video

Unlike animation, video requires a fast connection and a lot of bandwidth. Video is an evolving technology that is likely to continue to gain popularity on the Web. However, for now, video is plagued with low resolution, slow frame rate, small dimensions, and pixelated rendering. If you've seen video on the Web, you're familiar with these problems.

Similar to audio, video can be downloaded by the user, or viewed as a streaming medium. The most popular video players support streaming media, or can view downloaded files. To view video on the Web, a user is likely to use one of the following players:

✦ RealNetworks' RealVideo

✦ Apple's QuickTime

✦ Microsoft's Media Player

Compression is a primary factor in video quality. The more compressed the video, the more quality suffers. A compression tool can compress the following properties:

✦ Frame rate

✦ Image quality

✦ Sound quality

✦ Image size

Exam Tip

Because of bandwidth concerns, video should not be a mandatory element on your Web page. For video that is longer than a few minutes, the developer should allow users the option to stream or download the file. Streaming will help save bandwidth and download time.

Internet TV

The concept of Internet TV is supported by the big guns of Microsoft. Microsoft now owns WebTV, an access service that allows users to use a set-top box (similar to a cable TV box) to browse Web pages using a WebTV browser and a hand-held control. The controlling device is connected to the Internet with a modem or telephone line. Once connected, users can surf the Web using their TV. The functionality is similar to using a desktop machine. Users can see graphics, interact, fill out forms, and purchase products.

Microsoft acquired WebTV with the idea of enhancing the usefulness of the Internet for the consumer. WebTV is impressive and it might be the wave of the future. Find out more at www.webtv.net/index.html.

Choosing the Appropriate Media

 Selecting multimedia elements

The alphabet soup of multimedia offerings can be a bit much for most of us. With each new year (sometimes with each new month) comes new innovations, which sometimes add another multimedia file extension to the mix. To make matters worse, you have to worry about browser support and plug-ins. There's only so much screen space to fill, and that space is valuable, so do your research first. Selecting the appropriate multimedia element is of utmost importance.

As a designer, you have to be careful. First of all, you have to plan on some of your users not having plug-ins. This means that alternative instructions or entry points must be provided. Both Microsoft and Netscape have created auto detection of needed plug-ins or have created plug-in support pages, but don't rely on them to solve the problem. Be sure to supply alternative instructions when designing your site. For example, the following Web sites do just that:

✦ www.nylonmag.com

✦ www.humancode.com/index3.htm

Next, you need to avoid one of the common designer pitfalls: including something because you can. For example, if you're designing your navigation, do you really need expandable and collapsible JavaScript menus? Does the expandable/collapsible menu fit within your defined goals, or is it just fluff? Be careful here. Don't make more work than you have to.

There are many variables to consider when selecting a multimedia element. Figure 5-1 illustrates this concept. To the left of the scale, you have elements that have small file sizes and require less bandwidth, which translate into a quicker download time. On the right of the scale, you have the opposite: larger file sizes that require more bandwidth and a longer download time. You might be wondering why anyone would want to select multimedia elements on the right of the scale. This question is answered by the defined goals for the site. For example, if your company is offering online training, it might be helpful to have video of the instructor to illustrate key concepts. In this case, a simple GIF image wouldn't do the trick.

Figure 5-1: Multimedia elements in relation to size, bandwidth, and download time

There are even more variables to consider when selecting the appropriate multimedia element. For example, do you have the programming knowledge needed to produce the multimedia element of your choice? Do you have the necessary tools? How do the multimedia goals you mapped out work in relation to the goals for the entire Web site?

Multimedia authoring

After you've selected the appropriate multimedia element, you decide who will work with the technology. It's highly likely that you'll be working within a team environment, where several individuals are involved. For example, you might need a graphic designer, a programmer, and/or a design specialist, in addition to the person who actually knows the multimedia technology in question.

As the designer, it's important that the goals of the site are not lost and that you target your audience. This might limit your multimedia designs because it requires you to create a site that is interoperable between operating systems and hardware platforms. Browsers are working on making this easier for designers; however, it's important to evaluate all design-related issues before tackling the project.

As the multimedia author, there are plenty of options. Do you want to create animation, or would a video work better? Even if you decide on the appropriate media — for example, audio — you then have to decide on the format. Each format has advantages and disadvantages. For example, if you were to use a WAV file, it would sound great, but many users may have to wait a while for it to download. However, if you opted to convert the WAV file to an MP3, users would have quick access, but the quality would suffer a little. These decisions are crucial and should be evaluated when you're outlining the goals for your multimedia creation.

Designing anything from a plain HTML interface to a multimedia fanfare is not much different. Whether you're creating a simple HTML document or a complicated Flash file that will be embedded within an HTML document, you only have a few seconds to capture your user's attention. The look and feel of the screen plays an important role in engaging the user. Graphics enhance a user's experience. Think about your reaction to a site with only black and white text and your reaction to a site with some colorful graphics. The site with graphics (as long as it's usable) is more engaging and is likely to catch the user's eye.

Caution Don't get carried away with too many graphic files; you have to be careful with download time.

Plug-ins or applets?

The battle between plug-ins and applets has been around for some time now. After you decide which multimedia element you want to use, you have to decide just how to get it to the user. There are two common options:

✦ **Plug-in.** A program that is installed and recognized by the browser. When the browser does not recognize a file format, the browser uses a helper application (the plug-in) to interpret the file. The applications are used as part of the browser. In other words, they are "plugged into" the browser. When this method is used, the file is downloaded once.

✦ **Applet.** Created using Java, which is an object-oriented programming language, an *applet* is a small application that can be embedded within an HTML document. The Java applet can perform interactive animation, calculations, or other simple tasks. The applet requires that the user download the Java files each time the applet is played.

There are several advantages to both approaches, and of course, several disadvantages. Using the plug-in approach requires the user to download a plug-in. Although this practice is fairly common, there are many users who may be hesitant to download anything off the Web. Plug-ins have become easier to install, and many support a one-click installation process. However, that does not change the mind of those who don't trust downloading software.

Applets pose another set of problems. Although applets allow authors to send both the content and the engine that handles the content, there are those who feel Java suffers from a few security problems. There's also the issue of having to build that engine, which is a feat in its own right.

The debate of whether to use a plug-in or applet is interesting, and a lot of it comes down to what you're used to. When using plug-ins, you lose control of the user's environment. But then again, it's easier to send the file and hope for the best.

Visualize and understand your users

If you are familiar with your users, you can anticipate the hardware, software, and browsers they'll be using. For example, if you're on an intranet and you know that all of your users are using Internet Explorer 5.5 and have high-speed connections, you can plan accordingly.

If you can, try to visualize your users and identify the following information:

- ✦ **Monitor size.** For example, do they use a 15-inch or a 21-inch monitor?
- ✦ **Connection speed.** For example, do they use a cable or 56K modem?
- ✦ **Memory specifications.** For example, how much memory do they have: 10MB or 512MB?
- ✦ **Graphics accelerator card.** Do they have graphics accelerator cards?
- ✦ **Video card.** Do they have video cards?

If you're developing your site for the general public instead of an intranet, you should develop it with the lowest common denominator in mind; for example, a 15-inch monitor, a 28.8 Kbps modem, and so on.

> **Caution**   When working with video, there are still quality constraints that cannot be avoided. Digital video quality viewed via the Internet is likely to be pixilated and jerky.

Performance

Performance is always a concern when dealing with multimedia. One keyword that you need to be familiar with is *compression* (we'll say it again — compression, compression, compression). You can compress graphics, animation, video, and audio files with the help of tools. Compressed files are smaller, and therefore, download quicker. There can be some loss of quality, but if you're careful, you can keep quality loss to a minimum.

There are several file formats dedicated to compression. For audio files, you should look into converting your WAV files to an MP3 format. In this case, you could save your users over 30 minutes of download time. The compression rate for MP3s is phenomenal. For example, if you create a WAV audio file that consists of three minutes of music (which is typical of any of your favorite songs), it would consume about 30MB of space. However, if you compress that file size by converting to an MP3, the size is reduced to about 3MB. Now that's compression!

Another way to control your multimedia's performance is to store the necessary files locally. In this case, the markup would be located on the Internet, but the multimedia files would be housed locally. An example of this would be files that are located on a CD-ROM. Macromedia's Director supports this type of functionality.

Building User Interaction

    User interaction

You want your users to enjoy their experience. As a matter of fact, this concept is central to Web design. As with any design tactic, as the developer, it's important to engage the user. There are several different methods that developers use; however, the most successful of these methods is known as the *spiral* concept.

The spiral concept focuses on three stages:

✦ **Interest.** Peek the user's interest.

✦ **Activity.** Allow the user to interact with navigational elements.

✦ **Resolution.** The desired goal is attained.

To illustrate this concept, think of a product Web site. The first stage is to peek the user's interest. This might be accomplished by using interesting graphics or other multimedia. Next, you need to engage the user. This might be accomplished by providing navigational elements that allow the user to navigate to the product for which he or she is looking. The final stage is resolution. In this case, after the user locates and purchases the products, resolution is achieved.

Exam Tip   The spiral method uses three stages to engage users: interest, activity, and resolution.

Just how do you achieve the first two stages? It's important to focus on the user's experience. The more enjoyable that experience is, the more likely he or she will visit your site again. What's important to understand is that whatever multimedia elements you use, they must complement your Web site. In addition to complementing your Web site, they must serve a purpose. Just playing music to play music will not engage users. As a matter of fact, it's likely to drive them away. Be sure to identify and evaluate the goals of your multimedia elements, and then make sure those goals are in line with the goals of the entire site. When a user is engaged (or in a *heightened state*), they're more likely to reach the resolution stage, which means that your goals have been attained.

Exam Tip   When you engage a user, you're elevating the user to a heightened state. If a user becomes lost in a site and loses track of time, you've achieved that heightened state.

There have been studies that have examined user activity, and some of the common traits associated with a user experiencing a heightened state are:

✦ Users concentrate.

✦ Users are challenged.

✦ Users become mesmerized.

✦ Users lose self-consciousness.

✦ Users lose sense of time.

Use the previous information to focus on ways to encourage these characteristics. You might want to try an experiment of your own and go surf the Web in search of an engaging site.

In the Real World Although it would be wonderful to take users to a heightened state while they're shopping for a garden hose, this is not always likely. Business-oriented sites have to be careful to not add glam and glitz to engage their users. In this case, you would want usability and well-written text to engage the user.

Tools for Creating Multimedia

Multimedia tools range from the ridiculously expensive, to the wonder of being free. Selecting the right tool for the job has a lot to do with your multimedia requirements. For example, if you created an audio file that played show tunes in the background while your users surfed your site (which is not recommended by the way), you wouldn't need a state-of-the-art audio authoring program. However, if you worked for an orchestra and you were publishing some of its works on the Web to solicit fundraising support, you might consider investing in a professional audio authoring program.

The following sections define authoring tools for audio, video, and animation. And, of course, you have to know which plug-ins will play your multimedia extravaganzas, so we dedicate a section to media players.

Exam Tip The exam will not cover specific tools, except for those tools that have dedicated chapters in this book. However, the best way to learn about multimedia is to grab some tools and play.

Audio authoring, editing, and converting

When it comes to audio-editing tools, you have a lot to choose from. We have chosen our favorite three; however, we have left out some big names. For example, Pro Tools created by Digidesign (www.digidesign.com), sells for around $1000 dollars. Pro Tools is used by Hollywood and the MTV generation, and is most likely not necessary for those of you who just want to add a little music to your site.

In this section, we assume you're not a movie-making mogul, and stick with programs that are powerful and affordable. Note that (and we hate to state the obvious) you need a sound card to use any audio software.

Cool Edit Pro

URL: www.syntrillium.com/cep/

Platform: Windows 95/98/Me/NT/2000

Processor: 486 or better

RAM: 8MB (32MB or more recommended)

Syntrillium has created a wonderful audio editing package that provides the author with support for recording, editing, and mixing music. It offers a whopping 64 tracks of music, so if you're a musician, this tool packs a lot of punch. Unlike some of the other expensive audio authoring packages, there's no special hardware needed. Make sure you have a sound card, and some good speakers, and you should be ready to rock 'n' roll. Of course, you have to supply the music. But after the music's ready, you can edit, convert, and play. This tool also offers effects that can be applied to your music in case you want to make the vocals echo.

RealJukebox

URL: www.realnetworks.com

Platform: Windows 95/98/NT 4.0/2000

Processor: Pentium-200 MMX, Cyrix 6x86MX PR/233, or AMD K5 PR/200

RAM: 32MB

RealJukebox comes to us from RealNetworks, and as you might guess, can do most everything with your audio files. This package allows you to acquire, play, record, and manage your digital music collection right there from your PC. Your music can be saved as RealNetworks' proprietary format, as well as WAV, or MP3 formats. The Jukebox is more of a musical management tool; however, it does offer recording capabilities.

Sound Forge

URL: www.sonicfoundry.com

Platform: Windows 98SE/Me/2000

Processor: 200 MHz

RAM: 32MB

Sound Forge is a wonderful sound-editing software tool for Windows. As with Cool Edit Pro, Sound Forge allows authors to create and manipulate audio files. Creating Sound Forge files is easy and you can export them in almost every file format imaginable, from WAV to MP3. As an added bonus, it offers tons of cool effects to jazz up your audio files.

Video authoring and editing

Working with video is no easy feat. As a Web designer, you may contact someone to create video presentations for your Web site. Or, you may be the one who has to create the video footage. Either way, there are two tools you should know about: Final Cut Pro and Premiere. Both products are wonderful video editing packages and are worth looking at.

Final Cut Pro

> **URL:** www.apple.com/finalcutpro/
>
> **Platform:** Mac OS 9.1 or later
>
> **Processor:** 300MHz or faster
>
> **RAM:** 16MB

Final Cut Pro may cost a lot, but as far as video-editing software goes, this is one of the best. Not only does this program support the basic editing needs of any videographer, but it also supports complex editing techniques, as well as some cool special effects. You can even superimpose images. This is not a tool for amateurs; however, if you know your way around video, and you want the best, you'll want to check out this program.

Adobe Premiere

> **URL:** www.adobe.com/products/premiere/main.html
>
> **Platform:** Microsoft Windows 98/98SE/Me/2000/NT 4.0 with Service Pack 4, 5 or 6a
>
> **Processor:** Intel Pentium-30
>
> **RAM:** 64MB

As a cheaper alternative to Final Cut Pro, Adobe Premiere has provided users with a fairly affordable solution to video editing. In the beginning, Adobe Premiere was an easy tool built to edit QuickTime movies. It has come a long way to support complex editing and even some special effects. And as with Final Cut Pro, Premiere supports IEEE 1394 (FireWire/i.Link), so you can import your digital video faster than ever before.

Animation

From basic GIF animation to full-fledged Flash performances, animation can jazz up your site and keep your users interested. Beware: bad animation can drive your users away. Here are some of the tools that make animation work.

Exam Tip There are likely to be several questions about Flash on the exam. To prepare for these questions, also be sure to read Chapter 16.

Adobe After Effects

> **URL:** www.adobe.com/products/aftereffects/main.html
>
> **Platform:** Windows 98/Me/2000 or Mac OS v9.0.4/9.1/X
>
> **Processor:** Intel Pentium II or faster or Power PC processor (G4 recommended)
>
> **RAM:** 128MB (256 recommended) or 64MB (128 recommended)

Adobe After Effects allows authors to grab the images they created in Photoshop (or some other graphics editor) and transform them into wonders of animation. After Effects preserves layers, so you can manipulate each layer. This makes After Effects a powerful animation tool when used with Photoshop. Another benefit to using the Adobe family of products is that the integration does not end with Photoshop. After Effects also integrates nicely with Adobe Premiere and Illustrator. All in all, it's a wonderful tool for creating 2D or 3D composites, animation, or any other special effects needs.

Macromedia Flash

URL: www.macromedia.com/software/flash/

Platform: Windows 95/98/NT4/2000 Professional or Mac OS v8.5 and higher

Processor: 133 MHz

RAM: 32MB of free RAM

Flash has become such a Web powerhouse, that it is has its very own dedicated chapter in this book. As a program, Flash is wonderful. Macromedia has made it easy to use and the interface is flawless. The tool is fairly easy to learn and its Web site offers plenty of support.

If you want to create Flash animation, you have to use Macromedia's Flash program. With all of its bells and whistles, there are still some issues concerning how usable Flash animations can be. However, with careful planning, and some quality testing, it's possible to create usable Flash sites.

In the Real World Because Macromedia received so much flack about Flash animations not being a usable alternative to Web design, they published several articles and tips about creating usable Flash sites: www.macromedia.com/software/flash/productinfo/usability.

Macromedia Director

URL: www.macromedia.com/software/director/

Platform: Windows 95/98/2000/NT 4 with SP3/ME or Mac G3 or higher

Processor: Intel Pentium II

RAM: 64MB of free RAM

Director is a lot like Flash, as a matter of fact, there are many Flash users who might do better to take a look at Director. Macromedia is responsible for both of these products, and there are a few differences that should help guide you in your decision to use Director or Flash to create your animations. Director files must be viewed using a Shockwave player. Like the Flash plug-in, this player can be downloaded from Macromedia.

To begin with, Flash is a vector-based program, meaning that images can be resized without any loss of quality. Director images are bitmap images, and therefore, become distorted when resized. This means you really don't want to allow your user to change the window size when viewing the animation.

Director used to be at a disadvantage because it did not support streaming; however, that changed recently.

As for the interface, Director is the only Macromedia product that does not follow the standard Macromedia interface. This is likely to change in future versions, but for now, Director sticks with a theater metaphor, using labels such as stage, cast, and score. If you're a Flash user, it might take you a while to get used to Director's interface, but once you do, you might find you like it better than Flash.

Multimedia players

For users to hear your audio or see your video, they need a player. The browser does not recognize every file type, and when it comes to audio and video, it needs a helper application to interpret the unknown file types. There are three common players that support most of the same formats, they are:

✦ RealPlayer

✦ QuickTime

✦ Media Player

The following sections explore each player.

Players are important, because these are the applications that users use to play your multimedia elements. If a user has downloaded an older version of a player, or is using one that doesn't have support for most media types, that user might not be able to play your multimedia. Worse yet, they might be able to play it, but the quality might be poor.

One of the significant drawbacks to relying on your users to play your music with a player application is that you have no control over which player they use. If you offer multimedia, be sure to provide hyperlinks to player downloads. We suggest recommending one of the three defined in this section. If you fail to point users to download the necessary player, you might lose them. You should never assume that your users know what a player is, or where to find one. It's safe to assume that they have no idea that each player is different. Be sure to guide them, and they will be thankful. For a good example of guided multimedia, visit `www.cnet.com`. Select any of their video clips, and notice how they offer download information.

Another helpful tip is to be sure to test your multimedia on the three most common players, and check the performance at different connection speeds.

RealNetworks' RealPlayer

This free streaming media player is considered the best of the crop by most design-ers. Supporting more multimedia formats than any other player, it's no wonder most users choose this handy little application. The best part is that RealPlayer is easy to use. For audio, its streaming capabilities are nearly unmatched. It buffers faster than the previous version, which allows the user to listen to streaming audio without interruption. And for its video, RealNetworks claims that it's VHS quality, and from what we have seen, we can't disagree. You can find RealPlayer at www.realnetworks.com.

Apple's QuickTime

QuickTime has a dedicated following of Macintosh users, and there's good reason. This means whether you like it or not, some of your users will be using this player. The interface is Mac-friendly, which means that if you're a Mac user, you'll like how this tool feels. However, there are considerable drawbacks to this tool.

To begin with, QuickTime, like the Window's Media Player, doesn't support its competitors' file formats. This makes it difficult for you, as a developer, to create multimedia files that can be played in all players. Although QuickTime doesn't sup-port its competitors' formats, it does support most of the usual suspects, such as WAV, MIDI, AU, AIFF, and MP3.

As for performance, QuickTime is just not up to speed with the other two players listed in this section. As a designer, this might be all you have to read to encourage your users to opt for RealPlayer. You can read more about this player at www.apple.com/quicktime.

Microsoft's Windows Media Player

Although we like Microsoft's Windows Media Player and plenty of users out there use it, it doesn't support as many formats as RealPlayer. This is not to say that this is a bad tool. It has wonderful audio and video performance, and can even perform tasks such as recording and managing your audio collection. The interface is easy to use, and should look similar to your Windows environment. You can perform all sorts of tasks with this program. You can play, rip, encode, and even organize your audio files, in addition to playing video.

One advantage to using the Windows Media Player is that it provides a smoother video viewing experience because it doesn't buffer as often as RealPlayer. Users may be attracted to its wealth of information and online pointers to artists and Internet radio stations, in addition to its management capabilities.

This program allows you to record; however, because the Windows Media Player does not support MP3 recording, and instead opts for its own format (WMA), it can be problematic, especially if you plan to distribute your recordings to anyone else. There are also issues related to streaming. The Windows Media Player doesn't sup-port Real-formatted streams, which means the only way you can use the Windows

Media Player to view streaming media is if the site in question offers that media in a WMA format. Finally, this tool only works in Windows 98 and higher. You can read more about this tool at `www.microsoft.com/windows/windowsmedia/en/ default.asp`.

Copyright Law and Infringement

 Copyright issues

The Web is an open book. You can view and copy source code, steal images, and even download audio files. However, according to copyright law, it's illegal to use any published Internet material without permission from its creator or owner. This means you can't steal an image, use a song, or copy a video without permission from its owner. Currently, it's difficult to keep track of your property on the Web; however, this issue is gaining importance and you should be on the lookout for new ways to track your information on the Web.

Key Point Summary

This chapter focused on the current state of multimedia, and the tools used to create, edit, and play it. It covered the use of animation, audio, and video, and how you might be able to use these technologies to engage your users. Like any Web-related topic, there are design principles that you have to keep in mind to use multimedia effectively. Here are the key points:

✦ Like a movie, it's important to create a mental model for your site that users can interact with and relate to. There must be a common theme to your pages. Users have come to expect familiarity, and if your navigation or layout scheme changes from page to page, you might lose your audience.

✦ The three most common audio file formats are: MIDI, WAV, and MP3.

✦ The two ways an audio file can be delivered to users are the streaming and download methods.

✦ Animation is all over the Web. There are several animation techniques you can use to spice up your Web site, and engage the user, such as:

- Animated GIFs

- Rollovers

- Flash

- Director/Shockwave

✦ Because of bandwidth concerns, video should not be a mandatory element on your Web page. For video that is longer than a few minutes, the developer should allow users the option to stream or download. Streaming will help save bandwidth and download time.

✦ The spiral method uses three stages to engage users: interest, activity, and resolution.

✦ When you engage a user, you're elevating the user to a heightened state. If a user becomes lost in a site and loses track of time, you've achieved that heightened state.

✦ Multimedia tools range from the ridiculously expensive, to the wonder of being free. Selecting the right tool for the job has a lot to do with your multimedia requirements.

✦ From basic GIF animation to full-fledged Flash performances, animation can jazz up your site and keep your users interested. Bad animation, on the other hand, can drive them away.

✦ For users to hear your audio or see your video, they need a player. Browsers do not recognize every file type, and when it comes to audio and video, helper applications to interpret the unknown file types may be needed.

✦   ✦   ✦

STUDY GUIDE

This chapter covered the effective use of multimedia in Web sites. As a designer, you must be aware of how a media will react on different platforms. With a little planning, and a lot of patience, working with multimedia can be a worthwhile adventure. To make sure you have a firm grasp of all the topics in this chapter and to help you prepare for the exam, answer the following questions and spend some time on the scenarios and labs.

Assessment Questions

1. Which text animation technique should you avoid?

    A. Turning text

    B. Rounding text

    C. Pulling text

    D. Scrolling text

2. What are three of the most common audio file formats?

    A. AUFF, WAV, and MP3

    B. MIDI, WAV, and MP3

    C. AIFF, WAV, and MP3

    D. UA, WAV, and MP3

3. Which two factors inhibit rapid technology adoption?

    A. Processing speed and user training

    B. Browser support and bandwidth

    C. Authoring tools and processing speed

    D. User training and browser support

4. Which of the following is the technology type used to describe rollovers and Flash?

    A. Audio

    B. Streaming

    C. Animation

    D. Video

5. When planning a Flash site, which of the following should you consider including in your design?

    A. A Java applet

    B. Hyperlink pointing to a Flash plug-in download

    C. Tons of images

    D. A quit button

6. Which of the following is a disadvantage of using WAV files?

    A. Sound quality

    B. Compatibility issues

    C. Authoring tool availability

    D. File size

7. Why might you opt for streaming method delivery over a download method delivery for your video or audio files?

    A. Streaming allows files to be played while downloading; therefore, reducing the users' wait time.

    B. Streaming compresses file sizes; therefore, allowing for a quicker download.

    C. Streaming allows users to play the file directly from the Web site.

    D. Streaming provides a better sound quality.

Scenarios

1. You've been asked to create a Flash version of your company's Web site. Your boss asks you to present a proposal outlining all the possible concerns for building a Flash site. Make a list of the concerns you would raise.

2. You're creating audio files for your Web site. These files will be played as background music while your users visit your Web site. You have three formats to choose from: MIDI, WAV, and MP3. Which file type did you choose and why?

Lab Exercises

Lab 5-1: Visiting multimedia

For this lab, visit one of the following multimedia sites:

    ✦ www.wallpaper.com

✦ www.thesimpsons.com

✦ www.animated-teeth.com

Evaluate these sites according to the following goal-related questions:

✦ Who is their intended audience?

✦ Does the multimedia enhance the Web site?

✦ Does the multimedia engage the user?

✦ What is the message of the multimedia element?

Answers to Chapter Questions

Chapter pre-test

1. There are three main types of multimedia: audio, video, and animation. Audio and animation have become commonplace on the Web, but video is catching up.

2. Audio (and video) files can be delivered to a user using a streaming or download method. The streaming method allows users to play the audio file while it's downloading. The download method requires the user to completely download the audio file before they can begin playing it.

3. When a file is delivered to the user using the streaming method, it's broken into segments. The segments are then sent to a media player that contains a buffer. The buffer allows the file to begin to play as the segments arrive. As the segments arrive, the song is patched back together.

4. The "spiral" concept refers to a common method for elevating a user to a heightened state. This method follows three stages: interest, activity, and resolution.

Assessment questions

1. **D.** Scrolling text is the one type of animation that designers are warned about. Users tend to ignore scrolling text, and actually find it distracting at times. If you have important information, be sure it's not present it as scrolling text. See "Macromedia Flash files."

2. **B.** The three most common audio file formats are MIDI, WAV, and MP3. The WAV file format is used on most CDs. The MIDI file format doesn't contain any sounds, but rather information about those sounds. And finally, the MP3 file format is a compression format that drastically reduces file size while preserving sound quality. See "Audio."

3. B. Browser support and bandwidth hinder the rapid adoption of multimedia technology. The authoring tools are out there; however, bandwidth limits file size delivery. In addition, browsers and media players don't support all the possible file formats, requiring the designer to plan carefully. See "Multimedia Capabilities."

4. C. Rollovers and Flash are both types of animation. In addition to those two types of animation, you commonly see animated GIFs. See "Animation."

5. B. You should always provide users with a link to the appropriate plug-in or player needed to play your multimedia element. For Flash, your users need to download a Flash plug-in. See "Macromedia Flash files."

6. D. The WAV file has superb sound quality; just check out any CD from your favorite band. Although the sound is great, the file size is too large for Web use. One minute of play time translates into about 10MB of storage space. See "WAV."

7. A. Requiring your users to download audio files means, that depending on the file size, your users might have to wait a while. Streaming media has come a long way. If you offer streaming audio, the file is broken into segments, sent to a buffer, which then recreates the file. This process allows the file to begin playing before all the other segments have arrived. See "Streaming audio."

Scenarios

1. When considering using Flash animation, there are several questions you must ask yourself:

   - Are your users Web-savvy?

   - Will your users download a Flash plug-in if they don't already have it?

   - Will the Flash based site hinder usability?

2. If you're creating music that will only be used as background music, sound quality is not as important as it would be if you were trying to sell your music over the Web. If sound quality isn't as important, you can use the MP3 compression file format.

For More Information

✦ **Macromedia.** www.macromedia.com: Macromedia offers both Flash and Director, as well as trial versions of the programs. Macromedia also houses help files and pointers to information about using their products. Before searching the Web for help with using one of these products, check the Macromedia support pages.

✦ **Adobe.** `www.adobe.com`: Adobe offers tons of image and video tools, a couple of which were covered in this chapter. In addition to providing trial versions of each of its products, Adobe offers support files for each product.

✦ **RealNetworks.** `www.real.com`: As far as audio players go, RealPlayer takes the cake. RealNetworks offers plenty of support information about using its player, as well as editing, creating, conversion, and server tools.

✦ **Apple.** `www.apple.com`: Apple is the creator of QuickTime and this site provides information about its player.

✦ **Open Directory Project.** `http://dmoz.org/Computers/Multimedia/`: A large directory of multimedia resources.

✦ **Yahoo!** `http://dir.yahoo.com/Computers_and_Internet/Multimedia/`: Yahoo!'s multimedia resource index.

✦ **Scala's Multimedia Resources.**
`www.scala.com/multimedia/tutorials.html`: Provides a listing of multimedia resources.

✦ **Moving Picture Experts Group (MPEG).** `www.mpeg.org/MPEG/index.html`: MPEG is a family of standards used for compressing audio/video information. This site provides information about MPEG and provides resources to learn more.

The Development Process

CHAPTER PRE-TEST

1. How is the Web development process similar to a business model?

2. What are the three common areas of expertise that should be represented in a Web development team?

3. Why is it common for a team, rather than an individual to work on a Web project?

4. What is meant by the "bottom up approach?"

5. What are the five stages of the Web development process?

6. What is a metaphor?

✦ Answers to these questions can be found at the end of the chapter. ✦

In the beginning of the Web, the development process was rather ad hoc. However, there was indeed a common theme to most development processes: One individual did it all. This day and age, it's amazing to think that one person tackled everything from designing the concept, to creating the markup, to creating the graphics, to testing the environment, and so on. Today, the site development process involves a great deal of planning. This chapter covers the many variables that must be weighed before you dive into creating your first HTML document.

Site Development Process

 Site development methodology

Businesses in the non-Web sector have quite a different approach to achieving a goal. Think about business departments and titles, such as management, accounting, marketing, public relations, and development. These areas of expertise are divided into their own categories. This business model has been around for some time, and has proven to be effective.

Web design is starting to adopt a similar model and incorporate divisions of job responsibilities. This is not to say there aren't individuals out there who are still trying to be a Jack or Jill of all trades, but for the most part, you find individuals falling into one of several categories, such as:

✦ Graphic artists

✦ Multimedia artists

✦ Front-end gurus

✦ Project managers

✦ Programmers

These are just some of the divisions you might encounter. These divisions did not emerge to replace the individual mentality by accident. They were a deliberate step to learn from the business model and apply it to the Web sector. This model is an integral part of understanding the Web development process.

Not only does the Web development process involve several individuals that make up a team, but it also requires a lot of preparation. During the development phase, you should be asking questions such as:

✦ What is the vision statement?

✦ What are the client's expectations?

✦ How many developers will be involved?

✦ Do we need to seek outside consultant assistance?

✦ Who will be the project leaders for each expertise area?

✦ What is the project timeline?

These are only a small sample of questions that you, as a developer, are likely to ask yourself. In the following sections, you find out what's involved in the site development process — from defining a vision, to establishing a metaphor.

Design teams

From usability to creativity, it's beneficial to have input from more than one person. In addition, you need to assess this type of input, because it's beneficial as well as necessary to ensure that a Web project follows the same development cycle as other business projects. For example, a company preparing for a product launch would require participation in the development process from at least the following people:

✦ **Management.** To guide the development process

✦ **Engineering.** To build the product

✦ **Marketing.** To market the product

✦ **Sales.** To interest customers in purchasing the product

✦ **Technical support.** To assist customers after the product is available

This list is by no means exhaustive; however, you should begin to get the idea. Take a second to think of any other areas of expertise that would need to be covered in this scenario.

Like our product launch example, there are several areas of expertise that are used on Web projects. The most common are:

✦ Project management

✦ Graphic design

✦ Technology

✦ Marketing

✦ Writing and editing

✦ Information architecture

All members of the team are important; however, whether you're a designer that has been stuck with the task of project managing, or you're a project manager, it's important to understand all the roles.

For a project manager to be able to guide the process, he or she must understand the skills required for building and maintaining the site. A skill assessment can help determine what's needed for a project. For example, will Flash be involved in the project? If so, you need to make sure you have at least one Flash designer on your team. What about database integration? If you're working on a Web site that will be pulling data from a database, you need a few database experts. The same can be said about determining what front-end and back-end work needs to be done. For example, will you be using Java or Perl? How about XML? All of these questions, and more must be identified before creating the necessary team.

After you know the skill sets your project requires, it's time to take inventory of the available skills within your organization. Your client may want to use an Oracle database, but you don't have anyone in your company that knows Oracle. Alternatively, you might have a client that really needs to synchronize multimedia, but your organization doesn't have many multimedia gurus. In both of these cases, you'll likely need to seek the help of a consultant. There are many freelance contractors or consultants for almost any area of expertise that you may need. Don't be afraid to seek help outside of your organization. It's better to spend the money to have a job done right, than to try to shoehorn the skill set of someone within your organization into another category of expertise.

Our final piece of advice for any project manager is to be creative. We're not talking about contributing to the creative team's brainstorming efforts — although that would be helpful. We're talking about creative management. Try to inspire your group. That's the best way to get their creative juices flowing.

Development phases

The exam covers five phases to Web site development:

✦ **Conceptualization.** Defining the vision and strategy for the Web site

✦ **Design visualization.** Preparing the transactional, navigational, and hierarchical construction of content

✦ **Analysis.** Testing design concepts against site vision

✦ **Production.** Implementing the design plan, including the creation of all content and usability testing of the site

✦ **Evolution.** The ongoing process of refining and updating the site design

 Exam Tip   Be familiar with each of these phases. They are likely to appear on the exam.

Conceptualization

When working on a Web development project, you first must develop a vision and strategy for the Web site. By identifying a vision for the Web site, you can identify the basic objectives for the site. You can think of the vision as the company (or Web site) mission statement. As the Web site mission statement, you want your vision and strategy to provide information about the site's purpose.

Design visualization

Design visualization is the fun part. During this stage you identify and prepare for the site's functionality. For example, you should map the site's navigational and hierarchical construction. There are many constructs that will help you develop this process:

✦ **Mindmaps.** A way of using keywords and symbols to brainstorm for ideas

✦ **Storyboards.** A sketch of the possible pages in your Web site (the most fun for wannabe cartoonists)

✦ **Flow charts.** A logical outline of your site that shows which parts of your site link (flow) to other parts

Analysis

During the analysis stage, you test possible concepts that will help achieve the defined vision for the site. At this time, you need to evaluate any completed work, and decide whether modifications need to be made. Don't be worried if you find that you have to change some of the defined elements; this is expected. This stage wouldn't exist if everyone got it right the first time. It's common to have to go back to the drawing board, so be prepared to do so.

Production

After the design plan is created and has been analyzed, it's time to execute it. During this stage it's important to focus on usability testing. Throughout this book, we stress the need to understand usability.

Cross-Reference   Chapter 2 is where you can read more about defining and executing usability tests.

Evolution

This stage lasts for the remainder of the Web site's life. After you've created a Web site, tested for usability, and refined the site accordingly, it's ready for prime time. However, your work is not done yet. Think of all the sites you visit that contain outdated content. You don't want your Web site to be one of those; therefore, you must update and maintain it constantly. Not only do you have to be sure that content is not outdated, but you will also want to collect user data and use that data to determine if modifications need to be made to the Web site.

Creating Web sites from the bottom up

When the team first embarks on creating a Web site, there are many questions that are likely to be asked. As designers, one of our favorite questions is: how should the Web site look and feel? Designing the look and feel of a Web site is creative and fun. And for many first time designers, this is the first task completed. However, this approach is incorrect.

Take a few moments to think about the most important element of your Web site. Is it the technology or the navigational elements used? No, it's the user. Without the user, why even create a site? There are two important goals that must be covered when thinking about the user:

✦ Attracting the user

✦ Retaining the user

To achieve these two goals, you want to design your Web site from the bottom up. First, try to identify the users' expectations. You need to understand why users would visit your site, and what would keep them coming back. After you've identified the users' expectations, you're ready to tackle the look and feel of the site.

Design goals

One of the most important facets of the Web development process is defining the goals of the project. This allows the project manager (and team) to ensure that the expectations are understood and met. The project manager is expected to guide the development process. The project manager is not expected to be an expert in each area (see the "Design teams" section earlier in this chapter), but is instead expected to have the necessary understanding of the Web development process.

Although the project manager oversees the development process, you're also likely to find a project leader for each area of expertise. Each project leader is expected to oversee all team members relating to their expertise areas. This means that a Web development team is likely to have a project manager, a technical project leader, a creative project leader, and a content project leader, as well as other team members that work under each leader.

There are four basic design goal steps:

✦ Project analysis

✦ Client expectations and evaluation

✦ Milestones and sign-off stages

✦ Project transition

 Exam Tip   To prepare you for the answers to possible questions on the exam, be familiar with these four design goal steps.

Project analysis

The first step is to conduct a project analysis to assess the project's strengths and weaknesses. During this step, you should also assess the strengths and weaknesses of the team and establish a team hierarchy, which should define project leaders. Don't be surprised if you find that your team cannot cover every aspect of the project. It's not uncommon to seek outside consultants to fill the weak links.

There are several factors that affect the project analysis. For example, the project may be on a tight budget; therefore, you limit the number of team members or the amount of resources you can dedicate. Time may also be an important factor. If the project is on a tight timeline, you may have to reevaluate the scope of the project. During this step, you have to identify and assess all possible constraints.

Client expectations and evaluation

The next step involves talking to the client and obtaining a clear understanding of the client's expectations. Oftentimes, clients have unreal expectations or a lack of technological understanding. It's important that the team liaison identifies the project's expectations clearly to the client so the client is not disappointed in the end. You should also arrange for the client to evaluate the project after it's complete and be sure they're clear on what they're evaluating. This will help you ensure that you've met the client's expectations.

Milestones and sign-off stages

This third stage is to identify *milestones* and *sign-off stages* that eventually lead to the project's end date. When a project reaches a milestone (or a place where a significant step in the production process is completed), the project should be evaluated for possible modifications. For example, if a site utilized Flash technology, you would want to reevaluate the technology to see if Macromedia released a newer version of the software. The sign-off stage involves making sure the client is happy with the site as it appears at each milestone and getting the client to sign-off on the project up to that point.

Project transition

The final step defines just how and when the project will be submitted to the client. In this step, you decide which members of the team will be involved in the transition process. You also need to make sure that the client is ready to assume the responsibility of the Web site. This should be done near or at the final sign-off phase in the previous step.

Vision statements

Every plan needs a vision. The vision statement identifies the scope and intent of a Web site. The vision should be a concise statement that details a value and measurable goal for the project. For example, the following is a vision statement:

"We will become one of the best online training Web sites, recruiting at least 1,000 students a month by the end of the year."

In the previous statement, the value is "best online training Web sites" and the measurable goal is "at least 1,000 students a month by the end of the year."

Business requirements

The Internet is a business. Gone are the days of business brochures, where Web sites were mere informational structures. A Web site is not meant to merely provide information about a company; it's an integral part of its strategy to attain a defined goal for the company. For example, if you're hired by a company that sells CDs, chances are they'll want to sell CDs via the Web. However, allowing users to purchase CDs is not enough, because there are probably tons of other sites that sell the same CDs. Therefore, the purpose of the Web site should be to convince the user that he or she should purchase CDs from your client's Web site. As a result, you're not only developing a Web site with information pages, but you're also creating a marketing plan for that client. Strategy is important in developing a site that will engage the user.

There are two common types of electronically based companies:

✦ Those that sell products/services that depend on the Web, such as games or search engines

✦ Those that use the Web to sell their products

It's easy for either one of these types of companies to fail or succeed. However, all successful Web sites, whether they fit within the first or second category, have one common theme: to fulfill an unmet need for the user. If you can do that, you can be successful.

A Web Site as a Metaphor

 Web site as metaphor

A metaphor implies a likeness between two ideas or objects. In the beginning of the Web, most Web sites resembled brochures or catalogs. In this case, a brochure or catalog is the metaphor. Think of the MOMA.org (`http://moma.org`) Web site (for the Museum of Modern Art in New York City). In this case, the metaphor is a gallery. As you search through the pages, the environment almost feels like a gallery. In addition, most of the navigation resembles words that would be used in a gallery.

 Tip Also check out `http://thesimpsons.com` and `http://disney.go.com/` for more excellent sites that use some very obvious metaphors.

Learning from Success

A good example of a successful online store is Amazon.com, the largest book retailer on the Web. Amazon.com is a site that uses the Web to sell its products. There are bookstores in every city in every state, and most of those bookstores carry thousands of books (nowadays, they even offer café lattes and scones). However, there are plenty of times when you want to buy a book, but all of your local bookstores are out, or they just don't carry it. They can't possibly carry millions of titles at a time; however, Amazon.com can. When Amazon.com launched its Web site, it fulfilled a need for users. Now, instead of having to visit a bookstore only to find that they don't carry the book you're looking for, you can go to Amazon.com and have it delivered to you.

Another interesting case study is eBay.com, which also uses the Web to sell products. In this case, eBay allows users to buy and sell products on the Web. Before eBay, auctions like this didn't really exist. If someone had a sofa or camera to sell, he or she would list it in the city paper classifieds, or would try to sell the product through a consignment store. All in all, it was a hassle. Now, users can post their listings on eBay and have other users bid on those listings. The product then goes to the highest bidder.

Finally, we focus on another site that has taken off, CNET.com, which is a company that depends on the Web. At CNET.com, you find a wealth of resources; however, one of the most helpful of these resources is their hardware and software reviews. This service appeared just as the number of e-commerce outfits selling hardware and software were popping up. It's very useful because it provides valuable information to the user, such as which desktop to purchase, or what camera would best suit his or her needs. CNET is the consumer reports for Web technology.

In all of the previous examples, there's one common thread: Most of the business is with repeat customers. This is essential. For a business to be successful on the Web, users must be coming back for more. Think about Amazon.com. If each user visited the site, purchased a book, but never returned, the company would have gone under. In the world of e-tailing, it's all about the user. But then again, this isn't much different from any other business model. The customers are always right, and you can learn a lot from them.

Guidelines for working with metaphors

The Web has not been around for long. When users visit online stores, they need to feel at home and comfortable. You need to create an atmosphere where the user wants to experience the visit. Therefore, it's important to consider basing your Web site on a known metaphor. However, there are principles that guide this process.

Do *not:*

- ✦ Mix metaphors
- ✦ Overuse the metaphor
- ✦ Use a metaphor that may have negative connotations associated with it

Do:

✦ Choose a metaphor that is easy to remember

✦ Consistently utilize the metaphor in the design

✦ Use a metaphor that shares characteristics with your theme

✦ Use the familiar to explain the unfamiliar

✦ Chose a metaphor that is familiar to the chosen audience

Example metaphors

When users visit Web sites, they're likely to have a mental picture of that they expect based on prior experiences. As the designer, you can help establish a working metaphor; for example, a Web designer creating an online catalog that provides users with information about each product. The simple use of a "catalog" is a metaphor that helps the user understand your Web site.

Users' experiences are not limited to the non-Web world. As a matter of fact, as users wander through a site, they're making mental maps based on every action they make. However, problems are likely to arise if the users' mental maps are different from your design. At this point, users become frustrated and/or confused. Either way, the users will likely leave your site. The lesson here is that the closer your design resembles familiar situations, the more likely the users will be able to navigate through your site.

Defining the Mindmapping Process

 Objective   Mindmaps and Web site design

The concept of mindmaps has been around since the late 1960s. The concept was created by Tony Buzan, president of the Brain Foundation, as a way to represent ideas using words, images, symbols, and color. This concept had nothing to do with the Web; after all, it dates back to the late 1960's. However, you should already begin to see how it could apply to Web design. The concept is based on patterns identified in nature and human mind behavior.

 Exam Tip   Mindmapping is a concept you should map in your mind as a possible topic on the exam.

Mindmapping was created to help students take quicker notes by jotting down key words and images. This allowed the students to utilize both the left (creative) and right (logical) sides of the brain and it made the notes easier to remember and review.

So, just where do computers come into the picture? Because the mindmaps are not linear (they're made up of symbols and key words), they make it easier to link and cross-reference different elements on the map. See Figure 6-1. This very idea of linking and cross-referencing different elements is why hypertext was developed for the computer world.

The Fertilizer Initiative

Figure 6-1: A beginning sketch of a mindmap

Mindmapping has been applied to Web design and has proven to be a useful technique. For example, you're organizing a product launch for fertilizer. When you sit down to design a mindmap, you pull out a sheet of paper and create a symbol for the product launch and create a name for it. After you have these two items, jot them down in the center of the sheet of paper and circle it.

For our example, we'll call our product launch "the fertilizer initiative" and use "garden" as the symbol. Now, take a few seconds to think of components of the product launch and give them names. Think quickly and don't linger too long. When you have them in your mind, jot them down outside of your central circle. You will want to connect each word to the centerpiece, so it begins to look like a wheel with spokes. A few of the items you might come up with would be "PR," "Marketing," "Sales," and "Resellers."

You can begin to see your design as a "garden" of ideas. As you begin to work with symbols and keywords, you'll find ideas flowing like crazy. The first couple of times you work with mindmaps, you might be surprised at how creative you really are.

Site Implementation Factors

 Site implementation factors

When implementing a Web site, you're bound by certain constraints. This is true for anything you do in life. As a Web designer, you should begin to recognize the common types of constraints, so you can anticipate them and plan accordingly. The first few times you design a Web site, you're likely to make mistakes. Many of your mistakes will be because you're not yet familiar with the following common constraints (which are also covered in detail in the following sections):

✦ Scope

✦ Resource requirements

✦ Technology requirements

✦ Time constraints

Scope

The scope of the Web site is defined by the vision statement, which is a simple sentence or two that defines what the Web site is supposed to achieve. As stated previously in this chapter, Web sites are no longer just fancy brochures. Businesses are now seriously using the Web as an integral part of their business strategy. The scope of the Web site should drive the entire design.

Resource requirements

After you know what the Web site is to achieve, you have to focus on the design. You need to identify what will be needed to achieve the desired design. You have to identify which resources you'll need to complete the project — how many individuals will be working on your team and any budgetary constraints you may have.

Technology requirements

When you first map out what your site will do, you need to identify each technology requirement. For example, will your site use Flash? What programming language will be required, if any? Remember, Web sites are no longer simply HTML. From multimedia to programming, as the designer, you have to identify all requirements.

Time constraints

Time will most likely be working against you. Don't underestimate how much time will be needed for a project. If you're working with a client, you need to identify milestones, deadlines, and sign-off schedules before you even begin to work on the project. This means that your time schedule may not be flexible. In this case, you might have to alter the scope of the Web site to fit the timetable. Any decisions like these need to involve the client.

Moving from Vision to Strategy

If you have your vision down, and you know the steps in implementing a plan, it's time to implement your strategy. This short section identifies a few strategic guidelines that will help you reach your Web site's goals.

✦ The goal of your site should not be to create the best-looking site; it should be to attract and retain users.

✦ Use tactics to gather personal information from your users — it's common for Web sites to offer something in exchange for user information.

✦ Use tactics to reward users — it's common for Web sites to reward "first-time buyers."

Exam Tip   A tactic is a method defined to help implement your strategy. For example, you could offer your users free books in exchange for feedback on your Web site.

Key Point Summary

This chapter focuses on the theory of Web design and how these theories drive the development process. Each theory presented in this chapter has been developed over time as the best tactic for implementing a Web page from the bottom up. The key points covered in this chapter are:

✦ A design team is made up of individuals with varying areas of expertise. The six common areas of expertise are: project management, marketing, graphic design, technology, writing and editing, and information architecture.

✦ When defining a development strategy, there are five phases that the team should go through: conceptualization, design visualization, analysis, production, and evolution.

✦ The following steps should be taken to identify design goals: project analysis, client expectations and evaluation, milestones and sign-off stages, and project transition.

✦ A vision statement is used by the design team to drive the development process. Once the team identifies this measurable goal, the team can use it as the driving force behind the development strategy.

✦ Metaphors are used to help engage the users. A metaphor defines a familiar setting for a user.

✦   ✦   ✦

STUDY GUIDE

It's now time to study for your exam. Questions about design theory are not as cut and dried as those about general HTML topics; for example, when you're asked whether the `alt` attribute should be used with the `table` tag, you would quickly say no.

However, because the questions in this section are based on design theory, you should take a little more time choosing the correct answer. Scenarios and lab exercises are also included in this section to reinforce the theories.

Assessment Questions

1. What does a mindmap help Web designers do? (Choose the best answer.)

   A. Brainstorm for ideas

   B. Outline technologies needed

   C. Identify team members

   D. Publish Web sites

2. What are the five stages of Web design?

   A. Conceptualization, design, analysis, production, and evolution

   B. Conceptualization, design visualization, analysis, production, and evolution

   C. Conceptualization, deconstruct, analysis, production, and evolution

   D. Conceptualization, design visualization, analysis, patchwork, and evolution

3. Which of the following is not an area of expertise that would be included within a well-rounded Web development team?

   A. Public Relations

   B. Marketing

   C. Graphic Design

   D. Project Management

4. The bottom up approach begins with which of the following? (Choose the best answer.)

   A. Designing the look of the Web site

   B. Designing the feel of the Web site

   C. Defining the development process

   D. Developing user scenarios

5. As a Web designer, which of the following is the most effective way to use metaphors? (Choose the best answer.)

   A. Use multiple metaphors

   B. Select a unique metaphor because it might catch the user's attention

   C. Create a complex metaphor

   D. Create a metaphor that would be familiar to your users

6. According to this chapter, what is a metaphor? (Choose the best answer.)

   A. A visual suggestion to another thing or idea

   B. Using text in a Web site as a way to create literal comparisons

   C. A literary term

   D. A way to layout images on your Web site

7. Which of the following describes a good Web project vision statement? (Choose the best answer.)

   A. A statement that outlines financial and resource requirements

   B. A statement that lays out the team leaders

   C. A statement that defines a value and a measurable goal for a Web site

   D. A statement that defines technological requirements

8. Which of the following should be your main Web site strategy? (Choose the best answer.)

   A. Create the coolest site

   B. Create a site that is informative

   C. Create a site that attracts and retains users

   D. Create a site that refers users to other sites

Scenarios

1. Your company is about to redesign its Web site. Before the redesign starts, your boss has asked that you solicit feedback from users about the current Web site. Briefly describe at least one tactic you would use to implement a Web strategy that would accomplish this goal.

2. You have just been hired by a company that sells groceries online. Your first task is to create an effective metaphor for the company's new Web site. Briefly describe the metaphor you would choose and provide an explanation for your metaphor selection.

Lab Exercises

Lab 6-1: Examining Web sites that use metaphors:

For this lab, visit the following Web sites:

- **National Geographic's expedition site.** www.nationalgeographic.com/xpeditions/hall/index.html
- **Mama's Cucina site.** www.eat.com
- **International Olympic Committee's site.** www.olympic.org
- **HugeClick's site.** www.hugeclick.com

For each site, answer the following questions:

1. What metaphor is used?

2. Does each metaphor relate well to the goals of the site?

3. Is the metaphor easy for the user to understand?

Lab 6-2: Creating vision statements

Create a vision statement for a music CD online retailer. Before you are ready to write the vision statement, you need to identify each of the following:

1. A measurable goal

2. A value

Lab 6-3: Analyzing a Web site

For this lab, briefly visit a Web site and analyze it. As in Lab 6-2, you're working for an online music CD retailer. To learn more about your competition and to develop some ideas for your company's Web site, you need to visit www.cdnow.com and then do the following:

1. Define the services and products the Web site provides.

2. Define the features the Web site uses to engage users.

3. Define the features the Web site uses to encourage users to return to the site.

4. Define at least one change you would suggest to improve the Web site.

Lab 6-4: Defining your Web site

Now that you have defined a vision statement and taken a look at the competition, it's time to plan your fictitious Web site. Keeping with the theme, answer the following questions as if you were designing a Web site for an online music CD retailer:

1. What products will the Web site offer?
2. What services will the Web site offer?
3. What information will the Web site offer?

Answers to Chapter Questions

Chapter pre-test

1. In any business, teams are at the heart of getting anything done. For example, you work for a nonprofit organization responsible for an annual report that is distributed to donors at the end of each fiscal year. Although your accountant knows most of the numbers that need to go into that report, he wouldn't have any idea about the programmatic updates that need to be included. For this project, several individuals would have to be involved, and those individuals would make up a team — team member being an expert in a needed area.

2. Three common areas of expertise that should be represented in a Web development team are management, creative, and technical. Each area of expertise has its own skill set. A team needs a manager and team leaders to keep everyone on track and to guide the Web development process. The creative individuals come up with the ideas for the Web site, and the technical individuals are the ones who work with the technical side of the development process.

3. In a team structure, each area of expertise needed is represented by one or more individuals. Whereas it's important that they understand the other areas, especially in relation to their own area of expertise, they're not required to be experts execept in their specific area. For example, a graphic artist, should understand HTML, and maybe even know it. However, the most important factor the graphic artist should understand is how the images are embedded using HTML and what limitations that might pose.

4. Sometimes you might want to approach design by first designing the look and feel of a site, and then forcing users to conform to that design. As designers, we don't like limitations to what we can do creatively. However, users don't like to conform, and the result of forcing them to may prompt them to never come back to your site. If you use the bottom up approach, you first build user scenarios to determine what users will expect, and then you build the look and functionality according to your findings about user expectations.

5. The five stages of the development process are: conceptualization, design visualization, analysis, production, and evolution. Each phase builds on the one before it; therefore, it's not recommended to skip from conceptualization to production.

6. In the context of Web design, a metaphor is used to suggest identification with other things or experiences. There are many guidelines to using metaphors, such as: don't overuse a metaphor; don't mix metaphors; don't choose complicated metaphors; and use positive metaphors. Following the guidelines identified in this chapter will help you create effective metaphors for your Web sites.

Assessment questions

1. **A.** Mindmaps were originally tools for helping students take notes; however, they were quickly adopted by many disciplines as a way to brainstorms for ideas. See "Defining the Mindmapping Process."

2. **B.** The five stages to Web design are conceptualization, design visualization, analysis, production, and evolution. See "Development phases."

3. **A.** In this chapter, we identify six common areas of expertise for any Web development project team, none of which include public relations. They are: project management, graphic design, technology, marketing, writing and editing, and information architecture. Each of these areas has a vital role to the development and deployment of a Web site. See "Design teams."

4. **D.** Many first time Web designers tend to dive into to the Web development process by defining a look and feel for a Web site, but this is an incorrect approach. The most important function of a Web site is to encourage users to visit again. If this is the case, then the user is the most important element to consider when developing the site. See "Creating Web sites from the bottom up."

5. **D.** When working with metaphors, you want to create a metaphor that users are familiar with. See "A Web Site as a Metaphor."

6. **A.** A metaphor is a visual suggestion to another thing or idea that should resonate with a user. See "A Web Site as a Metaphor."

7. **C.** A vision statement is one that defines both a value and a measurable goal for a Web site. This is often like a simple mission statement for a company. See "Vision statements."

8. **C.** If you created a Web site, it's likely that you want users to see it. More than just that, you want users to come back. See "Moving from Vision to Strategy."

Scenarios

1. A tactic is a way to implement a strategy. In this case, you've been asked to design a tactic that would solicit feedback from users. One possible tactic would be to offer a free compilation CD to those that complete a feedback form on your Web site. Another tactic would be to allow users to enter a vacation giveaway. All they have to do to enter is complete a feedback form on your Web site.

2. The most obvious metaphor would be a grocery store. Choosing this metaphor would ensure that users would be familiar with keywords and images associated with your store. For example, the shopping cart could resemble a shopping cart you would find at your local grocery store. You could also use key words for users visiting each section: poultry, meats, fresh vegetables, canned soups, etc.

For More Information

✦ **CNET.com.** `http://builder.cnet.com`: CNET's builder site provides Web developers with up to date articles on tools and techniques for building Web sites.

✦ **A List Apart.** `www.alistapart.com`: At A List Apart, you will find articles by designers for designers. You will also find one of the best designer mailing lists around.

✦ **Webmonkey.** `http://hotwired.lycos.com/webmonkey/`: Hotwired's Webmonkey provides user with tons of articles on Web design. Be sure to check out their Top Ten Design Tips.

✦ **ZDNet's Developer site.** `www.zdnet.com/developer/`: Another developer site that provides tips and techniques for the Web designer.

✦ **Webreview.** `http://webreview.com`: Webreview provides the HTML community with articles about the business of creating Web pages. You're bound to find an article or two on the subject of Web design.

Understanding Web Site Design Technology

HTML Standards and Compliance

CHAPTER PRE-TEST

1. What does HTML stand for?

2. What is the origin of HTML?

3. What is the most recent version of HTML?

4. What is the World Wide Web Consortium?

5. What is the difference between HTML and XHTML?

✦ Answers to these questions can be found at the end of the chapter. ✦

This chapter introduces you to the origins and state of the HTML standard. Web technologies are constantly changing, and the HTML standard is no exception. This chapter not only introduces you to the current state of HTML, but it also provides you with information about how to keep up with HTML's evolution.

The Development of HTML

 The development of HTML

The Hypertext Markup Language (HTML) was first introduced by the Conseil Europeen pour le Recherche Nucleaire (CERN, which translates to The European Particle Physics Laboratory), and more specifically by Tim Berners-Lee, in 1992. The original and primary purpose of HTML was to allow access and retrieval of a large collection of documents using hypermedia. The main drive of HTML was focused on the idea of hypertext and hyperlinking, which would allow text documents to be *linked* or distributed over networks. Hyperlinks by themselves are instructions, and they are located in a text document that references another file. This allows an application to locate, or call, another file. These instructions are usually activated by the user. For example, when a user clicks the link with the mouse. In HTML, these links are created using the anchor (`<a>`) tag.

HTML is not a programming language. Although many HTML newcomers assume that it is, markup languages and programming languages are quite different. A *markup language* document consists of both the instructions and the data—everything that is needed for the application. However, a *programming language* document just consists of instructions, and the data resides in separate files. Furthermore, HTML doesn't provide the internal logic that is necessary for procedural programming languages (such as Pascal or C).

 Exam Tip HTML is not a programming language, so technically, it does not provide instructions. However, the exam materials refer to HTML markup as instructions; therefore, so do we.

Hyperlinking is the heart of the Web, but that is not all. Hypermedia allows you to reference more than just text documents (for example, image, video, audio, animation, and other multimedia files).

There are three HTML tags that govern hypermedia: the `a`, `img`, and `object` tags. The first tag (`<a>`) allows document authors to link to another document and is triggered by a user's mouse click. The `<img>` and `<object>` tags reference an external document, but embed the file when the document loads. Think about a Web page that has image files on it. Those image files are actually referenced and then embedded in the document when it's rendered.

Hypertext

Hypertext, the ability to distribute nonlinear text, is nothing new. As a matter of fact, Ted Nelson coined the term and introduced hypertext in 1965. Following Nelson, in 1987, Bill Atkinson (known for his work on MacPaint) introduced a commercial hypertext product called HyperCard. Apple Computer introduced HyperCard in 1987, and HyperCard allowed users to create graphical hypertext applications. The product featured support for forms, scripting, bitmap graphics, and full text searches. One problem with HyperCard was that its proprietary format only worked on Macintosh computers. Imitations were introduced during this time; however, nothing took off until Tim Berners-Lee introduced HTML.

In stark contrast to HyperCard (and other proprietary products), HTML is a cross-platform language, which allows users with Windows, Macintosh, and UNIX platforms to work with it. In addition, HyperCard did not work on client/server systems as HTML does. HyperCard only worked on standalone machines.

In the Real World   Some argue that the idea for hypertext was first introduced by Vannevar Bush (who called it memex) in a 1940s Atlantic Monthly article entitled "As We May Think." This article can be found on the Web at `www.theatlantic.com/unbound/flashbks/computer/bushf.htm`.

SGML

In 1969, Charles Goldfarb led a team of IBM researchers in a project that was designed to help the integration of law office information systems. From that project, Goldfarb, Edward Mosher, and Raymond Lorie invented the Generalized Markup Language (GML) as a means to allow formatted documents to be shared over different platforms. GML evolved into the Standard Generalized Markup Language (SGML) and was ratified as an International Organization of Standardization (ISO) standard in 1986.

SGML, unlike HTML, does not contain a defined tag set and there are no element or attribute names to mess with. Rather, SGML defines a set of syntax rules that other markup languages (such as HTML) must follow. Technically speaking, SGML is a meta-markup language that allows for the creation of markup languages. HTML is an application of SGML.

HTML

When Tim Berners-Lee created HTML he used SGML as the model for syntax. In essence, he defined HTML to follow SGML's syntax rules, but introduced HTML's own element and attribute names. In the beginning, HTML was designed as a document structure language (introducing tags such as `<body>` and `<head>`). However, it has quickly evolved to function as both a contextual and presentational language. For example, if you use the following markup, `<font color="green">text </font>`, the text following the opening `<font>` tag will be green. The `font` element explicitly defines how the browser should render the contained text, but doesn't tell you anything else.

Just what is HTML? First of all, HTML documents are plain-text files saved with a .htm or .html file extension that consist of markup and character data (also know as plain text). A document is marked up with tags that contain the actual data. Tags are delimited with a less than (<) and greater than (>) sign; for example, <tag>.

The previous example is just an opening tag; however, most data is contained by an opening and closing tag; for example, <tag>character data</tag>.

When you refer to the opening tag, closing tag, and the content in between, you call it an *element*. This is an important distinction. A tag is the individual piece of markup, whereas an element is the entire shebang.

Exam Tip

Throughout this book we refer to HTML markup as tags, such as the <p> tag or the <h1> tag. In addition, on the CIW exam (and in the real world) the terms tag and element are used interchangeably. So, to be consistent with the materials, we also use the terms interchangeably. However, this usage is not technically correct. The term tag should be used to describe the individual opening and closing tags and the term element should be used to describe the opening tag, closing tag, and the content.

To view your HTML documents, you have to use a special tool: browsers. Microsoft's Internet Explorer and Netscape's Navigator are the two most common browsers that interpret (and render) HTML. However, they are by no means the only browsers available to users. Other browsers include Opera and Amaya.

Tip

Browsers are not the only tools you can use to interpret HTML. For example, Netscape Communicator allows users to send and receive HTML messages.

An Overview of HTML Versions

Objective   HTML standards

HTML has seen many versions since its inception at CERN. It's easier to follow HTML's evolutionary path now that it's governed by the World Wide Web Consortium (W3C); however, the beginning of HTML is a little jumbled. In this section, we tackle each HTML evolutionary stage — one by one.

HTML 1.0 and 2.0

The first HTML specification, version 0, was used to test the implementation of the Web, using browsers such as Lynx from CERN. The HTML 1.0 standard, however, was basically the first version of HTML that was used by graphical browsers. It built on the first HTML specification (version 0) by adding support for graphics (the <img> tag).

HTML 2.0 built on HTML 1.0 and added form-related capabilities, such as support for user `input` fields. If you want to take a peak at HTML 2.0, visit `www.w3.org/MarkUp/html-spec/`.

HTML 3.0 and 3.2

The HTML 3.0 specification was never officially named a standard; instead, it evolved into HTML 3.2, which was officially named a W3C Recommendation. The need for a new version of HTML arose from a push from browser vendors. As browsers introduced proprietary markup, the standard was forced to keep up. This meant expanding the official tag set to include most of the proprietary tags introduced by browser vendors. This is one of the reasons HTML 3.0 was quickly updated, and HTML 3.2 was introduced.

Cross-Reference To read more about the W3C's process of ratifying standards and the introduction of proprietary markup, see later sections of this chapter.

HTML 3.2 was significant because it added many of the features Web developers now take for granted. The primary enhancements were:

✦ Figures

✦ Frames

✦ Improved tags

✦ Mathematical equations

✦ Tables

Take a look at HTML 3.2, found at `www.w3.org/TR/REC-html32`.

HTML 4.0 and 4.01

HTML 4.0 was the next addition to the HTML family. With it came some more enhancements, such as:

✦ Accessibility features

✦ Improved forms

✦ Enhanced tables

✦ Internationalization features (such as reading left to right)

✦ Scripting and multimedia features

✦ Support for Cascading Style Sheets (CSS)

Shortly after HTML 4.0 was introduced, the W3C fixed some grammatical and minor mistakes in the specification and renamed it HTML 4.01. There were no significant changes from HTML 4.0 to 4.01, just an attempt to clean house a bit.

There are three different variants of HTML 4.01. However, to understand the three different versions of HTML 4.01, you first have to understand what a Document Type Definition (DTD) is. A *DTD* is a document that outlines the rules that a markup language must follow; for example, what attributes can be used with which tags and what can be contained between opening and closing tags. Therefore, the three versions of HTML 4.01 use different DTDs and outline different rules.

HTML 4.01 Transitional

The most common version of HTML being used today (early 2001) is HTML 4.01 Transitional. Named for the DTD that this version adheres to, the HTML 4.01 Transitional DTD, this variant allows you to use most of the HTML elements, including all presentational elements. As the document author, you can use this version while using CSS and still use the HTML presentational elements. This is an important feature because older browsers don't support CSS, which is the most common Web style sheet language. Because of this support, Web developers are likely to use CSS to format pages, but still include some HTML presentational elements just in case some users are using browsers that don't support CSS.

Cross-Reference See Chapter 11 for more information on CSS.

The term transitional makes sense for this version because future versions of HTML will most likely not support HTML presentational elements, such as `<font>` and `<center>`.

HTML 4.01 Strict

This version doesn't allow you to get away with much—the name says it all. The HTML 4.01 Strict version, follows (you guessed it) the HTML 4.01 Strict DTD. Although rarely used, if you don't want to include presentational markup and use CSS style sheets instead, you're the perfect candidate for this version. But, be careful, you can only use document structure markup, such as the `<head>`, `<title>`, and `<body>` tags. This means you cannot use presentational markup, such as the `<font>` tag or `bgcolor` attribute. Most presentational elements are deprecated, which means that they will not be included in future versions of the HTML specification. Most deprecated elements are not allowed in this version. Deprecated elements are covered later in this chapter.

HTML 4.01 Frameset

The HTML 4.01 Frameset version is used for frameset documents, and only frameset documents. In case you're not familiar with frameset documents, they define the structure for a framed Web page layout (frames partition the browser window into separate windows).

Tip Take a look at the HTML 4.01 specification found at `www.w3.org/TR/html4/`.

Deprecated Tags

There are several tags and attributes that are on their way out of the HTML specification. What we mean is that future versions of HTML will not support a handful of tags and attributes. Ever since CSS was introduced, the W3C has been recommending that Web developers use the CSS as a way to separate style from structure. CSS allows you to define and store formatting information in a separate document and use HTML to define document structure. For example, you would still use the <head>, <body>, <p>, and <h1> tags, but you would define the color and font size of your text in the CSS document.

Tip   You can also define CSS style rules internally in the head of your HTML document using the <style> tag.

In favor of using style sheets, the most recent versions of HTML marks several tags and attributes as deprecated. The HTML standard does not recommend the use of deprecated tags and attributes. Although the W3C doesn't recommend that you use these deprecated tags and elements, there will be times that you will need to use them to format Web pages so they can be viewed in older browsers. Most deprecated elements are supported by the current browsers, so if you have to use them, you can.

The following tags are deprecated:

- ✦ <applet>
- ✦ <basefont>
- ✦ <center>
- ✦ <dir>
- ✦ <font>
- ✦ <isindex>
- ✦ <menu>
- ✦ <s>
- ✦ <strike>
- ✦ <u>

The following attributes are deprecated (only attributes that do not belong to the previous defined deprecated tags are listed):

- ✦ align (for most tags)
- ✦ alink
- ✦ background

- ✦ bgcolor
- ✦ border (for <img> and <object> tags)
- ✦ clear
- ✦ compact
- ✦ height (for the <td> and <th> tags)
- ✦ hspace
- ✦ language
- ✦ link
- ✦ noshade
- ✦ nowrap
- ✦ size (for the <hr> tag)
- ✦ start
- ✦ text
- ✦ type (for the <li>, <ol>, and <ul> tags)
- ✦ value (for the <li> tag)
- ✦ version
- ✦ vlink
- ✦ vspace
- ✦ width (for the <hr>, <pre>, <td>, and <th> tags)

Keep in mind that if a tag or attribute is deprecated, the W3C recommends you don't use it. This is not to say you can't use the deprecated tag or attribute; just that you need to avoid using deprecated tags and attributes if at all possible.

Standard vs. Proprietary HTML

 Proprietary HTML markup

Following the current HTML standard is always recommended; however, it is not always done by Web developers. Web developers can use HTML tags that aren't defined by the HTML standard because browsers often extend the HTML tag set by adding proprietary markup. The two main culprits are Microsoft's Internet Explorer and Netscape's Navigator. Proprietary markup, also known as extensions, is introduced and supported by an application, rather than by the World Wide Web Consortium (W3C).

Proprietary markup can be problematic. Although the application (a.k.a. the browser) introducing the new tags may offer support for them, other applications are not required to offer such support, and most likely will not. For example, Internet Explorer introduced a `bordercolordark` attribute that can be used with the `<table>` tag. This attribute allows you to control the lower and right borders of a table. Although this attribute is supported in Internet Explorer, Netscape browsers don't recognize it.

From the Web developer's perspective, it is nice to have more features; however, it makes it very difficult to create Web pages that render the same in each type of browser. This has become quite a problem for developers, forcing them to develop different, browser-specific versions of each Web site to ensure uniform rendering across a variety of browsers.

Web Browser HTML Support

Web browsers are HTML interpreters that are designed to understand and render hypermedia. Not only can browsers read HTML files, but they can also read graphic files, sound files, and other types of media formats. Because browsers are designed to render HTML documents, it's important that the browsers adhere to the current standards. This is not always as easy as one might think. The W3C can add features (tags) to HTML, but if the browsers don't support these features, the new tags won't be recognized and are relatively useless.

This has posed a problem for Web developers in the past. Although both major browsers, Netscape Navigator and Microsoft Internet Explorer, have promised to try to keep up with the current standards, they have yet to do so. Of the two power-houses, Microsoft has done a better job — until recently when Netscape released version 6. The most recent browser support is as follows:

- ✦ **Netscape Communicator 4.7.** Supports HTML 4.01, with buggy support for CSS1 and CSS2.

- ✦ **Netscape 6.** Reports support for HTML 4.01, CSS1, and CSS2; however, as of early 2001, Netscape 6.0 still has some bugs to iron out.

- ✦ **Microsoft Internet Explorer 5.0.** Supports HTML 4.01, with fairly good support for CSS1 and CSS2.

- ✦ **Microsoft Internet Explorer 5.5.** Supports HTML 4.01, and boasts better support (however, not full standard support) for CSS1 and CSS2 than Netscape 6.

Note that if a browser supports HTML 4.01, it also supports XHTML 1.0. After all, XHTML uses the exact same elements at HTML 4.01 and the syntax is backwards compatible.

HTML 4.01 and XHTML

 HTML 4.01 and XHTML

The most recent version of HTML doesn't have an HTML version number at all: it's called XHTML, the Extensible Hypertext Markup Language. There has been a lot of confusion over just what the X means. The X comes from the Extensible Markup Language (XML). If you recall from earlier sections in this chapter, HTML was created as an application of SGML. XHTML uses the same tag set; the only difference is that XHTML is an application of XML instead of SGML.

This difference doesn't amount to much except for a few stricter syntax and document rules. In this section, you find out what those rules are and where they come from.

An XML vocabulary

SGML has been around (formally) since 1986, and is not without its Web limitations. Because of these limitations (definitions of which are beyond the scope of this book), the W3C introduced a slimmed down version of SGML, and named it the Extensible Markup Language (XML). Therefore, XML is a direct descendant of SGML. Many say it contains 90 percent of the power, but only 10 percent of the complexity.

 There are many advantages gained from using XML, which are discussed in Chapter 19.

XHTML rules

This section is titled XHTML Rules, but it could very well be titled XML Rules, because, after all, XHTML follows XML syntax rules.

A document is well formed if it conforms to the syntax rules defined by the XML specification. According to the XHTML 1.0 specification, all XHTML documents must be well formed. That means they must adhere to the syntax rules described in the following sections.

All non-empty elements must contain an opening and closing tag

Don't let the term non-empty throw you off. Most elements are not defined as empty elements. An empty element is one that does not contain any character data (for example, the `<img>` element inserts an image file, but does not need an opening and closing tag to surround any data). An example of a non-empty element is the `<p>` tag, which should be used like this:

```
<p>character data</p>
```

All empty elements must be terminated

All empty elements require either a forward slash (/) within their tag or a closing tag. For example, `<img/>` and `<img></img>` are correct and `<img>` is not.

Technically, the previous example (`<img/>`) is correct; however, older browsers have trouble processing the syntax. To work around this, you must include a space before the forward slash. This will ensure that your XHTML documents are backwards compatible; for example, `<img src="file.gif" alt="text" />`.

All attributes must have values

According to XML's syntax rules, all attributes must be set to values. This is problematic for the HTML 4.01 specification, because it includes a handful of standalone attributes (Booleans that turn a function on when used). Because the XHTML 1.0 specification uses the exact same tag set (including attributes) as the HTML 4.01 specification, you need to make slight modifications to these standalone attributes. The solution seems a tad silly; however, you must set these attributes equal to themselves. This allows for backwards compatibility with browsers, while still following the XML syntax rules. For example, `<td nowrap="nowrap">...</td>`.

All attribute values must be contained by quotation marks

This rule is quite simple: All attribute values must be contained by quotation marks (single or double). This distinction is made because HTML 4.01 allows for some keyword attribute values to be free of quotation marks. This is not allowed for XHTML 1.0. For example, `<table width="75%">...</table>` is correct and `<table width=75%>...</table>` is not.

All elements must be nested correctly

Nesting is an important concept in XML, and also in HTML, although many Web developers tend to forget the concept. Nesting means that an element must contain another element completely; for example:

```
<p>This element <em>contains</em> the emphasis element</p>
```

In this example, the `<p>` element contains the `<em>` element. This case of nesting is easy to see, but what if you had the following example:

```
<p>The bold element is at the <b>end</p></b>
```

In this example, it's easy to close the `<p>` element before the `<b>` element, but this is incorrect because it violates the principles of nesting.

Element names are case sensitive

All element names are case sensitive. This means that `<p>` is not the same as `<P>`. Because strictly conforming XHTML documents must reference one of the three XHTML DTDs (according to XHTML document structure rules defined later in this section), all elements and attributes must adhere to the names defined in the DTDs. Because the XHTML DTDs define all the element and attribute names in lowercase, the elements and attributes you use in an XHTML document must be lowercase as well.

Document structure rules

That's it for the syntax rules; however, you must also adhere to the following document structure rules:

✦ You must reference one of the three XHTML DTDs: Strict, Transitional, and Frameset (see the "HTML 4.0 and 4.01" section earlier in this chapter).

✦ Remember that DTDs define rules about which elements and attributes can be used, and they even require a few rules themselves. So, before adding a document type (DOCTYPE) declaration referencing one of these DTDs, be sure to know what they allow and require. The three DOCTYPE declarations are as follows:

```
<!DOCTYPE html
    PUBLIC "-//W3C//DTD XHTML 1.0 Strict//EN"
    "http://www.w3.org/TR/xhtml1/DTD/xhtml1-strict.dtd">

<!DOCTYPE html
    PUBLIC "-//W3C//DTD XHTML 1.0 Transitional//EN"
    "http://www.w3.org/TR/xhtml1/DTD/xhtml1-
transitional.dtd">

<!DOCTYPE html
    PUBLIC "-//W3C//DTD XHTML 1.0 Frameset//EN"
    "http://www.w3.org/TR/xhtml1/DTD/xhtml1-frameset.dtd">
```

Internet and Web Standards Organizations

There are several bodies that control the standards that govern the Web. The HTML standard is just one of a handful of standards that keep the Internet going. The most influential standards organization that controls the way developers work is the World Wide Web Consortium (W3C). This organization controls the HTML, XML, and CSS standards, which serve as the backbone for any Web document.

Exam Tip

We don't expect there to be too many questions, if any, on this section; however, pay close attention to the section on the W3C. If there are questions, we expect them to be about the W3C.

World Wide Web Consortium

The W3C is a standards organization that controls the HTML standard (and therefore, its future). Formed in 1994, the W3C governs many important Web-related standards, including HTML, XHTML, XML, and CSS. These languages, among others, are published in the form of Recommendations. Before reaching this stage, each document, must go through a rigorous evaluation process.

An important thing to know about the W3C is that the technologies involved in the Internet, and therefore the standards they govern, are in a constant state of evolution. For this reason, it's important to keep on top of the latest versions. You must also be careful to not get too tied to a specification document before it reaches its final stages. The document is likely to see many revisions and changes before it's called a Recommendation.

The W3C stages of document development are as follows:

✦ **Working Draft.** The initial stage of a specification. It should be viewed as a work in progress. It goes through a Last Call stage that solicits feedback from working group members before moving on to the next stage.

✦ **Candidate Recommendation.** A stable Working Draft that the director has proposed to the community at large for implementation experience and feedback.

✦ **Proposed Recommendation.** A document that has been updated according to implementation experience and feedback and is then sent to the Advisory Committee for review.

✦ **Recommendation.** The document is fully supported by the W3C, rubber stamped by the W3C director, and is ready for widespread deployment.

The HTML 4.01 specification is a W3C Recommendation, as is the XHTML 1.0 specification. For more information, visit www.w3.org.

Internet Society

The Internet Society (ISOC) is international in scope and encompasses over 150 organizations and 6,000 individual members. The ISOC houses the Internet Engineering Task Force (IETF) and the Internet Architecture Board (IAB), and is a leader in addressing issues that deal with the future of the Internet. The members (both organizations and individuals) are joined "to assure the open development, evolution and use of the Internet for the benefit of all people throughout the world" (from the ISOC Mission statement — see www.isoc.org/isoc/mission/).

According to the ISOC, its main purpose "is to maintain and extend the development and availability of the Internet and its associated technologies and applications — both as an end in itself, and as a means of enabling organizations, professions, and individuals worldwide to more effectively collaborate, cooperate, and innovate in their respective fields and interests."

Internet Architecture Board

The Internet Architecture Board (IAB) is the technical advisory group of the ISOC. It provides the following:

✦ Oversight of the architecture for protocols and procedures used by the Internet

✦ Oversight for the process used to create Internet Standards

✦ Advice and guidance to the Board of Trustees and Officers of the ISOC

For more information, visit `www.iab.org`.

Internet Engineering Task Force

The Internet Engineering Task Force (IETF) is an international community of network designers, operators, vendors, and researchers that share a concern with the future of the Internet — more specifically the Internet's architecture. The work done at the IETF is primarily done by volunteers that have day jobs and a strong commitment to the future of the Internet.

The actual work of the IETF is done in its working groups, which are organized by topic into several areas (e.g., routing, transport, security, etc.). A lot of the work is handled through mailing lists (as is most Web-related standards work). For more information, visit `www.ieft.org`.

Internet Research Task Force

The Internet Research Task Force (IRTF) is composed of a number of small Research Groups. Research Groups are usually focused and long term — although short-lived task force-like Research Groups are possible.

The Research Groups work on topics related to Internet protocols, applications, architecture, and technology. Research Groups are expected to have the stable, long-term membership needed to promote the development of research collaboration and teamwork in exploring research issues. Participation is by individual contributors, rather than by representatives of organizations. For more information, visit `www.irtf.org`.

The Internet Corporation for Assigned Names and Numbers

The Internet Corporation for Assigned Names and Numbers (ICANN) is a nonprofit corporation (like most of the standards bodies listed in this section). Its primary responsibilities are governing IP address space allocation, protocol parameter assignment, domain name system management, and root server system manage-ment functions — all of which were previously performed under U.S. Government contract by Internet Assigned Numbers Authority (IANA)) and other entities. For more information, visit www.icann.org/.

Request for Comments

Request for Comments (RFCs) are formal documents that come from the IETF. These documents come from committees and are reviewed by interested parties. In the beginning, RFCs were simply *requests for comments*. Over time, RFCs have taken on a more formal nature (to the point people were referring to them as standards, even though they weren't). Currently, there are two types of RFCs:

✦ **FYIs.** Introductory documents overviews and topics

✦ **STDs.** RFCs that specify Internet standards

To locate an RFC, visit www.ietf.org/rfc.html. To learn more about RFCs, visit www.ietf.org/.

Key Point Summary

This chapter covered the origins and basics of the HTML standard. Some of the information you may have already known; other pieces may have been new to you. After reading this chapter, the following concepts should be clear:

✦ Tim Berners-Lee created HTML, while he worked at CERN, as a way to use hyperlinked documents.

✦ HTML has seen many revisions, the most recent being HTML 4.01. Each ver-sion introduced more advanced features, such as tables, forms, and frames.

✦ Proprietary markup makes it difficult for Web developers to create HTML doc-uments that will render the same in the different browsers.

✦ The HTML 4.01 specification defines several tags and attributes as depre-cated, which means that they will not be included in the next version of the specification.

✦ Although HTML 4.01 is the latest version of the HTML standard, there is another addition to the HTML family: XHTML. XHTML uses the same tag set defined by HTML 4.01; the only difference is that XHTML is an application of XML. (In other words, it follows XML's syntax rules.)

✦ The W3C controls the HTML standards, as well as other Web-related standards. The W3C has been around since 1994.

✦   ✦   ✦

STUDY GUIDE

This chapter was more like a history lesson than a tutorial. Instead of working through examples, you were asked to do a lot of reading. Take a few moments to quiz yourself on the material.

Assessment Questions

1. Which of the following languages predates HTML?

    A. DTD

    B. SGML

    C. XHTML

    D. XML

2. Which of the following concepts is at the heart of HTML?

    A. Video

    B. Audio

    C. Hyperlinking

    D. Image mapping

3. What is the most recent version of HTML?

    A. HTML 3.2

    B. HTML 4.0

    C. HTML 4.01

    D. HTML

4. Which of the following HTML 4.01 variations should be used for Web documents that contain deprecated tags?

    A. HTML 4.01 Transitional

    B. HTML 4.01 Specific

    C. HTML 4.01 Strict

    D. HTML 4.01 Frameset

5. What is the primary difference between HTML 4.01 and XHTML 1.0?

    A. XHTML 1.0 introduces new attributes.

    B. XHTML 1.0 does not allow developers to use deprecated tags.

    C. XHTML adheres to XML's syntax requirements.

    D. XHTML adheres to SGML's syntax requirements.

6. Proprietary markup was introduced by which of the following organizations?

    A. The World Wide Web Consortium

    B. Browser venders such as Netscape and Microsoft

    C. The Internet Society (ISOC)

    D. The Internet Corporation for Assigned Names and Numbers

7. Which of the following is the least troublesome problem associated with proprietary markup?

    A. Not all browsers support the same set of proprietary tags.

    B. Some browsers may ignore proprietary tags.

    C. Some tools require that you use proprietary tags.

    D. Proprietary tags might not be supported by the latest version of the HTML specification.

8. Which standards organization governs the HTML standard?

    A. CERN

    B. ISOC

    C. W3C

    D. IAB

Scenarios

1. Your company has asked you to take over the company Web site. You're told that it follows the HTML 4.01 Strict DTD. You have to decide what tags you can use in future updates to the site. Can you use document structure tags? Can you use presentation tags, such as the `<font>` tag?

2. You decide that you want to impress your boss and convert the company Web site to XHTML. What does this process entail? What advantages do you gain?

Lab Exercises

Lab 7-1: Examining and determining DTDs

Every Web site should reference the appropriate DTD; however, Web developers rarely include this line of markup in their documents. The reasons for excluding this markup range from laziness to a lack of knowledge on the subject. If you would like to examine a working example (a Web site that includes the DOCTYPE referenced to the appropriate DTD), visit `www.w3.org` and select View ⇨ Source from the Browser tool bar.

In this lab, you're expected to determine which DTD a given HTML document should reference, using the following steps:

1. Go to the following Web sites:

   • `http://hotwired.lycos.com/webmonkey/`

   • `www.cnet.com`

   • `www.projectcool.com/developer/tips/quickstart/index.html`

2. For each site, answer the following questions:

   a. Which DOCTYPE declaration should the Web page use?

   b. Why did you choose the DOCTYPE declaration above?

Answers to Chapter Questions

Chapter pre-test

1. HTML stands for the Hypertext Markup Language.

2. HTML was created by Tim Berners-Lee while he was with CERN. The idea was to add to the work done with hypertext and hypermedia and create a way to access a large universe of documents. HTML was created as an application of SGML.

3. The most recent version of HTML (4.01) has three different variants: Transitional, Frameset, and Strict. Each variant is governed by a separate DTD.

4. The World Wide Web Consortium (W3C) was introduced in 1994 and since then has governed the HTML standard. The W3C also governs the CSS, XML, and other XML-related standards.

5. XHTML is an application of XML, whereas HTML is an application of SGML. XML syntax rules are stricter, therefore, requiring Web developers to be more careful with XHTML documents.

Assessment questions

1. B. SGML predates HTML. After all, HTML is an application of SGML. See "The Development of HTML."

2. C. Hyperlinking is at the heart of HTML. The concept of linking documents, thereby allowing users access to a document universe, was the goal of HTML. Hyperlinking goes beyond just jumping to other HTML documents; it allows for the concept of hypermedia (accessing other data formats, such as audio and video files). See "The Development of HTML."

3. C. HTML 4.01 is the most recent version of HTML. We would like to point out that technically, XHTML is the most recent version. Although there's an X in the name, it still belongs to the HTML family of standards. However, most HTML materials define HTML 4.01 as the latest version, and consider XHTML 1.0 the beginning of a new language. See "An Overview of HTML Versions."

4. A. The HTML 4.01 Transitional DTD allows users to use deprecated presentational tags. According to the Transitional DTD, almost anything goes (except for most frame-related markup). See "HTML 4.01 Transitional."

5. C. The primary difference (and one of the only differences) between HTML 4.01 and XHTML 1.0 is that XHTML requires that you adhere to XML's syntax rules. This requires Web developers to use a stricter syntax, but that syntax still remains similar to that of HTML. So, in other words, there's not much difference other than syntax. See "HTML 4.01 and XHTML."

6. B. Both Netscape and Microsoft have been the leaders of introducing proprietary tags into the HTML language. Many of these tags have gone on to be incorporated into the formal standard; however, don't expect this trend to last. The future versions of HTML will be dumping most of the presentational tags (they are deprecated) and trimming the fat so to say. See "Standard vs. Proprietary HTML."

7. C. Proprietary markup introduces problems for Web developers because it is not consistent across all browsers. The tags that Netscape introduces will most likely not be supported by Internet Explorer, and the proprietary tags Internet Explorer uses will probably be ignored by Netscape. If you're a Web developer creating a Web site with a broad audience (one that uses both browsers), it makes it difficult to create a page that renders the same in both browsers. See "Standard vs. Proprietary HTML."

8. C. The W3C has governed the HTML standard since 1994. See "World Wide Web Consortium."

Scenarios

1. The Strict DTD allows you to use document structure tags; however, you can't use presentational tags. This means that you have to use CSS for defining presentation. This introduces a possible new problem: Most of the new browsers support CSS, but older browsers do not. For this reason, most Web developers are forced to use the HTML 4.01 Transitional DTD and use a combination of deprecated presentational tags, along with CSS.

2. The process of converting a Web site to XHTML just means that you have to follow the six syntax rules defined in this chapter. This can be done by hand or you can use a tool that does it for you. Either way, the process is fairly painless. Converting your site to XHTML provides the following advantages to both users and yourself as the Web developer:

- Because of the strict syntax, your code is cleaner, and therefore easier for browsers to download.

- Because your code is cleaner, and follows more regular syntax rules, it's easier to troubleshoot a problem. If your code is a mess (for example, you forget to use closing tags making it difficult to recognize element relationships), you'll have a harder time locating the problem.

Cross-Reference   More advantages to using XHTML are covered in Chapter 19.

For More Information

✦ **World Wide Web Consortium (W3C).** www.w3.org: As noted in this chapter, the W3C controls the HTML standard, as well as future versions of that standard. On their site, you have access to the standard itself, as well as an online validator that will check your documents for correct syntax and use of tags. As a Web developer, you should become cozy with the validator, it could be your best friend—it always tells you when you've messed up!

✦ **Zvon.** www.zvon.org: The Zvon Web site is a fairly new site that is adding Web-related reference guides almost every day. This site has an XHTML reference guide that provides information about the three XHTML DTDs, the tags allowed, and examples of most tags and attributes. This site is up to date, and a wonderful reference if you can't remember what tag is allowed where.

✦ **ZDNet's Developer site.** www.zdnet.com/developer/: The ZDNet developer site delivers timely articles on Web design, covering topics from Java programming to HTML Web design. The most notable tool on the site is a "Tag Reference" that defines each HTML tag, along with its attributes. It's easy to use and an essential reference for any Web developer learning HTML.

✦ **WebReview.com.** http://webreview.com: WebReview.com provides the HTML community with articles about the business. You'll find several how-to articles that focus on topics from usability to the HTML language itself.

HTML Tables and Page Structure

EXAM OBJECTIVES

- ✦ Understanding HTML tables
- ✦ Designing tables for page layout control
- ✦ Diagramming tables

CHAPTER PRE-TEST

1. Why are tables sometimes used to structure Web pages?

2. What are the two types of measurements that are commonly used to define the height and width of a table?

3. Which attribute is used to make the table "invisible"?

4. What is the outermost tag for any table?

This chapter looks at using table markup to define page layout (or structure). It's common practice for Web designers to use table markup to control the layout of objects on the page. If you need an image to be aligned a particular way, tables may be your only answer. In this chapter, you'll take a look at deciding whether you should use table markup to add structure, and if so, just how to go about using it to your advantage.

Overview of Table Markup Tags

 Understanding HTML tables

You should already be familiar with the table tags introduced in HTML 4.0. If you're not, please review the CIW Foundation materials or visit the W3C site at `www.w3.org/TR/html4/struct/tables.html`. Here's a brief rundown of the table tags:

✦ `<table>` — The table tag. This is the container tag for a table.

✦ `<tr>` — The table row tag. This tag defines a table row and is a child of the `<table>` tag.

✦ `<td>` — The table data cell tag. This tag defines a table data cell and contains the data of a table.

✦ `<th>` — The table header tag. This tag is used to define header cells for a table.

✦ `<tbody>` — The table body tag. Contains the `<td>` tags used for the body of a table.

✦ `<thead>` — The table head tag. Contains the `<th>` tags used for the header of a table.

✦ `<tfoot>` — The table foot tag. Contains the `<td>` tags used for the footer of a table.

✦ `<caption>` — The caption tag. Defines a caption for the table.

✦ `<col>` — The column tag. Defines properties for columns.

✦ `<colgroup>` — The column group tag. Defines properties for a group of columns.

You only need to know three of these tags when using table markup to define page layout. If you think about it, this makes sense. When you use table markup to position items on the page, you don't need a caption, table headers, or footers because you don't want the user to even know that a table exists. You don't even need to define the table body. Therefore, we don't discuss these tags in this chapter (`<caption>`, `<thead>`, `<tfoot>`, and `<tbody>`). Therefore, the only table tags you have to be concerned with are:

✦ `<table>` — To create the table

✦ `<tr>` — To define the rows for your table

✦ `<td>` — To house your content

Designing Tables for Page Layout Control

 Designing tables for page layout control

If you're not familiar with using table markup to define page layout, your first question may be, "Why should I use table markup to define page layout?" This isn't something Web designers want to do; however, using tables to define page layout has become a way of life for many designers.

 Exam Tip   Don't get confused if the exam uses uppercase for all element and attribute names. Both uppercase and lowercase element and attribute names are allowed. We use lowercase in this book because that is the way they're defined in the XHTML 1.0 specification.

Think about a basic Web page that contains `<h1>`, `<h2>`, and `<p>` tags and looks similar to the following:

```
<html>
  <head>
    <title>Boring Linear Document</title>
  </head>
  <body>
    <h1>Our first heading</h1>
    <p>An introduction paragraph</p>
    <h2>A subheading</h2>
    <p>Another paragraph</p>
  </body>
</html>
```

In this example, you have no control over element placement, except to decide which element comes first. In other words, all you have is linear control, as illustrated in Figure 8-1.

However, what if you want an image to appear in the upper portion of the page, with some navigation to the left of the page, and content paragraphs and more navigation to the right? (This is a common model found on many Web pages.) Figure 8-2 illustrates this design.

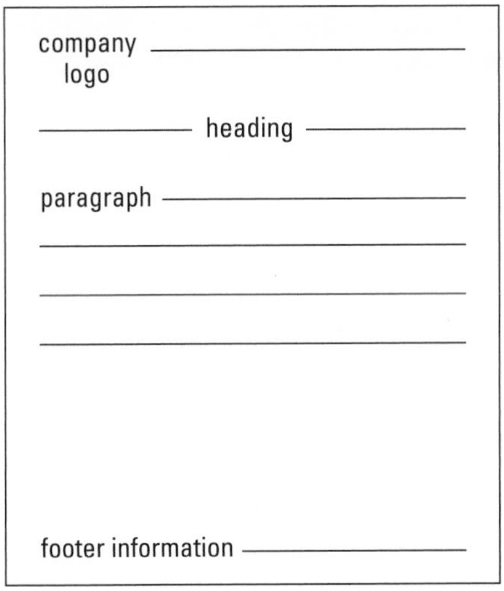

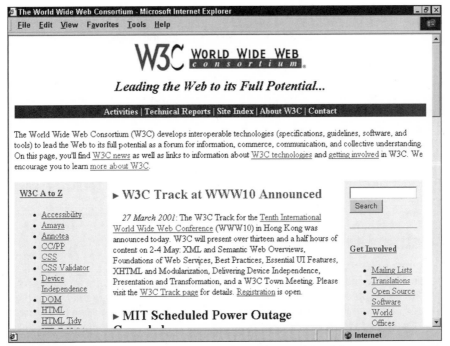

Figure 8-1: Linear control of a Web page document

Figure 8-2: A Web page with an image in the upper portion of the page, some navigation to the left of the page, and content paragraphs and more navigation on the right

Figure 8-2 abandons the idea of linear design by placing elements in various places on the page. There are currently three main ways to achieve this effect:

✦ **Frames.** You can define two frames. The left frame defines an image, followed by the navigation, and the right frame contains the content paragraphs.

✦ **CSS positioning.** More recently, Web developers have been able to use Cascading Style Sheets (CSS) positioning to define the left and top pixel positions of any element.

✦ **Tables.** And finally, what you're here to learn: Table markup can be used to define each section with <td> tags.

In the Real World   Many Web developers will tell you that frames are a big no-no, because some browsers don't support them. At the same time, CSS is not fully supported by all Web browsers either. Therefore, whether you like it or not, you'll probably have to resort to using table markup to define page layout.

Tables have one main advantage over frames: Users can bookmark Web pages defined with table markup. This may seem like a strange statement because you'd assume that users can bookmark any Web page. However, framed structure only lets you bookmark the frameset document, or the individual frame, but not all the possible frame combinations.

Cross-Reference   Frames are covered in Chapter 9 and CSS is covered in Chapter 11.

However, table markup also has a slight disadvantage: It requires the entire page to scroll (see Figure 8-3). Frames, on the other hand, allow you to define a navigation frame to the left that remains static, while allowing the content frame to scroll.

Table layout can be as complex as you want it to be. For example, Figure 8-4 uses three rows, and five columns.

Table markup can become even more complex with a concept called nesting, which we cover in detail in the following section.

Nesting tables

Nesting involves the placement of one table inside another table. Think of a set of boxes. You have a large box with a smaller box inside, with yet a smaller box inside that one, and so on. Nesting has become a common trait in page layout and a necessity for getting those elements just where you want them on the page. Figure 8-5 illustrates this concept.

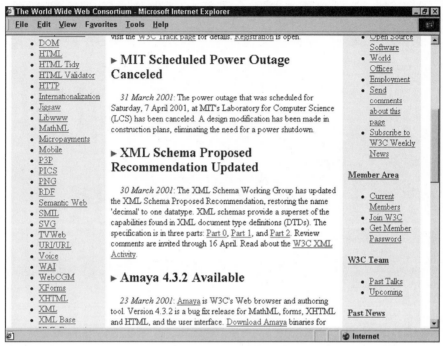

Figure 8-3: Tables do not allow the author to isolate navigation.

Figure 8-4: Table layout with three rows and five columns

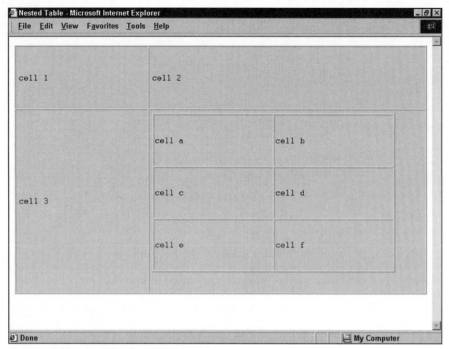

Figure 8-5: Nesting tables within tables

In the previous figure, you can see the borders of the table; however, when this is rendered in an actual Web page, you most likely want to define a borderless table. For example, Figure 8-6 contains a Web page using the same setup defined by Figure 8-5 — without borders.

Cross-Reference See the section later in this chapter, entitled "Dealing with Page Design Snags," for more information on how to turn table borders off and eliminate unwanted whitespace.

There's one primary rule you must live by when nesting tables: the nested table must be contained by the `<td>` tags. For example, the following snippet of markup is allowed:

```
<table>
  <tr>
    <td><img src="file.gif" alt="alternative text"></td>
    <td>
      <table>
        <tr>
          <td>Text for nested table</td>
        </tr>
      </table>
```

```
        </td>
      </tr>
    </table>
```

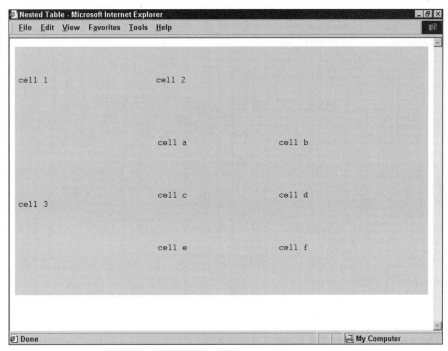

Figure 8-6: Figure 8-5 displayed without borders

However, the following markup is not allowed. Notice that the second table is nested within <tr> tags:

```
<table>
  <tr>
    <td><img src="file.gif" alt="alternative text"></td>
    <td>Text for the document</td>
        <table>
            <tr>
                <td>Text for nested table</td>
            </tr>
        </table>
  </tr>
</table>
```

Tip   Nesting tables is useful, but you have to be careful. Nesting tables can increase the amount of time your Web page takes to download; that's because the longer and deeper the table, the longer it takes for most browsers to read everything in the table (including other tables) before they render the markup.

Diagramming tables

Objective   Diagramming tables

Before you create your HTML table in your text editor, you need to map out your table by hand. In previous examples, you checked out simple table designs similar to the one shown in Figure 8-7.

Figure 8-7: A simple table design

However, a simple table is not the likeliest scenario. In the demanding world of Web design, companies request more complex table designs, such as the one shown in Figure 8-8.

Figure 8-8 contains nine cells. The cells in the upper-left and lower-left corners are used as spacers, and the other cells are designed to contain content for the page. In this example, you also see the concept of spanning, where the vertical cell in the center of the left column spans four rows.

Sketching out a table diagram requires that you know all the pieces and parts you want to include in your Web page. For example, the Web page in Figure 8-9 consists of an invisible table that governs page layout. Before the document author created that table, he or she sat down and took inventory of what needed to be included in the page. Then, the author sketched out a table diagram (as shown in Figure 8-10). Take a few seconds to create your own table diagram, noting cells that span rows or columns. We aren't talking about anything fancy, just a diagram that notes cell divisions.

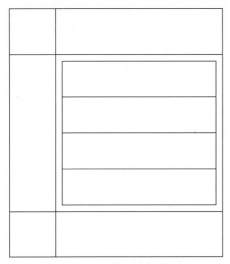

Figure 8-8: A complex table design

Figure 8-9: LANWrights' Web site uses tables for page layout.

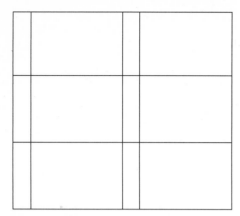

Figure 8-10: Diagram of LANWrights' table layout

Exam Tip

Remember that the colspan and rowspan attributes are used to allow a table data <td> cell to span both rows and columns. For example, <td rowspan="3"> creates a cell that spans three rows. This is sure to be on the exam, so take some time to map out some example tables using spanning cells.

Spanning rows and columns

A common trick of the table trade is to span rows and columns. As demonstrated in the previous section, you can instruct a cell to stretch across multiple columns or multiple rows. This is handy if you need your navigation column to stretch down the entire table, thereby spanning all other rows. You should already know the markup behind this trick; however, the following sections contain a refresher in case you forgot.

Spanning columns

If you plan to span columns, the markup used is simple:

```
<td colspan="number">
```

The colspan attribute is used within the <td> tag and the value should correspond with the number of columns you wish the cell to span (this number includes the cell itself). For example, if you have a simple table with two columns and two rows, but decide that you want the first row to span the entire width of the table (basically just the two columns), the markup would be:

```
<table>
  <tr>
    <td colspan="2">Cell that spans two columns</td>
  </tr>
```

```
  <tr>
    <td>cell</td>
    <td>cell</td>
  </tr>
</table>
```

Spanning rows

Spanning rows is not that much different from spanning columns. The syntax should look familiar:

```
<td rowspan="number">
```

Again, you're using an attribute with the `<td>` tag; however, this time, you use the `rowspan` attribute. The value of the `rowspan` attribute corresponds with the number of cells you want to span (including the cell defining the spanning). Take the previous example, a table with two columns and two rows. This time, you want to alter this table so that one column spans the entire table (two rows). The markup would be as follows:

```
<table>
  <tr>
    <td rowspan="2">Cell that spans two rows</td>
    <td>cell</td>
  </tr>
  <tr>
    <td>cell</td>
  </tr>
</table>
```

Dealing with Page Design Snags

The next step (after creating a table diagram) is implementing this design. Regardless of the amount of preparation you put into your table layout, chances are, you'll always run into a couple of snags. The following sections deal with two of the common issues you may encounter.

Unwanted whitespace

One of the most common snags you'll encounter is a small border of whitespace between the table and the top and left margins as shown in Figure 8-11.

This whitespace is not a problem with your table markup, but is instead a problem with the `<body>` tag. Believe it or not, the whitespace border is being applied to the body of the document, not the table. If you know your HTML elements and attributes, you know that the `<body>` tag (as defined by the W3C) doesn't have any attributes that will solve this problem. However, both Netscape and Internet Explorer introduced proprietary markup to solve it.

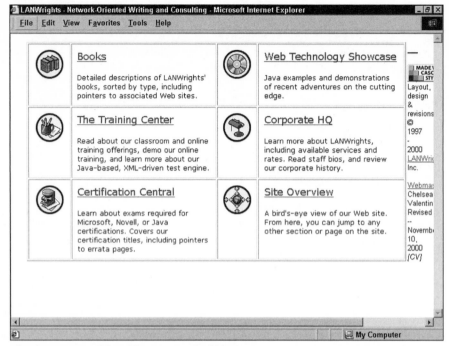

Figure 8-11: A table with unwanted whitespace

Although most Web designers dislike proprietary markup, this is one case in which it's beneficial and solves a problem for which there's no other solution. There are two attributes that Internet Explorer uses to correct this problem, and guess what? There are two very different attributes that Netscape uses. They are as follows:

✦ **Netscape.** `marginheight="0"` and `marginwidth="0"`

✦ **Internet Explorer.** `topmargin="0"` and `leftmargin="0"`

To align your page with the very top-left of the screen, add these four attributes to your `<body>` tag:

```
<body marginheight="0" marginwidth="0" leftmargin="0"
topmargin="0">
```

Turning table borders off

Now, on to the next possible snag: table borders. Table borders are easy to manipulate, and if you're creating a table that will be used for page layout, you want to turn the table border off. To turn the table border off, set the `border` attribute to zero (0), as follows:

```
<table border="0">...</table>
```

Working with Other Table Attributes

The `border` attribute is important to using tables for page layout; however, there are several other attributes that you have to be aware of as well:

✦ `width`

✦ `cellspacing`

✦ `cellpadding`

✦ `bgcolor`

Take a second to reacquaint yourself with these attributes, which are described in the following sections.

Table width

When using table markup to define page layout, you want your table to take up most of the page. To define the table width, you use the `width` attribute. However, when you use the `width` attribute, you need to decide whether the width will be in pixels or percentages. If you define a table with a set pixel width, the table takes up the exact number of pixels defined. For example, if your `table` tag looked like the following, your table would be exactly 550 pixels wide:

```
<table border="0" width="550">...</table>
```

If you define your table width using a percentage, however, your table will take up a percentage of the browser window. This allows the table to scale to the size of the browser window. This relative size can be defined like so:

```
<table border="0" width="90%">...</table>
```

You can also use the `width` attribute with the `<td>` tag to manipulate the width of an individual cell.

Cell spacing and padding

Another way designers can manipulate table layout is by altering the `cellspacing` and `cellpadding` attributes. Remember that the `cellpadding` attribute defines the amount of space (or padding) within the cell, whereas the `cellspacing` attribute defines the amount of space between cells. The following is an example of using the `cellspacing` and `cellpadding` attributes:

```
<table border="0" width="550" cellpadding="5"
cellspacing="0">...</table>
```

Adding color

You can assign color to your table in the `<table>` tag and the `<td>` tag. Both of these tags accept the `bgcolor` attribute and allow you to change the background color of a cell (or even the entire table). Using the `bgcolor` attribute with the `<td>` tag is a great way to define a visual separation between rows and cells, for example:

```
<table border="0" width="550" cellpadding="5" cellspacing="0">
  <tr>
    <td bgcolor="red">contents</td>
  </tr>
</table>
```

Key Point Summary

After reading this chapter, you should be familiar with table structures. The art of creating tables is a delicate balance of design and function, and this chapter has prepared you to enter that world. After reading this chapter, the following concepts should be clear:

✦ Tables can be used instead of a framed structure for page layout.

✦ The table tags you use to create basic table structures are the `<table>`, `<tr>`, and `<td>` tags.

✦ You can nest tables within tables; however, you must nest the second table within `<td>` tags.

✦ Borderless tables are used for page layout.

✦ ✦ ✦

STUDY GUIDE

If you enjoy solving problems, you probably enjoyed this chapter. Using tables to define your page layout is all about solving problems. Whether you're deciding to span a few rows, or to create a cell that is used as a spacer, table markup solves your layout problems. Now, it's time to apply what you learned from this chapter.

Assessment Questions

1. If you're nesting a table within another table, in which tag must the second table be nested?

   A. `<tr>`

   B. `<tbody>`

   C. `<td`

   D. `<table>`

2. Table data cells can span multiple:

   A. tables

   B. rows and columns

   C. frames

   D. pages

3. Which of the following attribute/value pairs is used to define a borderless table?

   A. `borders="0"`

   B. `borderless="1"`

   C. `border="1"`

   D. `border="0"`

4. The `width` attribute can define a table using which of the following measurements?

   A. Pixels and percentages

   B. Miles

   C. Inches and centimeters

   D. Feet and yards

5. What is the primary advantage of using frames over tables?

   A. Frames allow users to bookmark Web pages easily.

   B. Frames allow users to jump with pages.

   C. Frames allow users to manipulate objects on a page.

   D. Frames allow users to define a scrollable region, while supplying a static navigational frame.

6. Which of the following tags can you use within table markup?

   A. `<li>` and `<ul>`

   B. `<tr>` and `<td>`

   C. `<li>` and `<ol>`

   D. `<kbd>` and `<tt>`

Scenarios

Your company has asked you to redesign the company Web site. The company site must follow these specifications:

✦ The company logo must appear in the top left of the window.

✦ Navigation must appear to the left of the window.

✦ Content pages must appear in the middle of the page.

Before you create the site, you're required to provide a proposal to your boss. In that proposal, you must identify whether the site design will use frames or tables. What would your decision be, and why?

Lab Exercises

Lab 8-1: Diagramming a table

For this lab, you need to create a table that adheres to the following specifications:

✦ Contains four rows

✦ Contains three columns

✦ The first and last row spans three columns

✦ The first column spans four rows

The first step is to create your table diagram. It doesn't have to be anything fancy, just a sketch of where your content should go.

The next step is to dust off your text editor and begin to create your table. First create the `table` tag and set the `border` to 1. We know, you want the border to be invisible; however, when you first create a table, it's helpful to have the border visible. After the table is complete, you can change the `border` attribute value to 0.

This lab requires that you work with the `colspan` and `rowspan` attributes. Don't let this level of complexity confuse you. Take a few deep breaths and sketch it out in your table diagram first. When you're ready, add the attributes to your markup.

Lab 8-2: Diagramming Web sites with tables

For this lab, you need to visit `http://hotwired.lycos.com/webmonkey/` and view their source (View ⇨ Source or View ⇨ Source Code, depending on your browser). Webmonkey uses a table to control its layout. Take a peek at the markup to get a feel for how you might want to use tables to define your Web page structure. When you're ready, create a diagram that maps out the table used to create the Webmonkey Web site. Be sure to note when a cell spans columns or rows.

Lab 8-3: Creating a table

For this lab, you must create a table that could be used to emulate the Web page you viewed in Lab 8-2. Be sure to use the `colspan` and `rowspan` attributes, like you did in Lab 8-1.

The first step is to grab the diagram you created after viewing the source markup at `http://hotwired.lycos.com/webmonkey/` in Lab 8-2, and then add tags and attributes. As always, start by adding the `table` tag. For complex tables, we recommend that you work your way from the outside in. What we mean by that is that you create the `table` tags first, and then add the `tr` tags. After you have all the rows in place, go back and add the `td` tags. Notice that you add parent tags before their nested children—working your way outside in.

Because this lab requires you to create markup that already exists, you have an easy way to check your work—all you have to do is visit the Web site and view the source.

Answers to Chapter Questions

Chapter pre-test

1. Tables are used by Web designers to define Web page layout. Until recently, tables were one of the only ways to align objects on a page.

2. The two most common types of measurements used to define the height and width of a table are pixels and percentages. If you define the table width in pixels, no matter what the user's browser window size, the table will always remain the same width. However, if you define the table width in a percentage, the table will scale to always take up the same percentage of the user's browser window. So, when the user decreases the browser window size, the table decreases in size as well.

3. If the `border` attribute is set to 0, the table border is invisible.

4. The `<table>` tag is the outermost tag for any table.

Assessment Questions

1. **C.** When nesting tables within other tables, the second table must always be nested within the `<td>` tags. See "Nesting tables."

2. **B.** The `<td>` tag can span multiple rows and columns using the `colspan` and `rowspan` attributes. See "Diagramming tables."

3. **D.** Borderless tables are created using the `border` attribute and setting it equal to zero (0). See "Turning table borders off."

4. **A.** The two types of measurement used to define table width are pixels and percentages. See "Table width."

5. **D.** The main advantage frames have over tables is that they allow the Web designer to create a non-scrollable navigation region. This means the navigation remains present at all times, while the user can scroll the content region. See "Designing Tables for Page Layout Control."

6. **B.** Of the tags listed, `<td>` and `<tr>` are used to create tables. The `<tr>` defines a table row, and the `<td>` tag defines a table data cell. See "Overview of Table Markup Tags."

Scenarios

There's no right or wrong answer to this scenario. There are benefits and drawbacks to using either frame or table structures, as follows:

✦ **If you use frames.** You can define your navigation to always be present; however, you run the risk of alienating your audience, because navigating in a framed structure can be difficult, not to mention users will have a hard time bookmarking your site.

Cross-
Reference

See Chapter 9 for more information on frames and why navigating them is difficult.

✦ **If you use tables.** Users have no problem bookmarking your site, but if you want your navigation to always be present you either have to do some very careful planning, or you're forced to use dynamic HTML features to achieve the effect.

Bear in mind, these two choices will not always be the only ones. As browsers get up to speed with CSS, Web designers will be able to use CSS to define positioning of elements on the page, allowing designers to only use tables when they actually need to display a table of data (think Microsoft Excel type of table).

For More Information

✦ **World Wide Web Consortium (W3C) HTML 4.01 Tables.** www.w3.org/TR/html4/struct/tables.html: This is the section of the W3C HTML 4.01 Specification that discusses tables.

✦ **Webmonkey.** http://hotwired.lycos.com/webmonkey/: Hotwired's Webmonkey is a wonderful resource for catchy (and fun) tutorials on Web design. From programming to tables, you can find an article on almost anything you need. You can also view their source to see an example of a complex table used for layout.

✦ **ZDNet's Developer site.** www.zdnet.com/developer/: The ZDnet developer Web site provides designers with tons of articles on Web design related issues. You can bet that they have a few great articles on tables as well. Take a second to view the Web page source if you're interested in seeing a table in action.

✦ **WebReview.** http://webreview.com: WebReview provides the HTML community with articles about the business. You'll find several how-to articles on building tables on this site. You can also view the source code used in other Web sites and learn from how they use table markup.

HTML Frames and Site Design

EXAM OBJECTIVES

- ✦ Frames and usability
- ✦ Frames and framesets
- ✦ Simple page layout
- ✦ Complex page layout

CHAPTER PRE-TEST

1. What is a frameset document?

2. What tag does the `<frameset>` tag replace?

3. What can users view if their browser does not support frames?

4. What advantages do frames have?

5. What does "targeting" mean in relation to frames?

6. What does the `<base>` tag do?

✦ Answers to these questions can be found at the end of the chapter. ✦

This chapter examines HTML frame markup and defines the advantages and disadvantages to using a framed approach. In the past, most Web developers did not encourage frames; however, they have become more acceptable because of some improvements in frame markup and browser behavior. This chapter looks at how to take advantage of HTML frames.

Frames and Usability

 Frames and usability

A Web developer's initial reaction to the first mention of frames may be, "Yuck!" This is because, until recently, frames have not been very usable. *Usability* is the measure of how functional and usable a Web site is and should be one of the most important aspects of any Web design. Therefore, when usability is hindered by the incorrect use of frames, users may not revisit your Web site. If you know what you're doing with frames, however, it's possible to create a usable design.

In the beginning, the design of the Web was almost flawless. The design centered on several concepts:

✦ Users use hyperlinks to get from one document to another.

✦ Each document has an address that can be used on the Web.

✦ Users can bookmark a document.

✦ Documents are stored and maintained on a server.

These concepts allowed for a simple model that has grown into what we know as the Web. This design is in part responsible for the Web's rapid expansion.

Frames were introduced later in the HTML evolution. The way in which frames handle documents goes against the very model of the original design. In the original design, users viewed information in one screen full. With frames, a user's view is dependent upon a couple of navigational actions: first, the browser loads the frameset, and then the browser retrieves and loads the individual pages that populate each frame. These additional sequences of actions interrupt the original design model and can make navigation a nightmare.

Navigating within frames

The most obvious obstacle to useful navigation is the bookmark dilemma. For example, what if a user navigates to a different pairing of frames than the initial frameset defines? This happens when a user selects any internal navigation hyperlink within a framed structure. Now, if the user wants to bookmark this page, he or she has to right-click on the given frame and bookmark that individual page.

However, the user will then lose the other frames (some of which may define navigation). In addition, there may be users who aren't aware of this functionality; therefore, they're left bookmarking the main page only.

In the age of e-commerce and three-click navigation, making it difficult for users to bookmark pages deep within your site can cost you. Users want to find their information quickly and they don't want to have to search for it or go to extra steps to obtain it.

For example, go to `www.wola.org` (shown in Figure 9-1). You can easily bookmark this URL. However, if you select the About Us hyperlink, the browser jumps to the About Us page (shown in Figure 9-2), but the URL remains the same: `www.wola.org`.

Printing framed pages

There's yet another reason frames can get in the way of good design — printing. This is not an obstacle for the Web savvy, because most browsers let you select which frame you want to print from their print dialog boxes. However, for those of you who are not quite familiar with the way browsers print frames, most browsers only print one frame. For example, most users want to print the content-related frame page; however, they may get stuck printing the navigation frame or a frame containing the company logo.

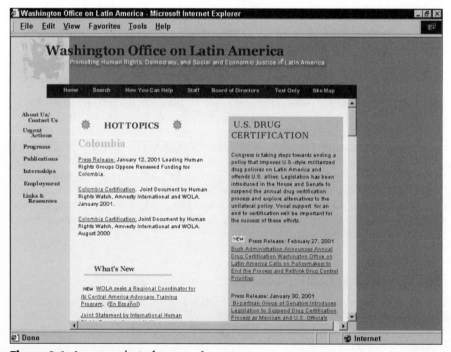

Figure 9-1: A screen shot of `www.wola.org`

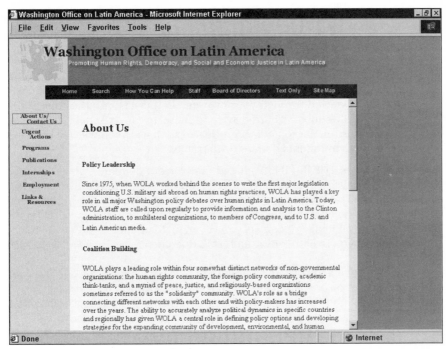

Figure 9-2: Navigating to the About Us page

If you do decide to use frames, we recommend that you always create printable versions of any content you think a user will want to print. If you host articles or informational tips, they would make prime candidates for a printer friendly icon that points to one HTML document that users can print without frustration.

When you should use frames

With all that has been written, you probably expect us to say that we never recommend using frames. That is not necessarily so. Although we don't jump up and down encouraging designers to use frames, there are some instances that warrant the use of them, such as the following:

✦ **Targeting carefully.** If you learn how to control hyperlinks within a frameset, you can use the `target="_top"` attribute with your `<a>` tags. This allows the browser to clear out all frames when loading the new page. Each pairing of documents would be controlled by its own frameset. This entails a lot of work, but it ensures that users can always bookmark a given pairing of documents.

Cross-Reference

An example of this is defined in the section "Hyperlinks in Frames."

✦ **Control environment.** If you're creating a set of documents that are not open to the Web, and you don't expect users to be jumping from your site to other sites during their visit, you have more control over users' navigation and are able to bypass many of the navigational concerns previously defined. One example can be seen with the help documents associated with many software products. After you download the product, you can access a help environment that is viewed through your browser. In this case, all the navigation is referencing files on your hard drive and there are no external hyperlinks to the Web. Most of Macromedia's products (such as Dreamweaver and Flash) have help environments defined with frames.

✦ **Inline frames.** HTML 4.0 introduced the concept of inline frames. In this case, you don't have to deal with frameset documents; the frame is embedded within an HTML document. This is new and not readily used, but it skirts all the navigation obstacles mentioned previously. Inline frames work much like embedding an image document; however, instead of embedding an image document, you're embedding an HTML document.

Although we've demonstrated why you shouldn't use frames, the Site Designer exam focuses on one advantage to using them: allowing a document author to combine static and dynamic information. By dynamic they mean that the one frame can remain static (commonly a navigation page), while another frame can change (commonly a content-related page) depending on user action. Although this is dynamic in nature — the content-related page is constantly changing — it does not require JavaScript and is not part of dynamic HTML.

Now it's time to turn your attention to the frame markup.

Overview of Frame Markup

    Frames and framesets

To understand frame design, you have to first understand frame markup. Although it's assumed you have some working knowledge of frame markup, you should take a few moments to reacquaint yourself with these tags:

✦ `<frameset>`

✦ `<frame>`

✦ `<noframes>`

✦ `<iframe>`

We cover these tags in more detail in the following sections.

The frameset tag

The most important piece of frame markup is the `<frameset>` tag. As the container tag for all frame markup, you can't define frames without it. A boilerplate for a frameset document is:

```
<html>
  <head>
     <title>Document Title</title>
  </head>
  <frameset>
     ...
  </frameset>
</html>
```

All frameset documents follow the basic HTML document structure using the `<html>`, `<head>`, and `<title>` tags. Although a frameset document is much like a regular HTML document, there are some exceptions:

✦ A frameset document does not contain the `<body>` tag.

✦ A frameset document must contain at least one pair of `<frameset>` tags.

✦ A frameset document is used to define the frame structure.

✦ A frameset document uses `<frame>` tags to reference content documents.

✦ You can nest `<frameset>` tags within the parent `<frameset>` tag pair.

Exam Tip For exam purposes, a frame is a scrollable region that contains an HTML document, and a frameset is an HTML document that defines a set of frames populated by other HTML documents.

Instead of using a pair of `<body>` tags to contain content, you use `<frameset>` tags to contain references to the content. The purpose of the `<frameset>` tag is to define the frame structure and to contain all other frame markup.

Caution Most browsers will ignore frame markup if it encounters a `<body>` tag. So, be sure to always omit the `<body>` tag when creating a frameset document. However, note that you can use the `<body>` tag within the `<noframes>` tag. See "The noframes tag" section later in this chapter.

The rows attribute

There are two ways you can define a frameset. First, you can define a horizontal set of frames (see Figure 9-3) or you can define a set of vertical frames (see Figure 9-4).

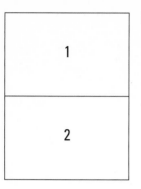

Figure 9-3: Horizontal frame structure

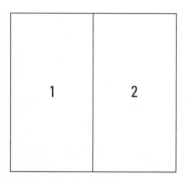

Figure 9-4: Vertical frame structure

Defining a set of horizontal frames is done using the rows attribute. For example, the following markup would create two horizontal rows: one with a height of 200 pixels, and one set to take up the remainder of the window:

```
<frameset rows="200,*">
```

Tip   The asterisk is used as a wild card; it tells the browser to fill the column or row with the remainder of the available space.

You can add as many frames as you would like. Just remember that each frame must have a corresponding row value, as follows:

```
<html>
  <head>
    <title>Document Title</title>
  </head>
  <frameset rows="25%,*,10%">
    <frame src="header.html">
    <frame src="content.html">
    <frame src="footer.html">
  </frameset>
</html>
```

The previous example is a frame structure with three horizontal frames. The first frame takes up 25% of the available browser space, the third frame takes up 10% of the available space, and the second frame takes up the remaining space (see Figure 9-5).

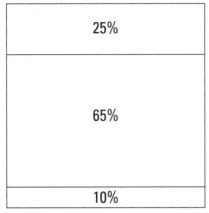

25%

65%

10%

Figure 9-5: A three-row frame structure

Tip The value of the `rows` attribute can be defined in relative or absolute terms. If you use percentages in the value, the frame structure is defined relative to the browser size. As the user makes his or her window smaller, the frames become proportionally smaller as well. If you use pixels to define a frame size, the frame size is set at that width and will not be scalable as the user shrinks his or her window size.

Now, let's try one with absolute widths:

```
<html>
  <head>
    <title>Document Title</title>
  </head>
  <frameset rows="250,450">
    <frame src="top.html">
    <frame src="bottom.html">
  </frameset>
</html>
```

This example is a frameset with the first frame spanning 250 pixels in height and the second frame spanning 450 pixels in height as shown in Figure 9-6.

The cols attribute

The `cols` attribute is a snap because it functions the same way as the `rows` attribute. The only difference is that the `cols` attribute defines a vertical frame structure.

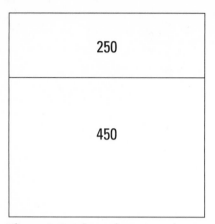

Figure 9-6: A framed structure that
will not scale with the browser window

The value of the `cols` attribute defines the width of each frame. A comma separates
each width value. For example, the following markup creates three columns: one
with a width of 200 pixels, the next with a width of 400 pixels, and the final column
is set to take the remainder of the window.

```
<frameset cols="200,400,*">
```

If you want to define the width using a percentage, and therefore allow the frames
to be scalable, create a document similar to the following:

```
<html>
  <head>
    <title>Document Title</title>
  </head>
  <frameset cols="25%,*">
    <frame src="nav.html" name="nav">
    <frame src="content.html" name="body">
  </frameset>
</html>
```

Remember that the asterisk is a wildcard and tells the browser that the second
frame can take the remainder of the browser window.

**Cross-
Reference**

For now, we keep our examples simple; however, later in this chapter in the
"Nested Framesets" section, you find out about nesting `<frameset>` tags to create complex frame structures.

Other frameset attributes

The attributes defined in this section are not formally a part of the HTML specification; however, both Netscape and Internet Explorer recognize them and they're commonly used by Web designers to define borderless frames.

The other attributes that you can use with the `<frameset>` tag are:

✦ `frameborder` — You can set the value to the following values: 1 (yes) or 0 (no — the frame border is invisible). Because this attribute is proprietary to both browsers, they define the values differently; however, both browsers recognize the other's defined values.

✦ `border` — This attribute globally defines the thickness of all frame borders. The value is in pixels to define the pixel width of the border.

✦ `framespacing` — This is a proprietary attribute defined by Internet Explorer to set the amount of space between frames. This works much like setting a thicker width using the `border` attribute. The value is defined in pixels.

✦ `bordercolor` — Later versions of both Internet Explorer and Netscape support this proprietary attribute to define a border color for all frames. The value can be a color name (for example, `green`) or a hexadecimal triple (for example, `#FFFFFF`).

The frame tag

The `<frame>` tag is an empty tag that references the HTML document that contains the content for each frame. It must be nested within `<frameset>` container tags, for example:

```
<html>
  <head>
    <title>Document Title</title>
  </head>
  <frameset rows="200,*">
    <frame src="top.html">
    <frame src="bottom.html">
  </frameset>
</html>
```

In the Real World

An empty tag does not contain character data. If you notice in the previous example, there is no character data outside of the `<frame>` tag. The only meaningful data is found in the attribute value position. Because of this, we refer to the `<frame>` tag as empty. Empty tags never have closing tag pairs. Also note that in XHTML empty tags are written with a closing space and slash at the end; for example, `<frame />`.

The src attribute

Each `<frame>` tag uses a `src` attribute to point to the content document. This means that any documents referenced must exist at the defined location (and they must also be well-formed HTML documents). The previous example defines a browser window that is partitioned into two horizontal frames. The content of each of those frames will be populated by the referenced source documents. For example, the following markup instructs the browser to pull the contents of top.html into the top frame and bottom.html into the bottom frame as shown in Figure 9-7.

```
<frameset rows="200,*">
    <frame src="top.html">
    <frame src="bottom.html">
</frameset>
```

```
┌─────────────────────────────────┐
│                                 │
│           top.html              │
│                                 │
├─────────────────────────────────┤
│                                 │
│                                 │
│          bottom.html            │
│                                 │
│                                 │
│                                 │
└─────────────────────────────────┘
```

Figure 9-7: The `src` attribute references the HTML files that are to fill each frame.

Tip   Keep in mind that the value of the `src` attribute must point to a local document or URL. Be sure to define a correct path to the source document, or the browser may be unable to locate the content for the frame.

The name attribute

You can also use the `name` attribute to name a particular frame. For example, the following markup would name the top frame `top` and the bottom frame `bottom`:

```
<frameset rows="200,*">
    <frame src="top.html" name="top">
    <frame src="bottom.html" name="bottom">
</frameset>
```

Naming a frame allows you to call the frame by name and target content into it. This is particularly handy if you use a frame design for a large Web site. For example, visit Project Cool's Web design tip's Web page at `www.projectcool.com/ developer/tips/design01_tips/index.html`.

If you visit this Web site, you'll notice that this window is divided into three parts. A right frame for navigation, a top-left frame for advertisements, and a bottom-left frame for content. This is a likely scenario; however, typically, you'll find navigation to the left.

If you visit the live document, you'll notice that every time you select one of the navigation hyperlinks, the browser loads the content into the bottom-left content frame. Well, the browser is not magical and it can't read minds, but it can interpret the `name` attribute.

In this case, the hyperlink is defined to open in a named frame: the bottom-left frame. It's always useful to name your frames, just in case you need to perform some targeted hyperlinking.

 Cross-Reference   We focus on this concept later in this chapter in the "Hyperlinks in Frames" section.

Other frame attributes

Similar to the `<frameset>` tag, the `<frame>` tag also has some additional attributes. The main difference is that the attributes defined in this section are formally a part of the HTML specification.

The attributes that you can use with the `<frame>` tag are:

✦ `frameborder` — Both browsers recognize the `frameborder` attribute. Like the `frameborder` attribute used with the `<frameset>` tag, you can set the value to one of the following values: 1 (yes) or 0 (no — the frame border is invisible).

✦ `scrolling` — Controls whether the scroll bar appears for a frame. If the value is set to `yes`, the scroll bar will always be present. If set to `no`, the scroll bar will not be present, even if the content of that frame is larger than its allotted space. If set to `auto`, the scroll bar appears only when needed. Netscape only supports the `auto` value. To achieve the same effect in Internet Explorer, omit the `scrolling` attribute altogether.

✦ `noresize` — This attribute is a standalone attribute, which means that it does not receive a value. It's a Boolean that when present, turns the function on, and when omitted, the function is assumed to be off. The `noresize` attribute explicitly sets the frame dimensions defined in the `<frameset>` tag. For example, if you define the frame as a certain width, users can still manually alter the size of a column or row. Adding the `noresize` attribute to a `<frame>` tag suppresses the user's ability to manually override the defined frame size.

✦ `marginwidth` and `marginheight` — It's normal for a browser to add a bit of space between the frame border and the content page filling that frame. You can set your own `marginwidth` or `marginheight` in pixels using these attributes.

Pulling it all together

Understanding frame markup is the initial step to understand how frames work. Take a second to look at the following example:

```
<html>
  <head>
     <title>Document Title</title>
  </head>
  <frameset cols="200,*" border="0" framespacing="0"
frameborder="0">
    <frame src="nav.html" name="nav" noresize scrolling="no"
frameborder="0">
    <frame src="content.html" name="body" scrolling="auto"
frameborder="0">
  </frameset>
</html>
```

This example creates two vertical frames. The first frame is 200 pixels wide and contains the document nav.html found in the same directory as our frameset document (note the relative path). The second frame contains content.html and fills the remainder of the browser window. The frames are named `nav` and `body`, respectively.

You probably also noticed that we threw in tons of attributes defining border behavior. This is part of the Web designer's plague — keeping up with browser support. Each browser recognizes different proprietary markup that you have to anticipate. To make sure that most versions of most browsers render in your pages as you want them to, you should add multiple border-related attributes as we did in the previous example.

The noframes tag

Frame markup is basically invisible to browsers that don't recognize it. These browsers don't produce error messages or freeze up; they just ignore the frame markup altogether.

So you don't leave people who depend on these browsers in the dark, use the `<noframes>` tag. Anything contained by the `<noframes>` tag pair is not displayed in frames-compatible browsers. However, browsers that don't support frames understand the tags contained within the `<noframes>` tag; for example:

```
<html>
  <head>
    <title>Document Title</title>
  </head>
  <frameset cols="200,*">
    <frame src="top.html" name="top">
    <frame src="bottom.html" name="bottom">
    <noframes>
        <body>
        <p>This site utilizes frame markup. You'll need a
3.0 or later browser to view the contents of this site. Please
visit our <a href="nonframes.html">no frames version</a> of our
Web site.</p>
        </body>
    </noframes>
  </frameset>
</html>
```

According to the XHTML 1.0 Frameset DTD, the `<body>` tag is a required child of the `<noframes>` tag. This isn't common usage, but for your document to validate, it's necessary.

The previous example creates a frameset document that will display beautifully in browsers that support frames. However, if a user tries to access the page using a browser that is not frames compatible, the browser renders everything within the `<noframes>` tag pair.

This is not always necessary because most browsers support frame markup. However, it never hurts to be on the safe side. If your Web site utilizes frames, you might want to offer a non-frame version of your site as well.

Inline frames

This entire chapter focuses on defined frames as a part of a frameset. The frameset follows its own DTD rules (such as the `<body>` tag being omitted) and has a distinctive function. The inline frame throws a wrench in the frameset functionality.

For a detailed discussion of the Frameset DTD, see the following section of this chapter.

An inline frame is a frame that is embedded within a plain HTML document. Because an inline frame is embedded like an image, there's no need for a frameset document. This is new to HTML 4 and is not supported by all versions of browsers. Internet Explorer 4 and higher, and Netscape 6 are the only browsers that support this function. As a designer, this means that you won't be able to reliably use this tag for a while.

However, this doesn't mean we don't want to give you a glimpse of what will be possible in the future. Here's an example of some code that contains an inline frame:

```
<html>
  <head>
    <title>Document Title</title>
  </head>
  <body>
    <h1>Inline Frame Example</h1>
    ...more HTML elements...
    <iframe src="nav.html" width="200" height="700"
align="left">Your browser does not support inline frames, to
view our navigation, please visit our other <a
href="file.html">version</a> of this Web site, or download a
more recent version of Internet Explorer or Netscape
Navigator.</iframe>
    ...more HTML elements...
  </body>
</html>
```

This code would produce a document that contains the nav.html document in a frame 200 pixels wide, 700 pixels high, and aligned to the left of the screen.

The Frameset DTD

In the previous section, "Overview of Frame Markup," you probably noticed a bunch of rules governing where and how you could use frame markup. The most interesting of those rules being that the <body> tag is omitted in a frameset document. Another rule is that <frame> tags must be nested within a <frameset> tag pair. These rules are not arbitrarily set; they come from the rules defined by a Document Type Definition (DTD).

Cross-Reference   To refresh your memory about DTDs, visit Chapter 7.

HTML 4.0 has three DTDs to choose from:

> ✦ Strict
>
> ✦ Transitional
>
> ✦ Frameset

The Transitional and Frameset DTDs are very similar. The primary difference is that the Frameset DTD requires that document authors use the <frameset> tag instead of the <body> tag.

The difference between the Frameset and Transitional DTD is a result of the functional difference between the two types of documents. The purpose of a frameset document is to define frame structure and reference the content pages to populate the frames. The purpose of a transitional HTML document is to present content — whatever that content may be — on the Web. However, you can use most of the tags used by transitional documents with frameset documents. Because some browsers do not support frames, the Frameset DTD also allows for a `<noframes>` tag to contain plain old transitional tags, such as the `<p>`, `<ul>`, `<li>`, and `<h1>` tags.

If you choose to use a DTD with your frameset document, you must use the Frameset DTD. The document type declaration (DOCTYPE) used to reference the Frameset DTD is:

```
<!DOCTYPE html PUBLIC "-//W3C//DTD HTML 4.01 Frameset//EN"
         "http://www.w3.org/TR/html4/frameset.dtd">
```

If you were to include the DOCTYPE declaration in a frameset document, the document would look something like this:

```
<!DOCTYPE html PUBLIC "-//W3C//DTD HTML 4.01 Frameset//EN"
         "http://www.w3.org/TR/html4/frameset.dtd">
<html>
  <head>
    <title>Document Title</title>
  </head>
  <frameset rows="200,*">
    <frame src="top.html" name="top">
    <frame src="bottom.html" name="bottom">
  </frameset>
</html>
```

The DOCTYPE declaration that we use must follow the syntax defined in the previous example. If you reference the Frameset DTD, you can use an HTML validator to make sure that you followed all the rules correctly.

We use the Frameset DTD in the rest of our examples, but please note that this is not a requirement for your frameset documents.

Hyperlinks in Frames

 Simple page layout

Hyperlinking within a frame setup can be a little tricky. If you're familiar with targeting, you have a head start. Most HTML documents contain hyperlinks to other HTML documents. In most cases, the new HTML document replaces the current document in the same browser window. For example, if you visit `www.w3.org` and select the HTML hyperlink found on the left-hand side of the page, a new page opens in place of the W3C's home page.

When you create a frame structure and include a hyperlink, the browser loads the new document in the current frame. This isn't very helpful if you're using one frame for navigation. Already, you've lost control of your Web site. What you want to be able to do is create a hyperlink that opens within a targeted frame. For example, if you have navigational hyperlinks about your company in a frame to the left of your page, you want the contents to always be displayed in the frame to the right. To do this, you follow these steps:

1. Define the frame name.

2. Use the <a> tag to define the hyperlink.

3. Use the target attribute to load a linked document into a defined frame.

We discuss these steps in more detail in the following sections as well as tell you how to use the <base> tag to define a default target.

Defining a frame name

In the previous section, "Overview of Frame Markup," you found out how to name your frames. This is an essential concept to grasp when dealing with targeting your hyperlinks. Take a second to refresh your memory with the following example:

```
<!DOCTYPE html PUBLIC "-//W3C//DTD HTML 4.01 Frameset//EN"
          "http://www.w3.org/TR/html4/frameset.dtd">
<html>
  <head>
     <title>Document Title</title>
  </head>
  <frameset cols="200,*">
     <frame src="nav.html" name="nav">
     <frame src="content.html" name="body">
  </frameset>
</html>
```

The previous example creates two frames: one named nav and the other named body. Because the frame named body is the content frame, you want to point most of your content-related documents to load in that frame.

Using the a tag

Now, you need to turn your attention to the content documents referenced by the <frame> tags and populate the frames. Targeting is all about how you define your hyperlinks. The <a> tag defines a hyperlink and creates some text that when selected, loads a new document in a browser window. The default behavior for loading the new document is to replace the current document window. However, targeting allows us to define hyperlink behavior.

For example, `nav.html` might contain several hyperlinks to documents about a company:

```
<!DOCTYPE html PUBLIC "-//W3C//DTD HTML 4.01 Transitional//EN"
          "http://www.w3.org/TR/html4/loose.dtd">
<html>
  <head>
     <title>Navigation Document</title>
  </head>
  <body>
   <h1>Site Map</h1>
   <ul>
      <li><a href="about.html">About Us</a></li>
      <li><a href="products.html">Products</a></li>
      <li><a href="employ.html">Employment</a></li>
      <li><a href="contact.html">Contact Us</a></li>
   </ul>
  </body>
</html>
```

This example creates four basic hyperlinks. In a framed structure, linked documents load in the frame of the current document. In this case, each linked document opens in the frame named `nav`. This doesn't do much for navigation and will have your users running in the other direction. If you recall, navigation is one of the primary drawbacks to using frames. However, targeting takes a step toward solving this problem.

Target values

When you use the `target` attribute, you can instruct the browser to load a linked document into a defined frame. Using targeting allows you to name a frame and then point to it. This functionality is gained by using the `target` attribute with the `<a>` tag. Take a second to look at our example (remember, we are still working with content documents):

```
<!DOCTYPE html PUBLIC "-//W3C//DTD HTML 4.01 Transitional//EN"
          "http://www.w3.org/TR/html4/loose.dtd">
<html>
  <head>
     <title>Navigation Document</title>
  </head>
  <body>
   <h1>Site Map</h1>
   <ul>
      <li><a href="about.html" target="body">About Us</a></li>
      <li><a href="products.html"
target="body">Products</a></li>
      <li><a href="employ.html"
target="body">Employment</a></li>
```

```
     <li><a href="contact.html" target="body">Contact
Us</a></li>
     </ul>
     </body>
</html>
```

Caution   If you modify your site, be sure to keep an eye on the targets and make sure they still go where you intended them to.

This example assumes that you have named a frame body (`<frame src= "content.html" name="body">`). Each `<a>` tag has a target attribute pointing to the frame named `body`. When selected, each new document would load in the content-related frame.

In the Real World   The Site Designer exam covers how to use the `name` attribute to name frames; however, you can gain the same functionality using the `id` attribute to identify each frame. The `id` attribute is a unique identifier.

Targeting is easy once you get the hang of it. Besides being able to target a named frame, the HTML specification provides us with four predefined target values: `_blank`, `_self`, `_parent` and `_top`.

The blank value

Using the `_blank` value tells the browser to load the linked document into a brand new window. After you've created a frame structure, there are many times that you'll want to link to another HTML document, but not force your users to leave your Web site.

The self value

The `_self` value tells the browser to load the linked document in the current window or frame. In the framed structure, the linked document would open within the same frame, not replacing the entire window. This is the default value assumed if you do not use the `target` attribute with the `<a>` tag.

The parent value

The `_parent` value tells the browser to load the linked document in the parent window (or frameset) as shown in Figure 9-8. In some cases, this results in the same functionality as setting `target="_self"`. For example, you create a frameset with one frame and one frameset (containing two frames).

If one of the frames in the nested frameset (for example, frame C) contained a hyperlink, you could instruct the browser to open the linked document in the parent frameset. In this case, the linked document would replace both B and C frames, leaving frame A alone.

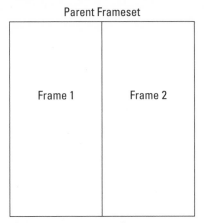

Figure 9-8: A parent frameset

The top value

Using the value _top can be the answer to many usability questions. For example, you create a frameset with two frames (one for navigation and one for content), and the navigation frame contains a link to the W3C. Instead of targeting that link to load in a new blank window, or to load in the content frame, you want to instruct the browser to replace all frames and load a Web page in the entire window. This can be achieved by setting target="_top".

In the Real World

This is not covered by the exam, but you can use the _top value to bypass most navigational problems associated with frames. In essence, you would have to create a frameset document for every pairing of documents. This is not easy to do if your Web site is over 100 pages; however, it's a convenient way to allow users to bookmark your Web pages.

The base tag

You can also control where your hyperlinks open by using the <base> tag to define a default target. If you're creating a frame for navigation, it will most likely contain tons of hyperlinks all with the same target value. Instead of specifying a target for every hyperlink, you can add a target attribute to a <base> tag in the head of your HTML document.

The <base> tag does not go in the frameset document, but is instead used in the HTML document that populates the frame and contains all the hyperlinks. For example, if you create a frameset document that looks like this:

```
<!DOCTYPE html PUBLIC "-//W3C//DTD HTML 4.01 Frameset//EN"
        "http://www.w3.org/TR/html4/frameset.dtd">
<html>
```

```
<head>
   <title>Document Title</title>
</head>
<frameset cols="200,*">
   <frame src="nav.html" name="nav">
   <frame src="content.html" name="body">
</frameset>
</html>
```

You can add the `<base>` tag to the nav.html document, as follows:

```
<!DOCTYPE html PUBLIC "-//W3C//DTD HTML 4.01 Transitional//EN"
         "http://www.w3.org/TR/html4/loose.dtd">
<html>
   <head>
      <title>Navigation Document</title>
      <base target="body">
   </head>
   <body>
    <h1>Site Map</h1>
    <ul>
       <li><a href="about.html">About Us</a></li>
       <li><a href="products.html">Products</a></li>
       <li><a href="employ.html">Employment</a></li>
       <li><a href="contact.html">Contact Us</a></li>
    </ul>
   </body>
</html>
```

This sets a default target attribute, which enables the browser to read the previous markup as:

```
<ul>
   <li><a href="about.html" target="body">About Us</a></li>
   <li><a href="products.html" target="body">Products</a></li>
   <li><a href="employ.html" target="body">Employment</a></li>
   <li><a href="contact.html" target="body">Contact Us</a></li>
</ul>
```

When selected, each linked document will be loaded in the frame named body.

Exam Tip You can also add an `href` attribute to the `<base>` tag to define a default `href` for your documents. For example, `<base href="http://www.yourdomain.com/" target="body">`.

Nested Framesets

Complex page layout

The previous examples in this chapter worked with simple frameset documents; however, you can also create some fairly complex frame structures. To do this, you will have to nest `<frameset>` tags within a parent `<frameset>` tag pair. Keep in mind that you must always have one top-level `<frameset>` tag pair that contains all other frame markup.

For example, to create a frame structure with two columns, with the first column divided into two rows, use the following markup:

```
<!DOCTYPE html PUBLIC "-//W3C//DTD HTML 4.01 Frameset//EN"
         "http://www.w3.org/TR/html4/frameset.dtd">
<html>
  <head>
     <title>Document Title</title>
  </head>
  <frameset cols="200,*">
     <frameset rows="220,*">
        <frame src="logo.html" name="bottom">
        <frame src="navigation.html" name="bottom">
     </frameset>
        <frame src="content.html" name="bottom">
  </frameset>
</html>
```

In this example, the initial `<frameset>` tag defines the two columns. The nested `<frameset>` tag divides the first column into two rows and the second `<frame>` tag defines the second column.

If you want to further divide the second column into three rows, you would change the markup as follows:

```
<!DOCTYPE html PUBLIC "-//W3C//DTD HTML 4.01 Frameset//EN"
         "http://www.w3.org/TR/html4/frameset.dtd">
<html>
  <head>
     <title>Document Title</title>
  </head>
  <frameset cols="200,*">
     <frameset rows="50%,50%">
             <frame src="frame1.html">
             <frame src="frame2.html">
       </frameset>
```

```
        <frameset rows="33%,33%,33%">
            <frame src="frame3.html">
            <frame src="frame4.html">
            <frame src="frame5.html">
        </frameset>
    </frameset>
</html>
```

Figure 9-9 illustrates this design.

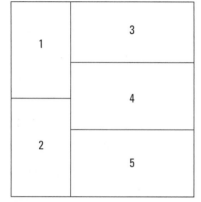

Figure 9-9: A frame design with five frames

Key Point Summary

In this chapter you learned about HTML frame markup and the advantages and disadvantages of using a framed approach. Here are the key points covered:

✦ Although most Web developers did not encourage the use of frames in the past, they have become more acceptable because of improvements in frame markup and browser behavior.

✦ If usability — the measure of Web site functionality — is hindered by the incorrect use of frames, users may not be able to easily revisit your site. If you know what you're doing with frames; however, it's possible to create a usable design.

✦ The most obvious obstacle to useful navigation is the bookmark dilemma. Bookmarks normally allow users to save a given location within a Web site; however, frames make this functionality difficult to achieve, usually allowing bookmarks only for the initial frameset document.

✦ A frame is a scrollable region that contains an HTML document. A frameset is an HTML document that defines a set of frames populated by other HTML documents.

✦ The Site Designer exam focuses on one advantage to using frames: They allow document authors to combine static and dynamic information (e.g., one frame — commonly a navigation page — can remain static, while another frame — usually a content related page — can change).

✦ The most important piece of frame markup is the `<frameset>` tag. As the container tag for all frame markup, you can't define frames without it.

✦ An inline frame is a frame embedded within a plain HTML document. Because an inline frame is embedded like an image, there's no need for a frameset document. This is new to HTML 4 and is not supported by all versions of browsers.

✦ If you choose to use a DTD with your frameset document, you must use the Frameset DTD — a document type declaration (DOCTYPE) used to reference the Frameset DTD.

✦ Hyperlinking within a frame setup can be a little tricky. If you're familiar with targeting, however, you have a head start.

✦ You can also create some fairly complex frame structures by nesting `<frameset>` tags within a parent `<frameset>` tag pair.

✦ ✦ ✦

STUDY GUIDE

This chapter contains material on why not to use frames; however, we understand that you may want to use them, or they're the best solution for you. For the exam, you must be prepared to answer questions regarding frame markup and how to use that markup. In this section, we present questions about frame markup, labs, and real world scenarios designed to prepare you for taking the exam.

Assessment Questions

1. Which tag is the parent tag for frame markup?

    A. `<frame>`

    B. `<frameset>`

    C. `<noframes>`

    D. `<frames>`

2. Which attribute would you use to define three vertical frames?

    A. `src`

    B. `rows`

    C. `cols`

    D. `width`

3. What is a frameset?

    A. An HTML document that defines a set of frames that are populated by other HTML documents

    B. An HTML document that includes subsets of other HTML documents

    C. A Web page that uses non-HTML tags to define the structure of a set of frames

    D. A Web page that embeds inline frames

4. How would you create a complex frame structure with three columns and two rows?

    A. Define a `<frameset>` tag with both the `cols` and `rows` attributes

    B. Define several `<frame>` tags with position information

    C. Define a `<frameset>` tag with the `cols` attribute, and then nest a `<frameset>` tag that uses the `rows` attribute

    D. Define several top-level `<frameset>` tags

5. What type of hyperlinking is required with frames?

   A. Accessing

   B. Targeting

   C. Referencing

   D. Pointing

Scenarios

1. Your Web site contains two frames (one for navigation and one for content). You're asked to add several hyperlinks pointing to another company's Web site. You are concerned with how the navigation will behave.

   a. How can you require the linked Web site to open in a new window?

   b. How can you require the linked Web site to open in a named frame?

2. You currently maintain a site that has two horizontal frames (a navigational and a content frame). You're asked to redesign your Web site so it has two vertical frames (a navigational and content frame).

   a. What document do you have to change?

   b. What do you have to change?

Lab Exercises

Lab 9-1: Creating a frameset document

For this lab, you need to create a frameset document that defines two vertical frames. The first frame should point to nav.html and the second frame should point to content.html.

1. Open a text editor.

2. Add the `<html>`, `<head>`, and `<title>` tags.

3. Add the `<frameset>` tag with a `rows` attribute set equal to two comma-separated values.

4. Add two `<frame>` tags as children of the `<frameset>` tag.

5. Each `<frame>` tag should have a `src` attribute pointing to either nav.html or content.html.

6. Save the file.

To view your result, you will have to create two simple HTML documents and save them as nav.html and content.html. Save all three documents in the same folder and then view the frameset document in a browser of your choice.

Lab 9-2: Creating targeted hyperlinks

For this lab, name your frames and add hyperlinks to the nav.html file.

1. Using a text editor, open the file you created in Lab 1.

2. Add a `name` attribute to each `<frame>` tag, `nav` and `body`, respectively.

3. Open nav.html (which you created in Lab 9-1).

4. Add three hyperlinks pointing to three Web sites of your choice (for example, `<a href="http://www.lanw.com">...</a>`).

5. Add `target="body"` to the first two `<a>` tags.

6. Add `target="_blank"` to the last `<a>` tag.

7. Save your frameset document and nav.html.

8. View the frameset document in a Web browser.

Lab 9-3: Nesting framesets

For this lab, add a nested frameset to the frameset document you created in Labs 9-1 and 9-2.

1. Using a text editor, open your frameset document.

2. Replace the second `<frame>` tag with a pair of `<frameset>` tags with a `rows` attribute with two comma-separated values. In this step, you're creating a nested frameset that will split the second column into two rows.

3. Add two `<frame>` tags as children of the nested `<frameset>` tag. The first `<frame>` tag should point to `http://www.w3.org`, and the second `<frame>` tag should point to content.html.

4. Save your frameset document.

5. View the frameset document in a Web browser.

Answers to Chapter Questions

Chapter pre-test

1. A frameset document uses frame markup to define a frame structure. The frameset document is an HTML document that defines a set of frames that are populated by other HTML documents.

2. According to the rules of the HTML Frameset DTD, the `<frameset>` tag replaces the `<body>` tag. A frameset document is not meant to contain data, but rather to define a document's frameset structure; therefore, the `<body>` tag is not needed.

3. It's wise to supply `<noframes>` content for users who are unable to view frame markup. Whereas most users use recent browser versions, there are still some who haven't upgraded yet. When you leave out a `<noframes>` tag, you're leaving some users in the dark.

4. Frames allow Web designers to create a static navigation page, while allowing the content page to dynamically change.

5. Targeting allows Web designers to have more control over navigational behavior. You can use the `target` attribute within the `<a>` tag to create hyperlinks that when selected, load the linked document in a defined frame or window. If you were to create a navigation document that defined hyperlinks to content pages about your company, you'd most likely want to target those linked pages to open in a separate frame, allowing one frame to remain static (navigation) and the other frame to dynamically change (content).

6. The `<base>` tag saves you time by allowing a Web designer to define default `href` and `target` values. For example, you can use `<base target="body">` to set a target default. Now, all `<a>` tags will assume this default unless you override the default target by adding the `target` attribute directly to the `<a>` tag.

Assessment questions

1. **B.** The `<frameset>` tag is always used as the parent tag for frame markup. In a frameset document, the `<frameset>` tag is used in place of the `<body>` tag. See "The frameset tag."

2. **C.** A `<frameset>` tag can define horizontal or vertical frames. The `cols` attribute defines vertical frames, and the `rows` attribute defines horizontal frames. See "The frameset tag."

3. **A.** A frameset is an HTML document that uses frame markup to define the frame structure. A frameset document uses `<frame>` tags to point to the documents that are to populate each frame. See "The frameset tag."

4. **C.** To create a complex frame structure with multiple rows and columns, you have to nest framesets within a parent frameset. One `<frameset>` tag can only define columns or rows, not both at the same time. The first step is to define the structure for your columns (or rows depending on which you want to do first), then to nest another `<frameset>` tag to define the structure for your rows. Just remember to always have a `<frame>` tag for every individual frame. See "Nested Framesets."

5. **B.** When you create a frame structure, you have to be careful with all your hyperlinks. Using the `target` attribute to define hyperlink behavior is essential to make sure that your users don't get lost in your Web site. See "Hyperlinks in Frames."

Scenarios

1. Adding hyperlinks to a frame structure must be handled with care. The first step is to add the hyperlinks. The next step is to add the appropriate `target` attribute value pair to each hyperlink.

   a. If you want the linked document to open in a new window, then you add `target="_blank"` to the corresponding `<a>` tag.

   b. If you want the linked document to open in a named frame, you set a target equal to the name of the frame, `target="body"`, for example.

2. If you want to change the structure of your frame, you have to do so in the frameset document. To change the frame structure from horizontal frames to vertical frames, you need to delete the `rows` attribute from the `<frameset>` tag and add a `cols` attribute. Because the frame's dimensions will likely change, you might have to reformat the HTML documents that populate each frame accordingly.

For More Information

✦ **The W3C's HTML 4.01 Frames information.** `www.w3.org/TR/html4/present/frames.html`

✦ **Webmonkey's frames information.** `http://hotwired.lycos.com/webmonkey/authoring/frames/`

✦ **Gettingstarted.net; Frames.** `www.gettingstarted.net/basics/frames/04-frames.html`

Metadata in HTML

CHAPTER PRE-TEST

1. Why should you use the <!DOCTYPE> declaration?

2. What is metadata?

3. What attributes are commonly used with the `<meta>` tag?

4. How is a directory different from a search engine?

5. What is meant by relevance and what are three common characteristics of it?

✦ Answers to these questions can be found at the end of the chapter. ✦

Metadata, also known as data about your data, is a concept worth mastering if you're looking to join the Web designers of the world. This chapter is dedicated to metadata and covers topics such as: how you can use metadata to enhance the searchability of your Web sites and how to redirect your Web sites.

Overview of Metadata

 Metadata and document identification

Metadata is an interesting concept to grasp. Many people will tell you that metadata is data about data. But, just what does that mean? The easiest way to understand what that means is to look at an example.

If you were to create a document describing all the surrealist artists, you could define some metadata that would be used to describe your content. In other words, the following keywords would be metadata: surreal, surrealists, artists, max ernst, and salvador dali. Each of these keywords is descriptive of the Web page's contents.

Metadata is used in both XML and HTML. In HTML, you can add metadata to your document with the `<meta>` tag. Although most metadata is added with the `<meta>` tag, there are other tags and markup that also supply metadata, such as the document type (DOCTYPE) declaration and the `<title>` tag. You take a look at all of these tags in the following sections.

Metadata serves specific functions within HTML, such as:

✦ The DOCTYPE declaration identifies to which version of HTML your document conforms.

✦ The `<title>` tag defines a descriptive title for your document.

✦ The `<meta>` tag defines keywords, document descriptions, author information, and document expiration data information.

Including a DOCTYPE declaration

In Chapter 7, you found out about the Document Type Definitions (DTDs) that are defined for HTML 4. If you need a reminder, there are three DTDs that can be used to define an HTML 4 document: Transitional, Strict, and Frameset. HTML 3.2 also has its own DTD. Most designers leave this information out of their documents. If you don't believe us, just take a second to cruise the Web and try to locate a document that actually includes a DOCTYPE declaration pointing to the appropriate DTD.

With that said, you might be wondering why you should care. There are a few reasons you should care:

✦ If you reference a DTD, you can use a validator to check your document for mistakes.

✦ DTDs provide information about to which version of HTML the document conforms.

✦ The HTML 3.2, 4.0, and XHTML 1.0 specifications require the DOCTYPE declaration if you want your document to be a strictly conforming (X)HTML document.

For this chapter, you're only concerned with the second point, because in essence, the DOCTYPE declaration provides metadata information. Take a look at an example:

```
<!DOCTYPE html PUBLIC "-//W3C//DTD HTML 4.0 Transitional //EN">
```

You might notice that this is an abbreviated version of the DOCTYPE declaration that only includes a reference to the uniform resource name (URN), and leaves the URL of the DTD out. From this markup, you know three things right off the bat:

✦ The document is an HTML document.

✦ The document conforms to HTML 4.0 specification.

✦ The document uses the tags defined by the Transitional DTD.

Exam Tip The exam and most designers refer to the DOCTYPE declaration (`<!DOCTYPE>`) as a tag. Do not let this terminology confuse you. Technically, it's a declaration.

The title tag

The `<title>` tag is a required tag that must be included as a child of the `<head>` tag. What you probably already know is that the `<title>` tag defines a title for your document that is displayed in the title bar of the browser window. What you may not know is that the content of the `<title>` tag is metadata that is used by search engines. The lesson here is to always include descriptive titles, and include a keyword or two in the `<title>` tag. For example, the following title is not recommended:

```
<head>
  <title>My document</title>
</head>
```

However, if you change your title to "Surrealist Artists," you would have descriptive title that would help search engines locate your document; for example:

```
<head>
  <title>Surrealist Artists</title>
</head>
```

Exam Tip The `<title>` tag is required and is a great way to add keywords that search engines can use to index your documents.

Using the meta tag

Objective Adding metadata to Web pages

Now you're ready to get to the meat of this chapter, the `<meta>` tag. The `<meta>` tag is an empty tag that requires the `content` attribute and either the `name` or `http-equiv` attribute. The `<meta>` tag can be used to:

✦ Define a document's expiration data

✦ Define author information

✦ Define keywords, which are used by search engines

✦ Define a description that is used by search engines

This list is not exhaustive, however, by the end of this chapter, you need to know how to use the `<meta>` tag to define each item in the previous list.

Exam Tip You need to know the main reasons why designers use the `<meta>` tag: to define author information, document expiration data, keywords, and descriptions.

There are two different types of `<meta>` tags: `name` and `http-equiv`. A `<meta>` tag that uses the `http-equiv` attribute defines information that needs to be attached to the HTTP header. For example, it might define cookie information that needs to be passed to the HTTP client. This relationship is discussed in the following sections.

The http-equiv attribute

The `http-equiv` attribute binds meta information to the HTTP header. As the browser reads a Web page with an `http-equiv` attribute, it grabs the content attribute value and attaches it to the document header, which is then sent prior to the rest of the page content. When processing the document, the browser or HTTP server may use the information defined by the `content` attribute, which is then attached to the header:

```
<meta http-equiv="expires" content="Tue, 01 Jan 2002 12:00:00
GMT">
```

The previous markup produces the following HTTP header:

```
expires: Tue, 01 Jan 2002 12:00:00 GMT
```

How HTTP Works

HTTP stands for the Hypertext Transfer Protocol and defines rules for exchanging resources identified by a URL on the Web. Each file can contain references to other files (think hyperlinks).

A browser (HTTP client) opens a connection with the Web server (HTTP server) by sending a request message. The server then sends a response message that normally contains the document that was requested. After the document is sent, the server closes the connection. Headers provide information pertaining to the request by the client or a response by the server.

Notice that the value of the `http-equiv` is not random; it's predefined. You should also notice that the `content` attribute provides the information that is passed onto the HTTP header. The value `expires` is one of five values that you'll look at in the following sections:

- ✦ `expires`
- ✦ `pragma`
- ✦ `refresh`
- ✦ `set-cookie`
- ✦ `window-target`

http-equiv="expires"

In many cases, when visiting a Web page, the browser will save a version of that page in its cache. The reason for this is because browsers use the cached version of a page if you decide to return to that page. If you use a `<meta>` tag with `http-equiv="expires"`, you can control when the browser uses a cached version, and when it visits the server for a fresh version.

Tip   A browser's cache is a temporary storage directory for Web pages. If you go back to a page that you've recently visited, the browser is likely to grab the page from the cache, rather than making another visit to the server. The purpose of this is to save you time, and save the server effort.

For example, to create a document that expires on August 8, 2000, you include the following `<meta>` tag in your document:

```
<meta http-equiv="expires" content="Tue, 08 Aug 2000 12:21:
57 gmt">
```

Take a look at just where it fits into an HTML document:

```
<!DOCTYPE HTML PUBLIC "-//W3C//DTD HTML 4.01 Transitional//EN"
   "http://www.w3.org/TR/html4/loose.dtd">
<html>
  <head>
     <title>Document title</title>
<meta http-equiv="expires" content="Tue, 08 Aug 2000 12:21:57
gmt">
  </head>
  <body>
     ...document content goes here...
  </body>
</html>
```

http-equiv="pragma"

This simple value prevents some browsers (namely Netscape Navigator) from caching the document. Similar to using the `expires` value, this is another way to control browser caching. The associated `content` attribute must be set equal to `no-cache`. When this is included in a document, some browsers are prevented from caching a page locally. You include it in a document as follows:

```
<!DOCTYPE HTML PUBLIC "-//W3C//DTD HTML 4.01 Transitional//EN"
   "http://www.w3.org/TR/html4/loose.dtd">
<html>
  <head>
     <title>Document title</title>
<meta http-equiv="pragma" content="no-cache">
  </head>
<body>
   ...document content goes here...
</body>
</html>
```

http-equiv="refresh"

As a designer, the odds are that your boss or client will ask that you redirect a Web page. For example, you've designed a new page for the contacts portion of your site. You know that there are a lot of outside sources that link to your contacts page. Therefore, you redirect the existing URL to a new URL so even people with the old link get to the new content. Redirecting a Web page is not magic; it's achieved by adding a `<meta>` tag. The `http-equiv` attribute must be set equal to `refresh` and the `content` attribute should be set equal to seconds and the new URL. The seconds should be defined first, followed by a semicolon. Next you type **URL=** followed by the URL of the new location. The contents of the entire string are in quotation marks — note that the value of the URL itself is not contained by quotation marks.

In the Real World   Internet Explorer and Netscape support this method of redirecting users, but not all browsers do. Therefore, be sure to always include a hyperlink to the new URL.

The syntax is important, so take a look at this example:

```
<!DOCTYPE HTML PUBLIC "-//W3C//DTD HTML 4.01 Transitional//EN"
  "http://www.w3.org/TR/html4/loose.dtd">
<html>
<head>
  <title>Document title</title>
  <meta http-equiv="refresh"
    content="5;URL=http://www.lanw.com">
</head>
<body>
...document content goes here...
</body>
</html>
```

 Caution

One word of warning, do not set the seconds to 0. Doing so prevents users from being able to use their browser's back button. There's nothing more frustrating than having a Web page disable a function that you rely on.

The exam does not cover this; however, you should be aware of this warning found in the HTML 4 Specification: "Some user agents support the use of meta to refresh the current page after a specified number of seconds, with the option of replacing it by a different URL. Authors should *not* use this technique to forward users to different pages, as this makes the page inaccessible to some users. Instead, automatic page forwarding should be done using server-side redirects."

http-equiv="set-cookie"

A Web site can place information on a user's hard drive using a cookie. The information is normally for future use and is stored by the server on the client side. There are many instances of cookies. For example, it's becoming common to find sites that provide personalized portals to their site. For example, you can set your own preferences at eBay.com. In these cases, a cookie is used to record the users' preferences. Some of the features provided by cookies won't work and may cause problems if you don't have cookies enabled on your browser.

As the user, you have access to information about the cookies stored on your hard drive. This is not to say that you'll understand what each cookie means, but you do have access to them. If you're using Netscape, you can locate a list of all cookies in a file named `cookies.txt`. Internet Explorer stores them each as a separate file in a subdirectory.

As the designer, you can use the `set-cookie` value to create a cookie to collect information. A cookie is created on the client side by including a set-cookie header as part of an HTTP response (typically generated by a CGI script).

As with all other `http-equiv` attributes, you must have an associated `content` attribute. In this case, the `content attribute` can contain several different values, one of which is an optional expiration date. If an expiration date is included, the cookie is saved on the user's hard drive until the expiration date, at which time, it's deleted. If an expiration date is not included, the cookie is discarded when the user exits his or her browser.

Take a look at an example:

```
<!DOCTYPE HTML PUBLIC "-//W3C//DTD HTML 4.01 Transitional//EN"
  "http://www.w3.org/TR/html4/loose.dtd">
<html>
<head>
  <title>Document title</title>
  <meta http-equiv="set-cookie"
  content="cookievalue=xxx;expires=Friday, 31-dec-99 23:59:59
GMT; path=/">
</head>
<body>
...document content goes here...
</body>
</html>
```

http-equiv="window-target"

The last http-equiv value covered in this chapter is window-target. Think back to frames for a second and you might remember the target attribute. Similar to the target attribute, defining a window-target http-equiv value can control the document window. For example, if you define content="_top", the <meta> tag forces the window to open in the top window, allowing it to escape frames. The content attribute can accept most values that the HTML target attribute can. For example, it can accept _blank or _parent. Take a look at an example:

```
<!DOCTYPE HTML PUBLIC "-//W3C//DTD HTML 4.01 Transitional//EN"
"http://www.w3.org/TR/html4/loose.dtd">
<html>
<head>
  <title>Document title</title>
  <meta http-equiv="window-target" content="_top">
</head>
<body>
...document content goes here...
</body>
</html>
```

The name attribute

Unlike the http-equiv attribute, the name attribute identifies information that does not correspond with HTTP headers. This is not to say that this information is not useful. You can define keywords, descriptions, and other information that is passed to search engines and directories, spiders, and other entities.

As with the `http-equiv` attribute, you must use a `content` attribute for every `name` attribute. The `content` attribute defines information that is relevant to the `name` value. The following are a few of the possible `name` values:

✦ **Author.** Specifies the name of the author of the document: `<meta name="author" content="Your Name">`

✦ **Copyright.** Defines copyright information: `<meta name="copyright" content="Copyright 2002, Your Company">`

✦ **Description.** Defines a description sometimes used by search engines to show with the results of searches: `<meta name="description" content= "A description of your company goes here.">`

✦ **Expires.** Defines an expiration date of the document: `<meta name="expires" content="Tue, 08 Aug 2000 12:21:57 GMT">`

✦ **Generator.** Specifies the name of the program that created the document: `<meta name="generator" content="Microsoft FrontPage 4.0">`

✦ **Keywords.** Defines keywords that are used by search engines: `<meta name="keywords" content="XHTML, XML, CSS">`

✦ **Owner.** Specifies the owner of the page or site: `<meta name="owner" content="Your Name">`

✦ **Reply-to.** Provides an e-mail address of contact for document: `<meta name="reply-to" content="name@domain.com">`

✦ **Robots.** Used to define pages to be excluded from robot indexing: `<meta name="robots" content="nofollow">`

If you add a few of these attributes and values to an HTML document, it should resemble the following:

```
<!DOCTYPE HTML PUBLIC "-//W3C//DTD HTML 4.01 Transitional//EN"
   "http://www.w3.org/TR/html4/loose.dtd">
<html>
  <head>
  <title>Document title</title>
   <meta name="author" content="Jane Doe">
   <meta name="copyright" content="Copyright (c) 1997-2001 Jane
Doe">
   <meta name="description" content="HTML and XHTML Tutorial">
   <meta name="generator" content="Microsoft FrontPage 4.0">
   <meta name="keywords" content="HTML, XHTML, Web pages">
   <meta name="robots" content="ALL">
  </head>
  <body>
    ...document content goes here...
  </body>
</html>
```

Exam Tip It's not necessary to memorize all of the possible values (previously listed) for the exam. The most important values are keywords, descriptions, and robots, and these are covered in the following sections.

Search engines

Objective

Metadata and indexing

Search engines index Web pages and allow access to users. Many search engines index all words in a Web page, excluding comments (`<!-- comment -->`). Some search engines will also use the first few sentences (about 250 characters) as an abstract for the Web page. So, in essence, most Web pages are searchable depending, of course, on the search engine you use. However, not all search engines use this method of indexing, and by using the `<meta>` tag, you can control how your Web page is indexed.

Using the `<meta>` tag is one of the primary ways to increase the probability that your site will be found by a user's query. This section covers some of the ways you can use metadata to increase the chances that your site is found by a user.

In the Real World Some search engines don't support `<meta>` tags at all. For example, Excite doesn't use them in an effort to save their users from unreliable searches.

Keywords and descriptions

One of the most important roles that the `<meta>` tag has is providing search engines with keywords and descriptions. As designers ourselves, it's puzzling to find that only about one in four Web sites use keywords and descriptions. Two lessons can be learned from that statistic. First, if you use keywords and descriptions, your site has a much better chance of being found; and second, other designers are foolish.

Remember that anything defined by the `<meta>` tag is not displayed by your browser — it's just metadata used by the browser, search engines, or the server. Although not all search engines recognize the `<meta>` tag, many do, and it's worth your time to take advantage of it.

Keywords are used by search engines to index your Web site. If you define "XHTML" as a keyword, and the search engine recognizes the `<meta>` tag, your site has a better chance of being found when a user searches on the string "XHTML." This is a simplified explanation; however, there are other factors involved that can help the searchability of your site, but those are covered later in this chapter.

To define keywords, you use the `<meta>` tag and set the name attribute equal to keywords. Next, you use the content attribute to define those keywords. Notice how the content and name attributes work hand in hand:

```
<meta name="keywords" content="XHTML, HTML, XHTML tutorial,
HTML tutorial, Web designer">
```

The keyword values contained by the `content` attribute are separated with commas. You probably also noticed the use of both individual words and similar combinations of words. You might think this a waste of time; however, your keywords need to match the types of searches users are going to enter when using search engines. This is not to say you need to go crazy with keywords. Some search engines will ignore a word if there are several occurrences of the same word. Keyword usage is limited to 1,000 characters, and although you're allowed up to 1,000 characters, it's rumored that some search engines don't pay attention to anything after the 255th character.

Exam Tip   You're limited to using 1,000 characters to define keywords; however, some browsers may only recognize the first 255 characters.

Now that keywords have been discussed, it's time to turn your attention to the sister of keywords, the description. Although the description is not recognized by all search engines, you should always include a short description of your Web site. Several search engines display this description when providing a search result that matches your Web page. Like the keyword syntax, you use the `name` and `content` attributes. For example:

```
<meta name="description" content="You enter your description
here.">
```

Exam Tip   It's important to keep the description short and concise. You're limited to 150 characters and you should use no more than 25 words.

With all of this keyword and description talk, let's take a look at an example:

```
<!DOCTYPE HTML PUBLIC "-//W3C//DTD HTML 4.01 Transitional//EN"
"http://www.w3.org/TR/html4/loose.dtd">
<html>
<head>
  <title>Document title</title>
  <meta http-equiv="expires" content="Tue, 08 Aug 2000 12:21:57
GMT">
  <meta name="keywords" content="HTML, XML, XSL, CSS, XSL,
style sheet, cascading, schema, XHTML, DOM, markup, tutorials,
online training, Web-based training, training">
  <meta name="description" content="Company A presents
tutorials, workshops, seminars and Web-based training on a wide
variety of topics such as HTML, XML, CSS, XSL and XSLT.">
</head>
<body>
...document content goes here...
</body>
</html>
```

Cross-Reference   Later in this chapter (in the "Adding keywords" section), you'll find tips on using keywords effectively.

Robots

There may be times when you don't want a particular page to be indexed by a search engine. In other words, you don't want your Web page included in a search engine's result list. If this is the case, you simply add a `<meta>` tag with a `name` attribute set equal to `robots` and a `content` attribute set equal to `noindex`. The syntax is simple:

```
<meta name="robots" content="noindex">
```

There are four common values for the `content` attribute that can be used in association with the `robots` value:

✦ `noindex` — Prevents the Web page from being indexed by a search engine.

✦ `nofollow` — Prevents the crawler from traversing the links on the Web page and then indexing the linked pages.

✦ `noimageclick` — Does not allow hyperlinks to be directed at images; only hyperlinks directed at the page itself are allowed.

✦ `noimageindex` — Prevents the images on a Web page from being indexed by the search engine; however, the text will still be indexed.

Search engine or directory?

Terminology can always get sticky. What do you think of when you read the term "directory"? What about when you read the term "search engine"? There's a distinction that needs to be made between these two terms. Most people in the Web world refer to both directories and search engines as simply search engines. However, there's a difference between the two.

Search engines use a spider, or robot, to find new Web pages. This process is automated and allows the spider to crawl through the Web following hyperlinks and then indexing the pages it finds. In other words, if Web sites exist that link to your site, a spider will find you sooner or later. The question is, just how long will that process take? The solution is for developers to submit their Web sites to search engines and request that they index the sites immediately. There are even groups that will do the dirty work for you and submit your Web site to the major search engines on the Web — for a fee, of course.

On the other side of the spectrum, a directory only lists Web sites that were submitted. In other words, if you don't submit your Web site, your site will never be included in its search results. After you submit your site, some directories will visit the site to verify the information submitted is correct. You may be wondering why any user would bother with searching with directories. Well, because they're more controlled — the search results tend to produce more quality matches to a user's query.

Exam Tip   The main difference between a directory and search engine is that the directories only index pages that are manually submitted, whereas search engines support manual submissions, as well as an automated process that crawls the Web indexing Web pages.

Relevance

You may have fooled around with search engines and wondered just how the ranking is decided. The criterion that decides the result ranking differs among searches and search engines; however, most adhere to the concept of *relevance*.

Search results are oftentimes ranked according to their relevance to the query itself. Although each search engine uses varied methods to define relevance, there are three common characteristics:

✦ **Document title.** Many search engines will first look to the contents of the `<title>` tag. If the contents match the search query, the odds are good that the site will have a high relevance.

✦ **Beginning content.** Many search engines will begin to scan the beginning of the document for the search query words.

✦ **Keyword frequency.** Many search engines will look at the number of times the query words were used in the document. In most cases, the more times the query words are used, the more relevant the page.

Although these characteristics are common among search engines, there's no set formula for deciding relevance. Some search engines use other techniques in addition to the ones previously noted. For example, some search engines also look at the number of times other sites link to a given Web page. You're also likely to find some search engines that do not support `<meta>` tags such as Excite and Lycos. You even have to be careful with frequency. Many browsers see that as a sign of relevance, but some browsers will penalize the overuse of words.

All in all, it's important to understand how relevance affects your Web site's chances of being found. It's also important to understand that relevance has different meanings to different browsers. Our recommendations are to make sure your `<title>` tag includes keywords, and be sure that relevant keywords are used in the beginning of your document.

Exam Tip   There are three common characteristics that search engines use to define relevance: `<title>` tag contents, beginning content, and keyword frequency.

Choosing a search engine or directory

As a designer, you should submit your Web site to several of the search engines or directories. However, it would be ridiculous to think that you could register with all of them; after all, there are hundreds of them on the Web. Here's a list of some of the more common search engines and directories used by most Web surfers:

✦ **AltaVista.** www.altavista.com

✦ **AOL Search.** http://search.aol.com

✦ **Ask Jeeves.** www.ask.com

✦ **Direct Hit.** www.directhit.com

✦ **Excite.** www.excite.com

✦ **Go.com.** www.go.com

✦ **Go2Net.** www.go2net.com

✦ **Google.** www.google.com

✦ **HotBot.** www.hotbot.com

✦ **Iwon.** www.iwon.com

✦ **LookSmart.** www.looksmart.com

✦ **Lycos.** www.lycos.com

✦ **Microsoft.** http://search.msn.com/

✦ **NBCi.** www.nbci.com

✦ **Netscape.** www.netscape.com

✦ **Northern Light.** www.northernlight.com

✦ **Open Directory Project.** http://dmoz.org/

✦ **RealNames.** www.realnames.com

✦ **WebCrawler.** www.webcrawler.com

✦ **Yahoo!** www.yahoo.com

If you register your site with all of these search engines and directories, you can rest assured that your site will be found.

Using Metadata Effectively

Many designers don't even use metadata, which is one of the reasons why it's almost impossible to find a particular Web page using search engines. However, if you use metadata, you need to be sure you're using it effectively, or you might as well not be using it at all. This section provides you with a few tricks of the trade.

Exam Tip   Know the tricks of the trade for effective metadata use, which are described in the following sections.

Adding keywords

Whether you register your site with the top 20+ search engines or not, you'll still want to include keywords that aid search engines in locating your document. Most designers assume that the only place to include keywords is in the `<meta>` tag. That is not true. There are many ways you can add keywords, and there are also ways *not* to add keywords.

✦ **Don't use misleading keywords.** Be sure that you use relevant keywords. There are some sites that are misleading, and there's nothing more frustrating than searching for a site on flowers and the search engine retrieving a page about fish. Take some time to think about the keywords users are likely to use.

✦ **Use a smart domain name.** First things first, don't choose a long domain name that doesn't make sense. Not only will it be impossible for users to remember, but search engines will also have no idea what it contains. If you can, include keywords in your domain name. Whether it's your company's name or a keyword that provides a hint about what it does (for example `www.paybills.com`). Search engines will pick up on keywords in your domain name.

✦ **Avoid frames.** Search engines have a difficult time indexing frameset documents, and your site may not show up in search engine results. See the sidebar titled "Frames and Usability."

✦ **Use smart file names.** If you can, use keywords to name your files. For example, if you sell grocery items, you might be able to name your files `grocery.html` or `grocerylist.html`.

✦ **Define combination keywords.** Some studies show that 60 percent of users search using two or more words. You should include combination words, such as "XHTML books," as well as including individual words, such as "XHTML" and "books," for example.

✦ **See what else is out there.** After you've decided on a few keywords, jump on a search engine and use them to see what type of documents they pull up. You should also visit some of the sites and view the source to see what other keywords they use.

✦ **Use a thesaurus.** Take a spin through a thesaurus to look up other words that users might search on.

✦ **Use acronyms, as well as spell them out.** Be sure to include any relevant acronyms; for example, if you create a Web site about the W3C, you should include "W3C" as a keyword, as well as "World Wide Web Consortium."

Developing link relationships

Some search engines look at the number of sites that link to a given site—the more the number, the higher the relevance. The more sites that are linked to yours also helps spiders (or robots) find your site. The lesson here is that it never hurts to have other sites link to your site. Just how do you achieve this? Well, you know you can't force other sites to provide a hyperlink to yours, but how about offering a trade. This is called link exchange and it's fairly common in the Web world. One nice way to foster link relationships is to create a list of Web sites that complement or benefit your site. Then contact the site owners and request that you both provide hyperlinks to each other's Web sites.

To find out more about link exchange, check out the following Web sites:

✦ **MS-Links Exchange.** http://ms-links.com/

✦ **Link Trader.** www.linktrader.com/

✦ **Link-Swap.com.** www.link-swap.com/

Frames and Usability

If you recall in Chapter 9 (HTML Frames and Site Design), frames are recommended for controlled environments. On the wide-open Web, frames can be a designer's nightmare. Most of the problems associated with frames can be summed up in one word: usability.

There's yet another problem with frames, and that is how a search engine indexes a Web site. When a search engine visits your site, it looks at the document, or metadata and begins to index it. However, when a search engine visits a frameset document, there's no content to index. The search engine doesn't really know what to do with the document because any indexing would not be helpful. For example, the following markup is a typical frameset document:

```
<!DOCTYPE html PUBLIC "-//W3C//DTD XHTML 1.0 Frameset//EN"
   "http://www.w3.org/TR/xhtml1/DTD/xhtml1-frameset.dtd">
<html xmlns="http://www.w3.org/1999/xhtml">
  <frameset rows="*,90">
    <frame src="contents.html" name="contents" />
    <frame src="ad.html" name="ad" />

  <noframes>
   <p>
    Because your browser doesn't support frames, click
    <a href="contents.html">here</a>.
   </p>
  </noframes>
  </frameset>

</html>
```

When the search engine tries to index the previous document, the <p> tag contains the only content it has to work with and that content doesn't contain any keywords. You can add <meta> tags to help search engines index your site; however, when it comes to creating searchable sites, frames are not recommended.

Key Point Summary

This chapter discussed metadata and how you use it to enhance the searchability of your Web site. The key points covered in this chapter are:

✦ Metadata is data about data.

✦ There are three elements used as metadata in HTML:

  • The DOCTYPE declaration

  • The `<title>` tag

  • The `<meta>` tag

✦ The main reasons why designers use the `<meta>` tag are to define author information, document expiration data, and keywords and descriptions.

✦ The `<meta>` tag takes the following attributes:

  • `content`

  • `name`

  • `http-equiv`

✦ Keywords are used by search engines to index your Web site and are limited to 1,000 characters to define keywords; however, some browsers may only recognize the first 255 characters.

✦ The main difference between a directory and search engine is that the directories only index pages that are manually submitted, whereas search engines support manual submissions, as well as an automated process that crawls the Web indexing found Web pages.

✦ There are three common characteristics used by search engines to define relevance:

  • Document title

  • Beginning content

  • Keyword frequency

✦   ✦   ✦

STUDY GUIDE

You're likely to encounter a few questions about `<meta>` tags or metadata in general on the exam. This chapter covered key concepts that should prepare you for those questions. But, before you move on to the next chapter, be sure to take a few moments to go through the chapter's study guide.

Assessment Questions

1. What is a required component of an HTML document?

   A. The `<p>` tag

   B. The `<b>` tag

   C. The `<title>` tag

   D. The `<temp>` tag

2. Which two `name` attribute values help search engines locate your site?

   A. keywords and robots

   B. keywords and description

   C. description and robots

   D. description and author

3. Which of the following requires designers to submit their site to be indexed?

   A. Web banks

   B. Search engines

   C. Directories

   D. Robots

4. Where should you not include keywords?

   A. In the `<title>` tag

   B. As part of a `<meta>` tag

   C. In the beginning of the document text

   D. In a separate metadata file

5. Which of the following attributes is required for the `<meta>` tag:

　A. `content`

　B. `http-equiv`

　C. `name`

　D. `meta`

6. The `<meta>` tag does all of the following except:

　A. Define a document's expiration data

　B. Define server information that is presented to the user

　C. Define keywords that are used by search engines

　D. Define a description that is used by search engines

7. Keywords defined by the `<meta>` tag are used by which of the following?

　A. Users

　B. Search engines

　C. Web banks

　D. W3C

Scenarios

1. Another company purchased your company, and you no longer need your Web site. Your boss is worried, however, that some of your customers may not know to go directly to the new parent company Web site. Your boss asks you to determine the easiest way to avoid this problem, and how to make it easy to redirect those who attempt to visit your old company site to the new site. Your challenge is to create a simple Web page that announces that your company has been bought. This page must provide a pointer to the new Web site that takes users there in less than five seconds.

　a. Which tag must you use to accomplish his request?

　b. What is the attribute(s) you have to use?

2. Your company is being clobbered by the competition. Your boss comes to you, the Web designer, and asks just what can be done to help. You then realize that your site never comes up in search engines. As the designer, you whisper "oops" under your breath and decide to fix the problem. What are three tactics that would increase your Web site's search result chances?

Lab Exercises

Lab 10-1: Using the meta tag to redirect a Web page

For this lab, you need to create one Web page and add a `<meta>` tag that uses the refresh attribute to redirect your Web page:

1. Create a basic Web page similar to:

```
<html>
  <head>
   <title>Document title goes here</title>
  </head>
  <body>
    <p>This is a temporary page.</p>
  </body>
</html>
```

2. Save the Web page as redirect.html.

3. Modify redirect.html and add a `<meta>` tag with a `refresh` attribute:

```
<html>
<head>
<meta http-equiv="REFRESH"
content="5;URL=http://www.lanw.com">
<title>Document title goes here</title>
</head>
<body>
  <p>This is a temporary page.</p>
</body>
</html>
```

4. Save redirect.html and open it in your browser.

5. After five seconds have passed, the browser should jump to the LANWrights Web site.

Lab 10-2: Using the meta tag to add keywords and a description

For this lab, you need to create one Web page and add two `<meta>` tags that describe the contents of your Web page:

1. Create a basic Web page similar to:

```
<html>
<head>
  <title>Document title goes here</title>
</head>
```

```
<body>
  <p>Content of your document goes here.</p>
</body>
</html>
```

2. Save the Web page as keywords.html.

3. Modify keywords.html and add two `<meta>` tags, one with a `name` attribute set equal to `KEYWORDS` and one with a `name` attribute set equal to `DESCRIPTION`. You'll also have to add `content` attributes with the appropriate values:

```
<html>
<head>
  <meta http-equiv="KEYWORDS" content="keyword, keyword,
keyword">
  <meta http-equiv="DESCRIPTION" content="Be sure to add your
description here. ">
  <title>Document title goes here</title>
</head>
<body>
  <p>If you want to create a page that is easily found by
search engines, be sure to use keywords in the title and in
the first few paragraphs of your document. Don't go crazy
with the keywords in your first few paragraphs; after all,
your users will be reading them too. </p>
</body>
</html>
```

4. Save keywords.html.

Tip   Please note that you won't be able to test your Web page using search engines unless you upload the page to a server.

Lab 10-3: Searching for other keywords

For this lab, you're going to surf the Web in search of keywords. You can either use the keywords you defined in Lab 10-2, or you can use any of the following:

✦ SGML

✦ Frogs

✦ Cats

✦ Cactus

Visit some of the major search engines and search on a keyword.

1. Open your browser.

2. Visit a search engine such as Yahoo! (www.yahoo.com) or HotBot (www.hotbot.com).

3. Enter in a keyword of your choice.

4. Visit at least 20 of the search engine results.

5. For each result document, view the document source and jot down any keywords that they used. Because about one out of four Web sites doesn't use `<meta>` tags, you might have to visit several sites before finding one that defines keywords. Jot down at least 10 other keywords that are similar to the one you first entered.

Answers to Chapter Questions

Chapter pre-test

1. Using the DOCTYPE declaration provides two functions. First, if you reference a DTD, you're able to use a tool called a validator to check your document for errors. This makes troubleshooting problems tons easier. The second benefit to using the DOCTYPE declaration is that it provides metadata information about the version of HTML to which the document adheres. Search engines do not use this information, but it's used by developers and designers.

2. Metadata is data about data. It provides additional information about the contents of your document. In the case of HTML, most metadata provides information that aids search engines in locating your document. Most metadata is added using the `<meta>` tag.

3. There are three attributes that are commonly used with the `<meta>` tag: `name`, `http-equiv`, and `content`. The `content` attribute is required and is used in conjunction with either the `http-equiv` or `name` attribute.

4. There's one major difference between a search engine and a directory. Whereas both allow designers to register their Web sites, only search engines employ an automated system that sends robots or spiders to crawl the Web and index any pages that they find. This is a helpful function, but as a designer, it's not recommended that you wait for the robots to find you. Be sure to register your site with the major Web browsers.

5. There's no strict definition of relevance, because it varies from search engine to search engine. There are, however, three common characteristics that most search engines use to determine a Web site's relevance. First, most search engines scan the contents of the `<title>` tag. Second, most search engines scan the top of a Web document for keywords. And finally, most search engines focus on the frequency of keywords.

Assessment questions

1. **C.** The `<title>` tag is a required child of the `<head>` tag. It's used by many search engines to determine relevance and is a good place to add keywords. See "The title tag."

2. **B.** Both keywords and descriptions (defined using the `name` and `content` attributes) are used by some search engines to determine a Web site's relevance. Descriptions are primarily used by search engines to provide users with a blurb about each search result. See "Keywords and descriptions."

3. **C.** Directories require that you register your site. Search engines offer this option as well, but it's not required because they also employ robots to automatically search the Web for Web sites to index. It is recommended that you register your Web site and not wait for the robots to find you. See "Choosing a search engine or directory."

4. **D.** You should include keywords just about everywhere you can in your HTML documents. Search engines primarily focus on the `<title>` tag and contents toward the beginning of the document. However, remember that users are reading your content and keep that in mind before you litter your document with keywords. See "Adding keywords."

5. **A.** The `content` attribute is required each time the `<meta>` tag is used. The value of the `content` attribute is associated with the present `http-equiv` or `name` attribute. See "Using the meta tag."

6. **B.** The `<meta>` tag can do a lot; however, it does not define or present server information to users. See "Using the meta tag."

7. **B.** Keywords are indexed by search engines and used to determine a site's relevance to a user's search query. It's important that you list as many relevant keywords that you can think of. You might even want to do some outside investigating to come up with more. You don't want to exceed the maximum allotted characters, and you should be aware that search engines might ignore the 256th character and higher. See "Keywords and descriptions."

Scenarios

1. In answer to the two parts of the first scenario:

   a. When you decide to redirect your Web site, all you have to do is add a simple tag to the head of your document:

   ```
   <meta http-equiv="REFRESH"
   content="4;http://www.company.com">
   ```

   b. In answer to the second part, you have to use two attributes: `http-equiv` and `content`. Remember that the `content` attribute is required for the `<meta>` tag.

2. The second scenario asks that you list a few of the ways you can increase your Web site's searchability. Lucky for you, there are several things you can do using simple keyword techniques:

   • Do not use misleading keywords

   • Use a smart domain name

   • Avoid frames

- Use smart file names
- Define combination keywords
- See what else is out there
- Use a thesaurus
- Use acronyms, as well as spell them out

For More Information

✦ **World Wide Web Consortium (W3C).** www.w3.org/DesignIssues/Metadata

✦ **Dublin Core Metadata Initiative.** http://dublincore.org/index.shtml

✦ **Search Engine Watch.** www.searchenginewatch.com

✦ **Search Engine Guide.** www.searchengineguide.org

✦ **Search Engine Showdown.** www.searchengineshowdown.com

✦ **Link Development Corporation.** www.linkdevelopment.com

Cascading Style Sheets

EXAM OBJECTIVES

- ✦ CSS versions
- ✦ CSS and site design
- ✦ Linking style sheets

CHAPTER PRE-TEST

1. Explain how style sheets separate style from structure, ensure consistency in display of Web pages, and make it easier to update their display.

2. Describe the differences between CSS1, CSS2, and CSS3.

3. What are the different components of a CSS style rule?

4. What are the four different ways to add style rules to a Web page?

5. How do inheritance and cascade affect the way style rules drive Web page display?

6. What are some elements you might find in a style guide?

✦ Answers to these questions can be found at the end of the chapter. ✦

Style sheets provide you with an easy way to consistently influence the way your Web pages look in Web browsers. Although style sheets took some time to catch on in the Web design community, their use is more prolific now, and they're regarded by professional Web developers and designers as the best way to define display rules for Web sites. In this chapter, you learn the fundamentals of style sheet design and development with particular focus on the topics the CIW Site Designer test places the most emphasis on. You leave this chapter with a solid understanding of how and why style sheets came to be, how Cascading Style Sheets — style sheets used on the Web — work, and the different ways you can use style sheets with your Web pages.

A Brief History of Style Sheets

A style sheet is nothing more than a set of rules that defines how a piece of a document should look in a particular display media. Style sheets can drive print display, display on the Web, or display in a variety of other devices. Each style rule in a style sheet includes all of the information that the display device needs to determine the correct way to present each piece of the document. When you combine text with a style sheet, the text is formatted when it's displayed. Usually, one style sheet drives the display of a particular document; but as pointed out later in this chapter, several style sheets may affect the final look and feel of a document.

The concept of a style sheet isn't a new one. The idea of a style sheet as a format guide to how text should be displayed in any medium has been around for quite some time. Word processing programs, such as Microsoft Word and WordPerfect, as well as page layout programs, such as FrameMaker and PageMaker, use style sheets to help users group display attributes into styles that can be reused across documents. The default Normal template style in Microsoft Word is just a style rule that specifies that standard paragraph text should be displayed in 12 point Times New Roman type, and the default Heading1 style specifies that first level heading text should be displayed in 18 point boldface Arial type.

The Standard Generalized Markup Language (SGML), the parent of the Hypertext Markup Language (HTML), uses style sheets to define how printers and computer monitors should display documents defined with SGML's extensive and complex markup tag system. SGML documents usually don't contain information about display; therefore, all formatting directives are included in style sheets that are written to go with each SGML document or type of document.

HTML was created to be display independent. In other words, the final look and feel of an HTML Web page should have to do with the way a Web browser interprets the HTML, and not what the Web page developer (page builder) does to affect that display. The Web page developer uses the appropriate HTML tags to define the pieces and parts of a document, and then the Web browser displays those pieces and parts based on the tags used to describe them. The structure of an HTML document was intended to be totally separate from its display. Despite the plans of the original creators of HTML, things didn't quite work out the way they intended.

As the Web has become a vehicle for mass information dissemination, the struggle to control the user experience and the display of Web pages has grown in leaps and bounds. Although HTML was never designed to be a page layout tool, it has become one. Of course, Web designers have to work in a world of many unknowns — different users have different browsers, monitors, computers, operating systems, settings, and so on. Therefore, Web designers constantly work to build Web pages that function well in a variety of settings.

A common solution to dealing with the many combinations of browser, computer, monitor, operating system, and user settings is to create different HTML pages for different common groups of settings — for example, one set of HTML for users on Macintoshes running Internet Explorer 3.0; another set of HTML for users on PCs running Netscape Navigator 4.0; and still another set of HTML for AOL users. Although this approach to Web design helps tailor the display and experience to the individual user, it requires a significant amount of work as well as complicated programming.

HTML was originally created to separate the structure of an HTML document from its display in a Web browser. However, this separation was not happening, so Cascading Style Sheets (CSS) was created. The goal of CSS is to provide Web designers with a mechanism for defining display styles for elements on a Web page that are: computer and browser independent, easily applied to large numbers of Web pages, and that preserve the user's ability to control the final display of a page in his or her own Web browser.

Tip If you're a history buff and want to know more about the origin of Cascading Style Sheets, you can read all about it online at `www.w3.org/Style/LieBos2e/history/`.

The Evolution of Cascading Style Sheets

Objective CSS versions

CSS is a style sheet mechanism designed specifically to work with HTML. Similar to other style sheets, CSS uses style rules to define how the different pieces and parts of a document should be displayed. Specifically, CSS attaches style rules to individual HTML elements. When you use an element to describe a piece of text in an HTML document, and the element has an associated style rule, the rule's display parameters are attached to that text. You can also create style rules for images and other non-text elements in a document.

Cross-Reference CSS provides a way to attach style rules to all instances of an element, specific instances of an element, combinations of elements, and more. The "CSS Syntax" section later in the chapter describes the different ways to assign style rules to elements in HTML.

Since its first appearance on the scene in the mid-1990s, CSS has been revised three times. Each version of CSS is aptly named CSS1, CSS2, and CSS3. Just as each new version of HTML includes new features, each version of CSS includes new features, such as support for new and more complex ways of defining style specifics for all aspects of a Web page. CSS2 and CSS3 even support style rules that define print parameters for Web pages and rules for how pages should be read by text-to-speech readers. You may very well be surprised at the depth and breadth of what you can do with CSS.

Caution　Just as the final display of a Web page is based on what a Web browser does with the HTML behind the Web page, the actual functionality of a style sheet is determined by which CSS conventions a particular Web browser supports. Although the most recent version of CSS, CSS3, includes a variety of sophisticated style functionality, most popular browsers don't support all of the functionality. To use CSS effectively, you need to know which versions of CSS (and consequently which functions) are supported by which browsers.

CSS1

The CSS Level 1 specification was released in December 1996 as the first style mechanism for Web pages. This version of CSS established the basic syntax for creating style rules to use with HTML and linking those rules to Web pages. CSS 1 allows you to assign basic design parameters to HTML elements. The different style aspects supported in CSS1 include:

✦ **Font specifics.** Face, size, styles, small-caps, color, and weight

✦ **Text specifics.** Word and letter spacing, alignment, indentation, and line height

✦ **Background specifics.** Background images, colors, positions, and alignment

✦ **Text block specifics.** Margins, padding, and borders

✦ **List specifics.** Bullets and number styles, and alignment

CSS1 was a solid set of style rules that was easy to apply to Web page styling. Although CSS1 was a good step towards providing Web designers with a new and better way to control the look and feel of a Web page, the Web browser vendors didn't buy into CSS immediately. The best support for CSS1 appeared in Internet Explorer (IE) 3.0 — with no support for CSS at all in Netscape Navigator 3.0. However, the support for CSS1 in IE 3.0 was far from complete and focused mainly on the font and color styling aspects of the specification. IE 4.0 saw better support for CSS1 but still not full support. That didn't appear until IE 5.0. Netscape Navigator's support for CSS1 lagged far behind IE's. CSS support didn't appear until Navigator 4.0. Over time, Navigator's support has become more complete and Netscape 6 has almost total support for CSS1.

Tip   For a complete rundown on which browsers support which aspects of CSS1, point your browser at WebReview's master browser compatibility list at `www.webreview.com/style/css1/charts/mastergrid.shtml`. In addition, the Leader Board at `www.webreview.com/style/css1/leaderboard.shtml` shows, at a glance, which browser has the best overall support for CSS.

Although it took CSS1 a while to catch on with developers and browser vendors, the W3C started revisions and additions to CSS1 almost immediately after its initial release. The result was CSS2.

Exam Tip   The differences between the various CSS specifications and how well they are supported in each of the browsers is a key topic on the exam. The browser compatibility lists at Web review are good tools to use to become familiar with which properties are supported in which browsers. The CSS specifications — listed at the end of the chapter — are the best resources for learning about the similarities and differences between the different specifications.

CSS2

The CSS Level 2 specification was released in May 1998 and added a substantial list of features to those already found in CSS1. The additions in CSS2 are:

✦ Support for different types of media. In CSS1, Web browsers are the only display media addressed. CSS2 includes support for a wider variety of media, including print, spoken translations, and on-screen presentations.

✦ Style rules to define tables.

✦ Methods for positioning elements in specific spots on the page.

✦ Methods for showing and hiding elements on a page.

✦ Support for bi-directional text so languages other than English — Hebrew for example — can be displayed on a Web page using CSS.

✦ Different kinds of cursors.

✦ Multiple sources for fonts including downloadable fonts.

The most significant CSS2 additions are the methods for positioning elements in specific spots on the page, and the methods to show and hide elements on the page. These two functions provide the basis for *dynamic HTML* — using client-side scripting such as JavaScript to control the behavior of a Web page.

Web developers combine JavaScript commands with the ability to place elements on a Web page to create flying blocks of text and other never-before-seen Web content. They use JavaScript and the capability to show and hide elements on a page to create expanding and contracting menus.

Once again, the browser vendors tightly controlled the way developers used the new additions to CSS by only implementing support for some aspects of the tool and not others. When CSS2 was released, both Netscape and Microsoft were contending for the position as "The dynamic HTML browser," so they only implemented those pieces of CSS2 that promoted that particular agenda. The result is that positioning and visibility are well developed in the 4.0 and later versions of the browsers, but cursors, tables, and different kinds of fonts are not well supported.

CSS2 is the current complete CSS specification from the W3C, and the one that the browser vendors continue to work to support. It's not surprising, however, that the next generation of CSS, CSS3, is in the works already.

CSS3

In its current iteration, CSS3 stands to rework the entire approach to style sheets that was originally defined in CSS1. Since the original release of CSS1, the Web and other information systems have grown and changed; therefore, the needs of Web designers have also grown and changed. Not only is Web content delivered via the Web, but it's also now available on cell phones, personal digital assistants (PDAs), and other wireless devices. In addition, as the Web becomes the vehicle of choice for delivery of services such as shopping and banking, there's a real need for more advanced Web sites with more advanced display and behavior requirements. CSS3 is being designed to meet the needs of the ever-changing Web, and give Web designers good tools for handling all aspects of a Web site's look and behavior.

CSS3 breaks the different pieces and parts of CSS into a collection of modules. Some of these modules reflect the basic grouping of style elements used in CSS1 and CSS2, including:

- ✦ Fonts
- ✦ Text
- ✦ Positioning
- ✦ Spoken media
- ✦ Tables
- ✦ Colors and backgrounds

In addition to these familiar groups of style elements, some new modules appear in CSS3:

- ✦ **Behavioral Extensions to CSS (BECSS).** Provides a way to attach user behaviors such as moving a mouse or pressing a key. When combined with a client-side scripting language such as ECMAscript (formerly known as JavaScript), the Web page can change dynamically based on user actions. Think of this as the new and improved dynamic HTML.

- ✦ **Multi-column layouts.** Provides a way to create multiple column layouts without using tables.

✦ **Scalable Vector Graphics (SVG).** Provides a way to use CSS to describe flexible vector graphics using the same simple CSS syntax that you use to create a style sheet.

The development of new modules in CSS3 depends on other work being done in other parts of the W3C. However, judging from the work already done on CSS3, it appears that the newest version of CSS3 will ensure that CSS keeps up with the demands of the Web. For a complete rundown on the newest additions to CSS and to track the progress of CSS3, visit the Cascading Style Sheets Working Group current work page at `www.w3.org/Style/CSS/current-work`.

Design Theory Behind CSS

CSS and site design

Even though CSS has evolved over time, the design theory behind each level of CSS has remained the same: Instead of adding tag upon tag upon tag to HTML to account for all of the different Web page layouts that a Web designer might want to put together, CSS creates a specific mechanism for defining the layout of Web pages. HTML should describe the pieces and parts of a document, and the style sheet should provide instructions to the Web browser on how the pieces and parts should look in a Web browser or other display device.

In other words, CSS attempts to separate the structure of an HTML document from its display. When you take this approach to Web development you're guaranteed to have a more consistent look and feel throughout your entire site. In addition, updates to the display of the site are far easier to make. The following three sections discuss the key aspects of the design theory in detail:

✦ Separate style from structure

✦ Ensure consistency in display

✦ Make updates and changes easier

Separate style from structure

As mentioned earlier in the chapter, HTML was never designed to be a Web layout tool. Instead, it was designed as a way to describe content so anyone with a Web browser could view it. This is the epitome of separating style from structure. HTML takes care of the structure and the display device takes care of the display. CSS is the mechanism for passing instructions to the browser to guide the display, so HTML can continue to just describe the pieces and parts of the document.

When you separate style from structure, you can divide the development of a page into two distinct parts:

✦ Describing the page's content as accurately as possible

✦ Defining a design for the display of the page

If Web pages only consisted of paragraphs or table cells, HTML would only need a couple of tags: paragraph and table cell tags. But a Web page is made up of many pieces and parts, including headings, lists, tables, code, and more. In addition, Web designers also mislabel content on a Web page to produce certain effects. For example, a Web designer may use paragraph (<p>) elements and images to create a bulleted list with graphical bullets instead of the default bullets and squares. The upside to this approach is that you can create bulleted lists that have great bullets; the downside is that you haven't accurately described the content on your page. Instead of a list of items, you have created a collection of paragraphs.

As you try to display Web pages on more and different kinds of devices, cell phones and PDAs for example, the more you want your HTML to accurately describe the content of your document. A cell phone won't display your cool image bullets, but it will display small standard bullets. If you use HTML correctly, a list will be a list on any device.

Even though you want your documents to function well in any device, you still want them to look good in a Web browser. The happy medium between using HTML correctly and being able to achieve a particular look and feel in a Web browser is using CSS and HTML together.

In addition to using HTML correctly and making your documents function well on a variety of devices, another benefit of using CSS to drive the display of Web pages is that a single style sheet can be applied to hundreds of Web pages. This ensures a consistent display across an entire Web site and makes updates and changes to the look and feel of the site easier.

Ensure consistency in display

If you've ever designed a large collection of Web pages — either by hand or using a popular Web development tool such as FrontPage or Dreamweaver — you know it can be difficult to ensure that each page has the same design elements. Although development tools and templates make this job a little easier, much of the job of ensuring consistency falls on the shoulders of the Web designer.

When you use style sheets to drive the display of a Web page or a Web site, you can create one style sheet that governs the look and feel of many pages. A single site may have a single style sheet or use a combination of style sheets. The display of a single page on a site may be driven by one or more style sheets. Even though the final look of an individual page is a combination of the HTML you use to create it and the style sheet assigned to it, you have a set list of HTML elements to work with and an established style sheet to work with.

When you use HTML alone to drive the display of a page, you should use the same combination of tags every time you want to achieve a particular effect. For example, if you want all of your first level headings to be displayed in maroon text in Arial font, you need to use both a font tag and a first level heading tag for every first level heading you create on your site:

```
<font color="maroon" face="Arial"><h1>Heading 1</h1></font>
```

The larger and more complex your site gets, the longer it will take to create your pages because you have to type two tags instead of one. In addition, you must remember to always use the `<font>` tag with the same attributes and the first level heading tag to ensure consistency or you'll end up with first level headings that don't match.

The LANWrights Web site (shown in Figures 11-1 and 11-2) uses a style sheet to drive the display of several elements on each Web page, including body text, headings, and different kinds of paragraphs. Notice that the font faces, colors, and other general design aspects are the same on both pages.

If ensuring consistency across pages isn't enough of a benefit to using style sheets, the separation of structure from display has yet another benefit: it's easy to update the look and feel of an entire Web site by simply changing its style sheet.

Figure 11-1: The LANWrights Web site uses CSS to ensure consistency of design across the site.

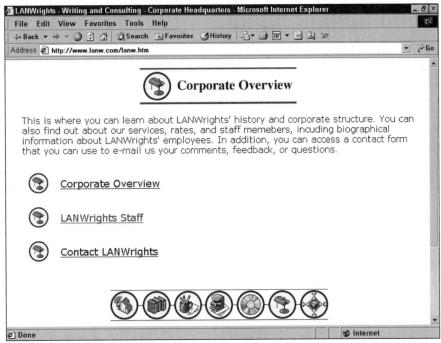

Figure 11-2: A different page on the LANWrights site has the same look and feel as the first, because they share the same style sheet.

Make updates and changes easier

The look and feel of the LANWrights Web site shown previously in Figures 11-1 and 11-2 is driven from a single style sheet. In its current iteration, the style sheet specifies that all paragraph text should be displayed in the Verdana font face and that all headings should be displayed in Arial. Because this single style sheet is attached to every page on the site, a change to the style sheet affects the display of every page to which it's linked.

When the site designer decides to change the paragraph text font from Verdana to Times New Roman and the heading text font to Tahoma, it's as simple as changing two style rules in the style sheet. The changes to the style sheet will affect all of the pages on the site the next time the pages are loaded into a Web browser.

In the previous section, you saw this bit of HTML code for creating first level headings with a particular color and font face attached to them:

```
<font color="maroon" face="Arial"><h1>Heading 1</h1></font>
```

If you needed to change the display of all first level headings to Comic Sans instead of Arial, you'd have to search every document on your site for the tag combination and change the value of face from Arial to Comic Sans. If you've only got a few pages on your site, this isn't a daunting task. However, if you have several hundred pages, it's a time-consuming activity. In addition, you can't be sure that you've caught every heading until you check every document (page) individually. If, on the other hand, you use CSS to style your Web pages, you only need to change a single style sheet and your work is done.

The larger a site is the more of a benefit style sheets can be. Even if you choose to use several different style sheets to drive the display of the various kinds of pages on your site, changing a few lines of style sheet code is more preferable than changing hundreds of Web site pages. You also don't have to worry about missing a page or two along the way when you use style sheets.

Cross-Reference

Using a collection of style sheets to guide the display of an entire Web site requires an understanding of how multiple style sheets can work together to guide the display of a single page. The section, "The Rules of Inheritance and Cascade," later in the chapter, discusses techniques for using several style sheets together on a single site.

CSS Syntax

A style sheet is nothing more than a collection of rules about how different elements on a Web page are displayed. To build style sheets, you simply need to know how to build style rules. The CSS syntax rules are fairly straightforward and easy to use. The basic syntax for a CSS rule is:

```
selector {property: value}
```

A `selector` is the HTML element to which you want the style rule to apply. The `property` defines which part of the element's style you want to affect, for example, `font-family`. The `value` specifies how you want to affect the property. A value for the `font-family` property might be `Times New Roman`. A simple style rule that sets the font type for all paragraphs to Times New Roman takes this form:

```
p {font-family: "Times New Roman"}
```

The selectors you can choose from are defined in the HTML specification. The properties and the values they can take are defined in the CSS specification. You can't make up your own selectors or properties, but you have so many to choose from that it won't matter.

Cross-Reference

The easiest part of creating style rules is learning the syntax. The hardest part is remembering what all of the CSS properties are and what values they take. Later in the chapter, in the "CSS Property Families Overview" section, you get a brief overview of the different groups of properties in the CSS1 specification, as well as links to useful resources that list all of the properties and the values that they can take.

Selector types

A property and value combination is applied to a single HTML element as shown in this code:

```
p {font-family: "Times New Roman"}
```

In this example, all paragraphs are displayed in the Times New Roman font face. However, what if you have different kinds of paragraphs throughout your Web pages that you want displayed differently?

For example, you have a footnote paragraph that you want displayed in Arial text and an introductory paragraph that you want displayed on the top of the page in Verdana. These different implementations of the generic HTML paragraph are called *classes* and you can use CSS to create different style rules to apply to each class.

To build a style rule that applies to a particular class of an HTML element, you simply add a period (.) and the name of the class after the selector in the style rule, like this:

```
p.footnote {font-family:Arial}
```

For the Web browser to know which paragraphs are footnotes and which aren't, you also have to add the class information to your HTML in the form of the `class` attribute, like this:

```
<p class="footnote">This is a footnote.</p>
```

The style rule for footnotes will only be applied to those elements in the Web page that have the `class` attribute value `footnote`. All other paragraphs will use the standard style for paragraphs. This snippet of code shows how you can create three separate styles for three kinds of paragraphs: a standard paragraph with no specific class, a footnote, and an introductory paragraph:

```
p               {font-family: "Times New Roman"}
p.footnote {font-family: Arial}
p.intro       {font-family: Verdana}
```

You can also create style rules that link to classes that aren't tied to a particular element. These styles are reusable across your document with any element. Create a class that doesn't have an associated element like this:

```
.highlight {background-color: yellow}
```

This particular rule creates a class rule called *highlight* that sets the background color of any element to which it's applied to yellow. This style rule can be used with any element using the `class` attribute, as shown in this bit of code:

```
<p class="highlight">This is a highlighted paragraph.</p>
<h1 class="highlight">This is a highlighted heading.</p>
```

The third and final way to better target the HTML to which a style rule is applied is by combining selectors so the rule is only attached to a particular set of HTML. In this example, the style rule is specifically defined for use with list items found within a numbered list:

```
ol li {font-family: Arial}
```

The style rules only apply to this specific combination of HTML tags:

```
<ol>
    <li>list item</li>
</ol>
```

This style rule only applies to list items found within a bulleted list:

```
ul li {font-family: Verdana}
```

This rule is linked specifically to this combination of HTML:

```
<ul>
    <li>list item</li>
</ul>
```

Tip   Because there are so many different ways to attach style rules to HTML elements or groups of elements, it pays to spend some time thinking through the different classes of elements you need as well as the different combinations of HTML to which you want to apply style rules. It's easier to build the rules if you already know what the HTML they are going to affect is.

Grouping selectors and declarations

One of the main goals of CSS is efficiency. You can create several different style rules to change several properties on a single selector, like this:

```
p {font-family: Arial}
p {color: navy}
p {left-margin: .5in}
p {font-size: 95%}
```

This isn't the most economical way to set all of the properties for a single element, but grouping declarations is. When you group declarations for a particular selector, all of the declarations live in a single set of curly braces and are separated by semi-colons:

```
p {font-family: Arial;
   color: navy;
   left-margin: .5in;
   font-size: 95%
   }
```

You can also group selectors if you want to apply the same set of declarations to more than one element or class of an element. To group selectors, simply separate the selectors with commas, like this:

```
p, li, td {font-family: Arial;
           color: navy;
           left-margin: .5in;
           font-size: 95%
           }
```

You can also break the declarations for a particular element into several rules. This allows you to create a base rule that several different elements share, and then create additional rules that apply specific formatting to individual elements in the original group, as in this code:

```
p, li, td {font-family: Arial;
           color: navy;
           left-margin: .5in;
           font-size: 95%
           }
p {font-weight: bold}
li {background-color: yellow}
td {background-color: green}
```

The final display of each element in the list is driven by a combination of all of the style rules set for it. In the previous example, the paragraph's style includes a bold, navy text with an Arial font face, a left-margin of half an inch, and a font size that is 95 percent of the standard display size of the browser.

The importance of punctuation

CSS syntax relies heavily on a very specific use of punctuation to separate selectors from declarations, properties from values, groups of selectors, types of selectors, and groups of declaration. If you inadvertently use a colon where a semi-colon should be, your style rule will not function correctly. Table 11-1 lists the punctuation marks used to build CSS rules and the role each one plays.

Table 11-1
CSS Punctuation

Punctuation mark	Description
curly braces ({ })	Contains the declaration in a style rule
colon (:)	Separates the property from the value in a declaration
period (.)	Precedes a class name in a selector
comma (,)	Separates multiple selectors in a single style rule
semi-colon (;)	Separates multiple declarations in a single style rule

Tip   When you compose long style sheets, it can be difficult to debug them and find small problems such as incorrect punctuation. A great tool for isolating problems in a style sheet is the CSS validator provided by the W3C at `http://jigsaw.w3.org/css-validator/`. You can download a copy of the validator to use on your computer or validate style sheets from across the Internet.

CSS Property Families Overview

The bulk of the CSS specification is devoted to defining which properties you can use to specify style information about elements on your page and which values each of those properties can take. To create CSS rules successfully, you have to abide by the rules set in the specification and use the exact property names and values those rules define.

The CSS1 specification breaks the different properties into *property families.* This is just a convenient way to classify and manage the many properties. These property families have evolved over time into the modules currently being developed for CSS3.

Table 11-2 lists the different CSS1 property families and the properties you can find in each one. Although CSS2 is the current specification, the best browser support for CSS still focuses on the CSS1 specification, which is why its property families are highlighted here.

Cross-Reference   The "For More Information" section at the end of the chapter includes links to the CSS1 specification and a couple of great CSS1 online resources so you can get the full details of what values the different properties take. The section also includes links to the CSS2 specification so you can compare the differences between the two specifications.

Table 11-2
CSS1 Property Families

Family name	Description	Properties

Font Properties	Contains all properties related fonts assigned to the text elements	`font-family`
		`font-style`
		`font-variant`
		`font-weight`
		`font-size`
		`font`

Family name	Description	Properties
Color and Background Properties	Contains all properties to text and background colors assigned to elements	color background-color background-image background-repeat background-attachment background-position background
Text Properties	Contains all properties related to the display of text	word-spacing letter-spacing text-decoration vertical-align text-transform text-align text-indent line-height
Box Properties	Contains all properties related to blocks of text (i.e., paragraphs,	margin-top margin-right margin-bottom margin-left margin padding-top padding-right padding-bottom padding-left padding border-top-width border-right-width border-bottom-width border-left-width border-width border-color border-style border-top border-right border-bottom border-left border width height float clear

Continued

Table 11-2 *(continued)*		
Family name	*Description*	*Properties*
Classification Properties	Contains all properties related to how text is defined in a document (Text can be classified as block text, such as paragraphs, or inline, such as bold and italic formatting, or as lists. These properties also control how lists are displayed.)	display white-space list-style-type list-style-image list-style-position list-style

The CSS properties values take a variety of forms. The `font-family` property takes a font name as a value, which is text, whereas the `margin-right` value takes a unit of measure as a value, which is a number. To make the values used in style rules more meaningful, CSS1 includes a variety of units of measure to use when setting values in a rule. The units in CSS1 are broken down into four categories:

✦ **Length units.** Hard-coded units of measure, such as inches and centimeters.

✦ **Percentage units.** Relative units of measure that depend on a variety of factors for their final value. For example, if you set the value for `font-size` to `95%`, the final display size of the font is 95 percent of the user's Web browser display font size. Percentage units are more flexible than length units because they account for the variety of display settings (such as font size, browser window size, and screen resolution) that a user can control.

✦ **Color units.** Color definitions based on the amount of red, green, and blue in a particular color.

✦ **URLs.** A special syntax for using URLs as values for properties. For example, the `background-image` property requires a link to a picture on the Web and uses the CSS URL syntax to specify that link.

Table 11-3 lists the specific units of measure in each measurement category.

Table 11-3
Units of Measure in CSS

Category	Specific units	Example
Length units	inches -- `in` centimeters -- `cm` millimeters -- `mm` points -- `pt` picas – `pc` ems (height of the element's font) -- `em` x-height (height of the letter x) -- `ex` pixels -- `px`	`p {font-size: 10in}`
Percentage units	Integer followed by the percent sign	`p {font-size: 75%}`
Color units	keywords -- `aqua`, `black`, `blue`, `fuchsia`, `gray`, `green`, `lime`, `maroon`, `navy`, `olive`, `purple`, `red`, `silver`, `teal`, `white`, **and** `yellow` RGB notation -- `#rrggbb`	`p {color: black}` `p {color: #000000}`
URLs	`url(url)`	`p {background-color:` `url(/graphics/bg.gif)`

To give you a good idea of how properties, values, and units all work together to define exactly how some aspect of an element on a page should look, Table 11-4 highlights some of the most commonly used CSS1 style properties. This table includes the property name, the aspect of the element that the property affects, the kind of value the property takes, and an example style rule that uses the property.

Exam Tip   The list of properties in Table 11-4 is non-inclusive. Be sure to review the CSS1 and CSS2 specifications before taking the exam so you're familiar with all of the properties and their values.

Table 11-4
A Sampling of CSS1 Properties and Values

Property	Element aspect affected	Value	Example
`font-family`	The font in which the element's text is displayed	Any font name	`p {font-family: Arial}`
`font-style`	The style in which the text is displayed	`normal`, `italic`, `oblique`	`p {font-style: italic}`
`font-weight`	How dark the text is	`normal`, `bold`, `bolder`, `lighter`	`p {font-weight: bold}`
`font-size`	The size of the element's text	A percentage or a length unit	`p {font-size: 12pt}`
`Font`	All aspects of the element's font display covered in the individual font family properties	Combine the values you can use with `font-family`, `font-style`, `font-weight`, `font-variant`, and `font-size` in one listing.	`p {font: Arial italic bold 12pt}`
`Color`	The color of the element's text	A color keyword or RGB code	`p {color: teal}`
`background-color #FFFF00}`	The background color of the element	A color keyword or RBG code	`p {background-color:`
`Background`	All aspects of the element's background	Combines the values you can use with all properties in the color and background property family	`p {background: #FFFF00 url(graphics/bg.gif) }`
`text-decoration`	Any line added to the element's text	`none`, `overline`, `underline`, `line-through`, `blink`	`p {text-decoration: blink}`
`vertical-align`	The vertical alignment of an element's text a percentage	`baseline`, `sub`, `sup`, `top`, `text-top`, `middle`, `bottom`, `text-bottom`,	`{vertical-align: sub}`
`text-align`	The horizontal alignment of an element's text	`left`, `right`, `center`, `justify`	`p {text-align: center}`

Property	Element aspect affected	Value	Example
text-indent	The indentation of the first line of a block of text	A percentage or a length unit	p {text-indent: 5px}
line-height	How much spacing appears between two lines of text on the page	A percentage or a length unit	p {line-height: 12pt}
margin-left	The length of the left margin of an element	A percentage or a length unit	p {left-margin: .5in}
border-top	The width, style, and color of an element's top border	Values used with the border-top-width, border-style, and color properties	p {border-top: .5pt, solid; navy}
Width	The width of the element	A percentage or a length unit	p {width: 150px}
Height	The height of the element	A percentage or a length unit	p {height: 150px}
list-style-image	The image used as a bullet for each item in a list	A URL	li {list-style-image: url(graphics/bullet.gif)

Notice that several of the properties in Table 11-4 combine the values other properties take. A good example of this is the `font` property, which combines the values of all of the other properties in the font property family. The properties that combine the values of other properties are a form of shorthand in CSS. They allow you to use a single property instead of one to set several similar values.

Cross-Reference

You may wonder what happens if you create two separate style rules for two separate elements and then combine those elements in your HTML document. How are the style rules for the two combined and applied? The answer to this question revolves around the concept of *inheritance.* In the section "The Rules of Inheritance and Cascade," you find out how elements that are nested inside of other elements pick up the styles from those elements.

The Different Ways to Use CSS in Web Design

Objective

Linking style sheets

After you learn the basics of CSS rule syntax, you can build entire style sheets that are as simple or complex as you want them to be. After you create a style sheet, you need to link it to a Web page so the styles can work with the HTML to drive design. The CSS developers recognized early on that for CSS to be useful to Web designers, it needed to be flexible and easy to use with HTML in a variety of ways. To that end, there are four different ways to add style sheets to a Web page:

✦ Internal style sheets

✦ External style sheets

✦ Imported style sheets

✦ Inline style declarations

The method you use to add styles to your Web pages depends entirely on the scope of the style — i.e. how many Web pages the style needs to apply to. In the following sections, you learn how each kind of style sheet affects a single page and an entire site, and we include some tips on when to use each kind of style sheet.

Exam Tip

Be sure you have a good understanding of the different ways to link to style sheets from your HTML pages. Be able to list the differences between the different methods.

Internal, or embedded, style sheets

Internal style sheets are sets of style rules that you list in a group directly within an HTML file. An internal style sheet only applies to the document in which it's housed. To include an internal style sheet in a Web page, place the style rules within the `<style>` tag in the document's header, for example:

```html
<html>
    <head>
        <style type="text/css">
            p, li, td {font-family: Arial;
                        color: navy;
                        left-margin: .5in;
                        font-size: 95%
                        }
            p  {font-weight: bold}
            li {background-color: yellow}
            td {background-color: green}
        </style>
    </head>

    <body>
        [the rest of the document]
    </body>
</html>
```

The benefit of using an internal style sheet is that your styles and the HTML that they work with are in the same document; therefore, it's easy to make changes and keep track of your document. The downside to using an internal style sheet is that you can't make the style sheet available to other documents without cutting and pasting the styles from one internal style sheet to the next.

We don't recommend the practice of cutting and pasting because if you need to make a change to a style, you have to make it in every document that uses the style sheet internally. If you want to link a single style sheet to a collection of documents, use an external style sheet.

External style sheets

An external style sheet keeps all of the style rules you want to use with a collection of HTML documents in a separate file saved on your Web site. The file only holds style rules and is usually saved with the file extension .css. Regardless of whether your style sheet is internal or external, you create the style rules the same way.

To link to an external style sheet, you use the link element in the head of your HTML document, for example:

```html
<html>
    <head>
        <link rel="StyleSheet" href="/site_style.css"
                type="text/css" />
    </head>

    <body>
        [the rest of the document]
    </body>
</html>
```

Tip

If you have styles that you want to apply to all pages of a Web site but also have styles specific to a single Web page, you can combine internal and external style sheets. Keep the styles that apply to all pages in the external style sheet and the ones specific to the page in the internal style sheet. This approach makes styles more manageable. The way the internal and external style sheets work together to affect the final display of the page is determined by the rules of inheritance and cascade, which are discussed in an upcoming section.

Imported style sheets

Another way to include external style sheets in your documents is to import them into your document. The affect of importing style sheets is the same as if you link to them, but the syntax is slightly different. To import style sheets into an HTML document, place the import statement in a `<style>` tag in the document's head:

```
<html>
    <head>
        <style type="text/css">
            @import url(/site_style.css)
        </style>
    </head>

    <body>
        [the rest of the document]
    </body>
</html>
```

Caution

The import statement isn't well supported across all of the major browsers. For maximum accessibility, link to external style sheets rather than import them.

Some designers prefer to use the import method when combining external and internal style sheets because it keeps all of the style information for the page within the `<style>` tags. This is really a matter of personal preference.

Tip

If you plan on importing more than one style sheet into your document, the order in which you list the import statements determines which one has precedence when the browser is trying to resolve conflicts. This topic is also discussed in further detail in the forthcoming inheritance and cascade section.

Inline styles

Inline styles are style rules written in the HTML markup itself and that apply to a single instance of an HTML element. To add an inline style to an HTML document, use the `style` attribute and the CSS properties and values:

```
<h1 style="font-family: Arial; color: teal; font-size: 24pt">
    This is a heading
</h1>
```

The benefit of using inline styles is that you can attach them at the very point in an HTML document where you need them. The downside to using inline styles is that you have to scour your HTML documents to update them and you can't reuse the style in the same document or in other documents without cutting and pasting it to other style sheets.

Of all of the methods for linking style rules to HTML documents, this is the least flexible. Although you do get the benefit of using CSS properties and values to change the look and feel of elements in a way that you wouldn't otherwise have with HTML elements, you can't take advantage of the ability to reuse styles or quickly update them.

Tip   Inline styles have precedence over all other styles applied to your document. If you need to override a standard page or site style just once, use the `inline` style with the element. If you use an inline style to override a standard style more than two or three times, you may want to think about making the inline style part of an internal or external style sheet to make it easier to manage.

The Rules of Inheritance and Cascade

We've referred to this section in the several other sections of this chapter. Whereas you have to know how to create style rules before you can create and link style sheets, you must understand how the rules of inheritance and cascade affect the final display of any Web page that uses HTML and style sheets.

Inheritance

The term inheritance in the context of style sheets refers to how the effects of style rules are passed down from a parent element to any child elements that it contains. For example, in the following snippet of code, the emphasis (`<em>`) element is a child of the paragraph (`<p>`) element:

```
<p>This is a paragraph with some <em>bold text</em>
   inside of it.</p>
```

The `<p>` element is the parent and the `<em>` element is the child. If a style rule is set on the `<p>` element that specifies that the element text font face should be Arial, the `<em>` element picks up that style, and the bold text will also be displayed in the Arial font face.

You can use the rules of inheritance to your advantage by setting the style definitions shared by many elements on a given page in the style rule for the `<body>` element. Because all other displayed elements are children of the `<body>` element, the style definitions you create for the `<body>` element are passed to every other element in the page. For example, this style rule defines font, color, and margin settings for the entire body of an HTML page:

```
body {font-family: Verdana;
      font-size: 95%;
      left-margin: .5in;
      top-margin: .25in;
      right-margin: .5in;
      background-color: white;
      color: navy
      }
```

Tip   When you use the `background-color` property, it's a good idea to set the `background-image` property to `none` so they don't conflict.

Figure 11-3 shows how this style rule and an associated HTML document might be displayed.

This is a first level heading.

This is some body text.

This is a second level heading.

1. This is the first item in a bulleted list.
2. This is the second item in a bulleted list.

Figure 11-3: Styles defined for the `<body>` element are inherited by all of the elements it contains.

Realistically, there will be times when you'll want to override some or all of an inherited style. In our previous example, all of the text on the page is displayed in Verdana. If you want to change the font face and color in which your headings are displayed, you simply create another style rule that changes the value of the `font-family` and `color` properties, like this:

```
h1, h2 {font-family: Arial;
        color: maroon;
        }
```

The new font face and color are defined for headings, but the other settings — margins and font size — are still inherited from the `<body>` element, as shown in Figure 11-4.

> ## This is a first level heading.
>
> This is some body text.
>
> ### This is a second level heading.
>
> 1. This is the first item in a bulleted list.
> 2. This is the second item in a bulleted list.

Figure 11-4: You can override inherited styles on a property-by-property basis.

Tip   Although the majority of properties are passed from parent elements to child elements, not every property in CSS1 or CSS2 is inherited. The CSS specifications (which can be accessed by checking out the sites listed in the "For More Information" section of this chapter) specify which elements are inherited and which aren't. In CSS2, you can control the inheritance of every element if you want to. When you're building style sheets, use the specifications as a guide to what is inherited and what is not.

As mentioned earlier, you can combine an external style sheet that drives the basic display of an entire Web site with an internal style sheet that governs the display of a specific page. When you combine style sheets in this manner, you end up with one style sheet for an individual page whose rules are stored in different places.

The rules of inheritance are in full force when you combine internal and external style sheets. You can use the internal style sheet to override any basic styles from the external style sheet based on the content of the page. You can also rely on the basic styles from the external style sheet to make the look and feel of the page consistent with other pages on the site.

Regardless of where you store your styles and how you use the rules of inheritance to control the look and feel of a particular element on the page, always remember that internal style sheets have precedence over external style sheets. If a style rule in your external style sheet and a style rule in your internal style sheet affect the same element and have different values for the same properties, the internal style sheet will prevail. The rules that determine how conflicting styles are resolved are referred to as the rules of cascade.

Cascade

The "C" in CSS stands for *Cascading* and refers to the way a set of style rules from different sources play together to define the final look and feel of a single Web page. The style definitions for a particular Web page come from many different sources:

✦ External style sheets

✦ Internal style sheets

✦ Imported style sheets

✦ Inline styles

✦ The Web browser's built-in style sheet

✦ The user's browser settings

✦ A user-written style sheet instructing the browser to display all pages a certain way

More often than not, these different sources of style rules will have conflicting settings. For example, the browser's default display font may be Times New Roman, the user's Comic Sans, and the Web site's Verdana. The rules of cascade specify how all of these conflicting rules are sorted. The general rules that CSS follows for resolving style rule conflicts are:

✦ The user's settings take precedence over all other settings. Most Web browsers provide a way for users to turn off a site's style sheets or font settings, as well as point to a set of CSS style rules that the user wrote themselves.

✦ Web site style rules override a browser's internal style rules. If a page's style sheet doesn't specify how to display a particular element, the browser's built-in style guides the element's display. If a page's style sheet only defines how certain parts of the element should be displayed — such as its font color and face but not its size — the browser guides the display of all undefined elements. Of course, the browser will only display those CSS style rules that it supports.

✦ Inline styles have precedence over internal style sheets.

✦ Internal style sheets have precedence over external and imported style sheets.

✦ If more than one style sheet is imported or linked in a page, the last style sheet listed has precedence over the ones before it.

Ultimately, adherence to the rules of cascade has everything to do with browsers and very little to do with the CSS specifications. It's up to the Web browser vendors to build browsers that follow the rules set out in the specifications, including the rules of cascade. In general, the browsers employ these rules well; however, only practice and experimentation with style sheets will ultimately provide you with the best understanding of how to implement style sheets in your Web pages.

Style Guides

Style sheets include all of the instructions that a browser needs to display a Web page. Before you write a style sheet, however, it's often useful to set down a few basic guidelines for how Web pages on your site will look and behave. This collection of guidelines is often referred to as a *style guide*.

Although style sheets go a long way towards making the display of your Web pages consistent across a site, style sheet builders need to have a good understanding of the general look and feel goals for the site before they start coding. A style guide can be as simple or as complex as you need for it to be. Usually, a style guide includes information such as:

✦ Standard colors, font faces, and sizes for the different kinds of text on the site (headings, paragraphs, news items, etc.).

✦ Suggestions or guidelines for including images in pages (size limitations, alternative text requirements, etc.).

✦ A standard set of templates for different kinds of pages (product pages, news briefs, customer testimonials, etc.).

✦ Required links and navigational components (standard logos, links to copyright information, standard footers, etc.).

Tip　If you have a style guide for print publications, you may be able to leverage it to get started on a Web site style guide. Many of the items covered in print style guides are similar to those you need in a Web style guide. There are a variety of style guides available on the Web for you to use as a reference. Our favorite is the Yale Web Style Guide, one of the original and most complete style guides available online. You can find it at `http://info.med.yale.edu/caim/manual/`.

Key Point Summary

This chapter presented a theoretical and technical overview of CSS. You learned the history of style sheets, the key role they play in Web design, how to create and link to them, and how the concepts of inheritance and cascade affect how style sheets work to drive the display of a Web page.

✦ The concept of a style sheet is not a new one. Style sheets are used in word processing applications to help users create and utilize standard formatting styles. SGML, the parent of HTML has its own style sheet reference. In 1996, CSS was created to work specifically with HTML to help Web designers better control the display of their pages in Web browsers.

✦ The primary design theory behind style sheets is to separate the instructions for styling a document from the markup that describes the content of the document to make the look and feel of pages across a site more consistent. You can also update the display properties of an entire Web site by simply updating the style sheets that define how the display should look.

✦ Style sheets are comprised of style rules that assign display properties to individual elements on a page. The syntax of a style rule is `selector {property: declaration}` where the selector is the element you want to style and the property and value define how the style should look. You can create selectors that point to specific classes of elements, combine a group of property and value combinations to a single element, or group selectors if they have the same properties and values.

✦ Punctuation in CSS is very important to creating style rules that function properly.

✦ There are four different ways to assign style rules to a Web page.

- You can save your style rules in an external style sheet and link that style sheet to a document using the `<link>` element or the `@import` statement.

- External style sheets can be reused across an entire Web site.

- Internal, or embedded, style sheets are kept entirely in the `<style>` element of an HTML document and apply only to that document.

- Inline styles are saved directly in an HTML element as an attribute and apply only to that instance of the element.

✦ Most properties in style rules are inherited by child elements from parent elements. You can override an inherited property by defining the property for the child element in a different style rule. You can also combine internal, inline, and external style sheets to drive the display of a page.

✦ The way conflicts in the style rules are resolved is decided by the rules of cascade. A user's browser settings have precedence over all other style rules, whereas inline styles have precedence over internal styles, and internal styles have precedence over external styles.

✦   ✦   ✦

STUDY GUIDE

In this chapter, you've learned a great deal about where style sheets come from, the many ways to use them with Web pages, and how a collection of style sheets work together to determine the final display of a Web page. This Study Guide provides you with the opportunity to test your knowledge by answering some assessment questions, thinking about how you might use style sheets to meet the needs of a real-world scenario, and creating a style sheet for a Web page you've already built.

Assessment Questions

1. Which of the following are ways to reference styles stored in external style sheets in a Web page? (Select all that apply.)

   A. Using the `@import` statement in the `style` element and the `link` element in the document's header

   B. Copying the style rules into the `style` element in the document's header

   C. Copying the style rules into the `style` element in the document's footer

   D. Adding the style rules directly to elements within the HTML document

2. As of April 2001, what is the most current full specification for CSS?

   A. CSS1

   B. CSS2

   C. CSS3

   D. CSS4

3. Which of the following is a correct style rule?

   A. `p,footnote {font-family; Arial}`

   B. `p.footnote [font-family: Arial]`

   C. `p.footnote {font-family Arial}`

   D. `p.footnote {font-family: Arial}`

4. What are some of the benefits of separating style from structure in your Web pages?

   A. You can use HTML to accurately describe your pages so they are accessible to different kinds of browsers.

   B. It is easier to update styles across a site when it is not embedded in the HTML.

   C. You can create a more consistent display across an entire site.

   D. All of the above.

5. Which of the following is a CSS2 feature that's also found in CSS1?

   A. Positioning of elements on the page

   B. Color and background properties

   C. Styles for tables

   D. Bi-directional text

6. When you combine a collection of external, internal, and inline styles, which has the highest precedence?

   A. Inline styles

   B. External styles

   C. Internet styles

   D. All have equal precedence

Scenarios

A client asks you to rework a large corporate Web site and use style sheets to do so. The site has a general look and feel that the client wants to maintain, but there are different kinds of pages on the site, each with its own particular display needs.

1. What steps would you go through to determine which style rules you need to create?

2. Where would you store those style rules?

Lab Exercises

Lab 11-1: Building your own style sheet

1. Select an HTML page that you have already built.

2. Analyze your HTML and find the markup you used to drive the display of the page, such as `<font>` tags.

3. Determine which other elements you'd like to change the display of but can't because HTML elements don't give you the ability to.

4. Create a short style guide for the page that lists the different elements you want to apply styles to and what those styles should be.

5. Remove all formatting HTML elements from the page.

6. Write an internal style sheet for the page.

7. Test the page's display in a collection of Web browsers to see how each responds to the style sheet.

8. Tweak your style sheet to further change the display of your page.

9. Try cutting the style rules from the Web page and save them in a separate, external style sheet.

10. Link your Web page to the external style sheet.

Answers to Chapter Questions

Chapter pre-test

1. Style sheets keep your HTML and the directions for displaying it in two separate places. You can reuse style rules across an entire Web site, ensuring that all pages use the same basic style rules. To update the display of all HTML pages that link to a style sheet, you only need to update the style sheet.

2. CSS1 was the original CSS specification and provided for the most basic formatting, including color and font settings, list style settings, and text formatting. CSS2 is the current CSS specification (as of April 2001) and it includes support for different kinds of media, positioning of elements, table formatting, cursors, and more. CSS3 is the future CSS specification and is still under development. It groups style functionality into modules and includes support for controlling behaviors, advanced graphics, and columnar layout, among others.

3. A style rule is made up of a selector, which identifies the HTML element to which the rule should be applied, and a declaration, which includes the specific property of the element the rule affects.

4. You can add style rules to a Web page via external style sheets, internal style sheets, inline styles, or imported style sheets.

5. Inheritance controls how style rules are passed from parent elements to child elements. The rules of cascade affect how conflicts in multiple style sheets applied to a single document are resolved.

6. A style guide documents the rules of how a site should look and feel. A guide may include definitions of how different text elements should look, the elements that are required on particular pages, how images may be used, and more.

Assessment questions

1. **A.** You can link to external style sheets using the `link` element or the `@import` statement. B, C, and D are incorrect because style rules stored in the `style` element or in any other element in a Web page are part of the document's internal style sheet. This is covered in the section titled "The Different Ways to Use CSS in Web Design."

2. **B.** Cascading Style Sheets Level 2 (CSS2) is the current specification for CSS. CSS1 was the original specification, CSS3 is the future specification, which is still in development, and there is no CSS4. This is covered in the section titled "The Evolution of Cascading Style Sheets."

3. **D.** The correct syntax for a style rule is `selector {property: value}`. If the selector has a class associated with it, such as `footnote`, the selector and the class are separated by a period. Properties and values are separated by colons, and the property-value combination is enclosed within curly braces. This is covered in the section titled "CSS Syntax."

4. **D.** Correct use of HTML, ease of update, and consistency of display are all benefits of separating structure from style. This is covered in the section titled "Design Theory Behind CSS."

5. **C.** Because color and background properties are part of the original CSS1 specification. A, B, and D are incorrect because positioning, tables, and support for bi-directional text are CSS2 features not found in CSS1. This is covered in the section titled "The Evolution of Cascading Style Sheets."

6. **A.** Inline styles have precedence over all other style rules applied to a document. This is covered in the section titled "The Rules of Inheritance and Cascade."

Scenarios

The exact path you take to upgrading a large corporate site to include style sheets will be different every time, but some of the decisions you have to make will be the same.

1. The steps you would take to answer the first part of this scenario are:

   a. The first step in the process is evaluating the current look and feel of the site, deciding which style rules you need to create, and then building a style guide to document the guidelines for the site.

   b. Next, you should look at the different styles and determine which should be applied globally and which are particular to an individual page or a particular kind of page, such as a news brief or a product page.

2. To decide on where to store the style rules, use the following guidelines:

- Global styles should be housed in an external style sheet that all pages reference.

- Whether you decide to create other external style sheets specific to the different kinds of documents depends on how many different kinds of documents there are and how many styles they need to share.

- Remember that you can have more than one external style sheet linked to any given page, so a product page might use a global style sheet and a product page style sheet.

- You may also need to create some internal styles specific to individual pages.

For More Information

- ✦ **The World Wide Web Consortium's CSS page.** www.w3.org/Style/CSS

- ✦ **The CSS1 specification.** www.w3.org/TR/REC-CSS1

- ✦ **The CSS2 specification.** www.w3.org/TR/REC-CSS2/

- ✦ **An overview of what is to come in CSS3.** www.w3.org/Style/CSS/current-work

- ✦ **The Web Design Group's CSS resources.** www.htmlhelp.com/reference/css/

Plug-Ins and Downloadable Files

EXAM OBJECTIVES

+ Plug-in technology
+ Linking to downloadable files
+ Downloading plug-ins

CHAPTER PRE-TEST

1. What are three different ways for a browser to handle non-native file types?

2. What kind of files are PDF and Flash?

3. What is the difference between streaming media and static media?

4. When you link to a non-native file, what information should you include for the user?

The Internet world is not made of HTML and graphics alone. Multimedia, word processing documents, spreadsheets, and other kinds of information are all abundant. These documents also need to be available via the Web from time to time; however, Web browsers by themselves don't always know what to do with the different and varying file formats.

In this chapter, you'll learn about plug-ins, which are additions to Web browsers that make alternative file formats available to users via the Web. You'll also learn about downloadable files, which are files that may not be displayed correctly by a Web browser or a plug-in, but that you need to distribute via the Web. The chapter includes information on the most popular plug-ins and the kind of content they display, how to link to downloadable files, how using alternative file formats affects the user experience, and how to install plug-ins.

Understanding Plug-Ins and Downloadable Files

 Plug-in technology

As a Web designer, you'll probably want to add content that a Web browser isn't prepared to handle on its own to your Web pages: for example, multimedia or word processing documents. You should decide up front which of the following ways you want browsers to handle this content:

✦ **Prompt users to save the file to their hard drives.** You can make a link to the file so users can download and open it on their hard drives with an application other than a Web browser, such as a Word processing application.

✦ **Use a plug-in to display the file within the browser window.** The file's content can be displayed within the Web browser as part of the page: for example, as an inline video clip or audio file.

A good understanding of how plug-ins and downloadable files are handled by Web browsers is all you need to include a variety of content in your pages for either display or download.

Plug-ins extend Web browsers and allow you to utilize a variety of file formats in your Web pages rather than converting all of your content to HTML or graphics. A *plug-in* is a small application that is downloaded and installed on the user's system. Each plug-in is designed to display a particular kind of file type. After the plug-in is installed, the browser automatically launches the plug-in when it encounters the associated file type.

When the Web was not as developed, there was a plethora of plug-ins that worked with very specific file types for displaying everything from multimedia, to calendars, to spreadsheets. Vendors tried to encourage Web developers to use certain proprietary file formats to store their non-standard Web content. Developers discovered very quickly that users don't like to have to stop and download a plug-in on every other page; as a result, the field of plug-ins has narrowed to a small set of common plug-ins and non-standard file types.

Exam Tip   The topic of plug-ins has a variety of facets that you need to know about as a Web designer in general and to successfully complete the CIW Site Designer exam. Pay special attention to the topics that are previewed in the folowing bulleted list.

In addition to understanding why you might use content in a Web page that requires a plug-in, this chapter also covers:

✦ The difference between a downloadable and displayable file and how a browser decides if it should display a file, launch a plug-in, or simply save a file to disk

✦ The common plug-ins and the kind of file types they support

✦ How to create links to files for display using plug-ins

✦ How to create links to download files to a user's computer

✦ How adding content that requires a plug-in to your Web site affects the user experience

Chances are that at some point during your Web design career, you'll need to include content that either requires a plug-in or that you want users to be able to download to their computers. The next several sections discuss the many facets of plug-ins and downloadable files so you'll have the knowledge you need to both pass the exam and use downloadable files and plug-ins successfully in your Web pages.

Downloadable vs. displayable files

You can group the content you serve over the Web and that is displayed in Web browsers into two different categories:

✦ Native file formats

✦ Non-native file formats

A *native file format* is one that the browser inherently supports, such as Hypertext Markup Language (HTML), Graphics Interchange Format (GIF), and Joint Photographic Experts Group (JPEG). The later versions of Web browsers have native support for a wider variety of files, including Extensible Markup Language (XML) documents, Cascading Style Sheets (CSS), and Portable Network Graphics (PNG). Even with this growing list of supported file formats, browsers can't possibly include native support for all file formats.

A *non-native file format* is one that the browser doesn't inherently support. Although you can view most multimedia files in many Web browsers, the browsers don't actually have native support for these files but instead utilize plug-ins to display the content. If the Web browser doesn't have a plug-in to use to display the file, the browser prompts users to download the file to their hard drives so they can use a different application to view the file.

Cross-Reference

There are three different ways to install plug-ins on your system. The section later in the chapter titled "Downloading and Installing Plug-Ins" describes each installation method in detail. The Lab Exercises towards the end of the chapter give you the opportunity to install two common plug-ins.

When you link to or embed a non-native file in a Web page, there are three things that may happen to that file:

✦ The browser launches the plug-in and the plug-in displays the file inside of the Web browser window.

✦ The browser recognizes the file type, doesn't have a plug-in installed to display the file type, but does know which application on the user's computer to use for the file and launches that application.

✦ The browser prompts the user to save the file to his or her hard drive.

Tip

Newer Web browsers running on the Windows platform are better at identifying the correct external application to automatically launch for non-native file formats. These browsers use the suffix of the file—.doc, .ppt, .vsd, etc.—and the Windows' settings that link file types to applications to choose which external application to run.

In summary, linked or embedded files saved in non-native file formats can either be displayed with a plug-in or another application, or saved to the user's hard drive. When you choose a non-native file format for your content and you want the content to be displayed by a plug-in in the browser, you should try to use the most common file formats. In other words, try to use the formats associated with the plug-ins that people are most likely to have installed on their systems already, as discussed in the following section.

Common plug-ins and the files they support

As the Web has matured, the number and variety of plug-ins has shrunk to a few standard ones that support most of the common non-native file formats. The most common plug-ins are:

✦ Adobe Acrobat Reader

✦ Macromedia Shockwave and Flash

✦ RealNetworks RealPlayer

The following sections take a closer look at each of these plug-ins and the file formats they can display.

Exam Tip   Be prepared to describe what kind of files each of the different plug-ins can process and display.

Adobe Acrobat Reader

Adobe Acrobat Reader is the plug-in that displays Portable Document Format (PDF) files. PDF is the standard for serving up highly formatted, lengthy documents that aren't good candidates for conversion to HTML, such as:

✦ Software documentation

✦ Brochures and marketing information

✦ Technical schematics

A PDF file is a digital representation of a document created in just about any word processing or page layout tool, from Microsoft Word to QuarkXpress. PDF files maintain the formatting and layout of a document exactly as it was in the original document and can include links between pages in the document. Graphics embedded in the document display as part of the PDF, and the PDF can be printed in the same way the original document would be. The Acrobat Reader plug-in, shown in Figure 12-1, provides a collection of tools for viewing a PDF document, including showing one or more pages at a time, zooming in and out, copying text, adding bookmarks, and more.

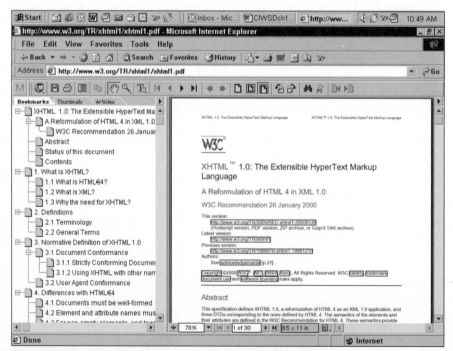

Figure 12-1: A PDF file as displayed in the Acrobat pug-in

PDF has become a popular format for sharing documents on CD-ROM as well as over the Internet and is frequently used for software documentation. A stand-alone version of the reader is also available so users can open and browse PDF files saved on their hard drives or on a CD without launching a Web browser.

Cross-Reference The CD that comes with this book includes a copy of Adobe Acrobat Reader. The complete (and searchable) text of this book is also included in PDF format.

The benefits of using PDF format over a standard Word Processing format for dissemination of complex or highly formatted documents are:

✦ Users only need to have the Acrobat Reader, plug-in or stand-alone application, installed on their computers to view PDF files. If you use a standard word processing format such as Microsoft Word, users must have Word installed to view documents.

✦ PDF files can be password protected, which prevents the copy of content from the PDF file to other documents. You can also password protect word processing documents, but it's difficult to prevent users from copying and pasting content. In general, PDF files are a more secure way to disseminate information than word processing documents.

✦ PDF files can be compressed as they are created, so they tend to have a smaller file size than their source documents.

Tip The Adobe Web site is the best resource for information on creating and serving PDF files. A good discussion of how to optimize PDF files can be found at www.adobe.com/epaper/tips/pdfgraphics/main.html.

The Acrobat Reader plug-in and application are both free downloads for any user. They work on major operating systems and with major browsers. To create PDF files, however, you must purchase a copy of Adobe Acrobat, Acrobat Capture, or a page layout tool such as Adobe PageMaker, which will save files in PDF format. It's very common for plug-ins to be free, but for the software developers to create files for those plug-ins, there's usually a licensing fee. Adobe Acrobat isn't an expensive tool, and if you have a need to disseminate long and complex documents via the Web or another distribution mechanism, you should consider Acrobat.

Macromedia Shockwave and Flash

As bandwidth increases around the Internet, there's more demand for interactive multimedia in Web pages. The Shockwave and Flash plug-ins from Macromedia provide a way for Web designers to deliver rich, interactive multimedia presentations to users via Web pages. The Shockwave and Flash plug-ins are designed to display files created with Macromedia's Director and Flash multimedia authoring tools.

Director is a multimedia-authoring environment originally designed as a tool for building multimedia CD-ROMs. Director is a high-end professional tool that is used in most professional multimedia development shops and has a wealth of functionality for combining all media from text to audio to digital video into complex presentations. Typically, a Director player, saved to a CD-ROM or local disk, drives the display of a Director presentation. Director presentations tend to have very large footprints and aren't optimized for the Web.

The Shockwave plug-in brings Director presentations to the Web. Director files that are optimized for Shockwave dissemination are compressed and include support for Web-specific actions like linking to files and Web pages with hyperlinks. To view Director files in a Web page, users must have the Shockwave plug-in installed in their browsers.

Flash is also a multimedia-authoring environment, but it was designed specifically for creating multimedia presentations for dissemination over the Web. Flash presentations include interactive components that respond to user events, such as mouse movements and key presses. Visit http://animal.discovery.com/ for a good example of an effective Flash presentation. Flash presentations are often used for adding interactive menus, product menus, and games to Web sites.

Although Flash isn't as complex as Director, it's still a sophisticated multimedia development tool that requires some knowledge to work with. The Flash plug-in is free, but you must purchase the Flash Development Studio from Macromedia to author Flash Presentations for your Web pages. More and more, Web sites are beginning to utilize Flash for advanced multimedia and it's becoming the accepted standard for multimedia content on the Web.

Cross-Reference   See Chapter 16 for more on using Macromedia Flash.

RealNetworks RealPlayer

The Web has become a favorite media for distributing audio and video files. Concerts, radio broadcasts, keynote presentations at conferences, and even short films are all prime candidates for distribution over the Web. There are a variety of file formats for audio and video files. Many of these formats are proprietary and require a special player that doesn't run within a Web browser but is installed as a separate application on your computer. Many vendors have developed plug-ins for listening to audio files and viewing video files on the Web — each with its own proprietary software for creating the files, of course — but the leader and recognized standard for audio and video is RealPlayer from RealNetworks.

RealPlayer is a browser plug-in that allows you to listen to audio files saved in a variety of file formats including:

✦ **.ra** — RealNetwork's proprietary audio and video format

✦ **.mp3** — MP3 audio files

✦ **.wav** — Legacy Windows audio files

✦ **.avi** — Microsoft's audio and video file format

✦ **SMIL** — (Synchronized Multimedia Integration Language, pronounced "smile") XML files that combine audio, video, and text into media presentations

RealPlayer not only allows you to play audio and video files, but it also supports streaming media. *Streaming media* are media files that start to play before the entire file has been downloaded to your system. The advantage of streaming media is that your users don't have to wait as long for large media files to download before they start to view them. Users want instant gratification, and streaming media helps satiate that desire.

Exam Tip   Be sure you know the difference between traditional media files — served using standard Web protocols (HTTP, or the Hypertext Transfer Protocol) — and streaming media: Traditional media files are downloaded in their entirety before they're viewed; streaming media files are downloaded and viewed simultaneously.

RealPlayer acts like any other plug-in: When the browser detects a media file that the player supports, the plug-in starts and plays the file. You can also run RealPlayer independent of a browser to access radio stations and play lists over the Internet.

Caution   Although the goal of streaming media is to listen to a song without interruption while it continues to download, high traffic times or low bandwidth can cause interruptions in play when the player catches up with the part of the song that hasn't downloaded yet. Users on slow modems and in high-traffic areas often can't benefit from streaming media.

There are several different versions of RealPlayer. The most basic is free and the most advanced is $30. Even though the cost of the plug-in is free or relatively inexpensive, authoring and serving streaming media is expensive. The current price for a streaming media starter kit from RealNetworks is $3,000. Tools for simply creating audio and video run from $90 and up.

In the Real World   Before you jump into any kind of a media delivery solution, be sure you spend a good deal of time analyzing what it takes to capture, process, and deliver media via the Web. Streaming media requires special server software and a certain bandwidth, and simply capturing video can require special equipment. The time you spend researching now may save you many hours and dollars later.

Linking to downloadable files

Objective   Linking to downloadable files

There are two ways to link to a downloadable file in a Web page. Both ways work for files you intend to display in a plug-in as well as those you want users to be able to download to disk. The methods are:

✦ Using the link (`<a>`) element

✦ Using the object (`<object>`) element

When you use the link (a) element, the browser attempts to load the document into a new window. When you use the object element, the browser attempts to embed the document within the current Web page display. With either method, if the browser has a plug-in or application associated with the file type, it launches the plug-in or the application. If it doesn't, it prompts the user to save the file to disk (as shown in Figure 12-2) or manually choose an application with which to open the file.

Figure 12-2: Saving a file to disk

When you link to a downloadable file that you expect to be displayed by a plug-in, you should include three key pieces of information along with the file:

✦ The file type so users know they're linking to a file saved in a non-native format

✦ What plug-in is required to view the file with a link to download the plug-in

✦ The file size so users know approximately how long the file will take to download

Even if you link to a file that you expect users to download but not view in a plug-in, you should include file type and size information, along with information about what kind of application the users might need on their systems to view the file: for example, Microsoft Excel for a spreadsheet or WinZip for a zipped archive.

Tip   Depending on how familiar you think your users are with plug-ins and the non-native file types you're using, you may need to provide detailed instructions on how to download and display files. A great example of a detail page can be found on the CliffsNotes site at www.cliffsnotes.com/store/sampledownload.html. Note that the site could more clearly state the file's type and size, however.

Most plug-in vendors have small icons or graphics that you can use to identify files of a particular type and that are designed to work with a particular plug-in. Adobe has an entire page of logos that you can use on your pages to let users know about links to PDF files. To access the logos, fill out the online license agreement (it's free) at `www.adobe.com/products/acrobat/distribute.html`. You can then download the Acrobat icon of your choice from the download page, which is available to everyone who fills out the agreement. The download page includes complete instructions on how to create a link to the Acrobat Reader on your pages and how to include a small Acrobat icon next to any PDF files you link to on your Web pages.

How plug-ins and downloadable files affect the user experience

The entire reason that plug-ins exist is because Web browsers aren't equipped to handle the wide spectrum of file types that developers want to store their content in. Although you can and should take advantage of the partnership between plug-ins and Web browsers, you should keep in mind that including files stored in non-native file types in your Web site can negatively affect the user's experience.

Even if you use common file types, your users still may not have the correct plug-in installed on their systems and may not want to wait to install the plug-in just to view a particular piece of content. In addition, some users are very careful about what they download and install and may simply be unwilling to download the plug-in.

Multimedia files and even the well-optimized PDF files are often large in size and can take a while to download. Although users are accustomed to some delays as they surf the Web, most expect information to be available very quickly. When you choose to create a link to large files, warn users about the file size and provide them with an estimated download time.

If possible, always create non-native files in common formats rather than using specialized plug-ins that many users may not have. Before creating your content, reevaluate it to be sure that you can't use a native file format such as HTML to store the data. Look for ways to break large files into smaller files. Read tutorials and articles on how to optimize each particular file format you're using and try to convert the files to the smallest possible size.

Before you release your site for public consumption, have others test your pages and give you feedback on how adding downloadable files to your site affects the user experience. Reduce or change the file formats if the additions adversely affect the quality of your site. The capability to link to or embed non-native files into Web pages is a powerful tool in site development. It's a tool that you should use carefully and only where appropriate.

Downloading and Installing Plug-Ins

 Downloading plug-ins

The three different ways for users to install or access plug-ins on their system are:

✦ **Online installation.** Downloading the plug-in file from the vendor's Web site

✦ **Offline installation.** Installing the plug-in from a CD (usually as part of a larger software package)

✦ **Preinstallation.** The plug-in is already installed in the browser

Of these, online installation usually takes the longest, because you have to download the plug-in from the vendor's Web site. Offline installation is faster, because the user is installing from a CD-ROM drive connected to a local computer. Of course, preinstalled plug-ins take no time at all to install, because they come with the browser. Most current browsers come with Adobe Acrobat Reader installed; however, users will need to install most other plug-ins themselves.

If your browser doesn't have Adobe Acrobat Reader installed, you can install the plug-in and stand-alone player all at once by following these simple steps:

1. Point your Web browser at the Adobe Acrobat main product page at `www.adobe.com/products/acrobat/main.html`.

2. Click on the Downloads ⇨ Free Acrobat Reader link.

3. At the bottom of the download Welcome screen, click the Get Acrobat Reader free link.

4. On the Download Acrobat Reader page, select the Acrobat version that meets your language, operating system, and location criteria. Type your name and e-mail address, and click the Download button.

5. From the File Download window, choose Save this program to disk and identify the location on your hard drive where you want the installation file to be saved. Click OK.

6. After the installation file is downloaded, double-click on it and follow the prompts in the installation window until the installation is complete.

The installation program automatically configures any Web browsers that you have installed on your system to use the plug-in so you don't have to install the plug-in more than once. You can view PDF documents in any of your installed browsers. Installing most other plug-ins is as simple as installing the Acrobat Reader.

Key Point Summary

In this chapter, you learned all about adding content saved in non-native file formats to your Web pages. Although you can easily link to or embed a non-native file in your Web page, there are a variety of issues associated with these kinds of files, including: how browsers handle non-native files, how these files affect the user experience, and the process of installing plug-ins to handle non-native file formats. They key points in the chapter are:

✦ Files that you want to disseminate over the Web fall into two categories: native and non-native. Native file formats such as HTML and JPEG are supported by the Web browser inherently. Non-native file formats such as Microsoft Word documents and PDF files require a plug-in or other application for display.

✦ Non-native files can either be displayed in the browser with a plug-in or in another application on your computer. If a browser doesn't recognize a file, it prompts users to download the file to their systems, so they can manually specify which application on their computer to use to open the file.

✦ The most common non-native file formats and their respective plug-ins are: PDF with Adobe Acrobat Reader, Macromedia Shockwave and Flash with plug-ins by the same name, and static and streaming media files with RealNetworks RealPlayer.

✦ When you link to downloadable files, or files you expect users to open with a plug-in, be sure to include the file size and type information with the file, as well as a link to the plug-in needed to view the file. If you expect users to download files to their computers and use another application to open the file, include the file type and size, as well as the application they need to view the file.

✦ Plug-ins can be installed online from a Web site or offline from a CD-ROM. Some plug-ins come preinstalled with a Web browser. Installing plug-ins is as simple as downloading the installer from the Web, or locating it on a CD, and following the installation prompts in the installer file.

✦ When you install a plug-in, it automatically configures itself to work with any browser you have installed on your system.

✦　　✦　　✦

STUDY GUIDE

This chapter included information on how browsers handle non-native file types, how you can link to non-native files. It also covered the most common plug-ins, the kind of files they support, and how to install plug-ins. In this study guide, you have the opportunity to apply the information you learned in this chapter via a collection of assessment questions, labs, and scenarios. Be sure to check the end of the study guide for solutions to the chapter pre-test questions, the assessment questions, and the scenarios.

Assessment Questions

1. Which of the following can you *not* view or play with the RealNetworks RealPlayer? (Choose the best answer.)

   A. Highly formatted and complex PDF documents

   B. Multimedia presentations written in XML

   C. Live concerts

   D. Live radio broadcasts

2. When a browser comes across a file that it doesn't have a plug-in for but whose file type it recognizes, what does it do?

   A. It trys to find a plug-in for the file.

   B. It prompts the user to save the file to their hard drive and then automatically opens the file for the user.

   C. It automatically launches the application the operating system has associated with the file.

   D. Nothing. The browser can only work with non-native files that it has plug-ins for.

3. Which plug-in is used to view PDF files?

   A. Macromedia Flash

   B. Adobe Acrobat Reader

   C. RealNetworks RealPlayer

   D. Macromedia Shockwave

4. When you link to a non-native file, what kind of information should you include for the user?

    A. The file type

    B. The file size

    C. A link to the plug-in or application that the user needs to view the file

    D. All of the above

5. Where do the installation files for an offline installation of a plug-in reside?

    A. On the vendor's Web site

    B. On a third-party Web site

    C. On a CD-ROM or other local media

    D. In the Web browser itself

6. Why were plug-ins developed?

    A. To help Web browsers display non-native file formats and to extend the range of content that developers could include on Web pages

    B. To give developers a new tool for creating Web content

    C. To allow developers to create multimedia files from within a Web browser

    D. To allow users to create files from within a Web page

Scenarios

You're building a Web site for your company's new product, and you want to include extensive documentation and interactive demonstrations. Which file formats would be best for each of these pieces of content, and what measures could you take to be sure that all visitors to your site could access important information?

Lab Exercises

Lab 12-1: Install the Macromedia Flash player

1. Point your Web browser at the Flash player download site at `www. macromedia.com/shockwave/download/index.cgi?P1_Prod_Version= ShockwaveFlash`.

2. Click on the Install Now button.

3. When the animation on the screen begins moving, the player is installed.

Answers to Chapter Questions

Chapter pre-test

1. When a browser comes across a non-native file type, it either displays it with a plug-in, launches another application on your computer to display the file, or prompts you to save the file to disk.

2. A PDF file holds complex or highly formatted documents, such as documentation and technical schematics, which aren't necessarily appropriate for conversion to native file formats. A Flash file is an interactive multimedia presentation.

3. Streaming media files begin to play before the entire file is downloaded, whereas static media files must be downloaded in their entirety before they can be played. To serve streaming media, you need special software, but static media can be served using standard HTTP protocols.

4. When you link to a non-native file, you should let the user know the file type, file size, and what plug-in or other application is necessary to view the file.

Assessment questions

1. **A.** Adobe Acrobat Reader is the plug-in that displays highly formatted and complex PDF documents. You can play live concerts, radio broadcasts, and XML-based multimedia presentations with RealNetworks RealPlayer. See "Common plug-ins and the files they support."

2. **C.** If a browser doesn't have a plug-in for a non-native file but knows which application on the user's system to use to view the file, the browser launches that application. A is incorrect because the browser doesn't attempt to locate another plug-in on the Internet. B is incorrect because the user doesn't have to save the file to disk first before the browser will launch the helper application. D is incorrect because the browser is able to work with non-native file types that it doesn't have a plug-in for. See "Common plug-ins and the files they support."

3. **B.** The Adobe Acrobat Reader is the plug-in you use to view PDF files. A is incorrect because Macromedia's Flash plug-in plays Flash presentations. C is incorrect because RealNetwork's RealPlayer plays audio and video presentations. D is incorrect because Macromedia's Shockwave plug-in plays Shockwave Director files that have been optimized for the Web. See "Common plug-ins and the files they support."

4. **D.** When you link to a non-native file you should include the file type, file size, and a link to the plug-in or application that supports the file. See "Linking to downloadable files."

5. C. Offline plug-in installation files are saved on a CD-ROM or other local media. A and B are incorrect because both describe online installation files available over the Internet. D is incorrect because it references a preinstalled plug-in. See "Downloading and Installing Plug-Ins."

6. A. Plug-ins were developed to help Web browsers support more kinds of content and for developers to utilize more kinds of content in site design. B, C, and D are incorrect because the plug-in itself isn't a development tool. See "Understanding Plug-Ins and Downloadable Files."

Scenarios

In this scenario, PDF files are probably your best bet for documentation, and Flash is a good format for online demonstrations. To make your information as accessible as possible, you might consider making your documentation available in both PDF and standard HTML versions so users without Acrobat or with text-only browsers can still access it. You might also think of creating a low-tech version of your demonstration using GIFs and HTML to give those without the Flash plug-in access to the basic functionality of the product.

For More Information

✦ **Acrobat information.** www.adobe.com/products/acrobat/main.html

✦ **Flash information.** www.macromedia.com/software/flash/

✦ **Shockwave information.** www.macromedia.com/software/flash/

✦ **RealPlayer information.** www.realplayer.com

✦ **Director vs. Flash tutorial at Webmonkey.** http://hotwired.lycos.com/webmonkey/99/27/index3a.html?tw=multimedia

✦ **Streaming Audio tutorial at Webmonkey.** http://hotwired.lycos.com/webmonkey/00/45/index3a.html?tw=multimedia

Using Web Site Development Tools

Microsoft FrontPage 2000

EXAM OBJECTIVES

- ✦ FrontPage navigation tools
- ✦ FrontPage standard elements
- ✦ FrontPage themes
- ✦ FrontPage advanced features

CHAPTER PRE-TEST

1. How does a FrontPage Web differ from "the Web"?

2. How do you import a Web site from the Web?

3. How do you tell FrontPage to use style sheets, instead of tables, to format your pages?

4. What are the advantages of using tables over style sheets to format your pages?

5. How do you select a theme?

6. What's the difference between a dynamic theme and a non-dynamic theme?

7. What must your Web server have to be able to accommodate FrontPage components?

8. What types of interaction does FrontPage permit with a database?

✦ Answers to these questions can be found at the end of the chapter. ✦

FrontPage 2000 is a powerful tool for creating and editing Web pages. It allows you to create and edit pages either using an interface similar to that of Microsoft Word (using buttons to create bold and italic text, as well as tables) or by directly editing the HTML. It's also loaded with features to create attractive, dynamic, and interactive Web sites using themes. In short, FrontPage 2000 is an excellent tool for creating dynamic Web pages.

Introduction to FrontPage 2000

FrontPage 2000 is an HTML editor that delivers almost immediate satisfaction. Almost anything you can imagine doing with a Web page can be done using FrontPage 2000. FrontPage 2000 relies on a point-and-click interface, and allows you to see what your pages look like as you're developing them. If you've never done anything with HTML, that's not a problem. You can use FrontPage 2000 without ever looking at what's behind the curtain. On the other hand, if you like to get your hands dirty and write your own code, you can do that as well.

FrontPage 2000 is rewarding software to use because you can use wizards to focus on just the content of the site. By using a wizard, the shell of a site can be created in just a few clicks. You can select a look and feel from the choices of themes, and then let FrontPage put the right buttons in the right places. Alternatively, you can create every graphic you need on your site yourself, and import them into FrontPage themes — either editing an existing one, or creating your own.

Whether you'd like to see animated graphics on your page (a lá PowerPoint), or whether you'd like butterflies to follow the visitor's mouse pointer when it moves around the page, FrontPage has the features to do this for you. Advanced features, including Dynamic HTML (DHTML), forms, reports, and other components can be added to permit a site to interact with a database.

FrontPage also understands that each Web site designer potentially has a different intended audience. Depending on the browsers you expect your visitors to have — perhaps you're working on an intranet on which everyone runs Internet Explorer 5, or you're developing a site for grade school teachers who'll be using Netscape 4 on a Mac — FrontPage can develop the same site for you using tables to force layout, using I-frames, or using Cascading Style Sheets (CSS). FrontPage is one Web development tool that has really thought of it all.

At any point during your Web creation, you can look at the bottom of the screen to see how long your page will take to load for a visitor coming to your site from a 28.8 Kbps connection (or at another connection speed, if you set it that way).

Finally, when you're ready to publish your site to the Web, you can use FrontPage's publishing features. If your Web server (or your Web hosting company's Web server) has FrontPage extensions installed, you can publish your site without requiring special File Transfer Protocol (FTP) software.

Exam Tip There's one important bit of FrontPage vocabulary that you need to master to fly through this exam. FrontPage refers to the files it creates related to a Web site — all the pages, the images, any tasks, any style sheets, and any scripts — as a *Web*. This can be very confusing if you don't know that a FrontPage Web is not the same thing as the World Wide Web. Before you can see your FrontPage Web on the World Wide Web, you have to publish it to your Web server.

WYSIWYG Editors vs. Text Editors

FrontPage is a WYSIWYG (pronounced WHIZ-ee-whig) editor, which means "what you see is what you get." FrontPage allows you to edit the page as it's going to look when it's published. The alternative to a WYSIWYG editor is a text editor. Supposedly, Web development purists prefer to code the HTML by hand in a text editor, but this method takes much longer.

In the early days of the Web, most Web developers used text editors, such as vi on UNIX, or Notepad or WordPad on Windows. The early WYSIWYG editors didn't let you both edit the page in WYSIWYG view, then see and modify the code. It was a strictly either/or proposition.

FrontPage opens in WYSIWYG mode, but text mode is only one click away.

There are a number of advantages to using a WYSIWYG Web editor:

✦ You can format text almost the same way you're used to doing in a word processor.

✦ Images are visible, so you can see exactly how much space they're going to take.

✦ There's no need to stage the page, or click over to a Web page and refresh.

✦ There shouldn't be any surprises when the page is published to a Web server.

There are also some advantages to using a text editor:

✦ You can reduce the size of the HTML file because there are no extraneous tags.

✦ You're not forced to include any extraneous attributes on the tags, such as height and width parameters on the `img` tag.

✦ If you know the visitors are coming from low-speed connections, you can keep the code as tight as possible to reduce download time.

Regardless of which way you prefer to work, FrontPage 2000 will accommodate it. Chances are, you'll appreciate the time saved by working in WYSIWYG mode, but you'll probably also want to have access to your HTML code to see how some of your page is implemented.

FrontPage Tools and Navigation

 FrontPage navigation tools

Just about everything you need to do to your Web site, from starting a page, to bolding text, to changing what links appear where, to selecting a theme, to adding interaction with a database, can be done from page view in normal mode, using menus and your mouse.

You interact with FrontPage in the following three ways (which are detailed in the subsequent sections):

✦ Menus

✦ Toolbars

✦ Views

Menus

Menus in FrontPage allow you to add most of the features you'll need in your site. The menus available in FrontPage appear at the top of the screen in this order:

✦ File

✦ Edit

✦ View

✦ Insert

✦ Format

✦ Tools

✦ Table

✦ Frames

✦ Window

✦ Help

 Tip   Note that you can customize the menu toolbar, so if you've done that, your toolbar may not have these same options. It may have other options such as Macros, New Menu, and more.

We discuss each of these in more detail in the following sections.

File menu

The File menu gives you most of the features you need to bring pages or entire sites into FrontPage. This menu also enables you to save them or publish them to a Web server. In all Office 2000 applications, the less frequently used items are low-lighted, and do not even show up in the list unless you either hold the menu open for more than a couple of seconds, or click on the double down-arrows that appear at the bottom of the brief list.

The file menu lets you do the following:

✦ Create new Web sites, Web pages, and tasks

✦ Open existing pages or Web sites in FrontPage, whether they come from a local file or the Web

✦ Save pages or Web sites you've been working on, either to your local file or to the Web (referred to as publishing)

✦ View and modify Web properties

✦ Print

The first four items in the preceding list are explained in detail in the following sections. Printing from FrontPage is the same as printing from Microsoft Word, so we won't belabor that here.

Creating Web sites, Web pages, and tasks

When you first enter FrontPage, chances are that the first thing you want to do is to create a new Web site.

To create a new Web, select File ➪ New ➪ Web.

When you select a Web site for a purpose, such as a corporate presence, FrontPage creates several things for you. First of all, FrontPage creates shell pages — typically, including a home page and any pages that are part of most sites of the type you selected.

FrontPage also creates a list of tasks that you'll probably want to accomplish before you complete the site. Finally, it creates a list of reports you'll want to run to make sure that both internal and external links all work, your images are all there, and there's no extra baggage in your Web (such as a theme you're not using).

In addition to creating a new Web, you can also use the File menu to add tasks to your list. To create a new task, select File ➪ New ➪ Task. Provide a task name, assign it to a person, indicate the priority, and provide a description in the appropriate box.

Opening Webs, pages, or Web sites

From the File menu, you can open existing Webs, Web pages, or even import entire Web sites from the Web. There are three ways to open an existing Web:

✦ Find the name of the Web on the Recent Webs list (File ➪ Recent Webs), and select it

✦ Click File ➪ Open Web to open a dialog box, find your Web on your local hard drive, and click Open

✦ Click the down-arrow next to the Open folder icon on the toolbar, select Open Web, select the Web you want to open from the dialog box, and click Open

There are also three ways to open a page:

✦ Select File ➪ Recent Pages, and click on the name of the page you want to open

✦ Click File ➪ Open to open a dialog box, find your page on your local hard drive, and click Open

✦ Click the Open folder icon on the toolbar to open a dialog box, find your page on your local hard drive, and click Open

If you already have a published Web site that you want to open in FrontPage, you can instruct FrontPage to pull it off the Web by following these steps:

1. Select File ➪ Import ➪ From Web. The Import Wizard appears.

2. On the first screen of the Import Wizard, indicate whether this site is on a local computer network or on the Web, and then provide either a path to the site or the URL of the Web site you want to import. If the site requires Secure Sockets Layer (SSL), check the appropriate box. Click Next.

3. On the second screen, shown in Figure 13-1, indicate:

   • Whether you want to limit the number of levels below the start page you want to download

   • If you want to limit the number of levels downloaded

   • Whether there's a limit to the amount of file space you want to download

   • If you want to limit the amount of file space, the number of megabytes (MB) you want to download

   • Whether to limit the download to text and images, or whether to download all media types associated with the site

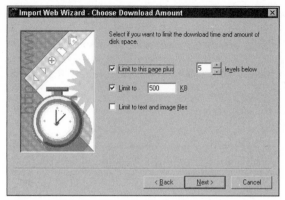

Figure 13-1: The second page of the Import Wizard is where you indicate how much of the Web site you want to import, by levels, by size, by media type, or by all of the above.

Saving pages and Webs locally or publishing to the Web

Each Web page is a separate .htm file. Additionally, each page is an integral part of a Web. Consequently, when you make changes in FrontPage, you need to save both the pages and the Web. By clicking File ➪ Save (or selecting Ctrl+S), you automatically save both. Alternatively, you can click on the diskette icon on the toolbar.

When you're ready to publish your site to the Web, you need to use the File ➪ Publish Web function. You must be connected to the Web or to your Web server for this to work. Additionally, the Web server to which you wish to publish your Web must have FrontPage extensions installed. If it does, FrontPage will ask you for your ID and password to publish on this server. If it does not, you'll be asked to provide a File Transfer Protocol (FTP) address with an ID and password for your Web server. You can indicate whether it should replace all files or only changed files. It will also query you as to whether it should remove files that are not used in the Web.

Tip   If you're developing with others who are not using FrontPage, be careful not to delete any files they may have uploaded that might be tied into the site, but not specifically linked to in your part of the site.

Viewing and modifying Web properties

By selecting File ➪ Properties, you can view and modify the properties of your Web. Almost everything you can modify in the properties dialog boxes, you can modify elsewhere in FrontPage. Depending on what you're looking at when you pull up the properties dialog box, you'll either see page properties, file properties, directory properties, or task properties.

Figure 13-2 shows the page properties dialog box for the GoodRepute Services page.

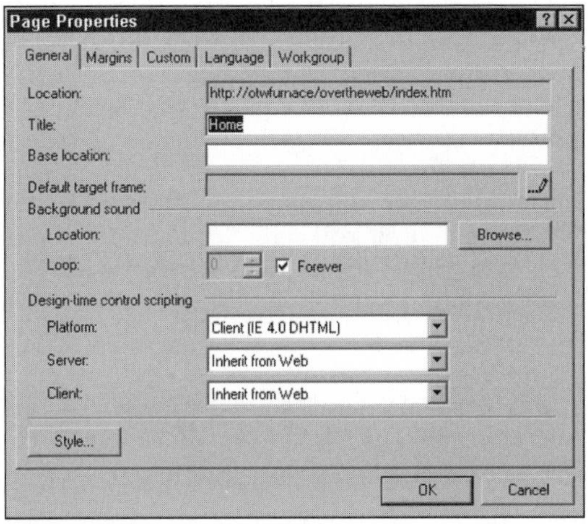

Figure 13-2: The General tab of the Page Properties dialog box allows you to edit properties relating to the page you've been editing, such as the page title and style sheets.

The General tab contains the following information:

✦ The physical location of the file, which cannot be edited.

✦ The title of the page, which is what will appear at the top of the browser window when the page is loaded in the browser by visitors; this can be edited.

✦ The base location, if you're using frames.

✦ The target frame name, if you're using frames.

✦ The location of the sounds file that plays upon loading the page, if you use one.

✦ The number of times the sound file plays (loops) or forever.

✦ The intended browser, which you can select from a list. This browser should be the minimum level browser that you would expect visitors to have. If you're developing for publishing on an intranet, you can probably say with certainty what the minimum browser level is; otherwise, you're relatively safe indicating version 4 browsers and above, since over 90% of Web visitors are running version 4 and above browsers.

✦ The intended server, which you can select from a list. If you don't know, select Other.

✦ The client, which will be dictated by your selection of intended browsers.

✦ A style button to add styles by hand into the style sheet for this page. If you're not comfortable typing style sheets by hand, click the Format button on the dialog box that opens when you click Style, and use the menu to select and format elements on the page, as you would with formatting styles in Microsoft Word.

The Margins tab of the Page Properties dialog box allows you to specify a top margin and a left margin for the page in pixels.

The Custom tab of the Page Properties dialog box allows you to add additional META tags to the head of your HTML document. If you want your site to be spidered and indexed by search engines, you can add robot and keywords META tags by clicking the Add button in the User variables section, and then specifying the tag names and the tag values.

If you need to change the language of the page you're creating, which actually dictates the HTTP-EQUIV values that are generated as part of the META tags, you can do that from the Language tab of the Page Properties dialog box.

If you're managing the Web with a team, you'll want to be able to assign a page to a person within a workgroup. You can edit the ownership of the file, as well as the status of the file, from the Workgroup tab of the Page Properties dialog box. You can also assign the page to categories, if you're managing assignments of pages in the Web based on categories. Finally, if you want a page to be excluded from publishing with the rest of the Web, click the checkbox to that effect at the bottom of the dialog box.

If you're looking at a file, rather than a page, and you click File ➪ Properties, you'll see a more restricted File Properties dialog box, which allows you to edit the page title from the General tab. You can also create or edit comments about the file from the Summary tab, which also shows when the file was created and by whom, and when it was last edited and by whom.

If you last clicked on the name of a folder (directory) in your Web, you'll see only a single General tab in the Directory Properties when you select File ➪ Properties. This dialog box allows you to indicate the permissions for that directory on the Web server. Your choices are: allow programs to be run, allow scripts to be run, and allow files to be browsed.

If you last clicked on a task when you select File ➪ Properties, you'll see the Task Details dialog box. This is the same dialog box you see when you create a new task using File ➪ New ➪ Task.

Edit menu

The Edit menu holds many of the same functions you'll find in the Microsoft Word Edit menu. The two areas of difference are Check-In/Check-Out and Task management. If you're working on a Web with a team, you can assign tasks and pages to individuals in a workgroup, from the Page Properties or File Properties dialog boxes as discussed previously. To prevent two or more people modifying a page at once, FrontPage allows you to check out a page to edit it, and then check it back in after you're done. Both of these tasks are accomplished from the Edit menu.

Additionally, tasks can be created, started, assigned, and marked as completed from the Task item on the Edit menu. Also, if you wish to see the history of the task, you can do that by highlighting the task, and selecting Edit ➪ Task ➪ Show History. When you choose to start a task, FrontPage automatically takes you to the correct page in Page view, and positions the cursor at the start of that page.

View menu

The View menu gives you menu access to the views that appear down the left side of the screen when you start FrontPage for the first time. If you want to use all the screen real estate for your page, you can disable the views on the left by unchecking the Views Bar from the View menu. You can also enable and disable the Folders List from the View menu. The six views that FrontPage offers are shown at the top of the View menu. They are:

✦ Page

✦ Folders

✦ Reports

✦ Navigation

✦ Hyperlinks

✦ Tasks

By selecting View ➪ Reports, you can see a list of all the reports available to you. Each of these views is discussed in detail in the later section on views.

The View menu also allows you to reveal tags, which is useful for seeing, while you're in Normal mode, where a tag begins and ends. If, when you choose to preview your page, the page isn't appearing as you expect it to, click View ➪ Reveal Tags to see whether your text is actually within the tag you think it ought to be in. When you enable Reveal Tags, you don't lose the WYSIWYG effects, but you do see yellow hexagons indicating where each tag begins and ends. Reveal Tags is an excellent diagnostic tool.

The View menu also gives you the ability to turn on or off the various toolbars. By selecting View ➪ Toolbars, you can see the many toolbars that FrontPage offers, and decide which to enable and which to disable.

Tip Be careful not to enable so many toolbars that your work space is compromised.

Insert menu

The Insert menu has many commands, which enable you to add many enhancements to your page and your Web, such as:

✦ **Break.** Inserting a break forces a line break (or soft return). If you're listing contact info, for example, you probably don't want each line to be its own paragraph. Use line breaks, instead, to create separate lines, without the white space between lines that results between paragraphs (hard returns).

✦ **Horizontal Line.** A horizontal line can be either a straight line or a graphic defined in the theme.

✦ **Date and Time.** Insert either the date and time of last edit or the date and time of last automatic modification.

✦ **Symbol.** Insert a symbol from the special characters permitted in HTML. Some symbols you might need include copyright (©) and registered (®).

✦ **Comment.** Comments allow you to document your page. Comments only appear to those viewing the source. If you want to leave instructions for someone who will be editing this page at a later date, use comments.

✦ **Navigation Bar.** You can insert a navigation bar anywhere on the page using Insert ⇨ Navigation Bar.

Tip   Your page will have better results with search engines if the first thing the search engine encounters on the page is not a navigation bar.

✦ **Page Banner.** Every page in a Web automatically has a page banner. If you're importing a page from outside the Web, you might need to insert a page banner to have the page conform with the rest of the Web. When you insert a page banner, you can indicate whether to include a picture or just text, and what the name of the page will be in the banner.

✦ **Component.** There are a number of FrontPage components you can insert. They are discussed in detail later in this chapter in the "Components" section.

✦ **Database.** If you have an Access database, you can instruct FrontPage to save form data to the database and read data from the database. Interacting with a database is discussed in detail later in this chapter in the "Reports" section.

✦ **Form.** Most developers want to collect some type of information from their Web site visitors, even if it's only a feedback form or a visitor guest book. If you even want visitors to be able to search your site, you'll have to provide a search form. These are discussed later in this chapter in the "Forms" section.

✦ **Advanced.** If you want to insert a Java applet, an ActiveX control, or a plug-in, you can do it by selecting Insert ⇨ Advanced, and then selecting the appropriate advanced feature you want to insert. You have to be able to direct FrontPage to the applet, ActiveX control, or plug-in. You also have to be able to instruct FrontPage as to what the parameters are for this advanced feature.

✦ **Picture.** To insert a picture into your Web, select Insert ➪ Picture, and then indicate where the picture is coming from. If you have a number of images you want to include in your site, you should probably copy them into the images folder of your Web, so they'll be there when you need to insert them. You can also include clip art.

✦ **File.** If you want to include a legal contract or terms and conditions, which have been created for you on your site, you can simply click Insert ➪ File to have the file opened, inserted, and formatted, directly into your page.

✦ **Bookmark.** Bookmark is FrontPage's terminology for Anchor Name (A Name). If you expect to want to link either from the top of a long page to a particular place in this page or from another page directly into the middle of this page, set a bookmark at that point so you can link deep into a page.

✦ **Hyperlink.** When you need to insert a hyperlink to another page or to a bookmark on this or another page, select Insert ➪ Hyperlink (or select Ctrl+K) and specify where you want to link. You can also hyperlink to a mail address from this dialog box.

Format menu

The Format menu gives you access to many of the formatting functions of FrontPage. The first four items on the Format menu resemble those found in the Format menu of Microsoft Word. They are Font, Paragraph, Bullets and Numbering, and Borders and Shading. The dialog boxes for these functions will also be familiar to Word users. The other formatting options require additional explanation, and they are:

✦ **Position.** If you're trying to position an element, such as a graphic so text wraps around it, select Format ➪ Position. The Position dialog box shown in Figure 13-3 appears. Within this box, you can specify the wrapping style, the positioning style, and the location and size for absolute and relative positioning. Finally, if you're developing for delivery primarily on Netscape Navigator, you can specify the Z-Order, which is the layer on the page (the third dimension) in which you want the graphic to appear. This is particularly useful if you're layering a sheer graphic over or under text. You can also position a paragraph or a table using this feature. The visitor's browser must have the ability to handle style sheets for this to work properly.

✦ **Dynamic HTML Effects.** When you select Dynamic HTML Effects from the Format menu, the Dynamic HTML effects toolbar appears. This toolbar is discussed in detail later in this chapter in the "Adding DHTML" section.

✦ **Style.** You can modify the style associated with any element by selecting Format ➪ Style. This feature is discussed in detail later in this chapter in the "Adding HTML Elements to a Page" section.

✦ **Style Sheet Links.** If you have a style sheet that defines styles for the entire Web or for an individual page, you can link to a style sheet from Insert ➪ Style Sheet Links. The style sheet file should have a .css extension.

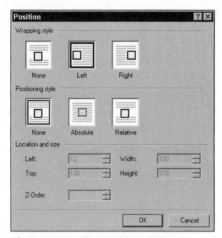

Figure 13-3: The Position dialog box
permits you to specify how an object
such as an image will be treated on
the page relative to text.

✦ **Theme.** A theme defines the look and feel of an entire Web or of pages within
a Web. Themes are one of the most powerful features of FrontPage. This feature is explained in detail later in this chapter in the "Themes" section.

✦ **Shared Borders.** Shared borders allow you to maintain certain functions, such
as navigation tools, and logos in the same place on every page, while only
having to create them once. Also, if you modify a shared border, your changes
will affect every page in the Web that shares this border. Figure 13-4 shows the
Shared Borders dialog box. Notice that FrontPage allows you to include navigation buttons only on the top and on the right. If you want navigation buttons on the left, you need to insert them using Insert ➪ Navigation Bar in the
right or bottom shared border.

✦ **Page Transition.** If you want the page to load or unload with a special effect,
such as vertical blinds, select the event and the effect in the Page Transitions
dialog box. You can also specify how many seconds over which you want the
page to load or unload.

✦ **Background.** If you're not using a theme, you can specify the background
image you want your page to use from the Background tab of the Page
Properties dialog box. If there's an image you want to use, you can select it
here. If you simply want the background to be a solid color, you can also specify that here. Finally, you can also tell FrontPage to get a background image
from another page. This is also where you can indicate the color of text hyperlinks, visited text hyperlinks, and active text hyperlinks, if you're not using
themes.

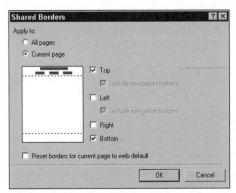

Figure 13-4: The Shared Borders dialog box permits you to specify where you want shared borders to appear.

✦ **Remove Formatting.** Sometimes it's just easier to remove all formatting from your site (particularly if you're trying to revamp it) than it is to modify the properties of each element on each page, one at a time. If you've imported your site from the Web and want to give it a facelift with a theme, remove all the formatting first, using Format ➪ Remove Formatting.

✦ **Properties.** This item, which has the Alt+Enter hotkey combination associated with it, is possibly the most valuable feature of FrontPage. Rather than clicking around to see what you can do to change the formatting or behavior of an element, always open its properties first to see how it's defined. The properties dialog box that opens depends on which item you have selected when you click Format ➪ Properties or Alt+Enter.

Tools menu

The Tools menu gives you access to several tools that will help you build a more professional Web, such as:

✦ **Spelling.** Spell check your Web by clicking Tools ➪ Spelling or pressing F7.

✦ **Thesaurus.** Find a synonym for a word by clicking Tools ➪ Thesaurus or pressing Shift+F7.

✦ **Recalculate Hyperlinks.** If you reorganize your files, or have made changes to file names, make sure everything works by selecting Tools ➪ Recalculate Hyperlinks.

✦ **Security.** The security menu allows you to create users and workgroups. To assign pages or tasks to people, you have to use Tools ➪ Security ➪ Permissions first to open the Permissions dialog box. Before you can assign permissions to individuals, you must indicate on the Settings tab of the

Permissions dialog box that you want to Use Unique Permissions for this Web, and then click Apply. Using either the Groups tab or the Users tab you can add and edit users or change the permissions of groups. Users must already be defined in your network for you to assign them permissions.

✦ **Macros.** You can define macros to automate tasks within FrontPage. Your macros can be written in Microsoft Macro language or VBScript.

✦ **Add-Ins.** You can add in COM objects via the Add-In dialog box.

✦ **Customize.** To customize the interface, select Tools ⇨ Customize, and then make changes to the toolbars or hotkey definitions.

✦ **Web Settings.** Most of the values you provided when you completed the New Web Wizard are stored in and modifiable from the Web Settings dialog box. You can also define databases in the Web Settings dialog box. Interaction with databases is explained in detail later in this chapter in the "Reports" section.

✦ **Options.** From the Options dialog box, you can configure editors to open and edit file types that FrontPage doesn't have the built-in ability to edit, such as images and sound files.

✦ **Page Options.** FrontPage can build the same Web a number of ways, depending on what you specify the target browser to be. You can define the target browser, as well as the Web server type, from the Compatibility tab of the Page Options dialog box. You can set many other options from the six tabs in this dialog box.

Table menu

The Table menu makes creating tables for the Web every bit as easy as it is to create tables in Microsoft Word. You can draw a table on the page, or select Table ⇨ Insert ⇨ Table. In FrontPage, it's easy to create nested tables, which can be necessary to achieve optimal formatting on older browsers.

Frames menu

The Frames menu gives you the ability to work with framed sites. A site with frames actually opens multiple HTML files, one in each frame. Make sure the text that visitors who come from non-frames-capable browsers can see is friendly, because this is the text that search engines typically pick up to use for your search engine listing.

Window menu

It's common to have multiple pages open at one time while you're working on your site. To go from one open page to another, select the page you want to be editing from the Window Menu. You won't lose your work on the other open pages.

Toolbars

Toolbars (such as the Navigation toolbar, Reporting toolbar, the Positioning toolbar, and the DHTML Effects toolbar) save you time by putting icons for the actions you want to take most frequently right in front of you. Toolbars can be invisible or visible. If visible, the toolbars can be docked at the top, bottom, left, or right sides of the page. They can also float.

To dock a toolbar, simply drag it to the perimeter where you want to dock it. To undock a toolbar, simply click on the handle bar at the left or top of it, and drag it where you want it to go. Figure 13-5 shows FrontPage with the DHTML Effects toolbar floating.

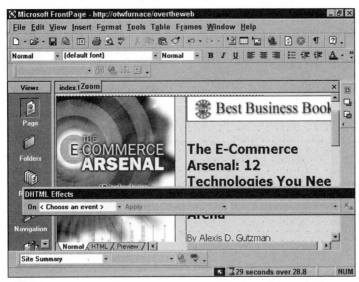

Figure 13-5: FrontPage with the DHTML Effects toolbar floating

The nine toolbars included in FrontPage 2000 are:

✦ **Standard.** The Standard toolbar includes many of the same icons you see in Microsoft Word and is one you probably don't want to close. Figure 13-6 shows the Standard toolbar. This toolbar gives you one-click access to opening, printing, and saving files, performing spell check, previewing a page in a browser, and a number of other useful actions. FrontPage also has the Format Painter icon, which you may recognize from Word or Excel. It's a powerful way of transferring formatting from one element to another. Just position your cursor on the item that has the formatting you want to share. Click on the Format Painter icon, and then highlight the element you want to format like the first element.

Figure 13-6: The Standard toolbar

✦ **Formatting.** The Formatting toolbar lets you select the style, font, size, appearance, and justification of text. It also gives you one-click access to aligning paragraphs, inserting bullets and numbering, and changing the text color.

✦ **DHTML Effects.** The DHTML Effects are a powerful feature of FrontPage. Using the toolbar, you can specify how and when you want an effect applied to text or a graphic. You can then preview the effect in Preview mode. Creating DHTML effects is discussed in detail later in this chapter in the "Adding DHTML" section.

✦ **Navigation.** The Navigation toolbar is only active when you're working in Navigation view. Using the toolbar, you can zoom into and out of a site layout, switch the relationships to horizontal or vertical, and perform other tasks associated with Navigation view.

✦ **Pictures.** The Pictures toolbar is convenient when you're inserting or editing an image to be included in your Web.

✦ **Positioning.** The Positioning toolbar allows you to modify the style of images, tables, paragraphs, or headings so text wraps around them.

✦ **Reporting.** The Reporting toolbar is only active when you're in Reports view.

✦ **Styles.** The Style toolbar gives you one-click access to the Style dialog box.

✦ **Tables.** The Tables toolbar allows you to perform most actions on a table with a single click.

Tip   All toolbars can be customized either by selecting View ➪ Toolbars ➪ Customize or by selecting Tools ➪ Customize. In either case, you see the Customize dialog box. By dragging an icon off the Commands tab on top of the toolbar you want to customize, you can add icons to toolbars.

Views

FrontPage offers six views. When the Views Bar is selected on the View menu, which it is by default, you see the views on the left side of the screen. The views allow you to navigate easily between the views. If you need the screen space, disable the Views Bar, and select the view you need from the View menu.

The six views are:

✦ **Page.** This is the view in which you'll spend most of your time. In Page view you can:

- Modify a page in WYSIWYG mode, which FrontPage calls Normal mode.

- You can also view and modify the HTML directly in HTML mode.

- You can preview the page and see how it will look in a browser in Preview mode. By clicking on the Preview in Browser icon, you can see how your page will look in whatever browser you have configured as your computer's default browser; however, you cannot edit in Preview mode.

- In Normal mode in Page view, the page doesn't look exactly as it does in Preview mode. Shared borders are delimited in Normal mode, so you know where the proprietary part of the page ends and where the shared part begins. Also, any element that's subject to a DHTML effect might be in a shaded box (this is something you can specify when you define DHTML effects).

- There's also a folder list displayed in Page view. You can turn the folder list on or off, depending on how much screen space you need to work on your page. You turn on display of the folder list by selecting View ➪ Folder List.

✦ **Folders.** This view is deceptive because you actually see files, as well as the folders. In Folders view you see the file or folder name, the page title, the file size, the file type, the last modified date, and who modified it last.

✦ **Reports.** This view shows the results of whatever report you've chosen to run. The default report that loads is the Site Summary report. From the Reporting toolbar you can select the report you want to see. When applicable, the second select list in the Reporting toolbar shows criteria for the report. For example, if you select Slow Pages from the Reporting toolbar, the second select list permits you to select the download time that you define as slow.

✦ **Navigation.** This view shows the site as a hierarchical structure, with the home page either at the top or on the right. Navigation view is very useful for seeing how deep your site is and where pages should and do link to other pages. A page isn't in your Web until you drag the file from the folder list to the Navigation view. You can also rearrange pages within your Web by dragging them from one place to another. If your site is getting too wide, switch from a vertical layout to a horizontal one, or adjust the zoom. Both of these can be accomplished from the Navigation toolbar. Figure 13-7 shows the Navigation view.

✦ **Hyperlinks.** If you want to see what links to a particular page, select that page, and then click on Hyperlinks view from the Views bar. Figure 13-8 shows the Hyperlinks view for a page that's a child to the home page. Notice that there's a JavaScript file that also links to this page. That file was created by FrontPage when a DHTML effect was added to this page.

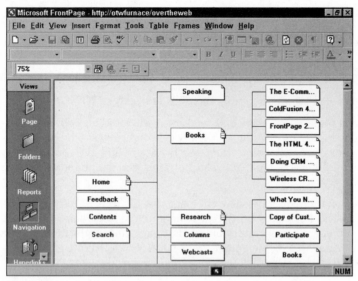

Figure 13-7: Navigation view lets you see how the pages in your Web link to each other.

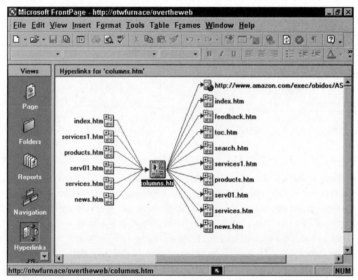

Figure 13-8: Hyperlinks view shows you what pages link to and from a selected page.

✦ **Tasks.** This view shows you any tasks that have not been completed. It shows the status, the task name, the person assigned to perform the task, the priority, the file it's associated with, the last date the task was modified, and a description. There are three ways to add a task:

- Right mouse click in Task view, below the listed tasks, and select New Task

- Select File ➪ New ➪ Task

- Select Edit ➪ Task ➪ Add Task

Creating and Managing Webs and Web Pages

The first part of this chapter explained what each of the menus, toolbars, and views do. In this and the following section of the chapter, you put that knowledge to work to create and manage Webs and Web pages.

Every Web site is unique, but Web sites can be divided into only a handful of different types. Rather than beginning a site with a single page, and growing it from there, it makes much more sense to let FrontPage generate all the pages it thinks you'll need in your site. FrontPage offers both Webs and wizards that create Webs for different types of sites. It's both fast and rewarding to take advantage of FrontPage's ability to generate the shell of your new site.

Creating a new Web

If the Web you need to create is a one-page Web, a personal Web, a customer support Web, or a project Web, it makes sense to let FrontPage generate the pages it thinks you need. You can then add pages, rename the pages it generates, and add content to every page. Although skipping the design phase of a Web project is never a good idea, FrontPage can save you many hours by creating the shells of the pages you're ultimately going to need.

To create a new Web without using a wizard, follow these steps:

1. Select File ➪ New ➪ Web.

2. Select the Web you want to create from the following choices: One-page Web, Customer Support Web, Empty Web, Personal Web, and Project Web.

3. Specify the location of the new Web. The name you give the final folder for your Web is really the name of the Web, so choose carefully.

4. If you want to make this Web a sub-Web of your current Web, check the box next to Add to Current Web.

5. If you're going to implement a secure connection for this Web using Secure Sockets Layer (SSL), check the box next to Secure Connection Required (SSL).

6. Click OK.

After you've clicked OK, it may take a couple of minutes for FrontPage to generate all the components of the Web. When it's done, you'll be looking at a shell of a new page that you can add to your Web. Before you do that, click on Navigation view to see all the pages in your Web and the hierarchy. Then, double-click on a page to begin editing that page in Page view.

If your new Web is either a corporate presence Web or a discussion Web, you can take advantage of FrontPage's wizards to create a highly customized Web.

To use a wizard to create a Web, follow these steps:

1. Select File ⇨ New ⇨ Web.

2. Select the wizard you want to use: Corporate Presence or Discussion Web.

3. Specify the location of the new Web.

Tip

As mentioned earlier, the folder name you choose will be how the Web is identified from here on out, so choose wisely. The default of MyWeb (or MyWeb1) is not very helpful later.

4. If you want to make this Web a sub-Web of your current Web, check the box next to Add to Current Web.

5. If you're going to implement a secure connection for this Web (using SSL), check the box next to Secure Connection Required (SSL).

6. Click OK.

7. You'll see a dialog box for the wizard you've chosen. Click Next to begin the wizard. At this point, the name you gave the Web has already been created in your file system.

8. Complete each screen of the wizard, selecting or deselecting the checkboxes next to the features you want or don't want. Depending on which wizard you select, you'll see different screens with different options.

9. Eventually you'll come to a screen that asks you to choose the Web theme. Click Choose Web Theme.

10. Select the theme you want from the Choose Theme dialog box. If you want to use vivid colors, active graphics, a background picture, or apply the theme using CSS, check those boxes in the lower left. When you're satisfied, click OK.

11. If you selected the Discussion Web, you have one more choice to make. Otherwise, you're almost done.

12. Click Finish to generate the custom Web created from your responses to the wizard. Wait patiently as FrontPage generates the pages.

Importing a Web

If you already have a Web, but you developed it using something other than FrontPage, you need to import it into FrontPage. You can do so using the FrontPage Import Wizard.

The instructions for using the Import Wizard appear back in the "Opening Webs, pages, or Web sites" section.

Adding a new page to an existing Web requires that you create a new page and that you link that page into your Web.

To add new pages to an existing Web:

1. Make sure your Web is open.

2. Select File ➪ New ➪ Page.

3. Select the page you want to add from the New Page dialog box. Note that in addition to the 26 choices on the General tab, there are also frames pages to choose from (via the Frames Page tab).

4. Select File ➪ Save As to save your page.

5. Provide a name and click Save.

6. Click on Navigation view (or select View ➪ Navigation).

7. Drag your new file from the folders list to the Navigation view and drop it where you want it to fall in the hierarchy.

Managing Webs and Web pages

A Web is old almost from the moment it's been published. After you've published your Web, you need to create a plan to keep the Web up-to-date. FrontPage's Task features (explained in detail earlier in this chapter) can help you stay on top of what needs to be done to keep your Web up-to-date.

If you find a folder that should be hidden because you don't need to access it from within FrontPage, name that folder something beginning with an underscore (_). FrontPage will work with that folder but hides it from view.

When it's time to publish your Web, FrontPage will upload your files using the Hypertext Transfer Protocol (HTTP), if the Web server has the FrontPage extensions running, or using FTP if it does not. Additionally, when you publish, you can indicate whether to upload every page or only those that have changed. If you don't know whether your Web server has FrontPage extensions installed, try to publish. If it does not, FrontPage will come back with a message asking you to provide an FTP address to upload the Web.

Adding HTML Elements to a Page

 FrontPage standard elements

Now that you have the shell of the Web and the shell of each page created, you can use the powerful tools in FrontPage to add essential elements to your pages. This section shows you how to modify page properties, add images, image maps, text, hyperlinks, tables, frames, forms, and style sheets.

Page properties

Page properties dictate what the all-important META tags will be that search engines use to index your site. From the Page Properties dialog box, you can indicate what the background color or image will be if you choose not to use themes. Finally, they dictate what the title of the page will be when it's loaded in a browser.

 For a complete discussion of page properties, please see the section titled "Viewing and modifying Web properties."

Images

No Web is complete without images. Inserting an image is a simple task in FrontPage. You simply:

1. Position the cursor where you want the image to appear.

2. Select Insert ➪ Picture ➪ From File. If you want to use clip art, select Clip Art instead of From File.

3. Find the image you want to insert either on a local drive or on the Web.

4. Click OK.

 Make sure you have permission to use an image if you're taking it from the Web. Just because you can copy an image off the Web doesn't mean you have a right to use it on your own site.

The image you've selected should appear where you had positioned your cursor. You can modify the image by revealing the Pictures toolbar and working with the picture editing functions — such as rotating the image, and changing the brightness and contrast. If you want to change the positioning of text relative to the image, select Format ➪ Position and indicate where on the page you want the image to appear and how you want text to behave with respect to that image.

Image maps

Image maps are powerful navigational tools. An *image map* is an image with multiple hyperlinks embedded in it. To create an image map, follow these steps:

1. Insert the image that will become the image map using the instructions in the previous section.

2. Turn on the Pictures toolbar by selecting View ⇨ Toolbars ⇨ Pictures.

3. Select the shape of hotspot you want to draw on top of the image from the Pictures toolbar. Figure 13-9 shows the hotspot icons on the Pictures toolbar.

 Figure 13-9: The hotspot icons are on the Pictures toolbar.

4. Draw the shape on top of the image where you want the first hyperlinked area to be. When you release the mouse button, a Create Hyperlink dialog box will open.

5. Select the page from this Web or the page on the Web you want this area to link to. If you want this hyperlink to send e-mail, click on the E-Mail icon and enter the e-mail address of the recipient. Click OK.

6. Repeat steps 3 through 5 for each hotlink in your image map.

FrontPage embeds the image map information directly into the Web page on which the image map appears.

Text

Inserting text into FrontPage is relatively straightforward. Just be careful not to try to insert a paragraph into another structure. For example, FrontPage uses definition lists. Most Web developers are only slightly familiar with the definition tags (DL, DT, and DD). FrontPage uses them to create unnumbered lists, such as a list of products. If you try to insert a paragraph of text within a definition list (DL), it will inherit the formatting of the previous item. To see whether you're typing text into an existing element, turn on Reveal Tags by selecting View ⇨ Reveal Tags, or pressing Ctrl+/ (forward slash). Figure 13-10 shows the shell page created by FrontPage in the Corporate Presence Wizard with tags revealed. The yellow hexagons tell you how each element on the page is defined.

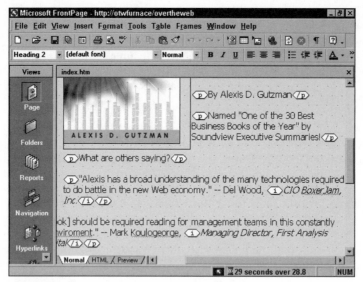

Figure 13-10: A page with Reveal Tags turned on

After you enter text, you can format it however you want, using bold, italics, font sizes, font colors, and paragraph formatting. However, rather than formatting text as you might in a Word document, consider applying a style to it. This will help ensure consistency within your page. To apply a style, follow these steps:

1. Enter the text where you want it to appear.

2. Highlight the text.

3. Select a style from the list of styles in the Style drop-down list on the Formatting toolbar.

If you don't see the style you want, create one. In theory, editing FrontPage's style features mirror CSS; in practice, however, FrontPage doesn't want you to create classes (styles) for elements, but simply wants you to create classes that can be applied to any element. To create a new class, follow these steps:

1. Click Format ➪ Style and click the New button.

2. Enter a name for the new style.

3. Click Format, and then select the attribute or attributes you want to modify for that element: Font, Paragraph, Border, Numbering, or Position. You can select more than one, but you have to select them one at a time.

4. Make all the necessary changes and then click OK.

Now that you've defined a style, that style appears in the User-Defined Styles list. The text on the right side of the Style dialog box shows the effect of using this style.

If you want to use a style in a later paragraph on the same page, highlight the text you want to format and then select the style from the Style select list. This style will not be available from another page. If you want to define a style to be accessible from all pages, you must edit the external style sheet to define the style there.

To change the style for the entire Web, you have to find the .css file linked to the Web, or create one if there isn't one, and edit that using either FrontPage or a style sheet editor such as TopStyle.

Links

A Web without links is just a page. There are four kinds of links you might want to create:

- ✦ External links to Web pages
- ✦ Links to e-mail
- ✦ Internal page links
- ✦ Internal bookmark (named) links

External links to Web pages

Frequently you'll want to link to other pages on the Web. To create an external link to a Web page:

1. Highlight the text or image you want to be the link.
2. Select Insert ⇨ Hyperlink (or press Ctrl+K). The Create Hyperlink dialog box opens.
3. Surf to the destination of the link.
4. Select Alt+Tab to return to FrontPage, or click on the FrontPage process running in your task bar on the bottom of your screen.
5. Click OK.

Links to e-mail

Sometimes you want visitors to be able to click on a link and have their e-mail software open automatically to send a message to someone related to the Web site. To accomplish this:

1. Highlight the text or image you want to be the link.
2. Select Insert ⇨ Hyperlink (or press Ctrl+K). The Create Hyperlink dialog box will open.
3. Click on the Make a Hyperlink that Sends E-Mail icon in the Create Hyperlink dialog box.
4. Enter the e-mail address of the recipient.

5. Click OK to close the Create E-mail Hyperlink dialog box.

6. Click OK to close the Create Hyperlink dialog box.

Internal page links

If you need to link to another page that is part of your Web, you can link to it by doing the following:

1. Highlight the text or image you want to be the link.

2. Select Insert ➪ Hyperlink (Ctrl+K). The Create Hyperlink dialog box opens.

3. Click on the Make a Hyperlink to a File on Your Computer icon in the Create Hyperlink dialog box.

4. Browse your local drive to find the destination page.

5. Click OK to close the Select File dialog box.

6. Click OK to close the Create Hyperlink dialog box.

Internal bookmark (named) links

If you have a particularly long page, it might be useful to put a table of headings at the top of the page, then link each heading to the part of the page where the heading is located. You often see this with FAQ, which will have a list of questions at the top of the page, then each question and answer further down the page. To get to the question and answer, you click on the question. To create a link to an internal bookmark:

1. Position your cursor at the place on the page you want to link to, and select Insert ➪ Bookmark.

2. Enter a name for your bookmark on this page. Make sure you use a name you'll easily recognize later. Click OK.

3. Highlight the text you want to be the hyperlink on the page from which you'll link.

4. Select Insert ➪ Hyperlink (Ctrl+K). The Create Hyperlink dialog box opens.

5. Click on the Make a Hyperlink to a File on Your Computer icon in the Create Hyperlink dialog box.

6. Browse your Web (or local drive or the Web, as instructed previously) to find the destination page.

7. Select the bookmark from the Bookmark select list.

8. Click OK to close the Create Hyperlink dialog box.

Tables

There are two reasons to use tables in your Web site. If you know your site will not format properly in visitors' browsers because you're using CSS, using tables makes sense. However, before you commit to using tables, realize that there are some disadvantages to using tables:

✦ Tables make the content of a page less accessible to the visually impaired. The W3C's Web Accessibility Initiative (WAI) recommends that tables only be used to format tabular data, not to format pages. Web pages formatted with tables are less readable by text-synthesizing browsers, than Web pages formatted by CSS.

✦ Table-formatted pages load slower than CSS-formatted pages.

✦ Table-formatted pages are less easily indexed by search engines.

✦ Tabbing around a table-formatted page is usually unintuitive. Because more people are accessing Web pages from wireless devices, the ability to tab around a page (or otherwise access a page without a mouse) is increasingly important.

Even with all those constraints in mind, most people are still formatting their pages with tables. There are three ways to insert a table into your page: drawing the table, clicking the Insert Table icon, or using the Insert Table dialog box. All three produce the same HTML code. Which one you use is a personal preference.

To insert a table by drawing it:

1. Select Table ➪ Draw Table. In addition to converting your mouse to a pencil, it will make the Tables toolbar visible.

2. Draw the table on your page. You cannot enclose already inserted text or images in your page. If you've already inserted the text or images into the page, you have to cut and paste them or highlight and drag them into the table.

3. To erase a line, click on the Eraser icon on the Tables toolbar, and drag the eraser over the line you wish to erase.

4. To format the table or any cell or cells in the table, highlight what you want to format, and select Format ➪ Borders and Shading.

5. Select the borders you want applied from the Borders tab and the shading you want applied from the Shading tab. If you want to include a background image inside a cell, you can select the image from the bottom of the Shading tab.

6. Click OK to save your formatting.

To insert a table from the Insert Table dialog box:

1. Position your cursor where you want the table to be inserted.

2. Select Table ⇨ Insert ⇨ Table to open the Insert Table dialog box shown in Figure 13-11.

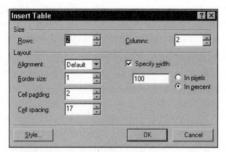

Figure 13-11: Inserting a table using the Insert Table dialog box

3. At a minimum, you must indicate the size of the table in rows and columns. The default is two rows and two columns.

4. You can also specify layout attributes such as:

- **Alignment of the table.** The table can be centered on the page, right justified, or left justified.

- **Width of the table.** You can set the width either as a percentage of the page or as a fixed size in pixels

- **Border size.** Increase this number to display a wider border.

- **Cell padding.** Increase this number to widen the borders of the cells. This must be set at the table level, even though it appears to be a property of cells.

- **Cell spacing.** Set the cell spacing higher if you want more space between the text or image in your cell and the inside border of the cells.

5. Click OK.

Tip

If you want to modify the table to any greater degree, such as defining a background image or color, border colors, or just about anything else, you need to create a new class for the table by clicking on the Style button and going into the Create Style dialog box and creating a new style as discussed in the "Text" section earlier.

To insert a table from the Insert Table icon:

1. Position the cursor where you want to insert the table.

2. Click the Insert Table icon on the Standard toolbar and hold it. It will expand to show a grid of cells.

3. Drag your mouse down and across until you've highlighted the number of cells you want your table to include. It will inherit the properties of the previously defined table on that page unless you specify otherwise by editing the table properties.

4. To edit the table properties, highlight the entire table then select Format ⇨ Properties (or press Alt+Enter). You'll see a Table Properties dialog box similar to the one shown in Figure 13-11. It has a few more properties that you can edit directly (without defining a style), such as border color, height, float, and background color or image.

Frames

The easiest way to use frames in FrontPage is to create a new page (or new Web) that's based on frames. A frame page with, for example, three frames actually represents four separate files: the frames page itself, which contains the definition of the framed page, and links to the pages that will populate each of the frames, and a NOFRAMES section, which dictates what will be seen by people who visit the page from non-frames-capable browsers (often including search engines). The contents of each of the three frames are held in separate pages. To create a frames page:

1. Select File ⇨ New ⇨ Page. You will see the New Page dialog box.

2. Select the Frames Pages tab. Note that the layout you're selecting is previewed on the right of the dialog box.

3. Click OK.

4. For each frame in the framed site, you need to either set the initial page by pointing to an existing page or instruct FrontPage to create a new page to populate that frame. To set the initial page as a page you've already created, click Set Initial Page.

5. You'll see the Edit Hyperlink dialog box. Select the page you want to use as the contents of that frame.

6. If you don't have a page that will provide content for that frame, select New Page to instruct FrontPage to create a new page to provide the content of that frame.

7. Repeat steps 4 through 6 for each additional frame in the site.

8. Create the page that will be seen by anyone who is coming to your site from a non-frame-capable browser. This includes most search engines. Make sure whatever keywords you hope to be indexed by search engines appear with frequency in the No Frames page. Click on the No Frames tab to enter Normal view for the no frames page.

Forms

Forms allow you to collect information from Web site visitors. That information can be stored on a file on the Web server, written to a database, or sent via e-mail. When you need to insert a page with a form, the quickest way will be to begin with the Form Wizard. To create a form page with the Form Page Wizard:

1. Select File ➪ New ➪ Page.

2. Select the Form Page Wizard.

3. Click OK.

4. You'll see the first page of the Form Page Wizard. Read it and click Next.

5. Click Add to collect a new category of information. Of course, initially there will be nothing on the list.

6. Select the type of information you want to collect from the list on top.

7. Phrase the question as you want it to appear in the bottom half of the dialog box. Figure 13-12 shows the dialog box for selecting the category of information and the question.

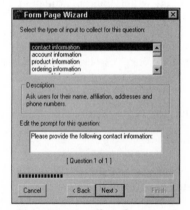

Figure 13-12: Select the type of information you want to collect and phrase the question you want to ask in the Form Page Wizard.

8. Click Next.

9. Check or uncheck boxes next to types of information you want to collect. For example, for contact information, you can select to include Name, Title, Organization, Postal Address, and much more.

10. Click Next.

11. Repeat steps 5 through 10 until all the information you want to collect is on the list. Click Next.

12. Indicate how you want the form to appear on the page, whether you'd like a table of contents for your form, and whether you want to use tables to align fields, as shown in Figure 13-13.

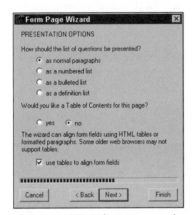

Figure 13-13: Select presentation options for your form.

13. Click Next.

14. Indicate where you want your form data to go. Your choices are saving the data to a Web page, to a text file, or using a Common Gateway Interface (CGI) script. If you want your data to go to a text file, provide a file name. If you want it to go to a CGI script, you'll have to edit the HTML later to put in the name of the CGI script.

15. Click Next.

16. Click Finish.

Style sheets

Style sheets are both the glory and the bane of HTML 4.01 (the current version of HTML). The advantages of using style sheets are numerous, but the disadvantages are not trivial. That said, most pages you see on the Web today do not utilize (or at least do not rely on) CSS, but most sites being built today do use CSS to some degree. CSS is one component of DHTML.

In the Real World

The Extensible Hypertext Markup Language (XHTML) deprecates many of the formatting elements found in HTML in favor of using style sheets. With this new implementation of HTML, and as more and more browsers support them, style sheets will become more commonplace and more the norm. So keep an eye out on the development of style sheets by checking out the W3C style pages at `www.w3.org/Style/CSS/`.

FrontPage makes it possible, but not easy to use style sheets. To create a style sheet in FrontPage, it's easier to start with one of the style sheets that FrontPage provides.

To create a style sheet in FrontPage:

1. Open the Web to which you want to apply the style sheet.

2. Open any page in the Web in Page view.

3. Select File ➪ New ➪ Page.

4. Click on the style sheet you want to use. Don't worry if it's not exactly what you want; you can edit it later.

5. Click OK.

6. You'll see the style sheet open in your Web. To edit it, select Format ➪ Style.

7. You'll see the styles that have been defined for this style sheet listed as user-defined styles. You can now either modify those styles or add new styles to the style sheet. By adding a new style, *while the style sheet is open in the background,* the style definition will become part of the style sheet and affect the entire Web, not just the page that's open when you define it.

8. If you click Hyperlinks view for any page in your site, you'll see that the style sheet is automatically associated with it.

If you already have a style sheet you like, you can associate it with your existing Web by following these steps:

1. Open a Web.

2. Select Format ➪ Style Sheet Links. The Link Style Sheet dialog box will open, as shown in Figure 13-14.

3. Select either All pages or Selected page(s). If you want the style sheet associated with every page, be sure to click All pages.

4. Click Add.

5. The Select Hyperlink dialog box will open. Browse the file system or surf the Web to find your .css file.

6. Click OK.

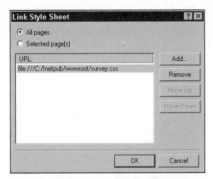

Figure 13-14: Associate style sheets to your Web from the Link Style Sheet dialog box.

7. Confirm that the .css file is associated with all pages by selecting Hyperlink view for more than one page. You should see the .css file you selected at the top on the right side of links into the page.

8. Save one of the pages in the Web to force FrontPage to copy the style sheet into the Web.

Themes

FrontPage themes

Themes give you the ability to change the face of your Web with just a few clicks. FrontPage offers many different themes for different occasions. For example, the theme Laverne is very 1950's looking, and Cactus is very Southwestern United States looking.

If none of the 67 themes that ships with FrontPage is what you want, consider buying a theme or a set of themes from a third party vendor such as Theme Mart.

To find out more about purchasing additonal FrontPage themes from Theme Mart, see the "For More Information" section at the end of this chapter.

Themes are the easiest way to change the look of your site. If you imported a site, you might have better results if you remove formatting before you apply a theme. If you built the Web in FrontPage, any theme should give you satisfactory results right from the beginning.

Themes work best when pages take advantage of the structural elements of HTML. For example, you should use blockquotes to block off text rather than tables. If you've created every page with tables and font tags to change the look of headings, you're in for a lot of work. If, however, you took advantage of definition lists and headings to format your page, themes should work well from the beginning.

To apply a theme, follow these steps:

1. Open the Web to which you want to apply the theme.

2. Select Format ⇨ Theme. You'll see the Themes dialog box, shown in Figure 13-15.

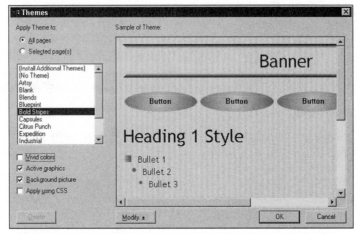

Figure 13-15: Select a theme to apply in the Themes dialog box.

3. Select the theme you want to apply. The Sample of Theme window on the right shows you how some of the elements of the theme will be formatted.

4. Indicate whether you want to apply the theme only to selected pages or to all pages. If you want to apply a theme (or a style, for that matter) only to selected pages, close the Theme dialog box, go into Folders view, select the pages to which you want the theme applied, and then resume the instructions at Step 2.

5. If you want vivid colors, check the box next to Vivid Colors.

6. If you want active graphics — i.e, the buttons to change when visitors roll a mouse over them — check the box next to Active Graphics.

7. If you want the theme to use a background picture, check the box next to Background Picture.

8. If you want the theme applied using CSS, check the box next to Apply using CSS.

9. Click OK.

To modify a theme, follow steps 1 through 8 in the previous instructions for applying a theme, and then follow these steps:

1. Click the Modify button at the bottom of the Themes dialog box.

2. Next, you can choose to modify the Colors, Graphic, or Text buttons, as described here:

   • When modifying colors, click the Custom tab and select a new color for any heading. You can't edit the color schemes from the Color Schemes tab. To edit the color scheme, click on the Color Wheel. Select a point on the color wheel and/or move the Brightness slider. Finish and click OK.

   • When modifying graphics, select the element you want to modify from the select list at the top of the dialog box. Click the Browse button next to the graphic(s) you want to replace (one at a time). Find the graphic on your local hard drive and click OK. Depending on whether you have Normal Graphics or Active Graphics checked, you'll see two or three graphics for some elements. For non-interactive elements, such as a horizontal rule, there is only one graphic.

   • To modify the font of graphics, click the Font tab. Select the font, size, style, and horizontal and vertical alignment for the element you selected. Figure 13-16 shows where you edit the font of graphic elements in a theme. If you have an element selected that does not have text associated with it, such as a horizontal rule, you won't be able to edit the font. Click OK when you're done editing the graphics and their fonts.

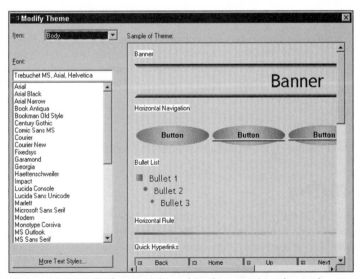

Figure 13-16: Edit the text of graphic elements in a theme from the Font tab of the Modify Theme dialog box.

• To modify the text of a theme, click the Text button. Select the item you want to modify from the item select list at the top of the dialog box. Select the font you want to use, and select the next item and font, until you're satisfied with the results. Click OK to save your changes.

3. Click Save to save the changes as the current theme. Click Save As to rename the theme.

Tip   When you click Save As and rename a theme, you're essentially creating a new theme.

4. Click OK to apply the theme to your Web.

Advanced FrontPage Features

    FrontPage advanced features

FrontPage has many advanced features that allow you to create truly sophisticated Web sites, such as:

✦ **DHTML.** Dynamic HTML effects, which make it possible to have activity on your site that doesn't require any action from the server, can be accessed in FrontPage with the click of a mouse.

✦ **Components.** Things like hover buttons, marquees (text that scrolls across the page), and hit counters, are easily added to FrontPage Webs.

✦ **Search forms.** If your Web is being published to a server with FrontPage server extensions installed, it's easy to add a search box on the pages of your Web, so visitors can look for pages containing specific words.

✦ **Reports.** Using the Database Results Wizard (a very powerful feature of FrontPage), you can generate a report on a Web page that displays the contents or a subset of the contents of your database.

The features are explored in detail in the following sections.

Adding DHTML

DHTML, Dynamic HTML, allows you to have activity on your site that doesn't require any action from the server. DHTML is event driven. For something to happen on a page, the visitor must take some action, such as move a mouse over an element, click, load a page, and so on.

Creating DHTML effects used to require knowledge of JavaScript or VBScript. This is no longer the case. FrontPage gives you access to many DHTML effects with the click of a mouse. Unfortunately, because it's so easy, people may get carried away. You should apply DHTML effects with discretion.

To add DHTML effects to an element on a page:

1. Enable the DHTML Effects toolbar by selecting View ➪ Toolbars ➪ DHTML Effects.

2. Highlight the element to which you want the DHTML effect applied.

3. Select the event that you want to cause the DHTML effect from the On select list on the DHTML Effects toolbar.

4. Select the effect you want to apply from the Apply select list on the DHTML toolbar.

5. If applicable, choose the next level of detail for that effect from the select list next to the Apply select list. For example, if you selected "fly in," you'd have to specify the place to fly in from, such as the top right, as shown in Figure 13-17.

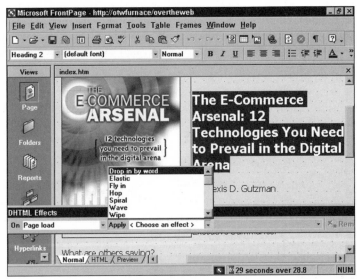

Figure 13-17: Inserting DHTML effects with the DHTML Effects toolbar

6. By default, any item that has a dynamic effect applied will be in a light blue box. You can turn off the box around elements to which dynamic effects have been applied by clicking the Highlight Dynamic HTML Effects box at the end of the DHTML Effects toolbar.

You cannot edit DHTML effects. If you're not happy with the effect, remove the effect using the Remove Effect icon on the toolbar and apply another effect.

To copy the DHTML effect from one element to another, position your cursor on the element with the DHTML effect, click on the Format Painter icon on the Standard toolbar, and then click on the element to which you want the effect applied.

Components

Components, such as a hover button, a marquee (text that scrolls across the page), and a hit counter, are easy to add to your FrontPage Web. The FrontPage components are interesting, but there are also purchased components you can add, such as enhanced navigation bars and scrolling text boxes. Components can be ActiveX controls, which run on the browser or server-side processing. The ones that require server-side processing require that FrontPage Extensions be installed on your Web server.

To insert a component into your Web:

1. Position the cursor on the page where you want to insert the component.

2. Select Insert ➪ Component, and select the name of the component you want to insert. Figure 13-18 shows the Hover Button Properties dialog box.

Caution   The components available to you depend on what you have installed from the CD, what you have indicated is the threshold browser, and what server you intend to publish your Web on. Some components require that FrontPage extensions be installed on the server to work. If you know your Web server does not have FrontPage extensions installed, and you've indicated this by selecting Tools ➪ Page Options ➪ Compatibility and unchecking the Enabled with FrontPage Server Extensions box, then you won't be offered any components that won't work.

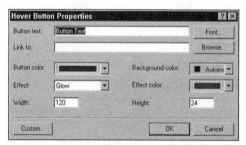

Figure 13-18: Inserting a hover button into a page

3. Provide the properties for the component you have chosen and click OK.

Search forms

It's often useful to have a search box on the pages of your Web to allow visitors to look for pages that contain specific words. FrontPage makes this easy if your Web is being published to a server with FrontPage server extensions installed. If your Web server does not have FrontPage server extensions installed, then work with your Web presence provider to see what kind of CGI scripts they have available to do this for you.

Exam Tip Know which features of FrontPage require FrontPage Server extensions. Many, but not all, of the more advanced ones do. This is a downside of FrontPage, because your Web presence provider must have them installed, and that's often beyond your control.

To insert a search form:

1. Position your cursor where you want to insert the search form.

2. Select Insert ➪ Component ➪ Search Form.

3. Provide the required properties in the Search Form Properties tab, as shown in Figure 13-19:

    - Label for form
    - Width of form
    - Label for start search button
    - Label for clear field button

4. Provide the required properties in the Search Results tab:

    - Word list to search; this defaults to All
    - Date and time formats if you've checked the Display File Date checkbox
    - Whether to display the score of the result
    - Whether to display the file date
    - Whether to display the file size

5. Click OK.

Figure 13-19: Supply properties for the Search Form Properties tab of the Search Form Properties dialog box.

Reports

To display the contents or a subset of the contents of your database in a Web page, you need to use the Database Results Wizard. This is a very powerful feature of FrontPage. For it to work, the Web server must allow .asp (Active Server Pages) scripts to run.

There are three steps involved in using the Database Results Wizard to generate a report on a Web page:

1. Assign an Open Database Connectivity (ODBC) datasource to the Web.

2. Run the Database Results Wizard.

3. Save your file as an Active Server Pages (.asp) file, and publish it to the Web server.

Each of these steps is explained in more detail in the following sections.

Assign an ODBC datasource to the Web

You must have an ODBC datasource defined for your database. If your Web server is hosted with a Web presence provider, you probably have to upload the database to their server and request that they create a Data Source Name (DSN) for you on their server. This DSN is what your database is called in FrontPage. You should create a DSN on your desktop computer as well, so you can set up FrontPage as follows:

1. Select Tools ➪ Web Settings ➪ Database.

2. Click Add to add a new datasource. You'll see the New Database Connection dialog box.

3. Assign a name to your database. Indicate the type of connection. If you have a DSN defined on your local computer, select System Data source on Web server. If the database is on a separate database server, select Network connection to database server. Click Browse to find the DSN. If you have to provide sign-in information, click on the Advanced button and provide that information there. Click OK.

4. You'll see your new data source on the list with a question mark next to it. Click Verify to confirm that the connection is a good one. The question mark will change to a check mark if the connection is good.

5. Click OK.

Run the Database Results Wizard

To run the Database Results Wizard, follow these steps:

1. Open the page where you want to display the database results.

2. Select Insert ➪ Database ➪ Results. Also, if you indicate on the Page Settings dialog box that your Web server does not support Active Server Pages, the Database item will be inactive because it creates ASP code.

3. Select the database connection, or create one by clicking the Create button. If you click the Create button, you'll go through the steps listed in the previous section, entitled: "Assign an ODBC Datasource to the Web."

4. Click Next.

5. In the second of five steps of the wizard, you must indicate where you want the records to come from. FrontPage automatically lists the name of every table and query in the database. Select the one you want to use from the select list, or click Custom Query, and then click Edit to create your own query. You must know the Structured Query Language (SQL) to create a query, as well as the field names and table names. For this example, we'll select the table and use the wizard to create the query for us.

6. Click Next.

7. In the third of the five steps of the wizard, you indicate which fields you want included in which order. By default, all fields are included. If you want to exclude some (possibly e-mail addresses and phone numbers, if this is going to be published in a public place), click Edit List.

8. Select each field you don't want to be displayed, and then click Remove. When you're satisfied with the fields remaining on the list, click OK.

9. To filter or sort the results, click More Options.

10. Click Criteria to specify which values of which fields will be returned.

11. For each field you want to limit, click Add, select the field name you want to limit, select the comparison you want to make, and then set the value you want to compare against. If you're planning to have multiple criteria, you also need to specify whether these criteria are cumulative (AND) or either/or (OR). When you're satisfied with the criteria you've entered, click OK.

12. If you want the results returned in a specific order, click Ordering. Select the field or fields you want sorted from the list of available fields. Change the sort order if you have multiple fields by highlighting a field, and then clicking Move Up or Move Down. When you're satisfied with the sort order, click OK.

13. Click OK to close the More Options dialog box and return to the third step screen of the wizard.

14. Click Next.

15. In the fourth step of the wizard, select your formatting options, including header rows, table borders, and other formatting options specific to the style of layout you select. Click Next.

16. In the fifth step, indicate how you want the records grouped, if at all. Click Finish.

Finally, you need to save your page with a file type of Active Server Pages (.asp) and publish it to a Web server with Active Server Pages running in order to see results.

Key Point Summary

FrontPage is a powerful tool for creating and managing sophisticated Web sites. By taking advantage of Web and page creation wizards, Web designers can create attractive, feature-rich sites without the sweat usually associated with Web site creation. The key points covered in this chapter were:

✦ Shared borders help you guarantee that all pages will have a uniform look.

✦ Navigation bars make sure that pages all link to each other properly. Rearranging a site is easy and visual through the Navigation view, just drag and drop pages where you want them. Navigation bars automatically reflect the latest design.

✦ By applying a theme, all elements of a site have a uniform look. From bullets to horizontal rules to vertical navigation buttons, every item on the page will contribute to creating a professional effect.

✦ Maintenance of sites is also facilitated with the Import Wizard. Reports show you in real-time whether any internal or external links are broken or whether any images are missing. Tasks help you keep track of what still remains to be done, and who needs to do it.

✦ Publishing a site takes only a few clicks. Whether your Web server has FrontPage Server Extensions loaded or not, you can publish using either HTTP or FTP. In either case, all files associated with the Web — .htm, .css, .asp, image files, and multimedia files — will all be uploaded.

✦ Components add impressive features such as scrolling marquees, hover buttons, and search forms. Depending on the server you plan to deploy your site on and the browsers you expect to be visiting your site, different components will be available to you. Most components require that FrontPage Server Extensions be installed on the Web server.

✦ Without knowing any programming at all, you can create forms that send data to a database. You can then use the Database Results Wizard to pull exactly the data you want from an existing database. To use database features, the Web server must permit Active Server Pages.

✦　　✦　　✦

STUDY GUIDE

This chapter packed in a lot of material. If you had never seen FrontPage when you started it, you sure know it now. If you've been using FrontPage for a while, perhaps it clarified a few mysteries, such as why Database is sometimes on the Insert menu and sometimes not, and helped you organize the material better. The following assessment questions and scenarios will help you gauge how well you've assimilated the material.

Assessment Questions

1. Which view of FrontPage lets you see how a Web is structured?

    A. Navigation view

    B. Hyperlinks view

    C. Folders view

    D. Reports view

2. What is the best way to have every page display the same logo at the top of the page and the same navigation buttons on the side? (Choose the best answer.)

    A. Use themes

    B. Use CSS

    C. Use DHTML effects

    D. Use shared borders

3. Which of the following methods will not allow you to modify the format of a table?

    A. The Insert Table dialog box

    B. The Style dialog box

    C. The Table properties dialog box

    D. None of the above

4. How do you apply a style sheet to your entire Web?

    A. Use the format painter icon

    B. Modify the theme

    C. Link the style sheet to the Web

    D. Open any page in the Web, select Format ⇨ Style, and click Apply to entire Web

5. How do you apply a theme to only part of a Web?

    A. Highlight the pages in the Web you want to apply it to from Folders view.

    B. Highlight the pages in the Web you want to apply it to in Navigation view.

    C. Highlight the pages in the Web you want to apply it to in the Folders list.

    D. You can't apply a theme to only some pages in a Web; you must apply it to the entire Web or to one page at a time.

6. Which of the following features of themes cannot be turned on and off?

    A. Vivid colors

    B. Active graphics

    C. Apply using tables

    D. Apply using CSS

7. What is it called when an element on the page appears after the page loads?

    A. DHTML effect

    B. Active graphics

    C. CSS

    D. Shared borders

8. To use the Database Results Wizard, which of the following must be the case?

    A. The Database component must be installed.

    B. The Web server must be able to execute Active Server Pages (.asp).

    C. The Web server must be able to execute Application Service Provider (.asp).

    D. FrontPage Server Extensions must be installed on the Web server.

Scenarios

1. You've been asked to create a Web site for a small law firm. What is the fastest way to do it? What would be the advantage of using a theme? Why would you or wouldn't you recommend the law firm have a feedback form? Where would you recommend storing the data collected by the form?

2. A construction company with a 20-page Web site that's been developed over the past three years comes to you requesting that you give them a new, integrated site that reflects their image, but uses all the content in the old site. What is the best way to get the content into FrontPage and create a re-vamped site for them? Would you recommend using a theme? DHTML effects? A search form?

3. An association that helps elderly people find appropriate in-home care wants a Web site. How would you format the site? Would you use themes? CSS? DHTML effects? A feedback form?

Lab Exercises

Lab 13-1: Create a Web using the Corporate Presence Wizard

1. Select File ➪ New ➪ Web.

2. Select the Corporate Presence Wizard, specify the location of the new Web, give the folder a memorable and relevant name, and click OK.

3. You'll see a dialog box for the Corporate Presence Wizard. Click Next to begin the Wizard.

4. Complete each screen of the wizard, selecting or deselecting the checkboxes next to the features you want or don't want. Use real values so you can see how it will all look when you're done.

5. When you come to a screen that asks you to choose the Web theme, click Choose Web Theme.

6. Select the theme you want from the Choose Theme dialog box. Indicate that you want to use active graphics and apply the theme using CSS. Click OK.

7. Click Finish to generate the custom Web created from your responses to the wizard. Wait patiently as FrontPage generates the pages.

8. Click around the Web. Look at it in each of the different views.

Answers to Chapter Questions

Chapter pre-test

1. A FrontPage Web is a collection of files and folders, which, when published to a Web server, becomes your Web site. The Web is the World Wide Web, which runs on the Internet, and is comprised of billions of interconnected pages.

2. Import a Web site from the Web using the Import Wizard.

3. When applying a theme, you can tell FrontPage to use style sheets. Most themes use tables to some degree. Shared borders also use tables.

4. Tables are viewable consistently by more browsers, but style sheets are more accessible for the visually impaired.

5. Select a theme from the Theme dialog box, where they're all listed.

6. A dynamic theme uses active graphics and a non-dynamic theme does not.

7. FrontPage components sometimes require that the FrontPage Server Extensions be installed. They also sometimes require that the visitor be browsing the page with Internet Explorer, rather than Netscape Navigator.

8. FrontPage allows you to save data to a database or read data from a database.

Assessment questions

1. **A.** Navigation view lets you see how visitors navigate from one page to another. Hyperlinks view shows you every page linked to and linking from the selected page. Folders view lists all files and folders in your Web. Reports view shows you diagnostic reports about your Web. See "Views."

2. **D.** Shared borders allow you to create the top of the page and the side of the page once, with navigation buttons, and then apply those borders to every page in the Web, automatically updating the navigation buttons as you build the Web. Themes determine how the Web will look. CSS affects the style. DHTML permits event-driven animation. See "Format menu."

3. **D.** You can format a table in one of three ways: from the Insert Table dialog box, the Style dialog box, or the Table properties dialog box. See "Tables."

4. **C.** You link the style sheet to the Web. The format painter icon applies formatting to only one element at a time. The theme does not necessarily even use a style sheet. There is no Apply to entire Web button in the Style dialog box. See "Style sheets."

5. **A.** Only in Folders view can you select more than one page. In the other views, you can only highlight one file at a time. See "Themes."

6. **C.** There is no Apply using tables checkbox in the themes dialog box. See "Themes."

7. **A.** Active graphics are only active when you roll the mouse over them. CSS affects the style of static elements. Shared borders merely insure that the same thing is on the top and sides (and bottom) of every page. See "Adding DHTML."

8. **B.** The Database Results Wizard requires you to be able to run Active Server Pages on the Web server. There is no Database component. Application Service Providers are not a scripting language. The Database Results Wizard does not require the FrontPage Server Extensions. See "Reports."

Scenarios

1. The fastest way to create the Web site is with the Corporate Presence Wizard. Using a theme will give you a consistent, professional look. There might be an advantage to a feedback form, if someone looked at the feedback. Sending the feedback by e-mail would probably make the most sense.

2. Import the existing Web site into FrontPage and remove all the formatting, then apply a theme. A search form is probably a good idea, but DHTML effects might look goofy for a construction company.

3. Format the site using CSS so visitors using text-synthesizing browsers won't have trouble getting at the information. Themes and DHTML effects would be secondary to accessibility. A feedback form is probably an excellent idea.

For More Information

✦ **Microsoft.** www.microsoft.com: Use the knowledge base for getting any questions answered

✦ **Microsoft FrontPage site.** www.microsoft.com/frontpage/: Use Microsoft's plethora of information on FrontPage to get all the help you'll need

✦ **Theme Mart.** www.thememart.com: Good place to purchase new themes

Macromedia Dreamweaver 3.0

+ Dreamweaver navigation tools

+ Dreamweaver standard elements

+ Dreamweaver templates

+ Dreamweaver JavaScript functions

+ Dreamweaver extended functionality

CHAPTER PRE-TEST

1. Can you name at least five common Dreamweaver inspectors or palettes?

2. What is a layer?

3. What are some of the Web page elements you can define using Dreamweaver?

4. What are library items?

5. How can a user define and apply a template to multiple Web pages?

6. What is the Macromedia Exchange?

✦ Answers to these questions can be found at the end of the chapter. ✦

Dreamweaver is quite possibly the premiere HTML editor on the market. Introduced by Macromedia, Dreamweaver marries a sleek and simple interface with functionality that is out of this world. Not only does Dreamweaver provide clean HTML markup, but it also supports JavaScript, Cascading Style Sheets (CSS), template creation, extended functionality via the Macromedia Exchange, and much more.

Dreamweaver Tools and Navigation

 Objective   Dreamweaver navigation tools

Dreamweaver, like all Macromedia products, uses a simple, yet powerful interface. If you're familiar with Fireworks or Flash, the interface will look familiar. Dreamweaver will not intimidate first time HTML developers. If you're a serious HTML developer that likes to work with JavaScript and CSS, you'll find everything you need in Dreamweaver, along with an easy to use interface.

Before you begin to work with Dreamweaver, you should take a tour of its interface. Dreamweaver is a powerful tool that provides the user with a wealth of options. Until you're familiar with its interface, it won't be as easy for you to take advantage of Dreamweaver's power.

 Exam Tip   It's important for you to understand the basic functionality of Dreamweaver for the CIW Site Designer exam.

Document window

Believe it or not, there's quite a bit to the document window. The main function of the document window is for you to enter the contents of the Web page. However, the document window also provides information about your document. There are four main components to the document window: content area, title bar, status bar, and menus. See Figure 14-1 to see the main document window.

Content area

The main part of the document window is made up of a blank page. This is where you can add HTML elements such as tables, hyperlinks, images, and text. All you have to do is place your cursor in the window and begin to type. If you want to add anything other than text, you can use Dreamweaver tools to create these objects, or you can add the source code yourself.

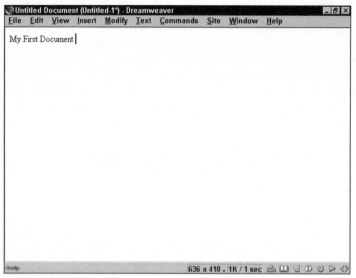

Figure 14-1: The Dreamweaver document window

Title bar

Similar to your favorite browser window, Dreamweaver displays a title bar that shows the title of the document. If you have not defined a title for your document, Dreamweaver will display "Untitled Document" as the default title name. Following the title of the document, Dreamweaver displays the name of the file. If you haven't named the file, Dreamweaver displays "Untitled-1." The number following Untitled will increase as you create additional documents.

While you're creating your first Web page, you'll notice an asterisk following the file name. This asterisk appears when a modified file contains elements that have not been saved. After you save the file, the asterisk disappears. The only purpose for the asterisk is to remind you to save your file.

Tip   Don't forget to put your document title in the source code within the title tags. The title of your document is important because it's used to label bookmarks and helps search engines find your Web site.

Status bar

The status bar also provides important information about your document. One main difference between the status bar and the title bar is that the status bar is interactive. From the left to the right, you'll find the following information on the status bar:

✦ **Tags.** Depending on which element is selected in the document window, the status bar provides the tag hierarchy for the selected item. This tag listing is interactive, which means that by selecting a tag from the list, you also select it from within the document window. This comes in handy when you need to modify individual elements on a page. If your document is blank, the status bar will only display the body tag as it does in Figure 14-1.

✦ **Window size.** The status bar displays the size of the current window in pixels. Although you can resize your window at any time using traditional minimize/maximize methods, you can also select precise dimensions. To do this, click the window size in the status bar and then select the precise dimensions from the menu presented (see Figure 14-2).

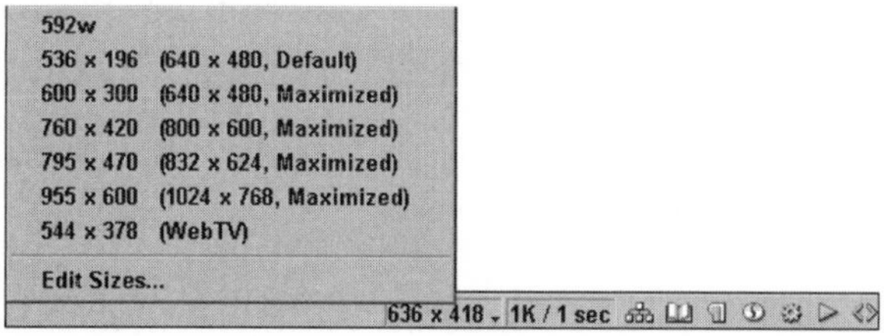

```
592w
536 x 196   (640 x 480, Default)
600 x 300   (640 x 480, Maximized)
760 x 420   (800 x 600, Maximized)
795 x 470   (832 x 624, Maximized)
955 x 600   (1024 x 768, Maximized)
544 x 378   (WebTV)

Edit Sizes...
                    636 x 418 ▾  1K / 1 sec
```

Figure 14-2: The menu that appears when you click the window size in the status bar

✦ **Document size/download time.** After the window size, the status bar provides information about the document size and download time. The document size is the combined file sizes of the document itself and all associated files. For example, if the document file size is 3K and three graphic files are associated, each 7K, the document file size displayed would be 24K. The download time assumes the user is using a 28.8 Kbps modem. You can always select another connection speed from the Preferences dialog box.

✦ **Mini-launcher.** The mini-launcher is interactive as well. In this case, the status bar provides shortcuts to all the options provided by the Launcher. From here, you can launch many of Dreamweaver's inspectors or palettes. The mini-launcher provides the following options: Site window, Library palette, HTML Styles palette, CSS Styles palette, Behavior inspector, History palette, and the HTML Source inspector.

Menus

There are many options to the menu bar. Although we cannot cover every option for each menu, we define the functionality for each menu:

✦ **File.** Similar to most of your favorite word processors, you can create, open, and save files from this menu. You can also import or export files, add design notes, check links, and preview the file in a browser.

✦ **Edit.** Allows you to undo and redo changes made, cut, paste, select, find, launch an external editor, and set Dreamweaver preferences.

✦ **View.** Shows or hides various Dreamweaver components, such as the status bar or head content.

✦ **Insert.** Allows you to insert objects, such as images, tables, and layers. Offers the same functionality as the Object palette.

✦ **Modify.** Allows you to alter or edit various elements on the Web page. For example, you can merge table cells, delete table rows, or split frames.

✦ **Text.** Provides spell check, as well as allows you to define attributes for your text elements.

✦ **Commands.** Allows you to format HTML source code, optimize images, record commands, and set color schemes.

✦ **Site.** Allows you to take advantage of Dreamweaver's powerful site management capabilities. You can open, define, and use sites, as well as view site maps and transfer files using FTP.

✦ **Window.** Shows or hides various inspectors and palettes. For example, if you select the Object palette, that palette is displayed within the document window.

✦ **Help.** Offers help pages that can be viewed through a browser window. You can launch these files locally using the help menu. You can also access Macromedia's Web site.

Tools

There are several inspectors and palettes that are ready to help you create well-designed Web pages. From inserting Flash files, to creating tables, the tools defined in this section can get the job done. We cover the most common of the inspectors and palettes first.

Launcher

To access the Launcher (shown in Figure 14-3), select Window ⇨ Launcher. The Launcher allows you to launch the most commonly used inspectors and palettes. The options are as follows:

✦ **Site window.** Opens the site dialog box that controls most of the Web site management capabilities.

✦ **Library palette.** Defines and uses elements that will be reused within the document, or between documents.

✦ **HTML Styles palette.** Defines or alters HTML font properties.

✦ **CSS Styles palette.** Defines or alters CSS styles for HTML elements.

✦ **Behavior palette.** Defines or alters JavaScript.

✦ **History palette.** Lists the history of all actions and allows you to undo and redo steps.

✦ **HTML Source inspector.** Allows you to view and edit the HTML source code.

Figure 14-3: The Launcher

Property inspector

The Property inspector is one of the most used windows in Dreamweaver. To access it choose Properties from the Windows menu. It allows you to add and modify attributes for various elements. The Property inspector changes depending on the element selected within the document window. For example, if text is selected, the Property inspector displays options such as font size, font color, bold, and italics (as shown in Figure 14-4). However, if an image is selected, the Property inspector doesn't display font options, but rather displays options for sizing, linking, and modifying the image.

Figure 14-4: The Property inspector displayed when text is selected

Object palette

If you need to insert objects into your Web page, you use this palette. To access it, choose Objects from the Windows menu. At first glance the Object palette can be a tad confusing because it only uses icons. You can change the palette to display text, icons, or both by selecting Edit ⇨ Preferences, choosing General, and selecting the appropriate option from the Object palette drop-down menu. We chose Icons and Text and the resulting Object palette is shown in Figure 14-5.

Figure 14-5: The Object palette

The Object panel (which can be accessed by selecting the pull-down menu at the top of the Object palette, as shown in Figure 14-5) is made up of six different panels, each of which defines a group of objects. The six panels are:

✦ **Character.** Inserts commonly used characters. The options are: Copyright, Trademark, Yen, Em Dash, Right Quote, Registered Trademark, Pound, Euro, Left Quote, and Other Character.

✦ **Common.** Defines the most frequently used objects. The options are: Image, Table, Horizontal Rule, Layer, E-Mail Link, Flash Movie, Generator, Java Applet, Plug-in, Rollover Image, Tabular Data, Navigation Bar, Line Break, Date, Shockwave Movie, Fireworks HTML, ActiveX Control, and Server-Side Include.

✦ **Forms.** Allows users to insert form objects. The options are: Form, Button, Radio Button, File Field, Hidden Field, Text Field, Check Box, List/Menu, Image Field, and Jump Menu.

✦ **Frames.** Allows document authors to create frames. The options are:

  • Left Frame

  • Top Frame

  • Right Frame

  • Bottom Frame

  • Split Frame Center

  • Left, Tip Left Corner and Top Frames

  • Top and Nested Left Frame

  • Left and Nested Top Frame

✦ **Head.** Defines objects that are specific to the head of an HTML document. The options are: Meta Tags, Description, Base, Keywords, Refresh, and Link.

✦ **Invisibles.** Inserts objects that are not visible to the user but that are a part of the Web page. The options are: Named Anchor, Script, Comment, and Nonbreaking Space.

History palette

The History palette was introduced in Dreamweaver 3, and allows you to gain access to a list of all your actions. To access it, choose History from the Windows menu. From here you can undo and redo actions with the click of a button. The benefit of using this palette is that you can select the action to undo or redo, rather than having to undo them one by one.

Layers

Before we tackle just how to work with layers, let's take a moment to define what a layer is. A *layer* is a definable region that can contain Web page elements such as text, images, and forms. The benefits of using layers are that you can define an exact location for them, as well as allow layers to overlap. The definition and functionality of layers has evolved over time. Currently, the most common approach to using layers is to use the CSS properties with the <div> and <span> tags. This technique is defined by the W3C and is supported by both Internet Explorer and Netscape Navigator.

Only the most recent browser versions support CSS and layering using the <div> and <span> tags. In the near future, browsers should introduce support for the layering of all HTML tags. Then, you can position an HTML element on the page.

There are two ways to introduce a layer to your Web page using Dreamweaver:

✦ **Menu.** The menu approach drops a new layer where the cursor is positioned. To use this method, place the cursor at the desired location, and select Insert ➪ Layer.

✦ **Object palette.** You can drag a layer to any spot on the Web page, or draw a layer using the Object palette. To drag a layer, select the Layer (Draw Layer) button and, while holding down the mouse button, drag the layer into the desired position on the page. The layer button will be active until you release the mouse button.

What layers are and how they are used (especially the Z-index) may be covered on the exam.

The Layers palette

The Layers palette helps users keep track of multiple layers (Window ➪ Layers). Within the Layers palette, each layer is defined in Z-order. A *Z-index* defines a layer's stacking order in relation to other layers. For example, a layer with a Z-index of 2 overlays a layer with a Z-index of 1. If you want to make changes to a layer, simply select it from within the document window, or select it from within the Layer palette. After it's selected, you'll notice the Property inspector changes to display properties specific to layers.

Adding content to a layer

The layer itself is like an invisible container. Without content, the layer doesn't do anything. To add Web page elements such as text to a layer, click inside the layer and type. You can add images, forms, and any other Web page elements that can appear within the body of an HTML document. You add these elements by clicking inside of the layer and then add elements as you would add them to the HTML page itself.

Positioning a layer

One of the perks to using layers is the advantage of positioning. Layers can be positioned absolutely, which means that you can define an exact pixel location on your page. This technique offers improved layout positioning in comparison to using HTML tables.

Dreamweaver provides you with two ways to position a layer:

✦ Select the layer's top left corner and drag it to the desired location. When it's close to the desired location, use the up, down, left, and right arrows to move it one pixel at a time.

✦ Use the Property inspector to define the exact pixel coordinates.

Modifying layer properties

Although the Layer palette helps you keep track of multiple layers, if you want to modify layer properties, you should use the Property inspector (Windows ➪ Properties). As with most elements on a Web page, the Property inspector can be used to define or modify specific properties relating to the element in question. You can use the Property inspector with a layer selected (see Figure 14-6) to modify many layer properties, such as:

✦ Pixel coordinates

✦ Width and height

✦ Z-index

✦ Name

✦ Visibility

✦ Background color

✦ Layer syntax

You must be sure the layer is selected to view these options in the Property inspector.

Figure 14-6: The layer Property inspector

Library items

There are two main ways to define information that can then be reused in multiple pages. The first option, using templates, is defined later in this chapter. Templates are useful for defining common elements found on each page of a Web site, such as logo branding, copyright information, or navigation. However, if you want to reuse information that might be used in the middle of a paragraph (such as your company's URL), you may want to define and use a Library item.

Using a Library item in a document inserts a copy of the HTML into the file and creates a reference to the original, external item. The reference to the external Library item makes it possible to update the content on an entire site all at once by changing the Library item and then using the update commands in the Modify ➪ Library menu.

Library items can be almost anything found in the document body. When you create a Library item from a selected portion of a document, Dreamweaver converts the selected area into a Library item. Library items can include any tag defined in the HTML body, including text, tables, forms, images, Java applets, plug-ins, and ActiveX elements.

To create a Library item, complete the following steps:

1. Select the item in the document that you wish to save as a Library item.

2. You then can complete one of the following:

   • Choose Window ⇨ Library and drag the selection into the Library palette. Press Control (Windows) or Command (Macintosh) to prevent the selection from being replaced by the new Library item.

   • Choose Modify ⇨ Library ⇨ Add Object to Library.

3. Enter a name for the new Library item.

If you want to use a Library item in a document, complete the following steps:

1. Place the cursor in the Document window.

2. Choose Window ⇨ Library or click the Library button on the Launcher.

3. Drag an item from the Library palette to the Document window, or select an item, and click Add to Page.

Tip　　Press Control (Windows) or Command (Macintosh) while dragging an item out of the Library palette to insert the item's content without creating an instance of the item in the Library palette.

HTML editing

Anytime you want to work directly with the HTML markup, you can launch the HTML Source window and enter changes by hand. You can open the HTML Source window using one of the following options:

✦ Select the HTML Source icon from the Launcher (see Figure 14-3).

✦ Select the HTML icon at the lower right corner of the screen (from the mini-launcher).

✦ Select Window ⇨ HTML Source.

The HTML Source window simply reveals the HTML markup. You can edit in the window, copy and paste the markup, or you can just watch the markup change as you're working in the document window.

When the HTML Source window is initially displayed, the window that contains the markup is displayed with a gray background. You remain in WYSIWYG mode until you click inside the HTML Source window. When the background of the window turns white, you can edit directly in the active HTML Source window (as shown in Figure 14-7). All you have to do is click the mouse one time in the HTML Source window and it will become active, if it's not already.

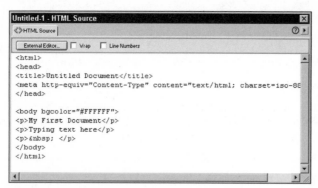

Figure 14-7: The active HTML Source window

After you've entered your changes into the HTML Source window, you have to click inside the Document window for those changes to be applied.

Tip   The HTML Source window, as well as most Dreamweaver windows, can be resized by dragging the lower left corner of the window.

Behaviors

Dreamweaver allows you to do just about anything you would want to do with your HTML page, which includes defining JavaScript behaviors. Dreamweaver supports many JavaScript behaviors, such as creating image rollovers or controlling a Shockwave movie.

Just what are JavaScript behaviors? A *behavior* is a specific JavaScript event that is applied to a defined HTML tag. You don't need to know JavaScript to use it in Dreamweaver; however, it's a good idea to be familiar with JavaScript.

Cross-Reference   Later in this chapter, we take a closer look at Dreamweaver's JavaScript support. For a comprehensive look at using JavaScript for client-side Web scripting, see Chapter 17.

Defining a site

Using Dreamweaver's site management tools could very well become a project manager's favorite thing about Dreamweaver. The Site window allows users to access site pages using FTP, check out documents, add design notes, and interact with other project team members. To get started using Dreamweaver's site management tools, you need to define a site. To define a new site, complete the following steps:

1. Open the Site Definition dialog box (choose Site ➪ New Site).

2. In the Local Info panel of the Site Definition dialog box (under Category and shown in Figure 14-8), do the following:

    • Enter a site name and click the Folder icon to browse to and select a local root folder.

    • If you want, select the Cache option to improve the speed of link and site management tasks.

    • Enter the URL of your site in the HTTP Address field.

3. Select Web Server Info and provide the following:

    • Select the Sever Access Option of FTP. This will set up a connection from your computer to the server.

    • Fill in the FTP Host name, the Host Directory, login information, and password.

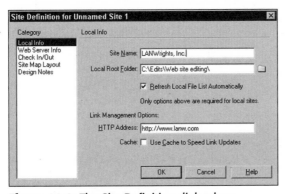

Figure 14-8: The Site Definition dialog box

Tip

A local site requires a name and a local root folder to tell Dreamweaver where you plan to store all of the site's files. You should create a local site for each Web site you work on.

HTML Elements in Dreamweaver

Dreamweaver standard elements

Dreamweaver is an HTML authoring tool and as you would expect, the tool provides users with a simple interface for adding HTML elements to a page. Instead of entering the markup by hand, you can use Dreamweaver inspectors and palettes to create HTML elements such as tables, frames, forms, and images. In this section, you find out how to add and modify common HTML elements in Dreamweaver.

Creating an HTML document

To create a blank HTML document, select File ➪ New. Dreamweaver opens a new, blank document window. Although the document window appears blank, if you view the source code (Window ➪ HTML Source), you'll see that the document is not blank; it contains the <html>, <head>, <title>, and <body> tags.

If you want to open an existing file, the process is similar to a common word processing application: select File ➪ Open. After the file is open, you can add, modify, and delete HTML elements.

After the document is open in the Document window, you're ready to add text or other HTML elements to your page.

Head properties

Some of the most important information in a Web page is defined within the <head> tags. A document's head defines its title, as well as metadata that provides definitions and keywords for search engines. If you're interested in getting your Web site to your audience, you should define both definitions and keywords appropriately.

See Chapter 10 for more information on metadata in HTML.

The <title> tag is also important because it names the document. The title of a document is used by the browser (displayed in the title bar), as well as used to name bookmarks. The information defined by the <head> tag is mostly invisible to the user. This is also true about Dreamweaver's document window. Unless you specify otherwise, the contents of the <head> tag are not displayed — with the exception of the document title, which appears in the title bar of both the browser and the Document window and is used as the label for bookmarks to the document.

The <head> tag also defines other important information such as the document type, style rules, the language encoding, JavaScript, and keywords for search engines. You can view the elements in the head by using the View menu or the HTML inspector.

To view elements in the head of a document choose View ➪ Head Content. An icon is used to represent each element allowed in the head of an HTML document. These icons are found at the top of the Document window.

If you wish to insert elements into the head of a document complete the following steps:

1. Select Head from the pop-up menu at the top of the Object palette.

2. Select one of the Head options in the Object palette. Your options are:

   - Meta

   - Keywords

   - Description

   - Refresh

   - Base

   - Link

3. Each Head option presents a dialog box in which you enter the appropriate information. Enter the appropriate information for the element in the dialog box that appears or in the Property inspector.

Images

You can insert images using a few different methods. Dreamweaver supports Joint Photographic Experts Group (JPEG) and Graphics Interchange Format (GIF) images.

Tip   In general, JPEG are used for photographs, and GIFs are preferred for most other images.

To insert an image, complete the following steps:

1. Choose one of the following three options to insert an image:

   - Place the cursor where you want the image to appear on the page and then choose Insert ➪ Image or click the Insert Image button on the Common panel of the Object palette.

   - Select and drag the Insert Image icon from the Object palette to the desired location on the page.

   - Highlight and drag an image from the desktop to the desired location on the page.

2. In the dialog box that appears, enter the path for the source file or select the Browse button to choose a file from your hard drive.

3. Define any image properties in the Property inspector. When the image is selected, the Property inspector provides properties specific to images as shown in Figure 14-9. (Click the down arrow in the lower-right corner to expand the image options.)

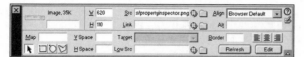

Figure 14-9: The Property inspector for an image

Image maps

Image maps allow you to define hotspots and add hyperlinks to those hotspots. To define an image map, complete the following steps:

1. Select the image from within the Document window.

2. Turn your attention to the Property inspector and name your map in the Map field.

3. Now you're ready to define hotspot regions by selecting one of the hotspot icons (see the blue shapes under the Map field in the Property inspector). Select the desired shape and drag around the area you would like to be a part of the hotspot. After the area has been drawn, the Properties inspector changes.

4. Enter the URL for the hotspot in the Link field. You can also add a target value in the Target field.

5. Repeat the process of defining a hotspot until you are done with the map.

Text

Working with text in Dreamweaver is as easy as typing in any word processor. Text is added to documents by typing in the Document window or by pasting text from other sources. If you type text directly into the document window, the default tag defined is the <p> tag. However, you can add text to table cells, or other defined HTML elements.

Images, horizontal rules, and other objects are added using the Object palette or commands on the Insert menu—choose Insert followed by the item you wish to insert. For example, Insert ⇨ Horizontal Rule.

As you add text, you can select and modify that text directly in the Document window. You have two main methods for modifying text:

✦ The most common way to modify text elements is to use the Text menu. From there, you can define items such as font properties, color information, alignment, indentation, and list item information.

✦ Use the Property inspector to define common text properties such as text alignment and font size.

Links

A Web page wouldn't be a Web page without hyperlinks. By using both relative and absolute URLs, designers are able to link documents. To add a link to text or an image, you can use one of the following methods:

✦ **Menu.** Select the text or image and choose Modify ⇨ Make Link. You can either choose a local file to which to link, or you can add the URL of the page to which you would like to link.

✦ **Properties inspector.** First, you need to make sure that the Property inspector is open. If the Property inspector is not open, open it. After the Property inspector is open, select the text or image and enter the filename that you would like to link to in the Link field of the Property inspector. If you do not remember the filename or path, you can select the yellow icon folder and navigate to the file that you would like to link to or add the URL of the page that you would like to link to externally.

As you may know, there are three main types of hyperlinks:

✦ **Absolute.** An absolute hyperlink is commonly used to link to external pages (pages that are not in your Web site). You must use the entire URL to reference external links. For example, `http://www.lanw.com/` is a well-formed, absolute URL, whereas `www.lanw.com` is not.

✦ **Relative.** When starting your site, you should think about the structure of it. It's common practice to store all your images in an images folder to keep the files organized. For example, you can point to a graphic file found in an images folder by using the following relative address: `graphics/file.gif`.

✦ **E-mail.** To link to an e-mail address, type **mailto:** into the Link field of the Property inspector (or using any of the methods previously discussed), followed by the e-mail address. For example the following value can be used to direct the hyperlink to an e-mail address: **mailto:name@domain.com**.

Tables

You're probably most familiar with using tables to organize data. As a Web designer, you should be aware that tables can also be used to control where text and graphics appear in a page. Dreamweaver allows authors to create tables with a few clicks of a button or drag of the mouse. After you've created a table, you can add content, copy and paste cells, and alter cell attributes. You can use the Object palette or the Insert menu to create a new table.

This book has an entire chapter dedicated to working with tables and page structure (see Chapter 8).

You have two options for creating a table using the Object palette. Your first option is to place the cursor where you want the table to appear on the page and click the Table button on the Common panel of the Object palette. The second option is to drag the Table button from the Object palette to the desired location on the page. Once you've done this, the Insert Table dialog box appears. You're asked to enter the following information:

✦ **Rows.** The number of table rows

✦ **Columns.** The number of table columns

✦ **Cell Padding.** The amount of spacing within the cell

✦ **Cell Spacing.** The amount of spacing between each table cell

✦ **Width.** The width of the table in pixels or as a percentage of the browser window

✦ **Border.** The width of the table border

If you don't want to work with the Object palette, you can alternatively choose Insert ➪ Table at which point you're also presented with the Insert Table dialog box.

Frames

Dreamweaver allows you to create frames with ease. You can use Dreamweaver to create basic framesets, to define nesting frames, and no frames content.

For detailed information on frames and site design, see Chapter 9.

To create a basic frameset document, do one of the following:

✦ Choose Modify ➪ Frameset ➪ Split Frame Left, Right, Up, or Down.

✦ Select View ➪ Frame Borders, and then hold down the Alt key (Windows) or Option key (Macintosh) and drag one of the borders to the desired location.

If you're creating a simple frameset document that only consists of two frames side by side, the task is easy. However, if you're creating a complex frameset, you need to know how to nest frames using Dreamweaver.

To define nested frames, select an existing frame and select Modify ➪ Frameset. You'll see the following options: Split Frame Right, Left, Up, or Down. When you make a selection, a new frameset is added to the original frame.

After your frames are in place, you should define specific frame properties. Dreamweaver allows you to define frame properties such as border color, border size, source file, scrolling behavior, and resizability. Like most HTML elements in Dreamweaver, you can modify the elements properties using the Property inspector. To use the frame Property inspector, select the frame in question. Once selected, the Property inspector (if visible) will display items relating to frames.

Tip The easiest way to select a frame is to open the Frames palette (Window ⇨ Frames), and click on the corresponding frame.

Because many older browsers do not display frames content, it's important to define alternative content for those users. To add NoFrames content, select Modify ⇨ Frameset ⇨ Edit NoFrames Content. When selected, a blank window appears in which you can define an alternate HTML page that will be displayed when users with older browsers visit your frameset document.

Forms

Forms are necessary for collecting data on the Web. The information collected can be sent to an application on your server or to your very own e-mail address. To create a form using Dreamweaver, complete the following steps:

1. Place the cursor where you want the form to appear and select Insert ⇨ Form. You can also use the Object palette to select or drag a form onto your page.

2. Define the action and method from within the Form Properties inspector. For example, you should specify an e-mail address or application location within the Action field.

3. After the form tags are defined, you're ready to add form objects. Place the cursor within the red dotted line to designate the form's boundaries. Select Insert ⇨ Form Object. You'll notice the following options:

   - Text fields
   - Buttons
   - Image fields
   - Checkboxes
   - Radio buttons
   - List/menus
   - File fields
   - Hidden fields
   - Jump Menu

4. After you've selected the form object you wish to enter, the Property inspector allows you to modify specific object properties.

Style sheets

The main drawback to using style sheets is compatibility. Style sheets aren't widely supported on multiple browser levels yet. However, if you can safely use style sheets, Dreamweaver allows you ample functionality for adding style rules. You can use CSS to define a wide range of formatting properties such as font family, word spacing, alignment, background color, line height, and margins.

Cross-Reference   See Chapter 11 for more about Cascading Style Sheets (CSS).

As you may know, most style sheet information is defined with `<head>` tags. There are three options for defining CSS style rules:

✦ Using an external style sheet

✦ Defining style rules within the `<style>` tag in the head of the HTML document

✦ Defining style rules inline

Use the Styles palette to add, modify, or delete style rules. You can access this palette by choosing Window ➪ CSS Styles. The Styles palette lists all of the available styles. To create a new style, click the document icon at the bottom right of the Style palette window.

To define a new style, you need to select one of the following options:

✦ **Make a Custom Style (class).** Allows you to define a class name, for example, `.intro`.

✦ **Redefine HTML Tag.** Allows you to define the HTML tag to be used as the CSS selector.

✦ **Use CSS Selector.** Allows you to define a predefined CSS selector.

After you've selected one of these options, click OK. From there, the Style definition dialog box appears as shown in Figure 14-10, and you're ready to define all CSS properties and corresponding values.

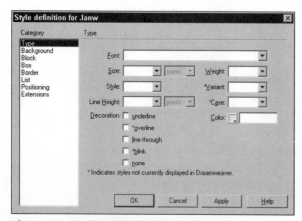

Figure 14-10: The Style definition dialog box

Dreamweaver Templates

 Dreamweaver templates

The first question to answer is just what is a Dreamweaver template. Most HTML editors allow authors to define templates. A template is similar to an outline of a document. When you create articles for a newspaper, there's information that doesn't change from page to page. In Dreamweaver, you can use that redundant information as the template that surrounds the changing content.

After you create the initial document, you can apply a template to any or all of the documents in your site; therefore, all of the pages share the information that doesn't change, although the content does change.

Creating a template

When creating a template you have two options. First, you can create a template from a blank HTML document. Or, you can save a page that you have already created as a template.

 Tip Templates are automatically stored in the Templates folder in the local, default root folder for the site (C:\Program Files\Macromedia\Dreamweaver 3\ Configuration\Templates). When you create a new template, the Templates folder is created if it does not already exist.

If you've already created a document that you would like to save as a template, you can do the following:

1. Select File ⇨ Open and select an existing document.

2. Select File ⇨ Save as Template.

3. In the dialog box that appears, select a site and enter a name for the template in the Save As box.

4. Save the template when you're done making modifications.

If you want to create a template from scratch, complete the following steps:

1. Choose Window ⇨ Templates.

2. In the Template palette, click New. A new, untitled template is added to the list of templates in the palette.

3. While the template is still selected, enter a name for the template.

Applying templates

In most cases, designers use a template as a starting point for a new document or apply it to an existing document. To apply a template to an existing document, you can do one of the following:

✦ Select Modify ➪ Templates ➪ Apply Template to Page. Choose a template from the list and click Select.

✦ Drag the template from the Template palette to the Document window.

✦ Select the template in the Template palette and click Apply to Page.

When you apply a template to an existing document, the content in the template is added to the document. If the document already has a template applied to it, Dreamweaver attempts to match editable regions that have the same name in both templates and insert the content from the editable regions into the editable regions in the new template.

If there are editable regions that do not match, or if an editable region in the previous template doesn't have a corresponding region in the new template, a dialog box appears prompting you to delete the extraneous regions or transfer them to the new template. If there are more editable regions in the new template, they will appear in the documents as place-holder content.

Updating templates

You can update or modify your templates at any time and the changes will be applied immediately to all of the pages that use that template. This functionality makes Dreamweaver very useful for Web site updates and redesigns.

To update or modify your template, complete the following steps:

1. Choose Modify ➪ Templates ➪ Update Pages. The Update Pages dialog box shown in Figure 14-11 appears.

2. From the Look in option, you can select one of the following options:

• Select Entire Site, and then select the site name. This updates all pages in the selected site to their corresponding templates.

• Select Files That Use, and then select the template name. This updates all pages in the current site that use the selected template.

3. From the Update option, make sure Templates is checked.

4. Click Start.

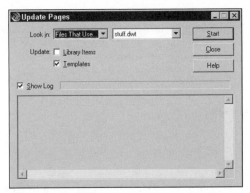

Figure 14-11: The Update Pages dialog box

JavaScript and Behaviors

Dreamweaver JavaScript functions

As we mentioned previously in this chapter, Dreamweaver allows you to work with several predefined JavaScript functions. It's easy to add these functions to your Web page, even if you don't know much about JavaScript. JavaScript behaviors can jazz up your Web page by defining image swaps (also known as rollovers), audio, pop-up messages, and plug-in detection. If you really know your JavaScript, you can add behaviors to timeline animations or add your own customized behaviors.

The Behaviors palette

JavaScript behaviors contain two definable parts: an event and an action. An event, such as a mouseover or click, triggers the action, such as a rollover. The Behavior palette (Windows ➪ Behaviors) defines a list of the events and actions that are pre-defined by Dreamweaver and available for use. As an added perk, Dreamweaver also organizes behaviors according to browser compatibility so you can easily see what will work on particular browsers.

Applying a behavior

To apply behaviors to objects such as links, images, form elements, layers, or even an entire document, select the element, open the Behaviors palette (select Windows ➪ Behavior), select from the list of available events (select the plus '+' sign), and then select any action. Depending on the action you select, you'll be presented with a dialog box for that action. For example, if you selected the Popup Message action, you're presented with a dialog box containing a text box in which you enter the text of the message. After you define the necessary properties for the action, you'll notice that the behavior is added to the Behavior palette. If you want to change the event (such as, `onClick` or `onMouseUp`), select the down arrow next to the event name, and select from the provided options.

The Macromedia Exchange

 Dreamweaver extended functionality

Dreamweaver, like many tools on the market today, allows its users to extend its functionality. At the Macromedia Exchange, you can get extensions, learn how to use them, and even create your own extensions. Although most of us think Dreamweaver is pretty darn near perfect, you might be surprised at how much further you can extend Dreamweaver. For each extension, you should find a page that includes the extension, provides a description for that extension, provides user reviews, and possibly even a discussion group for extension support.

One of the most interesting extensions that we found was the 508 Accessibility Suite. This extension checks your Web page to ensure that your page works within accessibility guidelines. The functionality is much like a word processing spell checker. The accessibility check can be conducted on one page for an entire site.

 Tip   To read more about Macromedia's extension program, visit `www.macromedia.com/exchange/dreamweaver/`.

Key Point Summary

This chapter was not meant to be a crash course in Dreamweaver, but rather a discussion of Dreamweaver's common functionality. With an easy interface and a powerful set of tools, Dreamweaver can be an asset to any Web designer. However, to take advantage of Dreamweaver, you have to know how to use it. This chapter covered the following key concepts:

✦ Dreamweaver is an HTML authoring tool that provides users with a simple interface for adding HTML elements to a page. Instead of entering the markup by hand, you can use Dreamweaver inspectors and palettes to create HTML elements such as tables, frames, forms, and images.

✦ Anytime you want to work directly with the HTML markup, you can launch the HTML Source window and enter any changes by hand. The HTML Source window simply reveals the HTML markup. You can edit in the window, copy and paste markup, or you can just watch the markup change as you're working in the document window.

✦ Library items can be almost anything found in the document body. When you create a Library item from a selected portion of a document, Dreamweaver converts the selected area into a Library item. Library items can include any tag defined in the HTML body, including text, tables, forms, images, Java applets, plug-ins, and ActiveX elements.

✦ Dreamweaver templates make it possible for you to apply a template to any or all of the documents in your site; therefore, all of your pages can share common information, although the content does change.

✦ JavaScript and behaviors can jazz up your Web page by defining image swaps (also known as rollovers), audio, pop-up messages, and plug-in detection.

✦ Macromedia exchange enables you to get extensions, learn how to use them, and even create your own extensions.

✦   ✦   ✦

STUDY GUIDE

The following questions are based on similar questions found on the CIW Site Designer exam. It's important for you to understand the basic functionality of Dreamweaver, and how to take advantage of concepts such as behaviors, templates, and extensions.

Assessment Questions

1. Which of the following is the best definition of a layer?

   A. A definable region that can contain HTML elements and be positioned absolutely

   B. A definable region that can contain HTML elements

   C. Part of a frameset

   D. An undefinable region that can contain HTML elements and be positioned absolutely

2. If a layer is defined with a Z-index of 3, which of the following is true?

   A. It will stack on top of a layer with a Z-index of 5.

   B. It will stack underneath a layer with a Z-index of 2.

   C. It will stack on top of a layer with a Z-index of 2.

   D. It will overlap a layer with a Z-index of 3.

3. Most attributes for a given HTML element can be defined using which tool?

   A. The Document window

   B. The Object palette

   C. The Property inspector

   D. The HTML Source window

4. Which of the following allow you to reuse redundant information?

   A. Templates and reusable items

   B. Templates and library items

   C. Reusable items and library items

   D. Only templates

5. Which of the following is not true about Dreamweaver templates?

   A. They can be created from scratch.

   B. A pre-existing HTML document can be saved as a template.

   C. They can be updated and reapplied to Web pages within a defined site.

   D. Templates can be applied to non-Dreamweaver HTML documents.

6. Which of following is true about Dreamweaver behaviors?

   A. JavaScript behaviors are not supported by Dreamweaver.

   B. Dreamweaver only allows you to define the action for a JavaScript behavior.

   C. You must know JavaScript to use Dreamweaver behaviors.

   D. Dreamweaver predefines several JavaScript behaviors for your use.

Scenarios

As a project manager, you're asked to define a site for your new project. The goal is to define a site that your entire team can use and interact with. Before defining remote access, your boss asks you to define a local site in Dreamweaver. You're asked to define a local site with the following characteristics using Dreamweaver:

✦ Name the site: Client Project One

✦ Name the URL: http://www.lanw.com/

✦ Name the local folder: Select a folder on your hard drive

Lab Exercises

Lab 14-1: Creating a Web page using Dreamweaver

For this lab, you create a simple HTML document:

1. Launch Dreamweaver.

2. If a blank document window does not appear, select File ➪ New.

3. Add two paragraphs of text and a table (Insert ➪ Table).

4. Save your document.

Lab 14-2: Adding a rollover to a Web page using Dreamweaver

For this lab, take the Web page you created in Lab 14-1 and add a rollover image. Most designers commonly call them rollovers, but Dreamweaver calls the behavior "Swap Image." Complete the following steps:

1. In Dreamweaver, open the HTML document from the previous lab.

2. Locate two images on your hard drive. It doesn't matter what these images are, you just need to locate two images you wish to swap.

3. Insert one of the images into your HTML document.

4. Select the image using your cursor or the tag selector at the bottom of the document window.

5. Name the image in the Property inspector.

6. Open the Behaviors palette.

7. Click on the Behaviors menu (the plus '+' sign) and select Swap Image.

8. The Swap Image dialog box appears (see Figure 14-12) that lists all the images on the page. Select the name of the image in your document.

9. In the dialog box, enter the path of (or browse for) the image to be swapped when the user mouses over it.

10. Check the boxes for Preload images and Restore on Mouseout. Preloading images will make sure that when the user mouses over the image there is no delay in the rollover effect.

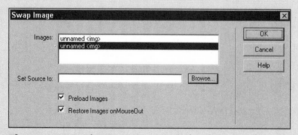

Figure 14-12: The Swap Image dialog box

Answers to Chapter Questions

Chapter pre-test

1. The one thing that Dreamweaver doesn't run out of is palettes and inspectors. Some of the most common ones are: the Property inspector, the Object palette, the Document window, the Site window, the Launcher, the Layers palette, and the CSS Styles palette.

2. A layer is a region on a Web page that can contain HTML elements and be positioned absolutely. A layer is used to help precisely lay out elements on a page. A specific region is defined as a layer, and then using CSS, you can define exact pixel coordinates. Layers can be overlapped.

3. You can create almost any HTML element using Dreamweaver, such as tables, frames, forms, text, and head information.

4. Library items are reusable chunks of information stored in external files. Library items are defined in and accessed from the Library palette. After an item is defined in the Library palette, it can be reused throughout your site. When you want to make changes to that item, for example, change the copyright date, you only have to change it in one location.

5. Users define a template by creating it from scratch or by saving a pre-existing HTML document as a template (File ⇨ Save As Template). After the template is created, you can create a page based on the template (File ⇨ New From Template) or you can apply the template to a pre existing HTML document (Modify ⇨ Templates ⇨ Apply Template to Page).

6. The Macromedia Exchange is a forum for exchanging extensions for Macromedia products. The forum also defines, describes, and rates known extensions.

Assessment questions

1. **A.** Layers can be used for layout purposes because they can be positioned absolutely (defining the exact pixel location). See "Layers."

2. **C.** If the Z-index of a layer is higher than the Z-index of another layer, it's stacked on top of the other layer. Therefore, a layer with a Z-index of 3 will overlap (stacked on top of) a layer with a Z-index of 2. See "Layers."

3. **C.** The Property inspector changes depending on the HTML element selected. The Property inspector is where you define most of the attributes for an HTML element. See "Property inspector."

4. **B.** Both templates and library items allow you to define reusable information. See "Library items."

5. D. Dreamweaver templates allow users to create a framework for related pages, as well as maintain that framework in the future. You can't apply them to non-Dreamweaver documents. See "Dreamweaver Templates."

6. D. Dreamweaver predefines several JavaScript behaviors for our use. You can also create and modify your own JavaScript functions. For each predefined behavior, you can modify both the action and event. See "JavaScript and Behaviors."

Scenarios

The first step in defining the New Site is to select Site ⇨ New Site. Doing so opens the Site Definition dialog box where the Local Info category should be selected. While in the Local Info category, enter the following information:

✦ **Site Name.** Enter a name for the site.

✦ **Local Root Folder.** Define the folder on your hard drive that should contain site files, templates, and library items.

✦ **Refresh Local File List Automatically.** Indicate whether to automatically refresh the local file list every time you copy files into your local site.

✦ **HTTP Address field.** Enter the URL for your Web site.

✦ **Cache option.** Indicate whether to create a local cache to improve the speed of link and site management tasks.

For More Information

✦ **Macromedia.** www.macromedia.com: Straight from the horse's mouth, Macromedia offers a wealth of information on using Dreamweaver.

✦ **Webmonkey.** http://hotwired.lycos.com/webmonkey/: Hotwired's Webmonkey provides a few good tutorials on Dreamweaver.

✦ **ZDNet's Developer site.** www.zdnet.com/developer/: Another developer site that provides articles on using Dreamweaver.

✦ **Webreview.** http://webreview.com: Webreview provides the HTML community with articles about the business of creating Web pages. You are bound to find an article or two on the subject of Web design.

Allaire HomeSite 4.5

EXAM OBJECTIVES

+ HomeSite standard templates
+ HomeSite tag tools
+ HomeSite file management

CHAPTER PRE-TEST

1. What are two ways you can work with tags in HomeSite?

2. How can you modify an existing HomeSite template to meet your particular needs?

3. Describe some of the items you can access from the Resource window.

4. How can you quickly create hyperlinks and embedded images in a document using HomeSite's file management features?

5. What role do wizards play in HomeSite?

6. What are some of HomeSite's file management features?

✦ Answers to these questions can be found at the end of the chapter. ✦

HomeSite 4.5 from Allaire is one of the better Web site development environments available today. Web designers should at least have minimal knowledge about this tool. HomeSite is an advanced HTML editor with support for a variety of advanced functions and an infinitely configurable interface. This chapter shows you how to use HomeSite to create Web pages using templates and HomeSite's various tag editing and document management tools.

Introduction to HomeSite 4.5

HomeSite is a tag-editing tool that requires a solid knowledge of HTML to use effectively. HomeSite isn't a WYSIWYG editor — although it does have a preview tool you can use to edit elements in a document without creating or changing HTML code. HomeSite's biggest strength as an advanced HTML development environment is as a powerful tag editing and document management tool.

Exam Tip　As you prepare for the exam, remember that HomeSite is not classed as a WYSIWYG editing tool — like FrontPage or Dreamweaver — but is instead a tag-editing tool. Other resources may also refer to HomeSite as an advanced text editor.

The HomeSite interface

The HomeSite interface is a rather complex setup, as shown in Figure 15-1, and allows for complete customization and access to frequently used tools.

In the Real World　Macromedia (the makers of Dreamweaver) and Allaire (the makers of HomeSite) have merged. There are no immediate changes in the software or the Web sites, but we predict there will be some eventually. In this chapter and throughout the book, we refer to HomeSite as an Allaire product.

HomeSite uses a collection of display components to manage its many functions, including:

✦ Menus for access to most components or component families

✦ An Editor toolbar for access to common editor functions such as closing documents and showing hidden characters

✦ An editing interface for creating and editing HTML documents

✦ An Editor tab for quick access to all currently open documents

✦ A Quick bar for access to frequently used tabs divided by type (common, fonts, tables, etc.)

✦ A Resource window (also called an Icon panel) for access to files on your local system, Web site projects, a diagram of the current site, snippets of frequently used code, help features, and a tag inspector to navigate the hierarchy of the tags that make up your page

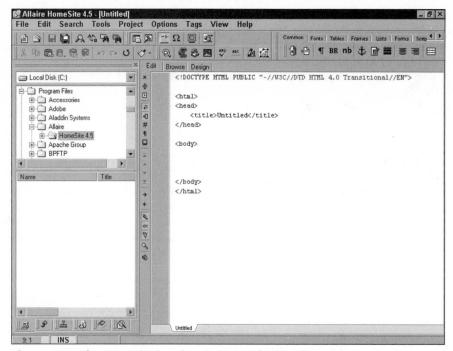

Figure 15-1: The HomeSite interface in its standard configuration

Exam Tip For purposes of the CIW Site Designer Exam, be sure to remember that the Resource window is also called the *Icon panel*.

To explore the standard interface features further, use the View menu to turn different features on and off. The Quick bar and Resource window are discussed in more detail later in the chapter. To customize what options appear in which menus and toolbars, choose Options ➪ Customize.

The Editing window

The central focus of the HomeSite interface is the Editing window. Its features include the Editor toolbar, which runs vertically down the window (between the editing space and the resources window), and following three tabs, which give you three different views of your Web page:

✦ **The Plain Text HTML or Edit view.** The default and most frequently used view

✦ **The Preview or Browse view.** Shows how your browser of choice will display your HTML document

✦ **The Design view.** For WYSIWYG-style editing

The ability to toggle back and forth between the Edit and Browse views makes it exceptionally easy to test any HTML code you create in a browser without having to actually launch the browser. HomeSite integrates the browser's display on the Browse tab for you. By default, HomeSite is configured to use Internet Explorer as its integrated browser, but you can easily change the configuration to any browser you like by selecting Options ➪ Configure External Browsers.

The Design view provides you with a WYSIWYG-style view of your Web page so you can edit it without having to write the HTML yourself. When you switch from the Edit view to the Design view, your HTML tags are hidden from you, and a new set of WYSIWYG toolbars appear in the editing window.

Caution HomeSite is not intended to be a flexible WYSIWYG design tool and it may alter any HTML you've already written when you switch from the Edit view to the Design view. If you choose to use HomeSite's Design view, save a copy of your original HTML with a different file name so you can return to it if you don't like the HTML HomeSite creates as you edit the page in Design view.

The Resource window

Next to the standard menus, the Resource window provides access to most of HomeSite's features in one location. The Resource window, shown in Figure 15-2, sits to the left of the Editing window by default.

Figure 15-2: The Resource window

Exam Tip The exam may refer to the different tabs in the Resource window as Icon panels. In this chapter, we refer to them simply as tabs.

By default, the Resource window has six different tabs that — in order from left to right — give you access to:

✦ **Files.** A hierarchical navigation tool that gives you access to all of the files on your local and networked drives to help you manage files associated with your Web site. This particular tool — called the Local tab on the test — is discussed a little later in the chapter in the "Managing Files" section.

✦ **Projects.** Provides access to any project — or collection of Web site files — that you define on your file system.

✦ **Site view.** A visual display of all of the files in a project or site.

✦ **Snippets.** A list of chunks of HTML code that you use regularly. Double-click on a snippet and it's added to your HTML file. We discuss creating and using snippets in more detail in the "Working with Tags" section later in the chapter.

✦ **Help.** Quick access to HomeSite's help. It's particularly well written and we recommend you browse through it to learn how to optimize HomeSite.

✦ **Tag inspector.** A run down of each and every tag in your document that includes all of the possible attributes you can have for that tag and the values for any attributes that you may have set. This feature is also discussed in more detail in the "Working with Tags" section later in the chapter.

Tip
You can customize which tabs appear in the Resource window. Choose View ➪ Resource Windows and uncheck those tabs that you don't want to see from the drop-down list that appears.

Other useful features

You've only just scratched the surface of HomeSite's many features in the discussion of its user interface. Some other tools to look out for are:

✦ A built in FTP client that allows you to associate an FTP site with a project and automatically or manually upload and update files on the FTP site with the files on your local system.

✦ A thumbnail view of all images associated with a particular Web page.

✦ Multiple ways to work with tags, including:

  • Type them by hand

  • Choose them from a list of tags via the Tag menus

✦ Snippets of frequently use code.

✦ A built in link verification tool that tests all of the links on a page or project — both internal and external — and reports errors back to you. You can check for broken links before deploying your site and without purchasing an additional link-checking tool.

✦ An HTML-aware spell checker that catches true misspelled words but knows that <html> and other tags aren't really words.

✦ A powerful search and replace tool that lets you find and replace text and markup in a single document or across an entire folder or project.

Exam Tip
For the exam, you should be able to list these other HomeSite features but you don't have to demonstrate your ability to use them.

HomeSite wizards

A part of HomeSite's feature set is a collection of wizards that move you through the basic steps of common Web development activities quickly. Some of the wizards in HomeSite's wizard collection are:

✦ **Quick Start wizard.** Gets your Web page started quickly. This wizard will collect and represent in HTML:

  • The document title and type (HTML version)

  • Document margins

  • Keywords and a description

  • Redirection information — new location and time until refresh — if necessary

✦ **Table wizard.** Helps you build complex or simple tables without hand-typing all of the necessary HTML. Using the table wizard, you can:

  • Define the number of rows and columns in the table

  • Specify all row and column spans you want in the table

  • Set the table alignment, cell padding, and cell spacing

  • Set the table width and background color

  • Set the table border and define the frames and rules for the table

  • Set layout and alignment properties for each cell in the table

  • Create content for each cell in the table

✦ **Frames wizard.** Helps you create a set of frames quickly. To create a set of frames with the wizard, you:

  • Specify the number of frames in the frame set and their arrangement

  • Identify a name and source URL for each frame in the set

  • Set the height and width for each frame

  • Set the border, scrolling properties, and resize rules for each frame in the set

✦ **Deployment wizard.** Helps you take an entire Web site that resides on your local system and deploy it to a live Web site via FTP. The wizard guides you through the basic steps of deployment, including:

  • Whether the deployment is a one-time activity or a repeated process for which you want to create a script in VBScript or Jscript.

  • Whether the deployment is to a system on your local network or to a remote site accessible via Remote Directory Services (RDS) or the File Transfer Protocol (FTP).

  • Whether you want the deployment to create missing folders, upload only new or all files, encrypt certain files, and force lowercase file names.

Exam Tip Know that HomeSite has wizards for creating tables and forms, and that wizards aren't always the best solution to a complex HTML problem.

To use the various wizards in HomeSite, you still need to know how HTML works and understand what kind of Web page or Web page element you're trying to create. Wizards just get you started, but they aren't flexible or detailed enough to provide a finished product on their own. They give you a good start but are no substitute for your own knowledge of HTML and Web design.

Caution The results of the wizards are often not what you expect from the code you would have written yourself. The wizard code can be unnecessarily complex and difficult to edit. You should experiment with the wizards and their output on a backup copy of your Web site to see if they provide code you can work with or code that is more trouble than it is worth to modify.

HomeSite Templates

Objective HomeSite standard templates

The basis of any new Web document in HomeSite is a template. Templates can be empty, or have a detailed collection of HTML already included in them to help you avoid recoding common structure elements. This section explores how you can use HomeSite's standard templates as a basis for your HTML documents and how you can create your own templates or modify existing ones to meet your particular needs.

What's in a template

A HomeSite template is a collection of predefined HTML tags grouped together to create a structure for an HTML document. The Default template includes the basic HTML structure tags:

```
<!DOCTYPE HTML PUBLIC "-//W3C//DTD HTML 4.0 Transitional//EN">
<html>
<head>
    <title>Untitled</title>
</head>
<body>
</body>
</html>
```

A more complex template, such as the Glossary of Terms template that comes with the standard HomeSite installation may have a larger collection of tags that represent standard structures in the document. In the case of glossary of terms, there are elements for headings and links to each letter of the alphabet in the glossary, definition list markup for defining glossary items, and links back to the top of the page. Figure 15-3 shows how a document created from the Glossary of Terms template appears in Preview view before any modifications are made to it.

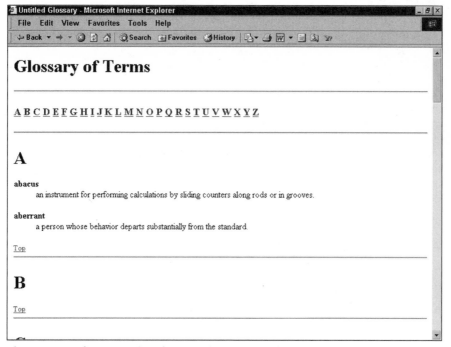

Figure 15-3: The HomeSite Glossary of Terms template

The Blank template that comes with HomeSite is simply a blank document with no markup included in it at all. If you want to start from scratch, this is the template to use.

Creating a new document from a template

You can create a new Web document in HomeSite in one of three ways:

✦ Choose File ➪ New

✦ Press Ctrl+N on the keyboard

✦ Click the New button on the Standard toolbar

If you use the short cut (Ctrl+N) or the New button, HomeSite automatically bases the document on the Default template stored in the system. If you open a new document using the menu, you can choose which template to use, as shown in Figure 15-4.

Figure 15-4: The New Documents window lists all available templates on which you can base your Web documents.

Modifying and creating templates

You can modify existing templates so they better meet your particular needs. To modify an existing template:

1. Create a new document that uses that template.

2. Edit the template to reflect the changes and additions you need included in your customized version of the template.

3. Choose File ⇨ Save As Template.

4. Type a name for the template in the Name dialog box, as shown in Figure 15-5, and click OK.

Figure 15-5: You can modify an existing template in just a few steps, the last of which is giving the template a new name.

Tip   All custom templates that you create, even those that are a modification of an existing template, are displayed in the Custom tab in the New Document window. To access your customized template, be sure to click the Custom tab and select the template from that collection of templates.

After you've saved the modified template, you can use it as the basis for new Web documents just like any other template. If you want to create a template from scratch, open a blank Web document in HomeSite, type the HTML you want to appear in the template, and choose File ➪ Save As Template to save the new HTML document as a template.

You can also make an existing HTML file into a template by simply changing the file's extension and moving it to the proper folder on your system. To turn a Web page into a HomeSite template, follow these steps:

1. From the Windows Explorer or from within a folder, make a copy of the HTML file and save it in the HomeSite 4.5\Wizards\HTML folder.

2. Change the file's extension from .html to .hst.

The file is now a HomeSite template and will behave like any other HomeSite template.

Working with Tags

   HomeSite tag tools

HomeSite is an advanced tag editor and its many features work to support the development of Web pages with HTML tags rather than a graphical interface. As part of its feature arsenal, HomeSite has a collection of methods you can use to create and modify HTML tags. The next several sections discuss the different methods you can use in HomeSite to work with tags as you build your HTML documents.

Tag Insight

Keeping a handle on all of HTML's tags and attributes can be a bit daunting, even for experienced Web developers. The goal of Tag Insight is to prompt you just when you need it and save you a few keystrokes along the way. Tag Insight provides drop-down lists right inside of the editing window that include lists of tags that you define, which you'll find out how to do in a couple of paragraphs. You define the tags or the attributes once you've added them to your page. Tag Insight also lists all predefined values for an attribute if they're available.

Exam Tip Know that Tag Insight is used to create an empty tag from the Tags menu, which you can fill in using the Tag Insight functionality.

When you type a less than sign (<) in a document and wait for a second or two, Tag Insight provides a list of tags for you to choose from. When the list of tags appears, you can begin to type the tag name to jump to all tags that begin with the character or characters you typed. If you want to jump to all of the table tags, as shown in Figure 15-6, type a **t** and the list fast forwards to all tags that begin with t.

After you specify a tag, hit the Space bar and wait for another second or two and a list of attributes for that tag appears in a drop-down list. Each attribute is prefaced by an icon, as shown in Figure 15-7. This icon indicates what kind of value — color, link, number, etc. — the attribute takes.

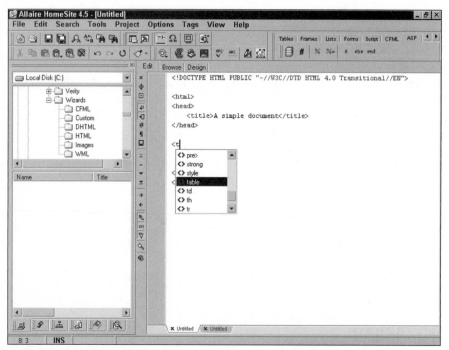

Figure 15-6: Tag Insight helps you find the tag you are looking for.

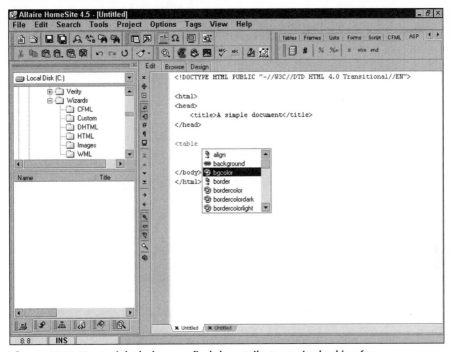

Figure 15-7: Tag Insight helps you find the attribute you're looking for.

Finally, if an attribute you've added to a tag has a list of predefined values — such as a color or alignment — a drop-down list appears that lists all of the predefined values, as shown in Figure 15-8.

If you're concerned that Tag Insight might be more of a hindrance than help, you can configure its settings to delay the amount of time it takes for the drop-down menus to appear. Therefore, they only appear when you really need them. You can also configure which tags appear in the tag list. To control the Tag Insight settings, including turning the feature off entirely, choose Options ➪ Settings and click on Tag Insight in the Editor list, as shown in Figure 15-9.

The Tags menu

The Tags menu gives you access to a variety of options for creating and editing tags, including:

✦ The ability to create a blank start or end tag (which you can fill using Tag Insight)

✦ Quick access to the most commonly used tags, including paragraphs, headings, formatting tags, and line breaks (along with shortcuts for those tags if they exist)

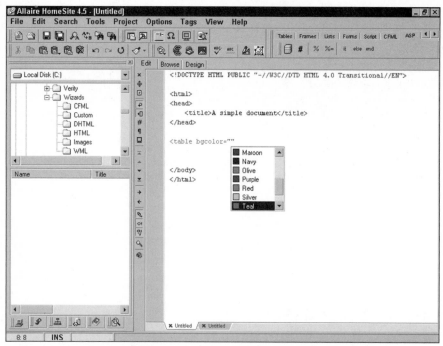

Figure 15-8: Tag Insight helps you find the attribute value you are looking for.

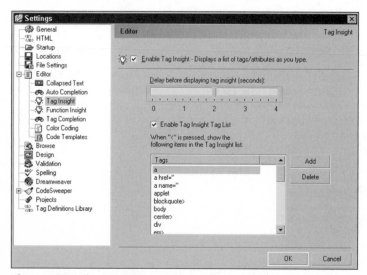

Figure 15-9: The HomeSite settings give you tight control over how Tag Insight behaves.

✦ A command to find a matching open or close tag somewhere in your document (particularly useful if you want to eliminate orphan tags)

✦ The ability to repeat the last tag you added to the document

✦ Links to edit or inspect the tag your cursor is positioned in (discussed in more detail in the "Tag Chooser" and "Tag Inspector" sections)

Tip   The Tag menu is generally the first place you go if you want to access tag options and work with tags. The Tag Chooser is next on the list of really useful tag tools.

Tag Chooser

The Tag Chooser is simply a list of tags that you can pick and choose from to add tags to your HTML documents. To access the Tag Chooser, select Tools ➪ Tag Chooser or click Ctrl+E. Before you open the Tag Chooser, position your cursor in your HTML document in the spot where you want your chosen tag to sit. The Tag Chooser, shown in Figure 15-10, isn't just limited to HTML tags; it also lists Extensible Markup Language (XML) tags (called elements) and Cold Fusion Markup Language (CFML) tags that are part of Allaire's Web application development tool, Cold Fusion.

Exam Tip   Be sure you know which shortcuts to use to access the different tag features such as the Tag Chooser and the settings for auto completion.

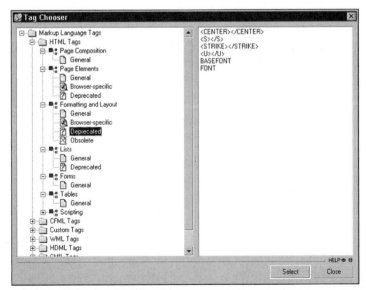

Figure 15-10: The Tag Chooser

Tags are organized into folders by markup language, with HTML at the top, and then further divided into other groups. Within each group, the tags are divided into categories:

✦ **General.** Part of the current HTML standard

✦ **Browser specific.** Proprietary browser tags

✦ **Deprecated.** Deprecated in the HTML 4 standard

✦ **Obsolete.** Identified as obsolete in the current HTML standard

To see all tags within a group, click on the group's name. To see the tags in a particular category, click that category. To add a tag to your document, simply click on the tag name in the Tag Chooser. Before HomeSite adds the tag to your document it launches the Tag Editor window specific to that tag so you can set any or all attribute values for that tag, as shown in Figure 15-11.

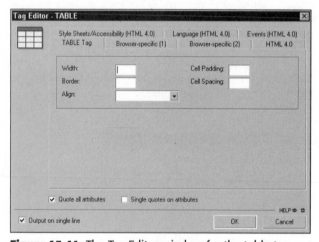

Figure 15-11: The Tag Editor window for the table tag

You can return to this edit window at any time for any tag. Position your cursor inside of the tag you want to launch the edit window for and Choose Tags ⇨ Edit Current Tag or click Ctrl+F4.

Automatic tag completion

Another useful HomeSite tag tool is Auto Completion. When this option is turned on, HomeSite will automatically complete tags, quotation marks, comments, and any other string that has a start and end. One of the elements of good page design is correctly nested, complete tag pairs. The Auto Completion function helps you to not forget closing tags, especially in lengthy and complex HTML constructs such as tables. Auto Completion also helps you avoid missing quotation marks, which can break the entire display of a page in a Web browser.

By default, Auto Completion is turned on. To turn it on or off, choose Options ⇨ Settings and select Auto Completion from the Editor list, as shown in Figure 15-12. You can also turn Auto Completion on or off for individual strings (quotation marks, tags, etc.) and add or delete strings for HomeSite to automatically complete. The keyboard shortcut to the Auto Completion settings is F8.

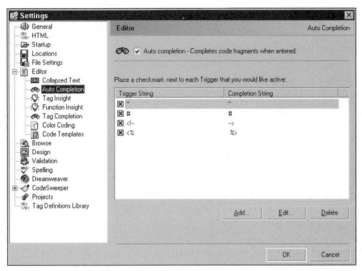

Figure 15-12: The Auto Completion window in the HomeSite Settings window

Exam Tip   Know the features of Tag Insight, the Tags menu, Tag Chooser, and the Auto Completion function discussed in this book.

Code snippets

As a designer, you most likely have chunks of HTML or JavaScript code that you reuse. Candidates include proven and well-tested client-side scripts for mouse rollovers or favorite HTML table designs. You can opt to keep this information stored in a collection of text files or even in one big text file, but HomeSite has a better option for storing and organizing these chunks of code — the Snippets feature.

A snippet is exactly what it sounds like: a small selection of HTML or other code that you want to be able to access and use repeatedly. You can create and store your code snippets in the Snippets tab of the Resource window, as shown in Figure 15-13. You can organize your snippets into folders, and, in fact, at least one folder must exist before you can create a snippet in the HomeSite system.

Figure 15-13: The JavaScript Snippets tab of the Resource window

To add a new folder to the Snippets tab, right-click anywhere in the tab and choose Add Snippet from the drop-down list that appears. To add a new snippet to a folder, right-click on the folder and choose Add Snippet from the drop-down list that appears. In the Snippet window, give the snippet a name as well as start and end code. To add a snippet to your document, position your cursor in the document where you want the snippet contents to appear and use one of two methods to access the snippet:

✦ Double-click on the snippet.

✦ Right-click on the snippet and choose Insert into document from the drop-down list that appears.

Tip   You can edit, delete, and rename snippets after you create them. You can't move them from one folder to another so think carefully about how you want to arrange and manage your snippets before you start creating folders and snippets.

Tag Inspector

The Tag Inspector is an in-depth look at the tags in any given document and the attributes you've set for each. You can access the Tag Inspector from a tab in the Resource window. The top pane of the Tag Inspector shows all of the tags in the current document as a hierarchical tree that you can expand and collapse. When you click on a tag, either in the top pane of the inspector or anywhere in the document, the bottom pane shows all of the possible attributes for that tag and any values you already have set for the attributes. Attributes that have a predefined list of values include drop-down lists from which you can choose a value, as shown in Figure 15-14.

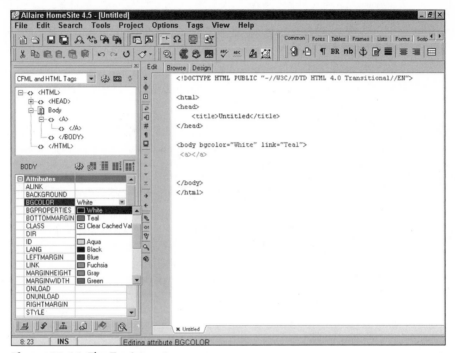

Figure 15-14: The Tag Inspector

If you want to know what all of the attributes are for a given tag or want a non-markup view of all of the values you've assigned to the attributes for a given tag, the Tag Inspector is a very useful tool. If you need to verify that your tags are nested correctly — especially in complex tables or other constructs — the upper pane of the inspector helps you walk the tree of your document to verify proper nesting and order.

The Tag Inspector completes HomeSite's well-rounded set of tag development tools. HomeSite's tag tools allow you to create and edit HTML documents in a variety of ways and has a tool or function to fit just about any designer's code development style.

Managing Files

HomeSite file management

One of HomeSite's other key functionalities is file management. Even a small Web site can have hundreds of HTML and image files, and it can be difficult to keep track of them outside of a development environment. The HomeSite Files tab in the Resource window presents you with hierarchical navigation of your entire site and makes it easy to work with files and their contents.

Exam Tip   The CIW Site Designer Exam calls the Files tab the Local tab. However, HomeSite's tool tips and help files all refer to this tab as the Files tab.

The display of your local system or a network drive looks and behaves much like the familiar Windows Explorer or other standard hierarchical navigation scheme. You can click folders to open and close them. Here's how HomeSite's file management features work in the Files tab:

✦ To quickly open an HTML file in HomeSite, simply double-click on it from the Files tab.

✦ To rename a file listed in the bottom pane of the Files tab, right-click on the file and choose Properties. You can change the file name in the Properties window.

✦ When you right-click on a folder in the upper pane, you see a drop-down list that is the same as the one you see in the Windows Explorer when you right-click on a folder. You can send the folder and its contents to a ZIP file, copy the folder, create a shortcut to the folder, view the folder's properties, and more.

✦ HomeSite's Files tab also supports Web page development. If you want to add a hyperlink to a particular file, simply drag that file from the bottom pane of the Files tab into the document where you want to make the link. HomeSite creates a relative hyperlink to the file.

✦ This same functionality also applies to images. To create a fully formed image tag in an HTML document, simply drag the image from the Files tab to the document where you want to create the image tag and HomeSite will build the tag with a relative link to the image for you.

The Files tab gives you access to all of your Web site documents from within your development environment. This makes them more accessible and easier to work with. The automatic hyperlink and image tag creation makes it particularly easy to link documents together and embed images on a page without having to worry about correct file and path names.

Combined with HomeSite's template and tag tools, file management rounds out the HomeSite feature set to create a strong Web site development environment. Remember that HomeSite is a tag editor, not a true WYSIWYG editor, and that it's designed to help you use your knowledge of HTML to create and manage Web sites.

Key Point Summary

This chapter introduced you to HomeSite, an advanced tag editor with complete template, tag, and file management tools. You learned how to create new documents from an existing template, how to modify an existing template, and how to create your own templates. You toured HomeSite's varied and feature-rich tag tool set and learned how to use Tag Insight, the Tags menu, Tag Chooser, and the Auto Completion tag feature to facilitate Web design. Finally, you discovered how HomeSite makes managing all of the files associated with a Web site easier and more efficient. Key information to take away from this chapter includes:

✦ The HomeSite interface is designed to provide immediate access to the application's different tools and features. The interface is fully customizable and includes a collection of menus, toolbars, and windows.

✦ The Resource window has six tabs that give you access to files, projects, a graphical view of a site, code snippets, help, and a tag inspector.

✦ HomeSite's advanced features include link verification, spell checking, a built-in FTP tool, and a strong search-and-replace tool.

✦ The HomeSite wizards make it easy for you to create a new Web page, tables, and framesets. The Deployment wizard even facilitates a one time or reoccurring Web site deployment.

✦ HomeSite templates are a collection of HTML tags that form the basis for a new HTML document. The default HTML template includes the standard HTML structure tags whereas the Blank template has no tags.

✦ You can modify an existing template by creating a new Web page based on the template, making changes to the tags created by the template, and then saving the page as a new template. You can make any existing HTML document a template by placing it in the HomeSite Wizards folder and saving it with the file extension .hst.

✦ HomeSite provides a variety of ways to create and edit HTML documents. Tag Insight has drop-down lists of tags, attributes, and attribute values to help you create HTML.

✦ The Tags menu provides access to all tools associated with tag development, including blank and most commonly used tags. You can access all other tag tools from the Tags menu.

✦ The Tag Chooser is a list of tags separated by type and category from which you can add a tag to an open document. After you select a tag from the Tag Chooser, an edit window specific to that tag pops up so you can set attribute values as necessary before HomeSite adds the tag to your document. Auto Completion simply finishes tags and quotation marks for you to help avoid missing or incomplete tags.

✦ HomeSite's file management system is located on the Files tab of the Resource window — sometimes called the Local tab. From the Files tab, you can navigate all of the files on your hard drive and networked drives and manage them as you would in Windows Explorer or any other hierarchical navigation system. You can quickly create hyperlinks and image tags in open HTML documents by dragging files from the File tab into your document.

✦ HomeSite automatically creates the HTML markup and relative URLs needed to link to the file or display it as an image.

✦   ✦   ✦

STUDY GUIDE

HomeSite is a complex and feature-rich application that can take time and practice to use effectively. The questions, scenarios, and lab exercises in the study guide are intended to help you practice what you've learned in this chapter in preparation for the test and to help you become a more proficient HomeSite user. Don't forget to check your work by looking up the correct answers to the chapter pre-test and the assessment questions in the Answers to Chapter Questions section toward the end of this chapter.

Assessment Questions

1. Which of the following accurately describes HomeSite?

   A. It is an advanced WYSIWYG editor.

   B. It is a beginner's WYSIWYG editor.

   C. It is an advanced tag editor with some WYSIWYG-style functionality.

   D. It is an advanced tag editor with no WYSIWYG functionality.

2. Which of the following is not accessible from the Tags menu?

   A. Tag Inspector

   B. Tag Chooser

   C. Empty start tag

   D. Tag Tips

3. Which keyboard shortcut brings up the Settings window for the Auto Completion function?

   A. F8

   B. F9

   C. F3

   D. F4

4. Which template in HomeSite includes basic HTML structure tags?

   A. A custom template you have to write yourself

   B. The Blank template

   C. The Default template

   D. None of the above

5. How can you turn a standard HTML file into a HomeSite template?

    A. Copy the contents of the file to HomeSite's proprietary template tool and save in their proprietary template language

    B. Move the file to the Wizards folder inside of the HomeSite folder

    C. Change the template's file extension from .html to .htm

    D. Change the template's file extension to .hst

6. Which HomeSite tag feature displays context-specific drop-down menus as you create tags?

    A. Tag Insight

    B. Tags menu

    C. Tag Chooser

    D. Auto tag completion

Scenarios

You're working with a group of Web developers to create a Web site that must adhere to precise design standards. Which HomeSite features can you use to help ensure that all pages use the same basic HTML design and that scripts and other HTML components are used consistently throughout the site?

Lab Exercises

Lab 15-1: Customizing the Default template

1. Launch HomeSite and choose File ➪ New.

2. Select the Default template from the New window and click OK.

3. In the new document, change the content of the title tag from "Untitled" to **My default template**.

4. Add `bgcolor="white"` and `text="navy"` to the `<body>` tag.

5. Choose File ➪ Save As Template.

6. In the Save As Template file name box, name the template **Default** and click OK.

7. To test your new template, choose File ➪ New.

8. Click the Custom tab in the New window, select the Default template, and click OK.

9. The markup in the new document should reflect the changes you made to the original Default template.

Answers to Chapter Questions

Chapter pre-test

1. HomeSite has several tools for working with tags, including Tag Insight, the various options on the Tags menu, the Tag Chooser, and the Auto Completion function.

2. You can modify an existing HomeSite template by creating a new document from the template, making your changes to the document, and saving it as a template using the Save As Template option in the HomeSite File menu.

3. The Resource window gives you access to HomeSite's file management system, projects, Site view, snippets, help, and the Tag Inspector.

4. You can create hyperlinks and embedded images in an open HomeSite document from the Files tab (also called the Local tab) in the Resource window by dragging the HTML file or image you want to link to or embed from the lower pane of the Files tab into your HTML document. HomeSite will create anchor or image tags with relative URLs.

5. Wizards provide a graphical front end for creating complex structures such as tables and forms, and for performing complex tasks such as deploying an entire Web site.

6. HomeSite has a hierarchical file management system that behaves much like Windows Explorer and provides access to all of the files on your local system and on any networked drives. From the file management system, you can move and copy files, as well as rename and delete them.

Assessment questions

1. **C.** HomeSite is an advanced tag editor with some WYSIWYG-style functionality. This information is covered in the section titled "Introduction to HomeSite 4.5."

2. **B.** The Tag Chooser is not accessible from the Tags menu but is instead accessible from the Tools menu. This information is covered in the section titled "The Tags menu."

3. **A.** F8 is the shortcut to bring up the Settings window for the Auto Completion function. This information is covered in the section titled "Automatic tag completion."

4. **C.** The Default template includes basic HTML structure tags. This information is covered in the section titled "HomeSite Templates."

5. **D.** You can turn an existing HTML file into a HomeSite template by changing the file's extension to .hst. This information is covered in the section titled "Modifying and creating templates."

6. **A.** Tag Insight displays context-specific drop-down menus as you create tags. This information is found in the section titled "Working with Tags."

Scenarios

You can use two of HomeSite's features to help drive consistency when a large number of developers are working on a site: templates and snippets. You can create customized templates for all of the different kinds of pages on your site so everyone starts building pages from the same set of base HTML. For frequently used components of code, such as JavaScript functionality, tables, copyright statements, and more, you can create a set of snippets to distribute to everyone so they can quickly add functionality and design without having to copy and paste from a sample page or make it up as they go along.

For More Information

- ✦ **HomeSite's home page.** `www.allaire.com/products/homesite/homesite.cfm`

- ✦ **HomeSite developer's center.** `www.allaire.com/developer/hsreferencedesk/`

- ✦ **HomeSite's a Smart Editor from Web Review.**
  `www.webreview.com/1998/02_20/webauthors/02_20_98_4.shtml`

Macromedia Flash 5.0 and Dynamic Media

CHAPTER PRE-TEST

1. How is animation created?

2. What is tweening?

3. What are symbols and why is it important to use them?

4. How are layers used in Flash?

5. How do you create buttons with rollovers and links?

I n this chapter, you find out as much about Flash as you need to know to pass the CIW Site Designer Exam. This is by no means complete coverage of Flash, but you do find out how to create animation, buttons, rollovers, and links, and you find out what tweening, symbols, and layers are.

Introduction to Flash

Flash is a time-based multimedia application that has changed the Web and how you experience it. Since its inception as Future Splash Animator in 1996, Flash has become the standard for Web animation, delivering highly interactive, rich media Web sites. With the release of version 5.0, Flash has taken a quantum leap forward from vector animation software to a fully integrated Web-development tool. Developers publish a Shockwave Flash movie (.SWF) via the application's authoring environment and distribute it by either embedding it into HTML, as a .SWF for playback in the Flash Player, or as a standalone executable file.

For complete coverage of Flash, check out the *Flash 5 Bible* by Robert Reinhardt and Jon Warren Lentz, also from Hungry Minds.

Exploring the Flash interface

The Flash authoring environment consists primarily of the work area, which houses the Stage, the Timeline (containing the Frames and Layers); a standard application main menu running across the top of the window with pull-down menus, the Library window (which stores Symbols), and the Toolbar and other floating panels for editing and controlling elements and behavior. In brief, the Flash application empowers its users in the following ways:

It's important that you know the basics of the Flash authoring environment. This information will likely be asked in the questions on the CIW Site Designer exam.

✦ **The Stage.** This is the visible area of your movie, where you place your buttons, symbols, and other elements. A movie's background color and size relate to the color and size of the Stage. You change your magnification of the Stage in the bottom left corner of your work area, with the Zoom tool from the Toolbar or from the main menu using the View commands. You can also move the Stage within the work area with the Hand tool from the Toolbar or by pressing the spacebar and dragging your cursor on the Stage.

✦ **The Timeline.** The Flash Timeline controls the pace of the movie and what is visible on the Stage. The Timeline is divided into snippets of time called frames. By moving the playhead through the frames, the Timeline simulates animation.

✦ **Templates.** In the Macromedia Flash 5/HTML folder, Flash has HTML publishing templates that you can modify. Flash templates can include any HTML content, JavaScript, or code. You can also create an image map or your own values for Flash `object` (Internet Explorer) and `embed` (Netscape) parameters.

✦ **The Flash window.** When you open a Flash file or create a new movie, the application window displays the Flash authoring environment that contains the Stage, Timeline, main menu, work area, Toolbar, and any open panels such as the Library, Info panel, and so on. This main window is also called the Edit Movie window. You edit buttons, movie clips, and other Symbols in the Edit Symbol window and switch back to Edit Movie mode to place them on the Stage and Timeline. The bottom of the application window also has a Launcher bar for panels on the right and a Zoom control.

✦ **The menu structure.** The Flash authoring environment has a standard application menu running across the top of the window consisting of pull-down menus.The menu headings, File, Edit, View, Insert, Modify, Text, Control, Window, and Help, and their corresponding menu list items, complement (and sometimes duplicate) the process of creating, working within, and publishing/ exporting your Flash movie.

✦ **Flash panels.** The 16 different Flash panels enable you to create, edit, and precisely control objects and their behavior. You can show, hide, group, and resize panels as you work, rearrange them any way you want, and save your panel layout. You can also show and hide several panels, including the Info, Mixer, Instance, Frame, and Actions panels, using buttons in the Launcher bar at the bottom of the application window.

✦ **The Flash Library.** The Flash Library stores and organizes a movie's symbols, imported art, and imported sounds. When you create a symbol or import a graphic or sound, these items are stored in the Library for reuse within your Flash movie, or you may open and use the symbols of other Flash movie Libraries in your current movie. To use a symbol in your movie, drag it from the Library's display window and drop it on the Stage.

✦ **The Toolbox.** The Flash toolbox has four compartments: Tools and Colors (for drawing and painting vector graphics, and selection for all elements); Options (for tool modifiers); and View (for zooming in and out of selected items or for changing the view of the entire Stage).

The Flash Player

The Flash Player, the plug-in that enables Web users to view Flash movies, boasts a user base of 350 million as of June 2001, while an estimated 700,000 developers create streaming Web sites, animations, and games within the Flash authoring application.

Cross-Reference   For more information on the Flash Player, see the "Testing for the Flash Player Plug-In" sidebar toward the end of this chapter.

The Timeline – Scenes, Frames, and Layers

 The Flash Timeline

Flash's Timeline is divided from left to right into segments called *Frames,* beginning with Frame 1, and from top to bottom into *Layers,* beginning with Layer 1 (see Figure 16-1). The Timeline is measured by the number of frames played per second, and controls the pace of the movie by moving the playhead (a red highlight and vertical line indicating the current frame) successively through the frames. By moving the playhead through the frames, the Timeline also controls what is visible on the Stage.

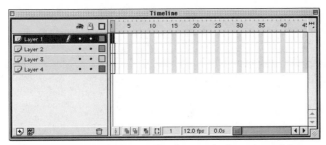

Figure 16-1: The Flash Timeline controls the pace of the movie and what is visible on the Stage.

Flash allows you to remove the Timeline and use it as a floating panel, or dock the Timeline on any side of the Stage. To remove the Timeline, click the gray area above Layer 1, drag the Timeline to the side or bottom of the Stage, and release it.

To keep the Timeline as a floating palette:

1. Go to Edit ➪ Preferences and choose the General tab.
2. Uncheck Disable Timeline Docking in the Timeline Options.

Using the Movie Properties dialog box

Both the Timeline's pace and the Stage's properties are set with the Movie Properties dialog box. To access the Movie Properties dialog box and set the Timeline's frame rate and the Stage properties, do one of the following:

✦ Double-click the Frame Rate in the Timeline's status bar

✦ Press Cmd+M (Mac) or Ctrl+M (Win)

✦ Select Modify ➪ Movie from the menu

You can edit a movie's properties in the Movie Properties dialog box, shown in Figure 16-2, in the following ways:

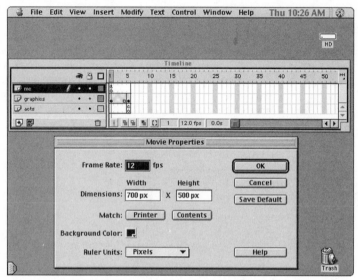

Figure 16-2: The Movie Properties dialog box sets your movie's frame rate, Stage size, background color, and measurement preference.

✦ Enter a number in the Frame Rate field. For Web animation, 12 fps (frames per second) usually works best.

✦ To change the Stage's dimensions, enter values in the Width and Height fields. The default movie size is 550 x 400 pixels.

✦ Select your movie's background color from the pop-up menu.

✦ Select which unit of measure you prefer from the Ruler Units pop-up menu. The default unit of measure is pixels.

✦ Click the Match Printer button to automatically set the Stage size to the maximum available print area.

✦ Click the Match Contents button to center the contents of the Stage and add equal margins around all four sides.

Exam Tip   Settings in the Movie Properties dialog box are Flash fundamentals that may be referenced in the exam.

Scenes

The Timeline also provides access to your movie's *Scenes,* which are sequential sections of your Flash movie. For example, you can make a brief introductory scene for a splash screen. Each scene has its own Timeline and Stage. Scenes are named and numbered by default, but you can change their name and playback order by choosing Modify ➪ Scene or Window ➪ Panels ➪ Scene from the main menu. The resulting dialog box is shown in Figure 16-3.

Figure 16-3: The Scene panel allows you to duplicate, add, delete, or rename a scene and change the order of how scenes play.

To add a new scene, choose Insert ➪ Scene from the main menu, or click the Plus Sign icon from the Scene panel. To remove a scene, choose Insert ➪ Remove Scene from the main menu, or click the Trash icon on the Scene panel. In the Scene panel, you can rearrange the playback order of scenes by clicking and dragging a scene's name up or down the list and dropping it under the scene you want it to play after. To rename a scene in the Scene panel, double-click the scene's name and type the new name. To duplicate a scene, choose a scene by its name and click the Scene panel's Duplicate icon.

Frames

Each frame in the Timeline represents a snippet of time. Starting with Frame 1 and continuing until the movie's end, each frame in the Timeline is played chronologically — unless the playhead is directed elsewhere by a script or user action. You can label keyframes (described in the following section) and then reference them through scripting.

This time-based, or frame-by-frame, animation is the basis of Flash (and traditional) animation. *Animation* is created by rapidly displaying a series of still images, each varying in position or with subtle differences in appearance. This process simulates movement and animates (gives life or movement to) an image.

Exam Tip   The CIW Site Designer exam may include questions on the basis of animation technique and on Flash's use of Scene, Layers, and Frames.

To add frames to your Timeline, choose Insert ➪ Frame from the main menu (the resulting dialog box is shown in Figure 16-4), press the F5 key, or access the Frame Context pop-up menu by Control-clicking the frame (Mac) or right-clicking the frame (Win) and selecting Insert Frame. To add more than one frame at a time, click ahead in a higher frame number and press the F5 key. The Timeline is then filled with frames to that frame number.

To delete or remove frames, select the frame by clicking it and pressing Shift+F5 on your keyboard, or access the Frame Context pop-up menu by Control-clicking the frame (Mac) or right-clicking the frame (Win) and selecting Remove Frames.

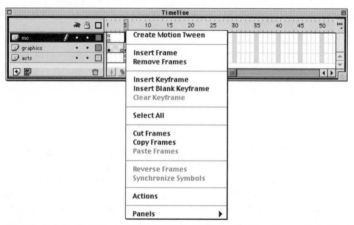

Figure 16-4: The Frame Context menu pops up by Control-clicking the frame (Mac) or right-clicking the frame (Win).

Keyframes

Flash uses keyframes to produce animation. A *keyframe* is frame that contains new content, and is indicated by a solid bullet in the Timeline. When you drag a symbol, button, or other element from the Flash Library (described in detail later in the chapter) onto an empty Stage, the current frame automatically becomes a keyframe. To create a keyframe from the main menu, choose Insert ➪ Keyframe, press the F6 key, or access the Frame Context pop-up menu by Control-clicking the frame (Mac) or right-clicking the frame (Win) and selecting Insert Keyframe.

A blank keyframe is a keyframe in which there's no content on the Stage, or one that removes the content of the previous frame. A blank keyframe is indicated by a solid black outline around the frame. To create a blank keyframe from the main menu, choose Insert ➪ Blank Keyframe, press the F7 key, or access the Frame Context pop-up menu by Control-clicking the frame (Mac) or right-clicking the frame (Win) and selecting Insert Blank Keyframe.

To clear either keyframes and blank keyframes from the main menu, choose Insert ⇨ Clear Keyframe, press Shift+F6 on your keyboard, or access the Frame Context pop-up menu by Control-clicking the frame (Mac) or right-clicking the frame (Win) and selecting Clear Keyframe. To move a keyframe or a blank keyframe to another frame number, click the keyframe and drag and drop it to another frame number. To label a keyframe, access the Frame panel or press Cmd+F (Mac) or Ctrl+F (Windows), and type a name in the Name field.

Editing multiple frames

Flash also allows you to edit multiple frames at the same time. This is especially important when moving animated objects with multiple frames and keyframes, because if you don't move the entire block of frames as a whole, your animation might become broken. This means that the visible result might not be what you originally intended.

To edit multiple frames at once:

1. Make sure the layer (described in the next section) that contains the frames you want to edit is unlocked. A locked layer displays a Lock icon.

2. Click the Edit Multiple Frames button in the Timeline status bar. Immediately, a shaded area bound by markers appears over the numbers in the Timeline (see Figure 16-5). These are the onion skin markers. One at a time, drag the onion skin markers so they cover all the frames you wish to edit, or click the Modify Onion Markers button and choose Onion All from the pop-up menu.

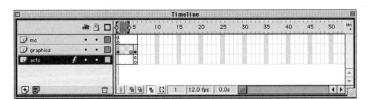

Figure 16-5: The Edit Multiple Frames button and the Onion Skin Markers

3. Select all the frames by pressing Cmd+A (Mac) or Ctrl+A (Win), or choose Edit ⇨ Select All from the main menu.

4. Position your cursor over the selected frames. Your cursor changes to a hand symbol. Click and drag the selected block of frames and drop them where you want them to appear on the Timeline.

Layers

The layers of a Flash movie are like clear sheets of film or plastic. You can paint or draw images, text, and buttons on these sheets, and then stack and rearrange them to produce different spatial effects and visual depth. By default, Flash always starts with Layer 1 and adds consecutive layers on top. If you have a large image on the top layer, it will obscure any smaller images on the bottom layer. By rearranging the stacking order of the layers, you can produce different perspectives. To change the stacking order of layers, click and drag the layer up or down the list and drop it where you want it. Figure 16-6 shows how the Timeline (discussed earlier in the "Timeline" section) provides quick access and control of a movie's layers.

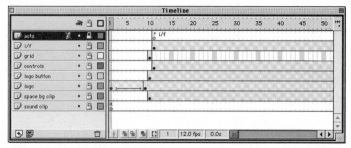

Figure 16-6: The Timeline provides quick access and control of a movie's layers.

Adding, deleting, and renaming layers

You can add or create a new layer using any of the following methods:

✦ Click the Insert Layer button at the bottom of the Timeline

✦ From the main menu, choose Insert ➪ Layer

✦ Access the Layer Context pop-up menu by performing a Control-click (Mac) or right-click (Windows) on a layer name, and then choosing Insert Layer

To rename a layer, do one of the following:

✦ Double-click the layer's name and type a new one

✦ Pop up the Layer Context menu — by Control-clicking (Mac) or right-clicking (Windows) on a layer name — choose Properties to access the Layer Properties dialog box (shown in Figure 16-7), and type a new name in the Name Field

✦ From the main menu, choose Modify ➪ Layer to access the Layer Properties dialog box, and type a new name in the Name Field

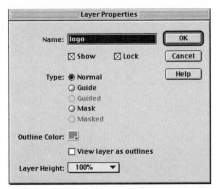

Figure 16-7: The Layer Properties dialog box provides many ways to edit layers.

To delete a layer, click on it to select it and:

✦ Click the Delete Layer button (Trashcan icon) in the Timeline

✦ Drag the layer to the Delete Layer button

✦ Access the Layer Context pop-up menu by performing a Control-click (Mac) or right-click (Windows) on a layer name and choosing Delete Layer

Tip　A quick way to access the Layer Properties dialog box from the Timeline is to double-click the Layer icon to the left of the layer name.

Locking and unlocking layers

While working in one layer, you may want to lock other layers to avoid inadvertently editing the wrong layer. Flash lets you lock or unlock one or more layers in any of the following ways:

✦ In a layer, click the bullet under the Lock icon column. A Lock icon appears, making the layer uneditable. Clicking a Lock icon unlocks the layer, and the Lock icon is replaced by a bullet to signify an editable layer.

✦ Click directly on the Lock icon in the bar above the top layer and all the layers will be locked. Click the Lock icon again and all the layers will be unlocked.

✦ Click and drag your cursor through multiple layers in the Lock column to lock or unlock layers.

✦ Access the Layer Context pop-up menu by performing a Control-click (Mac) or right-click (Windows) on a layer name and checking the Lock box.

✦ If you're working in one layer and want to lock all other layers, Option-click (Mac) or Alt-click (Win) the bullet in the Lock column of your current layer. To unlock all other layers, Option-click (Mac) or Alt-click (Win) the Lock column bullet again.

Displaying layers

Besides the Lock icon, there are two other icons in the bar above the top layer. These two icons control layers in the same way as the Lock icon. The Eye icon displays or hides layers, and the Outline icon displays a layer's content in outline form.

To show or hide layers, perform any of the following:

✦ In a layer, click the bullet under the Eye icon column. The bullet is replaced by a red X and the layer's content is hidden on the Stage. Click the red X again; the red X disappears, and the layer's content is visible on the Stage.

✦ Click directly on the Eye icon in the bar above the top layer and all the layers will be hidden. Click the Eye icon again and all the layers will be revealed.

✦ Click and drag your cursor through multiple layers in the Eye column to lock or unlock layers.

✦ Access the Layer Context pop-up menu by performing a Control-click (Mac) or right-click (Windows) on a layer name and check the Show box.

✦ If you're working in one layer and want to hide all other layers, Option-click (Mac) or Alt-click (Win) the bullet in the Eye column of your current layer. To show all other layers, Option-click (Mac) or Alt-click (Win) the Eye column bullet again.

To view a layer's content in outline form, do any of the following:

✦ In a layer, click the solid square under the Outline icon column. The solid square is replaced by an empty square and the layer's content is shown as outlines on the Stage. Click the empty square again; the solid square appears, and the layer's content is viewed normally on the Stage.

✦ Click directly on the Outline icon in the bar above the top layer and all the layers' contents will be in outline view. Click the Outline icon again to return to Normal view.

✦ Click and drag your cursor through multiple layers in the Outline column to display all content as outlines.

✦ Access the Layer Context pop-up menu by performing a Control-click (Mac) or right-click (Windows) on a layer name and checking the View layer as outlines box.

✦ If you're working in one layer and want to view all other layers as Outlines, Option-click (Mac) or Alt-click (Win) the square in the Outlines column of your current layer. To show all other layers, Option-click (Mac) or Alt-click (Win) the square in the Outlines column again.

Other settings in the Layer Properties dialog box allow you to change a layer's outline color with the Outline Color pop-up color picker, and change a layer's height in the Timeline by choosing 100%, 200%, or 300% in the Layer Height pop-up menu. You can also set the type of layer as Normal, Guided, or Masked in the Layer Properties dialog box.

Masking layers

Creating a mask layer in Flash is not unlike masking in other graphics applications. A solid filled-in shape on a masked layer is completely transparent, whereas any empty or blank space is opaque. First, create a solid, filled-in shape (a single shape, instance, or type object only) for use as a mask and place it on a layer. Then link the underlying layers you wish the mask to show by setting their layer property to masked. The mask layer hides any other unlinked layers beneath it.

For more information on the concept of *instances,* see the "Creating symbol instances" section, later in this chapter.

To create a mask layer:

1. Select the layer you want the mask to show.

2. From the menu, choose Insert ⇨ Layer. A mask layer must be directly on top of the layer you wish to mask.

3. Drop your shape, instance, or type object on the mask layer.

4. To make the layer a mask, double-click the Layer icon to the left of the layer name to access the Layers Properties dialog box and check the Mask box. The Layer icon changes to a down arrow, which is the Masked Layer icon.

5. To mask the layer immediately below, double-click the Layer icon to the left of the layer name to access the Layers Properties dialog box and check the Mask box. Now the masked layer has a Masked Layer icon, and the layer name is indented.

6. Lock both the mask and masked layer to view the masking effect (see Figure 16-8).

Now that you've created a mask layer, you can mask additional layers in any of the following ways:

✦ Click and drag a layer to place it directly below the mask layer.

✦ Add a new layer beneath the mask layer.

✦ Double-click the Layer icon of any layer below the mask layer to access the Layers Properties dialog box and check the Mask box.

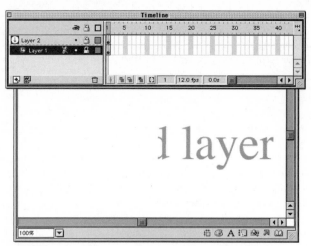

Figure 16-8: A layer mask reveals the contents of the linked layers directly beneath it.

To unmask layers:

1. Double-click the Mask Layer icon of the layer you want to unmask to access the Layers Properties dialog box and check the Normal box.

2. Click and drag the layer to anywhere above the mask layer.

Tip   A quick way to mask and unmask a layer is to Option-click (Mac) or Alt-click (Win) the Mask Layer icon.

Symbols

Objective   Creating button, graphic, and movie clip symbols

Symbols are the building blocks of Flash. By using vector graphics, always grouping your images, and turning buttons and animations into Symbols, you greatly reduce the file size (and download time) of your Flash movie. Another way to keep file size down is to use a symbol *instance*. You create an instance of a symbol when you drag a symbol from the Flash Library and drop it on the Stage. Each instance of a symbol is a representation of one symbol in a movie, but every instance can be named, scripted, or manipulated differently. Every symbol has its own Timeline, Stage, and layers. There are three kinds of symbol behaviors:

✦ **Graphic symbols.** These are static images (GIFs and JPGs) that can be reused repeatedly in a movie but don't add extra file size because they're only rendered once.

✦ **Button symbols.** These are for interactive graphical elements that a user manipulates — for instance, a mouse click or rollover. Buttons automatically have four predetermined frames: Up, Over, Down, and Hit.

✦ **Movie clip symbols (MCs).** These are like miniature Flash movies and contain everything a Flash movie can: sounds, symbols, buttons, and other MCs. Using an MC for animation saves more file size than animating a sequence directly on the Stage, and making an animation an MC allows you to reuse it throughout a Flash movie, including inside a button or another MC. *Smart Clips* are reusable MCs scripted to contain variables, values, and information passed from user actions. Although you build MCs in the Flash authoring environment, you cannot view their playback after you place them on your main movie's Stage. You can only view their playback after you publish or export your SWF file, or in Test Movie mode.

Exam Tip

Movie Clips (MCs) are used for complex interactions. Questions on how to use MCs may be included in the Exam.

Creating a new symbol

To create a new symbol:

1. From the main menu choose Insert ➪ New Symbol, or press Cmd+F8 (Mac) or Ctrl+F8 (Win).

2. The Symbol Properties dialog box shown in Figure 16-9 appears. Type a name, choose a symbol behavior from the radio buttons, and click OK. Automatically, Flash jumps to the Edit Symbol window. You can now edit the symbol.

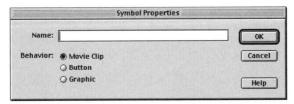

Figure 16-9: Create a button, symbol, or movie clip by choosing a symbol behavior in the Symbol Properties dialog box.

Tip

To quickly turn an image on your Stage into a symbol, select the image with the Arrow tool and press F8.

Creating button symbols

Buttons automatically have four predetermined frames: Up, Over, Down, and Hit, as shown in Figure 16-10. These frame states refer to a user's mouse actions. Where the user's mouse is positioned determines which view of the button is played, as follows:

✦ **The Up state.** A button's inactive view.

✦ **The Over state.** The button's view when the user's mouse rolls over it.

✦ **The Down state.** What a button looks like when a user clicks it.

✦ **The Hit state.** Defines a button's area and is invisible on the Stage.

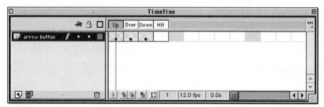

Figure 16-10: Buttons automatically have four predetermined frames: Up, Over, Down, and Hit.

To create a button, follow these steps:

1. From the main menu, choose Insert ➪ New Symbol, or press Cmd+F8 (Mac) or Ctrl+F8 (Win).

2. The Symbol Properties dialog box appears. Type a name, choose Button from among the Behavior radio buttons, and click OK. Automatically, Flash jumps to the Edit Symbol window. In the Timeline, frame numbers change to four frames, labeled Up, Over, Down, and Hit, with a blank keyframe already in the Up frame.

3. Create an Up state by placing an image, graphic, MC (movie clip), or symbol instance on the Stage.

4. Click in the Over frame, and press F6 to insert a keyframe.

5. Edit the image for the Over state.

6. Repeat steps 4 and 5 to create the Down frame.

7. Click in the Hit frame, and press F7 to insert a blank keyframe.

8. Draw a solid filled square, rectangle, or circle to enclose your button image and define your button's Hit state. To make sure your Hit state covers your button, click the Onion Skin button and view your other frames. Remember that the Hit frame is invisible on the Stage, so make sure it's big enough and solidly filled in.

9. Make sure every image in each Up, Down, Over, and Hit state is grouped. Select the image and choose Modify ⇨ Group from the main menu or press Cmd+G (Mac) or Ctrl+G (Win).

10. To return to the main Timeline and Stage, go to the main menu and choose Edit ⇨ Edit Movie. Drag the button symbol out of the Library window to create an instance of it in the movie. (If your Library is not open, choose Window ⇨ Library from the main menu.)

Tip

To quickly toggle between Edit Movie mode and Edit Symbol mode, press Cmd+E (Mac) or Ctrl+E (Win).

Creating symbol instances

To assign actions to a button, first you must create an instance of it by dragging it from the Flash Library and placing it on the Stage. An instance is like a snapshot of a symbol, and it can have its own name, behavior, and properties.

To create a new instance of a symbol:

1. Select the layer and frame in the Timeline in which you want your instance to appear.

2. If your Library is not open, choose Window ⇨ Library from the main menu or click the Library icon from the bottom right-hand corner of Flash's main window.

3. Click and drag your symbol from the Library window and drop it on the Stage. If the frame you want to place the instance in is not a keyframe, once you drop your symbol on the Stage, Flash automatically creates a keyframe as you're changing a frame's content.

Now your instance can be assigned an action, a new behavior, or an appearance change in color, opacity, etc. through the Instance panel (choose Modify ⇨ Scene, or Window ⇨ Panels ⇨ Instance from the main menu).

The Flash Library

The Flash Library stores and organizes a movie's symbols, imported art, and imported sounds. When you create a new symbol, it's automatically stored in the Library. Library items are represented by icons that indicate their file type, and a thumbnail view of the item is shown in the Library window (shown in Figure 16-11). Items can be put into folders, which you can name and organize any way you want.

To create a new folder in the Library window, click the New Folder button at the bottom of the window. You can click and drag items to move them from folder to folder. The Library window also has columns where you can sort items by name, type, modification date, usage number, or linkage status. The Library Options pop-up menu allows you to modify items in a variety of ways.

Figure 16-11: The Flash Library stores a movie's symbols.

A Flash file's Library can be opened and shared by other Flash files by choosing File ⇨ Open as Library or File ⇨ Open as Shared Library. You can also use Flash's built-in Libraries for sounds, MCs, buttons, and other items by choosing Window ⇨ Common Libraries. To use an item from any Library, simply drag its thumbnail image from the Library's window and drop it on the Stage.

To edit items in the library:

1. Select the item by clicking its name in the Library.

2. Choose an option in the Library Options pop-up menu.

 Tip   To rename a Library item, double-click its name and type a new name.

Tweening

 Objective   Working with tweening

Time-based or frame-by-frame animation is the basis of Flash (and traditional) animation. As mentioned earlier, animation is created by rapidly displaying a series of still images, each varying in position or with subtle differences in appearance. Flash has two methods of animation: frame-by-frame animation and tweened animation. *Frame-by-frame animation* creates a larger file size by having a keyframed image in every frame. *Tweened animation* creates a smaller file size by starting and ending with keyframes — and Flash automatically creates the tweened (between) frames. For example, Flash's tweening can scale and rotate an object to give it the appearance of moving closer or farther away.

Exam Tip   Tweening text and motion, or shape tweening questions might be on the CIW Site Designer Exam.

Motion tweening

To create a motion tween, follow these steps:

1. Create an instance by dragging and dropping a symbol on the Stage and positioning it where you want. This is your beginning keyframe.

2. Choose a frame number where you want your animation to end and create another keyframe.

3. Reposition your instance in this new position. Depending on the effect you want, scale, skew, or rotate your instance. You can also choose a transparency or color modification from the Effect panel.

4. Click on (select) your beginning keyframe.

5. In the Frame panel, choose Motion in the Tweening pop-up menu (shown in Figure 16-12). The Easing slider bar creates a slower tweened start or faster tweened start. Check the Scale box if you want your Tween's size to scale, and choose a Rotate option from the Rotate pop-up menu and enter the number of rotations in the times box. The Synchronization checkbox, when checked, controls the playback of MCs that may have a different frame rate or amount than the number of frames the tween is occupying in the main movie.

6. Press the Return key or choose Control ⇨ Play from the menu to watch your tween in action. Notice the dotted lines and arrow of tweened frames.

   **Figure 16-12:** The Frame panel's Motion Tweening options

Motion tweening on a path

To create a motion tween to follow a specific path:

1. Create an instance by dragging and dropping a symbol on the Stage and positioning it where you want. This is your beginning keyframe.

2. In the Frame panel, choose Motion in the Tweening pop-up menu. Check the Orient to Path box, and check the Snap box if you want the center (registration point) of the tweened instance to snap to the motion path.

3. Click your instance's layer, choose Insert ➪ Motion Guide, or click the Add Guide Layer button.

4. Draw a path with the Pen, Pencil, or Line tool. You can also choose an empty (no fill) Circle or Rectangle to draw a path.

5. Click your instance's layer and drag your instance over the path until a small circle appears. This indicates that your instance is recognizing the path. Keeping the small circle visible, drag your instance over the path to the desired place. Snap the center to the beginning of the line in the first frame and to the end of the line in the last frame.

6. Choose a frame number where you want your animation to end and create another keyframe.

7. Repeat step 5, snapping your instance on the end of the path or where you want it to stop.

8. Hide the motion guide layer by clicking its bullet in the Eye icon column.

9. Press the Return key or choose Control ➪ Play from the menu to watch your tween follow along a path. Notice the dotted lines and arrow of tweened frames.

Shape tweening

Shape tweening takes one shape and morphs, or changes, it into another shape. To tween a shape, the shape must not be a symbol and must not be grouped. Make sure to separate your shape by choosing Modify ➪ Break Apart, or press Cmd+B (Mac) or Ctrl+B (Win).

To tween a shape:

1. Click a layer and create a beginning keyframe.

2. Draw a shape.

3. Choose a frame a few frames away and create a keyframe.

4. Draw a second, differently shaped, image.

5. Click on (select) your beginning keyframe.

6. In the Frame panel, choose Shape from the Tweening pop-up menu (shown in Figure 16-13). The Easing slider bar creates a slower tweened start or faster tweened start. From the Blend pop-up menu, choose Angular for blending shapes with angled corners and straight lines, or Distributive for rounded shapes.

7. Press the Return key or choose Control ➪ Play from the menu to watch your shape tween in action. Notice the dotted lines and arrow of tweened frames.

Figure 16-13: The Frame panel's Shape Tweening options

Text tweening

You can motion tween a text item, but it will only be able to move, scale, skew, or rotate. To apply effects such as color or transparency to text, you must first make the text a symbol, and then tween an instance of it on the Stage.

To create a tween using text:

1. Create a new symbol. Type the text the way you want it and press Cmd+E (Mac) or Ctrl+E (Win) to return to the main Stage.

2. Create an instance by dragging and dropping the text symbol to the Stage and position it where you want. This is your beginning keyframe.

3. Choose a frame number where you want your animation to end and create another keyframe.

4. Reposition your instance in this new position. Depending on the effect you want, scale, skew, or rotate your instance. You can also choose a transparency or color modification from the Effect panel.

5. Click on and select your beginning keyframe.

6. In the Frame panel, choose Motion in the Tweening pop-up menu. The Easing slider bar creates a slower tweened start or faster tweened start. Check the Scale box if you want your tweens sized to scale, and choose a Rotate option from the Rotate pop-up menu and enter the number of rotations in the times box. The Synchronization checkbox, when checked, controls the playback of MCs that may have a different frame rate or amount than the number of frames the tween is occupying in the main movie.

7. Press the Return key or choose Control ➪ Play from the menu to watch your tween in action. Notice the dotted lines and arrow of tweened frames.

Actions

Working with actions

Flash uses ActionScript to write navigation and user interaction. You can use the Actions panel to script simple button actions or complicated programming actions. Many of the basic actions are prescribed for you, depending on the object to which you're applying an action. For instance, when you're assigning an action to a button, Flash automatically writes the On Mouse Event handler for you, because buttons are activated by user mouse events. You can also assign actions to MCs to make an action execute when the movie clip loads or reaches a certain frame.

Frame actions are actions that occur when the playhead enters that frame. You assign frame actions directly in the Timeline to a keyframe. For example, to stop the playhead in a movie in Frame 10, you create a keyframe in Frame 10 and add a Stop action in the Actions panel.

Tip   Note that the Action panels vary depending on the action you attach. In other words, if you select a button or movie clip, the Object Actions panel is displayed, and if you choose a frame, the Frame Actions panel is displayed. For convenience, we either refer to the specific Actions panel or simply call it the "Actions panel."

Frame actions

To assign an action to a keyframe:

1. Click the keyframe you want to assign an action to and choose Window ➪ Actions from the menu or click the Actions button on the bottom right side of the Flash window.

2. In the left side of the Frame Actions panel, click Basic Actions.

3. Double-click the action you want. The action appears highlighted and in code form on the right side of the panel.

4. Click the triangle in the lower-right corner of the Frame Actions panel to display the Parameters. (Which parameters appear depend upon which action you chose.) Set the parameters you need to complete your action.

5. Choose additional actions and parameters using the same process (repeat steps 2 through 4).

6. Choose Control ➪ Enable Simple Frame Actions from the menu, and then choose Control ➪ Play to play your movie and frame actions. Or you can test your actions by choosing Choose Control ➪ Test Movie.

Button actions

To assign an action to a button:

1. Select a button in the Library and drop it on the Stage to create an instance.

2. From the main menu, choose Window ➪ Actions or click the Actions button on the bottom right corner of the Flash window.

3. In the left side of the Object Actions panel (see Figure 16-14), click Basic Actions.

4. Double-click the On Mouse Event action. The On Mouse Event code appears highlighted on the right side of the panel.

5. Click the triangle in the lower-right corner of the Object Actions panel to display the Parameters. Choose the Mouse Event parameters you want your button to perform.

6. Repeat steps 3 and 4 to assign the additional actions you want.

7. Choose Control ➪ Enable Simple Buttons from the menu, and choose Control ➪ Play to play your movie and test your buttons. Or you can choose Choose Control ➪ Test Movie and test your buttons.

Figure 16-14: The Object Actions panel

Tell Targets and With action calls

The Tell Target action is deprecated in Flash 5's ActionScript, which now favors the easier With action. However, the basic idea of both Tell Target action and With action scripting is the same. To control a movie or MC, you first must identify a *controller* (a button, frame, or another MC) and a *target* (a movie or MC). The controller then calls the actions used to control the target. The Tell Target controls basic action. The With action can control multiple actions on the same target.

For a controller to recognize a target, your MC must be an instance on the Stage with a unique name. To name a MC instance, select the instance on the Stage and press Cmd+I (Mac) or Ctrl+I (Win) to access the Instance panel and type a name in the Name field.

To control a movie clip with Tell Target:

1. Select the MC instance that will be the controller.

2. From the main menu, choose Window ➪ Actions or click the Actions button on the bottom right side of the Flash window.

3. In the left side of the Object Actions panel, click Basic Actions and select the Tell Target action.

4. Choose the target MC by clicking the Insert Target Path button in the bottom right corner of the Object Actions panel. Click the instance name of your target MC and click OK.

5. In the left side of the Actions panel, select any additional actions you want your target MC to perform (for example, Play or Stop).

6. Choose Control ⇨ Test Movie to test your MC actions.

Audio

 Adding audio

The most common uses of sound in Flash are interactive buttons or loops for background sound tracks. The two types of Flash sounds are *event sounds* and *streaming sounds*. An event sound fully downloads before it begins playing, whereas a streaming sound can begin to play as soon as the first few frames download. Streaming sounds are used for animation voiceover and such, because they can be synchronized and controlled by the Timeline. You can import sounds or use Flash's built-in sounds, and then export them in a variety of ways, including MP3 compression. Also, Flash 5 has introduced better sound control with the use of the Sound Object in ActionScript. Sounds are symbols stored in the Library and can be reused like other symbols.

Compressing sound is important because sound can greatly add to your Flash movie's file size and download time. Flash lets you choose how you want to compress individual sounds via the Sound Properties dialog box shown in Figure 16-15, or you can choose a default setting for all your movie's sounds via the Publish Settings dialog box.

Figure 16-15: The Sound Properties dialog box

To add sound to a button:

1. Select a button in the library and double-click its name to jump to the Edit ⇨ Symbol mode.

2. Add a layer for sound in the button's Timeline.

3. Create a keyframe in the button state where you want the sound to play (i.e., the Down state).

4. From the main menu, choose Window ⇨ Common Libraries ⇨ Sounds.

5. Click a Sound's name in Flash's built-in Sound Library and drag its soundwave thumbnail from the Library's window and drop it on the Stage in your desired keyframe.

6. Choose the desired effects and options from the Sound panel.

7. To return to the Stage, press Cmd+E (Mac) or Ctrl+E (Win). Drag your button symbol out of the Library window and place it on the Stage.

8. Choose Control ⇨ Test Movie to test your buttons and their sounds.

To add a sound to a movie:

1. In the main Timeline, create a new layer for sound.

2. Create a keyframe where you want the sound to start playing.

3. Choose a sound from the Library or open Flash's built-in Sounds Library by choosing Window ⇨ Common Libraries ⇨ Sounds.

4. Click a sound's name in the Sound Library and drag its soundwave thumbnail from the Library's window and drop it on the Stage in your desired keyframe.

5. Choose the desired effects and options from the Sound panel.

6. Choose Control ⇨ Mute Sounds from the menu and make sure it's not active.

7. Choose Control ⇨ Play from the menu to play your movie and hear your sound.

To import sounds:

1. Choose File ⇨ Import from the menu or press Cmd+R (Mac) or Ctrl+R (Win).

2. In the Import dialog box, choose your WAV, AIFF, or MP3 sound file. The imported sound appears in your movie's Library.

Saving and Publishing Movies

 Objective   Making Flash movies

Publishing your Flash movie means exporting your .FLA (Flash movie) as a SWF (Shockwave Flash file) for playback on the Web. Through publishing, you can also automatically create an HTML document for your SWF file. Set your desired parameters in the Publish Settings dialog box (shown in Figure 16-16).

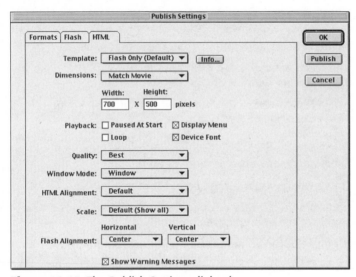

Figure 16-16: The Publish Settings dialog box

The Export function (File ⇨ Export Movie or File ⇨ Export Image) gives you the option of exporting either your movie, one or more frames, or a single image in a variety of formats, including GIF, JPEG, PNG, BMP, PICT, or AVI. You could also export your movie as a QuickTime file or as a series of animated GIFs and simultaneously generate the HTML needed for playback in a browser. Or you could create a standalone projector application in either a Windows executable file format (.EXE) or a Mac projector file.

 Exam Tip   Questions on how to publish or export your Flash movie may be on the CIW Site Designer Exam.

Testing your movie

Make sure you test your movie before you publish it on the Web. From the main menu, choose Control ⇨ Test Movie to check your movie's performance.

Testing for the Flash Player Plug-In

If you're proficient in JavaScript, there are a number scripts available on the Web (see the "For More Information" section at the end of this chapter) that you can add to your HTML page to check for various plug-ins, including the Flash Player.

Flash itself can generate a browser check by choosing the User Choice template from the Template pop-up menu in the HTML panel of the Publish Settings dialog box. This template automatically generates the code for browser detection, and writes a path back to Macromedia's site to direct a user to the right Player. The URL is:

```
www.macromedia.com/shockwave/download/index.cgi?P1_Prod_Version=S
hockwaveFlash
```

To publish a movie:

1. Save your Flash file.

2. Choose File ➪ Publish Settings from the main menu (see Figure 16-16).

3. Click the Formats tab and select the file formats you want to create.

4. For Filename, check Use Default Name or uncheck it and type a new name.

5. Click the Publish button.

Adding Flash movies to a Web page

When you publish your movie, you can simultaneously generate the HTML needed for playback in browsers, including the `object` and `embed` tags for both Netscape Navigator/Communicator and Internet Explorer. You choose the HTML parameters in the HTML tab of the Publish Settings dialog box. The HTML parameters define a movie's background color, size, and alignment in the browser window, among other things.

To create HTML for both Netscape and Explorer while publishing your Flash movie:

1. Save your Flash file.

2. Choose File ➪ Publish Settings from the main menu. The HTML tab is selected by default.

3. In the HTML panel, choose Flash Only from the Template pop-up menu. This template automatically generates the code for browsers.

4. Choose a Dimensions option to set the size of the movie.

5. Select Playback options to control how the movie plays.

6. For the fastest animation playback, select Window from the Window Mode pop-up menu so your movie will play in its own window on a Web page.

7. Pick an HTML Alignment option from the pop-up menu. Default is a good choice because it centers the movie in the browser window.

8. Choose a Scale option. Again, Default (Show All) is a good choice because it won't add borders or distort your movie's ratio, and will display your movie in its entirety.

9. If you select the Show Warning Messages, the user might get an error message when they hit your site.

10. Choose your desired Flash and Format settings and click OK.

Key Point Summary

The following key points were covered in this chapter:

✦ Flash is based on animation and uses a Timeline to control the pace of a movie.

✦ Keyframes denote a change in the content of the Stage or a frame script.

✦ All the elements of a Flash movie — animations, graphics, buttons, and sounds — are organized in layers. Layers can be locked, hidden, masked, viewed as outlines, or used as motion guides.

✦ By turning graphics, bitmaps, animations and buttons into symbols, you can use them repeatedly as instances, but not add significantly to your file size.

✦ You perform the creation and editing of a symbol in the Edit Symbol mode and then drag a symbol to the Stage to create an instance of that symbol.

✦ The Flash Library stores all of a movie's elements and symbols, and Flash has built-in sounds, symbols, etc. you can use in it's Common Library files.

✦ Tweened animation creates a smaller file size by starting and ending with keyframes. By setting up beginning and ending keyframes, Flash automatically renders motion or shape tweens.

✦ Actions can be scripted for buttons, MCs, frames, and sounds. MCs (movie clips) can call actions to control other MCs and the main Timeline.

✦ Sounds can be used in symbols or frames, and file size can be controlled by sound export settings.

✦ Flash movies get exported as SWFs through Publishing. The Publish Settings control all the playback options of your SWF and generate an HTML document to house your movie.

✦   ✦   ✦

STUDY GUIDE

Although Flash may seem complicated at first, after you become familiar with the application, you'll find authoring Flash movies to be rather straightforward. The basics of symbols, buttons, and animations can be quickly learned and applied to build Flash interfaces and presentations. This chapter is intended to help you get started and apply what you've learned in a practical way. The following questions, scenarios, and lab exercises are designed to test your aptitude. Check your work by consulting the "Answers to Chapter Questions" section at the end of the chapter.

Assessment Questions

1. What is a good frame rate for playback on the Web?

 A. 9 frames per second

 B. 100 frames per second

 C. 12 frames per second

 D. 50 frames per second

2. How do you change the Stage color?

 A. In the Toolbox, choose a color from the Color Picker and click the Stage with the Paint Bucket tool

 B. Choose Window ➪ Panels ➪ Fill, and pick a color

 C. In the Movie Properties dialog box (select Modify ➪ Movie), choose a color from the pop-up menu

 D. Choose a color from the Mixer Panel

3. How do you label a keyframe?

 A. Press Ctrl+M (Win) or Cmd+M (Mac) and type a name

 B. Press Ctrl+F (Win) or Cmd+F (Mac) and type a name in the Name field

 C. Assign a script to the frame and name it

 D. Click the frame and press F5

4. Why is the order of layers important?

 A. Layers organize a movie's content and can be used as masks or motion guides.

 B. Layers can be stacked and restacked to create different visual effects.

 C. Layers can be exported as SWF files.

 D. Layers can be saved as MCs.

5. How do you create a motion guide?

    A. Create an animation, save it as an MC, and drag it to the Stage.

    B. Create a new layer by clicking the Add Layer button and draw a path for your instance to follow.

    C. Option-click (Mac) or Alt-click (Win) the layer icon and check the Guide box.

    D. To create a motion guide, you click the Add Motion Guide button, draw a path for your instance to follow, and then snap your instance onto the beginning and end keyframes.

6. How do you mask a layer?

    A. To mask a layer, add a new layer immediately on top and place a filled shape. Option-click (Mac) or Alt-click (Win) the Layer icon and check the Mask box

    B. Click the Add Mask button, then snap your instance onto the beginning and end keyframes

    C. Assign a script to mask the layer in the beginning and end keyframes

    D. Create a symbol big enough to cover your layer and drag it to the Stage

7. Why can't you edit a symbol on the Stage?

    A. You cannot edit a symbol on the Stage because once you drag a symbol from the library and drop it on the Stage, it becomes an instance. The symbol can only be edited in the Edit Symbol mode.

    B. You cannot edit a symbol on the Stage because that creates a new keyframe.

    C. You cannot edit a symbol on the Stage unless you unlock the layer.

    D. You cannot edit a symbol on the Stage unless it is an MC.

8. Why do you need to make a Hit state for a button if the Hit state is invisible on the Stage?

    A. The Hit state determines whether a button contains an action.

    B. A button needs a Hit state or it will be invisible in your SWF.

    C. Although the Hit state is invisible, placing a filled shape around your button determines its active area.

    D. The Hit state is only invisible if your button is an MC.

9. How do you program a button to stop a movie's playback?

    A. Assign a script to Stop on a keyframe

    B. Assign a script to Stop on a mouse event

    C. Assign a script to Go to Frame 1

    D. Assign a script with a Tell Target action

10. What are the three kinds of symbols Flash uses?

   A. Strokes, shapes, and fills

   B. Frames, keyframes, and blank keyframes

   C. Vectors, bitmaps, and sounds

   D. Buttons, graphics, and MCs

11. Why would you turn a large animation into an MC?

   A. MCs can be used in buttons.

   B. MCs can be manipulated with Tell Target actions.

   C. An MC uses less file size and downloads quicker than animation on the Stage.

   D. All of the above.

12. How or where do you view an MC?

   A. In the Library window

   B. In the Edit Symbol window

   C. Perform a Test Movie function to view an MC's animation

   D. All of the above

13. What is an instance?

   A. An instance is automatically created when you import a bitmap.

   B. An instance is like a snapshot of a symbol, and it can have its own name, behavior, and properties.

   C. An instance is any item placed on the Stage with a keyframe.

   D. An instance is created and edited in the library.

14. When you import a sound, image, or bitmap, where does it go?

   A. Every time you import an element, sound, or image, it's instantly placed in the Library.

   B. Every time you import an element, sound, or image, it's instantly placed on the Stage.

   C. Every time you import an element, sound, or image, it's instantly created in the Edit Symbol mode.

   D. Every time you import an element, sound, or image, it's instantly placed in the Shared Library.

15. How do you motion tween a graphic?

   A. To create motion tween, you must name the instance of your MC and then control it with Tell Target or With scripting.

   B. To create a motion tween, add a new layer immediately on top and place a filled shape. Option-click (Mac) or Alt-click (Win) the layer icon and check the Tween box.

   C. To create a motion tween, you must save your animation as an MC and then place an instance in a beginning and end keyframe.

   D. To create a motion tween, you place an instance into a beginning and end keyframe, right-click the beginning frame to access the Frame pop-up menu, and then select Create Motion Tween.

16. How do you control an MC from the main Timeline?

   A. To control an MC from the main Timeline, you must create a button that is also an MC.

   B. To control an MC from the main Timeline, you must name the instance of your MC and then control it with Tell Target or With scripting.

   C. To control an MC from the main Timeline, you must use a keyframe script.

   D. To control an MC from the main Timeline, you must create buttons in your MC's Timeline and then control it with the main Timeline.

17. How do you create a SWF?

   A. SWF files are created in the Library.

   B. SWF files are created when you drag an MC onto the Stage.

   C. SWF files are created when you export or publish your FLA movie.

   D. SWF files are created when you save your FLA movie.

Scenarios

1. You need to make a left navigation bar with uniform buttons and different names, and you need to make the file size as small as possible. How would you use symbols to achieve this goal?

2. A sequence of animation on your main Stage has grown to 10 layers and 50 frames and has become too large. You know you need to turn it into a MC. How would you accomplish this?

3. Explain how to create a short animation for use as a splash screen to introduce your main movie.

Lab Exercises

Lab 16-1: Designing a splash screen

Design a small Flash site consisting of two scenes, a splash screen, and a main screen, and then link the two with scripts.

1. Create a new movie and choose Insert ⇨ Scene. Click the Edit Scene button or choose Window ⇨ Panels ⇨ Scene and double-click Scene 1.

2. Create a short animation in Scene 1, and in the last frame of the main Timeline in Scene 1, insert a keyframe by clicking in the frame and pressing F6.

3. Choose Window ⇨ Actions from the main menu or click the Actions button on the bottom right side of the Flash window.

4. In the left side of the Actions panel, click Basic Actions.

5. Choose Go To from the Basic Actions panel and Scene 2 from the Scene field. Check the Go to and Play box so the playhead will play through Scene 1 and then continue on to Scene 2 and play.

6. Click the Edit Scene button or choose Window ⇨ Panels ⇨ Scene and double-click Scene 2.

7. Create a navigation bar, interface, animation, or anything else you want in Scene 2. In the last frame of the main Timeline in Scene 2, insert a keyframe by clicking in the frame and pressing F6.

8. Choose Window ⇨ Actions from the main menu or click the Actions button on the bottom right side of the Flash window.

9. In the left side of the Actions panel, click Basic Actions.

10. Choose Go To from the Basic Actions panel and Scene 1 from the Scene field. Check the Go to and Play box so that the playhead will go to Scene 1 and play.

11. Choose Control ⇨ Enable Simple Frame Actions from the main menu, and choose Control ⇨ Play to play your movie and test your keyframe scripts. Or you can choose Choose Control ⇨ Test Movie.

Lab 16-2: Building navigation

Design and build a 10-frame movie and place a keyframe on frames 2, 4, 6, 8, and 10. Label each keyframe with a unique name, and script navigational buttons to jump to and pause at each frame.

1. Create a new movie.

2. In frames 2, 4, 6, 8, and 10, insert a keyframe by clicking in the frame and pressing F6.

3. Give each keyframe a different name by pressing Cmd+F (Mac) or Ctrl+F (Win), and type a name in the Name field.

4. In your first keyframe, drag a button from the Buttons Common Library (choose Window ➪ Common Libraries ➪ Buttons) and place it on the Stage. If you want, create some text or shapes as content for this keyframe as well.

5. From the main menu, choose Window ➪ Actions or click the Actions button on the bottom right corner of the Flash window.

6. In the left side of the Actions panel, click Basic Actions.

7. Double-click the On Mouse Event action. The On Mouse Event code appears highlighted on the right side of the panel.

8. Click the triangle in the lower-right corner of the Actions panel to display the Parameters. Double-click the On Mouse Event action and check the Release box under Event.

9. Choose Go To from the Basic Actions panel. Enter Frame Label in the Type field and enter the label name of your next keyframe in the Frame field. Uncheck the Go to and Play box so that the playhead will stop at the next keyframe.

10. Repeat steps 3 through 9 for each succeeding keyframe, and script your last keyframe to return to your first keyframe.

11. Choose Control ➪ Enable Simple Buttons from the main menu, and choose Control ➪ Play to play your movie and test your buttons. You can also choose Choose Control ➪ Test Movie and test your buttons.

Answers to Chapter Questions

Chapter pre-test

1. Animation is created by rapidly displaying a series of still images, each slightly different in appearance or position to give the simulation of movement.

2. Tweening is the process in Flash animation that automatically renders frames between keyframes.

3. Symbols are the building blocks of Flash. Every element, image, and object in Flash needs to be turned into a symbol in order to make it controllable by ActionScript and to conserve file size.

4. Layers organize a movie's content and can be used as masks or motion guides.

5. Buttons are created as four different images: Up, Over, Down, and Hit states. The Over state, for example, is portrayed when a user rolls his or her mouse over the button.

Assessment questions

1. **C.** The best playback quality over the Web is provided by 12 frames per second. See the "The Timeline—Scenes, Frames, and Layers" section.

2. **C.** To change a movie's background color, access the Movie Properties dialog box (select Modify ⇨ Movie) and choose a color from the pop-up menu. See the "The Timeline—Scenes, Frames, and Layers" section.

3. **B.** Press Ctrl+F (Win) or Cmd+F (Mac) and type a name in the Name field. See the "Keyframes" section.

4. **A.** How you stack layers determines what content is visible, masked, or contains a motion guide. See the "Layers" section.

5. **D.** To create a motion guide, click the Add Motion Guide button, draw a path for your instance to follow, and then snap your instance onto the beginning and end keyframes. See the "Tweening" section.

6. **A.** To mask a layer, add a new layer immediately on top and place a filled shape. Option-click (Mac) or Alt-click (Win) the Layer icon and check the Mask box. See the "Layers" section.

7. **A.** You cannot edit a symbol on the Stage because once you drag a symbol from the library and drop it on the Stage, it's then an instance. The symbol can only be edited in the Edit Symbol mode. See the "Symbols" section.

8. **C.** Although the Hit state is invisible, placing a filled shape around your button determines its active area. See the "Symbols" section.

9. **B.** Assign a script to stop on a mouse event. See the "Actions" section.

10. **D.** Flash uses buttons, graphics, and MCs as Symbols. See the "Symbols" section.

11. **D.** All of the answers are true. See the "Symbols" section.

12. **D.** All of the answers are true. See the "Symbols" section.

13. **B.** An instance is like a snapshot of a symbol, and it can have its own name, behavior, and properties. See the "Symbols" section.

14. **A.** Every time you import an element, sound, or image, it's instantly placed in the Library. See "The Flash Library" section.

15. **D.** To create a motion tween, you place an instance into a beginning and end keyframe, right-click the beginning frame to access the Frame pop-up menu, and then select Create Motion Tween. See the "Tweening" section.

16. **B.** To control an MC from the main Timeline, you must name the instance of your MC and then control it with Tell Target or With scripting. See the "Tell Targets and With action calls" section.

17. **C.** SWF files are created when you export or publish your FLA movie. See the "Saving and Publishing Movies" section.

Scenarios

1. Create a button Symbol with a different graphic for each Up, Over, Down, and Hit state. Add a layer and place your text labels in all three states. (Remember that the Hit state is not seen.) Then duplicate the button and just change the text label. Do this for as many buttons as you need.

2. Perform an Edit Multiple Frames action by unlocking all layers and clicking both the Edit Multiple Frames and Onion Skin buttons. Select all the frames and press the F8 key. Type a name for your symbol and hit OK. Delete the selected frames on the Stage, and place your MC where you want it.

3. Create a short (20-frame) animation on Scene 1. From the main menu, choose Insert ⇨ Scene and create a Scene 2 for your main movie. Place a keyframe in frame 20 of Scene 1 that tells the playback head to go to Scene 2.

For More Information

✦ **Macromedia's site.** www.macromedia.com

✦ **Macromedia's Flash Showcase site.** www.macromedia.com/showcase/

✦ **Flashcore.** www.flashcore.com

✦ **Flashkit.** www.flashkit.com

✦ **FlashPlanet.** www.flashplanet.com

✦ **ExtremeFlash.** www.extremeflash.com

Applying Advanced Design Technology

JavaScript and Client-Side Web Scripting

EXAM OBJECTIVES

+ Authoring vs. scripting vs. programming

+ Browser compatibility

+ JavaScript vs. Java

+ Create basic scripts

+ DHTML

+ Document Object Model (DOM)

CHAPTER PRE-TEST

1. What is the difference between the Web development tasks of authoring, scripting, and programming?

2. What is the difference between Java and JavaScript?

3. How do HTML and DHTML differ?

4. What is the Document Object Model?

5. Why are there DHTML compatibility issues between different browsers?

✦ Answers to these questions can be found at the end of the chapter. ✦

One of the key skills in the arsenal of a Web site designer is the ability to manipulate the Web page in response to user input. HTML is the appropriate tool for formatting Web page content to be displayed, but scripting the interactions between the user and the Web page opens an enormous realm of new possibilities for design. The first few sections in this chapter lay out the fundamentals of scripting and scripting languages with bits of code thrown in to demonstrate the various points, and then the chapter moves on to a discussion of the technology and practice of integrating JavaScript into Web pages. Whether you begin with the basics or jump right in to Web page scripting, you should come away with an understanding of the JavaScript language and how it can help you create more compelling Web pages.

Scripting Web Pages

 Authoring vs. scripting vs. programming

Web professionals are often forced to wear a number of different hats — graphic designer, network engineer, writer, editor, marketer, and, of course, developer. Over the past five years, there's been a gradual movement away from a single Webmaster in charge of the entire operation, and towards a team of professionals with different but overlapping roles in site design and development.

 Tip   If you can't wait to start scripting, you may want to skip ahead to the sections on "Introduction to JavaScript" and "Adding JavaScript to a Web Page."

The role of authoring and programming

Web professionals typically fall into one of the two following groups:

✦ **Front-end designers.** These individuals are responsible for *authoring* the site, which means they handle all aspects of the Web site that are visible to the end user. (If you're taking the CIW Site Designer Exam, you most likely fit into this category!) They perform or oversee graphic design and the development of rich media (audio, video, animation). Some focus on the usability of the site or quality assurance (QA). There are also writers and editors that create textual content. Marketing and advertising can also be a component of commerce-oriented or ad-supported sites. Regardless of the specific function, these designers all share some form of ownership over what the user sees.

✦ **Back-end developers.** This group of professionals are responsible for *programming* the site, which means they work behind the scenes with the infrastructure that supplies the services used by the front-end designers. One major role of back-end developers is computer (server) and network management, including security, reliability, and scalability. Another common role is the Web application developer, who uses tools ranging from UNIX shell scripts to commercial application servers to interact with databases and other enterprise services. There are also the analysts who provide the information used to make decisions about the site, and the database administrators (DBA) who keep the data infrastructure up and running efficiently.

In the Real World
Some media- and content-oriented Web sites also use the term "programming" to describe the process of scheduling content for users. This is a very different sense of the word than what is meant here. Programming the schedule on an Internet Radio station or on a Web site featuring animation shorts is clearly a front-end designer type of task!

In the realm of scripting

When you get right down to it, of course, things are rarely that cut-and-dried, especially at smaller companies and organizations. The sheer amount of technology out there means that many Web professionals tend towards one area of mastery or another. There is one area in between pure authoring and pure programming, however, where both extremes overlap: *scripting,* which is all about manipulation.

A *script* is simply a set of instructions performed by some entity or object. A movie script is not a bad analogy — actors perform a set of instructions based on the script, ranging from a simple raised eyebrow to a steamy love scene to unrestrained carnage with pithy dialogue. The actors are equivalent to scriptable objects in a Web page and the actions they perform are all methods that can be attributed to that object (bringing a whole new meaning to the phrase "method acting"). And just as actors can appear in a romantic thriller as the hero with the rippling biceps, and then later in an action movie as the villain with the rippling biceps, the methods of objects in a Web page can be used in very different ways or contexts on different pages.

The concepts of methods and objects can be related to Web scripting in the following ways:

✦ **Scripting languages.** There are a number of scripting languages, ranging from UNIX shell scripting languages (such as the Bourne shell) to the Microsoft Visual Basic for Applications scripting language that is used in client-server and desktop application development. All of these languages support a fairly standard set of programming conventions, which are discussed later in this chapter in the "Adding JavaScript to a Web Page" section. This chapter focuses on JavaScript, which is the standard language supported in all major browsers for scripting Web pages.

✦ **Client-side and server-side.** Web pages can be scripted in two distinct modes: client-side and server-side. This chapter focuses namely on client-side scripting, which is the most important area for designers. However, the following two sections discuss both types of Web page scripting in greater detail.

Client-side scripting

JavaScript was developed initially solely for the purpose of scripting Web pages in the Web browser. The JavaScript instructions are embedded in the Web page and are completely independent of any specific server or other network service — in fact, there's no need for a Web server. You could use client-side scripting to build a help application with indexing and search capability that runs from the computer hard drive or CD, an approach Macromedia took with the Help system for Dreamweaver, its flagship HTML design tool (discussed in Chapter 14).

Client-side scripting is focused on manipulating two broad kinds of objects:

✦ **Web page content.** Any type of content in a Web page is an object that can potentially be scripted using JavaScript. The text can be reformatted or replaced. Form elements such as buttons, text boxes, and drop-down lists can interact with user events. Content in rich media formats, such as audio or even Java applets, can be started, stopped, or changed. Potentially, any element of a Web page is accessible to JavaScript.

✦ **The browser itself.** A Web browser conceptually consists of a number of smaller components — such as frames, windows, status bars, menus, buttons, and the Web document itself. All of these objects can potentially be manipulated using JavaScript.

Web front-end designers take these two sets of objects, the JavaScript language, and a lot of imagination and produce graphical user experiences that are much more sophisticated than plain text and graphics sitting idly on a Web page.

An example may make all of this talk about manipulating objects clearer. Suppose you manage the Web site of a local civic youth group and you want to give each child his or her own Web page. It's easy to use plain HTML to create a text list of names that are hyperlinked to pictures you've take of each child as shown in Figure 17-1.

The simple approach certainly works, but there are a lot of ways to provide a better user experience by reducing screen clutter and improving organization of the page. This simple list method probably isn't the most efficient way to display 100 children's names, for example.

JavaScript gives us a number of tools for improving the user interface that also make the Web page more dynamic. Instead of a plain HTML list of hyperlinks, you could take the approach shown in Figure 17-2.

This time around, the list of children is available from an HTML list box element embedded in an HTML form. When the "Check Me Out!" button is pressed, the image and text are replaced by the content for that child. In this scenario, the JavaScript code is triggered by the button-press, which then scripts an `<img>` element on the page to load the image for the child selected in the list box.

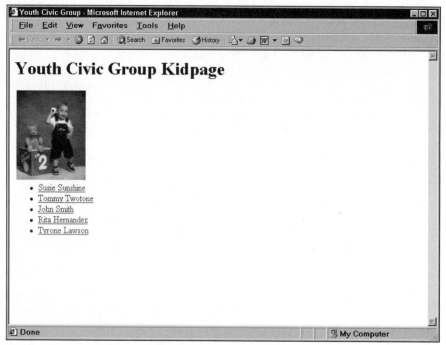

Figure 17-1: A simple Web interface using only HTML

Cross-Reference   The tools necessary to build this JavaScript application are covered in the following sections of the chapter, and the actual building of it is covered in Lab 17-1.

Server-side scripting

JavaScript, as well as a host of other technology options, can be used to script objects on the server-side in addition to the client-side. Server-side scripting provides the foundational infrastructure for building virtually any Web application that requires interaction with services other than those provided by the browser. Some of the most common reasons to use server-side scripting technologies include:

✦ **Form processing.** Any HTML form that collects information requires some way to do something with that information. Server-side scripting provides a tool for processing that data.

✦ **Database interactions.** Virtually every aspect of electronic commerce requires some sort of database interaction. These databases exist on the server-side and must be accessed using server-side scripting techniques.

✦ **File interactions.** Downloading files is easy on the Web, but uploading, moving, deleting, or any other sort of file manipulation requires server-side scripting.

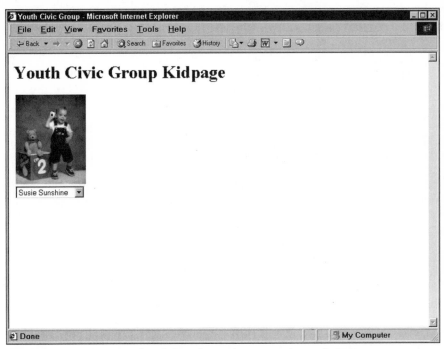

Figure 17-2: An improved Web interface using JavaScript and HTML

✦ **E-mail and other Internet services.** E-mail, File Transfer Protocol (FTP), and virtually any other Internet-oriented service can be provided through a Web interface by leveraging server-side scripting technologies.

✦ **State-management (persistence).** The Web is inherently stateless, so as users add items to a shopping cart or simply log in to a site with access restrictions, there needs to be some way to store that data and associate it with that user when he or she moves to the next page in the site. There are a number of approaches to state-management, but they always involve at least some amount of server-side scripting.

✦ **Any server-side executable.** Even if a particular service or application is not available to the Web server directly for scripting, the actual executable can be run through the appropriate server-side scripting technologies.

Clearly, server-side scripting opens a world of possibilities for Web application development. Although this chapter focuses on client-side script development, it's important to briefly cover the major server-side scripting technologies because they're commonly used and you'll almost certainly have to deal with them at some point in your design career.

In the Real World Many front-end designers actively work with back-end developers to create sophisticated designs that leverage the functionality of server-side scripting. One example is using Macromedia Flash to directly send and receive data to a database by using the network commands in Flash to send data and a server-side script to capture the data and write it to a database. This allows a "Web" application to consist solely of a Flash front-end instead of HTML.

CGI

In the beginning, the Web and HTML were principally designed to make it easier to markup and share research data between scientific researchers. Even in its earliest stages, HTML "coders" wanted to provide Web-based access to existing numerical and graphics programs as part of that sharing process. Capturing data from the Web was an even more important goal for other Web page authors. These pressures led to the creating of the Common Gateway Interface (CGI), which quickly became a standard component of all Web servers.

CGI provides a way to pass data from the Web to an application executing on the server. It also provides a way to pass data from an executing application back to the Web. This technology is one of the most fundamental developments leading to the birth of online commerce.

As the name suggests, CGI simply provides a gateway between the Web and applications(s) on the server. But what about the applications themselves? CGI applications can be developed using any development tools supported by the server operating system, but the overwhelming majority of CGI development is done using a language called PERL.

PERL scripts are typically small (a few to a few hundred) lines of code that provide a simple function such as putting a membership registration into a database or firing off an e-mail in response to an action on a Web page. PERL is an extremely rich and powerful, generally straightforward scripting language that runs on all operating systems and provides a stunning amount of capability with relatively little work.

Application servers

As Web development needs have matured, so have the available tools for server-side Web development. CGI is still used for many types of server-side Web application development, but newer application server platforms are often the choice for large-scale or sophisticated Web development projects. The tools do exactly what they say — they serve Web-based applications. They typically consist of a scripting language, components for common application functionality (such as database access or state-management), and a production environment that manages the execution of the pages and their interaction with the Web server and Web client. The application servers provide (in most cases) an alternative to CGI.

There are a large number of application server tools and platforms, but for all practical purposes, you'll most likely run into one of four different application server platforms, which are discussed in more detail in each of the following sections.

Active Server Pages

Microsoft includes Active Server Pages (ASP) as part of the Windows NT Internet Information Server (IIS) product line where it serves an integral role in building most types of Web applications. ASP provides a small set of scriptable objects for manipulating requests, responses, sessions, and even multi-step transactions. The most important component for most users however, is the database access object set. Even more importantly, it's possible to build custom objects that can be deployed on the server and scripted just like the included objects.

Tip   It's also possible to run ASP on Linux and other UNIX platforms using third party ASP application servers such as ChiliSoft or the fledging Apache mod for ASP. Although it's possible, it's rare in practice!

ASP can be scripted using either standard JavaScript, Microsoft's extended JScript implementation of JavaScript, and even esoteric languages such as REXX or PerlScript. However, the most common scripting language for ASP is Microsoft's own VBScript, which is (of course) based on their Visual Basic programming language.

ColdFusion

Allaire, which merged in early 2001 with Macromedia, offers a cross-platform application server that is focused on a tag-based approach to building applications. Allaire has its own JavaScript-like language for scripting ColdFusion (CF) objects, and an extensive set of tags for connecting to databases, interfacing with enterprise services, and security and state-management.

PHP

PHP (which stands for PHP Hypertext Preprocessor) is an extremely popular open-source scripting language for building Web applications. It provides all of the components its competitors do, but leans strongly towards integration with the MySQL open-source database platform. PHP and MySQL are a powerful combination that runs many Linux-hosted Web sites of all sizes.

JavaServer Pages

Sun's Java programming language (not JavaScript) includes a number of tools for Web development, but from a server-side scripting point of view, JavaServer Pages (JSP) is the most relevant. JSP is the Java equivalent of Microsoft's ASP product — Sun readily admits they "borrowed" from Microsoft's successes with the ASP metaphor in building the product. There are a number of commercial and open-source application servers that support JSP. The fact that there's a public JSP specification makes it possible for anyone to build a JSP-compliant server (for example, Allaire JRun) or integrate JSP into an existing server product (for example, Apache's Tomcat and Jakarta projects).

Basic Coding Concepts

Despite the fact that this chapter has been making a distinction between "scripting" and "programming" activities, both tasks share the same fundamental concept: *coding*, which is the use of a toolset — a language, set of libraries, objects, and any other components — to solve a problem. That problem could be as simple as "Register the number of visitors to my site" or as complex as "Create my site dynamically based on a user profile containing information divulged by the user and collected by this site on the user's past visits as to the user's habits, purchases, and interests." In either case, and in the many shadings in between, some sort of tool will need to be built to solve the problem. For the purposes of this chapter, our tool is JavaScript.

 Throughout this section of the chapter, as in real life, the terms "programming" and "coding" will be used to refer to the development of any kind of application using any kind of language. The terms "script" and "program" are used here as well. It seems that the biggest difference between scripting and programming is typically the paycheck!

Programming obviously involves computers, which means that you have to do a lot of work focused on breaking down the goal of the program into progressively smaller and smaller logical steps that can be explained to the computer using the target programming language. These steps need to be discrete and logical, but the computer must also have some way to control which steps happen when and in what order. In essence, writing a program comes down to issues of structure and control.

Structuring computer programs

Computer programs typically have a number of components that work together. These components are variously called *procedures, functions, subroutines, objects, classes,* or *libraries*, depending on the programming language. Most languages use some combination of these objects. In the JavaScript world, you deal mainly with functions and objects.

The elegance of components

There's an elegant logic to creating and arranging the elements of a program. The creators of the programming language created a set of components that they envision will be useful to program development — maybe a component that prints a block of text and a component that can handle basic math. Neither component does much by itself to solve problems, but if you need to print an invoice in a program, you can take those components and put them together to calculate the total price and print the invoice.

More importantly, instead of creating a program every time you need to print an invoice, you can take those basic components and create a higher-level component that prints an invoice from information on items and prices that are sent to it. Then you can take that invoice-printing component and plug it into a shopping cart application. You can then plug the shopping cart and invoicing components into a Web site that dynamically generates catalogs based on customer profiling — thereby pushing specific products you're certain they'll buy. This sort of structure can be represented by a pyramid, as shown in Figure 17-3.

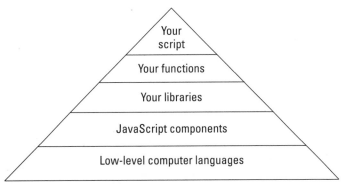

Figure 17-3: Pyramidal representation of the various layers of a program

The advantage of code reuse

An even more elegant aspect of the structural aspect of developing programs is *code reuse*, which, just like reusing components within the same application, allows you to code modules that can be reused in multiple applications. These modules can even be turned into products that can be bought and sold, because they save other programmers time (and thus the money) that would be wasted writing that code over and over in each application.

Here's a typical Web scripting scenario that will show you how code reuse can be valuable. The JavaScript specifics are avoided until later; for the purposes of this example, the focus is only on the process. As a Web designer, you'll be asked repeatedly to validate the contents of online forms. Specifically, you'll be asked to:

✦ Make certain fields in a form required

✦ Validate the contents of a given field to ensure it contains a properly formatted e-mail address, phone number, or Social Security number

✦ Limit the values of certain fields (particularly list boxes) based on the contents of another field

A representative form is shown in Figure 17-4 and the corresponding "pseudocode" for validation is shown in Listing 17-1.

Tip Pseudocode is a way of describing the function of a portion of a program without committing it to a specific programming language. Because all programming languages have similar concepts, the translation is usually straightforward.

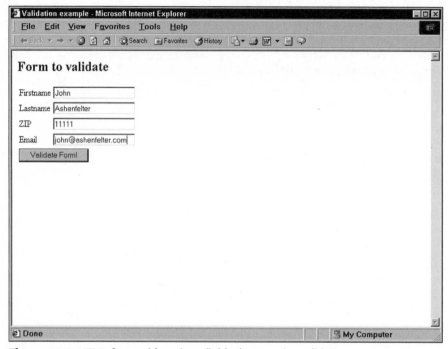

Figure 17-4: HTML form with various fields that require validation

Listing 17-1: **Pseudocode for data validation**

```
if length(lastname) is 0 then prompt "You must enter a last
name"
if length(firstname) is 0 then prompt "You must enter a first
name"
if length(zipcode) is 0 then prompt "You must enter a zipcode"
if length(zipcode) does not equal 5 then prompt "A zipcode must
be in the format 12345"
if e-mail does not contain "@" and at least 1 "." then prompt
"You must enter e-mail addresses in the mailto:name@host.com
format
if left character(1) ordernumber is not in [A-Z, a-z] then
prompt "Order number must start with an alphabetic character"
```

You translate this listing into JavaScript when you do Lab 17-2. Right now, you're just concerned with how to improve the structure of the program. Clearly the process outlined in Listing 17-1 would work. Frequently, you reuse components built into the language, such as some sort of function that determines the length of a text string, as the creators of the language intended. Also note, however, that in the previous code, the same thing is done three times when you check that firstname, lastname, and zipcode all have text values of at least one character. You could write the same piece of code three times with slightly different values, or you could take a lesson from the creators of the language and build your own component, which you'll call "checkExists." Now you can rewrite the code as shown in Listing 17-2:

Listing 17-2: Pseudocode for data validation using a custom function

```
if checkExists(lastname)
if checkExists(firstame)
if checkExists(zipcode)
```

This structure is much easier to understand. And not only can you reuse it in this instance, but you can also use the new checkExists capability in any of your other programs where you need the functionality. In JavaScript, checkExists would be a JavaScript *function*, which is discussed later in this section. The same sort of approach can be used to create JavaScript functions to validate e-mail addresses and the length of the zipcode that would finish our validation tasks for this (and potentially other) HTML forms.

Objects and the JavaScript Language

JavaScript, although not a full-fledged, object-oriented programming language, is at least an object-centric scripting language. The reason this fact is important is that the objects are, quite frankly, irrelevant to the JavaScript language. JavaScript contains all of the basic functionality of any traditional programming language—loops, control structures, variables, operators, and all the rest—but that's all it contains. What makes things interesting for JavaScript is the container that implements it.

The major Web browsers all implement JavaScript. More importantly, they also expose the internal elements of the browser, particularly the browser's internal roadmap of a Web page, to JavaScript as accessible objects. JavaScript-the-language is used to manipulate the browser objects to create useful applications. The browser is the container that runs the JavaScript program in this scenario. These browser objects are discussed later in this chapter as the Document Object Model (DOM).

Several server-side containers can also run JavaScript. Netscape Enterprise Web Server exposes a number of useful server-side objects that can be scripted using JavaScript. These objects can be used to connect to databases, authenticate users, and many other useful functions. IIS includes a number of server-side objects that provide the foundation for ASP. Although VBScript is the primary choice for scripting ASP objects, JavaScript can also be used effectively.

In theory, any application could be a container and run JavaScript to allow developers to manipulate its internal objects. In fact, Microsoft took this approach, although it chose Visual Basic as the scripting language for scripting Microsoft Office components. The point is that JavaScript is the language, not the objects.

Controlling computer programs

Although the structure of a computer program is important, controlling how those structures function with respect to each other is also crucial to developing useful applications. Computer programmers use conditional processing logic to model the complexities of real-world situations, as shown in a generic way in Figure 17-5.

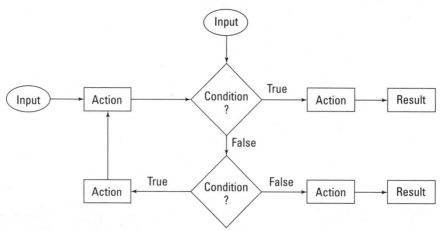

Figure 17-5: Conditional processing logic

Programming languages generally contain some set of tools that can be used to control the processing logic of an application. These tools fall into one of two categories:

✦ **Decision-making tools.** These tools allow the program to choose between two (or more) alternatives based on some sort of decision-making process.

✦ **Stepping (or repeating) tools.** These tools allow a program to repeat a given piece of code or an entire structural element one or more times.

These tools provide the fundamental building blocks for stringing together snippets of code and other structural elements to create useful applications. Table 17-1 lists the JavaScript control elements that are available.

Table 17-1
JavaScript Program Control Elements

Element	Function
If	Makes a decision based on some conditional expression that evaluates to either true or false.
Switch	Makes a decision among a number of possible values for a single expression.
For	Repeats a given code block for a specified number of times.
Do, while	Repeats a given code block while a conditional expression is true.

Each of the following sections discusses the specific JavaScript statements that can be used to control an application. You may wish to skip ahead to the "Introduction to JavaScript" section for a little more background or you can just jump right in.

The if ... else statement

One common goal of a script is to execute some code if (and only if) a certain condition is true. In JavaScript, as in many other programming languages, this control element takes the form of an if ... else statement. Listing 17-3 shows a simple JavaScript example:

Listing 17-3: The JavaScript if and if ... else statements

if statement

```
if(myPortfolioValue > 0) alert('Your stock portfolio is now
worthless!');
```

if else statement

```
if(myPortfolioValue > 0) alert('Your stock portfolio is now
worthless!') else alert('Your portfolio still has some value
left... for now.');
```

The specific syntax of JavaScript is discussed later in the chapter, but it should be pretty clear that this piece of code checks the value of myPortfolioValue and displays an alert message based on the value. The first example provides a single alternative — only if the expression in parentheses is true will the rest of the statement be executed. In the second example, one of the two alternatives will always be chosen.

The switch statement

Although the `if` statement works fine in many cases, there are clearly times where a choice has to be made based on a number of possible values for a given expression. In JavaScript, as in C and Java, the `switch` statement provides this functionality. Other programming languages, such as BASIC, use the equivalent `Select Case` statement. Listing 17-4 gives an example of the `switch` statement in action.

Listing 17-4: **The JavaScript switch statement**

```
switch (membershipLevel){
    case "Platinum":
        alert("This package will be shipped overnight!");
        break;
    case "Gold":
        alert("This package will be shipped 2nd day air.");
        break;
    default:
        alert("This package will be shipped by surface mail! ");
}
```

Caution   JavaScript will find the appropriate case based on the value of the expression in the `switch` statement, but will continue processing all of the code from that point forward. If you want to stop execution at the end of each `case` statement, you must include a `break` statement. In Listing 17-4, there is a `break` at the end of each case to stop further processing.

In this example, the type of shipping is determined by the user's membership level. The only special handling in this case is for "Platinum" and "Gold" members; everyone else gets normal shipping. Contrast this to using the `if` statement to get the same functionality. In this example, the amount of code is about the same, but imagine if there were 10 different membership levels — the `switch` statement works much better in that scenario.

The for statement

In some cases, a particular statement or block of code must be executed a specific number of times. The JavaScript `for` statement is used to guarantee that a block of code is executed a specific number of times. Listing 17-5 shows a very basic example.

Listing 17-5: **JavaScript for statement**

```
for (var x = 1; x =< 10; x++) {
document.write(x);
document.write('<BR>');
}
```

The parenthetical expression contains a lot of information—a variable name to serve as a counter with a starting value (x=1), a condition that signals a "stop" (x =<10), and an increment or step (x++). The rest of the example simply writes the value out followed by an HTML line break.

The while and do ... while statements

The for statement is guaranteed to execute the code a specific number of times, but in some cases, the code must be repeated until a specified condition occurs that can't be explicitly defined in a constant number of steps. The while statement can be used to execute a block of code as many times as necessary until a given statement evaluates to true. Listing 17-6 shows an example of both the while statement and the do ... while statement.

Listing 17-6: JavaScript while and do ... while statements

while statement

```
while (imageLoaded=false) {
    imageLoaded=checkImageLoaded(myImage);
}
```

do while statement

```
do {
    imageLoaded=checkImageLoaded(myImage);
} while (imageLoaded=false)
```

Tip   The major difference between the while and do while statements is that the do while statement will always execute the code block at least once, because the condition is not checked until after the code block has been executed. The while statement checks the value first, which means the code in between may never be executed.

In this example, the checkImageLoaded() custom function is used to determine if myImage has been loaded by the browser (ignore the inner workings of that function for now) and continues to loop through checking until myImage has finished loading.

Designing a program

There are a number of formal design methodologies for building programs, but most JavaScript applications are short and sweet. That does not, however, mean that you shouldn't spare at least a little thought towards the design of the JavaScript scripts that you'll build. Try the following simple steps:

1. **Define the goal of the script.** This could be as simple as saying to yourself "This script creates a pop-up box containing the user's name" or as complex as a written problem specification or needs analysis. Regardless of the exact format, don't skip this step. An explicit goal will help you keep on target as you build the application, even if it's very simple.

2. **Outline the steps to reach that goal.** A flowchart or simple sketch is a good starting point. Outlining the major pieces of functionality will help you pick the correct structures (JavaScript functions and objects) necessary to solve the problem in the next step. This step should not involve the computer — you may end up choosing another tool (Java, Flash) to solve the problem after you've outlined the necessary steps.

3. **Translate the steps into a rough script outline.** Here's where you start picking variable and function names as well as outlining specific JavaScript coding approaches. You might do this on paper or on the computer.

4. **Write and refine the JavaScript code.** Here's where you get your hands really dirty with the development effort. Your initial outline may have been a little off, or you may see a better way to create a function.

5. **Test the code in a browser.** Simply try things out. Keep track of any errors or weird behavior.

6. **Repeat Steps 4 and 5 until everything meets the goals you outlined in Step 1.** This is the debugging process — which is discussed in detail later in the chapter. Make sure that you test it in more than one browser, especially if you're doing anything complicated.

In the Real World One advantage of client-side JavaScript is that you can view the JavaScript of any publicly accessible Web site for your own use and education. There are also many online repositories of JavaScript code (some are listed in the "For More Information" section of this chapter). Odds are, you can find an existing approach to solving your problem or some part of it — and then use that script as a building block for your own efforts.

There's no magic formula or right way to solve a given problem. There are usually better and worse approaches, but only in the simplest cases is there a solitary way to use JavaScript to address a specific problem or goal. The best way to differentiate between better and worse approaches is to design and build a lot of code — the more you do, the better you'll understand the capabilities and pitfalls of JavaScript.

Variables and operators

Every programming language needs a way to store and manipulate data. *Variables* provide the containers to hold those data values. In Algebra, the infamous "x" can stand for different numbers in different situations. Sometimes "x" has a specific value, as in the equation $5x = 20$. In other cases, "x" represents a range of possible values as in the equation for a line: $y = 2x + 5$. Programming languages, even when they're not being used to solve mathematical problems, require the same sort of concepts.

Computers perform instructions literally and have little imagination, so each programming language includes a set of variable types that define the kinds of values that a particular variable will be able to hold. In Algebra, "x" typically held integer or decimal numbers; computer programs require a wider range of variable types. JavaScript has a relatively small number of variable types, which are listed in Table 17-2. Each of these variable types is actually a JavaScript object as well.

	Table 17-2 JavaScript Variable Types	

Type	Description
Number	Used for storing both decimal (floating point) and integer values.
String	Used for storing text of any kind.
Date	Used specifically for dates and times.
Boolean	Used for values that are either TRUE or FALSE.
Array	Used as a container to hold an ordered collection of any other kind of data type. Every element of the array must be of the same type, so you can have an Array of Strings or Numbers, but not a mix of both.

Caution

JavaScript is a *weakly typed* programming language, which means conversions between data types are handled automatically. If you assign a String value to the variable type Number, you will not get an error message and the JavaScript engine will do its best to make the conversion. *Strongly typed* languages, such as Java or C, require explicit conversions between data types. This may sound like a big advantage, but consider the String value "123 Main St."; when assigned to a Number variable, the conversion gives the variable the value "123" which is the "number-like" portion of the String. This sort of unwitting conversion can cause hard-to-find bugs. Always try to use the correct JavaScript data type for each variable in your application to avoid strange bugs.

Operators are the tools that let you do basic variable manipulation and comparisons. Table 17-3 lists the major categories of JavaScript operators and gives examples.

Table 17-3
JavaScript Operators

Type	Description
Mathematical	The standard set of symbols: +, -, *, and / as well as % for calculating the modulus (remainder) in a division.
Comparison	These come in three flavors: relational (<, >, <=, >=); equality (==, !=); and identity (===, !==). You're probably familiar with relational and equality. The difference between equality and identity is that equality operations first attempt to perform and data type conversion (number to string for example) if the two values are of different types. The identify operator assumes they are of the same type.
Logical	These operators are for performing logical AND (&&), OR (||), or NOT (!) operations.
Assignment	These operators perform a mathematical operation and then assign the result to the variable operated upon. For example, x += 5 is equivalent to x = x + 5. Each mathematical operator has an assignment equivalent.
Bitwise	These operators reach back to computing's roots to provide the ability to move the bits in a byte. If you're comfortable with binary math, you'll love these operators; otherwise, you'll probably never use them.
Special	Operators that are fairly specific to JavaScript. These include the NEW operator, which creates a new instance of a variable as well as the VOID operator, which returns the "undefined" value as the result of any operation. The TYPEOF operator is one of the most useful — the result of it operating on a variable is a text string describing the type of the variable — number, string, etc.

Operators perform simple manipulations and comparisons between variables of the same type. This is another area where JavaScript's weak variable typing can cause problems (see Caution above) — adding a string and an integer doesn't make much sense, but JavaScript will try and generate a result for you — just not the one you were probably expecting.

Statements and functions

Another component of every programming language is a set of *statements* that provide the framework for a program. You've already seen statements for controlling the execution of programs (e.g., the for loop) and for making decisions (e.g. the if decision) early in this chapter. There are a small number of other statements that flesh out the framework for building a JavaScript application that are shown in Table 17-4.

Table 17-4 **JavaScript Statements**	
Type	**Example**
Flow control	Controlling the flow of a script is crucial to any non-trivial script. Examples include do ... while; for, switch; continue; break.
Decisions	The decision-making functions enable scripts to branch or react to different situations. The only decision statement is if ... else.
Scripting	Scripts are read by human beings as well as computers. Most languages, including JavaScript include statements to help describe the code. Examples include label and comments (//, /* */).
Declarations	These statements deal with fundamental JavaScript capabilities. Examples include function and var.

During the design phase of a programming project, statements typically provide the bulk of the outline as code is generated from the design documents. The statements outline the structure of the application.

Functions are the programming components responsible for activity in your program. They're used to generate, transform, and manipulate other components of your application. More importantly, you can create your own JavaScript functions to encapsulate frequently used functionality in a single application, or to make it easier to reuse code between applications. Table 17-5 shows the major categories of JavaScript functions as well as common examples.

Table 17-5 **JavaScript Functions**	
Type	**Description**
Math	Typical mathematical functions ranging from trigonometric functions to square roots.
Date/Time	There are an astonishingly rich set of functions for converting and formatting virtually any kind of time or date.
String	Typical string functions are for slicing a string into pieces or finding particular characters in the string.
Browser	These functions access the browser and page elements. A new window may be opened or the content of a frame changed.
Custom	These are the functions that you create. A custom function could display an error message, perform an image swap for a mouseover, or anything else that your imagination and JavaScript permit.

It's important to realize that for both statements and functions, there's a difference in support between different versions of JavaScript and the Microsoft and Netscape implementations of JavaScript. This chapter sticks to the ECMAscript (JavaScript) 1.3 standard. The history and sordid details of various versions of JavaScript are discussed later in this chapter in the formal "Introduction to JavaScript" section.

Debugging

After you've got a well-designed plan for your programming project and a mastery of your toolset, you're still not quite ready to build the ultimate JavaScript application. The final, and in many ways the most crucial skill, is in techniques for debugging your application. The debugging process involves looking under the hood of your program to find out why portions produce incorrect or inconsistent results. Picture your car breaking down on the side of the road. There are two different scenarios for getting it moving again — one is to pop the hood, stare intently at the innards and jiggle a few things, and hope for the best; the other alternative is to systematically go through each system that could produce the symptoms your car exhibits, such as checking the radiator, distributor, battery, and all the other components of the car.

As you can probably guess, good debuggers use the second scenario in analyzing the problem application. The simplest advice is simply to break the program into small pieces to narrow down the problem, and then go through each area step-by-step until you find the problematic one.

JavaScript debugging requires a slightly different approach than compiled programming languages with sophisticated development tools — you basically must write the script in a text-editing or HTML tool of your choice and then open it in a browser. If it works, you may need to test it in other browsers to ensure that it works for your target audience. If it doesn't work, you need to track down the problem code. One of the most common techniques is to add statements to your JavaScript that write out variable values and other internal script information to the browser to help narrow down the problematic statement.

One powerful tool for debugging in Netscape is the JavaScript console, shown in Figure 17-6. If you type `javascript:` into the browser as a URL, you get a window that allows you to type JavaScript statements directly into the window and immediately see the value. This isn't quite as powerful as a real debugging environment, but it's quite useful. Microsoft provides a much more sophisticated tool if you install their Script Debugger application. The Script Debugger is very similar to the debugger in their VisualStudio product, but is much more complex to use than the Netscape tool. The disadvantage to either method is that you can only debug the JavaScript in that one browser — though in most cases that will be good enough.

Figure 17-6: The Netscape JavaScript console can be a useful debugging aid.

Introduction to JavaScript

This chapter has mentioned JavaScript in the discussions of client-side scripting; however, you haven't really had a formal introduction. This section covers everything from the development of the JavaScript language to the details of using it to script your Web pages.

Brief history of JavaScript

Although JavaScript does not have an especially long history, it has managed to trace out a path as complicated and convoluted as that of a typical European royal family. The reason for this crazy history rests squarely on the shoulders of two companies — Netscape and Microsoft.

In late 1995, early in the Web's history, Netscape was working on a scripting language for version 2 of the Netscape Navigator Web browser. This scripting language consisted of two flavors — a client-side scripting language called LiveScript and a server-side, database-oriented version called LiveWire. By December, in probably the most confusing marketing move in the Web world, Netscape and Sun announced a partnership on this scripting language and rechristened LiveScript as JavaScript — same language, new name. Thus begins the confusion between Java and JavaScript that lasts to this day and will continue well into the future.

 LiveWire still exists as Netscape Server-Side JavaScript, which is a component of the Netscape Enterprise Server. It's not as widely used as other competing server-side languages such as ASP, PHP, ColdFusion, and Java, but still exists in many enterprise settings.

The first browser that actually implemented client-side scripting was Netscape Navigator 2.0, released in February 1996. This put the Netscape browser product significantly ahead of Microsoft's rudimentary Internet Explorer browser. However, Microsoft rapidly moved to shore up their dominance in the emerging browser market and released Internet Explorer 3.0 in July of 1996, which supported two programming languages — Microsoft's own version of JavaScript, called JScript, and the Visual Basic-oriented VBScript.

Both Netscape Navigator 2.0 and Internet Explorer 3.0 supported JavaScript with nearly 100 percent compatibility between the two, so Web developers could now add JavaScript support to their pages that would work on both browsers. This version of JavaScript can be considered JavaScript 1.0. As Web developers adopted JavaScript to enhance the functionality of their Web pages, both Microsoft and Netscape responded by extending the JavaScript scripting language to gain market share.

By November of 1996, it was clear that there was a standards war brewing. Netscape Navigator 3.0 was on the way and Microsoft was working on its own enhancements to JavaScript for their 4.0 browsers. Netscape and Sun, as the originators of the JavaScript language, decided to put JavaScript in the hands of a standards body and chose the European Computer Manufacturers Association known as ECMA. While the standards process was slowly creeping along, Netscape 3.0 introduced what was effectively JavaScript 1.1. This version of JavaScript eventually became the core language standard endorsed by ECMA.

 To be completely accurate, JavaScript is now ECMAscript. Although not as snazzy a name as JavaScript, it certainly clearly differentiates it from Java. Of course virtually no one calls it ECMAscript. Even fewer people call it the ECMA-262 standard.

The version 4 browsers from both Microsoft and Netscape supported the ECMA JavaScript standard and extended beyond that core functionality to offer a remarkably consistent, cross-platform JavaScript implementation known as JavaScript 1.2. At this point, the ECMA scripting standards begin to overlap the areas involved in the W3C Document Object Model (DOM) standards as well as HTML, Cascading Style Sheets (CSS), and similar Web technology standards. This new conglomeration of technologies is typically referred to as Dynamic HTML (DHTML) and will be covered later in the chapter.

In the Real World Believe it or not, there are browsers other than Internet Explorer and Netscape Navigator. However, Netscape and Microsoft drive the development of JavaScript and are the browsers this chapter focuses on. Now that the ECMA nominally guides the standards process for JavaScript, the language should become more consistently supported across the browsers that typical users actually use.

JavaScript has remained fairly stable through the Netscape 4.x and the Internet Explorer 4.x and 5.x and higher browsers. Inconsistencies between the two have been virtually eliminated and more and more users have installed the newer browsers, so developing JavaScript is easier than it was when the browser wars were in full swing. The focus has now shifted to standardizing and improving the components that JavaScript manipulates to provide a more powerful application development platform (DHTML).

Strengths and weaknesses

Many developers dismiss JavaScript as simply a "scripting language," which demonstrates that they truly misunderstand the strengths of JavaScript:

✦ **Simplicity.** JavaScript is easy to learn. For many Web designers, it's their first programming language. There are only a few dozen statements and functions to learn and the objects are well documented and not that numerous.

✦ **Immediacy.** Developing in JavaScript means putting script in a Web document and viewing it in a browser. There's no linking, compiling, deploying, packaging, or any other complex script management.

✦ **Interactivity.** Web pages were dead before JavaScript. Now, there can be visual elements such as mouseovers or usability improvements such as data field validation in Web forms.

✦ **Control.** Modern browsers (4.x and higher) expose virtually every element of a page to the scripting engine for possible manipulating. Even Java applets and other media components can be manipulated with JavaScript in the browser environment.

✦ **Object-orientation.** Object-orientation is a powerful metaphor for a scripting language, which makes JavaScript a good platform for real-world development.

✦ **Resuability.** JavaScript can not only be easily reused within and between applications, but scripts can also be easily shared between sites or even borrowed from other locations on the Web.

Of course, there are also a number of problems with JavaScript. Many of the weaknesses have been addressed as the language has matured, but there are still a number of fundamental problems that remain:

✦ **Lack of Extensibility.** JavaScript includes a limited number of statements and functions that operate on whatever elements are exposed by the document object model of the browser. You cannot create your own objects, methods, or events — a feature of sophisticated programming languages.

✦ **Security.** JavaScript originally had a number of security holes, and the language can still be used to cause problems ranging from annoying (closing a browser window opens a new one) to dangerous (redirect from one site to another or collecting information in the background). Major problems can be avoided, however, because the scripting language can't really escape the browser (to access a file for example).

✦ **Cross-platform issues.** Despite the ECMA standardization, standards are still in motion and the various browser versions have differences. Even if JavaScript is the same across two browsers, the object model can differ significantly. The recent release of Netscape (Mozilla) 6, which supports the newer DOM standards without much backward compatibility, broke an enormous number of standard, cross-platform JavaScript scripts.

✦ **Limited development tools.** There are no integrated development environments of JavaScript debuggers that are truly effective. Microsoft offers a JavaScript debugger that can be used in Internet Explorer, but there are no tools comparable to the quality tools available for C++ or Java programmers.

✦ **Limited functionality.** JavaScript is missing many of the common functions found in other programming languages, many of them by design. Local file access, database connectivity, and running or interacting with files on the local computer are all impossible. This is a good thing for Web security, but a bad thing for a full-featured application development platform.

In a nutshell, JavaScript is a great way to quickly build client-side browser applications. It's well designed for the domain it's aimed towards — manipulating the objects contained in a document. It's not a replacement for C++ or Java as far as stand-alone application development goes, but it runs circles around either for client-side tasks on the Web, which are extremely complicated to create and deploy.

Syntax

One "feature" that JavaScript shares with Java is an extreme sensitivity to stylistic variations. In other words, JavaScript is very particular about how language elements are spelled, arranged, and even capitalized. The bad news is that this will be one of the biggest hurdles to get over as you start with JavaScript. The good news is that once you learn it, you'll have a hard time forgetting it.

The standard JavaScript syntax will look very familiar to Java programmers. For the rest of us, the syntax will seem draconian and complex but will soon become second nature. The basic syntax rules are:

✦ **Every line must end with a semicolon (;).** This is one of the first rules you learn and one of the most common (and annoying) mistakes that you'll make. Every single line, no matter how long or how short, must end with a semicolon.

✦ **Capitalization is essential.** Every object, method, property, variable, and operator in JavaScript must be capitalized appropriately. If a variable is named `myVar`, it's different from `MYVAR`, `myvar`, `myVAr`, and any other combination of those letters. All of the standard JavaScript language elements are implemented in all lowercase.

✦ **Blocks of code are demarcated by curly braces { }.** Any JavaScript functions that you create or blocks of code that are part of one of the control-flow statements require curly braces at the beginning and end; for example `{document.write(x);}`.

✦ **Text is marked by quotation marks.** Text in JavaScript can be delimited by either kind of quotation marks (single or double), as long as they match.

✦ **Any special character literals can be escaped in text by a slash (\).** If you need to embed a character with special meaning to JavaScript in a text field, particularly a quote mark, you can use the slash to "escape" the special character so it's interpreted as itself, not as the special meaning it has to JavaScript.

This list of syntax rules makes a lot more sense with some examples. Listing 17-7 shows these rules in action.

Listing 17-7: **JavaScript syntax examples**

Standard JavaScript statement
```
document.write("This is some text that includes an escaped \"
character");
```
JavaScript code block
```
do while (imageLoaded=false) {
    imageLoaded=checkImageLoaded(myImage);
}
```

That's all there is to it. Just remember that the JavaScript language elements are lowercase and that every line ends with a semi-colon, and you should be fine.

Tip   As Listing 17-7 demonstrates, many programmers use mixed case for variable names. One of the main reasons for this is that it makes it easier to find variables when you look at the code. Just remember that JavaScript is case-sensitive, so `imageLoaded` and `imageloaded` are two different variables.

Objects, methods, events, and properties

This chapter frequently discussed objects, methods, events, and properties without spending a lot of time defining what they are. Now is the time to remedy that omission. Purists argue over whether JavaScript is truly an "object-oriented" language, but it really doesn't matter — JavaScript uses all of the object metaphors so there's no way to escape some level of object-orientation with JavaScript. In brief:

✦ An *object* is simply a cohesive collection of methods, events, and properties.

✦ *Methods* are things that the object can do.

✦ *Events* are situations that the object can respond to.

✦ *Properties* are characteristics about the object.

There you go — the fundamental philosophy of object-oriented programming in a few short sentences.

An example of an object will help explain it more clearly. Take a moment and think about a real-world *object*, such as a car. What are its *properties*? A short list would include the make, model, year, color, and style of the car. How about the events it responds to? You could characterize starting the car, stopping the car, pressing the accelerator, and applying the brake all as situations that the car can respond to. And finally the *methods*. You can turn, accelerate, stop, roll down the windows, and play the radio among many other actions. Although this is not an exhaustive list of every conceivable method, event, and property of the object, it's a good example of conveying what the object is by assigning it these abstract properties — creating what Plato would call the idealized form of a car, ranging from a Chevy truck to a BMW convertible.

Exam Tip   It's important to understand and know what objects, properties, events, and methods are and what they do.

JavaScript can access two distinct types of objects:

✦ **Intrinsic objects.** These are part of the JavaScript language itself. They include some variable types, such as String and Number, each of which include a set of properties and functions for manipulating that variable type.

✦ **Scriptable objects.** These are the objects available inside the JavaScript container. For the purposes of our discussion, the *container* is a Web browser; therefore, objects available inside of that container include Web page elements such as images, blocks of text, and applets. The browser itself comprises a number of scriptable objects, such as windows, frames, the browser history, toolbars, and other related elements.

Each browser manufacturer can also include additional, non-standard objects in its version of JavaScript. One good example of a useful non-standard scriptable object is Microsoft's JScript implementation of a FileSystem object, which is useful (especially for server-side development) for manipulating files and streams of data to and from those files.

Browser support

 Browser compatibility

The most problematic issue in client-side Web development using JavaScript is compatibility across different browsers and operating systems. This problem is nowhere near as complex as it was in the late 1990s, but it's still an issue, as the recent release of Netscape Navigator 6.0 (the Mozilla browser) demonstrated. The simple truth is that the platforms are different and you need to take that into account as you develop and deploy JavaScript solutions.

This chapter doesn't list all the differences between the browsers as far as JavaScript goes — it would take a large book to reliably do that. However, you should support 4.0 browsers and above, because the installed base of those programs is huge. There are still cross-platform differences, but both 4.0+ browsers offer good capability and well-documented workarounds for their differences.

There are some options for ensuring browser compatibility. All can be used with some effect in appropriate situations, but none of them is optimal for large, public sites. The common methods used to overcome incompatibilities are:

✦ **Support a standard browser distribution.** This approach is typically used for enterprise intranets where the IT staff can ensure that all users have browser XYZ version 4.1 on their desktops. With a single browser to write for, your cross-platform problems disappear.

✦ **Least-common-denominator approach.** Pick a minimal browser requirement, say all 3.0 browsers and above, and only use functionality that is common to both. This limits your options, but guarantees your cross-platform functionality. This can be an approach to take on public sites if you can manage with the limited functionality.

✦ **Browser detection and custom scripting.** This is the most expensive option, but the most effective. It's not difficult to detect the browser information for a Web page visitor. That information can be used to execute browser-specific script to handle functionality that varies by platform. For example, you could write a dynamic menuing system that supports Netscape 4.x, another one for Internet Explorer 4.x, another one for Internet Explorer 5.x, and then add the new one for Netscape 6.0.

✦ **Cross-platform API.** This elegant approach uses traditional programming methodology to build an application programming interface that wraps the JavaScript. For instance, you build a number of functions for a dynamic menuing system — functions such as `findLocation()`, `createMenu()`, `gotoPage()`, and all the other abstract elements for creating the menu components. The individual functions are then each responsible for being cross-platform and can either take a least-common-denominator approach for simple functionality or custom scripting for complex interactions. More importantly, this method gives you a sophisticated toolbox for all of your JavaScript development.

Netscape 6.0 and Browser Support

The long-awaited release of Netscape 6.0, based on the now open-source Mozilla browser platform, was eagerly anticipated by most Web developers. One of its main draws is that it complies strictly with the dictates of the standards of the World Wide Web Consortium (W3C), particularly in its implementation of ECMAscript and the W3C DOM. After the days of cross-platform incompatibility, a standards-compliant browser seemed like the perfect tool.

The reality is that the W3C DOM is significantly different from the DOM implemented in both the older Netscape and Internet Explorer browsers. There's certainly a good degree of similarity, but properties, methods, events, and even objects have been changed. The result is that any sophisticated JavaScript is likely to break in Netscape Navigator 6.0. Those developers who spent significant effort building complex JavaScript-driven dynamic HTML menus found that their application would simply not work in Netscape 6.0.

Don't get our standpoint wrong; standards-compliant JavaScript is a good thing. The problem is that in complying with the standards, Netscape 6.0 doesn't support portions of JavaScript that have a huge installed base on Web sites around the world. As the W3C DOM becomes the standard for all newer browsers, and as older browsers are replaced by their 6.0 and higher counterparts, a long-awaited new era of cross-platform browser support should be ushered in.

The bottom line is that the only way to know your script works cross-platform is to test it on every platform you want to support. That requires a lot of work, but it's the only reliable way. As you become more comfortable with JavaScript and the capabilities of different platforms, knowing what does and doesn't work will become second nature. And as the browsers become more sophisticated, the hope is that the object models will meet a common standard to allow Web designers to focus on the functionality they desire instead of the quirks of each browser.

Common usage

By now, your head is probably reeling from the wide-ranging discussion presented on the ins-and-outs of the JavaScript language. It's not as complex or esoteric as it sounds. You've seen JavaScript used routinely without even knowing it if you spend much time on the Web. Here are some extremely common examples:

✦ **Mouseovers.** The one defining JavaScript script swaps one image for another as a mouse is moved across a graphic. This is typically used for an "On" and "Off" state of a button which adds emphasis to where the mouse is hovering.

✦ **Pop-up windows.** Regardless of whether it's a simple text pop-up or an entire browser window opening, pop-up windows are a way of life on the Web. They are especially common as an advertising tool to create a new browser window when a page is opened. Some annoying sites even recursively open a new window every time the existing one is closed to create an "unclosable" browser ad display.

✦ **Dynamic menus.** One of the most visually pleasing elements of the JavaScript world is the ability to dynamically open, close, and change menus on the fly. This is commonly used to increase the amount of screen real estate available for content by compressing the menu when it's not being actively used by the user.

✦ **Data validation.** Not particularly exciting, but data validation is where JavaScript becomes a true workhorse. Virtually all good Web-based forms use JavaScript to check the values of data before submitting it to the server for processing. In a similar manner, JavaScript can actively link form elements, such as linking the available subcategory choices in a drop-down list to only those subcategories that fall under the chosen value in the category drop-down list.

✦ **Controlling rich media.** Java applets and other plug-ins (Real, QuickTime, etc.) can be controlled by JavaScript to automatically do things such as start, stop, or load new content based on user activity on the Web page. This is extremely useful for sites with rich content.

There are many other examples of how you can use JavaScript in a Web page, but this covers the most common tasks you will be asked to perform. There are plenty of scripts that do all of these things out there for your taking on the Web, both from the JavaScript repository and tutorial sites, and from sites that simply implement JavaScript functionality you wish to emulate. These ready-made scripts are excellent learning aids, starting points for your own code, or even complete solutions to your existing problems or design challenges. Don't be afraid to try reusing someone else's code.

JavaScript vs. Java

 JavaScript vs. Java

One of the most frustrating events in the history of the online world was the late 1995 adoption of the name "JavaScript" for Netscape's scripting language, which was originally called "LiveScript." Marketers at both Sun and Netscape tied the nascent Sun Java language to the new Netscape JavaScript in a way that has caused confusion to the present day. It's important to start by saying very, very, very clearly that despite the fact that in some cases they look and even act the same, **JavaScript is NOT Java!**

Java is covered more thoroughly in Chapter 18, but it's covered a little here to help make the difference between Java and JavaScript a little clearer. The main differences come down to scope and extensibility, though Java also offers significantly more tools for building services than JavaScript.

Cross-Reference   Chapter 18 focuses on using client-side Java applets to provide a wide range of Web page functionality. Of particular interest to many designers is the ability to use Java applets to provide richer user interface components such as animated buttons, sortable data tables, and other advanced features common in traditional client-server application development.

Java is an object-oriented, enterprise-level programming language. It can be used to build stand-alone, client-server, or n-tier applications. It can be used to create *applets*, which are small programs that run in a browser. It can also be used to create *servlets*, Web pages that provide core functionality for Web applications. Java can further be used to create JSP pages for building dynamic Web content.

JavaScript, as discussed throughout the chapter, is a scripting language used to manipulate the contents of a Web page that has been rendered in a browser of some sort. JavaScript can be used to create simple client-side "applications" that run in a browser. It can also be used to script some server-side objects, particularly ASP and Netscape's Web server products.

Exam Tip   It's important to understand the basic differences between Java and JavaScript. This is a topic that's sure to be on the exam.

In the interest of making the difference even clearer, you can compare Java and JavaScript on a number of features:

✦ **Scope.** Java is typically used on the server-side and for stand-alone (non-browser) applications. JavaScript is normally used to manipulate browser content.

✦ **Extensibility.** Java is inherently extensible — developers can easily create new objects with properties, methods, and events. JavaScript has the capability to create custom objects with properties, but not much else.

✦ **Performance.** Java is compiled to bytecode and then executed by a Java Virtual Machine as it's run. It can be used for fairly high-demand applications. JavaScript is an interpreted language and runs in the browser process.

✦ **Complexity.** Whereas both languages have very similar syntax, constructs, and even objects, Java is a much richer language with literally thousands of objects available. This richness makes Java powerful, but more complex to learn. JavaScript is a simple language that operates on a small and closely restricted set of objects that cannot be extensively modified.

Probably the best distinction between the two is that JavaScript is best suited for interactive Web pages whereas Java is best suited for server-side development.

Adding JavaScript to a Web Page

 Create basic scripts

This chapter's covered a lot about JavaScript and how to write it, but you haven't spent much time actually *doing* scripting. Here's where that all changes. The first order of business involves how to embed scripts in a Web page. The next order is writing those scripts, and the remainder of this chapter goes through a few of the more useful scripting techniques to make sure you've got a good feel for the basics. You may want to refer back to the sections on syntax and programming where we discussed various details of the JavaScript language. You may also want to keep a JavaScript reference handy, several of which are listed at the end of the chapter.

 Exam Tip A knowedge of basic JavaScript scripting techniques is an exam topic with which you should have more than passing familiarity.

The script tag

HTML provides a special tag to identify blocks of code that should be interpreted as a runnable script. Not surprisingly, it's the `<script>` tag. The format of the tag is straightforward, as shown in the following block of code:

```
<script language="JavaScript">
    // some JavaScript code goes here
</script>
```

It's as simple as that. Note the `language` attribute of the `<script>` tag, which is used to specify which script language interpreter should be used to run the block of code. This is important, especially in Internet Explorer, which can run standard JavaScript, Microsoft JScript, or Microsoft VBScript.

A slightly more sophisticated version of the `<script>` tag is shown in the following block of code:

```
<script language="JavaScript" src="myfile.js"></script>
```

In this example, the JavaScript code is stored in another file and imported into the page when it loads. This is an excellent way to package commonly used code — data validation code, for example — so when you make improvements to the code it's reflected in every page that uses the file.

Very old browsers (3.x and lower) and some unusual browsers, such as text-based browsers, cannot handle JavaScript and will not be able to load a page that contains scripts, but there's an easy solution to the problem. In HTML page design, you learned that you can embed comments that are ignored by the browser using the

`<!-- some comment -->` syntax. You can use this technique, along with the scripting comment markup (//) to "hide" JavaScript from browsers that do not support it, as the following code example shows:

```
<script language="JavaScript">
<!--
   some JavaScript code goes here
// -->
</script>
```

This approach wraps all of the script code in an HTML comment. JavaScript browsers will ignore the HTML comment inside the `<script>` tags and execute the code properly, whereas non-JavaScript browsers ignore the entire block of code, because it looks like an unsupported tag and an HTML comment. Note the closing HTML comment symbol also starts with a JavaScript comment. This ensures that the JavaScript engine does not try to interpret the closing comment as JavaScript code.

Once you've got your `<script>` block, the next question is where do you put the block of code? The answer is, of course, "it depends." There are basically two places to put a chunk of JavaScript code — in the page itself (somewhere between the `<body>` tags) or in the `<head>` tag block at the beginning of a Web page. You can also put the JavaScript inline with the event that triggers it. All of these options are shown in Listing 17-8.

Listing 17-8: **Embedding JavaScript in a Web page**

Inline, between body tags.

```
<body>
<h1>Inline JavaScript example</h1>
The script will write text directly to the Web page on the next
line<br>

<script language="JavaScript">
<!--
document.write("Inline text.");
// -->
</script>
<p>Wasn't that cool?</p>
</body>
```

In the head

```
<head>
<script language="JavaScript">
<!--
function showText() {
alert("Page has finished loading!");
   }
```

```
// -->
</script>
</head>
<body onload="showText()">
This page automatically pops up a window when the page finishes
loading.
</body>
```

Inline with the event that triggers it

```
<body onload="alert('Page has finished loading!')"
```

The kind of script determines which location is correct. Scripts that execute immediately as the page loads should be placed in the page between the $\langle body \rangle$ tags.
Custom JavaScript functions that will be executed in response to an event or action
need to be stored in either the $\langle head \rangle$ (if they're long or frequently used in the
page) or in the triggering tag itself.

Exam Tip Be familiar with the $\langle script \rangle$ tag and how to use it to embed scripts in an
HTML document.

JavaScript event handlers

As you saw in the previous sections, JavaScript functions are commonly triggered
by an event. Remember that in JavaScript, you're scripting the object model of the
Web document, which means you can only respond to events relating to the document or the browser itself. Each HTML element has its own specific set of events it
can recognize. These events are dealt with by *event handlers*, which provide the
hook to allow you to integrate JavaScript into the page dynamically.

As shown in Listing 17-8, the $\langle body \rangle$ tag event handler onload is used to trigger a
JavaScript alert function. The code in the onload handler is executed whenever
the browser signals to the object representing the $\langle body \rangle$ tag that the page has finished loading. An exhaustive listing of page elements and their event handlers is
beyond the scope of this book, but Table 17-6 briefly lists some of the more common page elements and the useful event handlers associated with them.

Table 17-6
JavaScript Page Elements with Event Handlers

Page element	Event handlers
$\langle body \rangle$	onload, onunload
$\langle img \rangle$	onclick, onmouseover, onmouseout
$\langle form \rangle$	onsubmit, onreset
$\langle input \rangle$	onchange, onblur, onfocus, onkeypress

Most of those events should be self-explanatory. The `onblur` event handler is triggered when the element loses the focus of the user when they press the tab key or click somewhere else. The `onfocus` event handler triggers when the user tabs to or clicks on the page element. The useful event handlers are closely related to the typical use and function of the page element—pages are loaded, images are clicked on, input elements in a form are changed and interact with user navigation through the form.

Putting it all together

This is where you write some JavaScript, as promised. It may seem like you haven't done enough code so far, but what this chapter has done is give you all the useful fundamentals which will eventually coalesce into a real understanding of basic JavaScript. This section uses a data validation script to demonstrate the techniques discussed throughout the chapter.

Data validation with JavaScript

Picture an HTML form that simply contains a username field and a password field that is part of a registration form. Before the information is submitted to the server, where it will be processed by some server-side technology, you want to ensure that both fields are filled out and that the password is at least six characters. The code is shown in Listing 17-9.

Listing 17-9: **JavaScript registration form validation**

```
<html>
<head>
    <title>Registration Form JavaScript example</title>
    <script language="JavaScript">
        function checkForm(form){
            if (!form.username.value) {
                alert("Username is a required field.");
                form.username.focus();
                return false;
            }
            else if(!form.password.value) {
                alert("Password is a required field.");
                form.password.focus();
                return false;
            }
            else if(form.password.value.length <6) {
                alert("Password must be at least 6 characters
long.");
                form.password.focus();
                return false;
            }
```

```
        }
    </script>
</head>
<body>
<form action="register.cfm" method="post" onsubmit="return
checkForm(this);">

Username <input type="text" name="username"><br>
Password <input type="password" name="password">
<input type="submit">
</form>
</body>
</html>
```

Let's break down what happens in this script. The first thing to notice is that the only page element that is scripted is the form element, where the onsubmit event handler triggers the JavaScript function checkForm() that checks the values of the username and password form elements. It's important to understand that the checkForm function expects to receive a form element — and that the this keyword is used in the event handler to accomplish that. When the event handler is called, the form element is doing the calling, so the this keyword refers to the form element itself. The checkForm function receives the form element and navigates to the appropriate page element by navigating the document object model. You want to work with the username and password form elements that are part of the form. The checkForm function is passed a form element, which is called form, so form.username is the object representing the input text box named username in the form on the Web page. You then access the value property of that element to first check if it exists, and then in the case of the password, that the value is of the appropriate length.

Notice that the if statement is used to control which piece of the script is executed. Also note how the return keyword is used to produce a value for the function. The onsubmit event handler returns this value, so the event handler really becomes either true or false once the script executes — if it's false, the onsubmit event fails and the script ends. The final line of each validation test sets the focus to the problematic input box so the user gets both the pop-up information and the visual feedback he or she needs to correct the mistake. All of this happens without leaving the page — that's the beauty of client-side Web scripting.

Introduction to Dynamic HTML

 DHTML

Dynamic HTML (DHTML) is a buzzword that means far less than you might think. DHTML is the umbrella term under which all of the coolest new Web page technologies have gathered. You've got JavaScript (now ECMAscript, of course), HTML,

XHTML, CSS1, CSS-P, CSS2, and who knows what other technologies that fly the DHTML banner. Let's cut to the chase—DHTML is all about using scripting languages to do sophisticated, dynamic client-side page manipulation. You've already started down that road in this chapter, so you should now be ready to take the next step.

Exam Tip   Dynamic Hypertext Markup Language (DHTML) is a concept with which you should be familiar for the exam.

JavaScript

JavaScript is the core of DHTML, in fact it's the "D" in DHTML. The HTML, of course, stands for the standard Web page design language. With the addition of the technologies covered by the DHTML banner, you simply get more objects to manipulate. Cascading Style Sheets (CSS1 and CSS2) add the ability to change the formatting of page content on the fly. For example, you could change the typeface and font-size for different browsers to improve the cross-browser display of text. You could also use CSS to apply varying format to the page content depending on the path of the user to the information—using Times New Roman 12 pt font for those linking to the site from the *New York Times* and Arial 11 pt for those linking from the *Seattle News-Gazette*.

Cross-Reference   Chapter 11 includes an extensive discussion of Cascading Style Sheets.

Positioning HTML Elements with Cascading Style Sheets (CSS-P) makes dynamic HTML fun, but also gives rise to the majority of cross-platform 4.0 browser compatibility problems. CSS-P is a style sheet language for manipulating objects visually on the page—moving a block of text so it's always floating 10 pixels from the top and right margins for example. In one of the final major browser-compatibility fights, Netscape chose to use the `<layer>` tag and Internet Explorer and the W3C chose to embed it in the style information stored in the `<div>` and `<span>` tags.

Caution   CSS-P was incorporated into the CSS2 Recommendation, which you can find at www.w3.org/TR/REC-CSS2/.

Despite the fact there are these cool new objects to script and new attributes to apply to HTML tags, the JavaScript language remains the same. You already have all the tools to use JavaScript, DHTML just increases the number of scriptable objects.

Document Object Model

Objective   Document Object Model (DOM)

One of the key aspects of DHTML is an explicit, standard DOM. Both browsers are still heading towards that idea, but to be fair, it's a moving target as new standards emerge. A DOM is simply the internal representation of a Web page that the browser builds as it renders the page. The DOM defines what page elements are visible to the browser and how those elements can be manipulated by a scripting language. Figure 17-7 shows an example of a DOM for a browser.

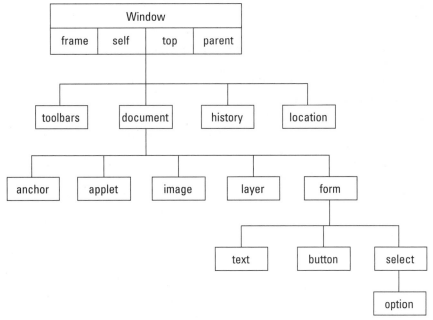

Figure 17-7: Example of a Document Object Model

As you may have inferred, the reason for cross-platform browser incompatibilities is differing DOMs between the browsers. The W3C standard DOM is fully supported by Netscape Navigator 6 and is very similar to the Microsoft DOM in Internet Explorer 5.x. As the next iteration of browsers comes out, there should be very few differences between the DOM of each.

Exam Tip   The DOM — its definitions and how it relates to DHMTL — are essential for your exam preparation.

Implementing DHTML

Implementing DHTML is no different than implementing JavaScript — you have the same choices to make about choosing supported browsers and dealing with incompatibilities between them. In some ways, DHTML makes things harder. Although Web developers had finally managed to start writing pretty good cross-platform DHTML with Netscape 4.x and Internet Explorer 5.x, there's now a third DOM to write for (the W3C standard), which is in Netscape 6.0 and will be in Internet Explorer 6. The only real upside is that instead of having to write new code for both Netscape 6 and Internet Explorer 6, you should only have to write it once for the "standard" W3C DOM that both fully support.

Key Point Summary

This chapter provided a broad overview of client-side Web scripting with JavaScript. It also covered various aspects of scripting as well as the Java vs. JavaScript debate.

✦ Client-side Web scripting is used to manipulate the elements of a Web page or the browser itself.

✦ Scripting crosses the boundaries between authoring front-end Web pages and programming back-end systems.

✦ JavaScript and Java are somewhat similar in syntax, but are completely different languages with different scopes of use. JavaScript excels at client-side browser manipulation, whereas Java is a full-fledged application development language.

This chapter also covered basic programming concepts that are relevant to scripting:

✦ JavaScript offers most of the functionality of traditional programming languages, including decision and flow-control statements, functions, operators, and variables.

✦ JavaScript is a language for manipulating objects — the browser contains the objects that JavaScript works with.

Finally, it covered JavaScript and introduced DHTML.

✦ JavaScript has a very specific syntax that must be followed exactly, particularly with respect to capitalization (lowercase for JavaScript objects and functions).

✦ Scripts can be inserted into Web pages either in the `<head>` element, the `<body>` element, or directly in the event handler of a page element.

✦ Scripts inserted in the body of the page will be executed as the page loads; scripts in the header of the file will only be executed when they are called from an event handler.

✦ Code that is inline with an event handler will execute immediately when that event handler is triggered.

✦ DHTML is simply the combination of JavaScript and Web technologies such as HTML, CSS, and the DOM.

✦ The DOM is the internal representation of a page created when the browser renders the page. It defines what objects are available to the scripting language.

✦   ✦   ✦

STUDY GUIDE

This chapter covered quite a bit of material related to JavaScript and client-side Web scripting. Take a deep breath (maybe a break), and then apply what you've learned to do the exercises and answer the following questions about this chapter. The answers to these questions are revealed in the "Answers to Chapter Questions" section, later in this chapter.

Assessment Questions

1. Which of the following tasks would be the most appropriate to address with client-side JavaScript?

   A. Reading from a database

   B. Writing a file to the user's local disk

   C. Validating a form

   D. Sending an e-mail

2. Objects have all of the following elements except one. Which is it?

   A. Values

   B. Methods

   C. Events

   D. Properties

3. Which of the following is not a JavaScript program control statement?

   A. `switch`

   B. `wend`

   C. `while`

   D. `for`

4. Which of the following variable types is not part of JavaScript?

   A. Array

   B. String

   C. Boolean

   D. Integer

5. What was the original name of the language that became client-side JavaScript in Netscape 2.0?

    A. JScript

    B. LiveWire

    C. LiveScript

    D. ECMAscript

6. Which of the following is not a true statement about the syntax of JavaScript?

    A. All text values must be enclosed in double-quotes.

    B. JavaScript is case-sensitive.

    C. Each line of JavaScript code must end with a semi-colon.

    D. Blocks of code are demarcated with curly braces.

7. Which of the following would not be a typical use of JavaScript?

    A. Data validation

    B. Pop-up window

    C. User registration

    D. Dynamic menu

8. If you want a script to execute automatically whenever the page is opened, where is the best place to put the script?

    A. In the `<head>` tag

    B. Directly in the page between the `<body>` tags

    C. Inline with the appropriate event handler

    D. In a linked script file

9. Which of the following is not an event handler for the `<img>` tag?

    A. `onclick`

    B. `onmouseover`

    C. `onsubmit`

    D. `onmouseout`

10. In the script, `this.form.password.value`, what is the object being manipulated?

    A. `document`

    B. `form`

    C. `password`

    D. `value`

11. Which of the following technologies is not part of DHTML?

   A. CSS

   B. HTML

   C. JavaScript

   D. HTTP

Scenarios

You're asked to create the client-side JavaScript to validate an order form. What kinds of JavaScript functions would you need to build to validate the data fields on a typical order form?

Lab Exercises

Lab 17-1: Creating a dynamic image viewer

Create a Web page that contains an HTML form, a list box, a button, and an ⟨img⟩ tag. Populate the list box with at least three people's names and the names of three images located in the same directory (for example, "Joe Smith", "smith.jpg"); you will also need those image (JPG and/or GIF) files accessible from the server. Use the onClick event of the button object to read the attributes of the list box that store the currently selected name and associated image name. Use the JavaScript load method to script the ⟨img⟩ tag to load the image associated with the name.

Lab 17-2: Building JavaScript validation functions

Starting from the process outlined in Listings 17-1 and 17-2, create a set of form validation routines. One should verify that a required field exists by checking that the length of the value in the text field is greater than 0. One should check an e-mail address field to ensure that both the at sign (@) is present as well as at least one period ".". If you're feeling inspired, you can also validate the e-mail address to make sure it ends in one of the valid top-level domains (.com, .org, etc.). Finally, create a field to validate a zipcode text field to ensure it contains five digits (or either 5 or 9 digits if you're on a roll). You'll use these functions in the real world again and again.

Answers to Chapter Questions

Chapter pre-test

1. Authoring activities are focused on creating client-side material that is immediately visible to the user. Programming tasks involve server-side functionality that is essentially invisible to the user. Scripting is a way of manipulating objects that exist on either the client-side or the server-side.

2. JavaScript is a simple scripting language primarily used to manipulate client-side content and user interaction in a browser. Java is a full-featured, enterprise-level object-oriented development language with many advanced features. Java can be used to build browser-based applets, server-side servlets, and stand-alone applications.

3. HTML is a text markup language used to create Web page content. DHTML is the combination of a variety of browser technologies, including JavaScript, the Document Object Model, and Cascading Style Sheets, in addition to HTML.

4. The DOM is the browser's internal map of the elements of a Web page. The objects contained in the DOM are accessible for scripting with JavaScript.

5. Competition between Netscape and Microsoft is the primary reason for compatibility issues between different browsers. Each browser implements its own object model, which means everything from supported HTML tags to the events, attributes, and methods of the objects can be different in different products, different versions of a single product, or even between the same product on two operating system platforms.

Assessment questions

1. **C.** JavaScript excels at client-side tasks such as validation and is not capable of interacting with databases, e-mail, or local files. See "Basic Coding Concepts."

2. **A.** Objects have properties, methods, and events. A property has a value. See "Objects, methods, events, and properties."

3. **B.** wend loops are part of Visual Basic and other languages, but not JavaScript. See "Controlling computer programs."

4. **D.** Integers in JavaScript are represented by the Number object. See "Variables and operators."

5. **C.** LiveScript was the original client-side language for Netscape. LiveWire was the server-side version. JScript is Microsoft's version of JavaScript and ECMAscript is the new, standardized version of JavaScript. See "Brief history of JavaScript."

6. **A.** Text in JavaScript can be delimited by either single or double quote marks. See "Syntax."

7. **C.** User registration requires some sort of storage and JavaScript has no direct access to either disks or databases, so there's no way to use it for an effective registration system. See "Common usage."

8. **B.** If you want JavaScript to execute immediately as part of the page, the script should be embedded between the `<body>` tags. See "The script tag."

9. **C.** The `onsubmit` event handler is for the form element, not an image. See "JavaScript event handlers."

10. **C.** The object of interest is password—which is probably an input text field. The first two elements are used to navigate the DOM to the correct object. The last element is the property (value) of the object (password). See "Statements and functions."

11. **D.** Although HTTP is the foundation for the Web, it's not necessary for DHTML. You can build complete browser-based client-side applications using DHTML that do not use the Web at all. See "Introduction to Dynamic HTML."

Scenarios

The most obvious validation test is that a field contains a value—this is needed for each required field. You may also want to validate phone numbers for the proper length and content, the zipcode for length, and if you really are interested, the credit card number to make sure it follows the mod10 algorithm—the standard for determining if a credit card number is real or fictional.

For More Information

✦ **JavaScript.com.** `www.javascript.com`: This is one of the central sites for everything JavaScript—scripts, how-to articles, and nearly anything else related to JavaScript.

✦ **Webmonkey.com.** `http://hotwired.lycos.com/webmonkey/`: Webmonkey is the technical side of Wired magazine's Web site. It's a great place to find articles and examples of JavaScript and other Web technologies.

✦ **DevGuru JavaScript reference.** `www.devguru.com/Technologies/ecmascript/quickref/javascript_intro.html`: This JavaScript reference, as well as the many other Web development references developed at DevGuru, are an excellent resource for Web development. The online version is free and there is a now small charge for a downloadable copy.

Java Applets in Web Pages

CHAPTER PRE-TEST

1. What is the purpose of a Java applet?

2. How is a Java applet related to the Java programming language?

3. What are some of the advantages to using Java in your Web page?

4. How do the terms client-side and server-side relate to a Java applet?

5. How do you create an applet?

6. How does an applet provide animation to a Web page?

7. How do you add an applet to a Web page?

8. How do you pass information to an applet?

✦ Answers to these questions can be found at the end of the chapter. ✦

ava applets are mini-applications written in the Java language and added to a Web page. Java is not JavaScript. Java is a full-featured, general purpose programming language. Java has many features that make it particularly useful for Web pages, such as the networking and security classes in its libraries and its portability. Applets have access to the full power of the Java language and libraries. Consequently, applets can provide application functionality unavailable to scripting languages, such as JavaScript.

The Difference between Scripts and Programs

 How scripts and programs differ

Chapter 17 describes the scripting language JavaScript extensively and discusses the difference between Java and JavaScript. It points out that Java, as a programming language, is much more powerful and complicated than JavaScript, a scripting language. In brief: All programming languages are more powerful and more complicated than all scripting languages, in the same way that Java is more powerful and complicated than JavaScript.

An additional major difference between scripting languages and programming languages is that programs written in programming languages are compiled before executing. To compile a program means to transform the program from source code to executable code. The source code is the program in the programming language, e.g., Java programming statements. Compiling the program transforms the source code into executable code, which are instructions that can be executed by the computer (a binary program). Because executable programs have been converted to instructions understood by the computer, executable programs run much faster than scripts, which are source code.

When discussing Java, the program source code file is named with a .java extension (for example, prog1.java and Clock.java). The executable program is called the *byte-code*. The Java program is converted into bytecode before it's executed. The bytecode of the Java program is named with a .class extension (for example, prog1.class or clock.class). The bytecode is downloaded to the browser that executes it.

 Knowing the basic differences between scripts and programs (such as Java applets) is something you should know for the exam.

Introduction to Java

Java is a relatively high-level programming language, related to C and C++. Java was developed in the 1990s by Sun Microsystems. Because it was developed during the growth of networking and the Web, it was designed with many features particularly well suited for network and Web-related applications. Consequently, its use has spread rapidly.

Java is a general-purpose, object-oriented language. Applications written in Java consist of one or more classes that define objects, which are independent modules. Once programmed, an object can be used in any application that requires the functionality represented by the object. The goal of object-oriented programming is to produce objects that can be moved from one program to another without changes, allowing programmers to reuse and share code. In addition, independent modules can be modified without requiring changes in other parts of the application.

Java is simpler to learn than many programming languages, but there's a great deal to it, so it takes time to become a proficient Java programmer. Java is compact, but powerful. To really program well in Java, you need to understand its object libraries. There are many, many libraries for Java. In fact, most of the major improvements to Java from version 1 to the present are improvements to the libraries, not improvements to the Java language, and the size of the libraries has approximately doubled. In addition to the basic libraries that are included, there are special-purpose and third-party libraries available for purchase or for free download on the Internet.

One of the most important features of Java is that it was designed from the beginning to be machine-independent. This is a feature that makes it very useful for network and Web applications. Java can run on all types of operating systems because it actually runs in the Java Virtual Machine (JVM), which is software that must be loaded on any machine before a Java program can run. The procedure for developing a Java program is as follows:

1. **Write the Java program using the Java language statements.** This is the source code. The source code is stored in a file with a .java extension.

2. **Compile the Java program.** The Java source code program is converted by the compiler to a binary program called bytecode. The bytecode is a language that the JVM understands. The bytecode is stored with a .class extension.

3. **Execute the program.** When the program is executed, the JVM interprets the bytecode to execute the program.

This is the procedure for executing a Java program that allows it to be machine independent. When a browser is said to be Java enabled, it means that the browser has a JVM built into it.

Java is fully object oriented. Almost everything in Java is an object. One type of Java object is an applet. An *applet* is a Java object that is designed specifically to run in a browser environment. Applets are client-side Java programs for use in Web pages. Applets provide many features that broaden the usefulness of Web pages. Applets can bring animation and interaction to Web pages.

Java also provides the capability of server-side programming. *Java servlets* are server-side Java programs for use in Web pages.

Brief History of Java

Java was developed by Sun Microsystems engineers to fill a specific need. Existing languages, such as C and C++, were not suitable when designing software for consumer electronics. The software needed to be very small and it needed to be more reliable than other software, because a software failure generally required the manufacturer to replace the entire product. In addition, the software needed to be independent of the architecture so it could run on new chips without recompiling, since manufacturers changed CPUs frequently, whenever new features were developed.

In 1990, the design of a new language to meet the needs of consumer electronics was begun by a group of Sun engineers, led by James Gosling and Patrick Naughton. Because the engineers came from a UNIX background, the language was based on C++. It was originally called Oak, but later it was discovered that an Oak language already existed, so the name was changed to Java.

The Green project was the first project using the new language. In 1992, the Green project delivered the "*7", an intelligent remote control with an animated, touch-screen user interface. The product helped develop the Java language, but was never turned into a consumer product by Sun.

During the next couple years, the Green project tried unsuccessfully to sell its new technology. The important features of Java (small size, security, architecture independence) were not considered valuable in the workstation environment. Then, in 1994, the World Wide Web began to gain prominence. The features deemed unimportant in a workstation environment looked very useful in a language for developing Web and Internet applications.

To show what Java could do, the Sun engineers developed a browser written in Java. Originally called WebRunner; it evolved into the HotJava browser. The technology was displayed at SunWorld in May of 1995. At the same exposition, Netscape announced that its next version, 2.0, would be Java enabled. This sparked the demand for Java. Java use has grown steadily ever since.

The first official release of Java was in January 1996, followed in a few months by 1.02. At this time, Java was not ready for serious application development. For instance, Java 1.02 was unable to print. Before the end of 1996, Java 1.1 was released with major enhancements in I/O, GUI development, security, networking, internationalization, and other features. In December 1998, Java 1.2 was released. Three days later, the release was named Java 2.

Strengths and weaknesses

Java has strengths and weaknesses as a Web language. Many of its advantages exist because it has been developed and enhanced specifically for use with network and Web applications. Other features of Java also make it suitable for Web site applications.

Some advantages of Java are:

✦ Java is a full-featured programming language. It has more capabilities than scripting languages, allowing you to provide Web pages with more functionality.

✦ Because Java was designed with networking in mind, Java has many capabilities that make writing network applications much easier than in many other languages. For instance, the applet feature of Java was specifically designed to allow Java to be included in Web pages.

✦ Because of Java's network orientation, security has been considered in its development, making Java relatively safe for interactive Web site applications.

✦ Java was designed to be portable; therefore, it can run on any operating system. Thus, a Java program can be downloaded from a Web page and run by any operating system, such as Windows, Mac, UNIX, etc., making a Web page with Java included accessible by all users that have Java-enabled browsers.

✦ Java runs faster than scripting languages.

✦ Java is popular, and many Java developers have made their Java applications freely available for anyone to use. With an abundance of Java applications available for download from the Web, you can often find exactly the Java application you need for your Web site without needing to write any Java code yourself.

✦ Java is *multithreaded*, which means Java can perform more than one task at a time, independently, such as interacting with several users at once or performing a computation in one thread while interacting with a user in another thread.

 In the Real World

Java's multithreading capabilities interact with the multitasking capability of the operating system, and the operating system may not support Java's multithreading technology. Thus, the Java program may not provide the same speed and efficiency it exhibits in stand-alone mode as it does when running as an applet on some operating systems, especially those with better multitasking capabilities.

Some disadvantages of Java are:

✦ Because Java is a full-featured programming language, it's more complicated and has more capabilities than scripting languages, making Java more difficult to learn than scripting languages. This disadvantage is somewhat offset by the availability of many Java applications that can be downloaded from the Web.

✦ The use of Java on a Web page requires that the user access the Web page with a Java-enabled browser. Most modern browsers are Java enabled, but some older browsers may not be able to run the Java application. In addition, a browser may be Java enabled, but use an older version than the version used for your Web application. In this case, the browser may see some parts of the Java program as errors.

✦ Although a Java program is small for a full-featured programming language, Java programs download slower than scripts and the entire applet must be downloaded before it can begin execution, making Java unsuitable for some uses when users are accessing via phone modems.

✦ Java applets are not cached in the browser cache. The Java program must be downloaded every time the user accesses it.

Applets

How applets work

Applets are Java programs. The name, applet, refers to small applications or mini-applications. An applet is a type of Java program designed specifically to be run inside a Web page. An applet can only be run using HTML code; it cannot be run as an independent, stand-alone Java program outside of the browser.

An applet is a client-side application. That is, the Java applet runs on the client computer. When the Web page that includes the Java applet is downloaded and parsed by the browser, the Java applet is also downloaded. After it's downloaded, an applet can interact with the user and perform tasks without requiring further resources from the server. The browser executes the applet and displays the results. Thus, the browser must be Java enabled to successfully run applets.

Applets are used to give the Web page more functionality than the static HTML code can provide. Applets can provide animated graphics for a Web page. Applets can be used to provide a user interface for dynamic, interactive Web applications. For instance, an applet might provide a GUI in which the user can interact with a database, displaying or updating data. An applet might allow the user to play an interactive game, setup and manage a calendar, operate a calculator, store and manipulate financial information, or interact with many other application programs.

Because applets are downloaded to the client, the potential exists for an applet to access, change, or damage information on the client computer. Consequently, security restrictions are placed on the applet's functionality to protect the user. By default, the applet:

✦ Cannot access files on the client computer

✦ Cannot start or run any other program on the client computer

✦ Can only communicate with the computer from which the HTML page containing the applet was downloaded

These default conditions can be changed using a *Java policy file*, which is an ASCII file that authorizes specific operations.

Java applets are Java bytecode, compiled Java programs. Java applets always have the .class extension (e.g., prog1.class and clock.class).

Exam Tip   All the information on how Java applets work is essential for answering certain questions on the CIW Site Designer exam.

Servlets

Servlets are sometimes referred to as applets that run on the server side. Servlets are server-side Java programs used for applications that need to run on the server, rather than on the client. For example, if data were needed by the application from a database located on another computer, a servlet could get data from the database and send it to the browser. A servlet could be used for displaying data or for interactive data update.

Servlets are alternatives to CGI programs. Servlets are faster than CGI programs because servlets are multithreaded, handling more than one client request at a time. This eliminates the need for the extensive start-up overhead required by CGI programs. Servlets are portable so if you move your application to a different operating system, you don't need to rewrite or recompile your Java program, as you would a CGI program. Servlets provide the benefits of the Java security features.

To use servlets on your Web server, you must have a servlet container or servlet engine installed. This is a separate piece of software that interacts with your Hypertext Transfer Protocol (HTTP) server to execute the servlets. Several third-party servlet engines are available for Apache Web Server, iPlant Web Server, Microsoft Internet Information Server (IIS), and others. Tomcat is one popular servlet engine that works with any Web server that supports servlets. Tomcat is an open source container developed at the Apache Software Foundation.

Cross-Reference   For more information on servlets, see the Java servlet page on the Sun Web Site (`http://java.sun.com/products/servlet/`). The remainder of this chapter discusses Java applets.

Creating Applets

The applet is created independently of the Web page. Applet creation includes the following steps:

1. The applet is programmed using the Java programming language.

2. The Java applet is compiled and stored in a separate file with a class extension (e.g., clock.class).

3. The applet is added to the Web page using an HTML tag.

Unless you already know Java, it's unlikely that you, as the Web designer, will create the applet yourself. Java is a full-featured, complicated programming language that is not learned in a few hours. A Java applet should be created by an experienced, competent Java programmer.

There are two ways that you can get the Java applet you need for your Web page:

✦ **Downloading an existing applet.** If the functionality of the applet you need is widely used, the applet you need may be available for download from the Internet.

✦ **Programming your own applet.** However, if you need an applet to perform operations that are specific and unique to your Web site, you'll need to work with a programmer to develop an applet with the functionality you need.

Using downloaded applets

If you decide to search for an applet to download from the Internet, you need to remember that the applet must do exactly what you require. You cannot alter the applet in any way. For instance, if it requires certain parameters, you need to have those parameters. You cannot alter the applet to use different parameters. You must use the parameters as programmed into the Java source code before it was compiled into a bytecode applet.

When downloading an applet for use in your Web page, be sure of the copyright and fee status of the applet. Many applets are available for free, with no copyright stipulations. However, some programmers place restrictions on the use of the applet. For instance, the programmer might make the applet available free to non-profit organizations, but not to commercial organizations. Or the programmer may require a link to his or her home page on any Web page that includes his or her applet. In some cases, a fee is required to use the applet. Be sure you're clear on the conditions of use for any applets you download.

When adding an applet to your Web page, you must use the name exactly as it existed prior to download. You cannot use a different file name for the applet or the browser will not be able to locate it for download.

There are several large archives of applets on the Internet that allow free download. In addition, there are many other small sites where developers make their applets available on their Web sites. A search on AltaVista entering "applet archive" as the search text resulted in over 28 million hits. The site at the top of the results list was Java Boutique, one of the better Java applet archives. Some applet archives are:

✦ **Java Boutique.** `http://javaboutique.webdeveloper.com/`

✦ **JavaPowered.** `www.javapowered.com/werks.html`

✦ **Spriteworks applet library.** `www.spriteworks.com/applets.html`

Working with programmers

If the exact applet you need cannot be found on the Internet, you'll need to work with a programmer to develop the applet you require. As the Web designer, it's your responsibility to determine the functionality and user interface design of the applet. It's the programmer's responsibility to advise you regarding the technical capabilities and limitations of Java with respect to the functionality and interface you design. It's very important to work closely with the programmer at every step of the program development. Here are some basic guidelines:

✦ **Create a design document.** The first step of a program design is to create a document that specifies exactly what the program should do. For instance, if you want a program that plays tic-tac-toe with the user, describe its operation in the document. Write the document without any assumption that the programmer understands tic-tac-toe. Where there are options, the document should provide information on selecting the options. Who is O and who is X? Who makes the first play? What rules does the computer use to make its play?

✦ **Discuss it with your programmer.** Provide this document to your programmer and go over it in detail. The programmer may point out some aspects of your design that are beyond the capability of Java. In most cases, the programmer will have questions that are not answered in the document. An experienced programmer may have suggestions for revisions to your design that will make the program easier, smaller, faster, or more efficient. After discussing the design with the programmer, revise the document to include the added or revised specifications. Continue with this process of reviewing the design with the programmer until you're both satisfied with the design specifications.

✦ **Create a functional GUI.** In addition to the functionality of the applet, you need to design the look of the graphical user interface (GUI) through which the user accesses the functionality of the applet. For this purpose, a drawing of the proposed GUI is useful, showing the buttons, text boxes, icons, and other components. This can be part of the above design document or a separate document. Again, review the GUI design in detail with the programmer, and remember: An experienced programmer may have very useful suggestions. Continue to revise the GUI design until both you and the programmer are satisfied with the results.

✦ **Test the applet.** In addition to designing the applet, you'll test the applet as well. If the applet is very complicated, the programmer can provide you with interim programs to test that have partial functionality. Testing is very important, and you should test as thoroughly as possible. Test all the functionality of the program. For some types of programs, it may be important to test the program features in different orders. Sometimes a program feature will fail when it's used after another feature but not fail if it's used before the other feature. If your Web site has a lot of traffic, you need to test the ability of the applet to handle a high volume of users.

Tip   Reload the page when testing an applet. Reloading the page will ensure that the browser reloads the applet, rather than just restarting it, so you'll see the changes. Newer browsers are less likely than older browsers to just restart the applet, but reloading the page each time the applet is changed avoids any possible problems.

✦ **Debug the applet.** No matter how carefully and thoroughly you test a Web page, a bug in the applet will often be discovered after it's added to your Web page. Because many more people are using it, often in ways that never occurred to you during testing, problems that were not uncovered in the testing phase can rise to the surface. Be sure that your agreement with the programmer includes fixing any additional bugs discovered after the applet is released and that the programmer will be available to do so in a timely manner.

✦ **Prepare for future revisions.** When the programmer has finished the applet, he or she should deliver the source code, as well as the bytecode applet. The applet is very likely to need revising or updating at some time in the future. The source code is required in order to make any changes to the applet. When applet updating is needed, the original programmer may not be able to locate the source code or may not be available. If you have a copy of the source code, you can provide it to the programmer, allowing a different programmer to revise the program if necessary.

Applet authoring tools

Objective   Applet development tools

If you're acquainted with Java, either as an experienced programmer, or with just a little knowledge, you may decide to write the applet yourself. Although any text editor can be used to write a Java applet program, Java applet authoring tools, which can greatly facilitate the creation of applets, are also available. Java authoring tools are aimed at different users. Some are useful for novices, whereas others are more difficult and require more experience.

Most authoring tools provide a visual environment for building Java applets. They provide visual tools and reusable components that can be inserted into the applet. The environment includes an editor, a debugger, and a compiler. Often, wizards are provided to assist in developing common components. Authoring tools can assist the novice by handling many of the programming details, thereby enabling the user to get by with less programming knowledge. Authoring tools can also assist the experienced developer by allowing faster program development and by automating programming tasks, such as assigning motion and hyperlinks to objects or creating events.

Exam Tip   A Java authoring tool might also be referred to as an Applet Development utility or an Interactive Development Environment (IDE). Make sure you have a grasp of all the applet development options covered in this portion of the chapter.

Some of the most widely used Java authoring tools are:

✦ **JBuilder by Borland.** A very comprehensive tool that provides many features of value to programmers. However, it requires some time to learn and some programming knowledge to use.

✦ **VisualAge for Java.** A comprehensive authoring tool by IBM.

✦ **VisualCafe.** This authoring tool, from WebGain, comes in three versions with varying degrees of complexity.

Several development tools can be found on the Sun Web site. See the "For More Information" section at the end of this chapter for details.

Java for animation

Java applets can be used to provide animation on your Web page. The applet can display an animated graphic alone or can add animation to any component of your GUI. You can animate the labels on your buttons, your icons, your menu items, or anything else.

Java has the capability of displaying a graphic image on the screen by reading it from a graphic file or by drawing a graphic image on the screen using its built-in library of drawing functions. Animation is achieved by displaying a series of graphic images at fixed time intervals, usually at a fairly high speed of 10-20 frames per second.

There are two basic ways to generate animation.

✦ **Create or obtain successive images of the entire scene, each slightly changed, and display them in sequence.** As an example, suppose you want to show an animation of a car moving away from a house. Using the first method, you create an image showing the house with the car next to the house, create a second image showing the house with the car a slight distance from the house, create a third image showing the house with the car slightly farther from the house, and so on. These images would be displayed in rapid succession to create the animation.

✦ **Create or obtain an image of the object that you wish to have moving and display it at different screen locations.** Using this method, for example, you create two separate images, a house and a car. You display the house as a static image in a fixed location. You display the car in a location next to the house, erase the car, display it in a location on the screen a slight distance from the house, erase it, display the car in a location slightly farther from the house, and so forth.

Animation in a Java applet uses the multithreading capabilities of Java. The animation generally runs continuously. To maintain the animation independently of any other part of the applet code, the animation function of the applet is implemented in a separate thread. The animation section of the program can be called the animation loop because it repeats until stopped by the user leaving the page or by an event that interacts with the applet. Because the animation is independent, more than one animation can be maintained simultaneously by an applet.

Adding an Applet to a Web Page

 Objective

Adding applets to Web pages

After you have the applet that you want on your Web page, you must add it to your Web page. Applets are added to a Web page in the same manner as any other component of the page — using an HTML tag.

There are two HTML tags that can be used to add an applet to your Web page: the ⟨applet⟩ tag and the ⟨object⟩ tag. According to the HTML 4.01 standard, the ⟨object⟩ tag should be used and the ⟨applet⟩ tag is deprecated. However, because not all browsers support the ⟨object⟩ tag yet, and the ⟨applet⟩ tag is still frequently used and is well supported by all browsers, you can use the ⟨applet⟩ tag to ensure that your Web page can be viewed in all browsers.

 Exam Tip   The ⟨applet⟩ **tag is discussed on the exam; not the** ⟨object⟩ **tag.**

The applet tag

The HTML ⟨applet⟩ tag allows you to add a Java applet to your Web page. When the browser encounters an ⟨applet⟩ tag, it sets aside a portion of the document display space for the applet. You can specify the size and location of the display area using attributes of the ⟨applet⟩ tag. The applet determines what will display inside the display area.

The simplest HTML statement for including an applet in your Web page is:

```
<applet code="clock.class">
</applet>
```

In this example, clock.class is the bytecode (compiled program) for the Java applet program. The applet is located in the same directory as the Web page. When using the ⟨applet⟩ tag, add a string that will display in browsers that are not Java enabled. For example:

```
<applet code="clock.class">
A Java-enabled browser is required.
</applet>
```

If this ⟨applet⟩ tag is parsed by a browser that is not Java enabled, it will display the statement so users can identify the problem.

The HTML statements are added to the Web page where the applet is to display. Listing 18-1 shows the HTML code for a Web page that includes an applet.

Listing 18-1: **HTML code that includes a Java applet**

```
<html>
<head>
<title>Testing an applet</title>
</head>
<body>
<p>This is a Java applet:</p>
<applet code="clock.class">
This feature of the Web page requires a Java-enabled browser.
</applet>
<p>This line will display after the Java applet.</p>
</body>
</html>
```

Be sure to include the extension, .class, when specifying the applet, although some browsers will automatically add the .class extension if it's missing.

When Listing 18-1 is displayed by the browser, it looks like the following:

This is a Java applet:

(The Java applet displays here)

This line will display after the Java applet.

The `<applet>` tag has several attributes. One useful attribute is `codebase`, which is used to provide a path to the applet when the applet is not in the same directory as the HTML code file. For example, suppose your home page is located at `http://www.mypage.com` and you have a subdirectory called applets. If the HTML page that includes the applet is located in your main directory, but the applet is located in the applet subdirectory, you need to use the `codebase` attribute. The following code will allow the applet to be located and downloaded.

```
<applet code="clock.class" codebase="/applets/">
</applet>
```

You could also use the following statement:

```
<applet code="clock.class"
codebase="http://www.mypage.com/applets/">
</applet>
```

Two additional attributes are frequently needed: `height` and `width`. These attributes are used to control the size of the area in which the applet is displayed. Use pixels to specify the size as follows:

```
<applet code="clock.class" height="100" width="100">
</applet>
```

The `<applet>` tag has several attributes, some of which are similar to attributes for other HTML tags. Table 18-1 shows all the attributes for the `<applet>` tag.

Table 18-1
Attributes for the Applet Tag

Attribute	Values	Purpose
Align	top, texttop, middle, absmiddle, baseline, bottom, absbottom, left, right	Aligns the applet display area with the surrounding text.
Alt	*text string*	Specifies text that will be displayed when the applet cannot be displayed.
Archive	*URL*. Filename must end in either .zip or .jar	Specifies a comma-separated list of the file(s) containing Java classes that will be cached before executing the applet. Useful when the applet relies on other Java classes.
Code	*applet path/name*	Specifies the location of Java applet bytecode.
Codebase	*URL or relative path*	Specifies an alternative (base) directory where the applet is located.
Height	*number of pixels*	Specifies the height of the applet display area.
Hspace	*number of pixels*	Specifies the horizontal space around the applet display area.
Mayscript	none	Allows Java applet to access JavaScript from within the applet. (Netscape only)
Name	*text string*	Specifies a label that uniquely identifies the applet.
Object	*text string*	Specifies the name of a resource that contains a serialized version of the applet. (Not supported by any browser)
Title	*text string*	Specifies a title that browsers may display or use in some other manner. (IE specific)
Vspace	*number of pixels*	Specifies the vertical space around the applet display area.
Width	*number of pixels*	Specifies the width of the applet display area.

The param tag

Some applets need information from the HTML page to execute correctly. For instance, the applet might need to know what type of browser it's running in. Or the applet might need to know which time zone to use in calculating time. Or the applet might need to know the name of a graphic to display. Information can be passed to an applet using the empty HTML tag, ⟨param⟩.

Because the ⟨param⟩ tag is an empty tag, if you're creating valid and well-formed Extensible Hypertext Markup Language (XHTML) documents, it needs to be written with a space and a closing slash, as follows: ⟨param /⟩.

The ⟨param⟩ tag is used to pass parameters to the Java applet. It's placed between the ⟨applet⟩ tag and its end tag. Each ⟨param⟩ tag requires two attributes: the name attribute and the value attribute, which are similar to the name and value attributes used when creating forms. The name attribute specifies a name for the parameter being passed and the value attribute specifies the value to be associated with the name. Using these attributes, the ⟨param⟩ tag passes a name/value pair to the applet. For example, the following code sample will pass a name/value pair.

```
<applet code="DisplayGraphics.class">
<param name="graphicname" value="image1.gif">
</applet>
```

In this case, the parameter name/value pair (graphicname/image1.gif) is passed to the applet named DisplayGraphics.class.

Note how the applet is named using uppercase letters for readability. Java programmers frequently name their programs in this manner. Be sure your code attribute references the applet file using the exact file name, correctly uppercased where required.

If you need to pass more than one name/value pair to the applet, use an additional ⟨param⟩ tag to pass each pair, as shown below:

```
<applet code="DisplayGraphics.class">
<param name="graphicname" value="image1.gif">
<param name="graphicheight" value="200">
</applet>
```

The object tag

The ⟨object⟩ tag is very similar to the ⟨applet⟩ tag, but it's more flexible. It can be used to add other types of objects to the Web page, in addition to applets. When used to add an applet, its simplest form is:

```
<object classid="clock.class">
</object>
```

The codebase attribute is used with the <object> tag in the same manner as for the <applet> tag.

The <object> tag has many attributes, some the same as the <applet> tag, but many are different or implemented differently. Table 18-2 shows all the attributes for the <object> tag that may be useful when adding applets to your Web pages. Attributes of the <object> tag that apply only to objects other than applets are not included in the table.

Table 18-2
Attributes for the Object Tag Relating to Applets

Attribute	Values	Description
Align	top, texttop, middle, absmiddle, baseline, bottom, absbottom	Aligns the applet display area with the surrounding text.
Archive	list of URLs	Space-separated list of directories containing Java classes that will be preloaded before executing the specified applet. Useful when specified Java applet relies on other Java classes.
Border	number of pixels	Specifies the width of the frame around the applet display area.
classid	applet path/name	Specifies the location of Java applet bytecode.
codebase	URL or relative path	Specifies an alternative directory where the applet is located.
codetype	application/Java	Required only if the browser cannot determine the MIME type of the applet.
data	path/filename	Specifies data file required by the applet.
height	number of pixels	Specifies height of the applet display area.
hspace	number of pixels	Specifies the horizontal space around the applet display area.
id	string	Specifies a label that uniquely identifies the applet. (Netscape specific)
name	string	Specifies a label that uniquely identifies the applet. (IE specific)

(continued)

Table 18-2 (continued) **Attributes for the Object Tag Relating to Applets**		
Attribute	*Values*	*Description*
standby	*string*	Specifies a message to display while the applet is downloading.
title	*string*	Specifies title that browser may display or use in some other manner. (IE specific)
type	*MIME type*	Used in conjunction with the `data` attribute. Indicates the MIME type of the data file specified by the `data` attribute.
vspace	*number of pixels*	Specifies the vertical space around the applet display area.
width	*number of pixels*	Specifies width of applet display area.

The `<param>` tag is used with the `<object>` tag to pass information to the applet in the same manner as it is used with the `<applet>` tag.

Key Point Summary

This chapter introduced you to Java applets. You learned that Java is a general-purpose programming language particularly suitable for network and Web applications. Applets are a particular type of Java program developed to be used in Web pages for the purpose of adding animation and interaction to the page. You learned how to create applets and how to add applets to your Web page. Some key points in this chapter are:

✦ Java is a general purpose programming language that can be used for a variety of applications.

✦ The strengths of Java for use in your Web page are:

- Java has more capabilities than scripting languages, with features designed specifically for network and Web applications.

- Java is fast, compact, secure, portable, platform independent, and multi-threaded.

- There are many existing Java programs available for free download from the Internet.

✦ The weaknesses of Java for use in your Web page are:

- Java is more complicated and difficult to learn than scripting languages.

- Java requires Java-enabled browsers.

- Java downloads slower than scripts and is not cached.

✦ Applets are a particular type of Java program designed specifically for use in a Web page.

✦ Applets are client-side programs that are downloaded and run on the client computer.

✦ Applets have limitations based on security considerations. They cannot access files on the client computer, run another program on the client computer, or communicate with any computer other than the computer from which it was downloaded.

✦ Servlets are Java programs that run on the server-side.

✦ Applets are created independently of the Web page and stored in a separate file with a .class extension.

✦ You can write your own applet in Java, work with a programmer who will write your applet, or find an appropriate applet to download from the Internet.

✦ Java authoring tools exist that can assist with creating an applet by providing a visual environment — with an editor, compiler, and debugger included — and with reusable components and wizards. Some authoring tools are JBuilder by Borland, VisualAge by IBM, and VisualCafe by WebGain.

✦ One use of applets is to provide animation. Animation is achieved by displaying a series of graphic images at fixed time intervals, usually at a fairly high speed of 10-20 frames per second.

✦ Applets are added to a Web page using an HTML tag. The `<applet>` tag adds applets to the Web page. The `<object>` tag from the HTML 4 standards was also mentioned, but because the `<object>` tag is not always supported by all browsers and the `<applet>` tag is still frequently used and well supported, the `<applet>` tag is preferred for browser independent Web page design.

✦ The `<applet>` tag has several attributes. The `code` attribute is required which provides the location of the applet. The `codebase` attribute is frequently used to specify an alternate location. The `height` and `width` attributes define the applet display area.

✦ The `<param>` tag is used to pass information to the applet that it requires to run correctly. The `<param>` tag passes name/value pairs, similar to those passed by elements of a form. A separate `<param>` tag is used for each name/value pair that is passed.

✦   ✦   ✦

STUDY GUIDE

Java applets are useful tools for the Web designer. To help you learn the information in this chapter and prepare for the test, the study guide provides useful exercises. Use the assessment questions, scenario, and lab exercises to test your knowledge and practice your skills. The answers for the questions and the scenario can be found at the end of the study guide.

Assessment Questions

1. Which of the following descriptions of Java is true?

    A. It's a powerful scripting language.

    B. It's a low-level programming language developed by the Java Corporation.

    C. It's an object-oriented programming language.

    D. It's a high-level programming language that only runs in a Web browser.

2. Which of the following statements is not an advantage of using Java in your Web pages?

    A. It runs faster than a scripting language.

    B. It's cached by the browser.

    C. It's multithreaded.

    D. It has more capabilities than a scripting language.

3. Which of the following descriptions of an applet is true?

    A. It's a client-side program that can be added to your Web page.

    B. It's a powerful scripting language.

    C. It's an alternative to a Java program.

    D. It's an alternative to a CGI program.

4. Which of the following is required to add an applet to a Web page?

    A. The `<param>` tag

    B. The `code` attribute or the `classid` attribute

    C. The `codebase` attribute of the `<object>` tag

    D. The `<applet>` tag

5. Which of the following descriptions of a Java applet animation is true?

   A. It's a set of graphic images that play concurrently.

   B. It's a graphic sequence that runs once in a Web page.

   C. It's an animation loop that must be the only element in the applet.

   D. It's an animation loop that runs in its own separate thread.

6. Which of the following is not an attribute of the `<applet>` tag?

   A. `height`

   B. `archive`

   C. `border`

   D. `object`

7. Which of the following statements about creating an applet is not true?

   A. Java authoring tools are useful.

   B. Java source code is compiled into bytecode.

   C. Writing a Java applet is generally more complicated and difficult than writing HTML code.

   D. After the applet is completed and tested, the class file should be renamed to an appropriate name.

8. Which of the following statements about the capabilities of an applet is true?

   A. It runs on the Web server.

   B. It can be a security risk.

   C. It can access the DOM model of the browser.

   D. It's compiled on the client computer before it executes.

Scenarios

You've been asked to add a calculator to an existing Web page. What are the steps you would follow to complete this task?

Lab Exercises

Lab 18-1: Write a design document for an applet

Write the design document discussed in the section "Working with programmers." The document will set out specifications for a tic-tac-toe game to be written as a

Java applet. The document does not cover any of the technical details of how to program the applet. It simply describes the functionality and the graphical user interface for the applet.

Lab 18-2: Add a Java animation applet to a Web page

The following steps take you through the procedures for adding a Java animation applet to a Web page:

1. Go to `http://javaboutique.internet.com/`.

2. From the Applets menu, click by Category.

3. Choose Visual Effects.

4. Select Sequential Animation.

5. Select an animation and click its link. JackhammerDuke is a simple animation.

6. The page for the animation provides instructions for downloading. It also provides the HTML code necessary to run the applet. It also shows any information you need to know, such as the author, any restrictions on the applet's use, etc. Download the files needed for the applet.

7. Create a skeleton HTML file to run the applet. It needs the `<html>`, `<head>`, `<title>`, and `<body>` tags.

8. Copy the HTML file and the applet and associated files into the same subdirectory. Many of the applet files are in a zip file. If so, unzip the files before copying them into the subdirectory.

9. Add the HTML code needed to run the applet. The quickest way is to use copy/paste to copy them from the Web page accessed in Step 6 and add them to your HTML file between the `<body>` tags.

10. Open the HTML file you just created from your browser. If the applet doesn't display, it may be that your browser is not Java enabled. Read some of the information on the Java Boutique Web site that provides troubleshooting instructions and hints.

Answers to Chapter Questions

Chapter pre-test

1. A Java applet allows you to extend the functionality of your Web page by using the powerful features of the Java programming language. Common uses are to provide animation or to provide an interactive application to the user.

2. The Java language is an object-oriented programming language. An applet is a specific type of Java object that is designed to be included in a Web page.

3. Some advantages of using Java in your Web pages are: 1) more capabilities than scripting languages, 2) features designed specifically for network and Web applications, 3) runs faster than scripts, 4) compact size, 5) built-in security features, 6) portable, 7) platform independent, 8) multithreaded, 9) many programs available to be downloaded free from the Internet.

4. The terms client-side and server-side refer to where the program runs. Java applets are client-side programs. The applet is downloaded by the browser and run on the client computer.

5. An applet is a Java program that is written and compiled into a bytecode file. As the designer, you can write the Java program yourself, work with a programmer to write the specific Java applet you need, or search the Internet to locate an appropriate applet and download it for use in your Web page.

6. Animation is achieved by displaying a series of graphic images at fixed time intervals, usually at a fairly high speed of 10-20 frames per second. The animation generally runs continuously. To maintain the animation independently of any other part of the applet code, the animation function of the applet is implemented in a separate thread.

7. An applet is added to a Web page using HTML tags. There are two tags that can be used. The HTML 4 standards specified the `<object>` tag, but because the `<object>` tag is not always supported by all browsers and the `applet` tag is still frequently used and well supported, the `<applet>` tag is preferred for browser independent Web page design.

8. Information is passed to an applet using the `<param>` tag. The `<param>` tag passes name/value pairs, similar to those passed by elements of a form. A separate `<param>` tag is used for each name/value pair passed.

Assessment questions

1. **C.** Java is an object-oriented programming language. It's not a scripting language or a low-level programming language. It's a general-purpose language, not a language that only runs in a Web browser. See "Introduction to Java."

2. **B.** The java program is not cached when it is downloaded. See "Strengths and weaknesses."

3. **A.** An applet is a client-side program that can be added to your Web page. It's not a scripting language; it's a type of Java program, not an alternative to a Java program. It's a client-side program, whereas CGI is server-side. See "Applets."

4. **B.** When adding an applet to a Web page, it's necessary to include the location of the applet. This is done in the `<applet>` tag with the `code` attribute or in the `<object>` tag with the `classid` attribute. Therefore, one of these attributes is necessary, depending on which tag is used. The `<applet>` tag is not necessary, because you could use the `<object>` tag instead, and vice versa. See "Adding an Applet to a Web Page."

5. D. Animation in a Java applet is a loop that needs to run in its own thread, independently. There can be more than one animation loop in an applet. The animation is a set of images that play sequentially, not concurrently. Most graphic sequences run repeatedly until stopped. See "Java for animation."

6. C. `border` is not an attribute of the `<applet>` tag. It is an attribute of the `<object>` tag. See "Adding an Applet to a Web Page."

7. D. The class file of an applet should never be renamed. If it is renamed, the `<applet>` tag will be unable to find it and the applet cannot be loaded. See "Adding an Applet to a Web Page."

8. B. Because the applet runs on the client computer, it can be a security risk if it's allowed to access files or run programs on the client computer. JavaScript accesses the DOM model, not applets. The applet is a compiled class file and the bytecode is downloaded, not the source code. See "Applets."

Scenarios

The steps to add a calculator to an existing Web page are:

1. Decide which would be the best way to add the calculator. Because a calculator requires interaction between the user and the Web page, a Java applet is a very appropriate object for this purpose.

2. Decide whether to create a new applet for the calculator functionality or download a calculator from the Internet. Because a calculator is a Web page feature that has probably been used many times before, it's very likely you can find one on the Internet.

3. Search for an existing calculator applet. The best place to search is Java Boutique, which has several calculator applets.

4. Download the applet file and store it in the same subdirectory with the HTML file for the Web page to which the calculator is being added.

5. Decide on the design of the new page with the calculator added. Where in the Web page will the calculator be added? How much screen space should the user interface for the calculator occupy?

6. Add the necessary tags to the HTML file in the appropriate location. The `<applet>` tag should be used with the `code` attribute. The `height`, `width`, and `align` attributes will also probably be needed.

7. Test the applet to be sure that it runs correctly.

For More Information

✦ **Java information.** `http://java.sun.com/`: A good site for general information about the Java language

✦ **Applet information.** `http://java.sun.com/applets/index.html`: The best place to look for information and resources regarding Java and Java applets, the Sun Web Site

✦ **Gamelan.** `www.gamelan.earthweb.com`: One of the most useful sites for Java documentation, free programs, tutorials, resources, links, and other useful information

✦ **Java Boutique.** `www.javaboutique.internet.com`: Another excellent source of Java documentation, free programs, tutorials, resources, links, and other useful information

Extensible Markup Language and Authoring

EXAM OBJECTIVES

- ✦ Role of XML in Web development
- ✦ XML vs. HTML
- ✦ XML document requirements
- ✦ Role of XHTML in Web development

CHAPTER PRE-TEST

1. What are some of the reasons that XML was developed?

2. What relationship does XML have to HTML and SGML?

3. What are some of the components of an XML document?

4. What rules does a well-formed XML document adhere to?

5. Define the terms meta-markup language, procedural markup, and logical markup.

6. Is XML designed to be a replacement for HTML?

✦ Answers to these questions can be found at the end of the chapter. ✦

The Extensible Markup Language (XML) isn't exactly a new kid on the block, but it still carries the cutting-edge technology label and is one of the hottest technologies in the Web world. XML is a markup language designed to let you create your own tags, and it isn't designed just for creating Web pages. In this chapter, you learn what XML is, where it comes from, why you need it, and what its relationship is to HTML. You also learn the basics of building XML documents, and delve into XHTML, the future of HTML. When you're done with this chapter, you'll have a good idea of the role XML plays in Web site design and be able to start thinking about how you might use XML in your own design activities.

Why XML?

Role of XML in Web development

The world of computers isn't a homogenous place with only one kind of operating system and one kind of software for each functional area of life. Hardware and software needs for individuals as well as organizations vary greatly; therefore, many combinations of hardware and software are used. In addition, it's sometimes difficult for everyone to share information because of these differences. There's a real need for a way to store and exchange information in a format that is platform and software independent — that is a format every computer and every application can use.

A markup language is a practical and established way to describe content in a way that is sharable across computer platforms and operating systems. HTML was originally designed as a mechanism for sharing data across computers and information systems. Unfortunately, HTML has been changed from a pure markup language to a formatting language. Therefore, the information world has been left without a true markup language to use as a standard data format. XML is designed to provide this much needed markup language, learning a few lessons from HTML along the way.

Inside the world of markup

As you know from your work with HTML, a markup language is simply a set of tags that you use to mark up your content. The tags say something about the content. In the following example, you may not be able to read any of the text — unless you're fluent in Latin — but the markup tags give you clues about the roles the different snippets of text play in the document:

```
<title>Oratio in Catilinam Altera<title>
<h1>Ad Populum</h1>
<h2>Argumentum</h2>
<p>Cum ea oratio, quam M. Tullius in senatu in L. Catilinam
praesentem a. d. VI Id. Novembres habuit, a senatoribus ita
audita esset ... orationem habuit.</p>
```

From a glance at the markup, you know that this fragment of text from Cicero's In Catilinam II has a title, a first level heading, a second level heading, and a paragraph.

Just as the markup tags provide a reader a good idea of what the different elements are in a block of content, the same markup tags can pass the same information to a computer. Although the computer can't be expected to read and comprehend Latin, it can be programmed to read and interpret markup tags.

The goal of a markup language is to provide a consistent, text-based method for describing content, so that a computer, or collection of computers, can do something with the content based on the description. The HTML markup language is designed to help computers display content on the screen, but that doesn't mean that markup languages can only be used to guide the display of content. Markup can be used to describe information that a computer may never display but that is necessary for the computer to complete some function. You can describe financial transactions, computer programming instructions, and just about any other kind of information using markup.

HTML is a perfect example of how markup facilitates the sharing of information across computer systems and software. You build Web pages using HTML and move them to a Web server so they're available to anyone with a Web browser. Users from around the world running any operating system on any computer with any Web browser should be able to view your Web pages. This universal access to Web pages is made possible by HTML. Every browser knows how to read HTML, and because HTML files are text-based, they're stored in a format that any computer can process.

Procedural vs. Logical Markup

The two most common reasons for using markup to describe content are to help a display device figure out how to display some content and to simply describe the content itself and let the computer system do what it will with that content. Markup that is designed to provide instructions to a computer about the display of a document is often called procedural markup. HTML tags such as bold (`<b>`), font (`<font>`), and underline (`<u>`) are examples of procedural markup.

Markup that is designed to simply describe content without having anything to say about layout is often referred to as logical markup or even descriptive markup. HTML tags such as paragraph (`<p>`), heading level 1 (`<h1>`), and address (`<address>`) are examples of logical markup. They give the processing application more information about content but don't include explicit instructions on how to format the content.

As HTML markup has become more procedural in nature, it has become less useful for describing data that can be used across a variety of systems. The goal behind XML is to move away from procedural markup and to logical markup.

Why HTML just isn't enough

There's already one ML (markup language) in town so why exactly do you need another? HTML is a booming success and is the foundation for millions of Web pages around the world. The reality is that HTML is doing far more than it was designed to do. HTML was created to describe research papers and simple documents, not drive e-commerce Web sites and Web-based applications for things like account management and internal company communications. HTML has been stretched to its limit and the holes are beginning to show.

 Exam Tip The limitations of HTML that have lead to the development of XML are an important topic on the exam.

The limitations that have driven the need for a new and different markup language include:

✦ HTML has been transformed by users and browser vendors from a true markup language to a formatting language.

✦ Serving Web pages built with HTML can be server intensive and require a great deal of bandwidth.

✦ Current HTML practices make it difficult to search for information on the Web efficiently and effectively.

We discuss these limitations in more detail in the following sections.

HTML has become a formatting language

Tim Berners-Lee's original vision for HTML was as a markup language that had nothing to do with formatting and everything to do with describing the structure of the document. The goal of HTML was for users to draw on HTML's collection of tags to describe the different pieces of content in their documents, and browsers would interpret those tags and drive the display of the documents. In Berners-Lee's world, different browser displays were good because users could tweak their display of Web pages any way they wanted to.

Unfortunately, as HTML became more popular, Web designers discovered that you could combine different HTML elements to get different results in browsers. As browser vendors began to create proprietary tags to try to lure designers to creating pages that worked best in a particular browser, the idea of a single HTML page functioning well in any browser was gone. HTML transitioned from a pure markup language to a tag-based formatting language.

Over time, the browser wars subsided, or at least moved onto different playing fields, so proprietary HTML tags aren't as abundant as they used to be. However, the practice of using HTML as a formatting language rather than as a pure markup language to describe the pieces and parts of a document is the status quo. HTML is no longer used to describe a document's structure. In fact, document structure may be relinquished in the name of display. For example, content that isn't tabular in nature is forced into HTML tables to meet display needs, and tags that don't describe structure at all, such as the `<font>` and `<center>` tags, abound to help define display rules for a page.

Serving HTML is server and bandwidth intensive

The limitations of HTML aren't only related to using it as a formatting language instead of as a true markup language. Although HTML documents are often very small in size — another benefit of text-based markup — the process of serving Web pages up to thousands of users a minute is very server and bandwidth intensive. Each time a user clicks a hyperlink in a Web page to view another Web page, a Web browser sends a request out over the Internet to a Web server and the Web server sends back a new Web page.

This constant request-response process is taxing on the servers, which have to answer all of the responses, and on the Internet, which has to carry all of the electronic traffic. As the Internet and Web grow, new technologies that transfer some of the burden of processing the huge amounts of data available on the Web from servers to clients is essential. Dynamic HTML — the combination of scripting and HTML — is a step towards this shift to the client side, but new and different technologies are also a necessity.

HTML doesn't facilitate productive Web searches

Because HTML has transitioned from a markup language that describes a document's structure to a formatting language, any information in the markup about the content of the document isn't really reliable. Programmers can't build search engines or other technologies that rely on consistent uses of HTML markup to describe a particular kind of content; therefore, search engines have to search on every kind of content. If you visit your favorite search engine to look for information on Web logging, you may very well find information on actual logging practices — cutting down trees and such — in addition to information on how to use the logs created by your Web server.

The amount of information on the Web grows exponentially every day and the only way the information can be useful is for it to be searchable. HTML's limited tag set and its role as a formatting language mean that it isn't the solution for describing easy-to-search content. A simple search on your favorite topic shows that there's an immediate need for new technologies that make sifting through the vast wealth of information on the Web practical and profitable.

XML: The new markup for the Internet age

XML is the answer to this need for a standard information format that any computer can create and read. Whereas HTML has a predefined set of markup tags that all content is supposed to fit into, XML is a set of rules that anyone can use to create their own markup elements to describe their content. You can describe everything from new articles to computer programming instructions in XML and share them with any other computer in the world, because XML documents, like HTML documents, are just plain text.

Because developers can create their own markup elements to describe their content, XML documents tell you a great deal about the content that is inside of them. If an article has an article head, byline, body, and footnotes, each piece of the document is described by a markup tag created especially for news articles, as shown in this snippet of code:

```
<article>
<article_title>XML saves the day</article_title>
<author>Joe Markup</author>
<body>
     XML has learned a variety of lessons from the
     trials and successes of HTML and is poised to be
     the next generation markup language for the Web.
</body>
</article>
```

An XML document written with tags that fit the content not only contains information, but it also contains descriptions of the information. If another person or another computer needs to work with the content of the document, the markup provides additional valuable information about the role each piece of content plays in the document.

From the get go, XML was designed to solve the growing information problems of the Internet. The goals of XML are defined neatly and succinctly in the W3C XML 1.0 Specification published in February 1998 (found at `www.w3.org/TR/1998/REC-xml-19980210#sec-origin-goals`). The goals as stated by the W3C are:

1. XML shall be straightforwardly usable over the Internet.

2. XML shall support a wide variety of applications.

3. XML shall be compatible with SGML.

4. It shall be easy to write programs which process XML documents.

5. The number of optional features in XML is to be kept to the absolute minimum, ideally zero.

6. XML documents should be human-legible and reasonably clear.

7. The XML design should be prepared quickly.

8. The design of XML shall be formal and concise.

9. XML documents shall be easy to create.

10. Terseness in XML markup is of minimal importance.

In a nutshell, XML provides a way to accurately describe information and save that information in a format that can be shared among computers and information systems. The descriptive markup provides clues to the different pieces of content and makes it possible for machines and people to process the content based on those descriptions. For example, newspapers around the world can receive news articles using the same XML descriptive elements and each one can then display the article differently based on the paper's style rules. Each paper knows what kind of information they're getting, what format it will be in (XML), and can choose how to deal with the information.

 Tip   A great introduction to what XML is and why you need it can be found on the W3C Web site in an article entitled "XML in 10 points." The article is short but to the point and touches on all of the basic ideas and methodologies behind the development and use of XML. It's highly suggested reading, and you can find it on the Web at `www.w3.org/XML/1999/XML-in-10-points`.

In the next several sections of this chapter, you find out where XML comes from and how it facilitates storing any kind of information in a standard format that is usable by any computer. You also find out about the role XML plays in Web site development and design. The best place to start is with a brief history of XML so you can understand how the need for XML came about and the steps that were taken to meet that need.

A Brief History of XML

The idea of using markup to describe content isn't a new one, and XML is really a happy medium between two other markup languages: the Standard Generalized Markup Language (SGML) and HTML. XML was developed in the mid-1990s well after HTML took hold of the Web world and developers were beginning to demand a way to deal with data that was more sophisticated and flexible than HTML. The first XML specification, XML 1.0, was released in 1998 and a massive development effort has surrounded the newest markup language ever since.

By itself, XML doesn't do anything other than provide developers with a standard way to create customized markup tags that describe particular sets of information. For XML to be useful beyond describing markup, these are just a few of the things you need:

✦ A way to process it

✦ A way to specify how XML-described content should be displayed in a particular media (Web browser, printed page, cell phone, etc.)

✦ A way to define links between XML documents

The list of supporting technologies for XML is long and growing every day. It currently includes:

✦ **Extensible Stylesheet Language (XSL).** A technology for creating style sheets to drive the display of XML documents in any kind of display media

✦ **XML Linking Language (XLink).** A technology for creating links among XML documents

✦ **XML Query.** A technology for searching XML documents using sophisticated search queries

✦ **Namespaces in XML.** A technology for reusing XML markup across documents

Even with all of the supporting technologies being developed for XML software, applications must exist that know how to process XML and work with the content that XML stores. The most recent versions of both Internet Explorer (5.5) and Netscape Navigator (6.0) have basic support for XML, but the real work with XML is being done in the software development world. Over time, more and more software applications have begun to support and even rely on XML as a way to store data. Web sites are beginning to use XML as a way to exchange data and even to store information that is later converted to HTML for display in a Web browser.

Tip   The best way to see the role XML plays in the information world is to learn more about how others are using XML. The XML Demos section at XML.com has some good examples. You can find the demos online at `www.xml.com/pub/rg/ Demos`.

Anyone who has used a markup language before is going to be curious about how XML relates to the two markup languages that preceded it: SGML and HTML. The developers of XML learned their markup lessons well and took the best of SGML and HTML when they created XML. They also worked hard to avoid the pitfalls and traps associated with earlier markup languages. Although XML isn't perfect, it does build on lessons learned from the past and the requirements of the Internet age.

XML and SGML

SGML is the grandfather of all markup languages. Both HTML and XML use the same basic markup syntax that is part of the SGML specification. HTML is an extremely simplified version of SGML and has one specific set of markup elements that you can use to describe content, whereas XML takes advantage of some of SGML's flexibility and power.

A brief history of SGML

In the 1960s, as computers were beginning to proliferate and were becoming common tools of the trade for many large organizations and research groups, a company called the Graphic Communications Association (GCA) developed a precursor to markup languages called GenCode. GenCode is a set of rules for describing the layout of a document, not its structure, but it was a beginning. Meanwhile at IBM,

Charles Goldfarb — often referred to as the father of SGML — built on the work done by GCA on GenCode and developed the Generalized Markup Language (GML), which was the first markup language and the ancestor of HTML.

GML is a comprehensive set of rules for creating markup tags to describe complex documents, including computer specifications, airplane specifications, and long and detailed documents. For almost a decade, GML was a language owned by IBM but used widely around the world — particularly in large organizations and in the government — to describe their documents in a way that was easily shared with others. In the late 1970s, the American National Standards Institute (ANSI) worked with Goldfarb to create a GML standard, called SGML, and released it in 1980. The SGML standard was revised over time and the final version of SGML was released in 1986.

Because large organizations and the government use SGML to describe their most complex documents, SGML has evolved over time to meet the needs of a variety of groups and content. The positive side of this evolution is that you can use SGML to describe virtually any kind of content — from submarine specifications to news articles. The negative side of this evolution is that SGML has become a large and complex beast that isn't really suitable for everyday use by anyone who isn't an SGML expert.

The SGML/XML connection

SGML, like XML, is a set of rules for creating custom markup tags. However SGML is extremely complicated to use and deploy. XML borrows much of its syntax for creating custom markup tags from SGML, but it isn't as complicated. SGML requires that all documents created using any set of SGML elements adhere to some standard document rules. XML also requires that all documents adhere to some standard document rules. Such documents are said to be *well formed.*

SGML is much more strict than HTML, which makes it less flexible but more predictable. One of the problems with HTML is that there are so many versions of it that it's difficult for a browser to know what to expect in a document or how to handle the HTML that it does get. XML leans toward the strictness of SGML to avoid the problems of ambiguity associated with the many versions of HTML. Although you may not know which markup tags a document is going to use, you do know that all documents will be built according to the same basic rules. This makes it easier to build tools to create and work with XML documents.

A key design theory behind SGML is that the description of the contents of a document and information about how it should be displayed should always be separated. This means that SGML documents don't use markup to drive the display of a document, but instead rely on style sheets for these display rules. XML subscribes to this same design theory, and good XML practice says that XML markup tags should simply describe the pieces and parts of a document. A style sheet language, such as Cascading Style Sheets (CSS) or Extensible Stylesheet Language (XSL) should include the display information.

Tip

Unlike both SGML and XML, many of the markup elements in HTML are designed specifically to drive the display of a document in a Web browser. Because browsers and user settings are different, this makes it difficult to create a Web page that looks good in multiple browsers. For more information on using CSS to separate structure from display in HTML pages, turn to Chapter 11.

In short, XML draws its rules for consistency from SGML and uses its syntax to provide developers with a way to create their own markup. XML is designed to keep the display of a document separate from its content, so the document can be shared across multiple computers regardless of how it will be displayed or processed. Whereas XML captures some of the better aspects of SGML that are lacking in HTML, it also draws heavily on HTML for ease of document creation and focus on use as a Web technology.

XML and HTML

Objective   XML vs. HTML

Different sources of information on the Web suggest that XML is here to replace HTML and this is not true. XML exists because HTML has been stretched to its limits and isn't suitable for information exchange, building complex applications, or any of the other complex functions that HTML is currently used to facilitate. The reality is that XML is designed to coexist peacefully and productively with HTML.

In the Real World

XML can be used to build Web pages, but older browsers don't support XML, so it's difficult to create backward-compatible Web pages with XML. Practical wisdom says that HTML will be around for quite some time and is the markup language of choice for creating Web pages, simply because it's better supported by a wider variety of browsers. In the real world, XML is being used for behind-the-scenes work instead of for defining how a Web page should look.

XML inherits as many attributes from HTML as it does from SGML. One of the reasons SGML didn't come back into style as soon as the need for something beyond HTML became apparent is because SGML is extremely complicated to work with, and most SGML tools are expensive and complex. The developers of XML realized that the overwhelming success of HTML stems from how easy it is to use, and they built that same usability into XML.

Although XML is more restrictive than HTML, and requires a little more knowledge than HTML, it's still fairly easy to learn and to build documents with. It incorporates standard markup elements such as tags and attributes that Web developers are accustomed to using, and you can use any text editor to create XML files.

The key difference between XML and HTML is that XML doesn't include a predefined set of tags that you have to use to describe each and every piece of data that you have. Instead, XML allows you to create your own tags. The advantage to creating your own tags is that you always have the best description of your content in any XML document you create. The disadvantage is that display devices don't automatically know how to treat your document.

Web browsers know — more or less — which HTML elements will make up a Web page, and the browser has default display rules for those elements. When a Web browser encounters XML, it doesn't know what elements to expect (because you create your own); therefore, it can't have built-in display rules for those elements. This means that for every XML document you send to a browser, you must also create a style sheet that tells it how to display the files. This isn't a step you have to go through with HTML. (Keep in mind, however, that some people do use style sheets to describe their HTML.)

Another important difference between XML and HTML is that XML files have to be well formed and HTML files do not. You can create HTML files that leave out quotation marks around the attributes, incorporate sloppy code, and use HTML elements that aren't part of the standard HTML 4.0 specification and still get pretty good results in a Web browser. Because the goal of XML is to help developers create consistent and predictable documents, such laxity isn't tolerated. XML documents must follow the basic rules of XML.

The rules of a well-formed XML document, however, are fairly simple to follow once you know what they are.

Cross-Reference   The section later in this chapter entitled "Well-Formed and Valid XML Documents" delves further into the discussion of what it takes for a document to be well formed.

XML is simpler than SGML, but not as simplistic as HTML. It incorporates the more rigid syntax conventions of SGML but is more flexible than HTML, because you can create your own tags.

It's important for Web designers to remember that markup is really designed to separate structure from display, and to understand how this important document-design theory can affect the way you create documents with XML.

The Benefits of Keeping Display and Structure Separate

You may be wondering why you should separate structure from format when, in reality, you're most concerned about the final delivery of your content in a Web browser. When you separate your document structure from display, you have a variety of benefits, including:

✦ Reusable content that can be coupled with display instructions for dissemination in just about any media. When structure is closely tied to display, it's more difficult to port a document to multiple display devices.

✦ You — and any computer reading your document — have a better idea of what kind of content you really have stored in a document. The markup element `<product_id>` is far more descriptive than `<li>`.

✦ You can share your document with other users or computer systems without worrying if your display parameters will work with their system. The content is up to you; the display is up to them.

Exam Tip   The benefit of separating structure from display is an important topic on the exam.

Another reason that it's important to separate display from structure is that not all content is meant to be displayed in the first place. Imagine that the following markup drives a Web-based online ordering system. The rules of the system say that only the product name and description should be displayed on a catalog page, and only if the produce is in stock. When a user clicks on a Buy link, the product ID is forwarded to an ordering system that processes the order. This bit of code contains a series of markup that describes a product:

```
<product>
     <product_id>087017395</product_id>
     <available instock="yes" />
     <name>The wonder widget II</product_name>
     <description>A widget you can't live without</description>
</product>
```

Of all the information in this chunk of markup, only the product name and description need to be seen by the end user. However, the product ID and availability information are still key to the success of the system. This combination of data for display and data to drive the behavior of a system is easy to achieve when you keep your markup focused on the content and not on the display.

To take this scenario one step further, imagine that a separate e-commerce site uses the same data and markup to describe products but has a different display. Site #2 displays all products, regardless of availability, and does list the product number for the user to see. Both sites can use the same XML format, and possibly draw from the same list of products, but they can maintain two separate displays.

Cross-Reference   Chapter 11 discusses the benefits of separating display from structure and how to do so using Cascading Style Sheets and XML.

Components of an XML Document

XML is really a meta-markup language, which means that it's a markup language designed to define other markup languages. You use XML's syntax and components to create the markup elements you need to define your own content. XML doesn't have any predefined markup tags, but instead has a whole series of rules about how you create and use your own tags.

Because HTML is also a markup language, you'll recognize the basic building blocks of an XML document. The primary components of an XML document include:

✦ A Document Type Definition (DTD)

✦ Elements

✦ Attributes

✦ Entities

We discuss these components in more detail in the following sections.

Every XML document begins with the following declaration, which specifies that the document is in fact an XML document and which version of XML the document is built with:

```
<?xml version="1.0" encoding="UTF-8"?>
```

The XML declaration also specifies which character encoding the document uses. The default is UTF-8, which is the standard 8-bit ASCII character set to which most Web pages built with Latin characters adhere. After you declare that you're building an XML document, you use XML's primary components to construct the rest of the document.

Exam Tip   Although our list of XML's components isn't 100% complete, it covers the basics you need to know for the exam. If you want to delve deeper into the syntax of XML, visit one of the resources listed in the "For More Information" section at the end of the chapter.

DTDs

When you create your own markup tags, it's a good idea to have a roadmap that specifies which tags you want to use in the document and how those tags should work together to define your content. A Document Type Definition (DTD) is the roadmap of an XML document and it specifies many things, including:

✦ Which markup tags you can use to describe your content.

✦ How you can combine those markup tags.

✦ Which attributes you can use with different markup tags.

✦ Which content elements are required and which are optional.

✦ What non-XML files, such as images and sound files, you can include in your document.

Although a DTD is designed to be a roadmap to an XML document, or to a whole collection of XML documents, you don't actually need to include a DTD for your documents to be complete. However, there are many reasons to include a DTD, such as:

✦ DTDs ensure consistency across a large number of documents by identifying the elements and attributes used in those documents. If you want to be sure that an entire group of like documents uses the same XML markup, you should create a DTD that can be used for all of them.

✦ DTDs help you plan how you want to describe your documents so you can be sure you've accounted for all of the pieces and parts in a document.

✦ Having a DTD allows you to verify that your XML documents play by the rules of the DTD when you process them. Properly created documents can often be the key to the success of a project, and being able to compare them to a DTD for accuracy is a benefit.

So if having a DTD is such a good thing, what are some reasons why you might not want a DTD? Two key reasons are:

✦ If you're developing a new set of markup tags to work with a particular kind of content, it often makes sense to add the markup directly to a few sample documents so you can decide the best way to define the markup rules for that content type. After you settle on standard markup conventions, you can build a DTD based on the markup used in your sample documents.

✦ If your content elements are constantly changing, it may be difficult to build a DTD for your documents. When your document doesn't have to conform to a DTD, you have more flexibility in the markup that you use to describe your content.

The general consensus is that it's worth the time and effort to develop a DTD or to build your documents based on an existing DTD. The consistency of description that you get when you work together with a DTD is valuable when you're trying to create Web sites and software that rely on constant data.

Tip   HTML 4.01 is actually a DTD for the way HTML markup should be used to build Web pages. Because Web browsers don't require that Web pages play by the rules of HTML, developers have been able to get away with breaking the rules of HTML. In the end, just because you have a DTD doesn't mean that the application that is going to process your documents requires that you adhere to its rules. A DTD can be either a suggestion or an ironclad requirement.

When you decide that you want a DTD to guide the description of your document's content, it's simply a matter of using XML's DTD syntax to define the markup rules for your documents and then using XML's markup syntax to build documents based on the DTD. In the following sections, you learn how to define XML components in a DTD and use them in a document.

In the Real World   Markup developers in the SGML and XML worlds often differ greatly in their opinions about the need for a DTD. Ultimately, the kind of content you're describing and the way it will be processed will determine whether you need a DTD.

Elements

Elements are the building blocks of XML documents and describe the different kinds of markup you find therein. An element is nothing more than a tag or set of tags that you put around some text in a document. In this example, from a previous section, XML elements are used to define product information:

```
<product>
    <product_id>087017395</product_id>
    <available instock="yes" />
    <name>The wonder widget II</product_name>
    <description>A widget you can't live without</description>
</product>
```

The elements at work in this snippet of a document are `product`, `product_id`, `available`, `name`, and `description`.

Tip   When working with markup, you often hear the words *tag* and *element* used interchangeably. Generally, we refer to tags as the markup you use around text to describe it and elements as the markup and the tag(s) combined.

Notice that the `product_id`, `available`, `name`, and `description` elements are all nested within the `product` element. A key part of using elements in XML, or any other markup language for that matter, is combining the elements to better describe content. By nesting all of the elements that describe a product within the `product` element, you know that they go together and refer to the same product. The way elements and text are combined to describe content is called a *content model*.

A DTD defines the elements you can use in a document with element declarations. The element declaration includes the element's name and the content model for that element. Content models are very specific and list which elements can be nested within the declared elements, how many times and in what order those elements should appear, and whether text can be the content for the element. The following code shows the element declarations for the elements used in the previous example to describe a product:

```
<!ELEMENT product (product_id, available, name, description)>
<!ELEMENT product_id (#PCDATA)>
```

```
<!ELEMENT available EMPTY>
<!ELEMENT name (#PCDATA)>
<!ELEMENT description (#PCDATA)>
```

Notice that every element declaration begins with `<!ELEMENT` followed by the element's name and the content model for the element in parentheses. The previous element declarations tell us a great deal about how to describe products using this markup. The declaration for the product element specifies that it must contain one and only one instance of the `product_id`, `available`, `name`, and `description` elements in that order. The `available` element can't contain any text because the content model doesn't specify that it can.

The `product_id`, `name`, and `description` elements just hold plain text, as specified by the `#PCDATA` content models. The `available` element is an empty element, which means that it can't have any content at all. It uses attributes to hold information instead of text. You may be familiar with empty elements in HTML, such as the image (`<img>`) and line break (`<br>`) tags.

Tip   Elements in XML are either made up of tag pairs or an empty (also called singleton) tag. An element can only be empty if the DTD specifies that it's empty; otherwise, all elements are assumed to be tag pairs.

Elements are designed to be reusable so they are often more generic than you might need them to be when you want to define a particular piece of content. In our example, the available element is required for every product, but the availability status is different from product to product. The element's goal is to hold availability information, but it needs a little more help to specify availability for each individual product. It gets that help from an attribute.

Attributes

Elements are designed to delineate the different pieces and parts of a document, but they don't work alone. Attributes make individual instances of an element more useful and meaningful. As discussed, the `available` element in our product sample earmarks availability information for each product, but it doesn't specify the actual availability for that product. To set that information on a product-by-product basis, the `available` element uses the `instock` attribute, which can be set to `yes` or `no`.

You use attributes regularly in HTML to define everything from table widths to URLs for hyperlinks and images. The HTML elements that take advantage of attributes, such as `table`, `a`, and `img`, are all designed to be used, in general, to define tables, links, and images, respectively. However, they use attributes to provide more information for an individual instance of each element. Attributes play the same role in XML.

In an XML DTD, you specify which attributes work with which elements using an *attribute declaration*. In our product markup, the only element that has an attribute is `available`. The DTD code to create that attribute looks something like this:

```
<!ELEMENT available EMPTY>
<!ATTLIST available
          instock (yes|no) yes #REQUIRED>
```

The attribute declaration starts with `<!ATTLIST` followed by the name of the element the attribute goes with, followed by a list of attributes for that element. In this example, the `available` element only has one attribute, `instock`. The attribute declaration specifies that this attribute can take one of two possible values, `yes` or `no`, with a default value of `yes`. The attribute is also required as specified by `#REQUIRED`.

You can create attributes that can take any text value, attributes that aren't required, and much more. Attributes should be a regular part of the markup that you create because they make elements more flexible and widely useable to describe different pieces of documents.

Entities

The last major components of XML are entities. An entity is a virtual storage unit in XML that can contain a variety of things, including:

✦ Chunks of XML and text that you want to use over and over again across several XML documents. Good examples of this are copyright statements, company names, and standard headers.

✦ Pointers to binary content including graphics, media files, word processing documents, and anything else that isn't a text or XML document.

✦ References to non-ASCII characters such as Icelandic characters, Cyrillic characters, Greek characters, and more.

Entities play a much larger role in XML than they do in HTML. In HTML, you use character and numeric entities to reference special non-ASCII characters such as copyright signs and accented characters in your documents. In XML, entities can hold just about anything you put into them. You have to reference all binary files in entities in the DTD before you can use them in a file. Two examples of entity declarations in a DTD, one binary and one text, are:

```
<!ENTITY corplogo SYSTEM "/graphics/corporate_logo.gif"
         NDATA GIF>

<!ENTITY copyright "Copyright Our Company, 2001">
```

The first declaration is a binary entity declaration that references a corporate_logo.gif file. The second declaration is a text entity. Both entity declarations begin with `<!ENTITY` and then list the entity's name (`corplogo` and `copyright`, respectively).

The keyword `SYSTEM` in the binary entity means that the actual file the entity references is saved on the file system somewhere. The file path immediately following the system reference, `/graphics/corporate_logo.gif`, actually points to the location of the file on the computer system. The value of the text entity is stored in the entity itself. The entity specifies that `copyright` is a shortcut to `Copyright Our Company, 2001`.

You reference entities in XML documents in two different ways. To use a text entity in a document, you include the entity name with an ampersand (&) before it and a semi-colon (;) after it, just like you create a character entity in HTML, and as shown in this code:

```
<footer>&copy;</footer>
```

When the document is processed, the entity `&copy;` is replaced with the text `Copyright Our Company, 2001`. You can reference text entities anywhere in an XML document that you want to. Binary entity references can only be included in the value of attributes and you don't have to put the ampersand and semi-colon around them, as shown in this snippet:

```
<picture src="corplogo" />
```

In this code, notice that the value of the attribute isn't the location of the file, but the name of the entity. The entity points to the file location and the attribute points to the entity.

Tip   You don't have to predefine elements and attributes in a DTD to create tags and attributes in an XML document. However, you do have to declare any entities you want to use in the document in a DTD for that document. This means that if you want to use entities in your document, you must have a small DTD that at least references those entities.

This section only scratched the surface of XML but it's enough to get you started and to get you through the XML questions on the exam. If you want more of the nitty-gritty behind XML, visit one of the several great resources listed in the "For More Information" section at the end of the chapter.

Well-Formed and Valid XML Documents

    XML document requirements

Regardless of whether you use a DTD and regardless of what combinations of elements, attributes, entities and such that you use to create your XML documents, every XML document has to be *well formed*, which means that it has to adhere to a specific set of rules as defined in the XML specification. If you want to be sure that your documents also play by the rules of a particular DTD, you'll also need to take steps to make them valid. Well-formed and valid XML documents are discussed in more detail in the following sections.

Well-formed XML documents

The rules of well-formedness aren't too difficult to follow, and the new class of XML development tools that have appeared on the scene go out of their way to make it easier to be sure your documents are well formed. The next few sections discuss what it takes for a document to be well formed.

Tip

HTML developers of all shapes and sizes have grown lazy over time because Web browsers don't require that they adhere closely to basic rules of document building. One of the most difficult parts of the transition from HTML to XML is following the basic rules of XML. Many of these rules apply equally well to HTML and it's a good idea to start using them in HTML as you prepare to use XML.

All open tags must be closed

If you open a tag, close it. In HTML, many Web authors use paragraph tags as stand-alone tags to create white space in their Web pages. This isn't acceptable in XML. If a closing tag is missing, the document isn't well formed. A complete HTML (and XML) element has a start tag and an end tag:

```
<p>...</p>
```

Empty elements are the exception to this rule.

Every empty element must have an ending slash

An empty tag is one that doesn't hold any content at all, like the image tag in HTML. If you're using a DTD, the tag must be defined in the DTD as empty. When you use empty tags in XML documents, you must include an ending slash in the tag just before the greater than sign, as follows:

```
<picture src="corplogo" />
```

Even if you don't use a DTD to guide the development of your documents, you still have to use the trailing slash in any empty element.

In the Real World

Note that it's also acceptable to close the empty tag by immediately following it with a closing tag; for example, `<img></img>`; however, it's more common to see the closing slash `<img />`.

All attribute values must be quoted

In HTML, you can often get away with not using quotation marks around your attribute values, but this is not true in XML. This rule is fairly straightforward: include all attribute values in quotation marks, as shown in this bit of code:

```
<available instock="yes" />
```

All elements must be completely nested

When you nest one element inside of another, the child element must be completely contained within the parent. In this example, the child element's closing tag comes after the parent's and is not well formed:

```
<product><product_id>087017395</product></product_id>
```

The correct way to nest the `product_id` element within the `product` element is:

```
<product><product_id>087017395</product_id></product>
```

Tip
A good trick to help you nest your elements correctly is to remember to: Always close the element first you opened last.

XML is case sensitive

Unlike HTML, XML is case sensitive. If you aren't using a DTD with your document, this isn't a big deal. However, if you're using a DTD to drive your document development, the case of the markup in your documents must match the case of the declarations in your DTD. You saw this entity declaration earlier:

```
<!ELEMENT description (#PCDATA)>
```

If you use the element in a document as `<DESCRIPTION>...</DESCRIPTION>`, your document won't be well formed. The correct usage is `<description>...</description>`.

In the Real World
When you're writing DTDs, it's generally a good idea to stick with one case or another. This makes it easier and less confusing to develop documents according to the DTD. Also, mixed case can be very difficult to use and we don't recommend it.

Following these basic rules of well-formedness will guarantee that all of your XML documents are well formed and can be read by any tool for processing XML.

Taking the next step: valid XML documents

A valid XML document is nothing more than a document that plays by the rules of a particular DTD. In our earlier product description example, our DTD specified that each `product` element must contain one instance of the `product_id`, `available`, name, and `description` elements, in that order. If you leave out one of the elements or put them in the wrong order, the document isn't valid because it disobeys the rules of the DTD.

Usually, the only reason a document absolutely must be valid is the processing system working with that document requires it to be valid. Web browsers don't require validity for any kind of markup—XML or HTML—but a financial transaction tool, for example, would most likely require valid documents to verify that all of the required information is present and in the correct form.

When you require that a document is valid, you constrain the way markup can be used to describe its content. At the same time, you guarantee that the document will have a particular structure and contain particular information. The more necessary consistent structure is, the more important validity becomes.

Browser Support for XML

Web browsers are the most common tools utilized by users to access information from the Web, and Internet browser support for XML is a practical, real-world concern for any Web developer. Currently, the following browsers support XML:

✦ Internet Explorer 5.0 and later

✦ Netscape 6

✦ Opera 4

Exam Tip   It's important to know which browsers support XML.

The best all around support for XML in a browser is currently found in Internet Explorer 5.0 and higher, but Netscape 6 is promising. Future browser releases should have even better support for XML, but only time will tell.

Tip   If you want more details about the support for XML in different browsers visit XML.com's Browser XML Display Support Chart at `www.xml.com/pub/a/2000/05/03/browserchart/index.html`. This Web-based chart gives you an overview of support for XML at a glance and links to more detailed articles on the different browser's support for XML.

XHTML

Objective   Role of XHTML in Web development

In an effort to move HTML under the XML umbrella, the W3C released XHTML 1.0 in January 2000. XHTML is not a new version of HTML with new elements and attributes, but rather is reformulation of HTML as XML. What this means to developers is that you should simply use the same HTML tags you're used to but create well-formed XML documents as discussed in the previous sections. For real-world Web page development, using XHTML means quoting all attribute values, nesting elements properly, adding trailing slashes to empty elements, and closing every element that you open. Although this is a slight departure from the more lax rules that developers are accustomed to, it isn't a difficult bridge to cross.

Tip

A key benefit to using XHTML instead of HTML is that you're creating a well-formed XML document so you can actually include other XML markup in your document as your particular content requires. With this approach, you get the best of both worlds: familiar markup tags and the ability to create any tags that your content requires.

XHTML also attempts to remove formatting-oriented tags from the HTML markup collection. There are three different flavors of XHTML that mirror the three different flavors of HTML:

✦ **XHTML Transitional.** Includes both structure and formatting tags. This is the flavor of XHTML most developers use right now.

✦ **XHTML Strict.** A formatting tag-free set of markup that focuses only on using markup to define Web page structure. If you opt for this flavor of XHTML, you need to use style sheets to drive the display of your pages.

✦ **XHTML Frameset.** Contains all of the elements related to creating frames in Web pages.

In the Real World

XHTML hasn't caught on like wildfire and the majority of Web developers are still using standard HTML to build their Web pages. Although XHTML is still a relatively new technology, it does represent the future of Web markup.

One of the reasons that XHTML hasn't been as widely accepted by developers as some might have hoped is because XHTML documents are XML documents, so they must be well formed, and it takes a bit more work to create well-formed documents. In addition, some of the well-formedness rules cause problems when browsers try to display XHTML documents. For example, in XML you don't need the trailing space before the slash at the end of empty elements; however, for backwards compatibility, you may need to use it in XHTML (`<img />` instead of `<img/>`).

Tip

A great resource for developers who want to start using XHTML, but want to avoid browser display problems, is the XHTML specification itself. Appendix C: HTML Compatibility Guidelines at `www.w3.org/TR/xhtml1/#guidelines` lists all of the different things you can do to make XHTML documents more browser friendly.

What the Future Holds for HTML

The most common question about XML is will it replace HTML, or will the two continue to play well together in the world of markup? The answer right now is unclear. HTML is still the most popular way to build Web pages, and until there are several versions of Web browsers that support XML, it simply isn't practical to create Web pages with XML.

Many of the current implementations of XML use it as a way to describe the data that drive computer systems and not necessarily Web pages. The default markup of choice for Web development is still HTML, but the default markup of choice for data exchange is XML.

For now, it's important for Web developers to have a good idea of what XML is and what it can be used for. Learning to work with XHTML is a good first step to becoming more comfortable with XML. Our advice: don't give up on HTML, but don't overlook XML.

Key Point Summary

In this chapter, you learned the basics of XML: Why you need it; where it came from; its basic components; and the affect it will have on HTML. In preparation for the test, be sure and have a good understanding of the basic theories and syntax of XML:

✦ A markup language is a text-based scheme for describing content in a text file using a tagging system. Most markup languages strive to separate the format of content from is description, so the content is reusable across many different platforms and media.

✦ HTML is a markup language and was originally designed to describe just the structure of a Web page and not its formatting. Over time, HTML has become a Web page formatting language, leaving the need for a strong markup language for the Internet unfilled. Serving HTML documents over the Internet is resource and bandwidth intensive and isn't the best solution for making information available to millions of people around the world.

✦ XML was developed to meet the markup language needs of the Internet. XML is a meta-markup language that you can use to define your own tags and use them to describe a particular kind of content. XML elements should describe your content accurately without including information about the way the content is displayed.

✦ XML strikes the middle ground between HTML and SGML. The HTML tag set is too limited to describe all of the different kinds of content that need to be passed around the Internet. SGML is too complex for everyday use. XML borrows ease of use from HTML and standardization of syntax from SGML.

✦ The primary components of an XML document include DTDs, elements, attributes, and entities. DTDs list the markup elements that should be used to describe a particular kind of content. Although DTDs aren't required for all XML documents, they are highly recommended.

✦ Elements are the markup tags that you use to describe your content.

✦ Attributes provide more information about a given element.

✦ An entity is a virtual storage unit and can hold either text or binary files. Any binary file that you want to use in your XML document needs to be declared in an entity.

✦ Every XML document must be well formed, which means that it must adhere to a basic set of document structure rules. Well-formed requirements include:

  • Including an XML declaration at the beginning of a document

  • Closing all elements

  • Adding a trailing slash at the end of empty elements

  • Quoting all attribute values

  • Nesting child elements completely within parent elements

  • Making sure that documents that use DTDs use the same case in the markup as used in the DTD

✦ A valid XML document is a well-formed document that plays by the rules of a particular DTD.

✦ Current browser support for XML is minimal. Internet Explorer 5.0, Netscape 6.0, and Opera 4 all have some support for XML. Future browser releases are likely to have more support for XML and make it easier for Web developers to begin using XML directly in their Web pages.

✦ XHTML is the reformulation of HTML in XML and the future of HTML. The goal of XHTML is to take advantage of the benefits of XML while still utilizing familiar HTML elements.

✦   ✦   ✦

STUDY GUIDE

In this chapter, you had the opportunity to learn about the basics of XML and what it means to you as a Web designer. In the study guide, you can test your knowledge by answering a series of assessment questions, working your way through a scenario, and completing a lab exercise.

Assessment Questions

1. Which of the following is not a limitation of HTML that makes it insufficient for describing Internet data?

    A. HTML has a finite set of elements and attributes.

    B. HTML has evolved into a formatting language.

    C. HTML has a variety of facilities for supporting detailed searches of Web content.

    D. Serving HTML pages is bandwidth intensive.

2. Which of the following is not a requirement for a well-formed document?

    A. All attribute values must be quoted.

    B. All elements must be empty.

    C. All empty elements must have a trailing slash.

    D. All elements must be nested correctly.

3. XML is the middle ground between which markup languages?

    A. XHTML and GML

    B. HTML and SGML

    C. GML and XLink

    D. SGML and XPath

4. Which of the following is true of valid XML documents?

    A. It is well formed and plays by the rules of a specific DTD.

    B. Elements and attributes must be in all uppercase.

    C. It doesn't play by the rules of any DTD.

    D. It isn't well formed.

5. Which of the following is true of XHTML?

    A. It is a new hybrid technology that is different from both XML and HTML.

    B. You can't use it to create Web pages.

    C. It is a reformulation of HTML in XML.

    D. It has totally replaced HTML as the tool for building Web pages.

6. Which of the following is a goal of XML as defined by the XML 1.0 Specification?

    A. It shall be easy to write programs which process XML documents.

    B. XML doesn't need to be compatible with SGML.

    C. XML documents can be difficult to create.

    D. XML documents don't need to be human-legible.

7. Which browsers have built-in support for XML?

    A. Internet Explorer 3.0 and Netscape 2.0

    B. Internet Explorer 5.0 and Opera 4

    C. Netscape Navigator 3.0 and Microsoft 2.0

    D. Opera 2 and Internet Explorer 3.0

8. Which of the following is not one of the flavors of XHTML?

    A. XHTML Strict

    B. XHTML Transitional

    C. XHTML Frameset

    D. XHTML Tableset

Scenarios

A client has asked you to help them build a Web-based application that is designed to collect loan application information and forward it to a processing center for approval. The processing center requires that the data they receive be valid XML. Which markup languages would you use for which parts of the site? Would you consider using XHTML in the solution? How might you be sure that the XML you send to the processing center is both valid and well formed?

Lab Exercises

Lab 19-1: Creating a well-formed XHTML document

The following steps offer you an opportunity to test your knowledge and practice the skills related to well-formed documents:

1. Select an HTML document you've already built.

2. Add an XML declaration to the top of the document.

3. Add this DOCTYPE declaration to the top of the document to specify that the document adheres to the XHTML Transitional DTD:

```
<!DOCTYPE html
     PUBLIC "-//W3C//DTD XHTML 1.0 Strict//EN"
   "DTD/xhtml1-strict.dtd">
```

4. Look for all instances of open tags missing closing tags, and add the closing tags to your document.

5. Add a trailing slash to every empty tag. Keep an eye out for the most common ones: images (`<img>`), line breaks (`<br>`), and hard rules (`<hr>`). Be sure there's a space between the last character in the tag and the slash.

6. Add quotation marks around all unquoted attribute values.

7. Be sure that all child elements are nested completely within their parent elements.

8. The XHTML DTD is written in lowercase. Convert all of your tags from uppercase to lowercase.

9. Save the document with an .html extension (browsers don't recognize the .xhtml extension).

10. Note how the change to a well-formed document affects the display of your Web page.

11. To see if your document is also valid, run it through the W3C validation tool at `http://validator.w3.org`.

Answers to Chapter Questions

Chapter pre-test

1. XML was developed because the HTML tag set is too limited to describe all of the different kinds of content on the Internet. In addition, HTML has become a formatting language and doesn't serve a purpose as a document structure definition language.

2. XML is based on both SGML and HTML. It borrows its ease of use and simple markup techniques from HTML. It also subscribes to SGML's basic theory that all documents should adhere to a basic set of rules, and that not all content can be described by a single set of tags.

3. An XML document can be guided by a DTD and uses elements, attributes, and entities to describe content.

4. A well-formed document must have complete tag pairs, empty tags with trailing slashes, quoted attribute values, properly nested elements, and use the correct case, as defined in the associated DTD.

5. A meta-markup language is a markup language used to define other markup. XML and SGML are meta-markup languages. Procedural markup is markup that directs a display device on how to display content. HTML is a procedural markup language. A logical markup language is one that describes the structure of a document irrespective of its display. Most XML markup should be logical markup.

6. XML is not designed to be a replacement for HTML but rather will work with HTML to meet the content description needs of the Internet. XHTML is a reformulation of HTML in XML that bridges the gap between the two.

Assessment questions

1. **C.** HTML doesn't support detailed Web searches well. XML is designed to make Web searching more effective. HTML's finite set of elements and attributes makes it difficult to use to describe all data. HTML has also become a formatting language over time and isn't viable for describing document structure. Serving HTML pages is both server and bandwidth intensive. See "Why HTML just isn't enough."

2. **B.** Not all elements in an XML document must be empty. An XML document can contain a combination of container and empty elements. Well-formed XML documents must have quoted attributes, trailing slashes in empty tags, and properly nested tags. See "Well-Formed and Valid XML Documents."

3. **B.** XML takes its syntax and theories from both SGML and HTML. See "A Brief History of XML."

4. **A.** A valid XML document is a well-formed document that also plays by the rules of a DTD. Elements and attributes must match the case specified in the DTD, valid documents must have a DTD to reference, and valid documents, like all other XML documents, must be well formed. See "Well-Formed and Valid XML Documents."

5. **C.** XHTML is a reformulation of HTML in XML. A is incorrect because XHTML isn't a separate technology from HTML and XML but rather is a combination of the two. See "XHTML."

6. **A.** "It shall be easy to write programs which process XML documents" is on the original list of goals for XML as listed in the XML 1.0 Specification. See "XML: The new markup for the Internet age."

7. **B.** Internet Explorer 5.0 and Opera 4 support XML. See "Browser Support for XML."

8. **D.** The three flavors of XHTML are Transitional, Strict, and Frameset. There is no such thing as XHTML Tableset. Table markup is part of all three flavors of XTHML. See "XHTML."

Scenarios

In this particular scenario, it probably makes the most sense to use HTML or possibly XHTML to create forms in Web pages that collect loan applications from users. The data collected from the forms could be converted on the server from raw data to data described with XML and then sent to the processing center in the required XML format. Because you know in which format the processing center wants its XML (a DTD gives you all the details), you can create an application on your server — using Perl, Java, or some other programming language — that saves the data gathered in the forms in valid XML markup. Tools called XML validators can help you verify that the XML you create is valid.

The decision to use XHTML to build the user-facing part of the site will be based on what browsers you want to support — the more browsers you need to support the less of a solution XHTML will be — and your client's willingness to use XHTML. A happy compromise might be to use some of the well-formedness requirements of XHTML — such as quoting attributes, closing and nesting elements correctly, and using lowercase tags — in an HTML document. Your pages would be well on their way to being well formed, but you could avoid some of the hassles associated with browsers and XHTML.

For More Information

✦ **The World Wide Web Consortium's XML page.** www.w3.org/XML.

✦ **The XML 1.0 Specification.** www.w3.org/TR/2000/REC-xml-20001006

✦ **XML.com – A Technical Introduction to XML.**
www.xml.com/pub/a/98/10/guide0.html

✦ **XML Info.** www.xmlinfo.com

✦ **The XML Cover pages.** http://xml.coverpages.org

HTTP Servers and Cookies

EXAM OBJECTIVES

- ✦ Servers and browser requests
- ✦ Server applications and dynamic Web sites
- ✦ The role of cookies in a stateless medium
- ✦ Working with cookies

CHAPTER PRE-TEST

1. What are the four steps in an HTTP communication between a Web browser and Web server?

2. What is a port?

3. How are ASP and JSP more processor efficient than CGI?

4. What is a cookie and how is it stored on your computer?

5. Describe how you can use cookies to maintain state between a Web browser and a Web server.

6. What are two ways you can control how cookies are stored on your system?

✦ Answers to these questions can be found at the end of the chapter. ✦

In this chapter, you learn how Web servers and Web browsers communicate, what it takes to perform basic administration tasks on some of the more popular Web servers, and how you can run applications on your server to add to the functionality of your Web site. You also learn about a topic that goes hand in hand with Web servers: cookies, which are snippets of user-specific information Web servers place on the user's hard drive. You find out where cookies come from, how to create and use them, and how to enable or disable them on your computer. We debunk some of the common cookie myths and discuss the pros and cons of using cookies so you can make an informed decision about what role cookies should play in the design of your Web site.

How Web Servers and Web Browsers Communicate

 Servers and browser requests

When you open or link to a Web page from your Web browser, you're requesting that particular page from a Web server somewhere on the Internet. Web servers are designed to hold Web pages, field requests from Web browsers for those pages, and deliver the pages back to the Web browser for display on the user's computer. The same Web server that answers requests from browsers over the Internet may also answer requests over an intranet.

 Tip The term "server" can be a bit misleading. Sometimes the term refers to the actual computer that serves up information. Other times it refers to the server software that runs on that computer and responds to requests for information stored on the computer. Unless we specify otherwise, when we use the term "server," we're referring to software running on a computer designated as a server, not just the computer.

Web servers use the Hypertext Transfer Protocol (HTTP) to communicate with Web browsers and serve up Web pages. The fact that a Web server is an HTTP server and that you preface all URLs with http:// is no coincidence. Web servers "listen" specifically for requests from browsers that are couched in the HTTP protocol — as opposed to other protocols such as File Transfer Protocol (FTP), Post Office Protocol (POP), or Telnet — and answer the requests as defined by the HTTP protocol.

An HTTP communication between a browser and a server has four steps:

1. The browser opens a connection to the HTTP server over a Transmission Control Protocol/Internet Protocol (TCP/IP) network using the open connection language specified in HTTP.

2. The browser requests a particular file from the HTTP server.

3. The server responds to the request.

4. The server closes the connection with the browser.

Most of the communication between browser and server via HTTP is transparent to the user. Steps 1 and 2 happen almost simultaneously when you click a hyperlink or type a URL into your browser's address field. The response from the server is fairly obvious but you don't even notice that the server shuts down the connection with the browser as soon as all of the pieces that you request are transferred to your system for display in a browser.

Every HTTP communication has these four steps, even the ones that don't result in the successful retrieval of a Web page by a Web browser. If a browser requests a URL that doesn't exist, the server still responds to the browser but with a 404 "File not found" error rather than actual Web content. The HTTP protocol contains built in responses that the server uses for various types of requests and problems it might encounter fulfilling those requests. Because both servers and browsers speak HTTP, the browser knows how to handle any response it gets from the server.

Ports

A single computer can serve up all kinds of information, from e-mail, to Web pages, to FTP files, and all of these server activities are defined by different protocols. This means that any server can respond to a variety of different requests couched in one of several different protocols. Ports help servers separate these different requests to make sure they're handled by the correct piece of server software that speaks the correct protocol.

A *port* is a logical connection point on a server that a client application — for example, a Web browser — can use to access a particular service such as a Web server or an FTP server. A port is labeled with a number, and a single computer can have port numbers that range from 0 to 65536. Each port on the computer has a unique identifying number and most services have a default number assigned to them. This number is usually between 0 and 1024.

Exam Tip   Be sure you're familiar with what ports standard HTTP servers and secure SSL servers use by default for the exam.

Standard, non-secure Web servers typically use port 80, whereas secure Web servers running the Secure Sockets Layer (SSL) protocol use port 443. SSL allows you to send and receive Web content securely. (See the sidebar titled "The Least You Need to Know about SSL.") By default, Web browsers and other HTTP clients know whether to access port 80 or port 443 — depending on the security requirements of the page — to request Web pages. The URLs `http://www.hungryminds.com:80/` and `http://www.hungryminds.com/` are, for all intents and purposes, identical. If you want to create a Web site for limited viewing, and that isn't immediately available to a browser, you can set up a Web server to use a different port than the standard 80, http://www.hungryminds.com:85/, for example. When a user tries to access the site, he or she must know the port to see the site.

If you want to put up a site with limited access, simply changing the port number on the site's sever isn't a complete method for protecting the site from prying eyes. A hacker with a modicum of understanding of how servers and ports work can diligently change port settings to try and find "hidden" sites. If you truly want to protect a site from those who shouldn't have access to it, password-protect it at the very least. You may even think of placing it behind a firewall or within the bounds of an extranet.

Common Web servers

To say that Web servers are a dime a dozen might be a little extreme, but there are definitely a wide variety of servers available to hold and deliver your Web pages. If you host your Web site at an Internet Service Provider (ISP), you may not get to choose which Web server you use. However, if you're still shopping for an ISP, and you can choose which Web server to use, you should know a bit about the more common Web servers.

For the exam, you need to know what the most common servers are, what platforms they run on, and if they are freeware, shareware, or commercial packages.

The Least You Need to Know about SSL

SSL is one of several different protocols designed to help Web browsers and Web servers communicate securely. As with any other protocol, both the Web client and the Web server have to speak and understand SSL to share information. The SSL protocol defines how a Web client requests a secure page from a Web server, how the client passes authentication information to the server so the server knows the client has permission to access the pages, and how the information passed back and forth between the client and server is encrypted so no one can intercept and read the transmissions.

All commerce activities should be done over a secure connection and you must have server software that supports encryption to create and manage a secure Web site. Most Web server packages and most 3.0 and later browsers support SSL, so it's a safe protocol to use for any secure site. Building a secure Web site is an adventure in itself, and you don't need to know the ins and outs of SSL or secure sites for the Site Designer exam. If you want to know more about SSL and Web security in general, you can read more about SSL in the Introduction to SSL tutorial on the iPlanet site at http://docs.iplanet.com/docs/manuals/security/sslin/index.htm.

Four of the most common Web server packages are:

✦ **Apache.** Apache is one of the most popular Web servers available, because it's free, reliable, and runs on both UNIX and Windows NT (common platforms for running Web server computers). However, Apache doesn't have as robust a user interface for administration as many other Web servers do. In fact, you have to use a command line to make changes and issue commands; however, it's still popular. A variety of Web sites and other references provide a plethora of information about Apache.

✦ **MS Personal Web Server 4.0.** The Microsoft Personal Web Server is a popular Web server with Windows users because it's freely available and integrates easily with most Windows platforms. Personal Web Server is not designed to handle heavy Web site traffic, but it's a good tool for serving up a small personal or business site that doesn't include complex server programming. Personal Web Server only runs on the Windows operating systems.

✦ **Netscape Enterprise Edition.** Netscape's enterprise-level server is a commercial product that can be purchased from Netscape and runs on both UNIX and Windows NT. Netscape Enterprise Edition was one of the first enterprise level server packages available and has a significant install base. The server has support for SSL and can handle heavy Web site traffic.

✦ **IIS.** Internet Information Server (IIS) is Microsoft's answer to the Netscape Enterprise Edition. IIS is an enterprise-level Web server that supports SSL and a variety of server programming options. IIS is built into Windows NT/2000 and only runs on Windows NT/2000. Organizations that have a mostly Microsoft infrastructure often run IIS simply because it integrates so well with Microsoft's other software products.

Over time, Web servers have become more user friendly and the software developers have worked to make it easier to administer and maintain the servers. Even if you aren't planning on administering your server yourself, it's a good idea to know a bit about how Web servers are administered.

Web server administration

There are two ways to administer a Web server:

✦ Via a Web browser and an HTTP connection
✦ Using the server's built-in administration tools

Not every Web server provides administration access in both ways, although many do. Web browser administration is an important tool for Web administrators because it allows them to access and control the Web server across the Internet or an intranet. If a Web server is housed at a hosting facility, the administrator does not have to visit the facility to administer the server. The administrator can also use any browser on any operating system to administer the server; regardless of the operating system the server machine is running. The benefit of a local administration tool that is only available from the server is that access to the server's administrative tools is more guarded and, therefore, more difficult to hack. Not all server software comes with a local administration tool that is installed as part of the server.

If a server allows administration from a Web browser via an HTTP communication, a specific port is designated for administration. The Web server doesn't come with a default administration port because that would give potential hackers the perfect place to start when they attempt unauthorized access to the server. Instead, the site Webmaster designates a port for Web server administration when he or she sets up the Web server software on the Web server computer. When a browser tries to access the site with the administration port appended to the URL, the server returns the standard server administration interface instead of the actual Web site. Of the four popular servers we discussed in the previous section, three come with different tools for administering them. Apache doesn't come with a graphical administration tool set of any kind, so to administer an Apache server, you either have to log or telnet into the server itself and make changes to one of several configuration files. The three that have graphical administration tools are:

✦ **MS Personal Web Server 4.0.** The Personal Web Server comes with an administration console built into the Windows operating system. There isn't a remote Web-based tool from Microsoft for administering this server.

✦ **Netscape Enterprise Edition.** The Netscape Enterprise Edition server relies solely on a browser-based interface to administer the server.

✦ **Internet Information Server.** IIS has both a browser-based administration interface and the Microsoft Management Console (MMC) that an administrator can use to access and control the site. Administrators can choose to enable the browser-based interface if they want access to the server over a TCP/IP network or disable it if they want to restrict administration to the local machine.

Tip

If your Web server only allows for local administration through a tool, and not browser-based administration, you can install a remote access tool such as Virtual Network Connection (VNC) or pcAnywhere to gain access to the server over the network and control it, as if you were sitting right in front of it.

A Web server can do much more than simply respond to a Web browser's request for Web pages, images, and multimedia files. A Web server can also host and call scripts and executable programs written in a variety of programming languages. In the following section, we take a high-level look at applications that run your Web server.

Server-Side Programming

Server applications and dynamic Web sites

Server-side programming can add extended functionality to your Web site that isn't supported by HTML or any of the different kinds of media you can incorporate into your Web site. HTML forms were developed specifically to gather information in a Web page from a user and pass that information to another application for processing on the server. HTML isn't capable of anything but gathering the data, but applications written in a variety of programming languages are.

An example of a Web form that gathers information for processing by a backend application is the new discussion form on the Frommer's Web site shown in Figure 20-1.

A visitor to the site fills in the information in the form and an application running on the server takes that information and turns it into a post available on the Web-based message board for other users to see. An HTML page alone could not process the information entered by the user to create a new Web page on the board. A program on the server side does the work instead.

Figure 20-1: A new discussion form on the Frommer's site collects information from users for display on a message board.

Plain HTML pages are relatively static, but programs that run on the server allow Web pages and Web sites to be more dynamic — that is, they change based on user input. In our previous example, the Web site changes when a user adds a new message posting. On complex commerce sites, personalized messages are tailored to each user and changed as the user shops.

A collection of technologies makes dynamic Web page creation possible, and there is no one standard for Web programming. The programming language you use for the applications you run on your Web server depends on what language you prefer, what language your server supports, and what you are trying to do. Some of the more common programming languages are:

✦ Common Gateway Interface (CGI)

✦ Active Server Pages (ASP)

✦ JavaServer Pages (JSP)

Cross-Reference

In addition to writing programs that run on the Web server, you can also write programs into your HTML pages that each user's Web browser runs locally. Client-side programming is often used in conjunction with server-side programming, and sometimes in lieu of it. Chapter 17 discusses client-side programming with the most popular language, JavaScript, in detail.

The following three sections discuss each of these common server-side programming languages in greater detail.

CGI

CGI is not really a programming language but is instead a protocol that Web servers use to share information gathered in HTML forms with applications that run on the Web server. You can write CGI applications in one of several different programming languages, including:

✦ Perl

✦ C++

✦ AppleScript

Of the three, Perl is probably the most popular programming language, but you can use just about any scripting language to create CGI applications. CGI is a good tool for server programming because it's cross-platform compatible. You can submit information from a Web browser running on a Macintosh to a Web server running on a UNIX box without worrying about platform compatibility.

CGI was the first Web programming protocol and is still the most popular. When you see simple guest books and counters on Web pages, they are usually made possible by a CGI script. CGI scripts can also access information stored in a database or in a file system. If you want to display information stored in databases or file systems, you can use CGI to extract that information and write HTML on the fly to display it.

All Web servers support CGI. To run CGI applications, all you have to do is put them in a directory on the server that has execute permissions and you're ready to go. The languages that each server supports may be limited to the language interpreters installed on the server. For example, chances are a UNIX server isn't going to have an interpreter for AppleScript. When you're setting up your server to run CGI, be sure to find out which CGI languages it supports.

ASP

ASP is a robust Web site delivery system developed by Microsoft and used heavily in the Web development world. ASP allows for the creation of database-based Web sites that react to user activities and preferences. ASP is perfect for commerce sites and database-driven sites.

ASP pages are a combination of special ASP code for accessing databases and processing user information, and programming logic and HTML. When a user requests an ASP page, the page and all of its code and HTML are processed by the ASP server and then delivered through the Web server to the user. The Web server is still a conduit for user requests and responses, but it passes all requests off to the ASP server to handle the complex processing that makes dynamic and personalized sites possible.

In the Real World Complex Web sites that are backed by databases and use advanced programming are often called Web applications instead of Web sites. Commerce applications drive online shopping, catalog applications drive online merchandise display, and university applications drive online learning sites—to name a few. Web applications utilize one or more server-side programming applications, such as CGI, ASP, or JSP.

ASP is a very powerful tool, but it's a Microsoft tool that requires a PC running Windows NT or 2000 and the IIS Web server software. When you choose ASP as an application programming language, you're committing to the Microsoft way of Web development.

JSP

JSP is an alternative to ASP that is Java-based rather than Microsoft-based. Because Java is platform-independent, you can run JSP on any kind of operating system that you want and with a larger variety of Web server software than with ASP. JSP strives to match ASP's functionality and does a good job. When a user requests a JSP page, the Web server routs the request to a JSP server, which processes the request and sends the final HTML back to the server to send to the browser.

The JSP server is Java-based, so it should be able to run on any operating system that has a Java Runtime Environment (JRE) installed on it. Although Java is a more open platform than Windows, it isn't always well implemented across all operating systems. In general, JSP is the choice of those who want to stay away from Microsoft products but want an application development environment that rivals ASP.

Choosing the right programming paradigm

If you're trying to choose between CGI, ASP, and JSP for your server-side programming environment, keep these things in mind:

✦ CGI is well established and well supported. You can find a plethora of free and tested CGI code on the Web just waiting to be reworked to meet your particular needs. Web servers have built-in CGI support and most Web hosting accounts (even the smallest ones) at ISPs include some level of CGI support.

✦ CGI supports several programming languages. If you or your programmers already know C++, shell scripting, Perl, or AppleScript, you can leverage those skills to build CGI applications without much of a learning curve. ASP and JSP are newer technologies and you may have to take some time to learn their syntax.

✦ ASP and JSP are multithreaded processes, whereas CGI is not. Each time a browser connects to your Web server and calls a CGI application, the server has to start a new process to handle the request. The busier the server gets, the more processes are running and the more overloaded the system gets. ASP and JSP use a single process to handle multiple requests, reducing the load on the system significantly. Although CGI is a great solution for a small to medium-size sites, ASP and JSP are more appropriate for enterprise-level sites.

The pros and cons of server-side programming

Server-side programming is an excellent technique for adding to the functionality of your Web site if you use it well. Keep in mind that server-side applications run on the server, so users have to wait for the application to process information and create a new HTML page before they get a response from the server. Server-side programming does slow down your site, but good programming techniques can reduce the slowdown.

The key benefit of server-side programming is that you only have to make the applications run on your Web server. You can use the best programming language and programming techniques based on the platform you choose and the database or file system you connect to. It's far easier to tweak a single application to run on a Web server than to write a client-side script to run in a thousand Web browsers. What you lose in speed, you make up for in functionality.

Ultimately, you must choose between the ease of implementation you have on the server side and the reduction in speed your users will encounter as they wait for a server-side application to process. An experienced Web programmer can help you balance functionality against speed and help you assess which functionality to leave on the server and which to move to the Web browser.

Web Servers and State

 The role of cookies in a stateless medium

In a traditional client-server network, servers know everything about their clients, including identification information. This built-in and constant connection between clients and servers is called *state*. The Web, however, is a *stateless* medium, which means that Web servers don't have this built-in means of keeping track of their Web clients. When you request a Web page from a Web server and then return to request another page, the server doesn't know that you are the same person or that your machine made both requests.

The Web was intentionally designed to be a stateless medium because it's much more efficient to ignore state than maintain it. Without state requests, Web pages can be routed from a browser to a server in any way necessary. Further, multiple Web servers, called *server farms*, can also handle requests to help balance the load across machines.

The problem with a stateless network, of course, is that the Web server doesn't know who you are. If you want to buy a collection of books from Amazon.com, the site needs to know that you're the same person who picked out the book on buying a home or this *CIW Site Designer Certification Bible*. When it comes time to check-out, however, the site needs to move everything from your virtual shopping cart to a purchase order and process your credit card information. For every piece of the process, the site needs to know who you are.

When it became obvious that the lack of state on the Web would be a problem, developers began to find ways to maintain state despite the Web's stateless status. One option is to use hidden form input values to pass unique user-identification keys from one page to the next as users move around the site. Information about users is stored in a database, like a virtual shopping cart, for example, so when you know who a user is after a site login or some similar feature, you can retrieve his or her personal data from the database.

However, the passing of an identification key only works during one session for the user. The moment the user closes his or her browser the key is lost. If the user comes back to the site, you have to start all over again or with the latest information stored in your database. You don't know who users are until they log in, and if they don't log in, you don't have any way of knowing who they are, period.

A solution to helping servers identify clients time after time is to use a *cookie*. A cookie is nothing more than a simple text file that a server places on the user's system to help identify them. Cookies have become a common tool — in combination with the unique identifiers and databases — for identifying unique users to a site and creating a personalized experience for each user.

An Overview of Cookies

 Working with cookies

Believe it or not, the term "cookie" doesn't have a special or hidden meaning, it was simply chosen at random by the developers of the technology and is short for *persistent client state HTTP cookies*. As the long name implies, a cookie helps an HTTP server maintain persistent state on a Web browser client. A server sets a cookie on a client system by sending the cookie information in the header of an HTTP response to the client's request for a page. You can't get a cookie from a Web site unless you first visit that Web site. If the browser accepts the cookie (and it doesn't always as you learn a bit later in the chapter), the text file that is the cookie is stored on the user's computer and can be accessed by the Web site that set it each time the user visits the site.

When you access a Web site that has set a cookie on your system, the browser sends the location of the cookie to the Web server so the server can decide if it wants to access the cookie and process the information stored there. Your browser only sends the cookie to the Web server if the Web server domain in the cookie matches the Web server domain of the site you're trying to access. This prevents other servers from accessing information in cookies that the server didn't set in the first place.

Using cookies

Earlier we mentioned that cookies are great for maintaining state in an otherwise stateless medium. The server can store information about the user in the cookie and find out each time the user visits exactly who they are. The server can match the user's identity with information in a database to present a unique view of the site for the user.

Normally, the information on a Web page is generic to any visitor to the site. Although it's interesting, it may not target the specific information or products the user is interested in. When you log in to a site, a cookie is set on your system, and updated by any subsequent visits, helps the server present a personalized view of the site based on your preferences and previous purchases.

In addition to delivering personalized sites, cookies can be used to:

✦ Store any information you supplied to a site in a Web-based form. This can keep the amount of data stored in the site's database to a minimum. Less-than-crucial information is stored on the user's system instead of in the server's database.

✦ Store encrypted information that only the server that set the cookie should have access to.

✦ Store browsing and buying information about a customer to target which banner ads and merchandise to display for that customer.

Web site personalization is by far the most common use for cookies. Users have made it very clear that privacy is of paramount importance on Web sites, and they do not appreciate having their private information used against them.

In the Real World   If you're going to gather information about your users to store in a cookie or to use to drive advertising and marketing on your site, it's always best to let the user know what you're doing and let them choose whether they want to participate. Users who feel like they are held hostage by a Web site and fed countless ads and targeted marketing are likely not to return. Be honest about why you're collecting personal information and use it carefully.

How cookies are built

Cookies are nothing more than a collection of name and value pairs, much like what is passed from an HTML form to a Web server. The standard cookie header has a collection of name value pairs used to store some basic information in the cookie, including:

✦ **The cookie's name.** `name=value`

✦ **The domain and location of the issuing server.** `path=path; domain=domain`

✦ **The expiration data for the cookie.** `expires=DD-Mon-YY HH:MM:SS GMT`

✦ **Whether the cookie should be sent securely.** `secure`

Of all of these name and value pairs, only the cookie's name is actually required to create the cookie. The rest are optional, and the server can also include other name and value pairs that are meaningful to it. The expiration date defines how long the cookie should stay on the user's system. If there's no expiration date, the cookie expires when the users close their browsers.

Tip   To expire a cookie with a future expiration date, reset the cookie on the user's system with an expiration date that occurs in the past and the cookie will expire as soon as the browser is closed.

A given server can only place 20 cookies on any one user's machine and a single user can only have 300 cookies set on his or her system. Browsers don't share cookies, so if a server sets a cookie on your system for one browser and you visit the site later with different information, the server won't have access to the cookie it originally gave you. If you're curious about how many cookies you have on your system take a look at the cookie files for the browsers you have installed. The various browsers keep cookies in different places. Here are the most common browsers and locations:

✦ **Internet Explorer.** In a subdirectory aptly named cookies

✦ **Netscape Navigator.** In a cookies.txt file in the application's User Profile

Tip   Because everyone's computer is configured a bit differently, we can't point you directly to your cookie files. A quick way to find all of the cookies on your system is to simply search for the word "cookies" and see what your system search brings up.

Debunking cookie myths

Almost from their first appearance on the Web, cookies have had a bad name. Many misconceptions about cookies make users afraid of them and worried that they can be used to gather and transfer private information to Web servers. This simply isn't true. To clear things up, here are a couple of truths about cookies:

✦ A cookie is just a plain text file. It isn't an application or even a script, so it can't read files from your hard drive or actively communicate with a Web server. It simply holds information that your Web browser sends to a Web server and that a Web server can add to or change. Because cookies are just text files, they can't contain viruses. Because cookies aren't active applications, they can't troll your computer for personal information or passwords.

✦ Other servers cannot access cookies on your system that they didn't set. A cookie is matched to a server and can only be shared with that server — remember the path and location information in the cookie parameters.

Caution   Some site developers choose to store a user's name and password in a cookie so the user doesn't have to enter the information every time he or she accesses the site. Although this is convenient, it makes your name and password available to anyone who can access your computer and open your cookie files with a text editor. Whereas saving passwords in cookies is a bit irresponsible on the site developer's part, it's a common activity. If you're worried about your passwords being accessed from your cookie files by another person, don't choose the option at a Web site to help you remember your password.

The general concerns about cookies revolve around their ability to gather and transfer information. If you remember that a cookie is nothing more than a text file, and it can't actively do anything on your system, your concerns about cookies should be minimized.

> **Tip**   When you design a site that uses cookies, be sure to include information in the help portion of your site that explains how cookies work — with links to independent and reputable sites with more information on cookies — and a brief description of what you use cookies for. Provide more information to your users than you think they'll ever want, and they will have more confidence in your site and your intentions.

The pros and cons of using cookies

If cookies weren't such a good thing, you wouldn't get one from just about every site you visit. Cookies are an easy way to track users, and they work with every major browser. However, cookies do have a downside. Users can set their systems to decline all cookies (as we show you in the following section), and users can delete their cookies at will. Although you can be relatively certain that a cookie you place on a user's system will be there the next time he or she visits, you can't be 100 percent certain.

When you choose to use cookies to track user information, think about the information you're tracking and how much of it is nice-to-have information and how much is must-have information. Anything that is must-have information should be stored on the server or in a database of some kind. Anything that is nice to have is a good candidate for cookies. If using and keeping cookies is a requirement for your site to work well for users, let them know up front when they register for the site that the site requires cookies.

> **Tip**   If possible, try to create your site so that cookies aren't required and then add cookie technology to make things easier for those users who do support cookies. It's always better to have a site that works for all users regardless of their settings than one that only works for those users who have their browser configured in a particular way.

Configuring a browser to work with cookies

Just about every browser available today has a tool for managing cookies. Managing cookies involves deciding whether you want to accept cookies at all and, if you do choose to accept them, picking what level of control you want to have over which cookies you accept and how frequently. In Internet Explorer 5, you control cookies from the Security Settings window, shown in Figure 20-2. To access the Security Settings window, choose Tools ➪ Internet Options, click on the Security tab, and click the Custom Level button.

The Cookies section of the Security Settings window addresses two different kinds of cookies: stored cookies and not stored (session) cookies. A stored cookie is one the computer leaves on your system with an expiration date sometime in the future. A session cookie is one that doesn't have an expiration date and expires when you close your browser. In general, both kinds of cookies behave the same way; however, session cookies tend to focus on current activities in the browser, whereas stored cookies keep information that the site can use over time.

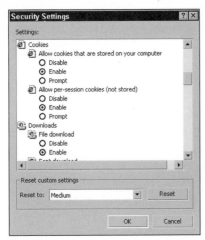

Figure 20-2: The Internet Explorer 5
Security Settings window

For both kinds of cookies, you have three options for accepting cookies:

✦ **Disable.** Don't accept cookies at all

✦ **Enable.** Accept all cookies

✦ **Prompt.** Ask before accepting cookies

If you choose the Prompt option, the browser will ask you each and every time a
server tries to set a cookie whether you want to accept the cookie. If you want to
see which servers are trying to set what cookies on your system, select this option.

Tip

> Although it's nice to know what sites are setting what cookies on your system,
> you'll quickly find that having to click a button each time a site tries to set a cookie
> can become annoying. Our experience says that choosing all cookies or no cook-
> ies is the most painless way to handle cookies.

Deleting cookies from your local computer

If you set your browser to accept cookies either at your prompting or across the
board, cookies will eventually begin to pile up on your system. Remember that
you're limited to 300 cookies and there may come a time when you have too many
cookies, especially if you spend a lot of time on the Web. You may also decide that
you want to get rid of the cookie for a particular site.

Once a cookie is set on your system, the only way to get rid of it (besides waiting
for it to expire) is to delete it. To delete cookies, you have to find where the cookies
are stored for your browser or browsers and delete them from your system. We

mentioned earlier in the "How cookies are built" section that in Internet Explorer 5, cookies are stored in a Cookies subdirectory on your system. To delete some or all of the cookies for IE 5, do the following:

1. Search for cookies

2. Open the Cookies folder

3. Choose those cookies that you want to delete

4. Delete the cookies

After you delete a cookie, the sites you previously visited that were tailored for you may not behave in the same way until you login to the site and another cookie is set on your system.

Key Point Summary

In this chapter, you learned how Web servers respond to requests from browsers. You also learned what cookies are, how they work, and how to enable and disable them on your system. Servers and cookies can work together to maintain state on the Internet and help Web sites provide content that is tailored to individual users. The key information in this chapter includes:

✦ Web servers respond to requests from Web clients — usually Web browsers — that use the HTTP protocol. The Web server always responds to a request from a client with some kind of a response. Even if the response is "file not found" or "access denied."

✦ A single server computer can host several different kinds of server software, including e-mail, FTP, and HTTP servers. To direct request traffic to the correct server software on the computer, each server has its own logical connection called a port that takes requests in a specific protocol.

✦ The default port for HTTP requests is 80, whereas the default port for SSL requests is 443. If you want to limit access to a server to a select group of users, you can change the port that the server listens on, and then only those who know the port information can access the server and its contents.

✦ There are many and varied Web servers available today. Some are freeware or shareware, whereas others are commercially licensed enterprise-level servers. There are servers available for every platform, and when you choose a server, you usually do so based on platform requirements, site traffic requirements, and cost.

✦ Apache is the most popular freeware server and it runs on both Windows NT and UNIX. Microsoft Personal Web Server is also a free server but it only runs on Windows NT. Both IIS and Netscape Enterprise Edition are commercially licensed, enterprise-level Web servers.

✦ Web servers can be administered in one of two ways: over the Web from within a browser and on the local server system using an application that came with the server. Some servers provide both kinds of administration, whereas others only provide one.

✦ Browser-based administration is more convenient, but local administration tools are more secure.

✦ You can create scripts and applications that run on a Web server to enhance your Web site and make it more dynamic. Server-side programs can be written in a variety of languages and run on any kind of server. Server-side programs can connect to databases and flat files so you can merge non-HTML content into HTML tags for display in a Web browser.

✦ CGI is a protocol for allowing Web pages to pass information to applications on the Web server. CGI applications can be written in one of several languages, including C++, Perl, and shell scripting.

✦ ASP and JSP are Web application development environments that combine specialized tags with HTML tags to create dynamic sites. When a user requests an ASP or JSP page, the request is passed to the ASP or JSP server, which processes the tags and HTML and sends completed HTML to the Web server to send to the user. A single instance of ASP and JSP can respond to a collection of requests, whereas a new instance of CGI must start each time a user requests a page supported by server-side programming.

✦ Cookies are text files that a server leaves on your browser to help it remember who you are the next time you visit the site and to track your movements through the site as you browse. Cookies were developed to help maintain state on the Web but have a variety of other uses as well. Cookies are not active applications, which means they cannot troll your hard drive for personal information nor transmit it back to the server that set it. Sites cannot read each other's cookies.

✦ You can enable or disable cookies or require that the browser prompt you to accept all cookies. You can also delete cookies from your system whenever you like. If you choose not to accept cookies or delete cookies from your system regularly, you may not be able to take advantage of the personalized content provided by many Web sites.

✦   ✦   ✦

STUDY GUIDE

The topics of Web servers and cookies are rather extensive and we only touched on both in this chapter. The study guide will give you a chance to practice with and test the knowledge you acquired, and to prepare yourself for the CIW Site Designer exam. Be sure to look for the answers to the chapter pre-test, assessment questions, and scenarios in the "Answers to Chapter Questions" section toward the end of this chapter.

Assessment Questions

1. An HTTP server is another name for what kind of sever?

   A. E-mail server

   B. A file transfer server

   C. A Web server

   D. A gopher server

2. Which of the following is a multithreaded server-side programming technology?

   A. SSL

   B. ASP

   C. JavaScript

   D. CGI

3. Why was the Web created as a stateless network?

   A. Because a network with state can only be maintained over a company LAN.

   B. To make it easier for Web developers to create personalized Web sites.

   C. To make client and server communications more efficient.

   D. To allow clients and servers running on different platforms to communicate.

4. Which ports on a server are the default ports for HTTP and SSL services?

   A. 443 and any port specified by the Web administrator

   B. 80 and 443

   C. 81 and 443

   D. 443 and 8080

5. In Internet Explorer, what are your options to control how cookies are saved to your system?

    A. Enable

    B. Disable

    C. Prompt

    D. All of the above

6. Which of the following is a drawback to using server-side applications to create dynamic content?

    A. Server-side programs can only be written in one programming language.

    B. Processing information and applications on the server can slow your Web site.

    C. Only certain specialized Web servers support server-side programming.

    D. Server-side programming only allows you to access special files on a file system and cannot connect with databases.

7. How can a cookie help maintain state between a Web server and Web client?

    A. By keeping track of the user's identity on the user's local system and passing that information to the server each time the user accesses the site.

    B. By directly saving personal information about the user to a database on the Web site.

    C. By reading other cookies set by other Web servers and passing that information to the Web server.

    D. By tracking user site visits to display targeted banner adds to the user.

8. A cookie is saved as which type of file?

    A. An executable

    B. A client-side script

    C. A database file

    D. A text file

9. Why would you want to delete cookies from your system? (Choose the best answer.)

    A. To prevent new Web sites from finding out about you.

    B. Because the cookies are sending personal information from your system to different Web servers.

    C. Because you can't have more than 300 cookies stored for a single browser.

    D. You should never delete cookies from your system.

10. Which of the following is true of cookies?

    A. Several different Web sites can share a single cookie.

    B. Cookies cannot troll your computer for personal information and send it to a different Web server.

    C. Cookies can contain viruses that can destroy other files on your computer.

    D. Cookies don't expire and cannot be deleted.

Scenarios

1. You're reworking your Web site and want to make it available over the Internet for a select group of users to see. How can you take advantage of your Web server's ports to limit which users have access to the site? What other measures should you implement to prevent unauthorized access to the site while it's under development?

2. You're building a corporate Web site, and your client wants you to create personalized content for the users that changes based on the parts of the site they visit and preferences that they select. Consider the following questions:

    a. How should you gather this information from the user, and how will you maintain it?

    b. How will you know who the user is as they move through the site and each time he or she returns to the site?

    c. Is there a way to guarantee that users won't have to log in again after the first time they register?

Lab Exercises

Lab 20-1: Analyzing cookies

1. Do a search on your system for cookies.

2. Locate your preferred browser's cookie file or folder.

3. Choose two or three cookies from Web sites you visit regularly and save copies of them to another folder or your desktop.

4. Open your Web browser and browse the sites whose cookies you made copies of.

5. Return to your browser's cookie file or folder and locate the cookies for the sites once again.

6. Open the original cookie you copied and the new version of the cookie in a text editor and compare the two. Notice what has changed and what remains the same. See if you can determine what information the cookie maintains.

Answers to Chapter Questions

Chapter pre-test

1. The four steps in an HTTP communication are: the client opens a connection to the server, the client requests a resource from the server, the server responds to the client's request, and the server closes the connection with the client.

2. A port is a logical connection on a server system that can be used to filter requests to different services, such as Web servers and e-mail servers.

3. ASP and JSP are more efficient than CGI, because they're multithreaded. A single process of an ASP or JSP server can handle several requests from clients. A CGI server must start a new thread each time a new request is submitted from a client.

4. A cookie is a text file that a server places on your computer in a designated cookie repository.

5. To maintain state on the Web, cookies can hold unique information about a user and pass that information back to the server each time the user visits a page on the server's site. The site then knows who a user is and can deliver content specific to that user.

6. You can control cookies by specifying whether you want to receive them at all and by deleting them from your system when you don't want them anymore.

Assessment questions

1. **C.** An HTTP server is a Web server. A is incorrect, because an e-mail server is usually an SMTP or POP server. An FTP server is a file transfer server and a gopher server hosts text-based hierarchical content. See "How Web Servers and Web Browsers Communicate."

2. **B.** ASP is a multithreaded server-side technology. SSL is a Web security protocol; JavaScript is a client-side programming technology; and CGI is an out-of-process server-side technology. See "The pros and cons of server-side programming."

3. **C.** The Web was created as a stateless medium to make communications between servers and clients more efficient. See "Web Servers and State."

4. **B.** Port 80 is the default port for an HTTP server and port 443 is the default server for an SSL server. See "Ports."

5. D. Your options for controlling cookies in Internet Explorer 5 include Enable, Disable, and Prompt. See "Configuring a browser to work with cookies."

6. B. Server-side processing can slow your Web site down. See "The pros and cons of server-side programming."

7. A. A cookie helps maintain state by keeping track of the user and passing that information to the server each time the user browses the server's site. See "Web Servers and State."

8. D. A cookie is saved as a text file. See "How cookies are built."

9. C. You might want to delete cookies from your system because you're limited to 300 cookies per browser. See "Deleting cookies from your local computer."

10. B. A cookie is just a text file, so it can't actively look for information on your system and send it to a Web server. See "Debunking cookie myths."

Scenarios

1. You can limit access to a Web site in development by setting the port for that site to a number other than 80, which is the default. If users want to access the site, they need to include the port information in the URL. Because curious hackers can easily get past this limitation, it's also a good idea to set a password on the site, so a user must know both the port and a password to access the site.

2. When you create a site with personalized content:

   a. You need to require that users register on the site so you can collect basic information about them as well as preferences for what kind of content they want to see. You should store the bulk of this information — especially mission critical information — in a database on your server. However, you can also store basic tracking information in a cookie on the user's system.

   b. Each time a user hits your site the server will pass the cookie to the server with information about the user (assuming he or she accepted the cookie in the first place). You can add information to the cookie to keep track of the user's last visited spot and changes to any nonessential information.

   c. You can save the user's login information in the cookie and use it to automatically log the user into the site. This isn't the best practice because it stores the user's name and password in plain, accessible text on the user's computer. If you do choose this method for auto-logging someone in, you can't guarantee that a user will never have to log into the site again, because the user may delete the cookie that your server set on his or her system or may use a different system or browser to visit the site again later.

For More Information

✦ **Serving Up Web Server Basics from Serverwatch.**
`http://webcompare.internet.com/webbasics/index.html`

✦ **Introduction to Active Server Pages from Webmonkey.**
`http://hotwired.lycos.com/webmonkey/98/39/index2a.html`

✦ **CGI Scripts for Fun and Profit from Webmonkey.**
`http://hotwired.lycos.com/webmonkey/99/26/index4a.html`
`?tw=programming`

✦ **Servlets and JSP from JavaBoutique.**
`http://javaboutique.internet.com/tutorials/JSP/`

✦ **Cookie Recipes – Client Side Persistent Data from iPlanet.** `http://devel-`
`oper.iplanet.com/viewsource/archive/goodman_cookies.html`

Web Site Publishing and Database Technology

EXAM OBJECTIVES

✦ The principles of good site design

✦ Web site hosting options

✦ Publishing sites with development and FTP tools

✦ Basic database structure

✦ Data extraction

✦ Database management systems

CHAPTER PRE-TEST

1. What are the two Web site hosting options?

2. What are the pros and cons of using a Web site development environment's site deployment tool instead of a standard FTP tool?

3. What services might an ISP provide?

4. What information about a database is contained in its schema?

5. What do the acronyms ODBC, JDBC, and BLOB stand for?

6. What are two common database applications?

✦ Answers to these questions can be found at the end of the chapter. ✦

All the elements of site design you've focused on in this book come together when you publish the site on the Web or an intranet. At its simplest, Web publishing is just a matter of moving your Web site files to a Web server. When you add more complex technologies, however, publishing requires good tools and a good plan for moving information from one place to another and for maintaining constant updates. Before you can move your files to a Web server, you also need to decide where that Web server resides and who maintains it. This chapter addresses all the key decisions you need to make in selecting a hosting solution for your Web site. It also illustrates what roles databases play when you design and publish a data-driven Web site.

Anatomy of a Well-Designed Site

 The principles of good site design

Have a conversation with three different Web design professionals and you'll get three different answers about how a well-designed site looks and behaves. Despite disparate opinions on the particulars that contribute to a well-designed site, there's general agreement in the design community about the principles that guide good site design, including:

✦ Treat the Web as its own unique media rather than a version of print or broadcast media. Take advantage of the Web's unique strengths to reinforce your site's message and brand.

✦ Keep the focus on content and avoid gratuitous graphics and multimedia. When the glitz gets in the way of the meat of the site, you risk the message, the brand, and a good interface.

✦ Stay focused on the users and give them what they want rather than what you think they want. It's your job to create a user experience that works for the user, not to force the user to have an experience that works for you.

✦ Be cognizant of bandwidth and its affect on your user's ability to access your site. Bandwidth is still very much an issue for many users, especially non-corporate users who access the Internet with modems at home. Think very carefully about who your audience is and what you know about its available bandwidth before you add too many high-bandwidth elements to your Web site.

✦ Keep the goal of building a usable and intuitive interface at the forefront of all other goals for the site. Your design is the mechanism by which a user will find his or her way through the site to the information or product he or she is looking for.

Cross-Reference These principles of good design form the cornerstone of the exam and this book. They're discussed in more detail in Chapter 1.

Each design that you create will be different and crafted to convey a specific message to a specific audience. A good way to test your design before you build the finished site is to create a prototype of the site that shows all of the following:

✦ A basic look and feel, including: colors, graphical styles, and other design elements

✦ A navigation plan to help users find their way through the site

✦ Layouts for different types of pages

✦ A general site map

✦ A sample of a high-bandwidth page

A prototype should not be a fully functional site but should represent the planned interface for the site and be complete enough for potential users to test it and provide feedback. A prototype also helps you identify project risks early on and identify possible solutions long before the inevitable time crunch that comes with launching any new Web site. All of the work you put into a prototype can be leveraged when you build the actual site itself.

A good user interface is a key component of a well-designed site, but it isn't the only one. Additional elements of a well-designed site are not necessarily visual but drive the design and development of the site. They include:

✦ **A vision statement for the site.** A vision statement defines the goals for the site and a concrete way to measure those goals. For example, if a goal of the site is to entice registered visitors to return to the site, the way to measure the success of the site against that goal is to keep count of how many times each registered user returns to the site and what percentage of registered users return in general.

✦ **Consistent and intuitive navigation.** Users should never wonder how to get around your site or how to find the information they're looking for. You should have a consistent and uninterrupted navigation that is always available to the user.

✦ **A unified theme.** When you design a site, you create an environment for the user to use to move around your site. All of the elements in the environment need to follow a common theme so users are in familiar territory when they move from page to page on your site. If your site needs to adhere to a particular branding scheme, that scheme needs to be incorporated into the theme.

✦ **Use images — both line art and photographic — to enhance your interface.** Although users tend to desert sites that use gratuitous graphics, they do expect judicious use of graphics to enhance the site's message. Use graphics on your site only where it makes sense — after all, color on the Web is free.

✦ **Integrate optional multimedia as appropriate.** There was a time when only a few users had support for multimedia because it took a significant amount of technical savvy to set up a Web browser to display multimedia. With the integration of multimedia viewers in the most popular browsers, multimedia is a reality for even the newest Web user, and Web developers are leveraging this reality. If multimedia helps support your brand and conveys your message, by all means integrate it into your site. However, be on the watch for gratuitous multimedia — that is multimedia for multimedia's sake. To make your site accessible to as many users as possible, be sure to include an alternative version — such as a text transcript — of your content.

When you and those who commissioned your Web site are satisfied that the site meets all the requirements of a well-designed site and effectively conveys your message and brand via a functional and attractive user interface, you're ready to take the site live to the world. Publishing a Web site involves more than simply moving some HTML pages and graphics to a Web server. It has to be facilitated with the right knowledge and toolset.

Publishing Your Site

When you're ready to publish your Web site, you must address two distinct issues:

✦ Where you're going to host your site.

✦ How you're going to manage the deployment of files to the host.

You don't have to wait to address these issues until you're ready to publish your site. In fact, part of your initial site plan should be solutions for both hosting and deployment strategies. The following two sections discuss defining your requirements for hosting and deployment tools, and choosing the right solution to meet your needs.

Choosing a Web site hosting option

 Web site hosting options

When you discuss Web site publishing and hosting, there are a few key terms that you need to be familiar with:

✦ **Web site host.** This is technically the computer — or server — that holds all of the components of your Web site.

✦ **Hosting provider.** A company that keeps and maintains a computer or server.

✦ **Development host.** The computer you use to create and test your Web site.

✦ **Production host.** The Web server that hosts your site when it's accessible to all users.

A host is more than just a PC that sits on your desktop and has Web server software installed on it. You can run Web server software on any PC, and you'll most likely do so for a development host. A PC that is suitable to be a production host needs to have a dedicated Internet connection that never goes down as well as enough RAM and disk space to handle the traffic that hits your Web site. You need to know two very important pieces of information about your production host:

✦ **An IP address or URL.** Either of these identifiers makes it possible for you and your users to access the files on the host system. Every host has an IP address but may not have a URL until you're ready to go live with the site. When you register for a domain name — for example, `www.lanw.com` — you match an IP address with that domain name and all URLs on that domain name. Until you've made that match, you'll need to access the host using its IP address. If you don't know the IP address, ask your hosting provider.

✦ **A username and password to access the host.** To publish a Web site, you need to be able to add and remove files from the host system, and for that level of access to the host, you'll need a username and password. Username and password systems protect your host from unauthorized access — an important consideration for any Web developer. If you expect that several people are going to need access to your host to publish content, be sure each user has his or her own username and password. It will be easier later on to track the actions of the different users if each one has to log onto the system with unique names and passwords.

Your Web hosting provider should always be able to provide you with all of the information you need about your production host and the help you need in publishing your site. A Web hosting provider is in the business of maintaining production-quality Web servers and many hosting providers are also Internet Service Providers (ISPs). In addition to hosting Web sites, they also provide Internet connections for individual users and organizations. When you're ready to choose a Web-hosting provider, you can select from one of two types:

✦ **Internal.** You or a department within your organization provide the hosting services for your Web site. Essentially, you become your own hosting provider.

✦ **External.** A secondary organization whose entire business is to provide Web site hosting and Internet connectivity.

Each type of hosting has its pros and cons and one of the most important decisions you will make about your Web site is where to host it. As you assess the benefits and risks of internal and external hosting you should address four different topics:

✦ **Cost.** Cost includes the human, technical, and financial resources required to host and maintain a production Web server.

   • **External.** An external hosting provider is able to share human and technical resources across several different hosts and clients and already has those resources in place when you're ready to host your site.

- **Internal.** Depending on what other Web sites you or your organization may already host, the cost of acquiring and setting up human and technical resources for a production host can be rather high. If you don't have a hosting infrastructure in place, you'll need to create one. You'll also need to pay for staff that can support that infrastructure over time.

✦ **Speed.** Speed is directly related to bandwidth. The more bandwidth you have, the more users your site can service at a fast rate. High bandwidth is expensive to set up and maintain.

- **External.** External hosting services count high bandwidth as a cost of doing business and already have high bandwidth connections in place.

- **Internal.** If you choose to host your site internally, you may need to acquire more bandwidth to support your site's traffic.

✦ **Reliability.** In a perfect world, your Web site would never be down; however, in the real world, it will be. If your site is unavailable on a regular basis, your users will consider it unreliable and go elsewhere for the information or products you have to offer.

- **External.** External Web hosts usually include a reliability clause in their contracts and have backup systems to take over when primary systems go down.

- **Internal.** If you host your site internally, you'll need to create and implement backup systems to maintain the reliability of your site.

✦ **Control.** When you do something yourself you have more control over it than when you rely on someone else.

- **External.** External Web hosting providers may have processes and standards that won't flex to meet your particular needs.

- **Internal.** Internal Web hosting providers can be flexible and focus entirely on your needs. You always have more control over all aspects of your production host if you host it internally.

When you're ready to choose a hosting solution — internal or external — you need to evaluate each aspect of hosting to see which kind of solution best meets your needs. Before you can compare the cost of hosting the site internally as opposed to externally, think through your hosting requirements. Make a list of all of the following questions and your answers to them:

✦ How many users do you expect will visit your site on a daily basis?

✦ About how much disk space will all of the files on your site take up?

✦ What Web site application server — Active Server Pages (ASP), ColdFusion, etc. — will you use to drive your site, if any?

✦ What database supplies the data to your site, if any?

✦ How often do you want your site backed up?

Caution You should always back up all of the components of your Web site, including HTML, images, multi-media, code, and databases. The kind and frequency of backups should be part of your overall publishing solution, and you should, at the very least, keep a separate copy of all of your files on your development system. If your production system crashes, you should be able to get it back up and running from the data in your backup within an hour or so.

After you define the requirements for your site hosting, figure out roughly what it would cost you to fulfill those requirements internally. Be sure to include human and computer resources and account for long-term maintenance of the site. After you have your own estimates, submit your requirements to two or three different external hosting providers for bids and compare the services offered in those bids with what you can provide for yourself internally. You'll eventually have to weigh the convenience and expertise of external hosting with the control you have with internal hosting.

In general, small Web sites with little or no advanced technologies — multimedia, databases, programming — can be easily maintained internally. Enterprise level organizations may also have the infrastructure to cost-effectively maintain Web sites internally rather than having to resort to an external hosting provider. Mid size Web sites often benefit the most from external hosting. Mid size companies have high bandwidth needs but not the resources to support internal hosting. The solution you choose will ultimately reflect your particular requirements and available resources.

Deploying your site

Objective Publishing sites with development and FTP tools

After you identify a host for your Web site, you can address how to deploy your site from your development host to your production host. Deployment is really nothing more than moving files from one place to another, but you want to be efficient when you move those files and be sure the correct version of each file is moved.

Exam Tip The industry standard term for publishing a Web site is *deployment*. The exam uses the phrase *publishing* in place of deployment. When we refer to deployment in this chapter, it's synonymous with the term publishing on the exam.

In addition to your knowledge of the Internet and Web servers, a good toolset is a prerequisite to a successful deployment strategy. Remember that deploying files to a production host isn't a one-time activity, but rather a regular function of site maintenance. Web sites should never be stale, so you should expect to deploy changes and updates to at least some of the elements of your site at least once a week if not more frequently. A good tool set will make regular deployment more efficient and manageable. When you select your deployment tools, you can choose from one of two types:

✦ A traditional FTP client

✦ A Web development tool — such as HomeSite, Dreamweaver, or FrontPage — that includes support for deployment

A Quick Review of FTP

FTP stands for File Transfer Protocol and it's a Transmission Control Protocol/Internet Protocol (TCP/IP) protocol that allows you to move files of any type from one place on the Internet to another. FTP is strictly for file transfer and isn't designed to display files as part of the transfer process.

To use FTP, you need an FTP client to communicate between two or more FTP servers to move files from point A to point B. FTP is an open and common standard that is the default method for transferring files on the Internet. Whether you use an FTP client, such as WS_FTP Pro, or a Web development tool, such as Dreamweaver, to deploy your site, the underlying protocol is usually FTP.

Many seasoned Web developers rely on their FTP client of choice to manage all deployment activities. Others prefer the deployment-specific functionalities that come with Web development tools. We recommend that you try both and see which best meets your needs. In the following sections, you learn the basics of how to deploy a site with WS_FTP Pro (a traditional FTP client) as well as with Dreamweaver and FrontPage 2000 (Web development tools with deployment features). Following the discussion of these three approaches to deployment are a few tips for choosing the deployment approach that best meets your needs.

WS_FTP Pro

WS_FTP Pro by Ipswitch, Inc. is a good example of a standard FTP tool and is the preferred FTP utility for many professional Web developers. WS_FTP Pro isn't part of any particular Web development environment and can be used in conjunction with or instead of a Web development environment's site publishing tools.

Tip

Most professional Web developers have more than a site-publishing tool in their bag of tricks. Sometimes you want to publish an entire site and other times just a document or a graphic. We recommend that you always have a good FTP tool, such as WS_FTP Pro, in your collection, so you can quickly and easily manage your Web site.

You can download a trial copy of WS_FTP Pro from the Ipswitch Web site at www.ipswitch.com. You can try the tool out for 30 days before you commit to a purchase.

Overview of WS_FTP Pro

WS_FTP Pro is a full-featured FTP tool that comes complete with a graphical interface and a collection of tools to facilitate the transfer of a single file or hundreds of files. If you're an experienced FTP user and worry that you'll lose some of the power of command-line FTP, you'll probably be pleasantly surprised by the access WS_FTP Pro gives you to all of the FTP commands you know and love. A quick tour of the WS_FTP Pro interface — shown in Figure 21-1 — gives you a good idea of how you can use the tool to meet your Web site publishing needs.

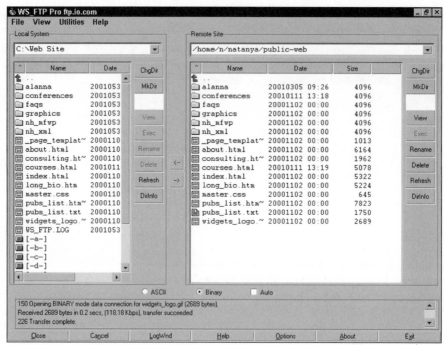

Figure 21-1: The WS_FTP Pro graphical interface

The main WS_FTP Pro window is split in half: the left side represents your local system and the right side represents the remote FTP server. Each window has buttons that you can use to create new directories, delete and rename files, and even view the files on either system. Use the buttons in the middle of the screen between the two windows to move files between your local system and the remote server.

The interface also supports drag and drop so you can drag a file or folder from one window to the other. When you move folders from one system to another, WS_FTP Pro automatically moves all of the files in the folder along with it. This feature makes it easy to move entire sites or groups of pages at once. Because not every FTP activity is the same, you can configure both your general application settings and individual FTP session settings in the Properties dialog box, shown in Figure 21-2. You access the Properties box by clicking the Options button in the main interface.

The Benefits of WS_FTP Pro

WS_FTP Pro is a good, all-purpose FTP tool that is designed to facilitate both simple and complex FTP tasks. Chances are that you'll need to FTP files to and from a variety of sites. You can save profiles for frequently visited sites so they're readily accessible. To add a new site to your list of saved sites, choose File ➪ Connect to launch the Connection window. In the Connection window choose File ➪ New Site and add all of the information about the site in the New Site dialog box. From the main interface, you can revisit recently visited sites. Choose File ➪ Recent Sites to view a list of FTP servers you've interacted with and to connect to one.

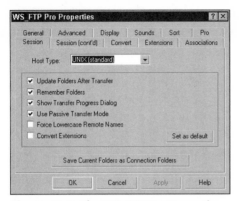

Figure 21-2: The WS_FTP Pro Properties

If you're an experienced FTP user and want to automate regular FTP activities with scripts, use the built in Scripting Utility to do so. The Scripting Utility provides you with command line access to WS_FTP Pro so you can create and manage your scripts. To access the utility, chose Utilities ➪ WS_FTP Scripting Utility.

Because not all FTP activities are alike, WS_FTP Pro has features that help guarantee successful transfers no matter which kind of file you're transferring or from where. You can choose whether a file is transferred in ASCII or binary mode on a file-by-file or site-by-site basis. Binary is a safe catchall format if you're unsure. The application can also auto-detect the file format or look at the file extension and use binary or ASCII transfer mode as appropriate. You can even transfer files from one remote server to another without using your local system as a middleman in the transaction. This feature speeds up transfer time and reduces the possibility of files being damaged during transfer.

A final and key benefit of WS_FTP Pro is that it's reasonably priced and maintained by an established software vendor, so it will be around for a while but not stretch your resources too thin. You can download a copy of WS_FTP Pro 7.0 for $39.95.

Deploying with WS_FTP Pro

If you want to transfer an entire site or just part of a site with WS_FTP Pro, follow this short list of steps:

1. Choose File ➪ Connect and set up the remote server information in the Connection window. You'll need the server name or IP address and login information.

2. Click the Connect button to make a connection to the server.

3. In the main window, navigate your local system to find the directory you want to transfer from, and then navigate the remote system to find the directory you want to transfer to.

4. Select the files you want to transfer from your local system and click the right arrow to upload them to the remote system. If you want to download from the remote system, select the files from the remote system window on the right and click the left arrow to initiate the download.

It's really that easy to move files to and from your local system to a remote FTP server. Before you transfer the files, you should be sure you know which files you need to transfer. If you need to transfer all of the files in a folder, transfer the whole folder instead of individual files. If you only need to move a file or two, transfer them individually.

As mentioned earlier, it's highly recommended that you have an FTP utility in your collection of tools. Most FTP utilities have feature sets and functions similar to WS_FTP Pro. The biggest differences among utilities are usually price, extra features (such as the Scripting Utility), and the interface.

Cross-Reference Check the "For More Information" section at the end of the chapter for a link to download WS_FTP Pro for a trial run.

Deploying with Dreamweaver

The Dreamweaver deployment toolset is built into the site management piece of the product. When you set up a site in Dreamweaver, you specify where the site files live on your local system, and you can also identify an FTP server to deploy the files to.

Tip You can only use Dreamweaver's built-in deployment tools if you take advantage of the site functionality. If you use Dreamweaver regularly for Web development, it's worthwhile to explore and utilize the site functionality.

You find all of the functionality associated with site management in Dreamweaver in the Site menu. To create a new site — based on existing Web files or in preparation for a new Web site — choose Site ➪ New Site. In the Site Definition Window, shown in Figure 21-3, give your site a name, point Dreamweaver at the folder on your local system that holds the site files, and click the OK button.

Figure 21-3: The Dreamweaver Site Definition window

After you set up a site, you can access it any time to tweak its settings. Choose Site ➪ Open Site and select the site you want to work with from the list of sites. To change the information you have stored about a site or to add more information about the site, choose Site ➪ Define Site, select the site you want to change from the site list, and click the Edit button to open the Site Definition window. To set up the FTP information for a particular site, choose Web Server Info from the left pane in the Site Definition Window, as shown in Figure 21-4.

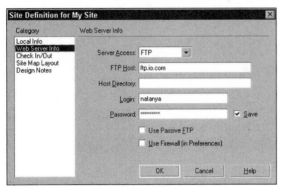

Figure 21-4: The Web Server Information fields in the Dreamweaver Site Definition Window

To configure the FTP site for your Dreamweaver site, simply fill in the name or IP address of the FTP server and type your name and password. Be sure to click the OK button to save your settings. To connect your local site to your remote FTP site, open the site from the Site menu and click the Connect button in the Site window. After Dreamweaver is connected to the remote site, the FTP server directory appears in the left column of the Site window, and your local site appears in the right, as shown in Figure 21-5.

You can move files to and from the FTP and local sites. To move files and folders, select the items you want to move and click the Get and Put buttons. Get downloads files from one server to another, and Put uploads files. A particularly useful feature in the Site utility is synchronize. You can synchronize your local site with your live site or vice versa. To activate the synchronize utility, chose Site ➪ Synchronize in the Site window.

In general, the Dreamweaver site management tools make deploying some or all of a Web site quick and easy. Although you don't have the same kind of direct control over the FTP process as you do with a standard FTP utility (you can't create automated scripts for example), you can use these types of tools for most common deployment activities. If you use Dreamweaver as your primary development tool, you should take advantage of its site management tools as well as its excellent page creation tools.

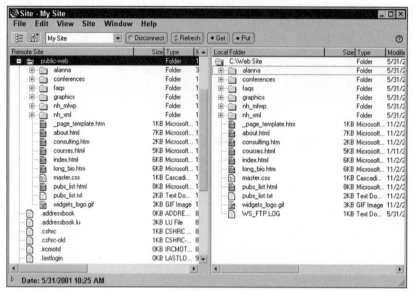

Figure 21-5: The Site window with both remote and local FTP sites displayed

Cross-Reference

See Chapter 14 for more about using Macromedia Dreamweaver 3.0.

Deploying with FrontPage 2000

FrontPage 2000 incorporates all the features you need to create, deploy, and manage a site into a single product. FrontPage is a Microsoft product that works especially well as a deployment tool when you deploy to a Microsoft Web server such as Internet Information Server (IIS). When you deploy a Web site (known simply as a Web in FrontPage) with FrontPage, you can use one of two different protocols to get the job done:

✦ **HTTP.** Only works with Web servers such as IIS that have FrontPage extensions installed on them

✦ **FTP.** For standard deployment to any Web server without FrontPage extensions installed

Tip

The Microsoft Web Publishing Wizard is designed to help you publish some or all of a Web site without much detailed knowledge of the inner workings of your Web server. The Wizard detects FrontPage extensions on any Web server you publish to and will use the correct protocol — HTTP or FTP — based on the presence of extensions or the lack thereof.

FrontPage 2000 manages Web sites by storing all files related to the site in a FrontPage Web. When you use the Web Publishing Wizard to deploy your site, the Wizard moves files from your local version of the Web to a remote Web server. If you're publishing a Web to a remote server with FrontPage extensions installed, you can use the FrontPage Folders feature to view and manage the files on the remote server as if they were local files. Be sure you know the URL or IP address of the Web server, as well as a username and password for the server, to take advantage of this feature.

Cross-Reference
For complete details on how to use Microsoft FrontPage 2000 to create and manage local Webs — and by extension Web sites on servers with FrontPage extensions installed — check out Chapter 13.

If you're deploying to a server with FrontPage extensions installed, FrontPage handles the process a bit differently than it does with a standard FTP deployment. FrontPage has more robust communications with a FrontPage-enabled server so it can be more efficient about deployment.

When you first publish a FrontPage Web to your Web server, FrontPage moves all of the Web files in one package, which helps you avoid losing or forgetting files. During any subsequent deployments, only new or updated files are moved to the server. This process ensures that your local system and remote system are in synch and that deployment takes as little time as possible. IIS comes with FrontPage extensions automatically installed. You can also install FrontPage extensions on an Apache server (see www.apache.org for more information).

The first time you publish a FrontPage Web to a server (with or without FrontPage extensions), you must identify the server you want to publish to. Choose File ➪ Publish Web to start the publishing process and click the Browse button to add a new publishing server. In the Publish dialog box, define your server by URL or IP address and include your username and password. If you want the Web files to be published in a specific directory, be sure to specify the directory in the dialog box. Without directory specifics the Web files will be published on the root directory of the server.

When you're ready to update an existing Web site with changed files from a FrontPage Web, choose File ➪ Publish and select the Web server from the list of servers you have already set up in the Publish dialog box. You can choose to republish the entire Web or just new or recently changed files. If your server has FrontPage extensions installed, FrontPage automatically knows which files are new or changed and will handle the update process for you. If your server doesn't have extensions installed and you want to move a subset of the Web files, you'll need to manually select the files to deploy.

Tip
Lab 21-1 includes step-by-step instructions for deploying a new Web site from FrontPage to a remote Web server.

Choosing the best deployment strategy

Your deployment strategy is an integral part of your overall site design and mainte-nance plans. If you can't quickly and easily get your Web files from your develop-ment system to your live site, your site won't have up-to-date and fresh content. Important issues surrounding deployment include:

✦ Who has permission to move files to your live site. You can control who has access to the site by limiting access to the site itself. Only give out usernames and passwords to those people who should be able to make changes to your live Web site.

✦ How often you deploy updates and changes to the site. You don't want to make wholesale changes to the site during peak traffic times. You also need to be sure any changes are reviewed before they move to the live site.

✦ What tool (or tools) you use for deployment.

The previous sections of this chapter looked at a variety of tools for publishing a site — from a standard FTP utility to tools built into popular Web development envi-ronments. After working with different deployment tools for a time, you'll find the tool or tools that best meet your needs. You may prefer to use a site development tool's deployment utility for significant changes to the site but use an FTP utility for quick fixes.

Typically, deployment utilities in tools constrain the way you publish a site and don't give you as much control over the deployment process. They are, however, easier to learn and help you avoid mistakes. Both FrontPage and Dreamweaver allow you to publish entire sites or a single file at a time. Of course, to take advan-tage of the publishing utility in a Web development environment, you must pur-chase that environment.

FTP utilities such as WS_FTP Pro are often reasonably priced and have friendly user interfaces. They don't require a development environment to use. You only have to be marginally familiar with FTP to use the tools successfully, but if you're an experi-enced FTP guru, you can leverage the utility to automate regular tasks and make your deployment more efficient.

The bottom line is that you have more control with FTP tools but less hassle with development environment utilities. FTP tools are usually less expensive than devel-opment environments, but if you already have a development environment, you should take advantage of its deployment toolset. Ultimately, your process and tools for deployment will be unique to your technology and site and will evolve over time. Identify your needs and processes carefully and the tool selection will be obvious.

Introduction to Databases

 Basic database structure

Databases play an important role in the lives of Web designers even though you don't need to know much about them to build a site that includes a database. When you integrate a Web site with a database, your site becomes dynamic, easy to personalize, and more powerful than a site created in static HTML. However, integrating a database into a Web site also requires Web programming skills and takes your site to a new level.

Information in databases is structured and organized in a way that's easy to access and manipulate. If a user's first and last name are stored in a database, you can call that information out of the database and use it to create different displays on your site. A home page might welcome the person by first name, and a site settings page might list both the first and last name of the user.

Databases can be very large or minimal in size. They can be stored on a single PC or across a collection of high-powered database servers (technically called a *distributed database*). There are a variety of different database software packages. Some are free or inexpensive (MySQL or Microsoft Access, for example); others are very expensive (such as Oracle or SQL Server). If you find that you need or want to integrate a database into your Web server, you should work with a database administrator or someone with database development experience to be sure that you choose the right database for your needs and configure it properly.

The remaining sections of this chapter briefly cover the very basic information you need to know about databases as a Web designer. If you want to learn more, the "For More Information" section at the end of the chapter includes URLs for further study.

 Exam Tip The Site Designer exam only requires that you understand databases. Don't feel like you need to be a database expert before you take the exam.

Database structure basics

The structure of a database is technically referred to as a *schema*. A schema defines what kind of information is stored in the database and how it is stored. Databases are broken into tables, which are further broken into columns and rows. A single table has several different columns to hold different information.

For example, a table that holds user information might have a column for the user's first name, last name, e-mail address, and phone number. A row in the table spans all of the columns and is usually referred to as a record. A single record (or row) in the user information table would include the first name, last name, e-mail address, and phone number for one user. The next row would contain that information for a different user. A single row and column intersect at a field. So in the user table, the field that holds John Doe's last name ("Doe") is where John Doe's record (or row) meets the last name column. Table 21-1 illustrates this.

Table 21-1 Database Example			
First name	*Last name*	*E-mail*	*Phone number*
John	Doe	johndoe@somewhere.com	555-555-5555
Jane	Doe	janedoe@somewhere.com	555-555-4444

Retrieving data from databases

 Data extraction

Database data isn't useful if you can't access and use it. You retrieve data from a database using a *query*, or search. In a query, you define a set of parameters that include what table(s) you want to search, what columns you want to look for, and any other rules you want to set on the query. For example, you could query a table of user information to get the e-mail addresses of all of the users in the table. Or you could narrow the search just to find e-mail addresses for users with the last name Doe.

Often, a database will have a user interface to help you with information queries. You can often choose a query from a list, or query menu, or you can specify values in a predefined query. These query methods are useful for those who are not familiar with databases, but they do not allow an experienced database user to fully harness the power of the database.

The most common method for accessing a database, and the one that provides the most control over the query, is the Structured Query Language (SQL). SQL was developed by IBM in 1974 and was originally called SEQUEL. The first commercial release of SQL was from Oracle in 1979. Each database vendor has developed its own particular "flavor" of SQL that works best with its database product. Database experts are very familiar with database design and general SQL syntax, but they often specialize in a particular flavor of SQL to work with a particular database.

When you hook your Web site to a database, you use Web programming to write SQL statements and gather data from the database. The Web application can then manipulate the data returned from the query and use it to build a Web page. Most Web applications such as ASP, JavaServer Pages (JSP), and ColdFusion come with the ability to access a SQL database built into the system.

Managing databases

 Database management systems

Although SQL is the method of choice for querying a database, a database administrator needs tools to manage and tune the database. A Database Management System (DBMS) is an interface — graphical or not — that an administrator can use to access data and manage the database. Most DBMSs (and the databases they manage) are one of the following types:

✦ **Relational Database Management System (RDBMS).** Helps not only maintain the rows and columns within the database, but also builds and manages relationships among the information in the tables.

✦ **Flat file.** Holds data in a single table with many rows and columns. Flat file DBMSs are not as powerful as RDBMSs but are less complex and easier to work with.

✦ **Multidimensional.** Maintains groups of records generated from a RDBMS.

Databases store data for everything from Web sites to intranets to traditional client-server applications. The code in the DBMS application — Web enabled or otherwise — has to be able to make a connection to the database and access the data in it. There's a whole collection of methods for connecting software code to databases, including:

✦ **ODBC (Open Database Connectivity).** By far the most common method for accessing a database and supported by every major database available. ODBC was originally developed by Microsoft, and applications use software utilities called drivers to speak with an ODBC-compliant database. The driver speaks both DBMS and the language of the code and translates the requests from the code into commands intelligible to the DBMS.

✦ **JDBC (Java Database Connectivity).** Developed by Sun Microsystems to support integration of Java applications with databases. JDBC translates database queries from Java code into SQL queries and can be used with any SQL-compliant database.

✦ **BLOB (Binary Large Object).** A method for storing and retrieving non-text information such as audio clips and images in a database.

Because databases are the most appropriate media for storing virtually every kind of data for retrieval by both people and machines, the database market has exploded in the last few years. Consequently, you have a variety of databases to choose from. Some of the most popular are:

✦ **Oracle.** The leader in Enterprise databases. Fortune 1000 companies use Oracle databases as a matter of course, but Oracle products are often not a practical choice for small or medium level applications.

✦ **Microsoft SQL Server.** A strong competitor to Oracle, SQL server is more affordable and more accessible to small and medium size organizations.

✦ **FileMaker Pro.** The leading Macintosh database.

✦ **SybaseSQL Anywhere.** Another popular medium to large application database.

You can connect a database to a Web site using Web programming and, specifically, a Web application development environment. Just about every Web application development environment supports ODBC, but some of the most popular are:

✦ **ASP.** Microsoft's Web programming environment, ASP works best with Microsoft's SQL database, SQL Server.

✦ **JSP.** Developed by Sun as a competitor to ASP, JSP uses JDBC connectivity to communicate with any SQL-compliant database.

✦ **CGI/Perl.** The original Web application environment, you can write CGI applications in Perl that connect to either SQL databases or flat file databases.

✦ **ColdFusion.** A popular Web application environment from Allaire, ColdFusion uses a tagging language to add logic and database connectivity to Web pages.

Although attaching a database to your Web site isn't always a simple undertaking, it can be a very beneficial one. Application environments such as ASP and JSP make it easier to build Web sites driven by databases. Large corporate Web sites are almost always backed by a database, and even if you never see the database, as a designer, you need to know what information on your site will be provided from the database so you can account for it in your design.

Key Point Summary

In this chapter, you learned about the last and crucial piece of designing a site — publishing it to the world. You also learned some basic but important information about how databases work. Important information to review for the exam includes:

✦ A Web site host publishes your Web site to the world.

✦ A hosting provider is usually an ISP and has many different levels of service you can purchase. You can also be your own hosting provider and manage your Web site yourself. When you host with an ISP, you can leverage the ISPs resources — technical, human, or otherwise — but you lose some control over your site. When you host your site yourself, you have total control and responsibility for the site.

✦ There are different tools that you can use to deploy your Web site to a live Web server:

   • FTP is the standard method for transferring files from your local system to a remote Web server, and utilities such as WS_FTP Pro provide a GUI for FTP activities.

   • Web development environments such as Dreamweaver and FrontPage 2000 have integrated deployment tools that make the deployment process easier but do not offer as much flexibility as a standard FTP utility.

✦ Databases hold data in an organized and structured way. You access databases with queries written in SQL.

✦ You manage databases with DBMS systems and you can choose from a variety of different database applications.

✦ You can integrate a database with a Web site using a Web application development environment such as ASP or ColdFusion.

✦   ✦   ✦

STUDY GUIDE

To reinforce what you've learned about deployment options and Web databases, work through the assessment questions, scenario, and lab in this study guide. Be sure you check your answers in the "Answers to Chapter Questions" section toward the end of the chapter. The concluding "For More Information" section, as usual, points you to resources for further study.

Assessment Questions

1. When you publish your Web site, what information do you need to know to connect to the Web server?

   A. The IP address or URL of the server

   B. A valid username

   C. A valid password

   D. All of the above

2. Which deployment tool allows you to publish using FTP or HTTP?

   A. FrontPage 2000

   B. Dreamweaver

   C. WS_FTP Pro

   D. All of the above

3. Which of the following is a standard FTP utility?

   A. FrontPage 2000

   B. Dreamweaver

   C. Allaire ColdFusion

   D. WS_FTP Pro

4. What is another term for a database row?

   A. Table

   B. Field

   C. Record

   D. Column

5. Which of the following is query language?

   A. ODBC

   B. SQL

   C. JDBC

   D. BLOB

Scenarios

As you plan to build a new Web site for a small business client, you need to help the client work through their Web hosting options and choose the one that best meets their needs. What questions should you ask the client, and what factors will affect the recommendation you make for their Web hosting solution?

Lab Exercises

Lab 21-1 Deploying a Web site with Microsoft FrontPage 2000

This lab references common FrontPage activities such as working with Webs or changing your view of a Web. To deploy a Web site using FrontPage, follow these steps:

 Cross-Reference   Chapter 13 includes the information you need to begin working with FrontPage. Be sure to review it before attempting this exercise.

1. Create a new Web in FrontPage or use an existing one.

2. Open the Web and select the Folders icon from the Views window.

3. Select File ➪ Publish Web.

4. In the Publish Web dialog box, type the URL or IP address of your Web server. If you don't have a Web server or want to publish to your local computer using the Personal Web Server that comes with FrontPage, type **http://localhost/folder** where *folder* is the name of the local Personal Web Server folder you want to publish to.

5. If you're publishing to a remote server, enter your username and password in the Name and Password Required dialog box. If you're publishing to your local system, you don't need to enter a name and password.

6. Monitor the status of the publishing process in the Publish Web dialog box. When the process is complete, a Web site published successfully dialog box appears with a link to your new site. Click the text "Click here to view your published web site" to automatically open your live site.

Answers to Chapter Questions

Chapter pre-test

1. Internal and external hosting are two options for Web site hosting.

2. A Web site development tool's deployment utilities make deployment fast and easy. They are not as flexible as a standard FTP utility.

3. An ISP may provide Web connectivity and e-mail services as well as Web site hosting services.

4. A database schema defines the tables in a database as well as what rows and columns those tables are broken into.

5. ODBC is an acronym for Open Database Connectivity, JDBC stands for Java Database Connectivity, and BLOB is short for Binary Lagre Object — three common methods of accessing database materials.

6. Some common database applications are Oracle, Microsoft SQL Server, Sybase SQL Anywhere, and FileMaker Pro.

Assessment questions

1. **D.** To connect to a Web server with any tool, you need to know the Web server's URL or IP address, a valid username, and a valid password for the server. See "Deploying your site."

2. **A.** Only FrontPage allows you to publish a Web site over FTP or HTTP. You can only use the HTTP option if you're publishing to a Web server with FrontPage Extensions installed. See "Deploying with FrontPage 2000."

3. **D.** WS_FTP Pro is a standard FTP utility. See "WS_FTP Pro."

4. **C.** Another name for a database row is a record. See "Database structure basics."

5. **B.** SQL stands for Structured Query Language and is used to query databases. See "Retrieving data from databases."

Scenarios

The client's internal resources and expertise will dictate the choice of an internal or external hosting solution. You should ask them:

✦ What skill sets they already have and which ones they are willing to acquire?

✦ What kind of connectivity they have and how much it would cost to buy more?

In light of the client's responses to these questions, you should then think about how complex their Web site can be and how much technical knowledge is required to keep the site new and fresh:

✦ If the client is a small business, chances are they do not have many extra hands around to support internal hosting. After you evaluate their resources and connectivity needs, work with the client to get quotes from external hosting sources.

✦ If, however, the client is a technical company with experienced network management and Web server support staff, it may make the most sense for them to host it internally. In this case, you can build a budget for internal hosting requirements.

After you have resource, connectivity, and cost information collected, sit down with the client and discuss the pros and cons of both internal and external hosting and work with them to find the hosting solution that is best for them. You'll most likely need to do some client education about the different hosting options and be sure they're making an informed decision that best meets the needs of their site and their business plan.

For More Information

✦ **WS_FTP.** www.ipswitch.com

✦ **Your First Database.** http://hotwired.lycos.com/webmonkey/99/13/index0a.html

✦ **Choosing the Right Database.** http://hotwired.lycos.com/webmonkey/98/24/index3a.html?tw=backend

What's on the CD-ROM

This appendix provides you with information on the contents of the CD-ROM attached to the inside, rear cover of this book, as well as sections on system requirements and use instructions for Windows, Linux, and the Mac OS. A brief troubleshooting guide is included at the end of this appendix.

An Overview of the CD's Content

A variety of site design-enabling software, source code, graphics, resources from the examples presented in the preceding chapters, an electronic, searchable version of the book — viewable with Adobe Acrobat Reader (also on the CD) — and a comprehensive testing engine, with questions similar to and formatted like the ones on the CIW Site Designer Exam, are all included on the CD.

Site design enabling software

The following programs are included on this CD:

- ✦ Adobe Acrobat Reader 5.0 (freeware)
- ✦ Adobe Photoshop 6.0 (trial version)
- ✦ BBEdit 6.1 (demo)
- ✦ BBEdit Lite 4.6 (freeware)
- ✦ Bobby 3.2 (freeware)
- ✦ Dreamweaver 4 (trial version)
- ✦ Expat XML Parser Toolkit 1.2 (GNU software)
- ✦ Flash 5 (trial version)
- ✦ GoLive 5.0 (trail version)
- ✦ Homesite 4.5 (trail version)

+ Internet Explorer 5.5 (trail version)

+ Paint Shop Pro 7.0 (evaluation version)

+ WS_FTP Pro 6.7 (trial version)

+ XML Pro 2.01 (demo)

The types of programs on the CD-ROM may be governed by certain rules and restrictions. Please observe the following:

+ **GNU and open source software.** These types are governed by their own licenses, which are included with the software. Such software is free and there are generally no restrictions on its distribution or use. See the software license for more details.

+ **Trial, demo, or evaluation versions.** These are usually limited either by time or functionality (such as being unable to save projects).

Source code, graphics, and resources

The CD contains source code and examples from several chapters. To find these elements on the CD, look in the Examples folder.

Electronic version of *CIW Site Designer Certification Bible*

The complete (and searchable) text of this book is on the CD-ROM in Adobe's Portable Document Format (PDF), readable with the Adobe Acrobat Reader (also included on the CD). For more information on Adobe Acrobat Reader, go to www.adobe.com.

Exam test engine

Included on the CD-ROM is a testing engine. This is a program that resembles the testing engine that will be used by the testing center where you will be taking your exam. The goal of the testing engine is to make you comfortable with the testing interface so that taking your exam will not be the first time you see that style of exam. The questions that will be used in the testing engine will cover all aspects of the exam, will be similar to the assessment questions that you will see in each chapter of this book, and will be similar to the questions that will be on your exam.

Using the CD

Before installing the CD, make sure your computer meets the minimum system requirements listed in the following sections. If your computer doesn't match most of these requirements, you may have a problem using the contents of the CD. You need at least 300MB of hard drive space to install all the software from this CD.

 System requirements vary depending on the software you install. The minimum system requirements listed here are intended as a guideline.

With Microsoft Windows

The system requirements for Microsoft Windows 9x, Windows NT 4.0, or Windows 2000 are:

✦ PC with a Pentium processor or equivalent

✦ 64MB RAM (128MB recommended)

✦ Internet connection

✦ A CD-ROM drive

To install the items from the CD on your hard drive, follow these steps:

1. Insert the CD into your computer's CD-ROM drive.

2. View the contents of the CD-ROM using Windows Explorer or by clicking the My Computer icon on your desktop.

3. Locate the software you wish to install.

4. Either double-click on the program's installation program to install it, or follow the directions contained in the `readme` file in the CD directory for the program.

With Linux

Although we've included Windows versions of the software on the CD, many of these products are also available for Linux. Refer to Table A-1 for a product-by-product breakdown of your options. The system requirements for Linux are:

✦ PC with a Pentium processor or equivalent

✦ 64MB RAM (128MB recommended)

✦ Internet connection

✦ A CD-ROM drive

Table A-1 **Options for Linux Users**	
Software	*Download URL*
Bobby 3.2	http://www.cast.org/Bobby/DownloadBobby316.cfm
XML Pro	http://www.vervet.com/demo.html

To open the items from the CD, follow these steps:

1. Log in as root.

2. Insert the CD into your computer's CD-ROM drive.

3. Mount the CD-ROM.

4. Launch a graphical file manager to view the items on the CD.

With Mac OS

Although we've included Windows versions of the software on the CD, many of these products are also available for Macintosh. Refer to Table A-2 for a product-by-product breakdown of your options.

Tip   Mac OSX is based on UNIX, so many products available for UNIX operating systems run on Macintosh computers with OSX installed.

The recommended system requirements for Macintosh users are:

✦ Macintosh with PowerPC processor

✦ 64MB RAM (128MB recommended)

✦ Internet connection

✦ A CD-ROM drive

Table A-2
Options for Macintosh Users

Software	Download URL
Adobe Photoshop 6.0	`http://www.adobe.com/products/photoshop/main.html`
Flash 5	`http://www.macromedia.com/software/flash/trial/`
BBEdit 6.1	`http://www.barebones.com/products/bbedit/bbedit-demo.html`
BBEdit Lite 4.6	`http://www.barebones.com/`
Bobby 3.2	`http://www.cast.org/Bobby/DownloadBobby316.cfm`
Dreamweaver 4	`http://www.macromedia.com/software/dreamweaver/`
GoLive 5.0	`http://www.adobe.com/products/golive/tryreg.html`

To open the items from the CD, follow these steps:

1. Insert the CD into your computer's CD-ROM drive.
2. Double-click the CD icon on your desktop.
3. Locate the item you wish to view.
4. Double-click the file you want to open, or use the Open command from the appropriate program.

Troubleshooting

If you have difficulty installing or using the CD-ROM programs, try the following solutions:

✦ **Turn off any anti-virus software.** Installers sometimes mimic virus activity and can make your computer incorrectly believe it's being infected by a virus. (Be sure to turn the anti-virus software back on later.)

✦ **Close all running programs.** The more programs you're running, the less memory is available to other programs. Installers also typically update files and programs; if you keep other programs running, installation may not work properly.

Tip If you still have trouble with the CD, please call the Hungry Minds Books Worldwide Customer Service phone number: (800) 762-2974. Outside the United States, call (317) 572-3993. Hungry Minds Books provides technical support only for installation and other general quality control items; for technical support on the applications themselves, consult the program's vendor or author.

✦　　✦　　✦

Objective Mapping

This appendix lists each of the topics covered in the CIW Site Designer certification and the skills measured by the CIW Site Designer exam (1D0-420). Each exam topic is referenced exactly as it appears in the Exam Objectives list at the beginning of each chapter. For easy reference, the section in that chapter pertaining to the objective is listed in the right column. As you'll note, there's a separate table for each chapter headed by the chapter's title.

Table B-1
Basic Design Concepts

Exam topic	Chapter	Section
Site design and Web development	Chapter 1	The role of site design in Web development
Tools and technologies in site design	Chapter 1	Choosing the right combination of tools and technology
Knowledge of HTML	Chapter 1	Why You Need to Know HTML
Emerging Web technologies	Chapter 1	The Future of Site Design

Table B-2
Page Layout and Design

Exam topic	Chapter	Section
Audience assumptions	Chapter 2	Web characteristics
HTML tags for structure and formatting	Chapter 2	HTML review
Web page layout	Chapter 2	Effective Page Design and Layout Components
Use of color in design	Chapter 2	Color basics
Use of fonts in design	Chapter 2	Implementing fonts
Web usability	Chapter 2	Defining and Executing Usability Tests

Table B-3
Site Navigation

Exam topic	Chapter	Section
Importance of Web site navigation	Chapter 3	Why is Navigation Important?
Primary and secondary navigation	Chapter 3	Primary and secondary
Navigation hierarchy	Chapter 3	Site structure and hierarchy
Site structure and information architecture	Chapter 3	Positional awareness

Table B-4
Graphics

Exam topic	Chapter	Section
Role of Web graphics in site design	Chapter 4	Images and Site Design
Color depth and resolution	Chapter 4	Image attributes
Graphic file formats	Chapter 4	Image File Formats
Image optimization	Chapter 4	Optimizing Images for the Web
Using Jasc Paint Shop Pro	Chapter 4	Using Jasc Paint Shop Pro

Table B-5
Multimedia

Exam topic	Chapter	Section
Multimedia design methodology	Chapter 5	Multimedia Design Methods
Current multimedia capabilities	Chapter 5	Multimedia Capabilities
Selecting multimedia elements	Chapter 5	Choosing the Appropriate Media
User interaction	Chapter 5	Building User Interaction
Copyright issues	Chapter 5	Copyright Law and Infringement

Table B-6
The Development Process

Exam topic	Chapter	Section
Site development methodology	Chapter 6	Site Development Process
Web site as metaphor	Chapter 6	A Web Site as a Metaphor
Mindmaps and Web site design	Chapter 6	Defining the Mindmapping Process
Site implementation factors	Chapter 6	Site Implementation Factors

Table B-7
HTML Standards and Compliance

Exam topic	Chapter	Section
The development of HTML	Chapter 7	The Development of HTML
HTML standards	Chapter 7	An Overview of HTML Versions
Proprietary HTML markup	Chapter 7	Standard vs. Proprietary HTML
HTML 4.01 and XHTML	Chapter 7	HTML 4.01 and XHTML

Table B-8
HTML Tables and Page Structure

Exam topic	Chapter	Section
Understanding HTML tables	Chapter 8	Overview of Table Markup Tags
Designing tables for page layout control	Chapter 8	Designing Tables for Page Layout Control
Diagramming tables	Chapter 8	Diagramming tables

Table B-9
HTML Frames and Site Design

Exam topic	Chapter	Section
Frames and usability	Chapter 9	Frames and Usability
Frames and framesets	Chapter 9	Overview of Frame Markup
Simple page layout	Chapter 9	Hyperlinks in Frames
Complex page layout	Chapter 9	Nested Framesets

Table B-10
Metadata in HTML

Exam topic	*Chapter*	*Section*
Metadata and document identification	Chapter 10	Overview of Metadata
Adding metadata to Web pages	Chapter 10	Using the meta tag
Metadata and indexing	Chapter 10	Search engines

Table B-11
Cascading Style Sheets

Exam topic	*Chapter*	*Section*
CSS versions	Chapter 11	The Evolution of Cascading Style Sheets
CSS and site design	Chapter 11	Design Theory Behind CSS
Linking style sheets	Chapter 11	The Different Ways to Use CSS in Site Design

Table B-12
Plug-Ins and Downloadable Files

Exam topic	*Chapter*	*Section*
Plug-in technology	Chapter 12	Understanding Plug-Ins and Downloadable Files
Linking to downloadable files	Chapter 12	Linking to downloadable files
Downloading plug-ins	Chapter 12	Downloading and Installing Plug-Ins

Table B-13
Microsoft FrontPage 2000

Exam topic	Chapter	Section
FrontPage navigation tools	Chapter 13	FrontPage Tools and Navigation
FrontPage standard elements	Chapter 13	Adding HTML Elements to a Page
FrontPage themes	Chapter 13	Themes
FrontPage advanced features	Chapter 13	Advanced FrontPage Features

Table B-14
Macromedia Dreamweaver 3.0

Exam topic	Chapter	Section
Dreamweaver navigation tools	Chapter 14	Dreamweaver Tools and Navigation
Dreamweaver standard elements	Chapter 14	HTML Elements in Dreamweaver
Dreamweaver templates	Chapter 14	Dreamweaver Templates
Dreamweaver JavaScript functions	Chapter 14	JavaScript and Behaviors
Dreamweaver extended functionality	Chapter 14	The Macromedia Exchange

Table B-15
Allaire HomeSite 4.5

Exam topic	Chapter	Section
HomeSite standard templates	Chapter 15	HomeSite Templates
HomeSite tag tools	Chapter 15	Working with Tags
HomeSite file management	Chapter 15	Managing Files

Table B-16
Macromedia Flash 5.0 and Dynamic Media

Exam topic	Chapter	Section
The Flash Timeline	Chapter 16	The Timeline – Scenes, Frames, and Layers
Creating button, graphic, and movie clip symbols	Chapter 16	Symbols
Working with tweening	Chapter 16	Tweening
Working with actions	Chapter 16	Actions
Adding audio	Chapter 16	Audio
Making Flash movies	Chapter 16	Saving and Publishing Movies

Table B-17
JavaScript and Client-Side Web Scripting

Exam topic	Chapter	Section
Authoring vs. scripting vs. programming	Chapter 17	Scripting Web Pages
Browser compatibility	Chapter 17	Browser support
JavaScript vs. Java	Chapter 17	JavaScript vs. Java
Create basic scripts	Chapter 17	Adding JavaScript to a Web Page
DHTML	Chapter 17	Introduction to Dynamic HTML
Document Object Model (DOM)	Chapter 17	Document Object Model

Table B-18
Java Applets in Web Pages

Exam topic	Chapter	Section
How scripts and programs differ	Chapter 18	The Difference Between Scripts and Programs
How applets work	Chapter 18	Applets
Applet development tools	Chapter 18	Applet Authoring Tools
Adding applets to Web pages	Chapter 18	Adding an Applet to a Web Page

Table B-19
Extensible Markup Language and Authoring

Exam topic	Chapter	Section
Role of XML in Web development	Chapter 19	Why XML?
XML vs. HTML	Chapter 19	XML and HTML
XML document requirements	Chapter 19	Well-Formed and Valid XML documents
Role of XHTML in Web development	Chapter 19	XHTML

Table B-20
HTTP Servers and Cookies

Exam topic	Chapter	Section
Server and browser requests	Chapter 20	How Web Servers and Web Browsers Communicate
Server applications and dynamic Web sites	Chapter 20	Server-Side Programming
The role of cookies in a stateless medium	Chapter 20	Web Servers and State
Working with cookies	Chapter 20	An Overview of Cookies

Table B-21
Web Site Publishing and Database Technology

Exam topic	Chapter	Section
The principles of good site design	Chapter 21	Anatomy of a Well-Designed Site
Web site hosting options	Chapter 21	Choosing a Web site hosting option
Publishing sites with development and FTP tools	Chapter 21	Deploying your site
Basic database structure	Chapter 21	Introduction to Databases
Data extraction	Chapter 21	Retrieving data from databases
Database management systems	Chapter 21	Managing databases

◆   ◆   ◆

Sample Exam

The CIW Site Designer exam consists of 60 questions. You must answer 45 (75%) of these questions correctly to pass. The following 60 questions are representative of the questions asked on the exam. Answers to the questions can be found at the end of this appendix. For further testing of your knowledge in preparation for the exam, see the comprehensive testing engine located on the CD that comes with this book.

Sample Questions

1. Why is site design important when developing a Web site?

   A. To create a site that is intuitive for the user to understand and navigate

   B. To implement the most complex technologies

   C. To analyze ways to add as much multimedia as possible to a site

   D. To create the HTML code

2. Which is important to Web site design?

   A. The selection of the appropriate development tools

   B. The selection of the appropriate Web site technologies

   C. Both tools and technology are important to site design

   D. Neither tools nor technology are important to site design

3. Why is knowledge of HTML important to site design? (Choose the best answer.)

   A. It's essential for incorporating XML.

   B. It allows the author to customize code generated by a WYSIWYG editor.

   C. It allows the author to develop Java applets.

   D. All of the above.

4. What screen size should you design a Web site for?

    A. 800x480

    B. 640x480

    C. 800x1200

    D. 800x600

5. What does the acronym RGB stand for?

    A. Read, Gage, Build

    B. Red, Green, Black

    C. Red, Green, Blue

    D. Ready, Go, Build

6. Which of the following is not a commonly used font?

    A. New York Times

    B. Courier

    C. Times New Roman

    D. Arial

7. Which of the following is not a usability element?

    A. Menu design

    B. Navigation strategy

    C. Use of white space

    D. Page content

8. Typically users will click how many times before giving up?

    A. 1

    B. 2

    C. 3

    D. 4

9. Identify two types of navigational elements?

    A. Menu and primary

    B. Main and sub

    C. Primary and menu

    D. Primary and secondary

10. Browser interfaces function on which level?

    A. Internet access layer

    B. Navigation layer

    C. Presentation layer

    D. All of the above

11. Which of the following are characteristic of a GIF file?

    A. The format is lossless.

    B. The color pallet is limited to 256 colors.

    C. None of the above

    D. All of the above

12. What are the two general types of digital images?

    A. Vector and dither

    B. Vector and bitmap

    C. Bitmap and transparent

    D. Bitmap and graphic

13. What is the disadvantage of using the JPEG format?

    A. JPEG files are lossless and decrease detail.

    B. JPEG files are not supported across multiple browsers.

    C. JPEG files can have a rich color pallet and that increases file size transfer time.

    D. All of the above.

14. Which is not an example of image optimization?

    A. Converting from JPEG to GIF

    B. Avoiding anti-aliasing and gradients

    C. Reducing the number of colors

    D. Cropping and scaling

15. What are three common audio file formats?

    A. UNIXA, WAV, and MP3

    B. AUDI, WAV, and MP3

    C. MIDI, WAV, and MP3

    D. UNIXA, WAV, and MIDI

16. Which is not an example of a multimedia player?

    A. QuickTime

    B. QuickPLAY

    C. RealPlayer

    D. Media Player

17. What is an advantage of using streaming audio over downloading an audio file?

    A. Streaming allows users to play the file directly from the Web site.

    B. Streaming compresses a file's size; therefore, allowing for a quicker download.

    C. Streaming provides better sound quality

    D. Streaming allows files to be played while downloading; therefore, reducing the users' wait time.

18. What is the purpose of a mindmap? (Choose the best answer.)

    A. To identify Web development team members

    B. To identify leading technologies

    C. To help Web developers brainstorm ideas

    D. To publish Web sites

19. What are the five stages of the Web design process?

    A. Conceptualization, design visualization, analysis, production, and evolution

    B. Conceptualization, design, layout, production, and evolution

    C. Conceptualization, layout, analysis, production, and evolution

    D. Conceptualization, design visualization, analysis, layout, and evolution

20. What is the most effective way to use metaphors in Web design?

    A. Create mixed metaphors

    B. Create multiple metaphors

    C. Create a metaphor that is familiar to your audience

    D. Create a metaphor that is not familiar to your audience

21. Which language predates HTML?

    A. XHTML

    B. DHTML

    C. GML

    D. XML

22. Which of the following statements contains some of the requirements for a well-formed document?

    A. All attribute values must be quoted, and all elements must be properly terminated and nested correctly.

    B. All elements must be empty and lack attribute values.

    C. All empty elements must have a slash immediately after the opening bracket (`</br>`).

    D. Element names must be in quotes and attributes must be in all caps.

23. What is another term for a database record?

    A. Column

    B. Field

    C. Heading

    D. Row

24. Who introduced proprietary HTML tags?

    A. Browser vendors such as Netscape and Microsoft

    B. The World Wide Web Consortium (W3C)

    C. The Internet Society (ISOC)

    D. A consortium of all the above organizations

25. Which standards organization governs the HTML standard?

    A. IEEE

    B. ISOC

    C. ACM

    D. W3C

26. The term cookie is short for which of the following?

    A. Persistent user state HTTP cookies

    B. Persistent HTTP cookies

    C. Persistent client state HTTP cookies

    D. Persistent server state HTTP cookies

27. Of the following options, which can table data span?

    A. Columns

    B. Rows

    C. Columns and rows

    D. Tables

28. What does the `cellspacing` attribute define?

    A. The amount of space between tables

    B. The amount of space between cells

    C. The amount of space within cells

    D. All of the above

29. What is the primary disadvantage of navigating with frames? (Choose the best answer.)

    A. Frames don't allow for the user to bookmark Web pages.

    B. Frames are not easy to navigate.

    C. Frames don't allow users to print pages.

    D. All of the above.

30. The `frameset` is what type of tag?

    A. Empty

    B. Nested

    C. Container

    D. None of the above

31. What type of hyperlinking is required with frames?

    A. Reference

    B. Absolute

    C. Recursive

    D. Target

32. Which of the following requires the Web designer to register the URL in order for it to be indexed?

    A. Meta sites

    B. Directories

    C. Search engines

    D. Robots

33. Where keywords are most likely to be ignored?

    A. In the `title` tag

    B. In the beginning of the document text

    C. At the end of the document

    D. In the `meta` tag

34. The `meta` tag is often used to perform which of the following?

    A. Embeds keywords indexed by search engines

    B. Defines a site description that is used by search engines

    C. May include a refresh parameter

    D. All of the above

35. Which of the following statements is true in describing the difference between a search engine and directory?

    A. A search engine automatically indexes a site whereas a directory requires that a URL be submitted to index the site.

    B. A directory automatically indexes a site whereas a search engine requires that a URL be submitted to index the site.

    C. A search engine can only index a site with a `meta`, tag whereas a directory can index a site without a `meta` tag.

    D. A directory can only index a site with a `meta` tag whereas a search engine can index a site without a `meta` tag.

36. As of April 2001, what is the most current CSS specification?

    A. CSS0

    B. CSS1

    C. CSS2

    D. CSS3

37. What is the benefit of using an internal style sheet?

    A. Your styles and the HTML that they work with are in the same document and it's easy to make changes and keep track of your document.

    B. It is easier to update a style across a site when it's in an internal document.

    C. None of the above.

    D. All of the above.

38. Which of the following are examples of plug-in technology?

    A. JavaScript

    B. Active Server Pages

    C. Shockwave and Flash

    D. Java

39. Creating a downloadable file link requires which of the following?

A. A plug-in

B. An FTP program

C. A Web browser

D. None of the above

40. In FrontPage, which of the following methods allows the table format to be modified?

A. The Insert Table dialog box

B. The Style dialog box

C. The Table Properties dialog box

D. All of the above

41. In FrontPage, how do you apply a style sheet to your entire Web?

A. Use the Format Style dialog box

B. Link the style sheet to the Web

C. Open any page in the Web, select Format Style, and click Apply to entire Web

D. Link to a theme

42. In FrontPage, you must do which of the following to use the Database Results Wizard?

A. Enable the Web server to execute Active Server Pages (.asp)

B. Install the Database component

C. Install FrontPage Server Extension on the Web server

D. All of the above

43. What is one of the primary purposes of HTML tables?

A. Site structure

B. Page structure

C. Complexity

D. All of the above

44. What is a Library item in Dreamweaver?

A. A reusable chunk of information that defines the structure for a Web page

B. A reusable chunk of information that is stored in a Dreamweaver template

C. A reusable chunk of information that is used with HTML elements such as paragraphs

D. A reusable chunk of information that can only be used in tables

45. The Dreamweaver Property Inspector defines which of the following?

   A. Tag names

   B. Attribute values

   C. JavaScript behaviors

   D. CSS styles

46. Which of the following choices is accessible from the Tools menu in an Allaire HomeSite 4.5?

   A. Tag Chooser

   B. Container tag

   C. Empty start tag

   D. Tag generator

47. How can you turn a standard HTML file into an Allaire HomeSite 4.5 template?

   A. Change the template's file extension to .htm

   B. Move the file to the Wizards folder inside of the HomeSite folder

   C. Change the template's file extension to .hst

   D. All of the above

48. The Macromedia Flash 5.0 Timeline is measured in which of the following?

   A. The number of pixels displayed per frame

   B. The number of frames played per minute

   C. The number of frames played per second

   D. The number of Tweens per second

49. A Scene in Macromedia Flash 5.0 is best described as which of the following?

   A. A way of breaking up your movie into sequential sections

   B. An Action

   C. A masking layer

   D. Multiple Tweens

50. What is an advantage of tweened animation over frame-by-frame animation in Macromedia Flash 5.0?

   A. Tweened animation provides higher resolution.

   B. Tweened animation creates a smaller file size by starting and ending with keyframes.

   C. None of the above.

   D. All of the above.

51. Macromedia Flash 5.0 uses ActionScript for which of the following?

   A. To write navigation and user interaction

   B. To script simple button actions

   C. To build program logic into scenes

   D. All of the above

52. What must you do to publish your Flash movie?

   A. Export your FLA as a SWF for playback on the Web

   B. Export your FLA as an HTM for playback on the Web

   C. Export your FLA as a .asp for playback on the Web

   D. Any of the above

53. Which of the following tasks would be the most appropriate to address with client-side JavaScript?

   A. Submitting a Web form

   B. Validating a Web form

   C. Communicating between a database and server

   D. Creating a MAILTO

54. JavaScript is embedded in Web pages using which HTML tag?

   A. <embed>

   B. <language>

   C. <script>

   D. All of the above

55. What is the Microsoft version of JavaScript referred to as?

   A. JScript

   B. LiveWire

   C. LiveScript

   D. VBScript

56. JavaScript language properties most closely correspond to which type of language?

   A. Authoring

   B. Java

   C. Programming

   D. Scripting

57. Which of the following descriptions of Java is true?

    A. Java is a powerful scripting language.

    B. Java is an object-oriented programming language.

    C. Java is a programming language that only runs in a Web browser.

    D. Java is an object-based programming language.

58. Which of the following statements is an advantage of using Java in your Web pages?

    A. It executes faster than a scripting language.

    B. It's portable.

    C. It's multithreaded.

    D. All of the above.

59. Which of the following descriptions of an applet is true?

    A. It's a client-side program that can be added to your Web page.

    B. It's an alternative to XML.

    C. It's an alternative to a CGI program.

    D. It's an alternative to a DHTML.

60. To add an applet to a Web page, which HTML tag should be used?

    A. `<applet>`

    B. `<script>`

    C. `<language>`

    D. Any of the above will work

Answers to Sample Questions

    1. A. The most important goal of designing a Web site is to create a site that is intuitive for the user to navigate and understand, and to be able to perceive the message of the site. See Chapter 1.

    2. C. The combination of the right tools and the right technologies are important to good Web site design. See Chapter 1.

    3. B. It allows the HTML author to have enough knowledge to modify code generated by an HTML development tool. See Chapter 1.

    4. B. 640x480 is the most commonly used screen size resolution and affords a faster download time than larger resolutions. See Chapter 2.

5. C. RGB stands for Red, Green, Blue; the three primary color elements. See Chapter 2.

6. A. New York Times is not a commonly used screen font. See Chapter 2.

7. D. Page content is not a usability element. See Chapter 2.

8. C. Usability studies have shown that users give up searching for a particular piece of information after three clickthroughs. Therefore, your navigational structure should allow users to locate any information on your Web site in three clicks or less. See Chapter 3.

9. D. Most navigational elements fall within two categories: primary and secondary. Secondary navigational elements are those that are specific to a particular page. Primary navigation can be found on most pages in your Web site and are relevant to the entire site. See Chapter 3.

10. D. All of the above. All three are levels on which a Web browser functions. See Chapter 3.

11. D. All of the above. The GIF format is lossless and has a limited pallet of 256 colors. See Chapter 4.

12. B. The two general types of digital image files are vector and bitmap. The majority of Web graphics are bitmap images; however, vector images are becoming more prominent as new technologies emerge. See Chapter 4.

13. C. The risks of using the JPEG format are that rich color depth can cause file size to increase, and JPEG files aren't lossless, which can lead to degradation of image quality. See Chapter 4.

14. A. Converting files from one format to another is not an example of image processing. See Chapter 4.

15. C. The three most common audio file formats are MIDI, WAV, and MP3. The WAV file format is used on most CDs. The MIDI file format doesn't contain any sounds, but rather information about those sounds. And finally, the MP3 file format is a compression format that drastically reduces file size while preserving sound quality. See Chapter 5.

16. B. QuickPLAY is not a multimedia player. QuickTime, developed by Apple Computer, is a popular player, as well as RealPlayer from Real Networks and MediaPlayer from Microsoft. See Chapter 5.

17. D. Requiring your users to download audio files means, depending on the file size, your users might have to wait awhile. See Chapter 5.

18. C. Mindmaps were originally tools for helping students take notes; however, they were quickly adopted by many disciplines as a way to brainstorm for ideas. See Chapter 6.

19. A. The five stages to Web design are conceptualization, design visualization, analysis, production, and evolution. See Chapter 6.

20. C. A metaphor is a visual suggestion to another idea that should resonate with a user. See Chapter 6.

21. C. GML predates HTML. HTML derived from SGML, which is derived from GML. See Chapter 7.

22. A. All attribute values must be quoted, and all elements must be properly terminated and nested correctly. These are requirements for a well-formed XML document. See Chapter 19.

23. D. Another name for a database record is a row. See Chapter 21.

24. A. Netscape and Microsoft have been the leaders of introducing proprietary tags into the HTML language. Many of these tags have gone on to be incorporated into the formal standard. The future versions of HTML will be eliminating most of the proprietary tags. See Chapter 7.

25. D. The W3C has governed the HTML standard since 1994. See Chapter 7.

26. C. The term *cookie* is short for persistent client state HTTP cookies. See Chapter 20.

27. C. Table data can span multiple rows and multiple columns but not between tables. See Chapter 8.

28. B. Cellspacing defines the amount of space between cells. See Chapter 8.

29. A. The most obvious obstacle to frames and navigation is the difficulty of using bookmarks. Users can only bookmark the initial frameset document. See Chapter 9.

30. C. The `frameset` tag is a container tag that embeds the `frame` tag. See Chapter 9.

31. D. When you create a frame structure, you have to be careful with all your hyperlinks. Using the `target` attribute to define hyperlink behavior is essential to making sure that your users don't get lost in your Web site. See Chapter 9.

32. B. Directories require that you register your site. Search engines offer this option as well, but it's not required, because they also employ robots to automatically search the Web for Web sites to index. It's recommended that you register your Web site and not wait for the robots to find you. See Chapter 10.

33. C. Keywords are most likely to be ignored at the end of a document. The only exception is robots that do full text retrieval and indexing. See Chapter 10.

34. D. The `meta` tag embeds keywords indexed by search engines, defines a site description that is used by search engines, and may include a refresh parameter to update the page at preset intervals in the user's browser. See Chapter 10.

35. A. Search engines automatically index a site whereas directories require that a URL be submitted to index the site. See Chapter 10.

36. C. CSS2 is the current specification for CSS. CSS1 was the original specification and CSS3 is the future specification, which is still in development. There is no CSS0. See Chapter 11.

37. A. The benefit of using an internal style sheet is that your styles and the HTML that they work with are in the same document; therefore, it's easy to make changes and keep track of your document. The downside to using an internal style sheet is that you can't make the style sheet available to other documents without cutting and pasting the styles from one internal style sheet to the next. See Chapter 11.

38. C. Shockwave and Flash are examples of plug-in technologies that extend the functionality of a Web browser. See Chapter 12.

39. D. Creating a downloadable file only requires a hyperlink to the Web file itself. A plug-in is not required to create a link. A browser or FTP application is required to download a file, not to create a downloadable file link. See Chapter 12.

40. D. All of the above. You can format a table in one of three ways including the Insert Table dialog box, the Style dialog box, and the Table Properties dialog box. See Chapter 13.

41. B. You link the style sheet to the Web. See Chapter 13.

42. A. The Database Results Wizard requires you to be able to run Active Server Pages on the Web server. See Chapter 13.

43. B. One of the greatest advantages of using tables is for page display and page structure. Tables are often used to display tabular information or information that best lends itself to display in rows and columns. See Chapter 8.

44. C. A Library item allows you to define reusable information such as a domain name or company name. The item itself is stored in an external file, and then referenced from multiple Web pages. See Chapter 14.

45. B. The Property Inspector allows you to modify the attributes for a selected HTML tag. The options provided by the Property Inspector change depending on the item selected. See Chapter 14.

46. A. The Tag Chooser is accessible from the Tools menu. See Chapter 15.

47. C. You can turn an existing HTML file into a HomeSite template by changing the file's extension to .hst. See Chapter 15.

48. C. The Timeline is measured by the number of frames played per second; it controls the pace of the movie by moving the playhead (a red highlight and vertical line indicating the current frame) successively through the frames. See Chapter 16.

49. A. Each scene has its own Timeline and Stage; therefore, sequential sections. See Chapter 16.

50. B. Tweened animation creates a smaller file size by starting and ending with keyframes. See Chapter 16.

51. D. Flash uses ActionScript to write navigation and user interaction, script simple button actions, or complicated programming actions. Flash automatically writes the On Mouse Event handler for you, because buttons are activated by user mouse events. See Chapter 16.

52. A. Publishing your Flash movie means exporting your FLA as a SWF for playback on the Web. See Chapter 16.

53. B. JavaScript is best used for error checking and form validation. See Chapter 17.

54. C. The `<script>` tag in HTML is used to embed JavaScript statements in a Web page. See Chapter 17.

55. A. The Microsoft version of JavaScript is referred to as JScript. See Chapter 17.

56. D. The JavaScript language is a scripting language that allows program logic but in a viewable non-compiled format. See Chapter 17.

57. B. Java is a powerful object-oriented programming language. See Chapter 18.

58. D. All statements are true. Java executes faster than a scripting language, is portable, and is multithreaded. See Chapter 18.

59. A. Java is a client-side program referred to as an applet that can be added to increase the functionality of a Web page. See Chapter 18.

60. A. To add an applet to a Web page the `<applet>` tag should be used. Note that in XHTML, the `<applet>` tag is deprecated in favor of the `<object>` tag. See Chapter 18.

✦　　✦　　✦

Exam Tips

This appendix covers many of the concerns you may have about signing up for and actually taking the CIW Site Designer exam (1D0-420). Each issue, in addition to useful tips, is dealt with in a separate section — everything from prerequisites for the test, where to take it, how much it costs, and what to do after you've gotten the results.

What Are the Prerequisites?

The CIW Foundations exam (1D0-410) is the prerequisite to the Site Designer exam. To achieve CIW certification, you must at least take the Foundations exam along with the Site Designer exam. Passing the Site Designer exam alone does not result in certification.

Tip You can also get credit for the Foundations exam if you've taken the CompTIA i-Net+ exam. See `www.ciwcertified.com/exams/examcredit.asp?comm=home&llm=10` for more information.

Where Can I Take the Test?

Like all CIW exams, the Site Designer exam is available worldwide through VUE and Prometric. Exam candidates must register with either VUE or Prometric, schedule an exam appointment, and pay the candidate fee — which is the price of the test.

Information on VUE and Prometric locations can be found at their Web sites. VUE's URL is `www.vue.com` and their CIW registration page is `www.vue.com/ciw/`. For information on Prometric, visit their registration site at `www.2test.com`.

Tip For the latest information from CIW on taking the test, visit `www.ciwcertified.com` and click on Exams and then on Taking the Exam.

How Do I Register?

As mentioned in the previous section, you can register through VUE or Prometric as follows:

✦ **VUE.** To register with VUE, visit `http://www.vue.com/ciw/index.html`. From this page, you can get a VUE username and password if you don't have one or register for an exam if you do have one.

✦ **Prometric.** To obtain a Prometric Web User Login, visit `www.2test.com/ GetAptcCustomerData.jsp`. When you have your login information (username and password), return to the home page at `www.2test.com` and choose Information Technology Certifications from the drop-down menu. Click the Go button to register for the exam.

How Do I Cancel My Exam Appointment?

After you've registered for the exam, you'll receive a confirmation along with instructions on how to cancel the exam appointment. General cancellation information is included in the following sections. Please refer to the instructions in your exam appointment confirmation materials in case of any discrepancies.

VUE

After you've registered for the exam, you can cancel it on the VUE Web site *if the appointment is more than 24 hours away.* Visit `www.vue.com/ciw/` and click on Register, reschedule, or cancel an exam online.

If your exam appointment is less than 24 hours away, you need to contact the testing center or a VUE agent directly. To locate the VUE agent closest to you, check out the VUE Telephone Directory at `www.vue.com/contact/vuephone.html`.

Prometric

Exams can be canceled one business day prior to your scheduled exam appointment, before 7:00 p.m. CST. That's all the information currently available regarding Prometric cancellations.

How Much Does It Cost?

The fee for a CIW exam in the United States and Canada is U.S. $125. The exam fee outside the United States and Canada is approximately U.S. $125, depending upon local currency exchange rates. Contact your testing center to determine the exact rate in your local currency.

How Long Is the Test?

The test consists of 60 questions. You're given 75 minutes to complete the exam.

 Cross-Reference For a good idea of what the test will be like and to help prepare yourself in advance, see the sample exam in Appendix C. Also check out the comprehensive testing engine included on the CD that comes with this book.

Can I Bring Anything with Me into the Testing Center?

You're not allowed to bring any materials into the testing center. A pencil and scratch paper are available upon request.

How Do I Get My Results?

After you complete the exam, the results are displayed on your testing station computer screen. A printed copy of your exam score is also available from the testing center staff. Be sure to save this copy for your records.

What Happens if I Pass?

If you've already passed the Foundations exam (1D0-410), you're awarded Certified Internet Webmaster Professional (CIWP) status. You'll receive your certificate four to eight weeks after passing the exam.

What Do I Do if I Fail?

If you fail the exam, we recommend that you immediately take some notes on the exam topics you found especially difficult. Study these topics closely until you feel prepared to take the exam again.

 Tip If you fail the exam, you may retake it as many times as you like. But, you have to pay the candidate fee ($125) each time you take it, so be sure to be prepared before you schedule another appointment.

What if I Have a Problem with the Test, or a Question on the Test?

Thorough information on all CIW exams can be found at the CIW Web site, www.ciwcertified.com.

Tip   If you can't find the answer to your question there, contact the CIW Exam and Certification Department at exam@CIWcertified.com, or choose the appropriate contact from the CIW Contacts page (select Contacts from the CIW home page: www.ciwcertified.com).

What's the Next Step (the Next Exam to Take)?

After you've passed the Foundations exam (1D0-410) and the Site Designer exam (1D0-420), you can take the E-Commerce Designer exam (1D0-425) to achieve Master CIW Designer certification.

✦   ✦   ✦

HTML 4.01 Elements and Attributes

In this appendix, we've included the tables of elements and attributes from the W3C site. These tables are copyrighted by the W3C. You can access the copyright document at `www.w3.org/Consortium/Legal/copyright-documents-19990405`. You can use these tables to access information on the various tags and attributes, such as whether the tag or attribute is deprecated, whether the element's an empty element, which tags an attribute can be used with, and more.

Table of Elements

This section presents you with the HTML 4.01 table of elements, in all its glory, direct from the W3C site at `www.w3.org/TR/html401/index/elements.html`. This is a very handy reference to have, and we guarentee you'll use it often. The columns in Table E-1 contain the following information:

- ✦ **Name.** The name of the element.

- ✦ **Start Tag.** Tells you whether the start tag is optional or not. If there's an **O** in the cell, the start tag is optional.

- ✦ **End Tag.** Tells you whether the end tag is optional (**O**) or forbidden (**F**). If the end tag is forbidden, the element is an empty element.

- ✦ **Empty.** Tells you whether the tag is an empty element (**E**). Empty elements only have one tag; not a start tag and an end tag.

- ✦ **Depr.** Tells you whether the element is deprecated (**D**). If an element is deprecated, you should try to avoid using it because it will be phased out of the next implementation of XHTML.

✦ **DTD.** Tells you which DTD the element can be used with. There are three HTML DTDs: Strict (empty), Transitional (which is the loose DTD, **L**), and Frameset (**F**).

See Chapter 7 for more information on the three types of DTDs.

✦ **Description.** Provides you with a description of the element when necessary.

Although the start and end tags for certain elements may be optional, you should follow the new XHTML well-formed rules and always use both a start tag and an end tag for every element (unless it's an empty element). In addition, empty elements in XHTML are formatted as follows: `<img />`. Using these conventions will ensure that your documents are ready for the next phase of HTML.

Table E-1
Table of the HTML 4.01 Elements

Name	Start Tag	End Tag	Empty	Depr.	DTD	Description
A						anchor
Abbr						abbreviated form (e.g., WWW, HTTP, etc.)
Acronym						
Address						information on author
Applet				D	L	Java applet
Area		F	E			client-side image map area
B						bold text style
Base		F	E			document base URI
Basefont		F	E	D	L	base font size
Bdo						I18N BiDi over-ride
Big						large text style
Blockquote						long quotation
Body	O	O				document body
Br		F	E			forced line break
Button						push button

Name	Start Tag	End Tag	Empty	Depr.	DTD	Description
Caption						table caption
Center				D	L	shorthand for DIV align=center
Cite						citation
Code						computer code fragment
Col		F	E			table column
Colgroup		O				table column group
Dd		O				definition description
Del						deleted text
Dfn						instance definition
Dir				D	L	directory list
Div						generic language/style container
Dl						definition list
Dt		O				definition term
Em						emphasis
Fieldset						form control group
Font				D	L	local change to font
Form						interactive form
Frame		F	E		F	subwindow
Frameset					F	window subdivision
h1						heading
h2						heading
h3						heading
h4						heading
h5						heading
h6						heading
Head	O	O				document head
Hr		F	E			horizontal rule

Continued

Table E-1 *(continued)*

Name	Start Tag	End Tag	Empty	Depr.	DTD	Description
Html	O	O				document root element
I						italic text style
Iframe					L	inline subwindow
Img		F	E			embedded image
Input		F	E			form control
Ins						inserted text
Isindex		F	E	D	L	single line prompt
Kbd						text to be entered by the user
Label						form field label text
Legend						fieldset legend
Li		O				list item
Link		F	E			a media-independent link
Map						client-side image map
Menu				D	L	menu list
meta		F	E			generic meta information
noframes					F	alternate content container for non frame-based rendering
noscript						alternate content container for non script-based rendering
object						generic embedded object
ol						ordered list
optgroup						option group
option		O				selectable choice
p		O				paragraph
param		F	E			named property value

Name	Start Tag	End Tag	Empty	Depr.	DTD	Description
pre						preformatted text
q						short inline quotation
s				D	L	strike-through text style
samp						sample program output, scripts, etc.
script						script statements
select						option selector
small						small text style
span						generic language/ style container
strike				D	L	strike-through text
strong						strong emphasis
style						style info
sub						subscript
sup						superscript
table						
Tbody	O	O				table body
td		O				table data cell
textarea						multi-line text field
tfoot		O				table footer
th		O				table header cell
thead		O				table header
title						document title
tr		O				table row
tt						teletype or monospaced text style
u				D	L	underlined text style
ul						unordered list
var						instance of a variable or program argument

Table of Attributes

This section presents you with the HTML 4.01 table of attributes; also from the W3C site. This table is a little more complicated than the element table, so we've modified some of the information to make it more understandable. Therefore, if you look at this table on the W3C site at `www.w3.org/TR/html401/index/attributes.html`, it will look slightly different. But never fear, the information is all the same. The columns in Table E-2 contain the following information:

+ **Name.** The name of the attribute.

+ **Related Elements.** Tells you with which elements you can use the attribute.

+ **Type.** This column tells you the type of value. Note that these values are taken from the DTDs so consult the specification if you have any questions.

+ **Default.** Tells you the default value of the attribute if there is one.

+ **Depr.** Tells you whether the attribute is deprecated (**D**).

+ **DTD.** Tells you with which DTD the attribute can be used. There are three HTML DTDs: Strict (empty), Transitional (which is the loose DTD, **L**), and Frameset (**F**).

+ **Comment.** Additional information about the attribute if there is any.

Table E-2
Index of HTML 4.01 Attributes

Name	Related Elements	Type	Default	Depr.	DTD	Comment
Abbr	td, th	Plain text	#IMPLIED			abbreviation for header cell
accept-charset	form	A space-separated list of character encodings, as per RFC2045	#IMPLIED			list of supported charsets
Accept	form, input	Comma-separated list of media types, as per RFC2045	#IMPLIED			list of MIME types for file upload
Accesskey	a, area, button, input, label, legend, textarea	A single character from ISO10646	#IMPLIED			accessibility key character
Action	form	A Uniform Resource Identifier	#REQUIRED			server-side form handler
Align	caption	(top | bottom | left | right)	#IMPLIED	D	L	relative to table
Align	applet, iframe, img, input, object	(top | middle | bottom | left | right)	#IMPLIED	D	L	vertical or horizontal alignment
Align	legend	(top | bottom | left | right)	#IMPLIED	D	L	relative to fieldset
Align	table	(left | center | right)	#IMPLIED	D	L	table position relative to window
Align	hr	(left | center | right)	#IMPLIED	D	L	
Align	div, h1, h2, h3, h4, h5, h6, p	(left | center | right | justify)	#IMPLIED	D	L	align, text alignment

Continued

Table E-2 (continued)

Name	Related Elements	Type	Default	Depr.	DTD	Comment
Align	col, colgroup, tbody, td, tfoot, th, thead, tr	(left | center | right | justify | char)	#IMPLIED			
Alink	body	A color using sRGB: #RRGGBB as Hex values	#IMPLIED	D	L	color of selected links
Alt	applet	Plain text	#IMPLIED	D	L	short description
Alt	area, img	Plain text	#REQUIRED			short description
Alt	input	CDATA	#IMPLIED			short description
Archive	applet	CDATA	#IMPLIED	D	L	comma-separated archive list
Archive	object	CDATA	#IMPLIED			space-separated list of URIs
Axis	td, th	CDATA	#IMPLIED			comma-separated list of related headers
Background	body	A Uniform Resource Identifier	#IMPLIED	D	L	texture tile for document background
Bgcolor	table	A color using sRGB: #RRGGBB as Hex values	#IMPLIED	D	L	background color for cells
Bgcolor	tr	A color using sRGB: #RRGGBB as Hex values	#IMPLIED	D	L	background color for row
Bgcolor	td, th	A color using sRGB: #RRGGBB as Hex values	#IMPLIED	D	L	cell background color
Bgcolor	body	A color using sRGB: #RRGGBB as Hex values	#IMPLIED	D	L	document background color
Border	table	Integer representing length in pixels	#IMPLIED			controls frame width around table
Border	img, object	Integer representing length in pixels	#IMPLIED	D	L	link border width

Name	Related Elements	Type	Default	Depr.	DTD	Comment
Cellpadding	table	nn for pixels or nn% for percentage length	#IMPLIED			spacing within cells
Cellspacing	table	nn for pixels or nn% for percentage length	#IMPLIED			spacing between cells
Char	col, colgroup, tbody, td, tfoot, th, thead, tr	A single character from ISO10646	#IMPLIED			alignment char, e.g. char=':'
Charoff	col, colgroup, tbody, td, tfoot, th, thead, tr	nn for pixels or nn% for percentage length	#IMPLIED			offset for alignment char
Charset	a, link, script	A space-separated list of character encodings, as per RFC2045	#IMPLIED			char encoding of linked resource
Checked	input	(checked)	#IMPLIED			for radio buttons and check boxes
Cite	blockquote, q	A Uniform Resource Identifier	#IMPLIED			URI for source document or msg
Cite	del, ins	A Uniform Resource Identifier	#IMPLIED			info on reason for change
Class	all elements **but** base, basefont, head, html, meta, param, script, style, title	CDATA	#IMPLIED			space-separated list of classes
Classid	object	A Uniform Resource Identifier	#IMPLIED			identifies an implementation
Clear	br	(left | all | right | none)	none	D	L	control of text flow
Code	applet	CDATA	#IMPLIED	D	L	applet class file

Continued

Table E-2 (continued)

Name	Related Elements	Type	Default	Depr.	DTD	Comment
Codebase	object	A Uniform Resource Identifier	#IMPLIED			base URI for classid, data, archive
Codebase	applet	A Uniform Resource Identifier	#IMPLIED	D	L	optional base URI for applet
Codetype	object	Media type, as per RFC2045	#IMPLIED			content type for code
Color	basefont, font	A color using sRGB: #RRGGBB as Hex values	#IMPLIED	D	L	text color
Cols	frameset	Comma-separated list of MultiLength	#IMPLIED		F	list of lengths, default: 100% (1 col)
Cols	textarea	Number	#REQUIRED			
Colspan	td, th	Number	1			number of cols spanned by cell
Compact	dir, dl, menu, ol, ul	(compact)	#IMPLIED	D	L	reduced interitem spacing
Content	meta	CDATA	#REQUIRED			associated information
Coords	area	Comma-separated list of lengths	#IMPLIED			comma-separated list of lengths
Coords	a	Comma-separated list of lengths	#IMPLIED			for use with client-side image maps
Data	object	A Uniform Resource Identifier	#IMPLIED			reference to object's data
Datetime	del, ins	Date and time information. ISO date format	#IMPLIED			date and time of change
Declare	object	(declare)	#IMPLIED			declare but don't instantiate flag
Defer	script	(defer)	#IMPLIED			UA may defer execution of script

Name	Related Elements	Type	Default	Depr.	DTD	Comment
Dir	all elements but applet, base, basefont, bdo, br, frame, frameset, iframe, param, script	(ltr | rtl)	#IMPLIED			direction for weak/neutral text
Dir	bdo	(ltr | rtl)	#REQUIRED			directionality
Disabled	button, input, optgroup, option, select, textarea	(disabled)	#IMPLIED			unavailable in this context
Enctype	form	Media type, as per RFC2045	"application/x-www-form-urlencoded"			
Face	basefont, font	CDATA	#IMPLIED	D	L	comma-separated list of font names
For	label	IDREF	#IMPLIED			matches field ID value
Frame	table	(void | above | below | hsides | lhs | rhs | vsides | box | border)	#IMPLIED			which parts of frame to render
Frameborder	frame, iframe	(1 | 0)	1		F	request frame borders?
Headers	td, th	IDREFS	#IMPLIED			list of id's for header cells
Height	iframe	nn for pixels or nn% for percentage length	#IMPLIED		L	frame height
Height	td, th	nn for pixels or nn% for percentage length	#IMPLIED	D	L	height for cell
Height	img, object	nn for pixels or nn% for percentage length	#IMPLIED			override height
Height	applet	nn for pixels or nn% for percentage length	#REQUIRED	D	L	initial height

Continued

Table E-2 (continued)

Name	Related Elements	Type	Default	Depr.	DTD	Comment
Href	a, area, link	A Uniform Resource Identifier	#IMPLIED			URI for linked resource
Href	base	A Uniform Resource Identifier	#IMPLIED			URI that acts as base URI
Hreflang	a, link	A language code, as per RFC1766	#IMPLIED			language code
Hspace	applet, img, object	Integer representing length in pixels	#IMPLIED	D	L	horizontal gutter
http-equiv	meta	Name	#IMPLIED			HTTP response header name
Id	all elements but base, head, html, meta, script, style, title	ID	#IMPLIED			document-wide unique id
Ismap	img, input	(ismap)	#IMPLIED			use server-side image map
Label	option	Plain text	#IMPLIED			for use in hierarchical menus
Label	optgroup	Plain text	#REQUIRED			for use in hierarchical menus
Lang	all elements but applet, base, basefont, br, frame, frameset, iframe, param, script	A language code, as per RFC1766	#IMPLIED			language code
Language	script	CDATA	#IMPLIED	D	L	predefined script language name
Link	body	A color using sRGB: #RRGGBB as Hex values	#IMPLIED	D	L	color of links

Name	Related Elements	Type	Default	Depr.	DTD	Comment
Longdesc	img	A Uniform Resource Identifier	#IMPLIED			link to long description (complements alt)
Longdesc	frame, iframe	A Uniform Resource Identifier	#IMPLIED		F	link to long description (complements title)
Marginheight	frame, iframe	Integer representing length in pixels	#IMPLIED		F	margin height in pixels
Marginwidth	frame, iframe	Integer representing length in pixels	#IMPLIED		F	margin widths in pixels
Maxlength	input	Number	#IMPLIED			max chars for text fields
Media	style	Single or comma-separated list of media descriptors	#IMPLIED			designed for use with these media
Media	link	Single or comma-separated list of media descriptors	#IMPLIED			for rendering on these media
Method	form	(GET | POST)	GET			HTTP method used to submit the form
Multiple	select	(multiple)	#IMPLIED			default is single selection
Name	button, textarea	CDATA	#IMPLIED			
Name	applet	CDATA	#IMPLIED	D	L	allows applets to find each other
Name	select	CDATA	#IMPLIED			field name
Name	form	CDATA	#IMPLIED			name of form for scripting
Name	frame, iframe	CDATA	#IMPLIED		F	name of frame for targeting

Continued

Table E-2 (continued)

Name	Related Elements	Type	Default	Depr.	DTD	Comment
Name	img	CDATA	#IMPLIED			name of image for scripting
Name	a	CDATA	#IMPLIED			named link end
Name	input, object	CDATA	#IMPLIED			submit as part of form
Name	map	CDATA	#REQUIRED			for reference by usemap
Name	param	CDATA	#REQUIRED			property name
Name	meta	NAME	#IMPLIED			metainformation name
Nohref	area	(nohref)	#IMPLIED			this region has no action
Noresize	frame	(noresize)	#IMPLIED		F	allow users to resize frames?
Noshade	hr	(noshade)	#IMPLIED	D	L	
Nowrap	td, th	(nowrap)	#IMPLIED	D	L	suppress word wrap
Object	applet	CDATA	#IMPLIED	D	L	serialized applet file
Onblur	a, area, button, input, label, select, textarea	Script expression	#IMPLIED			the element lost the focus
Onchange	input, select, textarea	Script expression	#IMPLIED			the element value was changed
Onclick	all elements but applet, base, basefont, bdo, br, font, frame, frameset, head, html, iframe, isindex, meta, param, script, style, title	Script expression	#IMPLIED			a pointer button was clicked

Name	Related Elements	Type	Default	Depr.	DTD	Comment
Ondblclick	**all elements but** applet, base, basefont, bdo, br, font, frame, frameset, head, html, iframe, isindex, meta, param, script, style, title	Script expression	#IMPLIED			a pointer button was double clicked
Onfocus	a, area, button, input, label, select, textarea	Script expression	#IMPLIED			the element got the focus
Onkeydown	**all elements but** applet, base, basefont, bdo, br, font, frame, frameset, head, html, iframe, isindex, meta, param, script, style, title	Script expression	#IMPLIED			a key was pressed down
Onkeypress	**all elements but** applet, base, basefont, bdo, br, font, frame, frameset, head, html, iframe, isindex, meta, param, script, style, title	Script expression	#IMPLIED			a key was pressed and released

Continued

Table E-2 (continued)

Name	Related Elements	Type	Default	Depr.	DTD	Comment
Onkeyup	**all elements but** applet, base, basefont, bdo, br, font, frame, frameset, head, html, iframe, isindex, meta, param, script, style, title	Script expression	#IMPLIED			a key was released
Onload	frameset	Script expression	#IMPLIED		F	all the frames have been loaded
Onload	body	Script expression	#IMPLIED			the document has been loaded
Onmousedown	**all elements but** applet, base, basefont, bdo, br, font, frame, frameset, head, html, iframe, isindex, meta, param, script, style, title	Script expression	#IMPLIED			a pointer button was pressed down
Onmousemove	**all elements but** applet, base, basefont, bdo, br, font, frame, frameset, head, html, iframe, isindex, meta, param, script, style, title	Script expression	#IMPLIED			a pointer was moved within

Name	Related Elements	Type	Default	Depr.	DTD	Comment
Onmouseout	**all elements but** applet, base, basefont, bdo, br, font, frame, frameset, head, html, iframe, isindex, meta, param, script, style, title	Script expression	#IMPLIED			a pointer was moved away
Onmouseover	**all elements but** applet, base, basefont, bdo, br, font, frame, frameset, head, html, iframe, isindex, meta, param, script, style, title	Script expression	#IMPLIED			a pointer was moved onto
Onmouseup	**all elements but** applet, base, basefont, bdo, br, font, frame, frameset, head, html, iframe, isindex, meta, param, script, style, title	Script expression	#IMPLIED			a pointer button was released
Onreset	form	Script expression	#IMPLIED			the form was reset
Onselect	input, textarea	Script expression	#IMPLIED			some text was selected
Onsubmit	form	Script expression	#IMPLIED			the form was submitted
Onunload	frameset	Script expression	#IMPLIED		F	all the frames have been removed

Continued

Table E-2 *(continued)*

Name	Related Elements	Type	Default	Depr.	DTD	Comment
Onunload	body	Script expression	#IMPLIED			the document has been removed
Profile	head	A Uniform Resource Identifier	#IMPLIED			named dictionary of meta info
Prompt	isindex	Plain text	#IMPLIED	D	L	prompt message
Readonly	textarea	(readonly)	#IMPLIED			
Readonly	input	(readonly)	#IMPLIED			for text and passwd
Rel	a, link	Space-separated list of link types	#IMPLIED			forward link types
Rev	a, link	Space-separated list of link types	#IMPLIED			reverse link types
Rows	frameset	Comma-separated list of MultiLength	#IMPLIED		F	list of lengths, default: 100% (1 row)
Rows	textarea	Number	#REQUIRED			
Rowspan	td, th	Number	1			number of rows spanned by cell
Rules	table	(none | groups | rows | cols | all)	#IMPLIED			rulings between rows and cols
Scheme	meta	CDATA	#IMPLIED			select form of content
Scope	td, th	(row | col | rowgroup | colgroup)	#IMPLIED			scope covered by header cells
Scrolling	frame, iframe	(yes | no | auto)	Auto		F	scrollbar or none
Selected	option	(selected)	#IMPLIED			
Shape	area	(rect | circle | poly | default)	Rect			controls interpretation of coords

Name	Related Elements	Type	Default	Depr.	DTD	Comment
Shape	a	(rect | circle | poly | default)	Rect			for use with client-side image maps
Size	hr	Integer representing length in pixels	#IMPLIED	D	L	
Size	font	CDATA	#IMPLIED	D	L	[+|-]nn e.g. size="+1", size="4"
Size	input	CDATA	#IMPLIED			specific to each type of field
Size	basefont	CDATA	#REQUIRED	D	L	base font size for FONT elements
Size	select	Number	#IMPLIED			rows visible
Span	col	Number	1			COL attributes affect N columns
Span	colgroup	Number	1			default number of columns in group
Src	script	A Uniform Resource Identifier	#IMPLIED			URI for an external script
Src	input	A Uniform Resource Identifier	#IMPLIED			for fields with images
Src	frame, iframe	A Uniform Resource Identifier	#IMPLIED		F	source of frame content
Src	img	A Uniform Resource Identifier	#REQUIRED			URI of image to embed
Standby	object	Plain text	#IMPLIED			message to show while loading
Start	ol	Number	#IMPLIED	D	L	starting sequence number

Continued

Table E-2 (continued)

Name	Related Elements	Type	Default	Depr.	DTD	Comment
Style	all elements but base, basefont, head, html, meta, param, script, title	Style sheet data	#IMPLIED			associated style info
Summary	table	Plain text	#IMPLIED			purpose/structure for speech output
Tabindex	a, area, button, input, object, select, textarea	Number	#IMPLIED			position in tabbing order
Target	a, area, base, form, link	Render in this frame	#IMPLIED		L	render in this frame
Text	body	A color using sRGB: #RRGGBB as Hex values	#IMPLIED	D	L	document text color
Title	all elements but base, basefont, head, html, meta, param, script, title	Plain text	#IMPLIED			advisory title
Type	a, link	Media type, as per RFC2045	#IMPLIED			advisory content type
Type	object	Media type, as per RFC2045	#IMPLIED			content type for data
Type	param	Media type, as per RFC2045	#IMPLIED			content type for value when valuetype=ref
Type	script	Media type, as per RFC2045	#REQUIRED			content type of script language
Type	style	Media type, as per RFC2045	#REQUIRED			content type of style language

Name	Related Elements	Type	Default	Depr.	DTD	Comment
Type	input	(TEXT | PASSWORD | CHECKBOX | RADIO | SUBMIT | RESET | FILE | HIDDEN | IMAGE | BUTTON)	TEXT			what kind of widget is needed
Type	li	DISC | SQUARE | CIRCLE or 1 | a | A | i | I	#IMPLIED	D	L	list item style
Type	ol	1 | a | A | i | I	#IMPLIED	D	L	numbering style
Type	ul	DISC | SQUARE | CIRCLE	#IMPLIED	D	L	bullet style
Type	button	(button | submit | reset)	Submit			for use as form button
Usemap	img, input, object	A Uniform Resource Identifier	#IMPLIED			use client-side image map
Valign	col, colgroup, tbody, td, tfoot, th, thead, tr	(top | middle | bottom | baseline)	#IMPLIED			vertical alignment in cells
Value	input	CDATA	#IMPLIED			specify for radio buttons and checkboxes
Value	option	CDATA	#IMPLIED			defaults to element content
Value	param	CDATA	#IMPLIED			property value
Value	button	CDATA	#IMPLIED			sent to server when submitted
Value	li	Number	#IMPLIED	D	L	reset sequence number
Valuetype	param	(DATA | REF | OBJECT)	DATA			how to interpret value
Version	html	CDATA	%HTML	D	L	constant

Continued

Table E-2 (continued)

Name	Related Elements	Type	Default	Depr.	DTD	Comment
Vlink	body	A color using sRGB: #RRGGBB as Hex values	#IMPLIED	D	L	color of visited links
Vspace	applet, img, object	Integer representing length in pixels	#IMPLIED	D	L	vertical gutter
width	hr	nn for pixels or nn% for percentage length	#IMPLIED	D	L	
width	iframe	nn for pixels or nn% for percentage length	#IMPLIED		L	frame width
width	img, object	nn for pixels or nn% for percentage length	#IMPLIED			override width
width	table	nn for pixels or nn% for percentage length	#IMPLIED			table width
width	td, th	nn for pixels or nn% for percentage length	#IMPLIED		L	width for cell
width	applet	nn for pixels or nn% for percentage length	#REQUIRED	D	L	initial width
width	col	Pixel, percentage, or relative	#IMPLIED			column width specification
width	colgroup	Pixel, percentage, or relative	#IMPLIED			default width for enclosed COLs
width	pre	Number	#IMPLIED	D	L	

◆   ◆   ◆

CSS2 Properties and Values

This appendix contains a table of the CSS2 properties and values from the W3C site. This table is copyrighted by the W3C and can be found at `www.w3.org/TR/REC-CSS2/propidx.html`. You can access the copyright document at `www.w3.org/Consortium/Legal/copyright-documents-19990405`.

The columns in Table F-1 contain the following information:

◆ **Name.** The name of the property.

◆ **Values.** The possible values for the property. Values that appear between the less-than and greater-than signs are placeholders.

◆ **Initial Value.** The default value for the property.

◆ **Applies to.** Defines to which elements the property applies.

◆ **Inherited?** Defines whether the property is inherited or not.

◆ **Percentages.** If the property can use a percentage as a value, this column explains what that percentage affects.

◆ **Media groups.** Describes to which media group the property belongs.

Table F-1
CSS Properties and Values

Name	Values	Initial Value	Applies to (Default: all)	Inherited?	Percentages (Default: N/A)	Media groups
'azimuth'	<angle> | [[left-side | far-left | left | center-left | center | center-right | right | far-right | right-side] || behind] | leftwards | rightwards | inherit	center		yes		aural
'background'	['background-color' || 'background-image' || 'background-repeat' || 'background-attachment' || 'background-position'] | inherit	XX		no	allowed on 'background-position'	visual
'background-attachment'	scroll | fixed | inherit	scroll		no		visual
'background-color'	<color> | transparent | inherit	transparent		no		visual
'background-image'	<uri> | none | inherit	none		no		visual
'background-position'	[[<percentage> | <length>]{1,2} | [[top | center | bottom] || [left | center | right]] | inherit	0% 0%	block-level and replaced elements	no	refer to the size of the box itself	visual
'background-repeat'	repeat | repeat-x | repeat-y | no-repeat | inherit	repeat		no		visual
'border'	['border-width' || 'border-style' || <color>] | inherit	see individual properties		no		visual

Name	Values	Initial Value	Applies to (Default: all)	Inherited?	Percentages (Default: N/A)	Media groups
'border-collapse'	collapse | separate | inherit	collapse	'table' and 'inline-table' elements	yes		visual
'border-color'	<color>{1,4} | transparent | inherit	see individual properties		no		visual
'border-spacing'	<length> <length>? | inherit	0	'table' and 'inline-table' elements	yes		visual
'border-style'	<border-style> {1,4} | inherit	see individual properties		no		visual
'border-top' 'border-right' 'border-bottom' 'border-left'	['border-top-width' || 'border-style' || <color>] | inherit	see individual properties		no		visual
'border-top-color' 'border-right-color' 'border-bottom-color' 'border-left-color'	<color> | inherit	the value of the 'color' property		ino		visual
'border-top-style' 'border-right-style' 'border-bottom-style' 'border-left-style'	<border-style> | inherit	none		no		visual
'border-top-width' 'border-right-width' 'border-bottom-width' 'border-left-width'	<border-width> | inherit	medium		no		visual
'border-width'	<border-width>{1,4} | inherit	see individual properties		no		visual
'bottom'	<length> | <percentage> | auto | inherit	auto	positioned elements	no	refer to height of containing block	visual

Continued

Table F-1 (continued)

Name	Values	Initial Value	Applies to (Default: all)	Inherited?	Percentages (Default: N/A)	Media groups
'caption-side'	top | bottom | left | right | inherit	top	'table-caption' elements	yes		visual
'clear'	none | left | right | both | inherit	none	block-level elements	no		visual
'clip'	<shape> | auto | inherit	auto	block-level and replaced elements	no		visual
'color'	<color> | inherit	depends on user agent		yes		visual
'content'	[<string> | <uri> | <counter> | attr(X) | open-quote | close-quote | no-open-quote | no-close-quote]+ | inherit	empty string	:before and :after pseudo-elements	no		all
'counter-increment'	[<identifier> <integer>?]+ | none | inherit	none		no		all
'counter-reset'	[<identifier> <integer>?]+ | none | inherit	none		no		all
'cue'	['cue-before' | 'cue-after'] | inherit	XX		no		aural
'cue-after'	<uri> | none | inherit	none		no		aural
'cue-before'	<uri> | none | inherit	none		no		aural

Name	Values	Initial Value	Applies to (Default: all)	Inherited?	Percentages (Default: N/A)	Media groups
'cursor'	[[<uri> ,]* [auto | crosshair | default | pointer | move | e-resize | ne-resize | nw-resize | n-resize | se-resize | sw-resize | s-resize | w-resize | text | wait | help]] | inherit	auto		yes		visual, interactive
'direction'	ltr | rtl | inherit	ltr	all elements, but see prose	yes		visual
'display'	inline | block | list-item | run-in | compact | marker | table | inline-table | table-row-group | table-header-group | table-footer-group | table-row | table-column-group | table-column | table-cell | table-caption | none | inherit	inline		no		all
'elevation'	<angle> | below | level | above | higher | lower | inherit	level		yes		aural
'empty-cells'	show | hide | inherit	show	'table-cell' elements	yes		visual
'float'	left | right | none | inherit	none	all but positioned elements and generated content	no		visual

Continued

Table F-1 (continued)

Name	Values	Initial Value	Applies to (Default: all)	Inherited?	Percentages (Default: N/A)	Media groups
'font'	[['font-style' || 'font-variant' || 'font-weight']? 'font-size' [/ 'line-height']? 'font-family'] | caption | icon | menu | message-box | small-caption | status-bar | inherit	see individual properties		yes	allowed on 'font-size' and 'line-height'	visual
'font-family'	[[<family-name> | <generic-family>],]* [<family-name> | <generic-family>] | inherit	depends on user agent		yes	yes	visual
'font-size'	<absolute-size> | <relative-size> | <length> | <percentage> | inherit	medium		yes, the computed value is inherited	refer to parent element's font size	visual
'font-size-adjust'	<number> | none | inherit	none		yes		visual
'font-stretch'	normal | wider | narrower | ultra-condensed | extra-condensed | condensed | semi-condensed | semi-expanded | expanded | extra-expanded | ultra-expanded | inherit	normal		yes		visual
'font-style'	normal | italic | oblique | inherit	normal		yes		visual
'font-variant'	normal | small-caps | inherit	normal		yes		visual
'font-weight'	normal | bold | bolder | lighter | 100 | 200 | 300 | 400 | 500 | 600 | 700 | 800 | 900 | inherit	normal		yes		visual

Name	Values	Initial Value	Applies to (Default: all)	Inherited?	Percentages (Default: N/A)	Media groups
'height'	`<length>` | `<percentage>` | auto | inherit	auto	all elements but non-replaced inline elements, table columns, and column groups	no	see prose	visual
'left'	`<length>` | `<percentage>` | auto | inherit	auto	positioned elements	no	refer to width of containing block	visual
'letter-spacing'	normal | `<length>` | inherit	normal		yes		visual
'line-height'	normal | `<number>` | `<length>` | `<percentage>` | inherit	normal		yes	refer to the font size of the element itself	visual
'list-style'	['list-style-type' | 'list-style-position' | 'list-style-image'] | inherit	XX 'display:	elements with list-item	yes		visual
'list-style-image'	`<uri>` | none | inherit	none	elements with 'display: list-item'	yes		visual
'list-style-position'	inside | outside | inherit	outside	elements with 'display: list-item'	yes		visual
'list-style-type'	disc | circle | square | decimal | decimal-leading-zero | lower-roman | upper-roman | lower-greek | lower-alpha | lower-latin | upper-alpha | upper-latin | hebrew | armenian | georgian | cjk-ideographic | hiragana | katakana | hiragana-iroha | katakana-iroha | none | inherit	disc	elements with 'display: list-item'	yes		visual

Continued

Table F-1 (continued)

Name	Values	Initial Value	Applies to (Default: all)	Inherited?	Percentages (Default: N/A)	Media groups
'margin'	<margin-width>{1,4} | inherit	XX		no	refer to width of containing block	visual
'margin-top' 'margin-right' 'margin-bottom' 'margin-left'	<margin-width> | inherit	0		no	refer to width of containing block	visual
'marker-offset'	<length> | auto | inherit	auto	elements with 'display: marker'	no		visual
'marks'	[crop || cross] | none | inherit	none	page context	N/A		visual, paged
'max-height'	<length> | <percentage> | none | inherit	none	all elements except non-replaced inline elements and table elements	no	refer to height of containing block	visual
'max-width'	<length> | <percentage> | none | inherit	none	all elements except non-replaced inline elements and table elements	no	refer to width of containing block	visual
'min-height'	<length> | <percentage> | inherit	0	all elements except non-replaced inline elements and table elements	no	refer to height of containing block	visual

Name	Values	Initial Value	Applies to (Default: all)	Inherited?	Percentages (Default: N/A)	Media groups
'min-width'	`<length>` | `<percentage>` | inherit	UA dependent	all elements except non-replaced inline elements and table elements	no	refer to width of containing block	visual
'orphans'	`<integer>` | inherit	2	block-level elements	yes		visual, paged
'outline'	['outline-color' | 'outline-style' | 'outline-width'] | inherit	see individual properties		no		visual, interactive
'outline-color'	`<color>` | invert | inherit	invert		no		visual, interactive
'outline-style'	`<border-style>` | inherit	none		no		visual, interactive
'outline-width'	`<border-width>` | inherit	medium		no		visual, interactive
'overflow'	visible | hidden | scroll | auto | inherit	visible	block-level and replaced elements	no		visual
'padding'	`<padding-width>`{1,4} | inherit	XX		no	refer to width of containing block	visual
'padding-top' 'padding-right' 'padding-bottom' 'padding-left'	`<padding-width>` | inherit	0		no	refer to width of containing block	visual
'page'	`<identifier>` | auto	auto	block-level elements	yes		visual, paged
'page-break-after'	auto | always | avoid | left | right | inherit	auto	block-level elements	no		visual, paged

Continued

Table F-1 (continued)

Name	Values	Initial Value	Applies to (Default: all)	Inherited?	Percentages (Default: N/A)	Media groups
'page-break-before'	`auto | always | avoid | left | right | inherit`	`auto`	block-level elements	no		visual, paged
'page-break-inside'	`avoid | auto | inherit`	`auto`	block-level elements	yes		visual, paged
'pause'	`[ [<time> | <percentage>] {1,2} ] | inherit`	depends on user agent		no	see descriptions of 'pause-before' and 'pause-after'	aural
'pause-after'	`<time> | <percentage> | inherit`	depends on user agent		no	see prose	aural
'pause-before'	`<time> | <percentage> | inherit`	depends on user agent		no	see prose	aural
'pitch'	`<frequency> | x-low | low | medium | high | x-high | inherit`	medium		yes		aural
'pitch-range'	`<number> | inherit`	50		yes		aural
'play-during'	`<uri> mix? repeat? | auto | none | inherit`	auto		no		aural
'position'	`static | relative | absolute | fixed | inherit`	static	all elements, but not to generated content	no		visual
'quotes'	`[<string> <string>]+ | none | inherit`	depends on user agent		yes		visual
'richness'	`<number> | inherit`	50		yes		aural
'right'	`<length> | <percentage> | auto | inherit`	auto	positioned elements	no	refer to width of containing block	visual

Name	Values	Initial Value	Applies to (Default: all)	Inherited?	Percentages (Default: N/A)	Media groups
`'size'`	`<length>`{1,2}	auto | portrait | landscape | inherit	auto	the page context	N/A		visual, paged
`'speak'`	normal | none | spell-out | inherit	normal		yes		aural
`'speak-header'`	once | always | inherit	once	elements that have table header information	yes		aural
`'speak-numeral'`	digits | continuous | inherit	continuous		yes		aural
`'speak-punctuation'`	code | none | inherit	none		yes		aural
`'speech-rate'`	`<number>` | x-slow | slow | medium | fast | x-fast | faster | slower | inherit	medium		yes		aural
`'stress'`	`<number>` | inherit	50		yes		aural
`'table-layout'`	auto | fixed | inherit	auto	`'table'` and `'inline-table'` elements	no		visual
`'text-align'`	left | right | center | justify | `<string>` | inherit	depends on user agent and writing direction	block-level elements	yes		visual
`'text-decoration'`	none | [underline || overline || line-through || blink] | inherit	none		no (see prose)		visual
`'text-indent'`	`<length>` | `<percentage>` | inherit	0	block-level elements	yes	refer to width of containing block	visual
`'text-shadow'`	none | [`<color>` || `<length>` `<length>` `<length>`? ,]* [`<color>` || `<length>` `<length>` `<length>`?] | inherit	none		no (see prose)		visual

Continued

Table F-1 (continued)

Name	Values	Initial Value	Applies to (Default: all)	Inherited?	Percentages (Default: N/A)	Media groups
'text-transform'	capitalize | uppercase | lowercase | none | inherit	none		yes		visual
'top'	\<length> | \<percentage> | auto | inherit	auto	positioned elements	no	refer to height of containing block	visual
'unicode-bidi'	normal | embed | bidi-override | inherit	normal	all elements, but see prose	no		visual
'vertical-align'	baseline | sub | super | top | text-top | middle | bottom | text-bottom | \<percentage> | \<length> | inherit	baseline	inline-level and 'table-cell' elements	no	refer to the 'line-height' of the element itself	visual
'visibility'	visible | hidden | collapse | inherit	inherit		no		visual
'voice-family'	[[\<specific-voice> | \<generic-voice>].]* [\<specific-voice> | \<generic-voice>] | inherit	depends on user agent			yes	aural
'volume'	\<number> | \<percentage> | silent | x-soft | soft | medium | loud | x-loud | inherit	medium		yes	refer to inherited value	aural
'white-space'	normal | pre | nowrap | inherit	normal	block-level elements	yes		visual
'widows'	\<integer> | inherit	2	block-level elements	yes		visual, paged

Name	Values	Initial Value	Applies to (Default: all)	Inherited?	Percentages (Default: N/A)	Media groups
'width'	`<length>` | `<percentage>` | auto | inherit	auto	all elements but non-replaced inline elements, table rows, and row groups	no	refer to width of containing block	visual
'word-spacing'	normal | `<length>` | inherit	normal		yes		visual
'z-index'	auto | `<integer>` | inherit	auto	positioned elements	no		visual

Design Resources, Style Guides, and References

It's no secret that the Web is an environment that quickly changes. Therefore, by the time you get to this appendix (or this book for that matter), some of the URLs listed here may not work anymore. If you come across a non-functional URL, try going to its root and verifying that the information you seek is still on the site. For example, if you're looking for the Books section of the LANWrights Web site at www.lanw.com/books and it's not there, try going to www.lanw.com and checking if there's still a Books link listed.

Web Site Design Resources Online

The following is a list of Web site design resources, separated by topic, that you can visit to learn more about the technologies, concepts, and products we discussed in this book. You can also find this list in an HTML file on the CD that comes with this book. You can even import these links into your Internet Explorer favorites or your Netscape Navigator bookmarks if you like.

Web site design

✦ **lynda.com.** www.lynda.com

✦ **webmonkey.** http://hotwired.lycos.com/webmonkey/

✦ **World Wide Web: Design and Application.** www.inx.net/catalog/wwwdes.htm

✦ **Cabrillo College Library Web Design Pointers.** `http://libwww.cabrillo.cc.ca.us/html/depts/S01dm160.html`

✦ **Internet.com's Web Developer Channel.** `www.internet.com/sections/webdev.html`

✦ **Web Professional Research Center.** `www.cio.com/forums/careers/getting_started.html`

✦ **Web Developer's Virtual Library. Web Site Design.** `http://wdvl.internet.com/Seminars/Design/`

✦ **WebVoodoo's Web Design Clinic — Color Theory 101.** `www.webdesignclinic.com/ezine/v1i1/color/`

Web site usability

✦ **Advanced Common Sense: Steve Krug's Web site.** `www.sensible.com` (Read his book: "Don't Make Me Think!")

✦ **Alertbox: Jakob Nielsen's Column on Web Usability.** `www.useit.com/alertbox/`

✦ **Interview: Web Usability Past, Present, and Future.** `http://webword.com/interviews/nielsen.html`

✦ **Usable Web.** `www.usableweb.com`

✦ **goodexperience.com.** `www.goodexperience.com`

✦ **WebWord.com Usability and Human Factors for the Internet.** `http://webword.com`

Information architecture

✦ **Information Architecture.** `http://uncle-netword.com/articles/writeweb3.html`

✦ **Web Review – Web Architect.** `http://webreview.com/universal/previous/arch/index.html`

✦ **O'Reilly's Information Architecture for the World Wide Web, Chapter 2: Introduction to Information Architecture.** `www.oreilly.com/catalog/infotecture/chapter/ch02.html`

HTML Style Guides Online

What follows is a list of HTML style guides you can find online. Remember: You can also find this list in an HTML file on the CD that comes with this book, and you can import those links into your Internet Explorer favorites or your Netscape Navigator bookmarks.

✦ **Admiral Gandalf's HTML Style Guide.** `www.wybble.demon.co.uk/user/gandalf/GCHTMLStyle.HTML`

✦ **Alan Trachtenberg's HTML Style Guide.** `http://www.trachtenberg.com/styleguide.html`

✦ **Art and the Zen of Web Sites.** `www.tlc-systems.com/webtips.shtml`

✦ **Basic HTML Style Guide.** `http://guinan.gsfc.nasa.gov/Style.html`

✦ **CSU San Marcos HTML Style Guide.** `http://public.csusm.edu/public/guests/history/netinfo/html/`

✦ **David Siegel's "High Five" Archive.** `www.highfivearchive.com/core/index.html`

✦ **Electric Pages.** `www.electric-pages.com/`

✦ **HTML Style Guide.** `http://erebus.bentley.edu/empl/c/rcrooks/toolbox/style/index.html`

✦ **HTML Style Guide & Test Suite.** `www.charm.net/~lejeune/styles.html`

✦ **IWA's HTML Resources.** `www.iwanet.org/member/resources/authoring/html_stuff.html`

✦ **Jakob Nielsen's "Writing for the Web."** `www.sun.com/980713/webwriting/index.html`

✦ **Links2Go's List of HTML Style Guides.** `www.links2go.com/more/guinan.gsfc.nasa.gov/Style.html`

✦ **Systems Magic HTML Style Guide.** `www.sysmag.com/web/html-style-old.html`

✦ **W3C's Style Guide for Online Hypertext.** `www.w3.org/Provider/Style/Overview.html`

✦ **Web Developer's Virtual Library List of Style Guides.** `http://wdvl.internet.com/Seminars/Style/`

✦ **WebStandards Resouces.** `www.webstandards.org/general.html`

✦ **What Makes a Great Web Site?** `http://webreference.com/greatsite.html`

✦ **Wired Style.** `http://hotwired.lycos.com/hardwired/wiredstyle/`

✦ **Yale Center for Advanced Instructional Media Style Guide.** `http://info.med.yale.edu/caim/manual/index.html`

XML Reference Materials

This section contains a list of Web sites with more information on XML, separated by topic. Again, this list is also available in an HTML file on the CD. We also provide a short and sweet bibliography of choice XML titles for your further education on this fascinating topic.

Online sources

✦ **W3C.** The home of specifications for most XML-related initiatives, the W3C is the right place to start looking for information on this large, complex subject. For that reason, we provide multiple pointers here:

- **Main XML page.** www.w3.org/XML/
- **XML Schemas.** www.w3.org/XML/Schema
- **XPath.** www.w3.org/TR/xpath
- **XPointer.** www.w3.org/XML/Linking
- **XSL and XSLT.** www.w3.org/Style/XSL/

✦ **XML.com.** A great site for XML news, information, opinions, examples, and pointers to useful resources galore: www.xml.com

✦ **Oasis.** An acronym for the Organization for the Advancement of Structured Information Standards, Oasis is home to all kinds of useful standards-related information, including Robin Cover's excellent collection of XML resource information, standards, and pointers: www.oasis-open.org/cover/xml.html

✦ **Microsoft XML.** XML is a key ingredient in Microsoft's future development strategy, which is why it's featured prominently on the Microsoft Developer Network (MSDN) Web site, in conjunction with great free tools, information, training materials, and so forth: www.microsoft.com/xml/ or http://msdn.microsoft.com/xml/

✦ **Finetuning.** An interesting collection of XML pointers, resources, and information from Lisa Rein: www.finetuning.com

✦ **XML: Recommended Reading.** A slightly dated, but ever-so-useful compendium of books and online articles relevant to a broad range of XML concepts and technologies: www.cs.caltech.edu/~adam/local/xml.html

✦ **ZVON.org.** A gang of eclectic and productive XML experts from the Czech Republic. You'll find all kinds of useful tools as well as information and pointers on XML at this site: www.zvon.org

✦ **XMLInfo.com.** Noted XML experts James Tauber, Jamie Rice, and Daniel Krech, have teamed up to provide an excellent collection of pointers to XML-related information at: www.xmlinfo.com

✦ **XML Magazine.** A monthly online and printed publication (be sure to subscribe to the print version if you still like reading magazines the old-fashioned way): www.xmlmag.com

A short XML bibliography

✦ Aviram, Maria: *XML For Dummies Quick Reference*, Hungry Minds, Indianapolis, Indiana, 1998. ISBN: 0764503839.

✦ Eddy, Sandra, et al.: *XML in Plain English*, Second Edition, Hungry Minds, Indianapolis, Indiana, 2000. ISBN: 0764547445.

✦ Harold, Elliott Rusty: *XML Bible*, Second Edition, Hungry Minds, Indianapolis, Indiana, 20010764547607. ISBN: 0764532367.

✦ Harold, Elliott Rusty: *XML: Extensible Markup Language*, Hungry Minds, Indianapolis, Indiana, 1998. ISBN: 0764531999.

✦ Mengle, Rev and Emily Vander Veer: *XML: Your Visual Blueprint for Building Expert Web Pages*, Hungry Minds, Indianapolis, Indiana, 2000. ISBN: 0764534777.

✦ St. Laurent, Simon: *XML: A Primer*, Hungry Minds, Indianapolis, Indiana, 2001. ISBN: 0764547771.

✦ St. Laurent, Simon and B.K. DeLong: *XHTML: Moving Toward XML*, Hungry Minds, Indianapolis, Indiana, 2000. ISBN: 0764547097.

✦ Tittel, Ed and Frank Boumphrey: *XML For Dummies*, Second Edition, Hungry Minds, Indianapolis, Indiana, 2000. ISBN: 0764506927.

Alphabetical Listing of References

Here's an alphabetical listing of all the companies and products mentioned in this book, including the URL for the company or product, as well as the chapter in which it was discussed.

A

✦ **A List Apart.** Articles by designers for designers. `www.alistapart.com`: See Chapter 6 (the "For More Information" section)

✦ **Adobe.** Acrobat icon download. `www.adobe.com/products/acrobat/distribute.html`: See Chapter 12

✦ **Adobe.** Acrobat main product page. `www.adobe.com/products/acrobat/main.html`: See Chapter 12

✦ **Adobe.** Adobe products. `www.adobe.com`: See Chapter 5 (the "For More Information" section)

✦ **Adobe.** PDF file optimization. `www.adobe.com/epaper/tips/pdfgraphics/main.html`: See Chapter 12

✦ **Adobe.** SVG viewer. `www.adobe.com/svg/viewer/install/main.html`: See Chapter 4 (the "For More Information" section)

✦ **Adobe After Effects.** Animation tool by Adobe. `www.adobe.com/products/aftereffects/main.html`: See Chapter 5

✦ **Adobe Premiere.** Video authoring and editing tool by Adobe. `www.adobe.com/products/premiere/main.html`: See Chapter 5

✦ **Allaire.** HomeSite developer's center. `www.allaire.com/developer/ hsreferencedesk/`: See Chapter 19 (the "For More Information" section)

✦ **Allaire.** HomeSite's home page. `www.allaire.com/products/homesite/ homesite.cfm`: See Chapter 15 (the "For More Information" section)

✦ **AltaVista.** Search engine. `www.altavista.com`: See Chapter 10

✦ **Amazon.com.** Online retailer (Web site personalization). `www.amazon.com`: See Chapter 1

✦ **Animated-Teeth.com.** Site used to illustrate a concept. `www.animated-teeth.com/`: See Chapter 5

✦ **AOL Search.** Search engine. `http://search.aol.com`: See Chapter 10

✦ **Apache.** Apache server information. `www.apache.org`: Chapter 21

✦ **Apple.** Apple products. `www.apple.com`: See Chapter 5 (the "For More Information" section)

✦ **Ask Jeeves.** Search engine. `www.ask.com`: See Chapter 10

✦ **Atlantic Monthly.** As We May Think. `www.theatlantic.com/unbound/ flashbks/computer/bushf.htm`: See Chapter 7

B

✦ **Beck.** Site that informs you that you need a plug-in. `www.beck.com`: See Chapter 5

C

✦ **CDNOW.** Online retailer. `www.cdnow.com`: See Chapter 6 (Lab 6-3)

✦ **CliffsNotes.** Corporate Web site (company brand example). `www.cliffsnotes.com`: See Chapter 1

✦ **CliffsNotes.** Example of a detail page. `www.cliffsnotes.com/store/ sampledownload.html`: See Chapter 12

✦ **CNET Builder.com.** Spotlight on Web Graphics. `www.builder.com/ Graphics/Spotlight/`: See Chapter 4 (the "For More Information" section)

✦ **CNET.com.** CNet's builder site. `http://builder.cnet.com`: See Chapter 6 (the "For More Information" section)

✦ **CNet.com.** Example of guided multimedia. `www.cnet.com`: See Chapters 5 and 7 (Lab 7-1)

✦ **Cool Edit Pro.** Audio authoring, editing, and converting tool by Syntrillium. `www.syntrillium.com/cep/`: See Chapter 5

D

✦ **DeBabelizer.** Software optimizer from Equilibrium. `www.debabelizer.com`: See Chapter 4

✦ **DevGuru.** JavaScript reference. `http://www.devguru.com/Technologies/ecmascript/quickref/javascript_intro.html`: See Chapter 17 (the "For More Information" section)

✦ **Direct Hit.** Search engine. `www.directhit.com`: See Chapter 10

✦ **Disney.** Example of a metaphor. `http://disney.go.com/`: See Chapter 6

✦ **Doctor HTML.** Online Web site that tests for load time. `www2.imagiware.com/RxHTML`: See Chapter 4

✦ **Dublin Core Metadata Initiative.** Metadata information. `http://dublincore.org/index.shtml`: See Chapter 10 (the "For More Information" section)

E

✦ **Excite.** Search engine. `www.excite.com`: See Chapter 10

✦ **ExtremeFlash.** Flash information site. `www.extremeflash.com`: Chapter 16 (the "For More Information" section)

F

✦ **Final Cut Pro.** Video authoring and editing tool by Apple. `www.apple.com/finalcutpro/`: See Chapter 5

✦ **Flashcore.** Flash information site. `www.flashcore.com`: Chapter 16 (the "For More Information" section)

✦ **Flashkit.** Flash information site. `www.flashkit.com`: Chapter 16 (the "For More Information" section)

✦ **FlashPlanet.** Flash information site. `www.flashplanet.com`: Chapter 16 (the "For More Information" section)

G

✦ **Gamelan.** Java documentation, free programs, tutorials, resources, links, and more. `www.gamelan.earthweb.com`: Chapter 18 (the "For More Information" section)

✦ **Gettingstarted.net.** Frames information. `http://www.gettingstarted.net/basics/frames/04-frames.html`: See Chapter 9 (the "For More Information" section)

✦ **GIF Cruncher.** Software optimizer from Spinwave.com. `www.spinwave.com`: See Chapter 4

✦ **GIF Wizard.** Online optimizer from OptiView Technologies. `www.gifwizard.com`: See Chapter 4

✦ **GifBot.** Online optimizer by NetMechanic Inc. `www.netmechanic.com/accelerate.htm`: See Chapter 4

✦ **GifLube.** Online optimizer from Netscape. `http://websitegarage.netscape.com/0=wsg/turbocharge/gif_lube/index.html`: See Chapter 4

✦ **Go.com.** Search engine. `www.go.com`: See Chapter 10

✦ **Go2Net.** Search engine. `www.go2net.com`: See Chapter 10

✦ **Google.** Search engine. `www.google.com`: See Chapter 10

H

✦ **HotBot.** Search engine. `www.hotbot.com`: See Chapter 10

✦ **HugeClick's site.** `www.hugeclick.com`: See Chapter 6 (Lab 6-1)

✦ **Human Code Inc.** Site that informs you that you need a plug-in. `www.humancode.com/index3.htm`: See Chapter 5

✦ **Hungry Minds.** Corporate publisher Web site. `www.hungryminds.com`: See Chapter 1

I

✦ **IETF.** Request for Comments (RFCs). `www.ietf.org/rfc.html`: See Chapter 7

✦ **ILearning.** Training and education services (navigation example). `www.ilearning.com`: See Chapter 3

✦ **International Olympic Committee's site.** `www.olympic.or`: See Chapter 6 (Lab 6-1)

✦ **Internet Architecture Board (IAB).** Technical advisory group of the ISOC. `www.iab.org`: See Chapter 7

✦ **The Internet Corporation for Assigned Names and Numbers (ICANN).** Governs IP addresses. `www.icann.org`: See Chapter 7

✦ **Internet Engineering Task Force (IETF).** International community of network designers, operators, vendors, and researchers. `www.ieft.org`: See Chapter 7

✦ **Internet Research Task Force (IRTF).** Internet research groups. `www.irtf.org`: See Chapter 7

✦ **Internet Society.** ISOC Mission statement. `www.isoc.org/isoc/mission/`: See Chapter 7

✦ **iPlanet.** Cookie Recipes — Client Side Persistent Data. `http://developer.iplanet.com/viewsource/archive/goodman_cookies.html`: See Chapter 20 (the "For More Information" section)

✦ **iPlanet.** Introduction to SSL. `http://docs.iplanet.com/docs/manuals/security/sslin/index.htm`: See Chapter 20

✦ **Ipswitch.** Trial copy of WS_FTP Pro. `www.ipswitch.com`: Chapter 21

✦ **Iwon.** Search engine. `www.iwon.com`: See Chapter 10

J

✦ **Java Boutique.** Java applet archive. `http://javaboutique.webdeveloper.com/`: Chapter 18

✦ **Java Boutique.** Java documentation. `www.javaboutique.internet.com`: Chapter 18 (the "For More Information" section)

✦ **Java Boutique.** Servlets and JSP. `http://javaboutique.internet.com/tutorials/JSP/`: See Chapter 20 (the "For More Information" section)

✦ **JavaPowered.** Java applet archive. `www.javapowered.com/werks.html`: Chapter 18

✦ **JavaScript.com.** JavaScript reference. `http://www.javascript.com`: See Chapter 17 (the "For More Information" section)

✦ **JPEG.** JPEG 2000-Links. `www.jpeg.org/JPEG2000.htm`: See Chapter 4 (the "For More Information" section)

K

✦ **KPNQuest.** Site that informs you that you need a plug-in. `www.kpnqwest.com/intra/default.htm`: See Chapter 5

L

✦ **LANWrights, Inc.** Network-oriented consulting and writing (site structure example). `www.lanw.com`: See Chapter 3

✦ **Link Development Corporation.** `www.linkdevelopment.com`: See Chapter 10 (the "For More Information" section)

+ **LookSmart.** Search engine. `www.looksmart.com`: See Chapter 10

+ **Lycos.** Search engine. `www.lycos.com`: See Chapter 10

+ **Lynda.com.** The Browser-Safe Color Palette. `www.lynda.com/hex.html`: See Chapter 4

M

+ **Macromedia.** Extension program. `www.macromedia.com/exchange/dreamweaver/`: See Chapter 14

+ **Macromedia.** Flash information. `www.macromedia.com/software/flash/`: See Chapter 12 (the "For More Information" section)

+ **Macromedia.** Flash player download site. `www.macromedia.com/shockwave/download/index.cgi?P1_Prod_Version=ShockwaveFlash`: See Chapter 12 (Lab 12-1) and Chapter 16

+ **Macromedia.** Macromedia products. `www.macromedia.com`: See Chapters 5, 14, and 16 (the "For More Information" sections)

+ **Macromedia.** Shockwave information. `www.macromedia.com/software/flash/`: See Chapter 12 (the "For More Information" section)

+ **Macromedia.** Flash Showcase site. `www.macromedia.com/showcase/`: Chapter 16 (the "For More Information" section)

+ **Macromedia CONTACT _Con-4954D95F2.** Animation tool by Macromedia. `www.macromedia.com/software/flash/productinfo/usability`: See Chapter 5

+ **Macromedia Director.** Animation tool by Macromedia. `www.macromedia.com/software/director/`: See Chapter 5

+ **Mama's Cucina site.** `www.eat.com`: See Chapter 6 (Lab 6-1)

+ **Microsoft.** FrontPage site. `www.microsoft.com/frontpage/`: Chapter 13 (the "For More Information" section)

+ **Microsoft.** Knowledge base for getting any questions answered. `www.microsoft.com`: Chapter 13 (the "For More Information" section)

+ **Microsoft.** Search engine. `http://search.msn.com/`: See Chapter 10

+ **MPEG.org.** The Moving Picture Experts Group (MPEG). `www.mpeg.org/MPEG/index.html`: See Chapter 5 (the "For More Information" section)

+ **Museum of Modern Art.** Example of a metaphor. `http://moma.org`: See Chapter 6

N

✦ **National Geographic's expedition site.** `www.nationalgeographic.com/ xpeditions/hall/index.html`: See Chapter 6 (Lab 6-1)

✦ **NBCi.** Search engine. `www.nbci.com`: See Chapter 10

✦ **Netscape.** Search engine. `www.netscape.com`: See Chapter 10

✦ **Northern Light.** Search engine. `www.northernlight.com`: See Chapter 10

✦ **Nylon.** Site that informs you that you need a plug-in. `www.nylonmag.com`: See Chapter 5

✦ **Nylon.** Site with heavy animation and video. `www.nylonmag.com/04/ index.html`: See Chapter 5

O

✦ **Open Directory Project.** Multimedia resources. `http://dmoz.org/ Computers/Multimedia/`: See Chapter 5 (the "For More Information" section)

✦ **Open Directory Project.** Search engine. `http://dmoz.org/`: See Chapter 10

P

✦ **Paint Shop Pro.** Image software from Jasc Software. `www.jasc.com/ product.asp?pf%5Fid=001`: See Chapter 4

✦ **Project Cool.** Web design tips. `http://www.projectcool.com/developer/ tips/design01_tips/index.html`: See Chapter 9

✦ **Project Cool Developer.** `http://www.projectcool.com/developer/tips/ quickstart/index.html`: See Chapter 7 (Lab 7-1)

Q

✦ **Quicktime.** Multimedia player by Apple. `www.apple.com/quicktime`: See Chapter 5

R

✦ **RealJukebox.** Audio authoring, editing, and converting tool by RealNetworks. `www.realnetworks.com`: See Chapter 5

✦ **RealNames.** Search engine. `www.realnames.com`: See Chapter 10

✦ **RealNetworks' Real.com.** RealNetworks products. `www.real.com`: See Chapter 5 (the "For More Information" section)

✦ **TUCOWS.** Image Editors section. `http://tucows.surfus.net/win2k/imgedit2k.html`: See Chapter 4

U

✦ **useit.com.** Jakob Nielsen's Web site (breadcrumb example). `www.useit.com`: See Chapter 3

W

✦ **W3C.** Cascading Style Sheets information. `www.w3.org/Style/LieBos2e/history/`: See Chapter 11

✦ **W3C.** Cascading Style Sheets Working Group. `www.w3.org/Style/CSS/current-work`: See Chapter 11

✦ **W3C.** Getting Started with HTML. `www.w3.org/MarkUp/Guide/`: See Chapter 1 (the "For More Information" section)

✦ **W3C.** HTML 2 Specification. `www.w3.org/MarkUp/html-spec/`: See Chapter 7

✦ **W3C.** HTML 3.2 Specification. `www.w3.org/TR/REC-html32`: See Chapter 7

✦ **W3C.** HTML 4 Specification. `www.w3.org/TR/html4/`: See Chapter 7

✦ **W3C.** HTML 4.01 Frames information. `www.w3.org/TR/html4/present/frames.html`: See Chapter 9 (the "For More Information" section)

✦ **W3C.** HTML Compatibility Guidelines. `www.w3.org/TR/xhtml1/#guidelines`: See Chapter 19

✦ **W3C.** Metadata information. `www.w3.org/DesignIssues/Metadata`: See Chapter 10 (the "For More Information" section)

✦ **W3C.** PNG site (Find links to image editors that support PNG). `www.w3.org/Graphics/PNG/`: See Chapter 4 (the "For More Information" section)

✦ **W3C.** SVG site. `www.w3.org/Graphics/SVG/Overview.htm8`: See Chapter 4 (the "For More Information" section) and Chapter 5

✦ **W3C.** Style pages. `www.w3.org/Style/CSS/`: See Chapter 13

✦ **W3C.** Synchronized Multimedia (SMIL) site. `www.w3.org/AudioVideo`: See Chapter 5

✦ **W3C.** Table information. `www.w3.org/TR/html4/struct/tables.html`: See Chapter 8

✦ **W3C.** The CSS1 specification. `www.w3.org/TR/REC-CSS1`: See Chapter 11 (the "For More Information" section)

✦ **W3C.** The CSS2 specification. `www.w3.org/TR/REC-CSS2/`: See Chapter 11 (the "For More Information" section)

- **W3C.** XML 1.0 Specification. `www.w3.org/TR/1998/REC-xml-19980210#sec-origin-goals`: See Chapter 19

- **W3C.** XML in 10 points. `www.w3.org/XML/1999/XML-in-10-points`: See Chapter 19

- **W3C.** XML page. `www.w3.org/XML`: See Chapter 19 (the "For More Information" section)

- **W3C Jigsaw.** CSS validator. `http://jigsaw.w3.org/css-validator/`: See Chapter 11

- **Wallpaper.com.** Site with heavy animation and video. `www.wallpaper.com`: See Chapter 5

- **Washington Office on Latin America (WOLA).** Example of bookmarking Frames. `www.wola.org/`: See Chapter 9

- **Web Design Group.** CSS resources. `www.htmlhelp.com/reference/css/`: See Chapter 11 (the "For More Information" section)

- **Web site garage.** Online Web site that tests for load time. `http://websitegarage.netscape.com`: See Chapter 4

- **WebCrawler.** Search engine. `www.webcrawler.com`: See Chapter 10

- **Webmonkey.** CGI Scripts for Fun and Profit. `http://hotwired.lycos.com/webmonkey/99/26/index4a.html?tw=programming`: See Chapter 20 (the "For More Information" section)

- **Webmonkey.** Choosing the Right Database. `http://hotwired.lycos.com/webmonkey/98/24/index3a.html?tw=backend`: Chapter 21 (the "For More Information" section)

- **Webmonkey.** Director vs. Flash tutorial. `http://hotwired.lycos.com/webmonkey/99/27/index3a.html?tw=multimedia`: See Chapter 15 (the "For More Information" section)

- **Webmonkey.** Frames information. `http://hotwired.lycos.com/webmonkey/authoring/frames/`: See Chapter 9 (the "For More Information" section)

- **Webmonkey.** Graphics articles. `http://hotwired.lycos.com/webmonkey/design/graphics/`: See Chapter 4 (the "For More Information" section)

- **Webmonkey.** Information Architecture Tutorial. `http://hotwired.lycos.com/webmonkey/design/site_building/tutorials/tutorial1.html`: See Chapter 1 (the "For More Information" section)

- **Webmonkey.** Introduction to Active Server Pages. `http://hotwired.lycos.com/webmonkey/98/39/index2a.html`: See Chapter 20 (the "For More Information" section)

- **Webmonkey.** Streaming Audio tutorial. `http://hotwired.lycos.com/webmonkey/00/45/index3a.html?tw=multimedia`: See Chapter 15 (the "For More Information" section)

✦ **Webmonkey.** The Foundations of Web Design. `http://hotwired.lycos.com/webmonkey/design/site_building/tutorials/tutorial3.html`: See Chapter 1 (the "For More Information" section)

✦ **Webmonkey.** The Web developer's resource. `http://hotwired.lycos.com/webmonkey/`: See Chapters 3 and 6 (the "For More Information" sections), 7 (Lab 7-1), 8 (Lab 8-2 and the "For More Information" section), Chapter 14 (the "For More Information" section), and Chapter 17 (the "For More Information" section)

✦ **Webmonkey.** Your First Database. `http://hotwired.lycos.com/webmonkey/99/13/index0a.html`: Chapter 21 (the "For More Information" section)

✦ **WebReview.com.** Back to Basics: A compilation of basic Web design development articles. `www.webreview.com/1998/08_28/index.shtml`: See Chapter 1 (the "For More Information" section)

✦ **WebReview.com.** Cross training for Web Teams. `http://webreview.com`: See Chapters 3, 6, 7, 8, and 14 (the "For More Information" section)

✦ **WebReview.com.** HomeSite's a Smart Editor. `www.webreview.com/1998/02_20/webauthors/02_20_98_4.shtml`: See Chapter 19 (the "For More Information" section)

✦ **WebReview.com.** Introducing Web Accessibility. `www.webreview.com/2001/03_02/webauthors/index03.shtml`: See Chapter 4 (the "For More Information" section)

✦ **WebReview.com.** Leader Board. `www.webreview.com/style/css1/leaderboard.shtml`: See Chapter 11

✦ **WebReview.com.** Master browser compatibility list. `www.webreview.com/style/css1/charts/mastergrid.shtml`: See Chapter 11

✦ **WebTV.** From Microsoft. `www.webtv.net/index.html`: See Chapter 5

✦ **Windows Media Player.** Multimedia player by Microsoft. `www.microsoft.com/windows/windowsmedia/en/default.asp`: See Chapter 5

✦ **World Wide Web Consortium (W3C).** Markup language standards. `www.w3.org`: See Chapters 1, 2, 7 (Lab 7-1), and Chapter 9

X

✦ **The XML 1.0 Specification.** `www.w3.org/TR/2000/REC-xml-20001006`: See Chapter 19 (the "For More Information" section)

✦ **XML.com.** A Technical Introduction to XML. `www.xml.com/pub/a/98/10/guide0.html`: See Chapter 19 (the "For More Information" section)

✦ **XML.com.** Browser XML Display Support Chart. `www.xml.com/pub/a/2000/05/03/browserchart/index.html`: See Chapter 19

✦ **XML.com.** XML Demos section. `www.xml.com/pub/rg/Demos`: See Chapter 19

✦ **The XML Cover pages.** XML Resource. `http://xml.coverpages.org`: See Chapter 19 (the "For More Information" section)

✦ **XML Info.** XML resource. `www.xmlinfo.com`: See Chapter 19 (the "For More Information" section)

Y

✦ **Yahoo!** Multimedia resource index. `http://dir.yahoo.com/Computers_and_Internet/Multimedia/`: See Chapter 5 (the "For More Information" section)

✦ **Yahoo!** Search engine. `www.yahoo.com`: See Chapter 10

✦ **Yahoo!** The Animated GIFs page. `http://dir.yahoo.com/Entertainment/Comics_and_Animation/Animation/Computer_Animation/Animated_GIFs/`: See Chapter 4

✦ **Yale Web Style Guide.** Online style guide. `http://info.med.yale.edu/caim/manual/`: See Chapter 11

Z

✦ **ZDNet's Developer site.** Web design site. `www.zdnet.com/developer/`: See Chapters 3, 6, 7, 8, and 14 (the "For More Information" section)

✦ **Zvon.** Markup language reference. `www.zvon.org`: See Chapter 7 (the "For More Information" section)

✦   ✦   ✦

Glossary

animated GIF A sequence of GIF image files that are displayed one at a time to create a movie-like display.

animation Rapidly displaying a series of still images, each varying in position or with subtle differences in appearance to produce the illusion of movement.

anti-aliasing A process that smoothes the edges of each letter, thereby increasing readability.

applet A small Java application that can be embedded within an HTML document. An applet is also a client-side program that is downloaded and run on the client computer.

ASP (Active Server Pages) A Microsoft technology that provides a small set of scriptable objects for manipulating requests, responses, sessions, and even multi-step transactions.

attributes A component of an XML or (X)HTML document that provides more information about a given element.

bitmap image A collection of squares, called pixels, of different colors that when merged create an image. The larger a graphic is, the more squares of color it needs to create the image.

BLOB (Binary Large Object) A method for storing and retrieving non-text information such as audio clips and images in a database.

branding The consistency in look and feel of a Web site with the look and feel standards of the organization it represents.

bytecode In Java, it's the executable program.

cable modem A modem that works with your cable TV connection.

cascade The way a set of style rules from different sources work together to define the final look and feel of a single Web page.

CGI (Common Gateway Interface) A protocol that Web servers use to share information gathered in HTML forms with applications that run on the Web server.

cookie A simple text file that a server places on the user's system to help identify the user.

CSS (Cascading Style Sheets) An advanced tool for defining the look and feel of a Web page using style rules to define how the different pieces and parts of a document should be displayed.

DBMS (Database Management System) An interface — graphical or not — to the database that an administrator can use to access data and the database.

DHTML (Dynamic HTML) DHTML combines HTML and client-side scripts written in JavaScript or VBScript to create HTML that users can interact with after the page is downloaded to their systems.

dithering When a browser approximates the color to the closest browser safe color that it supports. It simply replaces colors in the image's pallet with system colors.

DOM (Document Object Model) The internal representation of a Web page that the browser builds as it renders the page. The DOM defines what page elements are visible to the browser and how those elements can be manipulated by a scripting language.

DSL (Digital Subscriber Line) A high-speed Internet connection typically provided to consumers by telephone companies.

DTD (Document Type Definition) A document that outlines the rules that a markup language must follow; for example, what attributes can be used with which tags and what can be contained between opening and closing tags.

dynamic When an action occurs when it's needed by the user instead of when the page loads. For example, a mouseover occurs when the user puts the mouse pointer of the object with the appropriate properties assigned, creating a particular effect on demand.

e-commerce 1) Commerce conducted via any electronic medium. 2) The integration of communication, data management, and security capabilities that allows organizations to exchange information about the sale of goods and services.

elements The building blocks of XML documents that describe the different kinds of markup you find therein. Sometimes called tags in HTML.

entity A virtual storage unit in an XML or (X)HTML document that can hold either text or binary files.

events In programming, situations to which the object can respond.

external style sheet A style sheet that keeps all of the style rules you want to use with a collection of HTML documents in a separate file saved on your Web site.

extranet An extension of an intranet that allows select users outside of the organization to access the resources and information on an intranet.

frame An HTML element that allows Web designers to create a static navigation page, while allowing the content page to dynamically change.

frameset A component of a Web page that displays multiple Web pages at the same time in the same window. An HTML document that defines a set of frames that are populated by other HTML documents.

FTP (File Transfer Protocol) A Transmission Control Protocol/Internet Protocol (TCP/IP) protocol that allows you to move files of any type from one place on the Internet to another.

function The programming component responsible for activity in your program.

GIF (Graphics Interchange Format) Created by CompuServe as a tool for displaying images in their pre-Web Internet access software. GIF files are platform independent and work in any graphical browser your users might come across.

GUI (Graphical User Interface) Any computer interface that utilizes graphics (such as mouse pointers and menus) instead of command lines.

hexadecimal code Defines colors using a pound sign followed by six characters.

HTML (Hypertext Markup Language) Created by Tim Berners-Lee while he was with CERN. The idea was to add to the work done with hypertext and hypermedia and create a way to access a large universe of documents. HTML was created as an application of SGML.

HTTP (Hypertext Transfer Protocol) Defines rules for exchanging resources identified by a URL on the Web. It's an application layer protocol in the TCP/IP stack that provides Web-based services using the default port 80.

hyperlink Instructions in a text file created using markup that allow you to connect to information in a separate file.

hypertext The ability to distribute nonlinear text.

IAB (Internet Architecture Board) The technical advisory group of the ISOC.

ICANN (The Internet Corporation for Assigned Names and Numbers) A nonprofit corporation with the primary responsibility of governing IP address space allocation, protocol parameter assignment, domain name system management, and root server system management functions—all of which were previously performed under U.S. Government contract by IANA and other entities.

IETF (Internet Engineering Task Force) An international community of network designers, operators, vendors, and researchers that share a concern about the future of the Internet—more specifically the Internet's architecture.

image map An image with multiple hyperlinks embedded in it.

inheritance In the context of style sheets, refers to how the effects of style rules are passed down from a parent element to any child elements that it contains.

inline frame A frame embedded within a plain HTML document.

inline style Style rules written in the HTML markup itself and that apply to a single instance of an HTML element. Inline styles have precedent over all other styles applied to your document.

internal style sheets Sets of style rules that you list in a group directly within an HTML file.

intranet A TCP/IP-based network that uses standard Internet services and applications within the confines of a particular organization to create a sort of "in-house Internet."

intrinsic objects Objects that are part of the JavaScript language itself.

IRTF (Internet Research Task Force) An organization composed of a number of small research groups that work on topics related to Internet protocols, applications, architecture, and technology. Research groups are usually focused and long term, although short-lived task force-like research groups are possible.

ISOC (Internet Society) An international organization with over 150 organizations and 6,000 individual members. This organization houses the Internet Engineering Task Force (IETF) and the Internet Architecture Board (IAB) and is a leader in addressing issues that deal with the future of the Internet.

Java An object-oriented, enterprise-level programming language.

Java applet *See* applet.

JavaScript A scripting language used to manipulate the contents of a Web page that has been rendered in a browser of some sort.

JDBC (Java Database Connectivity) A standard programming interface developed by Sun Microsystems to support integration of Java applications with databases. JDBC translates database queries from Java code into SQL queries and can be used with any SQL-compliant database.

JPEG (Joint Photographic Experts Group) One of the standard image file formats most widely supported by Web browsers. JPEG was created as a way to overcome the color depth limitations of the GIF format. Image files are automatically compressed when they're saved as JPEG files, and Web browsers decompress the images before they display them.

JSP (JavaServer Pages) Sun's Java programming language (not JavaScript) that includes a number of tools for Web development, but from a server-side scripting point of view, JSP is the most relevant. JSP is the Java equivalent of Microsoft's ASP product.

JVM (Java Virtual Machine) Software installed on a machine that processes Java bytecodes, converts the bytecodes to a machine language, and then executes the bytecodes.

LAN (Local Area Network) One of a variety of communications technologies used to connect computers in a single building, business, or campus environment.

logical markup language Describes the structure of a document irrespective of its display.

metadata Data about data. In reference to HTML, it provides additional information about the contents of your document within the `<meta>` tags.

meta-markup language A markup language used to define other markup. XML and SGML are meta-markup languages.

method In programming, it's something that the object can do.

MIDI (musical instrument digital interface) A digital audio standard originally created to allow sounds created on one keyboard to be played on another without losing any quality. MIDI is now used for electronic instruments and sound cards to communicate.

MP3 (MPEG 1, audio layer 3) Compression files that can compresses a CD-quality file to about 10 times its original size (this value is variable and can be as high as 17 times).

native file format A file format inherently supported by the browser, such as Hypertext Markup Language (HTML), Graphics Interchange Format (GIF), and Joint Photographic Experts Group (JPEG).

non-native file format A file format that the browser doesn't inherently support.

object In programming, a cohesive collection of methods, events, and properties.

ODBC (Open Database Connectivity) The most common method for accessing a database and supported by every major database available. ODBC was originally developed by Microsoft and applications use software utilities called drivers to speak with an ODBC-compliant database. The driver speaks both DBMS and the language of the code and translates the requests from the code into commands intelligible to the DBMS.

operators In JavaScript, these are the tools that let you do basic variable manipulation and comparisons.

PDF (Portable Document Format) A digital representation of a document created in just about any word processing or page layout tool, from Microsoft Word to Quark Xpress. PDF files maintain the formatting and layout of a document exactly as it was in the original document and can include links between pages in the document.

PHP (PHP Hypertext Preprocessor) An extremely popular open-source scripting language for building Web applications.

pixel This is an abbreviation for picture element and is one point on a graphic.

plug-in A small application that is downloaded and installed on the user's system and recognized by the browser. Each plug-in is designed to display a particular kind of file type.

PNG (Portable Network Graphics) Is the latest Web graphic file format and is a W3C specification. It was developed with the needs of designers and the drawbacks of GIF and JPEG in mind.

port A logical connection point on a server that a client application.

primary navigation Used to define navigational elements that are located on most pages in a Web site.

procedural markup Markup that directs a display device on how to display content. HTML is a procedural markup language.

property In CSS, it defines which part of the element's style you want to affect.

RGB (red, green, blue) A color scheme that consists of red, green, and blue. This combination of color is known as additive. Each RGB value works within base-10 numbers that range from 0 to 255.

ripping The process of converting WAV files to MP3s.

rollover Actions triggered by a mouseover.

sans-serif Fonts that do not have serifs — the decorative strokes at the end of the letter's main strokes.

schema Referring to databases, it's the structure of a database that defines what kind of information is stored in the database and how it is stored.

script A set of instructions performed by some entity or object.

scriptable objects Objects available inside the JavaScript container.

secondary navigation All those hyperlinks on an interior page that are specific to that page (or subset of pages).

selector In CSS, it's the HTML element to which you want the style rule to apply.

serif fonts Fonts defined by small decorative strokes at the end of a letter's main strokes.

servlets Server-side Java programs used for applications that need to run on the server, rather than on the client.

SGML (Standard Generalized Markup Language) Defines a set of syntax rules that other markup languages (such as HTML) must follow. Technically speaking, SGML is a meta-markup language that allows for the creation markup languages. HTML is an application of SGML.

shell scripting A command programming language used to supply UNIX operating systems with an interface, including variables, parameter passing, control-flow primitives, and more.

site map Detail of a Web site's structure used as navigation.

SMIL (Synchronized Multimedia Integration Language) This W3C standard allows authors to create presentations that integrate varying multimedia elements.

SSL (Secure Sockets Layer) One of several different protocols designed to help Web browsers and Web servers communicate securely. The SSL protocol defines how a Web client requests a secure page from a Web server, how the client passes authentication information to the server so the server knows the client has permission to access the pages, and how the information passed back and forth between the client and server is encrypted so no one can intercept and read the transmissions.

statement An instruction provided in some type of markup language or programming language that instructs the computer to perform a specific action.

stream A technology that allows audio files to be played as they arrive.

streaming media Media files that begin play before the entire file has downloaded to your system.

style guide Documents the rules of how a site should look and feel. A guide may include definitions of how different text elements should look, the elements that are required on particular pages, how images may be used, and more.

style sheet A set of rules that defines how a piece of a document should look in a particular display media.

SVG (Scalable Vector Graphics) Graphics that use XML to describe the mathematical equations that make up vector graphics. SVG is being developed by the W3C.

tag *See* elements.

transparent GIF An image that blends in with its background.

TrueType font A font that can be rendered in any font size without suffering from poor image quality. Developed by Apple Computer, TrueType is now used by both the Windows and Macintosh platforms. A few examples of TrueType fonts are Arial, Times New Roman, Georgia, and Verdana.

tweening The process in Flash animation that automatically renders frames between keyframes.

URL (uniform resource locator) The primary naming scheme used to identify Web resources, URLs define the protocols to be used, the domain name of the Web server where a resource resides, the port address to be used for communication, and the directory path to access a named Web file or resource.

usability The measure of how functional and usable a Web site is and should be one of the most important aspects of any Web design.

user interface The design of a Web site.

value In CSS, it specifies how you want to affect a specific CSS property.

vector image A collection of lines that is defined by mathematical equations. A vector image viewer interprets the mathematical equations and displays the image accordingly.

W3C (World Wide Web Consortium) A standards organization that controls the HTML standard (and therefore, its future) as well as other Web-related standards.

WAN (Wide Area Network) A network that covers a large geographical area.

WAV format A sound format developed by Microsoft and IBM to store audio files on a PC. The CDs you purchase of your favorite band use a WAV file format.

Web The World Wide Web, which runs on the Internet and is comprised of billions of interconnected pages. A FrontPage Web is a collection of files and folders, which, when published to a Web server, becomes your Web site.

WYSIWYG (what you see is what you get) An HTML editing tool that allows you to edit the file as it would appear in the browsers; therefore, bypassing the HTML markup all together.

XHTML (Extensible Hypertext Markup Language) The reformulation of HTML in XML and the future of HTML.

XLink (XML Linking Language) A technology for creating links among XML documents.

XML (Extensible Markup Language) A set of rules that anyone can use to create their own markup elements to describe their content.

XML Query A technology for searching XML documents using sophisticated search queries.

XSL (Extensible Stylesheet Language) A technology for creating style sheets to drive the display of XML documents in any kind of display media.

Index

Continued

Continued

Continued

Continued

Hungry Minds, Inc.
End-User License Agreement

READ THIS. You should carefully read these terms and conditions before opening the software packet(s) included with this book ("Book"). This is a license agreement ("Agreement") between you and Hungry Minds, Inc. ("HMI"). By opening the accompanying software packet(s), you acknowledge that you have read and accept the following terms and conditions. If you do not agree and do not want to be bound by such terms and conditions, promptly return the Book and the unopened software packet(s) to the place you obtained them for a full refund.

1. **License Grant.** HMI grants to you (either an individual or entity) a nonexclusive license to use one copy of the enclosed software program(s) (collectively, the "Software") solely for your own personal or business purposes on a single computer (whether a standard computer or a workstation component of a multi-user network). The Software is in use on a computer when it is loaded into temporary memory (RAM) or installed into permanent memory (hard disk, CD-ROM, or other storage device). HMI reserves all rights not expressly granted herein.

2. **Ownership.** HMI is the owner of all right, title, and interest, including copyright, in and to the compilation of the Software recorded on the disk(s) or CD-ROM ("Software Media"). Copyright to the individual programs recorded on the Software Media is owned by the author or other authorized copyright owner of each program. Ownership of the Software and all proprietary rights relating thereto remain with HMI and its licensers.

3. **Restrictions On Use and Transfer.**

   (a) You may only (i) make one copy of the Software for backup or archival purposes, or (ii) transfer the Software to a single hard disk, provided that you keep the original for backup or archival purposes. You may not (i) rent or lease the Software, (ii) copy or reproduce the Software through a LAN or other network system or through any computer subscriber system or bulletin-board system, or (iii) modify, adapt, or create derivative works based on the Software.

   (b) You may not reverse engineer, decompile, or disassemble the Software. You may transfer the Software and user documentation on a permanent basis, provided that the transferee agrees to accept the terms and conditions of this Agreement and you retain no copies. If the Software is an update or has been updated, any transfer must include the most recent update and all prior versions.

4. **Restrictions on Use of Individual Programs.** You must follow the individual requirements and restrictions detailed for each individual program in Appendix A of this Book. These limitations are also contained in the individual

license agreements recorded on the Software Media. These limitations may include a requirement that after using the program for a specified period of time, the user must pay a registration fee or discontinue use. By opening the Software packet(s), you will be agreeing to abide by the licenses and restrictions for these individual programs that are detailed in Appendix A and on the Software Media. None of the material on this Software Media or listed in this Book may ever be redistributed, in original or modified form, for commercial purposes.

5. **Limited Warranty.**

   (a) HMI warrants that the Software and Software Media are free from defects in materials and workmanship under normal use for a period of sixty (60) days from the date of purchase of this Book. If HMI receives notification within the warranty period of defects in materials or workmanship, HMI will replace the defective Software Media.

   (b) **HMI AND THE AUTHOR OF THE BOOK DISCLAIM ALL OTHER WARRANTIES, EXPRESS OR IMPLIED, INCLUDING WITHOUT LIMITATION IMPLIED WARRANTIES OF MERCHANTABILITY AND FITNESS FOR A PARTICULAR PURPOSE, WITH RESPECT TO THE SOFTWARE, THE PROGRAMS, THE SOURCE CODE CONTAINED THEREIN, AND/OR THE TECHNIQUES DESCRIBED IN THIS BOOK. HMI DOES NOT WARRANT THAT THE FUNCTIONS CONTAINED IN THE SOFTWARE WILL MEET YOUR REQUIREMENTS OR THAT THE OPERATION OF THE SOFTWARE WILL BE ERROR FREE.**

   (c) This limited warranty gives you specific legal rights, and you may have other rights that vary from jurisdiction to jurisdiction.

6. **Remedies.**

   (a) HMI's entire liability and your exclusive remedy for defects in materials and workmanship shall be limited to replacement of the Software Media, which may be returned to HMI with a copy of your receipt at the following address: Software Media Fulfillment Department, Attn.: *Microsoft Application Center 2000 Configuration and Administration*, Hungry Minds, Inc., 10475 Crosspoint Blvd., Indianapolis, IN 46256, or call 1-800-762-2974. Please allow four to six weeks for delivery. This Limited Warranty is void if failure of the Software Media has resulted from accident, abuse, or misapplication. Any replacement Software Media will be warranted for the remainder of the original warranty period or thirty (30) days, whichever is longer.

   (b) In no event shall HMI or the author be liable for any damages whatsoever (including without limitation damages for loss of business profits, business interruption, loss of business information, or any other pecuniary loss) arising from the use of or inability to use the Book or the Software, even if HMI has been advised of the possibility of such damages.

(c) Because some jurisdictions do not allow the exclusion or limitation of liability for consequential or incidental damages, the above limitation or exclusion may not apply to you.

7. **U.S. Government Restricted Rights.** Use, duplication, or disclosure of the Software for or on behalf of the United States of America, its agencies and/or instrumentalities (the "U.S. Government") is subject to restrictions as stated in paragraph (c)(1)(ii) of the Rights in Technical Data and Computer Software clause of DFARS 252.227-7013, or subparagraphs (c) (1) and (2) of the Commercial Computer Software - Restricted Rights clause at FAR 52.227-19, and in similar clauses in the NASA FAR supplement, as applicable.

8. **General.** This Agreement constitutes the entire understanding of the parties and revokes and supersedes all prior agreements, oral or written, between them and may not be modified or amended except in a writing signed by both parties hereto that specifically refers to this Agreement. This Agreement shall take precedence over any other documents that may be in conflict herewith. If any one or more provisions contained in this Agreement are held by any court or tribunal to be invalid, illegal, or otherwise unenforceable, each and every other provision shall remain in full force and effect.

CD-ROM Installation Instructions

The contents of this page will give you a quick start in installing the CD-ROM included with this book. The CD contains a variety of site design-enabling software, source code, graphics, resources from the examples presented in the preceding chapters, an electronic, searchable version of the book — viewable with Adobe Acrobat Reader (also on the CD) — and a comprehensive testing engine, with questions similar to and formatted like the ones on the CIW Site Designer Exam.

Cross-Reference For detailed information on the contents of the CD-ROM — as well as specific options for users of Windows, Linux, and the Mac OS — see Appendix A. Troubleshooting guidelines, notes on the software restrictions, and system requirements are also included in Appendix A.

Before installing the CD, make sure your computer meets the minimum system requirements listed in Appendix A. Although we've included Windows versions of the software on the CD, many of these products are also available for Linux and the Mac OS. Refer to Tables A-1 and A-2 in Appendix A for a product-by-product breakdown of your options. You will need at least 300MB of hard drive space to install all the software from this CD.

+ **Microsoft Windows.** To install the items from the CD on your hard drive, follow these steps:

  1. Insert the CD into your computer's CD-ROM drive.

  2. View the contents of the CD-ROM using Windows Explorer or by clicking the My Computer icon on your desktop.

  3. Locate the software you wish to install.

  4. Either double-click on the program's installation program to install it, or follow the directions contained in the readme file in the CD directory for the program.

+ **Linux.** To open the items from the CD, follow these steps:

  1. Log in as root.

  2. Insert the CD into your computer's CD-ROM drive.

  3. Mount the CD-ROM.

  4. Launch a graphical file manager to view the items on the CD.

✦ **Mac OS.** To open the items from the CD, follow these steps:

1. Insert the CD into your computer's CD-ROM drive.

2. Double-click the CD icon on your desktop.

3. Locate the item you wish to view.

4. Double-click the file you want to open, or use the Open command from the appropriate program.